Making Friends in Mexico

A Spanish Phrasebook

Rodnik Publishing Company

Seattle, Washington

2003

Making Friends in Mexico; A Spanish Phrasebook

Compiler: **Robert F. Powers**
Translator: **Hugo J. Gomez Padilla**
Editor: **Lillian Levy Guevara**
Graphics editor: **Marvin Powers**
Technical assistants: **Thu Hien Powers**
                     Thanh Thao Pham

Published by:

Rodnik Publishing Company
P.O. Box 46956
Seattle, WA 98136-0956

Library of Congress Control Number: 2003092617
ISBN 1-929482-05-1

Cover photo courtesy of Saron Llistosella and Jon Reyes.

Printed in the United States of America

to
Hong-Oanh
ever there when I need you

Table of Contents

INTRODUCTION

The main goal of this phrasebook is to help you make new acquaintances -- hopefully leading to friendships -- with people in Mexico. Whereas most phrasebooks set their sights (and yours) on brief, to-the-point exchanges with customs officials, taxi drivers, hotel employees, store clerks, waiters, and mechanics, this phrasebook equips you with the phrases and vocabulary to meet people, learn about them, carry on conversations, have fun, and even pursue romance. (However, just in case you need it, we've included a good helping of that mundane stuff, too.)

Something else we think you'll like about this phrasebook is that it's quick and easy to find what you want to say. Phrases and terms are group under their key words, and the key words are in alphabetical order (not in categories that often leave you guessing what's where). Got a phrase or term in mind? Go to it's key word, the same as you would in a dictionary, and chances are good that it'll be there. Total elapsed time: six seconds.

Because the phrases and vocabulary in this book cover a wide spectrum of interests, activities and situations, there is a rich supply of friendship material for people of all ages, male or female, married or single. We sincerely hope that, whoever you are, whatever your age, you'll be able to put this phrasebook to the purpose for which it's intended -- making friends among the wonderful Mexican people.

How to Use the Phrasebook

Main words

All phrases and terms in the phrasebook are grouped under the "**main words**," which they contain. For example, the phrase "**We'll call you later.**" is listed under the main word "**call**."

Some phrases appear in the dictionary more than once, because they contain more than one important main word. For example, the phrase "**Could you show me around the city?**" is listed once under the main word "**city**" and a second time under "**show**."

Parts of speech

Each listed main word is followed by its abbreviated part of speech, such as *n* for "noun," *vt* for "verb transitive," etc. (See "**Abbreviations Used in the Dictionary**" on page 10.)

Tilde substituting main word

For all terms, a **tilde** ~ substitutes for the main word of the term. For example, under the main word **cake**, "**wedding cake**" is listed as **wedding** ~. Similarly, "**call back**" under the main word "**call**" is given as ~ **back**.

Slash = or

Throughout the phrasebook a **slash** / is used to mean "**or**," i.e., that you can choose one or the other. The choices are numbered, in parentheses, both on the English side and the Spanish side. Hence, the term "*(1,2)* **curly hair** cabello *(1)* rizado / *(2)* ondulado" can be said as either "cabello rizado" or "cabello ondulado". Sometimes the choices differ in meaning, sometimes they are the same.

The same is true of parts of phrases that are numbered and separated by a **slash** /. These will sometimes be preceded or followed -- or both -- by three dots. For example, in the phrase "**I enjoy *(1)* ...being (together).... / *(2)* ...talking... / *(3)* ...doing things... with you.** Disfruto *(1)* ...estar (juntos)... / *(2)* ...platicar... / *(3)* ...de hacer cosas... *con usted (Fam: contigo).*" you can choose to say "**I enjoy being together with you.** Disfruto estar juntos *con usted (Fam: contigo)."* or "**I enjoy talking with you.** Disfruto platicar *con usted (Fam: contigo)."* or "**I enjoy doing things with you.** Disfruto de hacer cosas *con usted (Fam: contigo)."*

Parentheses = optional

Words or parts of phrases in **parentheses** are **optional**. In the phrase **"No one can match you (in any way). Nadie se puede igualar contigo (de ninguna manera).",** you could include or omit the words **(in any way)** in both English and Spanish. In a very few cases, an English word in parentheses is optional in English, but has no counterpart in Spanish: the sentence in Spanish will be the same either way.

Feminine forms of words

For individual Spanish words, only the ending of the feminine form is given, preceded by a hyphen. In phrases, the feminine ending of a word appears in italics in parentheses. For more explanation of feminine forms, see **Appendix 2: Spanish Grammar** on page 409.

Polite and familiar forms of words

In phrases, the polite form of pronouns and verbs appears in the open, in italics, and the familiar form that can replace it is given in parentheses, in italics. For more explanation of polite and familiar forms, see **Appendix 2: Spanish Grammar** on page 409.

Spanish pronunciation

The basic rules of Spanish pronunciation may be found in the **Alphabet** appendix on page 407. Additionally, notes on pronunciation are given throughout the phrasebook in footers at the bottom of pages.

Spanish Usage

In using this phrasebook, please bear in mind that the Spanish phrases in many cases represent the best translation we could provide of the English phrases and, although they will be easily understood by a Mexican, they are not necessarily what Mexicans themselves would think of to say for those particular ideas.

Abbreviations Used in the Dictionary

abbrev	abbreviation	*pers.pron*	personal pronoun
adol.	adoloscent(s)	*phr prep*	phrasal preposition
adj	adjective		
adv	adverb	*phys.*	physical
anat.	anatomy	*pl*	plural
automot.	automotive	*Pol:*	polite
coll.	collective	*polit.*	political
colloq.	colloquial	*poss.*	possessive
comm.	communications	*pp*	past participle
comp.	computers	*prep*	preposition
conj	conjunction	*pron*	pronoun
dem.	demonstrative	*sing.*	singular
elec.	electrical	*s.o.*	someone
etc	etcetera	*s.th.*	something
f, F	feminine	*transp.*	transportation
Fam:.	familiar	*univ.*	university
fig.	figurative	*vi*	verb intransitive
gram.	grammar	*vt*	verb transitive
imp.	imperative		
interj.	interjection		
m, M	masculine		
mech.	mechanical		
med.	medical		
mil.	military		
n	noun		
naut.	nautical		
org.	organization		

A

ble: be ~ ser capaz de, poder **Will you** *(1,2)* **be able to** *(3)* **change it?** /
(4) **come?** / *(5)* **do it?** / *(6)* **fix it?** / *(7)* **get it?** / *(8)* **get off work?** / *(9)* **go?**
/ *(10)* **meet** *(11)* **me?** / *(12)* **us?** *(1)* ¿Será usted *(Fam: ¿Serás)* capaz
de... / *(2)* ¿Podrá usted *(Fam: Podrás)*... *(3)* cambiarlo? / *(4)* venir? / *(5)*
hacerlo? / *(6)* arreglarlo? / *(7)* conseguirlo? / *(8)* salir del trabajo? / *(9)* ir?
/ *(10)* reunirse *(Fam: reunirte)* *(11)* conmigo? / *(12)* con nosotros? **I
wasn't able to** *(1)* **call you.** / *(2)* **change it.** / *(3)* **come.** / *(4)* **do it.** / *(5)*
find it. / *(6)* **get it.** / *(7)* **get off work.** No pude *(1)* llamarle a usted
(Fam: llamarte). / *(2)* cambiarlo. / *(3)* venir. / *(4)* hacerlo. / *(5)* encontrarlo.
/ *(6)* conseguirlo. / *(7)* salirme del trabajo.

bout *adv (approximately)* casi, poco más o menos, alrededor de **~ an hour**
casi una hora **~ a kilometer** casi un kilómetro **~ a week** casi una semana **~
a month** casi un mes **~ a year** casi un año **It's about 2 kilometers from
here.** Queda como a dos kilómetros de aquí. *(1)* **I'll** / *(2)* **We'll be back
about 7:00.** *(1)* Regreso / *(2)* Regresamos como a las siete.

bout *prep* acerca de, sobre **What are you talking about?** ¿De qué *está
usted (Fam: estás)* hablando? **What is the** *(1)* **book** / *(2)* **movie about?**
¿De qué se trata *(1)* el libro? / *(2)* la película? **How about...?** ¿Qué te
parece...?

bsent *adj* ausente *m&f* **~ from school** ausente de la escuela

bsent-minded *adj* distraído *m*, -da *f*

bsolute *adj* total *m&f*, absoluto *m*, -ta *f*

bsolutely *adv* totalmente, completamente, absolutamente **~ impossible**
completamente imposible *(1-3)* **Absolutely!** *(1)* ¡Sí! / *(2)* ¡Sin lugar a
dudas! / *(3)* ¡Completamente! *(1,2)* **Absolutely not!** *(1)* ¡No! / *(2)*
¡Terminantemente no!

bsurd *adj* absurdo *m*, -da *f* **That's absurd!** ¡Eso es absurdo! **That's the**

A slash always means "or".

most absurd thing I've ever heard. Eso es lo más absurdo que haya oido jamás.

academy *n* academia *f*

accent *n* acento *m* **My accent is terrible.** Mi acento es terrible. **I love your accent.** Me encanta tu acento.

accept *vt* aceptar **I accept your invitation.** Acepto *su (Fam: tu)* invitación

access *n* acceso *m* **internet ~** acceso a Internet **Do you have access to** **computer?** ¿Tiene usted *(Fam: Tienes)* acceso a una computadora?

accessories *n, pl* accesorios *mpl*

accident *n* accidente *m* **car ~** accidente automovilístico *(1)* **I /** *(2)* **We had a accident.** *(1)* Tuve / *(2)* Tuvimos un accidente. *(1)* **He /** *(2)* **She was** *(3* **injured /** *(4)* **killed in a(n) (car) accident.** Resultó *(1:3)* lesionado / *(2:3* lesionada *(1:4)* muerto / *(2:4)* muerta en un accidente (automovilístico). **was injured in a(n) (car) accident.** Resulté lesionado *(-da)* en un accident (automovilístico).

accommodations *n, pl* hospedaje *m* **Can** *(1)* **I /** *(2)* **we get accommodations there?** *(1)* ¿Puedo / *(2)* ¿Podemos conseguir hospedaje ahí? **How are the accommodations there?** ¿Cómo es el alojamiento en ese lugar?

accompany *vt* acompañar **May I accompany you?** ¿Puedo *acompañarle* *usted (Fam: acompañarte)*?

according to según **According to the schedule the train arrives at 4 PM** Según el itinerario el tren llega a las cuatro de la tarde.

accordion *n* acordeón *m*

account *n* cuenta **bank ~** cuenta bancaria **take into ~** tomar en cuenta **You have to take into account...** Usted tiene *(Fam:Tienes)* que tomar en cuenta... **Do you have a bank account?** ¿Tiene usted (*Fam: Tienes)* cuenta bancaria?

accurate *adj* exacto *m*, -ta *f* *(1)* **That clock... /** *(2)* **My watch... is no** **accurate.** *(1)* Ese reloj... / *(2)* Mi reloj ... no es exacto.

ace *n (cards)* as *m*

ache *vi* duele **It aches (terribly).** Duele (muchísimo). **My heart aches with love for you.** Me duele el corazón de amor por ti.

acquaintance *n (person)* conocido *m*, -da *f* *(1)* **He /** *(2)* **She is an (old)** **acquaintance of mine.** *(1)* Él es un (viejo) conocido mío. / *(2)* Ella es una (vieja) conocida mía.

acquainted *pp* conocido *m*, -da *f* **We're (already) acquainted.** (Ya) Nos conocemos.

acrobat *n* acróbata *m&f* **You're a real acrobat.** Usted es *(Fam: Tú eres)* un(a) acróbata verdadero *(-ra)*.

acrobatic *adj* acrobático *m*, -ca *f*

Spanish "v" is pronounced like a soft "b".

cross *adv* al otro lado **go ~** ir al otro lado **swim ~** cruzar a nado, nadar al otro lado

cross *prep* por, a través de **~ the river** al otro lado del río **~ the street** al otro lado de la calle

act *vi* 1. *(behave)* actuar; 2. *(drama: perform)* actuar **I'm sorry I acted the way I did.** Lamento haber actuado de esa manera.

act *n* 1. *(deed)* acto *m*; 2. *(of a play)* acto *m* **in the** *(1)* **first** / *(2)* **second** / *(3)* **last ~** en el *(1)* primer / *(2)* segundo / *(3)* último acto. **I caught you in the act!** ¡Te atrapé con las manos en la masa! *(an expression)*

active *adj* activo *m*, -va *f* **You're quite an active person.** Usted es (*Fam: Tú eres*) una persona bastante activa. **I like an active lifestyle.** Me gusta llevar una vida activa.

activity *n* actividad *f* **What sort of activities do they have here?** ¿Con qué tipo de actividades cuentan aquí?

actor *n* actor *m*

actress *n* actríz *f*

actually *adv* verdaderamente, en realidad, de verdad **Actually, I'm not working right now.** En realidad, ahora no estoy trabajando. **Do you actually believe that?** ¿De verdad cree usted (*Fam: crees*) eso?

ad *(advertisement) n* anuncio *m* **personal ~** anuncio personal **place a personal ~** (*[1]* **in the paper.** / *[2]* **on the web.**) colocar un anuncio personal (en *[1]* el periódico. / *[2]* la red.) **want ~** anuncio clasificado **I read your ad** *(1)* **in the paper.** / *(2)* **in a magazine.** / *(3)* **on the Internet.** Leí *su* (*Fam: tu*) anuncio en *(1)* el periódico. / *(2)* una revista. / *(3)* Internet. **Your ad was very interesting.** *Su* (*Fam: Tu*) anuncio era muy interesante.

Adam's apple *n* nuez *f* de Adán

adapter *n* adaptador *m* **I need an adapter for my** *(item)*. Necesito un adaptador para mi ___.

add *vt* agregar **Add it to** *(1)* **my** / *(2)* **our (room) bill.** *Agréguelo* (*Fam: Agrégalo*) a *(1)* mi / *(2)* nuestra cuenta (de la habitación).

addicted *pp* adicto *m*, -ta *f* **I'm completely addicted to you.** Soy adicto a ti por completo.

addition *n* además **in ~ to** además de **In addition, ...** Además, ...

address *n* domicilio *m* ; dirección *f* **business~** dirección comercial **complete ~** dirección completa **correct ~** dirección correcta **e-mail ~** dirección electrónica **father's ~** domicilio del padre *(1,2)* **friend's ~** domicilio *(1)* del amigo *m* / *(2)* de la amiga *f* **home ~** domicilio personal **hotel ~** dirección del hotel **Internet ~** dirección de Internet **mailing ~** dirección postal **mother's ~** domicilio de la madre **my ~** mi domicilio **new ~** domicilio nuevo **office ~** dirección de la oficina **old ~** domicilio viejo **our ~** nuestro domicilio

---

Time expressions are given on page 413.

parents' ~ domicilio de los padres **permanent** ~ domicilio permanent **return** ~ domicilio del remitente **right** ~ domicilio correcto **temporary** domicilio temporal **work** ~ dirección del trabajo **wrong** ~ dirección equivocada **your** ~ *su (Fam: tu)* dirección **What's your address?** ¿Cual e *su (Fam: tu)* dirección? **My (new) address is** *(address)*. Mi (nuev. dirección es ___. **Please write (down) your address for me.** Por fav. anóteme *su (Fam: anótame tu)* **dirección. Let me write down** *(1)* **my /** *(. **your address.** Déjame anotar *(1)* mi / *(2)* su *(Fam: tu)* dirección. **Write** me **at this address.** Escríbeme a esta dirección. **I** *(1)* **forgot /** *(2)* **lost you address.** *(1)* Olvidé / *(2)* perdí *su (Fam: tu)* dirección.

adjacent *adj* adyacente *m&f* **It's adjacent to** *(what)*. Es adyacente a ___.

adjoining *adj* colindante *m&f* ~ **room** habitación colindante

administration *n* administración *f* **I work in administration.** Trabajo e la administración.

administrative *adj* administrativo *m*, -va *f* **I do administrative work.** Y hago trabajo administrativo.

admiration *n* admiración *f* **I have a lot of admiration for you.** Tengo much admiración por *usted (Fam: ti)*.

admire *vt* admirar **I admire** *(1,2)* **you.** *(1)* Lo *m* / *(2)* La *f (Fam: Te)* admir. **I admire many things about you.** Admiro muchas cosas de *usted (Fam ti)*.

admirer *n* admirador *m*, -ra *f* **You have a new admirer – me.** *Usted tien* *(Fam: Tienes)* un nuevo admirador, yo.

admit *vt* aceptar **C'mon, admit it – you're crazy about me.** Vamos, acéptal. estás loca por mí.

adopt *vt* adoptar *(1)* **I /** *(2)* **We plan to adopt a child (here).** *(1)* Planeo / *(2* Planeamos adoptar un niño (aquí). **I was adopted (when I was** *[age]***).** M adoptaron (cuando tenía ___ años).

adoption *n* adopción *f* **What can you tell** *(1)* **me /** *(2)* **us about adoptio** **(over here)?** ¿Qué *puede usted (Fam: puedes)* *(1)* decirme / *(2)* decirno. acerca de la adopción (en este lugar)?

adorable *adj* adorable *m&f* **You are (absolutely) adorable.** Tú eres (com. pletamente) adorable.

adore *vt* adorar **I adore** *(1)* **you. /** *(2)* **everything about you.** *(1)* Te adoro / *(2)* Adoro todo lo tuyo.

adult *adj* adulto *m*, -ta *f* ~ **movie** película *f* para adultos ~ **video** video *m* para adultos

adult *n* adulto *m*, -ta *f* **It's for adults only.** Es sólo para adultos. **Two adult** **and one child, please.** Dos adultos y un menor, por favor.

advantage *n* ventaja *f* **I would never try to take advantage of you.** Nunc.

Spanish "qu" is pronounced like "k".

intentaría sacar ventaja de *usted (Fam: ti)*.

dventure *n* aventura *f* **Life is boring without a little adventure, don't you think?** La vida sin un poco de aventura es aburrida, *¿no cree usted (Fam: crees)?* **I like adventure** *(1)* **movies.** / *(2)* **novels.** / *(3)* **stories.** Me gustan las *(1)* películas / *(2)* novelas / *(3)* historias de aventuras.

dventurous *adj* audaz *m&f*, aventurero *m*, -ra *f* **You're an adventurous soul.** Usted es (*Fam: Tú eres*) un espíritu audaz.

dverb *n* adverbio *m*

dvertise *vt & vi* anunciar

dvertisement *n* anuncio *m* publicitario *(See phrases under* **ad***)*

dvertising *n* publicidad *f* **I work in advertising.** Trabajo en publicidad.

dvice *n* consejo *m* *(1)* **I** / *(2)* **We need your advice.** *(1)* Necesito / *(2)* Necesitamos *su (Fam: tu)* consejo. **May I give you some advice?** ¿Puedo *darle (Fam: darte)* un consejo? **Thank you for the advice.** Gracias por el consejo.

dvise *vt* aconsejar **What would you advise?** ¿Qué *aconsejaría usted (Fam: aconsejarías)?* **I advise you...** *Le (Fam: Te)* aconsejo…**I advise you not to** *(1)* **do it.** / *(2)* **go there.** / *(3)* **try it.** *Le (Fam: Te)* aconsejo *(1)* que no lo *haga (Fam: hagas).* / *(2)* que no *vaya (Fam: vayas).* *(3)* no intentarlo.

erobic *adj* aeróbico *m*, -ca *f* **~ dance** baile aeróbico **~ workout** ejercicio aeróbico

erobics *n* aerobics *mpl* **I do aerobics (3 or 4 times a week).** Yo hago aeróbicos (tres o cuatro veces a la semana). **I do low-impact aerobics.** Practico aeróbicos de bajo impacto.

esthetic *adj* estético *m*, -ca *f*   ★   **aesthetics** *n* estética *f*

far *adv* lejos **I** *(1)* **noticed** / *(2)* **saw you from afar.** Lo *(Fam: Te)* *(1)* observé / *(2)* ví desde lejos.

ffair *n* 1. *(matter)* asunto *m* ; 2. *(love)* aventura *f*, amorío *m* **business ~(s)** negocio(s) *m (pl)* **love ~** aventura (amorosa), amorío **I'm not interested in just an affair.** No me interesa sólo una aventura.

ffect *vt* afectar **It doesn't affect my feelings for you.** Eso no afecta lo que siento por ti.

ffection *n* afecto *m*, cariño *m* **I crave affection. (And I have so much to give.)** Anhelo cariño. (Y tengo tanto qué dar.) **I love the way you show me affection.** Me encanta la manera en que me demuestras tu cariño.

ffectionate *adj* afectuoso *f*, -sa *f*, cariñoso *m*, -sa *f* **You're very affectionate.** Eres muy cariñoso *(-sa).* **I've never known anyone as affectionate as you are.** Nunca he conocido a nadie tan cariñoso *(-sa)* como tú.

fficionado *n* aficionado *m*, -da *f*, fanático *m*, -ca *f*

ffidavit *n* declaración *f* **~ of support** declaración de sostenimiento

---

Words in parentheses (not italicized) are optional.

afford *vt* darse el lujo *(1)* **I** / *(2)* **We can't afford it.** *(1)* No puedo… / *(2)* No podemos… darnos ese lujo. **I'm not sure I can afford it.** No estoy seguro de poder darme ese lujo.

afraid *adj:* **be ~** tener miedo **Are you afraid?** ¿Tiene (*Fam: ¿Tienes*) miedo? **I'm (not) afraid.** (No) Tengo miedo. **What are you afraid of?** ¿De qué tiene (*Fam: tienes*) miedo? **Don't be afraid.** No *tenga (Fam: tengas)* miedo.

after *prep* después **~ all** después de todo **day ~ day** día tras día **the month ~ next** el mes que sigue después del siguiente **the week ~ next** la semana que sigue después de la siguiente **I'll meet you after you get off work.** Me reuniré *con usted (Fam: contigo)* después de que salga de *su (Fam: tu)* trabajo. **After dinner let's go dancing.** Vamos a bailar después de cenar. **After that, we visited the Aztec temples.** Después de eso, visitamos los templos aztecas. **I was named after my** *(1)* **grandfather.** / *(2)* **grandmother.** Me pusieron el nombre de mi *(1)* abuelo. / *(2)* abuela. **It's ten minutes after six.** Son las seis y diez. **You came after all!** ¡Viniste después de todo! *(1)* **I** / *(2)* **We decided to come after all.** *(1)* Decidí / *(2)* Decidimos venir después de todo.

afternoon *n* tarde *f* **every ~** todas las tardes **in the ~** en la tarde **Saturday ~** sábado en la tarde **this ~** esta tarde **tomorrow ~** mañana en la tarde **yesterday ~** ayer en la tarde **Good afternoon!** ¡Buenas tardes!

afterward(s) *adv* después **Afterwards, we can have dinner (at the** *[restaurant]***).** Después, podemos cenar (en ___).

again *adv* de nuevo, otra vez

against *prep* contra **The two of us will play against you two.** Nosotros dos jugaremos contra ustedes dos. *(1)* **I** / *(2)* **We don't want to do anything against the law.** *(1)* No quiero… / *(2)* No queremos… hacer nada ilegal. **Why are you against the idea?** ¿Por qué *está usted (Fam: estás)* en contra de esa idea?

age *n* edad *f* **What's your age?** ¿Qué edad *tiene usted (Fam: tienes)*? **You look (much) younger than your age.** *Usted se ve (Fam: Te ves)* (mucho) más joven que la edad que *tiene (Fam: tienes).* *(1)* **Your age...** / *(2)* **Our age difference... doesn't matter to me.** *(1)* Tu edad... / *(2)* Nuestra diferencia de edades... no me importa. **Do you know someone (around) my age?** ¿*Conoce usted (Fam: ¿Conoces)* a alguien que sea (más o menos) de mi edad? **You have a beauty that age can never diminish.** *Usted tiene (Fam: Tienes)* una belleza que la edad no puede deslucir.

agency *n* agencia *f* **introduction ~** agencia de presentaciones **travel ~** agencia de viajes

agenda *n* orden *m* del día **What's our agenda for today?** ¿Cuál es el

---

A single Spanish "r" should be lightly trilled;
double "r" ("rr") should be strongly trilled.

orden del día para hoy?

agent *n* agente *m&f* **real estate** ~ agente de bienes raíces **travel** ~ agente de viajes **You can be my publicity agent.** *Usted puede (Fam: Tú puedes)* ser mi agente publicitario.

aggressive *adj* agresivo *m*, -va *f*

agile *adj* ágil *m&f* **You're as agile as a cat.** Eres tan ágil como un gato.

ago *adj* hace *m&f* **How long ago did you come here?** ¿Hace cuánto tiempo *llegó usted (Fam: llegaste)* **aquí? I arrived here three weeks ago.** Llegué aquí hace tres semanas. **That was a long time ago.** Eso fue hace mucho tiempo.

agree *vi* estar de acuerdo **Do you agree?** ¿Está usted *(Fam: ¿Estás)* de acuerdo? **I (don't) agree.** (No) Estoy de acuerdo. **I agreed.** Yo estuve de acuerdo. **Did** *(1)* **he /** *(2)* **she agree (to it)?** ¿Estuvo *(1)* él / *(2)* ella de acuerdo (con eso)? *(1)* **He /** *(2)* **She agreed.** *(1)* Él / *(2)* Ella estuvo de acuerdo. **Did** *(1)* **they /** *(2)* **you agree (to it)?** ¿Estuvieron *(1)* ellos / *(2)* ustedes de acuerdo (con eso)? *(1)* **We /** *(2)* **They agreed.** *(1)* Nosotros / *(2)* Ellos estuvieron de acuerdo.

agreeable *adj* agradable *m&f*

ahead *adv* 1. *(in front)* adelante; 2. *(winning)* ganando **You go ahead.** *Adelántese (Fam: Adelántate).* **Go ahead.** *(=Do it.)* Adelante. **Who's ahead?** *(game)* ¿Quién va ganando? *(1)* **I'm /** *(2)* **He's /** *(3)* **She's /** *(4)* **We're /** *(5)* **You're /** *(6)* **They're ahead.** *(game)* *(1)* Yo voy… / *(2)* Él / *(3)* Ella va… / *(4)* Nosotros vamos… / *(5)* Ustedes / *(6)* Ellos van… ganando.

aid *n* 1. *(assistance)* ayuda *f*, auxilio *m*; 2. *(device)* aparato *m* **first** ~ primeros auxilios **first** ~ **kit** equipo *m* de primeros auxilios **hearing** ~ aparato *m* de audición **I wear a hearing aid.** Yo uso un aparato de audición.

air *n* aire *m* **fresh** ~ aire fresco **Let's get some fresh air.** Vamos a tomar un poco de aire fresco. **The air is really nice, isn't it?** El aire está de verdad agradable ¿no?

air force *n* fuerza *f* aérea **I'm in the Air Force.** Estoy en la fuerza aérea. **I'm a** *(1)* **Sergeant /** *(2)* **Lieutenant /** *(3)* *(rank)* **in the Air Force.** Soy *(1)* sargento / *(2)* teniente / *(3)* ___ de la fuerza aérea. **I served four years in the Air Force.** Presté servicios en la fuerza aérea por cuatro años.

air-conditioned *adj* con aire acondicionado *(1)* **I /** *(2)* **We want an air-conditioned room.** *(1)* Quiero… / *(2)* Queremos… una habitación con aire acondicionado.

air conditioning *n* aire *m* acondicionado **Does the room have air conditioning?** ¿Tiene aire acondicionado la habitación?

airmail *n* correo *m* aéreo **by** ~ por correo aéreo

airplane *n* avión *m* *(See terms under* **plane***)*

Familiar "tu" forms in parentheses can replace italicized polite forms.

airport *n* aeropuerto *m (1)* **I'll /** *(2)* **We'll meet** *(3,4)* **you at the airport.** *(1)* Yo *(3)* lo *m* / *(4)* la *f (Fam: te)* veré… / *(2)* Nosotros *(3)* lo *m* / *(4)* la *f (Fam: te)* veremos… en el aeropuerto. **Can you come with** *(1)* **me /** *(2)* **us to the airport?** *¿Puede usted (Fam: ¿Puedes)* venir *(1)* conmigo / *(2)* con nosotros al aeropuerto? *(1)* **I'll /** *(2)* **We'll go with you to the airport.** *(1)* Yo iré… / *(2)* Nosotros iremos… *con usted (Fam: contigo)* al aeropuerto. *(1)* **I'll /** *(2)* **We'll take you to the airport.** *(1)* Yo *(3)* lo *m* / *(4)* la *f (Fam: te)* llevo… / *(2)* Nosotros *(3)* lo *m* / *(4)* la *f (Fam: te)* llevamos… al aeropuerto. *(1)* **I'll /** *(2)* **We'll take** *(3)* **a bus /** *(4)* **a taxi /** *(5)* **the train to the airport.** *(1)* Yo tomaré… / *(2)* Nosotros tomaremos… *(3)* un camión / *(4)* un taxi / *(5)* el tren al aeropuerto.

alarm *n* alarma *f* **False alarm!** ¡Falsa alarma!

alarmed *pp* alarmado *m,* -da *f* **Don't be alarmed.** No *se alarme (Fam: te alarmes).*

album *n* álbum *m* **Could I look at your (photo) album?** ¿Podría ver *su (Fam: tu)* álbum (de fotos)?

alcohol *n* alcohol *m (1)* **I /** *(2)* **We don't drink alcohol.** *(1)* Yo no tomo… / *(2)* Nosotros no tomamos… alcohol. **I can't drink any alcohol. Doctor's orders.** No puedo tomar nada de alcohol. Órdenes del doctor. **No alcohol for me. I'm driving.** Nada de alcohol para mí. Vengo manejando.

alcoholic *adj* alcohólico *m,* -ca *f* ★ *n* alcohólico *m,* -ca *f*

alibi *n* coartada *f* **No alibis!** ¡Sin coartadas!

alike *adj* parecido *m,* -da *f,* similar *m&f* **You and I are very much alike.** *Usted (Fam: Tú)* y yo somos muy parecidos. **You two are just alike. (Both - imps!)** Ustedes dos se parecen. (¡Ambas traviesas!) **You** *(1)* **men /** *(2)* **women are all alike.** *(1)* Ustedes los hombres son todos iguales. / *(2)* Ustedes las mujeres son todas iguales.

alive *adj* vivo *m,* -va *f* **You make me feel (vividly) alive.** Usted me hace *(Fam: Tú me haces)* sentir (intensamente) vivo *(-va).* **Hey, is anybody alive here?** ¡Hola! ¿Hay alguien por aquí?

all *adj* todo *m,* -da *f* ~ **day** todo el día ~ **month** todo el mes ~ **night** toda la noche ~ **the time** todo el tiempo ~ **week** toda la semana ~ **year** todo el año **All my love is yours.** Todo mi amor es tuyo.

all *pron s* todo *m,* -da *f (pl:* todos *m,* -das *f)* ~ **of us** todos nosotros **Is that all?** ¿Eso es todo? **That's (not) all.** Eso (no) es todo. **Tell me all about it.** *Cuéntemelo (Fam: Cuéntamelo)* todo.

all *adv* totalmente, completamente **Are you all alone?** ¿Está usted *(Fam: Estás)* totalmente solo *(-la)*? **I'm all worn out.** Estoy completamente agotado *(-da).*

allergic *adj* alérgico *m,* -ca *f* **I'm allergic to** *(1)* **cats. /** *(2)* **dogs. /** *(3)* **smoke.**

Spanish "ll" is pronounced like "y" in "yes".

/ *(4)* **work.** Soy alérgico *(-ca) (1)* a los gatos. / *(2)* a los perros. / *(3)* al humo. / *(4)* al trabajo.

alley *n* callejón *m*; sendero *m* **bowling ~** pista *f* de bolerama **dark ~** callejón oscuro **Is there a bowling alley around here?** ¿Hay alguna pista de bolerama por aquí?

all right *(idiom)* está bien **All right!** *(Exclamation of praise or pleasure.)* ¡Qué bien! **Are you all right?** ¿Está usted (Fam: ¿Estás) bien? **I'm all right.** Estoy bien. **All right, we'll walk there.** Está bien, caminaremos hasta allá. **Is that all right (with you)?** ¿Le *(Fam: ¿Te)* parece bien *(a usted? [Fam: a ti?])*? **It's all right (with [1] me / [2] us).** Está bien (para *[1]* mí. / *[2]* nosotros.). **That's all right, don't worry about it.** Está bien, no *se (Fam: te)* preocupes por eso.

all-terrain vehicle (ATV) vehículo *m* todo terreno

alluring *adj* fascinante *m&f*, atrayente *m&f*, seductor *m*, -tora *f*

almost *adv* casi **I almost left.** Casi me voy. **It's almost time (to [1] go / [2] leave).** Ya casi es hora (de *[1]* ir / *[2]* salir).

alone *adv* a solas, solo *m*, -la *f* **Are you (here) alone?** ¿Estás solo *(-la)* (aquí)? **I'm (here) alone.** Estoy solo *(-la)* (aquí). **Do you live alone?** ¿Vive usted *(Fam: Vives)* solo *(-la)*? **I live alone.** Vivo solo *(-la)*. **I'm tired of being alone.** Estoy cansado *(-da)* de vivir solo *(-la)*. **Life is too short to spend it alone.** La vida es demasiado corta para pasarla a solas. **Leave me alone!** ¡Déjeme *(Fam: ¡Déjame)* en paz!

along *adv* acompañar, llevar consigo **Can I *(1,2)* come along?** ¿Puedo *(1)* acompañarlo *m* / *(2)* acompañarla *f (Fam: acompañarte)*? **You can come along (if you want to).** Puede *(Fam: Puedes)* acompañarme (si *usted quiere [Fam: si quieres]*). **You'd better take along a(n) *(1)* coat.** / *(2)* **sweater.** / *(3)* **umbrella.** Será mejor que *se lleve (Fam: te lleves)* un *(1)* abrigo. / *(2)* suéter. / *(3)* paraguas.

along *prep* por, a lo largo de **Let's walk along the beach.** Vamos caminando por la playa.

alphabet *n* alfabeto *m* **Please teach me how to pronounce the alphabet.** Por favor, *enséñeme (Fam: enséñame)* a pronunciar el alfabeto.

already *adv* ya **We're already acquainted.** Ya nos conocemos. **I've already *(1)* finished it.** / *(2)* **graduated (the university).** / *(3)* **read it.** / *(4)* **seen the movie.** Ya *(1)* lo terminé. / *(2)* me gradué (de la universidad). / *(3)* lo leí. / *(4)* ví la película.

also *adv* también

altogether *adv* en conjunto, en general **How much will it cost altogether?** ¿Cuánto costará en conjunto? **Altogether it will cost *(amount)*.** En conjunto costará ___.

Common professions are listed on pages 415-416.

always *adv* siempre *(1)* **I** / *(2)* **We will always remember** *(3,4)* **you.** Siempre *(3)* lo m / *(4)* la f *(Fam: te)* *(1)* recordaré. / *(2)*) recordaremos. *(1)* **I** / *(2)* **We will always remember** *(3)* **your kindness.** / *(4)* **your wonderful hospitality.** Siempre *(1)* recordaré / *(2)* recordaremos *su (Fam: tu)* *(3)* amabilidad. / *(4)* maravillosa hospitalidad. **I feel as though I've always known** *(1,2)* **you.** Siento como si *(1)* lo m / *(2)* la f *(Fam: te)* conociera desde siempre. **I will always cherish the memory of these times together with you.** Siempre apreciaré el recuerdo de estos momentos junto a ti.

amateur *n* aficionado *m*, -da *f* **Actually, I'm not allowed to play against amateurs.** Realmente, no me permiten jugar contra aficionados. **I'm an amateur photographer.** Soy fotógrafo aficionado.

amaze *vt* asombrar **You (constantly) amaze me.** *Usted me asombra (Fam: Me asombras)* *(constantemente).*

ambition *n* ambición *f* **My ambition in life is to become** *(1)* **a cosmonaut.** / *(2)* **obscenely rich.** / *(3)* **your husband.** Mi ambición en la vida es ser *(1)* cosmonauta. / *(2)* escandalosamente rico. / *(3)* tu esposo.

ambitious *adj* ambicioso *m*, -sa *f* **You certainly are ambitious.** En verdad *es usted (Fam: eres)* ambicioso *(-sa).*

ambulance *n* ambulancia *f* **Call an ambulance.** Llama una ambulancia.

America *n* Estados Unidos *f* **from** ~ de Estados Unidos **in** ~ en Estados Unidos **to** ~ hacia Estados Unidos

American *adj* norteamericano *m*, -na *f* ★ *n* norteamericano *m*, -na *f*

among(st) *prep* entre **You're among friends.** *Usted está (Fam: Estás)* entre amigos *(-gas).* **Amongst all those girls, you're (by far) the prettiest.** De entre todas esas muchachas, *usted es (Fam: tú eres)* la más bonita (por mucho).

amorous *adj* apasionado *m*, -da *f* **You're too amorous.** Eres demasiado apasionado *(-da).*

amount *n* cantidad *f* **huge** ~ muchísimo *m*, -ma *f* *(of what = + noun)*

amuse *vt* divertir **You (really) amuse me.** *Usted (Fam: Tú)* (de verdad) me *divierte (Fam: diviertes).*

amused *pp* divertido *m*, -da *f* **I'm not amused.** No estoy divertido *(-da).*

amusing *adj* divertido *m*, -da *f* *(1,2)* **That's very amusing.** *(1)* Eso es muy divertido *m*. / *(2)* Esa es muy divertida *f*.

angel *n* ángel *m* **beautiful** ~ ángel hermoso **little** ~ angelito *m* **sweet** ~ ángel dulce **You are my special angel.** Tú eres mi ángel especial. **You have the face of an angel.** *Usted tiene (Fam: Tienes)* cara de ángel.

angelic *adj* angelical *m&f*

angry *adj* enojado *m*, -da *f* **Are you angry?** ¿Estás enojado *(-da)*? **I'm (not) angry.** (No) Estoy enojado *(-da).* **I hope you're not angry.** Espero que no

---

Spanish "y" is "ee" when alone or at the end of words.

estés enojado *(-da)*. **Please don't get angry.** Por favor, no te enojes. **Why are you angry?** ¿Por qué estás enojado *(-da)*? **That makes me angry.** Eso me hace enojar.

animal *n* animal *m* **stuffed ~** animal de peluche

announcement *n* anuncio *m* **What was that announcement?** ¿Qué decía ese anuncio?

another *adj & pron* otro *m*, -ra *f* **Perhaps another time.** Quizás en otra ocasión. **Would you care for another one?** *(drink)* ¿Le gustaría a usted *(Fam: Te gustaría)* tomar otra? **There's another** *(1)* **bus /** *(2)* **flight /** *(3)* **train at** *(time)*. Hay otro *(1)* camión / *(2)* vuelo / *(3)* tren a las ___. **Please give me another chance.** Por favor, dame otra oportunidad.

answer *vt* contestar, responder **Answer me.** Contéstame. **I can't answer (the question).** No puedo contestar (la pregunta).

answer *n* respuesta *f* **What's the answer?** ¿Cuál es la respuesta?

ant(s) *n (pl)* hormiga(s) *f (pl)* **There are too many ants around here.** Hay demasiadas hormigas por aquí.

antique *n* antigüedad *f (1)* **I'm /** *(2)* **We're interested in antiques.** *(1)* Me / *(2)* Nos interesan las antigüedades.

antiquing *n* dar apariencia de antigüedad a objetos *(1)* **I /** *(2)* **We enjoy antiquing.** *(1)* Me / *(2)* Nos gusta dar apariencia de antigüedad a objetos.

anxious *adj* 1. *(worried)* preocupado *m*, -da *f* ; 2. *(eager)* ansioso *m*, -sa *f* **You must be very anxious (about** *[1]* **her /** *[2]* **him /** *[3]* **it /** *[4]* **them).** *Usted debe (Fam: Tú debes)* estar muy preocupado *(-da)* (por *[1]* ella / *[2]* él / *[3]* eso / *[4]* ellos). *(1)* **I'm /** *(2)* **We're anxious to meet** *(3)* **her. /** *(4)* **him. /** *(5)* **them.** *(1)* Estoy ansioso *(-sa)*... / *(2)* Estamos ansiosos... por *(1)* conocerla. / *(2)* conocerlo. / *(3)* conocerlos.

any *adj & pron* un, uno(s) *m (pl)*, una(s) *f (pl)*, alguno(s) *m (pl)*, -na(s) *f (pl)*, algo de **Do you have any** *(1)* **playing cards? /** *(2)* **coins? /** *(3)* **matches? /** *(4)* **money? /** *(5)* **stamps? /** *(6)* **tissues?** ¿Tiene usted *(Fam: ¿Tienes)* (1) algunas cartas para jugar? / *(2)* unas monedas? / *(3)* unos cerillos? / *(4)* algo de dinero? / *(5)* unas estampillas? / *(6)* unos pañuelos de papel? **I'm sorry, I don't have any.** Lo lamento, no tengo. **Do any of you speak English?** ¿Alguien de ustedes habla inglés?

anybody *pron* alguien, cualquiera *(See expressions under* **anyone***)*

anyhow *adv* de cualquier modo *(See expressions under* **anyway***)*

anymore *adv* no más *(1)* **I /** *(2)* **We don't need it anymore.** *(1)* No lo necesito... / *(2)* No lo necesitamos... más.

anyone *pron (questions)* alguien; *(negative sentences)* nadie **Are you attached to anyone?** ¿ Tiene usted a alguien? **I'm not attached to anyone.** No tengo a nadie. **There could never be anyone else for me except you.**

Feminine forms of words in phrases
are usually given in parentheses (italicized).

Nunca podría haber para mí nadie más que tú. **Please don't tell anyone (about this).** Por favor, no le digas a nadie (de esto). **I promise I won't tell anyone.** Te prometo que no le diré a nadie.

anyplace *adv* en cualquier lugar *(See expressions under* **anywhere***)*

anything *pron (questions)* algo; *(negative sentences)* nada; *(whatever)* lo que sea; cualquiera **Do you want anything (to [1] drink / [2] eat)?** *¿Quiere usted (Fam: ¿Quieres)* algo *([1]* para tomar / *[2]* de comer)? **I don't want anything.** No quiero nada. **You can tell me anything (and I'll understand).** *Puede usted (Fam: Puedes)* decirme lo que sea (y yo lo entenderé). **I love you more than anything (in this whole world).** Te amo más que nada (en todo este mundo). **Anything is** *(1)* **okay.** / *(2)* **fine with me.** Lo que sea está *(1)* bien. / *(2)* bien para mí. **Is there anything I can do?** Hay algo que pueda hacer? **I didn't do anything.** Yo no hice nada.

anytime *adv* en cualquier momento, a cualquier hora **Call me anytime.** Llámame a cualquier hora.

anyway *adv* de cualquier manera, en todo caso, de todos modos **I don't feel like going anywhere. It's raining, anyway.** No tengo ganas de ir a ninguna parte. De todos modos, está lloviendo. **Anyway, to make a long story short, ...** En todo caso, para decirlo en pocas palabras, ... **Where did you get that, anyway?** *¿A todo esto: dónde consiguió usted (Fam: conseguiste)* eso?

anywhere *adv (questions)* algún lugar; *(negative sentences)* ningún lugar; *(wherever)* cualquier lugar **We can go anywhere you want.** Podemos ir a cualquier lugar que *usted quiera (Fam: quieras)*. **Is there anywhere around here where we can use a computer?** *¿Hay algún lugar por aquí donde podamos usar una computadora? **I can't find it anywhere.** No lo encuentro por ningún lugar.

apart *adv* por separado, separado **live** ~ vivir por separado **Time and distance will never keep us apart.** El tiempo y la distancia nunca podrán separarnos. **I don't want to be apart from you.** No quiero separarme de ti.

apartment *n (See also phrases under* **come** *and* **go***.)* apartamento *m,* departamento *m* **This is a** *(1)* **beautiful /** *(2)* **big /** *(3)* **nice apartment.** Este es un departamento *(1)* hermoso. / *(2)* grande. / *(3)* bonito.

apologize *vi* disculparse **I apologize for** *(1)* **what I did. /** *(2)* **what I said. /** *(3)* **being late. /** *(4)* **not calling.** Me disculpo por *(1)* lo que hice. / *(2)* lo que dije. / *(3)* llegar tarde. / *(4)* no llamar.

apology *n* disculpa *f* **Please accept my (humble) apologies.** Por favor, *acepte usted (Fam: acepta)* mis (humildes) disculpas. **I accept your apology.** Acepto *sus (Fam: tus)* disculpas.

appeal *vi* atraer **You appeal to me (in so many ways).** *Usted me atrae*

Spanish "c" before "e" and "i" is pronounced like "s".

(Fam: Me atraes) (de tantas maneras). **The idea appeals to me.** Me atrae la idea. **The idea doesn't appeal to me.** No me atrae la idea.

appetite *n* apetito *m* **Good appetite!** ¡Buen provecho!

application *n* solicitud *f* **submit an** ~ remitir una solicitud *(1)* **I** / *(2)* **You** / *(3)* **We need to fill out an application.** *(1)* Necesito... / *(2)* Usted necesita *(Fam: Necesitas)*... / *(3)* Necesitamos... llenar una solicitud.

apply for *vi* solicitar ~ **a job** solicitar un trabajo ~ **a marriage license** solicitar una licencia de matrimonio ~ **a visa** solicitar una visa ~ **admission into a university** solicitar ingreso en una universidad

appreciate *vt* apreciar **I really appreciate it.** De verdad lo aprecio. **I really appreciate** *(1)* **everything you did for me.** / *(2)* **your (kind) hospitality.** / *(3)* **your giving me a ride.** De verdad aprecio *(1)* todo lo que *usted hizo (Fam: hiciste)* por mí. / *(2)* su *(Fam: tu)* amable hospitalidad. / *(3)* que me haya *(Fam: hayas)* llevado.

appreciation *n* aprecio *m* **I want to show my appreciation.** Quiero demostrar mi aprecio. **As a small token of my appreciation, I'd like to** *(1,2)* **invite you to dinner.** Como pequeña muestra de mi aprecio, me gustaría *(1)* invitarlo *m* / *(2)* invitarla *f (Fam: invitarte)* a cenar.

approve *vi* aprobar **I hope your parents will approve of me.** Espero que tus padres me aprobarán. **I hope your** *(1)* **mother** / *(2)* **father will approve of me.** Espero que tu *(1)* madre / *(2)* padre me aprobará.

approximately *adv* aproximadamente

April *n* abril *m* **in** ~ en abril **on** ~ **first** el primero de abril

aquarium *n* acuario *m*

Aquarius *(Jan. 20 - Feb. 18)* Acuario

archery *n* tiro *m* con arco

architecture *n* arquitectura *f*

area *n* área *f* **picnic** ~ zona de picnic **safe** ~ área segura **Do you know this area?** ¿Conoce usted *(Fam: Conoces)* esta área? **I (don't) know this area (well).** (No) Conozco (bien) esta área.

argue *vi* discutir **I don't want to argue (with you).** No quiero discutir (contigo). **I don't like to argue.** No me gusta discutir. **Let's not argue.** No discutamos.

argument *n* discusión *f* **big** ~ gran discusión **get into an** ~ meterse en una discusión **small** ~ pequeña discusión **start an** ~ comenzar una discusión **I hate arguments.** Odio las discusiones. **Let's not have an argument.** No tengamos una discusión.

Aries *(Mar. 21 - Apr. 19)* Aries

arm *n* brazo *m* ~ **in** ~ del brazo **muscular** ~**s** brazos musculosos **slender** ~**s** brazos delgados **strong** ~**s** brazos fuertes **I** *(1)* **want** / *(2)* **love to hold you**

Numbers in Spanish are given on pages 411-412.

in my arms. *(1)* Quiero… / *(2)* Me encanta… tenerte en mis brazos. **I lost my arm in** *(1)* **the (Vietnam) war.** / *(2)* **an accident.** Perdí mi brazo en *(1)* la guerra (de Vietnam). / *(2)* un accidente.

army *n* ejército *m* **I'm in the Army.** Estoy en el ejército. **I'm a** *(1)* **Sergeant** / *(2)* **Lieutenant** / *(3)* *(rank)* **in the Army.** Soy *(1)* sargento / *(2)* teniente / *(3)* ____ del ejército. **I served three years in the Army.** Presté tres años de servicio en el ejército.

aroma *n* aroma *m* **intoxicating** ~ aroma embriagador **sweet** ~ aroma dulce **wonderful** ~ aroma estupendo

around *prep* alrededor de, cerca de, por **look** ~ mirar alrededor **turn** ~ voltear **Do you live around here?** *¿Vive usted (Fam: Vives)* por aquí? **Is there a** *(1)* **bank** / *(2)* **bus stop** / *(3)* **coffee shop** / *(4)* **copy shop** / *(5)* **Internet café** / *(6)* **money exchange around here?** ¿Hay *(1)* algún banco… / *(2)* alguna parada de camiones… / *(3)* algún café… / *(4)* alguna copiadora… / *(5)* algún café de Internet… / *(6)* alguna casa de cambios… por aquí? *(1)* **I** / *(2)* **We walked all around the town.** *(1)* Caminé / *(2)* Caminamos por toda la ciudad. **I looked all around.** Vi todo. **I'd really like to travel around together with you.** De verdad me gustaría viajar contigo. **I'd love it if you would show me around (the town).** Me encantaría que me *mostrara (Fam: mostraras)* los alrededores (la ciudad). **There's no one around (except you and I).** No hay nadie a la redonda (excepto tú y yo). **It costs around 50 pesos.** Cuesta unos cincuenta pesos.

arouse *vt* provocar **You don't know how you arouse me.** No sabes cuánto me provocas.

arrangement *n* arreglo *m* **That sounds like a good arrangement.** Eso parece un buen arreglo. **Can you make the arrangements?** *¿Puede usted (Fam: Puedes)* hacer los arreglos? *(1)* **I'll** / *(2)* **We'll make…** / *(3)* **I** / *(4)* **We made… (all) the arrangements**. *(1)* Yo haré… / *(2)* Nosotros haremos… / *(3)* Yo hice… / *(4)* Nosotros hicimos... (todos) los arreglos.

arrive *vi* llegar **What time will the** *(1)* **bus** / *(2)* **train** / *(3)* **flight arrive?** ¿A qué hora llegará el *(1)* camión? / *(2)* tren? / *(3)* vuelo? **The** *(1)* **bus** / *(2)* **train** / *(3)* **flight will arrive at** *(time)*. El *(1)* camión / *(2)* tren / *(3)* vuelo llegará a las ____. **When did you arrive?** ¿Cuándo *llegó usted (Fam: llegaste)*? *(1)* **I** / *(2)* **We arrived** *(3)* **today.** / *(4)* **yesterday.** / *(5)* **two days ago.** / *(6)* **last week.** *(1)* Llegué / *(2)* Llegamos *(3)* hoy. / *(4)* ayer. / *(5)* hace dos días. / *(6)* la semana pasada.

art *n* arte *m* **fine** ~**s** bellas artes **martial** ~**s** artes marciales **Are you interested in art?** *¿Le interesa a usted (Fam: Te interesa)* el arte? **What kind of art do you like?** ¿Qué tipo de arte *le (Fam: te)* gusta? **I'm interested in** *(1)* **Egyptian** / *(2)* **medieval** / *(3)* **Renaissance** / *(4)* **modern** / *(5)* *(type)*

Spanish "h" is always silent.

art. Me interesa el arte *(1)* egipcio. / *(2)* medieval. / *(3)* renacentista. / *(4)* moderno. / ___. *(Names of most types of art are close to English.)* **I have a passion for art and music.** Soy apasionado del arte y la música.

articulate *adj* elocuente *m&f*

artist *n* artista *m&f* con ~ timador *m*, -dora *f* **I'm an artist.** Soy artista. **Who's your favorite artist?** ¿Quién es *su (Fam: tu)* artista favorito? **My favorite artist is** *(name)*. Mi artista favorito es ___.

artistic *adj* artístico *m*, -ca *f* **You're very artistic.** *Usted es (Fam: Eres)* muy artístico *(-ca)*.

as *conj* tan; como **You're as cute as can be.** Eres lo más lindo *(-da)* que hay. **I've never known anyone as nice as you.** Nunca conocí a nadie tan bueno *(-na)* como usted *(Fam: tú)*. **As you know, I have to return soon.** Como *usted sabe (Fam: tú sabes)*, tengo que regresar pronto.

ashamed *adj* avergonzado *m*, -da *f* **I'm (really) ashamed (to tell you).** (De verdad) Me avergüenza (decirte). **You should be ashamed.** Debiera darte vergüenza.

ashore *adv (direction)* a tierra; *(location)* en tierra **Are you going ashore?** ¿*Va usted (Fam: ¿Vas)* a bajar a tierra? *(1)* **I'm** / *(2)* **We're going ashore.** *(1)* Voy / *(2)* Vamos a bajar a tierra. **Let's go ashore.** Bajemos a tierra.

ask *vt* preguntar **I'll go ask.** Iré a preguntar. **Could you ask them for me?** ¿*Podría usted (Fam: Podrías)* preguntarles por mí? **May I ask you a question?** ¿Puedo *hacerle (Fam: hacerte)* una pregunta? **Feel free to ask me anything.** *Siéntase usted (Fam: Siéntete)* en libertad de preguntarme lo que sea.

★ **ask for** *idiom* pedir **I'll go ask for** *(1)* **one.** / *(2)* **some.** Voy a pedir *(1)* uno. / *(2)* unos.

asleep *adj* dormido *m*, -da *f* **be ~** estar dormido *(-da)* **fall ~** dormirse **He's asleep.** Él está dormido. **She's asleep.** Ella está dormida. *(1,2)* **They're asleep.** *(1) (M's & both:)* Ellos están dormidos. / *(2) (F's:)* Ellas están dormidas. **Are you asleep?** ¿Estás dormido *(-da)*? **I fell asleep.** Me quedé dormido *(-da)*.

aspirin *n* aspirina *f*

assure *vt* asegurar **I assure you.** Le *(Fam: Te)* lo aseguro.

asthma *n* asma *f* **I have asthma.** Tengo asma.

astounded *adj* asombrado *m*, -da *f* **I'm (truly) astounded.** Estoy (de verdad) asombrado *(-da)*.

astrology *n* astrología *f* **Do you believe in astrology?** ¿Cree usted *(Fam: ¿Crees)* en la astrología? **I (don't) believe in astrology.** (No) Creo en la astrología.

at all *adv* en absoluto, de ninguna manera, en modo alguno, del todo **I don't**

Questions about the metric system? See page 417.

mind at all. No me importa en absoluto. **There are no seats left at all.** Ya no hay asientos del todo. **If at all possible, I'll be there.** Si hay algún modo, ahí estaré.

athlete *n* atleta *m&f* **armchair** ~ atleta de sofá, atleta de sillón

athletic *adj* atlético *m*, -ca *f* **You're very athletic.** *Usted es (Fam: Eres)* muy atlético *(-ca)*.

athletics *n, pl* atletismo *m*

atmosphere *n* atmósfera *f*, ambiente, *m* **cozy** ~ ambiente acogedor **friendly** ~ atmósfera amigable **intimate** ~ atmósfera íntima **lively** ~ ambiente animado **pleasant** ~ atmósfera agradable **romantic** ~ ambiente romántico

attach *vt (e-mail)* adjuntar

attached *pp* casado *m*, -da *f* ; unido *m*, -da *f* **May I ask you a personal question? Are you attached?** ¿Puedo *hacerle (Fam: hacerte)* una pregunta personal? ¿Es usted casado *(-da)*?

attachment *n (e-mail)* archivo *m* adjunto

attention *n* atención *f* **attract (my)** ~ atraer (mi) atención **pay** ~ poner atención **I'm glad I caught your attention.** Me alegra captar *su (Fam: tu)* atención.

attire *n* atuendo *m* **formal** ~ atuendo formal

attitude *n* actitud *f* **bad** ~ mala actitud **good** ~ buena actitud **laid-back** ~ actitud tranquila y relajada **negative** ~ actitud negativa **philosophical** ~ actitud filosófica **positive (mental)** ~ actitud (mental) positiva

attract *vt* atraer **What first attracted me to you was your** *(1)* **beautiful / eyes.** / *(2)* **bright smile.** Lo que primero me atrajo de ti *(1)* fueron tus ojos hermosos. / *(2)* fue tu radiante sonrisa.

attraction *n* atracción *f* **instant** ~ atracción instantánea **mutual** ~ atracción mutua **physical** ~ atracción física **powerful** ~ atracción poderosa **strange** ~ atracción extraña **strong** ~ atracción fuerte **I've never felt such a(n) (powerful) attraction to anyone.** Con nadie he sentido (tan poderosa) atracción.

attractive *adj* atractivo *m*, -va *f* **You're very attractive.** *Usted es (Fam: eres)* muy atractivo *(-va)*. **You make me feel attractive.** *Usted me hace (Fam: Tú me haces)* sentir atractiva *f*.

attribute *n* atributo *m* **You have so many attributes that I admire.** *Usted tiene (Fam: Tienes)* tantos atributos que admiro.

ATV *abbrev* = **all-terrain vehicle** vehículo *m* todo terreno

audacious *adj* audaz *m&f*

audacity *n* audacia *f* **You really have a lot of audacity.** De verdad tienes mucha audacia.

August *n* agosto *m* **in** ~ en agosto **on** ~ **first** el primero de agosto

---

The letter "ñ" sounds like the "ny" in "canyon".

aunt *n* tía *f*

Australian *adj* australiano *m*, -na *f*; *n* australiano *m*, -na *f*

author *n* escritor *m*, -tora *f*, autor *m*, -tora *f*

automatic *adj* automático *m*, -ca *f*

automatically *adv* automáticamente

autumn *n* otoño *m* **in the** ~ en el otoño **last** ~ el otoño pasado **next** ~ el otoño próximo **Autumn is the best time to** *(1)* **come here.** / *(2)* **travel.** El otoño es la mejor época para *(1)* venir aquí. / *(2)* viajar.

available *adj* disponible *m&f* **Is there a room available?** ¿Hay algún cuarto disponible? **Nothing is available.** No hay nada disponible.

avenue *n* avenida *f*

average *adj* medio *m*, -dia *f*, promedio *m&f*; *n* promedio *m* **on the** ~ en promedio

avoid *vt* evitar

away *adj* lejos de *m&f*, fuera *m&f* **How long will you be away?** ¿Cuánto tiempo *va usted (Fam: vas)* a estar fuera? *(1)* **I'll** / *(2)* **We'll be away for** *(amount of time)*. *(1)* Estaré / *(2)* Estaremos fuera durante ___. **I can't bear the thought of being away from you.** No puedo soportar la idea de estar lejos de ti.

away *adv* lejos *(1,2)* **Go away!** *(1)* ¡Aléjate! / *(2)* ¡Vete! **I don't want you to** *(1,2)* **go away.** No quiero que te *(1)* alejes. / *(2)* vayas.

awesome *adj* formidable *m & f*, espléndido *m*, -da *f* **totally** ~ completamente formidable **It's awesome!** ¡Es formidable!

awful *adj* malo *m*, -la *f*, horrible *m&f*, desastroso *m* , -sa *f*, atroz *m&f*

awfully *adv* 1. *(very)* muy; 2. *(terribly)* terriblemente

awhile *adv* por un momento

awkward *adj* torpe *m&f*

ax(e) *n* hacha *f*

Aztec *adj* azteca *m&f*

B

baby *n* bebé *m&f* ~ **bottle** biberón *m* ~ **carriage** carriola *f* ~ **crib** cuna *f*
~ **food** comida *f* para bebés ~ **seat** asiento *m* para bebé ~ **stroller** carriola
f **Don't be such a baby!** ¡No seas niño *(-ña)*!
babysit *vi* cuidar niños **Could you babysit for us (tonight)?** Podría cuidarnos
al niño (esta noche)? **Do you know someone who could babysit for us?**
Conoce usted a alguien que pudiera cuidarnos al niño?
babysitter *n* baby sitter *m&f*
bachelor *n* soltero *m*
bachelorette *n* muchacha *f* soltera
back *n* 1. *(body part)* espalda *f* ; 2. *(rear)* trasero *m* **little** ~ espalda chica
smooth ~ espalda suave **Let me rub your back.** Déjame frotarte la espalda.
back *adv* 1. *(backward)* hacia atrás; 2. *(returned)* devuelto **get** ~ *(return
home)* regresar, volver a casa **give** ~ devolver *(una cosa)* **go** ~ regresar,
volver **Step back (a little).** Retroceder (un poco). **Please give it back.** Por
favor, regrésalo. **When do you have to go back?** ¿Cuándo *tiene usted*
(Fam: tienes) que regresar? **When will** *(1)* **he** / *(2)* **she be back?** ¿Cuándo
va a regresar *(1)* él? / *(2)* ella? *(1)* **I'll** / *(2)* **We'll be back** *(3)* **by** *(time).* /
(4) **soon.** *(1)* Regreso / *(2)* Regresamos *(3)* a las ___. / *(4)* pronto. *(1)* **I** /
(2) **We have to go back at** *(time).* *(1)* Tengo que... / *(2)* Tenemos que...
regresar a las ___. **When I get back, I'll** *(1)* **call** / *(2)* **e-mail** / *(3)* **write
you.** Cuando regrese, *le (Fam. te)* *(1)* llamo. / *(2)* mando un correo
electrónico. / *(3)* escribo. **When we get back, we'll** *(1)* **call** / *(2)* **e-mail** /
(3) **write you.** Cuando regresemos, *le (Fam. te)* *(1)* llamamos. / *(2)*
mandamos un correo electrónico. / *(3)* escribimos.
backgammon *n* backgammon *m*
backpack *n* mochila *f*
backpacking *n* excursionismo *m* de mochila **go** ~ viajar con mochila

Spanish "o" is pronounced like "o" in "note".

backward(s) *adv* 1. *(rearward)* hacia atrás; 2. *(back to front)* al revés
  You've got it on backwards. Lo *tiene usted (Fam: tienes)* puesto al
  revés.
bad *adj* mal *m&f*, malo *m*, -la *f* ~ **cold** fuerte resfriado ~ **headache** fuerte
  dolor de cabeza ~ **idea** mala idea **That's too bad.** Qué lástima. **Not bad!**
  ¡No está mal! **Don't feel bad.** No te sientas mal. **I feel bad about it.** Me
  siento mal por eso.
badly *adv* mal, malamente **I played badly.** Jugué mal. **I want badly to go.**
  Tengo muchas ganas de ir.
badminton *n* badminton *m (See phrases under* **like, love** *and* **play.**)
bag *n* 1. *(suitcase)* maleta *f*; 2. *(sack)* bolsa *f*, costal *m* ; 3. *(purse)* bolsa *f*
  overnight ~ bolsa de viaje, bolsa de fin de semana **paper** ~ bolsa de papel
  plastic ~ bolsa plastica **shoulder** ~ bolsa *f* **sleeping** ~ bolsa para dormir
  How many bags do you have? *(suitcases)* ¿Cuántas maletas *tiene usted
  (Fam: tienes)*? **Where are your bags?** ¿Dónde están *sus (Fam: tus)*
  maletas? **Can I help you carry your bag?** *(suitcase)* ¿Puedo *ayudarle
  (Fam: ayudarte)* a llevar *su (Fam: tu)* maleta?
baggage *n* equipaje *m*
bait *n* carnada *f*
bakery *n* panadería *f*
balcony *n* balcón *m*
bald *adj* pelón *m*, -ona *f*, calvo *m*, -va *f*
ball *n* 1. *(for games)* bola *f*, pelota *f*; 2. *(dance)* baile *m* **have a** ~ divertirse
  de lo lindo *(1,2)* **You're on the ball.** *(1)* Tú eres capaz. / *(2)* Tú estás en lo
  tuyo. *(1)* **I'd** / *(2)* **We'd** / *(3)* **You'd better get on the ball.** Será mejor que
  (1) me ponga / *(2)* nos pongamos / *(3)* se pongan ...a darle.
ballad *n* balada *f*
ballet *n* ballet *m (See phrases under* **go, like** *and* **love.**) **watch** ~ ver el ballet
balloon *n* 1. *(toy)* globo *m* ; 2. *(hot-air)* globo (aerostático) *m*, aeróstato *m*
  hot-air ~ globo (aerostático) de aire caliente
ballooning *n* aerostación *f* **go** ~ ir a pasear en globo
band *n* 1. *(ribbon; tie)* cinta *f*; 2. *(ring)* anillo *m* ; 3. *(orchestra)* banda *f*
bangs *n, pl (hair on forehead)* flequillos *mpl*
bank *n* banco *m* ~ **account** cuenta *f* del banco ~ **card** tarjeta *f* del banco
banquet *n* banquete *m*
bar *n* bar *m* **I don't like bars.** No me gustan los bares. *(1)* **I** / *(2)* **We stay out
  of bars.** *(1)* Me mantengo... / *(2)* Nos mantenemos... fuera de los bares.
barbecue *n* 1. *(meat)* carne *f* asada; 2. *(activity)* barbacoa
bare *adj* desnudo *m*, -da *f* ~ **arms** sin mangas ~ **breasts** sin sostén ~ **feet**
  descalzo *m*, -za *f* ~ **legs** sin medias

Numbers in parentheses always signal choices.

bare-breasted *adj* sin sostén *m&f*

bare-chested *adj* pecho descubierto *m&f*

barefoot *adj* descalzo *m*, -za *f*

barefoot *adv* descalzo *m*, -za *f* **go around** ~ andar descalzo *(-za)*

barely *adv* apenas **I barely know** *(1,2)* **you.** Apenas *(1)* lo *m* / *(2)* la *f (Fam: te)* conozco.

barhop *vi* andar de bar en bar

barn *n (for cows)* establo *m* ; *(for crops)* granero *m*

barracks *n, pl* barracas *fpl* **I live in the barracks.** Vivo en las barracas.

barrier *n* barrera *f*, muro *m* **language** ~ barrera idiomática

base *n* 1. *(mil.)* cuartel *m* militar, base *f* ; 2. *(baseball)* base *f* **air force** ~ cuartel de la fuerza aérea **army** ~ cuartel del ejército **navy** ~ cuartel de la marina **I live on base.** *(mil.)* Vivo en el cuartel.

baseball *n* béisbol *m (See phrases under* **like, love** *and* **play**.*)*

based *past part*: **be** ~ *(mil.)* estar encuartelado **I'm based at** *(name of [1] base / [2] city)*. Estoy encuartelado en *([1,2] ___)*.

bashful *adj* tímido *m*, -da *f*, vergonzoso *m*, -sa *f* **You don't have to be bashful with me.** No tienes que ser tímido *(-da)* conmigo. **Don't be (so) bashful.** No seas (tan) vergonzoso *(-sa)*.

bashfulness *n* timidez *f*

basically *adv* básicamente

bask *vi* 1. *(in the sun)* asolearse; 2. *(enjoy)* complacerse **I love to bask in the sunshine.** Me encanta asolearme.

basket *n* 1. *(for carrying)* canasta *f* ; 2. *(basketball)* canasta *f* **make a** ~ *(basketball)* anotarse una canasta **picnic** ~ canasta para día de campo **Do you want to shoot some baskets?** *(basketball)* ¿Quieres lanzar unas canastas?

basketball *n* baloncesto *m (See phrases under* **like, love** *and* **play**.*)*

bath *n* baño *m* **take a** ~ tomar un baño (juntos), bañarse

bathroom *n* baño *m* **I have to go to the bathroom.** *(toilet)* Tengo que ir al baño.

battery *n (radio, flashlight, etc)* pila *f* ; *(car)* batería *f*

be *vi* estar, ser **I'm glad.** Estoy contento *(-ta)*. **He's nice.** Él es agradable. **She's pretty.** Ella es bonita. **It's okay.** Está bien. **We're ready.** Estamos listos. **You're very kind.** *(1) Usted es (Fam: Tú eres)* muy amable. **They're** *(1)* **busy.** Están ocupados *(-das)*. **I was** *([1]* **here** / *[2]* **there)**. Yo estaba *([1]* aquí. / *[2]* allá). *(1)* **He** / *(2)* **She was** *([3]* **here** / *[4]* **there)**. *(1)* Él / *(2)* Ella estaba *([3]* aquí. / *[4]* allá). **You were** *([1]* **here** / *[2]* **there)**. Usted estaba *(Fam: Tú estabas)* *([1]* aquí. / *[2]* allá). **We were** *([1]* **here** / *[2]* **there)**. Nosotros estábamos *([1]* aquí. / *[2]* allá). **They**

Spanish "a" is mostly like "a" in "mama".

were (*[1]* **here** / *[2]* **there**). Ellos estaban (*[1]* aquí. / *[2]* allá). **I'll be there.** Yo estaré allá. *(1)* **He** / *(2)* **She** / *(3)* **It will be there.** *(1)* Él / *(2)* Ella / *(3)* Eso estará allá. **We'll be there.** Nosotros estaremos allá. **Will you be there?** *¿Estará usted (Fam: ¿Estarás)* allá? **They'll be there.** Ellos estarán allá. **I'll be there in 15 minutes.** Estaré allá en quince minutos. **How long do you plan to be here?** ¿Cuánto tiempo *planea usted (Fam: planeas)* estar aquí? *(1)* **I** / *(2)* **We plan to be here** *(3)* **for** *(number)* **days.** / *(4)* **for two weeks.** / *(5)* **until** *(day / date)*. *(1)* Planeo / *(2)* Planeamos estar aquí *(3)* por __ días. / *(4)* por dos semanas. / *(5)* hasta __. **Have you ever been** *(1)* **there?** / *(2)* **in** *(place)***?** / *(3)* **to** *(place)***?** ¿Nunca *ha estado usted (Fam: has estado)* *(1)* allá? / *(2,3)* en __? *(1)* **I've** / *(2)* **We've (never) been** *(3)* **there.** / *(4)* **in** / *(5)* **to** *(place)*. *(1)* Yo (nunca) he... / *(2)* Nosotros (nunca) hemos... estado *(3)* allá. / *(4,5)* en __. **I'm a** *(job title)*. Yo soy __.
★ **be over** *idiom* 1. *(come over)* pasar, venir; 2. *(be finished)* terminar
    Wait, I'll be right over. Espera, ya llego. *(1)* **I** / *(2)* **We will be over about** *(time)*. *(1)* Acabo / *(2)* Acabamos como a las __. **What time will it be over?** ¿A qué hora termina?
beach *n* playa *f* **beautiful ~** playa hermosa **crowded ~** playa atestada, playa llena de gente **long ~** playa larga **nude ~** playa nudista **quiet ~** playa tranquila **popular ~** playa popular *(1,2)* **rocky ~** playa *(1)* rocosa / *(2)* pedregosa **sandy ~** playa de arena **secluded ~** playa apartada **topless ~** playa seminudista **wide ~** playa ancha **Let's go lie on the beach.** Echémonos en la playa. **Let's go for a walk on the beach.** Vamos a caminar por la playa. **I love to take long walks on the beach.** Me encanta dar largas caminatas por la playa.
beachcomber *n* raquero *m*, beachcomber *m*
beachcombing *n* beachcombing *m*
bear *n* oso *m* **teddy ~** osito de peluche
bear *vt* soportar **I can't bear the thought of leaving you.** No puedo soportar la idea de dejarte.
beard *n* barba *f* **You look (very)** *(1)* **good** / *(2)* **distinguished** / *(3)* **handsome** / *(4)* **scholarly** *(5)* **in** / *(6)* **with a beard.** *Usted se ve (Fam: Te ves)* (muy) *(1)* bien / *(2)* distinguido / *(3)* guapo / *(4)* docto *(5,6)* con barba.
beautiful *adj* hermoso *m*, -sa *f*, precioso *m*, -sa *f* **You are** (*[1]* **exceptionally** / *[2]* **incredibly** / *[3]* **so** / *[4]* **very) beautiful.** *Es usted (Fam: Tú eres)* (*[1]* excepcionalmente / *[2]* increíblemente / *[3]* tan / *[4]* plenamente / *[5]* muy) preciosa. **You're the most beautiful** *(1)* **girl** / *(2)* **woman** *(3)* **here.** / *(4)* **in the room.** / *(5)* **I've ever met (in all my life).** *Es usted (Fam: Tú eres)* la *(1)* muchacha / *(2)* mujer más preciosa *(3)* en este lugar. / *(4)* en

---

Articles: m = el, f = la, mpl = los, fpl = las

el cuarto. / *(5)* que haya conocido (en toda mi vida). **You are beautiful beyond words.** *Es usted (Fam: Tú eres)* hermosa más allá de las palabras. **I don't think you (even) know how beautiful you are.** No creo que *usted sepa (Fam: sepas)* (siquiera) lo hermosa que *es usted (Fam: eres).* **How beautiful you are!** ¡Qué hermosa *es usted (Fam: eres)*! **How beautiful you look!** ¡Qué hermosa *se ve usted (Fam: te ves)*! **I can't believe how beautiful you are.** No puedo creer lo hermosa que *es usted (Fam: eres).* **You have such a beautiful** *(1)* **face.** / *(2)* **figure.** / *(3)* **mouth.** / *(4)* **smile.** *Tiene usted (Fam: Tienes)* una *(1)* cara / *(2)* figura / *(3)* boca / *(4)* sonrisa tan hermosa. **You have such (a) beautiful** *(1)* **hair.** / *(2)* **body.** *Tiene usted (Fam: Tienes)* un *(1)* cabello / *(2)* cuerpo tan hermoso. **You have such beautiful** *(1)* **eyes.** / *(2)* **legs.** / *(3)* **lips.** *Tiene usted (Fam: Tienes) (1)* unos ojos *(2)* unas piernas / *(2)* unos labios tan hermosos. **What a beautiful** *(1)* **face** / *(2)* **figure** / *(3)* **smile you have!** ¡Qué *(1)* cara / *(2)* figura / *(3)* sonrisa tan hermosa *tiene usted (Fam: tienes)*! **What a beautiful** *(1)* **dress!** / *(2)* **hairdo!** / *(3)* **necklace!** / *(4)* **outfit!** ¡Qué *(1)* vestido / *(2)* peinado / *(3)* collar / *(4)* traje tan hermoso! **What beautiful** *(1)* **earrings** / *(2)* **fingernails** / *(3)* **legs (you have)!** ¡Qué *(1)* aretes *m* / *(2)* uñas *f* / *(3)* piernas *f* tan hermosos *(-sas)* *(tiene usted [Fam: tienes])*! **That's a (very) beautiful** *(1)* **dress** / *(2)* **gown** / *(3)* **outfit** / *(4)* **suit** / *(5)* **sweater** / *(6)* **swimsuit.** Ese es un *(1)* vestido *(2)* vestido de gala / *(3)* atuendo / *(4)* traje / *(5)* suéter / *(6)* traje de baño (muy) bonito. **That's a (very) beautiful.** *(1)* **blouse.** / *(2)* **skirt.** / *(3)* **necktie.** Esa es una *(1)* blusa / *(2)* falda / *(3)* corbata (muy) bonita.

beautifully *adv* bellamente, de maravilla, maravillosamente **Your hair is so beautifully done.** *Su (Fam: Tu)* cabello está bellamente peinado. **You play beautifully.** *(piano, guitar, etc)* Usted toca *(Fam: Tú tocas)* de maravilla. **You sing beautifully.** *Usted canta (Fam: Tú cantas)* de maravilla.

beauty *n* 1. *(quality)* belleza *f* ; 2. *(woman)* belleza *f* **I am (totally) captivated by your (radiant) beauty.** Estoy (plenamente) cautivado por *su (Fam: tu)* belleza (radiante) **You have a beauty that** *(1)* **age** / *(2)* **time can never diminish.** *Tiene usted (Fam: Tienes)* una belleza que *(1)* la edad / *(2)* el tiempo nunca podrá empañar. **Your beauty** *(1)* **takes my breath away.** / *(2)* **is like some thing out of a dream.** *Su (Fam: Tu)* belleza *(1)* me deja sin aliento. / *(2)* es como salida de un sueño.

because *conj* porque *conj (1)* **I** / *(2)* **We can't go (with you), because** *(3)* **I'm** / *(4)* **we're already signed up for a tour.** *(1)* No puedo... / *(2)* No podemos... ir *(con usted [Fam. contigo])*, porque ya *(3)* ...me anoté... / *(4)* ...nos anotamos... en una gira turística.

Spanish "z" is pronounced like "s" in "safe".

become *vi* llegar a ser **What do you want to become?** ¿Qué *quiere usted (Fam. quieres)* llegar a ser? **I want to become a** *(profession).* Quiero llegar a ser ___.

bed *n* cama *f* **double ~** cama doble **get in ~** acostarse **twin ~s** camas gemelas **water ~** cama de agua **I'm going to bed.** Me voy a la cama.

bedding *n* ropa *f* de cama

bedroom *n* recámara *f* **Which window is your bedroom?** ¿Cuál es la ventana de tu recámara?

bedtime *n* hora *f* de ir a la cama **It's ([1] my / [2] our) bedtime.** Es *([1]* mi / *[2]* nuestra) hora de ir a la cama. **It's (1) her / (2) his / (3) their bedtime.** Es *(1-3)* su hora de ir a la cama.

beer *n* cerveza *f* **bottle of ~** botella *f* de cerveza **case of ~** caja *f* de cerveza **glass of ~** vaso *m* de cerveza **six-pack of ~** un seis de cerveza **I'm thirsty for a beer. How about you?** Se me antoja una cerveza. ¿Y a tí? **Would you like a beer?** ¿Le *(Fam. ¿Te)* gustaría tomar una cerveza? **What kind of beer do you have?** ¿Qué tipo de cerveza tienen? **I'll go buy a (1) case / (2) six-pack of beer.** Voy a comprar *(1)* una caja... / *(2)* un seis... de cerveza.

before *adv* antes **What kind of job did you have before?** ¿Qué tipo de trabajo *tenía usted (Fam. tenías)* **antes?**

before *prep* antes de **Before that, I worked as a** *(job title).* Antes de eso, trabajé como ___.

beg *vt* rogar **I beg you (with all my heart) to (1) forgive me. / (2) give me one more chance. / (3) stay. / (4) let me see you (tonight).** *Le (Fam: Te)* ruego (de todo corazón) que *(1)* me *perdone (Fam: perdones).* / *(2)* me *dé (Fam: des)* otra oportunidad. / *(3) se quede (Fam: te quedes).* / *(4)* me *deje verlo (-la) (Fam: dejes verte)* (esta noche).

begin *vi* comenzar **What time does it begin?** ¿A qué hora comienza? **It begins at** *(time).* Comienza a las ___ . **I'm beginning to fall in love with you.** Estoy comenzando a enamorarme de ti.

behave *vi* comportarse **I promise to behave like a gentleman.** Prometo comportarme como un caballero. **I'm sorry for the way I behaved.** Lamento la manera en que me comporté. **Behave yourself.** Compórtate.

behind *adv* atrás, detrás, a la zaga *(1)* **I'm / (2) We're / (3) You're behind by 10 points.** *(1)*Yo voy... / *(2)*Nosotros vamos... / *(3) Usted va (Fam: Tú vas)*... atrás por diez puntos.

behind *prep* detrás, atrás de *(1)* **I'm / (2) We're right behind you.** *(1)* Estoy / *(2)* Estamos justo atrás de *usted (Fam: ti).*

being *n* ser *m* **fellow human ~** prójimo *m* **for the time ~** por el momento

---

A tilde ~ in terms stands for the main entry word.

human ~ ser humano

belief *n* creencia *f* ~ **in God** creencia en Dios **beyond** ~ de no creerse **firm** ~ creencia firme **religious** ~**s** creencias religiosas **sincere** ~ creencia sincera

believe *vt* creer **Please believe me.** Créeme por favor. **Don't you believe me?** ¿No me *cree usted (Fam: crees?)*? **I (don't) believe** *(1)* **that.** / *(2)* **you.** (No) *(1) Lo / (2) Le (Fam: Te)* creo. **I can't believe how beautiful you are.** No puedo creer qué hermosa *es usted (Fam: eres)*. **It's hard to believe (that you're not married).** Es difícil creer (que *usted no esté [Fam: no estés]* casado *[-da]*).

belly *n* panza *f*, barriga *f* **pot** ~ barriga *f*

bellybutton *n* ombligo *m*

belly dance *n* danza *f* del vientre

belong *vi* pertenecerle a alguien, ser de alguien **Does this belong to you?** ¿Es esto de *usted (Fam: tuyo)*? **That belongs to me.** Eso es mío. **It doesn't belong to me.** Eso no es mío. **We belong together.** Somos el uno para el otro.

beloved *adj* querido *m*, -da *f*, amado *m*, -da *f* **My beloved darling.** Mi amado tesoro. **My beloved** *(name)* Mi amado *(-da)* ___ .

belt *n* cinturón *m*, banda *f*

berth *n (train)* litera *f* **lower** ~ litera baja **upper** ~ litera alta

beside *prep* al lado de, junto a **I like having you beside me.** Me gusta tenerte a mi lado.

besides *adv* además **Besides, the walk will do us good.** Además, la caminata nos hará bien.

best *adj* mejor *m&f* ~ **man** *(wedding)* padrino *m* de bodas **Which one is best?** ¿Cuál es el mejor? **That one is the best one.** Ese es el mejor. **They have the best pastries you've ever eaten.** Tienen la mejor repostería que hayas probado. **Where's the best place to stay?** ¿Cuál es el mejor lugar para quedarse? **Let's see who's the best** *(1)* **swimmer.** / *(2)* **tennis player.** Veamos quién es el mejor *(1)* nadador. / *(2)* jugador de tenis. **You're the best.** Tú eres el *(la)* mejor. *(1)* **I** / *(2)* **We wish you all the best.** Te *(1)* deseo / *(2)* deseamos todo lo mejor.

bet *vt* apostar **Let's bet** *(amount)* **on horse number four.** Apostemos ___ al caballo número cuatro. **I'll bet you must be tired.** Apuesto a que *usted está (Fam: estás)* cansado *(-da)*. **You bet!** ¡Por supuesto!

betray *vt* traicionar **I would never betray you.** Nunca te traicionaría.

better *adj* mejor *m&f* **Is it better?** ¿Es mejor? **It's better.** Es mejor. **Which one is better?** ¿Cuál es mejor? **That one is better.** Ese es mejor.

better *adv* mejor **do** ~ hazlo mejor **get** ~ aliviarse **I want to get to know** *(1,2)* **you better.** Quiero *(1) conocerlo m / (2) conocerla f (Fam: conocerte)*

Spanish "ch" is pronounced like ours
(e.g., "cheese," "charge").

mejor. **I should have known better.** Debí haberlo sabido. **Do you feel better?** ¿*Se siente usted (Fam.* ¿*Te sientes)* mejor? **I feel better (now).** (Ahora) Me siento mejor. **I'd better** *(1)* **ask (them).** / *(2)* **do it (now).** / *(3)* **find out.** / *(4)* **get it.** / *(5)* **go.** / *(6)* **hurry.** Será mejor que *(1)* (les) pregunte. / *(2)* lo haga (ahora). / *(3)* lo averigüe. / *(4)* lo consiga. / *(5)* vaya. / *(6)* me apresure. **We'd better** *(1)* **ask (them).** / *(2)* **do it (now).** / *(3)* **find out.** / *(4)* **get it.** / *(5)* **go.** / *(6)* **hurry.** Será mejor que *(1)* (les) preguntemos. / *(2)* lo hagamos (ahora). / *(3)* lo averigüemos. / *(4)* lo consigamos. / *(5)* vayamos. / *(6)* nos apresuremos. **You'd better** *(1)* **ask (them).** / *(2)* **do it (now).** / *(3)* **find out.** / *(4)* **hurry.** Será mejor que *(1)* (les) preguntes. / *(2)* lo hagas (ahora). / *(3)* lo averigües. / *(4)* te apresures.

between *prep* entre **It's between Mexico City and Monterrey.** Es entre la Ciudad de México y Monterrey.

beverage *n* bebida *f*

bewildered *adj (confused)* desconcertado *m*, -da *f*, perplejo *m*, -ja *f* **You look bewildered. Can I help you?** *Usted se ve* (*Fam. Te ves*) desconcertado, *(-da).* ¿Puedo *ayudarle (Fam. ayudarte)*?

bewitch *vt* hechizar **You bewitch me with your beautiful smile.** *Usted me hechiza con su (Fam: Me hechizas con tu)* hermosa sonrisa.

bewitching *adj* hechizante *m&f*

beyond *prep* más allá **It's beyond that.** *(location)* Es más allá.

Bible *n* Biblia *f*

bicycle *n* bicicleta *f* ~ **race** carrera *f* de bicicleta **Do you have a bicycle?** ¿*Tiene usted (Fam.* ¿*Tienes)* bicicleta? **I (don't) have a bicycle.** Yo (no) tengo bicicleta. **Where can we rent bicycles?** ¿Dónde podemos rentar bicicletas?

bicycling *n* andar en bicicleta **Would you like to go bicycling (with** *[1]* **me?** / *[2]* **us?)?** ¿*Le gustaría a usted (Fam: Te gustaría)* andar en bicicleta (*[1]* conmigo? / *[2]* con nosotros)? **Let's go bicycling (together).** Vamos a pasear en bicicleta (juntos).

big *adj* grande *m&f*, largo *m*, -ga *f* **This is a big vacation for** *(1)* **me.** / *(2)* **us.** Estas son vacaciones grandes para *(1)* mí. / *(2)* nosotros. **That's a big** *(1)* **pack.** / *(2)* **suitcase.** Ese es una *(1)* mochila / *(2)* maleta grande. **This is the biggest trip** *(1)* **I've** / *(2)* **we've ever taken.** Este es el viaje más largo que *(1)* he / *(2)* hemos hecho.

big-hearted *adj* de buen corazón *m&f*

bike *vi* 1. *(bicycle)* andar en bici; 2. *(motorcycle)* andar en moto

bike *n* 1. *(bicycle)* bici *f*; 2. *(motorcycle)* moto *f* **mountain** ~ bicicleta de montaña

biking *n* ciclismo *m* **mountain** ~ ciclismo de montaña

Stress rule #1: The last syllable is stressed if the word ends in a consonant (except "n" and "s").

bikini *n* bikini *m*

bill *n* cuenta *f* (1) **I'll** / (2) **We'll take care of the bill.** (1) Yo me hago cargo... / (2) Nosotros nos hacemos cargo... de la cuenta. **How much is the bill?** ¿Cuánto es de la cuenta?

billfold *n* billetera *f*

billiards *n* billar *m* **I'll show you how to play billiards.** Yo te enseño a jugar billar.

bindings *n, pl (skis)* sujetadores *mpl*

bird *n* pájaro *m*, ave *f* **love ~** tórtolo *m*, -la *f*

birding, birdwatching *n* observación de aves, observar aves **One of** (1) **my** / (2) **our favorite pastimes is birdwatching.** Uno de (1) mis / (2) nuestros pasatiempos favoritos es observar aves.

binoculars *n, pl* binoculares *mpl*

birth *n* nacimiento *m* **at ~** al nacer **give ~ to** dar a luz, parir

birthday *n* cumpleaños *m* **~ party** fiesta *f* de cumpleaños **~ present** regalo *m* de cumpleaños **Happy birthday!** ¡Feliz cumpleaños! **This is for your birthday.** *(gift)* Esto es por tu cumpleaños. **When is your birthday?** ¿Cuándo es *su (Fam: tu)* cumpleaños? **My birthday is (on)** *(day / date)*. Mi cumpleaños es el ___. (1) **Today** / (2) **Tomorrow is my birthday.** (1) Hoy / (2) Mañana es mi cumpleaños. **We have to celebrate your birthday.** Tenemos que celebrar tu cumpleaños. **What do you want for your birthday?** ¿Qué quieres para tu cumpleaños?

birthmark *n* mancha *f*, marca *f* de nacimiento *f*, lunar *m*

bit *n (piece)* pedazo *m*, trozo *m* **a ~** *(somewhat)* un poco **a little ~** un pedacito **I think** (1) **I've** / (2) **you've drunk a little bit too much.** Creo que (1) he / (2) has tomado demasiado.

bite *vt & vi* morder **I'm not going to bite you.** No te voy a morder. **Are the fish biting?** ¿Están mordiendo los peces?

bite *n* bocadillo *m* **Let's get a bite to eat.** Vamos a buscar algo para comer.

bitter *adj* amargo *m*, -ga *f*

black *adj* negro *m*, -gra *f*

black *n (person)* negro *m*, -gra *f*

blackmail *n* chantaje *m* **That's blackmail!** ¡Eso es chantaje!

blame *vt* echar la culpa, culpar **I don't blame** *(1,2)* **you.** No (1) lo *m* / (2) la *f (Fam: te)* culpo. **Don't blame me!** ¡No me culpes!

blanket *n* manta *f*, cobija *f*

bless *vt* bendecir **Bless you!** *(When someone sneezes)* ¡Salud!

blessing *n* bendición *f* **What a blessing to have met** *(1,2)* **you.** Qué bendición (1) haberlo *m* / (2) haberla *f (Fam: haberte)* conocido.

blind *adj* ciego *m*, -ga *f* **partially ~** parcialmente ciego **They say love is**

Spanish "i" is mostly "ee", but can also be shorter, like "i" in "sit," when together with other vowels.

blind. Dicen que el amor es ciego.

bliss *n* dicha *f* **This is bliss.** Esto es dicha.

blissful *adj* de gozo *m&f*, de gran felicidad *m&f*

blithe *adj (happy, carefree)* alegre *m&f*, risueño *m*, -ña *f* **You have such a blithe spirit.** Tienes un espíritu tan risueño.

blond *n* rubio *m* ; **blonde** *n* rubia *f*

blonde *adj* rubio *m*, -a *f*

blood *n* sangre *f*

blouse *n* blusa *f* **That's a (very) beautiful blouse.** Esa es una blusa (muy) bonita. **You make that blouse very beautiful.** Tú haces que la blusa se vea muy bonita.

blow out *idiom* apagar (de un soplido) **Make a wish and blow out all the candles (in one breath).** Pide un deseo y apaga todas las velas (de un soplido).

blow up *idiom (inflate)* inflar **Blow up the** *(1)* **air mattress.** / *(2)* **ball.** / *(3,4)* **rubber boat.** Infla *(1)* el colchón de aire. / *(2)* la pelota. / *(3)* el bote de hule. / *(4)* la balsa de caucho.

blue *adj* 1. *(color)* azul *m&f* ; 2. *(sad)* triste *(See phrases under* **sad***)* ~ **eyes** ojos azules

blue grass *(music)* blue grass *m*

blues *n, pl* 1. *(music)* blues *m* ; 2. *(sadness)* tristeza *f* **have the** ~ estar triste

bluff *vi* fanfarronear **(I think) You're bluffing.** (Creo que) Estás fanfarroneando.

bluff *n* farsa *f* **I'm going to call your bluff.** Voy a desenmascararte.

blunder *n* error *m* garrafal, metida *f* de pata *(1)* **I've** / *(2)* **We've made a terrible blunder.** *(1)* He / *(2)* Hemos cometido un terrible error.

blush *vi* sonrojarse **I've made you blush.** Hice que *usted se sonrojara (Fam: te sonrojaras)*.**You make me blush.** *Usted hace (Fam: Haces)* que me sonroje.**You're blushing.** *Usted se está (Fam: Te estás)* sonrojando. **Why are you blushing?** ¿Por qué *se sonroja usted (Fam: te sonrojas)*?

board *vt* abordar **It's time to board (the** *[1]* **plane.** / *[2]* **ship.** / *[3]* **train.).** Es hora de abordar (el *[1]* avión. / *[2]* barco. / *[3]* tren.).

board *n* 1. *(announcements)* tablero *m* ; 2. *(games)* tablero *m*, marcador *m* ; 3. *(surfing)* tabla *f* ; 4. *(plank)* tabla *f* **diving** ~ trampolín *m* **on** ~ a bordo **Is there a bulletin board around here?** ¿Hay algún tablero de avisos por aquí? **Let's check the bulletin board.** Vamos a chequear el tablero de avisos. **It's time to get on board.** Es hora de abordar. **We'd better get on board.** Será mejor que abordemos.

boast *vi* presumir **I don't mean to boast (but I'm the greatest).** No quiero

---

presumir (pero soy el mejor).

boat *n* lancha *f*, barco *m*, bote *m* **launch a** ~ botar un bote **motor** ~ lancha de motor, lancha motorizada *f* **pedal** ~ lancha de pedales **rubber** ~ bote de hule, balsa de caucho. **Let's rent a boat.** Rentemos una lancha. **How much does it cost to rent a boat?** ¿Cuánto cuesta rentar una lancha?

boating *n* dar un paseo en lancha **Would you like to go boating (with *[1]* me / *[2]* us)?** ¿Le gustaría a usted (Fam:¿Te gustaría) dar un paseo en lancha (*[1]* conmigo / *[2]* con nosotros)?

body *n* cuerpo *m* **athletic** ~ cuerpo atlético **beautiful** ~ cuerpo hermoso **gorgeous** ~ cuerpo estupendo **little** ~ cuerpo menudo **lovely** ~ cuerpo bello **nice** ~ buen cuerpo **perfect** ~ cuerpo perfecto **petite** ~ cuerpo menudo **sexy** ~ cuerpo sensual **shapely** ~ cuerpo bien torneado **slender** ~ cuerpo delgado **small** ~ cuerpo pequeño **whole** ~ cuerpo entero **wonderful** ~ cuerpo maravilloso **You have a (really)** *(1)* **beautiful /** *(2)* **great /** *(3)* **nice body.** Tienes un cuerpo (realmente) *(1)* precioso. / *(2)* fabuloso. / *(3)* bello. **What a beautiful body (you have)!** ¡Qué cuerpo tan precioso (tienes)!

bodyrub *n* masaje *m* corporal **sensual** ~ masaje sensual

bold *adj* atrevido *m*, -da *f* **Forgive me for being so bold.** Perdóneme (Fam. Perdóname) por ser tan atrevido (-da).

bond *n* vínculo *m*, lazo *m* **~s of friendship** lazos de amistad **~s of marriage** lazos conyugales **love ~s** lazos de amor **spiritual** ~ vínculo espiritual **This is a symbol of the bond between our souls.** Este es un símbolo de la unión de nuestras almas.

bonehead *n* estúpido *m*, -da *f*, imbécil *m&f*

book *vt* reservar *(1)* **I'll book...** / *(2)* **I booked... a** *(3)* **room /** *(4)* **flight (for us).** *(1)* Reservaré... / *(2)* Reservé… *(3)* una habitación / *(4)* un vuelo (para nosotros).

book *n* libro *m* **address** ~ libreta *f* de direcciones **phone** ~ directorio *m* telefónico **What's the book that you're reading?** ¿Qué libro está usted (Fam: estás) leyendo? **Is that a good book?** ¿Es un buen libro?

bookshop, bookstore *n* librería *f*

bookworm *n* ratón *m*, -na *f* de biblioteca

boot(s) *n* bota(s) *f (pl)* **high ~s** botas altas **hiking ~s** botas para montaña **ski ~s** botas para esquiar

border *n* frontera *f*

bore *vt* aburrir **I don't want to** *(1,2)* **bore you.** No quiero *(1)* aburrirlo *m* / *(2)* aburrirla *f* (Fam: aburrirte). **I hope I** *(1)* **am not** *(2,3)* **boring...** / *(4)* **don't** *(5,6)* **bore...** / *(7)* **didn't** *(8,9)* **bore... you.** Espero *(1)* no estar *(2)* aburriéndolo *m* / *(3)* aburriéndola *f* (Fam: aburriéndote). / *(4)* ...no *(5)* aburrirlo *m* / *(6)* aburrirla *f* (Fam: aburrirte). / *(7)* ...no *(8)* haberlo *m* /

Spanish "j" is pronounced like "h".

(9) haberla f (Fam: haberte) aburrido. **You're not boring me (at all).** *Usted no me está (Fam: No me estás)* aburriendo (para nada).

bore *n* pesado *m*, -da *f*, aburrido *m*, -da *f* **Forgive me for being such a bore.** *Perdóneme (Fam. Perdóname)* por ser tan pesado *(-da)*.

bored *adj* aburrido *m*, -da *f* **Are you bored?** ¿*Está usted (Fam: ¿Estás)* aburrido *(-da)*? **I'm (not) bored.** (No) Estoy aburrido *(-da)*. **Are you bored with this?** ¿*Le (Fam:¿Te)* aburre (esto)? **I'm (really) bored with this.** Estoy (de verdad) aburrido *(-da)* de esto. **It's impossible to be bored around you.** Es imposible aburrirse estando contigo. **You look bored.** *Usted se ve (Fam: Te ves)* aburrido *(-da)*. **I was so bored until I met you.** Estaba tan aburrido *(-da)* hasta que te conocí.

boredom *n* aburrimiento *m* **I know a way to relieve the boredom.** Conozco un modo de quitarse el aburrimiento.

boring *adj* aburrido *m*, -da *f (1)* **This is...** / *(2)* **It is...** / *(3)* **That is...** / *(4)* **It was...** (*[5]* **rather** / *[6]* **really** / *[7]* **so** / *[8]* **terribly** / *[9]* **very**) **boring.** *(1)* Esto es... / *(2)* Es... / *(3)* Eso es... / *(4)* Fue... (*[5]* algo / *[6]* de verdad / *[7]* tan / *[8]* terriblemente / *[9]* muy) aburrido. **Life seemed so boring until I met you.** La vida parecía tan aburrida hasta que te conocí.

born: be ~ nacer **Where were you born?** ¿Dónde *nació usted (Fam: naciste?)*? **I was born in** *(place)*. Nací en ___.

borrow *vt* prestar **Could I borrow** *(1)* **your pen?** / *(2)* **100 pesos until tomorrow?** ¿Me *puede usted (Fam: puedes)* prestar *(1)* su *(Fam: tu)* lapicero? / *(2)* cien pesos hasta mañana?

bosom *n* seno *m*, pecho *m*, busto *m*

boss *n* jefe *m*, -fa *f*

both *adj* ambos *m*, -bas *f* **Use both hands.** Usa ambas manos.

both *pron* ambos *m*, -bas *f* **~ of them** ellos *m*, *(ellas f)* dos **~ of us** nosotros *m (-tras)* dos **~ of you** ustedes dos *m & f*

bother *vt* molestar **Am I bothering** *(1,2)* **you?** *(1)* ¿Lo *m* / *(2)* ¿La *f (Fam: ¿Te)* estoy molestando? **I hope I'm not** *(1,2)* **bothering you.** Espero no estar *(1)* molestándolo *m* / *(2)* molestándola *f*, *(Fam: molestándote)*. **I'm sorry to** *(1,2)* **bother you.** Siento *(1)* molestarlo *m* / *(2)* molestarla *f (Fam: molestarte)*. **I don't want to** *(1,2)* **bother you.** No quiero *(1)* molestarlo *m* / *(2)* molestarla *f (Fam: molestarte)*. **I didn't mean to** *(1,2)* **bother you.** No quise *(1)* molestarlo *m* / *(2)* molestarla *f (Fam: molestarte)*. **You're (not) bothering me.** (No) Me *está usted (Fam: estás)* molestando. **Please don't bother me (anymore).** Por favor, (ya) no me *moleste (Fam: molestes)*.

bottle *n* botella *f* **water ~** botella *f* de agua; *(canteen)* cantimplora *f* **Bring along a water bottle.** Trae una botella de agua.

Familiar "tu" forms in parentheses can replace italicized polite forms.

bottom *n* 1. *(of a container)* fondo *m* ; 2. *(buttocks)* trasero *m (1,2)* **Bottoms up!** *(1)* ¡Al centro y pa'dentro! / *(2)* ¡Fondo blanco!

bouquet *n* ramo *m* ~ **of flowers** ramo de flores

bowl *vi* lanzar bolos, jugar boliche **I'll teach you how to bowl.** Yo te enseño a jugar boliche.

bowl *n* bolo *m*

bow-legged *adj* patizambo *m*, -ba *f*, zambo *m*, -ba *f*

bowling *n* jugar boliche **Would you like to go bowling?** ¿Le *(Fam. ¿Te)* gustaría ir a jugar boliche?

box *n* caja *f* ~ **of candy** caja de dulces ~ **office** taquilla *f* **cardboard** ~ caja de cartón **post office** ~ apartado *m* (de correos) **wooden** ~ caja de madera

boxing *n* boxeo *m* ~ **match** pelea *f* de box

boy *n (child)* niño *m*, chiquillo *m* ; *(adol. up)* muchacho *m* ; chico *m (1)* **bashful** ~ *(child)* chiquillo penoso **cute** ~ *(child)* chiquillo mono **good** ~ *(child)* buen chiquillo **handsome** ~ *(child)* chiquillo guapo; *(adol. up)* chico guapo **naughty** ~ *(child)* chiquillo travieso **nice** ~ *(child)* chiquillo simpático; *(adol. up)* chico simpático **quiet** ~ *(child)* chiquillo tranquilo **shy** ~ *(child)* chiquillo tímido **smart** ~ chiquillo listo **I** / *(2)* **We have** *(3)* **a boy.** / *(4)* **two boys.** *(1)* Tengo / *(2)* Tenemos *(3)* un niño. / *(4)* dos niños.

boyfriend *n* novio *m* **former** ~ novio anterior **previous** ~ novio anterior **This is my boyfriend** *(name)*. Este es mi novio ___. **Do you have a boyfriend?** ¿Tiene usted *(Fam: ¿Tienes)* novio? **I (don't) have a boyfriend.** Yo (no) tengo novio. **I have a lot of friends, but no boyfriend.** Yo tengo muchos amigos, pero novio no.

bra *n* sostén *m*, brasier *m*

bracelet *n* brazalete *m* **ankle** ~ ajorca *f*

brag *vi* fanfarronear **I don't mean to brag.** No me gusta fanfarronear.

braid *n* trenza *f* **Your hair looks good in braids.** Se *le ve bien a usted (Fam: te ve bien)* el pelo trenzado.

brain *n* cerebro *m* ; mente *f* **sharp** ~ mente aguda

brainwaves *n, pl* pensamientos *mpl*, ondas *fpl* mentales **I was sending you brainwaves (- real nice ones -) for the past hour.** Te estuve enviando ondas mentales (- realmente bonitas -) durante la última hora.

brand-new *adj* nuevecito *m*, -ta *f*

brave *adj* valiente *m&f* **You're really brave, you know it?** Eres de verdad valiente, ¿lo sabías?

break *vt* romper **I'm sorry I broke it. (Please let me pay for it.)** Lamento haberlo roto. (Por favor, déjeme pagarlo.) **I'm glad you broke the ice.** Me da gusto que *usted rompiera (Fam: rompieras)* el hielo. **How did you break it?** ¿Cómo *lo rompió (Fam: rompiste)*?

Spanish "e" is pronounced like English "e" in "get".

★ **break down** idiom descomponerse; averiarse *(1)* **My /** *(2)* **Our car broke down.** Se descompuso *(1)* mi / *(2)* nuestro carro.

★ **break up** idiom *(end a relationship)* terminar **We broke up** *(number)* *(1)* **months /** *(2)* **years ago.** Terminamos hace __ *(1)* meses. / *(2)* años.

break n 1. *(rest period)* descanso m ; 2. *(school vacation)* vacaciones fpl **spring** ~ vacaciones de primavera **winter** ~ vacaciones de invierno *(1,2)* **Let's take a break.** *(1)* Vamos a tomarnos... / *(2)* Tomémonos... un descanso. **Give me a break!** ¡Déjame en paz!

breakfast n desayuno m **Let's meet for breakfast tomorrow**. Juntémonos a desayunar mañana.

breast(s) n pecho(s) m(pl) **bare** ~s pechos desnudos *(1,2)* **beautiful** ~s pechos *(1)* preciosos / *(2)* hermosos **big** ~s pechos grandes **lovely** ~s pechos bellos **magnificent** ~s pechos magníficos **What beautiful breasts (you have)!** ¡Qué pechos tan preciosos (tienes)!

breath n aliento m, respiración f **You're like a breath of fresh air in my life.** Eres como una oleada de aire fresco en mi vida. **Your beauty takes my breath away.** *La belleza de usted (Fam: Tu belleza)* me quita el aliento. **Does my breath smell bad?** ¿Me huele mal el aliento?

breathless adj *(very impressed)* sin aliento m&f **You leave me absolutely breathless.** Me dejas completamente sin aliento.

breath-taking adj impresionante m&f, imponente m&f

bribe n soborno m **That's what's called a bribe. (I'll take it.)** A eso se le llama soborno. (Lo tomo.)

bride n novia f

bridegroom n novio m

bridesmaid n dama f de honor

bridge n 1. *(span)* puente m ; 2. *(card game)* bridge m **We'll cross that bridge when we come to it.** Ese problema lo resolveremos cuando llegue el momento.

brief adj breve m&f ~ **message** mensaje m breve

briefcase n portafolios mpl

briefly adv brevemente m&f **To put it briefly,...** En pocas palabras,…

bright adj 1. *(luminous)* brillante m&f ; 2. *(smart, clever)* listo m, -ta f **Your smile makes a bright day even brighter.** Tu sonrisa hace que un día soleado brille más. **My days are brighter because of you.** Mis días son más brillantes por ti.

brighten vt animarse, alegrarse, iluminarse **Your smile brightens up even a sunny day.** Tu sonrisa ilumina hasta a un día soleado. **You brighten my life with your sweet smile and loving ways.** Alegras mi vida con tu dulce

---

Stress rule # 2: The next-to-last syllable is stressed in words ending in "n", "s" or a vowel.

sonrisa y tus modos cariñosos.

bright-eyed *adj* de ojos vivos *m&f*, de ojos vivarachos *m&f*

brilliant *adj (very smart)* brillante *m&f*

bring *vt* traer **I brought you this.** *Le (Fam: te)* traje esto. **I'll bring** *(1)* some wine. / *(2)* **a picnic lunch.** Yo traeré *(1)* algo de vino. / *(2)* un almuerzo campestre. **Bring back a lemonade for me.** Tráeme una limonada. **Don't forget to bring** *(1)* **your camera.** / *(2)* **an umbrella.** / *(3)* **a swimsuit.** No olvide usted *(Fam: olvides)* traer *(1)* su *(Fam: tu)* cámara. / *(2)* un paraguas / *(3)* un traje de baño. **Bring a friend.** *Traiga usted (Fam: Trae)* un*(a,* amigo *(-ga).* **You bring me a lot of happiness.** Tú me traes mucha felicidad ★ **bring up** *idiom (raise, rear)* criar, educar **I was** *(1,2)* **brought up in** *(place).* Me *(1)* criaron / *(2)* educaron en ___.

brisk *adj* brioso *m,* -sa *f*, vigoroso *m,* -sa *f* ~ **walk** marcha vigorosa

broad *adj* ancho *m,* -cha *f* ; amplio *m,* -plia *f*

broad-minded *adj* de mentalidad abierta, de mente amplia

brochure *n* folleto *m*

broke *adj (without money)* quebrado *m,* -da *f*, pelado *m,* -da *f*, bruja *m&f* **I'm (just about) broke.** Estoy (más o menos) quebrado *(-da).*

broken *adj* roto *m,* -ta *f*, quebrado *m,* -da *f* **It's** *(1,2)* **broken.** Está *(1)* roto. / *(2)* quebrado.

broken-hearted *adj* destrozado *m,* -da *f* **I'm going to be broken-hearted if** *(1)* **I don't see** *(2,3)* **you again.** / *(4)* **you don't call me.** Se me va a romper el corazón *(1)* si no *(2)* lo *m* / *(3)* la *f* veo a usted *(Fam: te veo)* de nuevo. / *(4)* si no *me llama usted (Fam: llamas).*

brother *n* hermano *m* **older** ~ hermano mayor **oldest** ~ el mayor de los hermanos **middle** ~ hermano de en medio **younger** ~ hermano menor **youngest** ~ el menor de los hermanos **This is my brother** *(name).* Este es mi hermano ___.

brother-in-law *n* cuñado *m*

brown *adj* marrón *m&f*, castaño *m,* -ña *f*, café *m&f*

brunette *n* morena *f*

brush *n* cepillo *m* **paint** ~ brocha *f*

b.s. *(vulgar slang: nonsense)* pendejadas *fpl*, babosadas *fpl* **That's a lot of** *(1,2)* **b.s.** Esas son puras *(1)* pendejadas. / *(2)* babosadas.

buddy *n (colloq: friend)* amigo *m,* cuate *m*

buff *n (fan, enthusiast)* aficionado *m,* -da *f* **fitness** ~ entusiasta del ejercicio y la salud **movie** ~ cinéfilo *m,* -la *f* **sports** ~ aficionado a los deportes **tennis** ~ aficionado al tenis

buffet *n (meal)* bufet *m*

buggy *n (for babies)* cochecito *m* **dune** ~ buggy *m*

Spanish "x" is always like "ks", as in our word "taxi".

build *vt* construir **I hope we can build a strong friendship together.** Espero que podamos construir una sólida amistad.

build *n* complexión *f* **You have a nice build.** *Usted tiene (Fam: Tienes)* una bonita complexión.

builder: body ~ fisiculturista *m&f*

building *n* *(structure)* edificio *m* **body** ~ fisiculturismo *m*

bull *n* 1. *(zool.)* toro *m* ; 2. *(slang: nonsense)* pendejadas *fpl*, babosadas *fpl*

bullfight *n* corrida *f* de toros **Let's go to a bullfight.** Vamos a una corrida de toros.

bum *n* *(loafer, idler)* vago *m*, -ga *f* **beach** ~ vago de la playa

bum around *(slang)* vagabundear, deambular **I'm just bumming around the country.** Nomás ando vagabundeando por el país.

bummer *n* *(slang: unlucky / bad experience / situation)* mala onda

bump into *(idiom)* toparse con alguien **I'm glad I bumped into you.** Me alegra haberme topado *con usted (Fam. contigo)*.

bun *n* 1. *(pastry)* bolillo *m* ; 2. *pl: (slang: buttocks)* nalgas *fpl*

bunch *n* montón *m* ~ **of junk** montón de basura ~ **of papers** montón de papeles ~ **of people** montón de gente ~ **of stuff** montón de cosas

bungalow *n* bungalow *m*, cabaña *f*

bunny *n* *(slang: little darling)* conejita *f*, amorcito *m* **honey** ~ *(sweetheart)* amor *m&f*, querido *m*, -da *f* **snuggle** ~ amorcito apapachón *m&f*

burn *vi* arder, quemarse **Something is burning!** ¡Algo se está quemando!

burning *adj* *(fig.)* ferviente *m&f*

bus *n* autobús *m*, camión *m* ~ **schedule** horario *m* de autobuses ~ **station** estación *f* de autobuses ~ **stop** parada *f* de autobuses ~ **terminal** terminal *f* de autobuses **Does this bus go to** *(place)*? ¿Va este autobús a ___? **What time will the bus** *(1)* **arrive?** / *(2)* **depart?** ¿A qué hora *(1)* llega / *(2)* sale el autobús? **The bus will** *(1)* **arrive** / *(2)* **depart at** *(time)*. El autobús *(1)* llega / *(2)* sale a las ___. **Is there another bus to** *(place)* **today?** ¿Hay otro autobús para ___ el día de hoy? **How much is the bus fare (to** *[place]*)? ¿Cuál es la tarifa del autobús (para ___)?

bushed *adj* *(slang: exhausted)* hecho *m* polvo **I'm bushed.** Estoy hecho *(-cha)* polvo.

business *n* negocio *m*, asunto *m* ~ **trip** viaje *m* de negocios **company** ~ negocio corporativo **establish a** ~ constituir un negocio **manage a** ~ administrar un negocio **open a** ~ abrir un negocio **operate a** ~ operar un negocio **personal** ~ negocio personal **run a** ~ dirigir un negocio **start up a** ~ iniciar un negocio **urgent** ~ asunto urgente *(1)* **I** / *(2)* **We have some business to attend to (**[3] **first** / [4] **today** / [5] **tomorrow).** *(1)* Tengo / *(2)* Tenemos un asunto que atender (*[3]* primero. / *[4]* el día de hoy. / *[5]*

Stress rule # 3: Syllables with accent marks have the stress there.

mañana.).

businessman *n* hombre *m* de negocios, comerciante *m*

businesswoman *n* mujer *f* de negocios, comerciante *f*

bust *n* busto *m (See terms under* **bosom** and **breast**)

busy *adj* ocupado *m*, -da *f* **Are you busy?** ¿Está usted (Fam. ¿Estás) ocupado *(-da)*? **I'm (***[1]*** not /** *[2]* **very) busy.** Yo (*[1]* no) estoy (*[2]* muy) ocupado *(-da)*. **Are you busy** *(1)* **after work?** */ (2)* **tonight?** */ (3)* **tomorrow (***[4]* **morning?** */ [5]* **afternoon?** */ [6]* **evening?)?** */ (7)* **on Saturday?** */ (8)* **right now?** ¿Está usted (Fam. ¿Estás) ocupado *(-da) (1)* después del trabajo? */ (2)* por la noche? */ (3)* mañana (en la *[4]* mañana? */ [5]* tarde? */ [6]* noche?)? */ (7)* el sábado? */ (8)* ahora? **I won't be busy.** No estaré ocupado *(-da)*. **I'm busy** *(1)* **after work.** */ (2)* **tonight.** */ (3)* **tomorrow (***[4]* **morning.** */ [5]* **afternoon.** */ [6]* **evening.).** */ (7)* **on Saturday.** */ (8)* **right now.** Estoy ocupado *(-da) (1)* después del trabajo. */ (2)* esta noche. */ (3)* mañana (en la*[4]* mañana. */ [5]* tarde. */ [6]* noche.). */ (7)* el sábado. */ (8)* ahora.

but *conj* pero, sino

butt(ocks) *n* nalgas *fpl*

buxom *adj* bustona *f*, pechugona *f*

buy *vt* comprar **What do you need to buy?** ¿Qué *necesita usted (Fam. necesitas)* comprar? *(1)* **I /** *(2)* **We need to buy** *(3)* **a few things.** */ (4)* **some batteries.** */ (5)* **some film.** */ (6)* **some gifts for** *(7)* **my /** *(8)* **our** *(9)* **friends.** */ (10)* **relatives.** */ (11)* **some souvenirs.** */ (12)* **some stamps.** */ (13)* **something.** */ (14) (item).** *(1)* Necesito /** *(2)* Necesitamos comprar *(3)* unas cuantas cosas. */ (4)* unas baterías. */ (5)* película. */ (6)* unos regalos para *(7)* mis /** *(8)* nuestros *(9)* amigos. */ (10)* parientes. */ (11)* unos recuerdos. */ (12)* unos timbres. */ (13)* algo. */ (14)* ___. *(1)* **I'd /** *(2)* **We'd like to buy** *(item)*. *(1)* Me /** *(2)* Nos gustaría comprar ___. **Where can** *(1)* **I /** *(2)* **we buy** *(item)*? ¿Dónde *(1)* puedo /** *(2)* podemos comprar ___? **Where did you buy that?** ¿Dónde *compró usted (Fam: compraste)* eso? *(1)* **I /** *(2)* **We bought it** *(3)* **at /** *(4)* **in** *(place)*. Lo *(1)* compré /** *(2)* compramos en ___. **I'll buy it (from you).** Yo lo compro. (Te lo compro). *(1)* **I /** *(2)* **We want to buy** *(3)* **it /** *(4)* **them for you.** *(1)* Quiero /** *(2)* Queremos *(3)* comprarlo */ (4)* comprarlos para ti. **I'll buy** *(1)* **it /** *(2)* **one /** *(3)* **them for you.** *(1)* Lo compraré... /** *(2)* Compraré uno... /** *(3)* Los compraré... para ti. **We'll buy** *(1)* **it /** *(2)* **one /** *(3)* **them for you.** *(1)* Lo compraremos... /** *(2)* Compraremos uno... /** *(3)* Los compraremos... para ti. *(1)* **I /** *(2)* **We bought** *(3)* **this /** *(4)* **these for you.** *(1)* Compré /** *(2)* Compramos *(3)* este /** *(4)* estos para ti. **Let's buy** *(1)* **it.** */ (2)* **one.** */ (3)* **them.** Hay que *(1)* comprarlo. */ (2)* comprar uno. */ (3)* comprarlos.

bye-bye *interj* adiós

Spanish pronunciation rules are on pages 407-408.

C

cabaret *n* cabaret *m*, centro *m* nocturno, café *m* cantante

cabin *n* 1. *(hut)* cabaña *f*, choza *f*; 2. *(ship)* camarote *m* ; *(small boat)* cabina *f* **rent a ~** rentar una cabaña

cable *n (elec., naut., mech.)* cable *m* **~ car** 1. *(suspended)* teleférico *m* ; 2. *(on rails)* funicular *m* **jumper ~** cable de arranque

cactus *n* cactus *m*

caddy *n (golf)* caddy *m&f*, ayudante *m&f*, portador *m* de palos de golf

café *n* café *m* **Internet ~** café de Internet **seaside ~** café de la costa

cafeteria *n* cafetería *f*

cake *n* pastel *m* **birthday ~** pastel de cumpleaños **wedding ~** pastel de bodas

calculator *n* calculadora *f*

calendar *n* calendario *m*

calf *n* **(calves** *pl*) 1. *(of the leg)* pantorrilla *f* (pantorrillas *fpl*); 2. *(zool.)* ternero *m*, -ra *f*

call *vt* llamar **~ a taxi** llamar un taxi **~ back** regresar la llamada **~ each other** llamarse entre sí **Could I call you?** ¿Podría *llamarle (Fam: llamarte)*? **What time shall I call (you)?** ¿A qué hora *le llamo a usted (Fam: te llamo?)*? *(1)* **I'll** / *(2)* **We'll call you** *(3)* **later.** / *(4)* **tonight.** / *(5)* **tomorrow** *([6]* **morning** / *[7]* **afternoon** / *[8]* **evening).** / *(9)* **at** *(time)*. *Le (Fam: Te) (1)* llamaré / *(2)* llamaremos *(3)* más tarde. / *(4)* esta noche. / *(5)* mañana *([6]* por la mañana / *[7]* por la tarde / *[8]* por la noche). / *(9)* a las ___. **Please call** *(1)* **anytime.** / *(2)* **whenever you have time**. Por favor *llámeme usted (Fam: llámame)* a *(1)* cualquier hora. / *(2)* cuando *tenga (Fam: tengas)* tiempo. **Please call me at** *(1)* **this number:** *(number).* / *(2)* **home.** / *(3)* **my office.** / *(4)* **work.** Por favor *llámeme usted (Fam: llámame) (1)* a este numero: ___. / *(2)* a mi casa. / *(3)* a mi oficina. / *(4)* al trabajo. **Please don't call me at** *(1)* **home**. / *(2)* **my office.** / *(3)* **work**. Por favor no me *llame usted (Fam: llames) (1)* a mi casa. / *(2)* a mi oficina. / *(3)* al trabajo.

Some Spanish words have accented and unaccented forms to differentiate their meanings (e.g., el = the, él = he).

Please don't call *(1)* **before 9:00 AM.** / *(2)* **after 10 PM.** Por favor no m
llame (Fam: llames) (1) antes de las nueve de la mañana. / *(2)* después d
las diez de la noche. **If you call and I'm not there,** *(1)* **please try agai**
later. / *(2)* **leave a message.** Si *usted llama (Fam: tú llamas)* y no m
encuentro *(1)* por favor *intente (Fam: intenta)* de nuevo más tarde. / *(2*
deje (Fam: deja) un recado. **I'm really glad you called.** Me alegra qu
usted haya (Fam: hayas) llamado. **Did you call me?** ¿Me *llamó uste*
(Fam: llamaste?)? **I waited for you to call me (but you didn't).** Esperé *
que *usted me llamara (Fam: tú me llamaras)* (pero no *llamó [Fam*
llamaste]). *(1)* **I** / *(2)* **We called you, but you weren't there.** Le *(Fam*
Te)(1) llamé / *(2)* llamamos, pero no *estaba usted (Fam: estabas)* ahí. *(1,*
I / *(2)* **We tried many times to call you.** *(1)* Traté / *(2)* Tratamos mucha:
veces de *llamarle a usted (Fam: llamarte.)*. **I** *(1)* **didn't** / *(2)* **couldn't ca**
you, because *(reason)*. *(1)* No *le (Fam: te)* llamé..., / *(2)* No pude *llamarl*
(Fam: llamarte)... , porque ___. **I'm sorry I didn't call you. (I lost you**
number.) Lamento que no *le llamé (Fam: te llamé)*. (Perdí *su [Fam: tu,*
número). **I intended to call you.** Intenté *llamarle (Fam: llamarte)*. **Wh**
didn't you call me? ¿Por qué no me *llamó (Fam: llamaste)*? **Could yo**
please call a taxi? ¿*Podría usted (Fam:¿Podrías)* llamar un taxi por fa
vor? **Let's call a taxi.** Llamemos un taxi. **I'll call a taxi.** Voy a llamar un
taxi. **I called a taxi.** Llamé un taxi. *(1)* **My friends call...** / *(2)* **Everybody**
calls... / *(3)* **You can call...** / *(4)* **Please call... me** *(name)*. *(1)* Mis amigo·
me llaman... / *(2)* Todos me llaman... / *(3)* Usted puede llamarme... / *(4,*
Por favor llámeme... ___. **What do you call** *(1)* **this** / *(2)* **that in Span**
ish? ¿Cómo se llama *(1)* esto / *(2)* eso en español? **In English we call** *(1,*
this / *(2)* **that** *(name)*. En inglés *(1)* esto / *(2)* eso se llama___.

★ **call off** *idiom* cancelar

call *n* llamada *f* **I'll give you a call** *(1)* **tomorrow.** / *(2)* **on Friday.** / *(3)* **on**
Saturday. / *(4)* **on Sunday.** Le llamaré a usted *(Fam: Te llamaré) (1,*
mañana. / *(2)* el viernes. / *(3)* el sábado. / *(4)* el domingo. **Please give me**
a call *([1]* anytime / *[1]* sometime). Por favor *llámeme usted (Fam.*
llámame) ([1] a cualquier hora. / *[1]* alguna vez). **I need to make a long·**
distance call. Necesito hacer una llamada de larga distancia. **How do I**
make a long distance call? ¿Cómo hago una llamada de larga distancia;
Were there any calls? ¿Hubo llamadas? **Did I get any calls?** ¿Hubo
alguna llamada para mí?

calm *adj* tranquilo *m*, -la *f* **Just stay calm.** Sólo mantenga la calma.

camera *n* cámara *f* **digital** ~ cámara digital **disposable** ~ cámara desechable
video ~ cámara de video **Do you have a camera?** ¿Tiene usted (Fam.
¿Tienes) cámara? **I (don't) have a camera.** Yo (no) tengo cámara.

> *Spanish "g" is pronounced like "h" in front of "e" and "i".*
> *In front of other vowels it sounds like our "g" in "gun".*

camp *vi* acampar **Can we camp** *(1)* **here?** / *(2)* **there?** ¿Podemos acampar *(1)* aquí / *(2)* allá? **Where can** *(1)* **I** / *(2)* **we camp?** ¿Dónde *(1)* puedo / *(2)* podemos acampar? **We can camp at** *(place)*. Podemos acampar en __.

campfire *n* fogata *f* **Let's make a campfire.** Hagamos una fogata. **Did you put out the campfire?** ¿Apagaste la fogata?

campground *n* terreno *m* para acampar **Is there a campground around here?** ¿Hay algún terreno para acampar por aquí?

camping *n* campamento *m (See phrases under* **go,** *like and* **love**.*)* **go ~ (over-night)** ir a acampar (por la noche)

can: Can you? ¿*Puede usted (Fam:* ¿*Puedes)*? **I can.** Yo puedo. **I can't.** No puedo. **We can.** Nosotros podemos. **We can't.** No podemos. **Can** *(1)* **he?** / *(2)* **she?** ¿Puede *(1)* él? / *(2)* ella? *(1)* **He** / *(2)* **She can(not).** *(1)* Él / *(2)* Ella (no) puede. **Can they?** ¿Ellos pueden? **They can(not).** Ellos (no) pueden. **Could you?** ¿*Podría usted (Fam:* ¿*Podrías)*? **I could.** Yo podría. **I couldn't.** No podría.

can *n* lata *f* **~ opener** abrelatas *m*

Canada *n* Canadá *m* **from ~** de Canadá; desde Canadá **in ~** en Canadá **to ~** hacia Canadá

Canadian *adj* canadiense *m&f* ★ *n* canadiense *m&f*

canal *n* canal *m*

cancel *vt* cancelar **It's been cancelled.** Se ha cancelado.

Cancer *n (zodiac) (Jun. 21 - Jul. 22)* Cáncer

candle *n* vela *f*

candlelight *n* luz *f* de las velas *(1)* **Let's have...** / *(2)* **I love... dinner by candlelight**. *(1)* Vamos cenando... / *(2)* Me encanta cenar ... a la luz de las velas.

candy *n* dulce *m* **piece of ~** dulce **Would you care for some candy?** ¿Le *(Fam:*¿*Te)* apetece algo dulce?

canoe *vi* remar en canoa **I'll teach you how to canoe.** Yo *le enseño a usted (Fam: te enseño)* a remar en canoa.

canoe *n* canoa *f*

canoeing *n* canotaje *m* **Let's go canoeing!** ¡Vámonos a hacer canotaje!

canteen *n* cantimplora *f* **Bring your canteen**. *Traiga usted su (Fam: Trae tu)* cantimplora.

canyon *n* cañón *m*

cap *n* cachucha *f* **You'd better wear a cap. (The sun is strong.)** Será mejor que *se ponga usted (Fam: te pongas)* una cachucha. (El sol está fuerte.)

capacity *n* capacidad *f* **I have a great capacity for love.** Tengo una gran capacidad para el amor.

English-Spanish and Spanish-English glossaries
of food and drink are on pages 420-427.

Capricorn *n (zodiac) (Dec. 22 - Jan. 19)* Capricornio
capable *adj* capaz *m&f*
capricious *adj* caprichoso *m*, -sa *f*
captivate *vt* cautivar **You have captivated my heart.** Has cautivado mi
corazón. **Your beautiful eyes have captivated me completely.** *Sus (Fam:
Tus)* bellos ojos me han cautivado por completo.
captivated *past part* cautivado *m*, -da *f* **I'm captivated by your beauty.**
Estoy cautivado *(-da)* por *su (Fam: tu)* belleza.
capture *vt* capturar **You captured my attention the moment** *(1)* **I saw you.**
/ *(2)* **you walked in.** Capturaste mi atención al momento en que *(1)* te vi.
/ *(2)* entraste caminando.
car *n* 1. *(auto)* carro *m*, coche *m* ; 2. *(train)* coche *m*, vagón *m* *(1,2)* **drive a**
~ *(1)* manejar / *(2)* conducir un carro **rent a ~** rentar un carro **rental ~**
carro de renta **Do you have a car?** ¿Tiene usted *(Fam: ¿Tienes)* **carro?**
(1) **I** / *(2)* **We (don't) have a car.** *(1)* (No) Tengo / *(2)* Tenemos carro. **Can**
you drive a car? ¿Sabe usted *(Fam: Sabes)* manejar? **I can(not) drive a**
car. (No) Sé manejar. **Does someone in your family have a car?** ¿Alguien
de tu familia tiene carro? **Do you know someone with a car?** ¿Conoce
usted *(Fam: ¿Conoces)* a alguien que tenga carro? **We can go there in** *(1)*
my / *(2)* **our car.** Podemos ir allá en *(1)* mi / *(2)* nuestro carro. **Where can**
(1) **I** / *(2)* **we rent a car?** ¿Dónde *(1)* puedo / *(2)* podemos rentar un carro?
card *n* tarjeta *f* **ATM ~** tarjeta para el cajero automático **business ~** tarjeta
comercial **calling ~** tarjeta de presentación **cash machine ~** tarjeta para
máquina de efectivo **credit ~** tarjeta de crédito **ID / identification ~** tarjeta
de identificación **Green Card** *(U.S. immigration document)* Tarjeta Verde
telephone ~ tarjeta telefónica **Where can I buy a telephone card?** ¿Dónde
puedo comprar una tarjeta telefónica?
cards *n, pl* cartas *f, pl,* naipes *m, pl (See also phrases under* **like, love** *and*
play.*)*
care *vi* 1. *(be interested)* interesarle a uno 2. *(have feelings for)* importarle a
uno **I don't care.** No me importa. **I care about you very much.** Me
importas muchísimo.
  ★ **care for** *idiom (like)* gustarle a uno **Would you care for a** *(1)* **cup of**
    coffee? / *(2)* **glass of wine?** / *(3)* **beer?** / *(4)* **coke?** ¿Le *(Fam: ¿Te)*
    gustaría una *(1)* taza de café? / *(2)* copa de vino? / *(3)* cerveza? / *(4)*
    coca?
care *n* ciudado *m* **take ~ of** cuidar de, encargarse de **Could you** *(1,2)* **take**
care of this (for a few minutes)? ¿Podría usted *(Fam: ¿Podrías)* *(1)*
cuidar / *(2)* encargarse *(Fam: encargarte)* de esto (por unos minutos)? *(1)*
I'll / *(2)* **We'll take care of it for you.** *(watch over)* *(1)* Yo *se (Fam: te)* lo

---

A phrasebook makes a great gift!
Use the order form on page 432.

cuido. / (2) Nosotros *se (Fam: te)* lo cuidamos. **Thanks for taking care of it for me.** Gracias por cuidármelo. *(1)* **I'll /** *(2)* **We'll take care of it.** *(pay the bill) (1)* Yo me encargo de eso. / (2) Nosotros nos encargamos de eso. **I promise to take very good care of you.** Prometo que te cuidaré muy bien. **I want to give you lots of tender, loving care**. Quiero cuidarte **con** mucho cariño y ternura.

career *n* carrera *f* **What kind of career do you want?** ¿Qué clase de carrera quieres?

carefree *adj* despreocupado *m*, -da *f* **You seem like a carefree person.** Parece que *usted es (Fam: eres)* una persona despreocupada.

careful *n* cuidadoso *m*, -sa *f* **Please be careful.** Por favor, ten cuidado. **We have to be careful.** Tenemos que ser cuidadosos *(-sas)*. **I promise I'll be careful.** Te prometo que seré cuidadoso *(-sa)*.

carefully *adv* con cuidado; cuidadosamente

careless *adj* descuidado *m*, -da *f*

caress *vt* acariciar ~ **gently** ~ acariciar suavemente **I love to caress you.** Me encanta acariciarte. **I could spend endless hours caressing you.** Podría pasarme horas enteras acariciándote.

caress *n* caricia *f* **gentle ~es** suaves caricias **loving ~es** amorosas caricias **soft ~es** tenues caricias **I love your caresses.** Me encantan tus caricias. **Your caresses are pure magic.** Tus caricias son magia pura.

caring *adj* solícito *m*, -ta *f* ~ **person** persona *m&f* solícita **You're such a good, sweet, caring person.** Eres una persona tan buena, dulce y solícita.

carnival *n* carnaval *m* **Let's go to the carnival!** ¡Vamos al carnaval!

carry *vt* llevar **I'll carry it (for you).** Yo *(se [Fam: te])* lo llevo. **Let me carry it (for you)**. *Déjeme llevárselo (Fam: Déjame llevártelo).*

cart *n* carro *m*, carreta *f*

carving *n (object)* talla *f* **wood** ~ talla de madera

case *n* 1. *(large box)* cajón *m* ; 2. *(small box)* cajita *f* ; 3. *(event)* caso *m* ; 4. *(grammar)* caso *m* **in** ~ en caso **just in** ~ por si acaso

cash *vt* cambiar **Where can I cash traveler's checks?** ¿Dónde puedo cambiar cheques de viajero?

cash *n* dinero *m* en efectivo ~ **machine** máquina *f* de efectivo **I don't have enough cash (with me).** No traigo suficiente efectivo . **Is there a discount for cash?** ¿Hay algún descuento por pago en efectivo?

casino *n* casino *m*

cassette *n* casete *m* ~ **player** toca-casetes *m* ~ **tape** tocacintas *m* **video** ~ cartucho de video

castle *n* castillo *m*

casual *adj* 1. *(informal)* informal *m&f* ; *(superficial)* superficial *m&f* ; 2.

A slash always means "or".

(nonchalant) despreocupado *m*, -da *f* ~ **clothes** ropa *f* informal

casually *adv (nonchalantly)* con aire despreocupado; con toda tranquilidad

cat *n* **gato** *m*, -ta *f* ~ **lover** amante *m&f* de los gatos

catch *vt* 1. *(ball, objects)* agarrar, cachar; 2. *(capture, trap)* atrapar; 3. *(fish)* pescar; 4. *(attract)* atraer; 5. *(become infected)* atrapar; contraer; 6. *(buses, trains)* tomar *(1,2)* **Catch!** *(1)* ¡Cacha! / *(2)* ¡Agarra! **I'm so glad I caught your attention.** Estoy tan contento de que pude captar *su (Fam: tu)* atención. **I think I caught a cold.** Creo que atrapé un resfriado. **Where can I catch the bus to** *(place)*? ¿Dónde puedo tomar el camión que va a ___?

catch *n (game)* lanzar la pelota *f* **Let's play catch.** Juguemos a lanzarnos la pelota.

cathedral *n* catedral *f*

Catholic *adj* católico *m*, -ca *f* ★ *n* católico *m*, -ca *f*

cause *vt* ocasionar, causar, producir, provocar **What caused it?** ¿Qué lo causó? *(1)* **I** / *(2)* **We don't want to cause you any** *(3)* **inconvenience.** / *(4)* **trouble.** *(1)* No quiero / *(2)* queremos ocasionarle *(Fam: ocasionarte)* *(3)* ninguna incomodidad. / *(4)* ningún problema.

cause *n* causa *f*

caution *n* cautela *f*, prudencia *f* **We have to use caution.** Tenemos que ser cautelosos.

cautious *adj* prudente *m&f*, cauto *m*, -ta *f*, cauteloso *m*, -sa *f*

cave *n* cueva *f* **Are there any caves in this area?** ¿Hay cuevas en esta área?

cavort *vi* retozar **Come cavort with me.** Ven a retozar conmigo.

celebrate *vt* celebrar **Let's celebrate** *(1)* **the day.** / *(2)* **the evening.** / *(3)* **the holiday.** / *(4)* **the holidays.** / *(5)* **the occasion.** / *(6)* **being together.** Celebremos *(1)* el día. / *(2)* la velada. / *(3)* el día festivo. / *(4)* las vacaciones. / *(5)* la ocasión. / *(6)* que estamos juntos. **We're going to celebrate your birthday.** Vamos a celebrar tu cumpleaños.

celebration *n* celebración *f* **This calls for a celebration.** Esto amerita una celebración.

celebrity *n* celebridad *m&f* **I'm a celebrity travelling incognito. I can't stand the media.** Soy una celebridad que viaja de incógnito. No soporto a los medios.

celibacy *n* celibato *m* **Celibacy is painful, but it can be cured.** El celibato es doloroso, pero se puede curar.

celibate *adj* célibe *m&f* **I've been celibate a long time. (Since 9 o'clock last night.)** He sido célibe por mucho tiempo. (Desde las nueve en punto de anoche.)

cellphone *n* teléfono *m* celular **Could I please use your cellphone?** Por

---

Spanish "v" is pronounced like a soft "b".

favor, ¿podría usar *su (Fam: tu)* teléfono celular?

cemetery *n* cementerio *m*

center *n* centro *m* **amusement** ~ centro de diversiones **city** ~ centro de la ciudad **fitness** ~ centro de acondicionamiento físico **shopping** ~ centro comercial

ceremony *n* ceremonia *f* **civil** ~ *(wedding)* ceremonia civil **graduation** ~ ceremonia de graduación **religious** ~ *(wedding)* ceremonia religiosa **wedding** ~ ceremonia de matrimonio

certain *adj* seguro *m*, -ra *f* **Are you certain?** *¿Está usted (Fam: ¿Estás)* seguro *(-ra)*? *(1)* **I'm** / *(2)* **We're (not) certain.** *(1)* (No) Estoy seguro *(-ra)*. / *(2)* (No) Estamos seguros.

certainly *adv* por supuesto, seguro, claro *(1,2)* **Certainly!** *(1)* ¡Seguro! / *(2)* ¡Claro! *(1,2)* **Certainly not.** *(1)* Seguro / *(2)* Claro que no.

certificate *n* certificado *m* ; acta *f* **birth** ~ acta de nacimiento **marriage** ~ acta de matrimonio **You need to have your birth certificate translated.** Es necesario que se traduzca su *(Fam: tu)* acta de nacimiento.

chain *n* cadena *f* **gold** ~ cadena de oro **silver** ~ cadena de plata

chair *n* silla *f* **beach** ~ silla de playa **deck** ~ silla de playa **lounge** ~ sillón de jardín **easy** ~ sillón *m*, poltrona *f* **We need** *(1)* **another chair.** / *(2)* **more chairs.** Necesitamos *(1)* otra silla. / *(2)* más sillas.

challenge *vt* retar, desafiar **I challenge you to a game of** *(1)* **chess.** / *(2)* **cribbage.** / *(3)* **tennis.** Te reto a un juego de *(1)* ajedrez. / *(2)* baraja. / *(3)* tenis.

challenge *n* reto *m*, desafío *m* *(1)* **I** / *(2)* **We accept the challenge.** *(1)* Yo acepto... / *(2)* Nosotros aceptamos... el reto.

challenging *adj* desafiante *m & f*, provocativo *m*, -va *f* ; emocionante *m&f* **Your** *(1)* **career** / *(2)* **job** / *(3)* **profession sounds very challenging.** *Su (Fam: Tu)* *(1)* carrera / *(2)* empleo / *(3)* profesión suena muy emocionante.

champagne *n* champaña *f or m* **This calls for some champagne.** Esto amerita un brindis con champaña. **Bring out the champagne!** ¡Traigan el champaña!

champion *n* campeón *m*, -ona *f* **new** ~ nuevo *(-va)* campeón *(-peona)* **world** ~ campeón *(-peona)* mundial

championship *n* campeonato *m* **This is for the (world) championship.** Esto es para el campeonato (mundial).

chance *n* 1. *(opportunity)* oportunidad *f* ; 2. *(occasion)* ocasión *f* ; 3. *(risk)* riesgo *m* **another** ~ otra oportunidad **big** ~ gran oportunidad **give** *(1)* **you** / *(2)* **me a** ~ *(1)* dar te / *(2)* darme una oportunidad **good** ~ buena oportunidad **last** ~ última oportunidad **miss the** ~ perder la oportunidad **only** ~ la única oportunidad **second** ~ una segunda oportunidad **take a** ~ correr el riesgo

Time expressions are given on page 413.

I'm so glad I had the chance to meet you. Me complace haber tenido ocasión de conocerte. **We're so glad we had the chance to meet you.** Nos alegra haber tenido ocasión de conocerte. **If you have the chance ([1] tonight / [2] tomorrow), call (3) me / (4) us.** Si tiene usted (Fam: tienes) ocasión ([1] esta noche / [2] mañana), (3) llámame. / (4) llámanos. **Is there any chance that (1) I can see (2,3) you (4) tonight? / (5) tomorrow? / (6) this weekend? / (7) you can get off work (8) today? / (9) tomorrow? / (10) you can take vacation? / (11) you can come with me?** ¿Hay alguna oportunidad de que (1) pueda (2) verlo m / (3) verla f a usted (Fam: verte) (4) esta noche? / (5) mañana? / (6) el fin de semana? / (7) pueda usted (Fam: puedas) salir del trabajo (8) hoy? / (9) mañana? / (10) pueda usted (Fam: puedas) tomar unas vacaciones? / (11) pueda usted (Fam: puedas) venir conmigo? **You'll never have any fun in life if you don't take a chance.** Nunca te divertirás en la vida si no corres el riesgo. **I thought I would never have a chance for love (in my life).** Pensé que nunca (en mi vida) tendría la oportunidad de amar. **A chance like this comes only once in a lifetime.** Una oportunidad como esta sólo ocurre una vez en la vida. **Please give me (1) another / (2) a second chance.** Por favor, dame (1) otra / (2) una segunda oportunidad.

change vt cambiar ~ **channels** (TV) cambiar canales ~ **clothes** cambiar la ropa ~ **diapers** cambiar pañales ~ **partners** (games) cambiar de compañeros ~ **places** (seats) cambiar de lugar **Do we have to change trains?** ¿Tenemos que cambiar de tren? **We (don't) have to change trains.** (No) Tenemos que cambiar de tren. **(1) I / (2) We need to change some money. (1)** Necesito / (2) Necesitamos cambiar dinero. **Where can (1) I / (2) we change money?** ¿Dónde (1) puedo / (2) podemos cambiar dinero?

change n 1. (alteration) cambio m ; 2. (small money) cambio m ; morralla f **small** ~ pequeño cambio **This is such a (1) nice / (2) refreshing change (from my [work] routine).** Este es un cambio tan (1) agradable / (2) refrescante (en mi rutina [de trabajo]).

channel n (TV) canal m **Do you mind if I change the channel?** ¿Te importa si cambio el canal?

chapel n capilla f

chaperon(e) vt chaperonear

chaperon(e) n chaperón m, -na f

character n 1. (nature) carácter m ; 2. (movie, novel) personaje m **easygoing** ~ de carácter sencillo **fine** ~ de bonito carácter **good** ~ de buen carácter

charge vt 1. (ask a price) cobrar; 2. (apply to credit) cargar; 3. (battery) cargar **How much do (1) you / (2) they charge (per [3] hour / [4] day)?**

Spanish "qu" is pronounced like "k".

¿Cuánto *(1)* ...cobra usted... / *(2)* ...cobran... (por *[3]* hora / *[4]* día)? **Can I charge it (to my credit card)?** ¿Puedo cargarlo (a mi tarjeta de crédito)?

charge *n* 1. *(price, fee)* cobro *m*, cargo *m* ; 2. *(command, leadership)* mando *m* **be in ~** estar al mando **free of ~** gratis, sin cargo **take ~** tomar el mando **What is this charge?** ¿De qué es este cargo? **Is there a charge (for that)?** ¿Se cobra (por eso)?

charisma *n* carisma *m* **You have a lot of charisma.** *Usted tiene (Fam: Tienes)* mucho carisma.

charm *vt* cautivar, embelesar **You could charm the socks off a police commissioner.** Tú podrías cautivar al más pintado.

charm *n* encanto *m*, atractivo *m* **I'm captivated by your charm.** Estoy cautivado por *su (Fam: tu)* encanto. **You dazzle me with your charm, beauty, and blithe spirit.** Me *deslumbra usted (Fam: deslumbras)* con *su (Fam: tu)* encanto, *su (Fam: tu)* belleza y *su (Fam: tu)* espíritu risueño.

charming *adj* encantador *m*, -dora *f*

charter *vt (hire)* fletar **~ a boat** fletar un bote **~ a bus** fletar un autobús

charter *n (hire)* (contrato *m* de) flete *m*

chase *vt* cazar **~ rainbows** cazar arcoiris

chat *vi* platicar, charlar, chatear **~ on the Internet** chatear por Internet **Let's sit and chat for awhile.** Sentémonos y platiquemos un rato.

chat *n* plática *f*, conversación *f*, charla *f* **~ room** *(Internet)* sala de chateo **long ~** una larga plática **Let's go someplace and have a chat.** Vamos a algún lugar a platicar.

chatterbox *n* parlanchín *m*, -china *f*, tarabilla *m&f*

chauvinist *n* chovinista *m&f*

chauvinistic *adj* chovinista *m&f*

cheap *adj (inexpensive)* barato *m*, -ta *f*

cheapskate *n* tacaño *m*, -ña *f*, agarrado *m*, -da *f*, mezquino *m*, -na *f*

cheat *vt* engañar, estafar, hacer trampa **That's not fair! You cheated!** ¡No es justo! ¡Hiciste trampa! **I would never *(1,2)* cheat on you.** Nunca te *(1)* engañaría. / *(2)* estafaría.

cheating *n* trampa *f*, engaño *m* **No cheating!** ¡Sin trampas!

check *vt* verificar, revisar, checar **Could you please check the *(1)* brakes? / *(2)* engine? / *(3)* oil? / *(4)* transmission?** ¿Podría revisar por favor *(1)* los frenos? / *(2)* el motor? / *(3)* el aceite? / *(4)* la transmisión?

check *vi* verificar, revisar **I'll go check.** Voy a verificar. **Check and see if...** Ve a ver si …

check *n* 1. *(bill)* cuenta *f*; 2. *(payment)* cheque *m* **traveller's ~(s)** cheque(s) de viajero *(1)* **I'll /** *(2)* **We'll take care of the check.** *(1)* Yo me hago... / *(2)* Nosotros nos hacemos... cargo de la cuenta. **Do *(1)* you /** *(2)* **they**

Words in parentheses (not italicized) are optional.

accept traveller's checks? *(1)* ¿Acepta usted... / *(2)* ¿Aceptan... cheques de viajero?

check in *idiom* registrar la entrada

check out *idiom* registrar la salida **What time do we have to check out?** ¿A qué hora tenemos que registrar la salida?

checkers *n, pl* damas *fpl* **Want to play some checkers?** ¿Quieres jugar damas?

cheek *n* mejilla *f*, cachete *m* **You have such** *(1)* **smooth /** *(2)* **soft cheeks.** Tienes unas mejillas tan *(1)* tersas. / *(2)* suaves. **Your cheeks are getting red.** Se te están poniendo rojas las mejillas.

cheerful *adj* alegre *m&f* **I like your cheerful nature.** Me gusta *su (Fam: tu)* naturaleza alegre. **You're such a cheerful person.** *Usted es (Fam: Eres)* una persona tan alegre.

cheerfulness *n* alegría *f* **Your cheerfulness is so refreshing.** *Su (Fam: tu)* alegría es tan refrescante.

Cheers! *(toasting expression)* ¡Salud!

cheer up *vt* animar *(1)* **I /** *(2)* **We want to cheer you up.** *(1)* Yo quiero / *(2)* Queremos *animarlo a usted (Fam: ...animarte)*. **Maybe this will help cheer you up.** Tal vez esto *le ayude a animarse (Fam: te ayude a animarte)*.

cheer up *vi* animarse **Cheer up, everything will be okay.** *Anímese (Fam: Anímate)*, todo saldrá bien.

chemistry *n* 1. *(science)* química *f*; 2. *(attraction)* química *f* **We have such good chemistry between us.** Hay tan buena química entre nosotros.

cherish *vt* apreciar mucho, valorar, estimar **I cherish you.** Te aprecio mucho. **I will always cherish the memory of** *(1)* **these days... /** *(2)* **this time... (with you).** Siempre atesoraré el recuerdo de *(1)* estos días... / *(2)* este momento... (contigo).

chess *n* ajedrez *m* ~ **set** juego *m* de ajedrez **Do you know how to play chess?** *¿Sabe usted (Fam: Sabes)* jugar ajedrez? **I'll teach you how to play chess.** Yo *le (Fam: te)* enseño a jugar ajedrez. **Let's play a game of chess.** Juguemos una partida de ajedrez.

chessboard *n* tablero *m* de ajedrez

chest *n* 1. *(breast)* pecho *m* ; 2. *(box, trunk)* cofre *m* **bare ~** pecho descubierto **beautiful ~** pecho hermoso **big ~** pecho grande **nice ~** pecho bonito **You are a(n) (absolute) treasure chest of** *(1)* **beauty. /** *(2)* **delights. /** *(3)* **fun.** / *(4)* **love. /** *(5)* **pleasure. /** *(6)* **sweetness.** Tú eres todo un tesoro de *(1)* belleza. / *(2)* delicias. *(3)* diversión. / *(4)* amor. / *(5)* placer. / *(6)* dulzura.

chewing gum *n* chicle *m*, goma *f* de mascar

chic *adj* elegante *m&f* **My! How chic you look!** ¡Caramba! ¡Qué elegante *se ve usted (Fam: te ves!)*! **You look very chic in that** *(1)* **dress. /** *(2)*

A single Spanish "r" should be lightly trilled;
double "r" ("rr") should be strongly trilled.

outfit. *Se ve usted (Fam: Te ves)* muy elegante con ese *(1)* vestido. / *(2)* atuendo.

child *n (boy)* niño *m* ; *(girl)* niña *f* ; *(son)* hijo *m* ; *(daughter)* hija *f* **Do you have any children?** ¿Tiene usted hijos? *(1)* **I** / *(2)* **We have** *(3)* **one child.** / *(4)* **two** / *(5)* **three** / *(6)* **four children.** *(1)* Yo tengo... / *(2)* Nosotros tenemos... *(3)* un*(a)* hijo *(-ja)*. / *(4)* dos / *(5)* tres / *(6)* cuatro hijos. *(1)* **I** / *(2)* **We don't have any children.** *(1)* Yo no tengo... / *(2)* Nosotros no tenemos... hijos. *(1)* **My** / *(2)* **Our children are grown.** *(1)* Mis / *(2)* Nuestros hijos ya están grandes. **How old are your children?** ¿Que edad tienen sus hijos? **I love children.** Me encantan los niños. **Can you recommend something for children?** ¿Me puede recomendar algo para los niños?

childhood *n* niñez *f* **in my ~** en mi niñez

childish *adj* infantil *m&f*, pueril *m&f*

chilly *adj* frío *m*, fría *f* **It's chilly!** ¡Hace frío! **Why are you so chilly toward me?** ¿Por qué eres tan frío *(fria)* conmigo?

chin *n* barbilla *f*, mentón *m* **I love the dimple on your chin.** Me encanta ese hoyuelo en tu mentón.

chips *n, pl (snack)* frituras *f, pl* **corn ~** frituras de maíz **nacho ~** nachos **potato ~** papas *f, pl* fritas

chivalrous *adj* cortés *m&f*, caballeroso *m*, -sa *f*, gentil *m&f* **How chivalrous you are!** ¡Qué gentil es usted!

chocolate *n* chocolate *m* **box of ~s** caja *f* de chocolates **hot ~** chocolate caliente **Do you like chocolates?** ¿Te gustan los chocolates?

choice *n* elección *f*, selección *f* **bad ~** mala elección **first ~** primera elección **good ~** buena elección **lucky ~** elección afortunada **make a ~** elegir, escoger, decidir **second ~** segunda elección **Coming here was the best choice I ever made.** Venir acá fue la mejor decisión que he tomado jamás.

choir *n* coro *m* **church ~** coro de la iglesia **I sing in a choir.** Yo canto en un coro.

cholesterol *n* colesterol *m* **I have to watch my cholesterol.** Tengo que vigilar mi colesterol.

choose *vt* elegir **I'll let you choose.** Te dejaré elegir. **Go ahead and choose one.** Anda y elige uno.

choosy *adj* exigente *m&f*, difícil *m&f* de complacer

chord *n (music)* acorde *m* **play a few ~s** tocar unos cuantos acordes

chorus *n* coro *m*

Christian *adj* cristiano *m*, -na *f*

Christian *n* cristiano *m*, -na *f* **born-again ~** que volvió a nacer en Cristo

Christianity *n* cristiandad *f*

---

*Familiar "tu" forms in parentheses can
replace italicized polite forms.*

Christmas *adj* de (la) Navidad, navideño *m*, -ña *f* ~ **card** tarjeta de Navidad ~ **Day** el Día de la Navidad ~ **Eve** la Víspera de la Navidad ~ **gift** regalo de Navidad *(1,2)* ~ **shopping** compras *(1)* navideñas / *(2)* de la Navidad ~ **tree** árbol de Navidad ~ **vacation** vacaciones de Navidad

Christmas *n* Navidad *f* **Merry Christmas!** ¡Feliz Navidad! **I want to spend Christmas together with you.** Quiero pasar la Navidad junto a ti.

chubby *adj* regordete *m*, -ta *f*, rechonchito *m*, -ta *f*, gordito *m*, -ta *f*, rellenito *m*, -ta *f* **I like it that you're a little chubby.** Me gusta que seas un poco gordito *(-ta)*. **I hope you don't mind it that I'm a little chubby.** Espero que no te importe el que sea un poco gordito *(-ta)*.

church *n* iglesia *f* **Do you go to church (often)?** ¿*Va usted (Fam: ¿Vas)* (mucho) a la iglesia? *(1)* **I** / *(2)* **We (don't) go to church (**[3] **often.** / [4] **regularly.** / [5] **every Sunday.).** (No) *(1)* Voy / *(2)* Vamos a la iglesia (*[3]* mucho. / *[4]* con regularidad. / *[5]* todos los domingos.). **Let's go to church together on Sunday.** Vamos juntos a la iglesia el domingo.

chutzpah *n (audacity, nerve)* desfachatez *f*, audacia *f*, atrevimiento *m*

cigarette *n* cigarrillo *m*

circle *n* círculo *m* ~ **of friends** círculo de amistades **go around in** ~s dar la vuelta en círculos

circulation *n* circulación *f* **It's good for your circulation.** Es bueno para *su (Fam: tu)* circulación. **I've been out of circulation for a long time.** He estado fuera de circulación por mucho tiempo.

circumstance *n* circunstancia *f* **difficult** ~s circunstancias difíciles **financial** ~s circunstancias financieras **unfortunate** ~s circunstancias desafortunadas

circus *n* circo *m*

citizen *n* ciudadano *m*, -na *f* **become a** ~ hacerse ciudadano *(-na)* **senior** ~ persona mayor **I'm a(n)** *(1)* **American** / *(2)* **Australian** / *(3)* **British** / *(4)* **Canadian** / *(5)* **Irish** / *(6)* **New Zealand citizen.** Soy ciudadano *(-na)* *(1)* estadounidense. / *(2)* australiano *(-na)*. / *(3)* británico *(-ca)*. / *(4)* canadiense. / *(5)* irlandés *(-desa)*. / *(6)* neozelandés *(-desa)*.

citizenship *n* ciudadanía *f* **apply for** ~ solicitar la ciudadanía **get** ~ obtener la ciudadanía

city *n* ciudad *f* ~ **map** mapa *m* de la ciudad **What city are you from?** ¿De qué ciudad es usted? **Do you know this city well?** ¿*Conoce usted (Fam: ¿Conoces)* bien esta ciudad? *(1)* **I** / *(2)* **We (don't) know this city (very) well.** (No) *(1)* Conozco / *(2)* Conocemos (muy) bien esta ciudad. **Could you show** *(1)* **me** / *(2)* **us around the city?** ¿*Podría usted (Fam: ¿Podrías)* *(1)* mostrarme / *(2)* mostrarnos la ciudad? **That was really nice of you to show** *(1)* **me** / *(2)* **us around the city.** Fue muy amable de *su (Fam: tu)* parte *(1)* mostrarme / *(2)* mostrarnos la ciudad.

Spanish "ll" is pronounced like "y" in "yes".

clairvoyant *adj* clarividente *m&f* **You must be clairvoyant.** Tú debes ser clarividente.

clam(s) *n (pl)* almeja(s) *f (pl)* **dig ~s** sacar almejas

class *n (*1. *school group;* 2. *category;* 3. *style)* clase *f* **business ~** clase comercial **economy ~** clase económica **first ~** primera clase **graduating ~** clase de graduados **second ~** segunda clase **tourist ~** clase turista

classmate *n* compañero *m*, -ra *f* de clase

classy *adj* con clase

clean *adj* limpio *m*, -pia *f*, aseado *m*, -da *f*

clean *vt* limpiar **The maid hasn't cleaned the room yet.** La recamarera no ha limpiado el cuarto todavía.

★ **clean up** *idiom* asearse *(1)* **I'm / (2) We're going to go clean up.** *(1)* Me voy... / *(2)* Nos vamos... a asear.

clear *adj (1. easily visible; 2. easily understandable)* claro *m*, -ra *f*

clearly *adv (1. easily visible; 2. undoubtedly)* claramente

clerk *n* dependiente *m*, -ta *f* **office ~** oficinista *m&f* **store ~** tendero *m*, -ra *f*

clever *adj* listo *m*, -ta *f*, inteligente *m & f* **How clever!** ¡Qué listo! **Oh, you are a clever one!** ¡Ah, tú eres de los listos!

client *n* cliente *m*, -ta *f* **I have to meet with a client.** Tengo una reunión con un*(a)* cliente *(-ta)*.

cliff *n* precipio *m* ; *(seacoast)* acantilado *m*

climb *vt* escalar **I like to climb mountains.** Me gusta escalar montañas. **Have you ever climbed a mountain?** ¿Alguna vez has escalado montañas?

climbing *n* montañismo *m* **(mountain) ~ equipment** equipo de montañismo **go mountain ~** ir de montañismo

clock *n* reloj *m* **alarm ~** reloj despertador **Don't forget to set the alarm clock.** No se te olvide poner el despertador. **Is that clock right?** ¿Está bien ese reloj? **The clock is** *(1)* **fast. / (2) slow. / (3) right.** El reloj está *(1)* adelantado. / *(2)* retrasado. / *(3)* correcto.

close *adj* cercano *m*, -na *f* **~ resemblance** gran semejanza **That was a close call.** Se salvó por un pelo.

close *adv* cerca **I like to have you close to me.** Me gusta tenerte cerca. **Come (a little) closer.** Ven (un poco) más cerca.

close *vt* cerrar **Close your eyes (and hold out your hands).** *Cierre (Fam: Cierra)* los ojos (y *extienda [Fam: extiende]* las manos).

close *vi* cerrar **What time does it close?** ¿A qué hora cierra? **It closes at** *(time)*. Cierra a las ___.

closed *pp* cerrado *m*, -da *f* **It** *(1)* **is / (2) was closed.** *(1)* Está / *(2)* Estaba cerrado.

clothes *n, pl* ropa *f* **change ~** cambiarse la ropa **comfortable ~** ropa cómoda

---

Common professions are listed on pages 415-416.

dirty ~ ropa sucia **put** ~ **on** ponerse la ropa **take** ~ **off** quitarse la ropa **warm** ~ ropa calientita **wash** ~ lavar la ropa

clown (around) *vi* payasear, hacer payasadas **Stop clowning around!** Deja de andar payaseando.

clown *n* payaso *m*, -sa *f*

club *n* club *m* **dance** ~ club de baile **fitness** ~ gimnasio **gay** ~ club de gays **health** ~ club de salud **music** ~ club de música **private** ~ club privado **Do you know any clubs?** ¿Conoce usted clubes? **I know a great club we can go to.** Yo conozco un club fenomenal al que podemos ir.

clubbing *n*: **go** ~ andar de club en club

clubs *n, pl (card suit)* tréboles *mpl*

clumsy *adj* torpe *m & f* **I'm sorry, that was very clumsy of me.** Lo siento, fui muy torpe.

coach *n (sports)* entrenador *m*, -dora *f*

coast *n* costa *f* **East Coast** *(USA)* la Costa Este **West Coast** *(USA)* la Costa Oeste

coat *n* abrigo *m* **sport** ~ abrigo deportivo **suit** ~ abrigo **warm** ~ abrigo calientito **winter** ~ abrigo de invierno

cockroach(es) *n (pl)* cucaracha(s) *f (pl)*

cocoa *n (drink)* cocoa *f*

coffee *n* café *m* **How about a cup of coffee?** ¿Que tal una taza de café? **Let's (go somewhere and) have a cup of coffee.** Vamos (a algún lugar) a tomarnos un café.

coin *n* moneda *f* **collect** ~**s** coleccionar monedas

cold *adj* frío *m*, fría *f* **get** ~ **feet** acobardarse; echarse para atrás ~ **heart** corazón frío ~ **look** mirada fría **Are you cold?** ¿Tiene usted (Fam: ¿Tienes) frío? *(1)* **I'm** / *(2)* **We're (not) cold.** (No) *(1)* Tengo / *(2)* Tenemos frío.

cold *n (ailment)* resfriado *m*, -da *f* **I have a (slight) cold.** Estoy (algo) resfriado *(-da)*.

cold-hearted *adj* de corazón frío

collect *vt* coleccionar **Do you collect anything?** ¿Colecciona usted (Fam: ¿Coleccionas) algo? **I collect** *(1)* **banknotes.** / *(2)* **coins.** / *(3)* **dolls.** / *(4)* **postcards.** / *(5)* **stamps.** / *(6)* **telephone cards.** Colecciono *(1)* billetes. / *(2)* monedas. / *(3)* muñecas. / *(4)* postales. / *(5)* timbres. / *(6)* tarjetas telefónicas.

collection *n* colección *f* **coin** ~ colección de monedas **doll** ~ colección de muñecas **stamp** ~ colección de timbres

collector *n* coleccionista *m & f* **coin** ~ coleccionista de monedas **doll** ~ coleccionista de muñecas **stamp** ~ coleccionista de timbres

college *n* universidad *f* ~ **education** educación universitaria **Do you go to**

Spanish "y" is "ee" when alone or at the end of words.

college? ¿Va usted (Fam: ¿Vas) a la universidad? **I go to college.** Voy a la universidad. **I graduated from college (in _[year]_).** Me gradué de la universidad (en ___). **I'm going to graduate from college _(1)_ this year. / _(2)_ next year.** Me voy a graduar de la universidad _(1)_ este año. / _(2)_ el próximo año.

color n color m **What color is it?** ¿De qué color es? **It's ([_1_] dark / [_2_] light) _(3)_ black. / _(4)_ blue. / _(5)_ brown. / _(6)_ green. / _(7)_ grey. / _(8)_ maroon. / _(9)_ orange. / _(10)_ pink. / _(11)_ purple. / _(12)_ red. / _(13)_ white. / _(14)_ yellow.** Es ([_1_] oscuro / [_2_] claro) _(3)_ negro. / _(4)_ azul. / _(5)_ café. / _(6)_ verde. / _(7)_ gris. / _(8)_ marrón. / _(9)_ naranja. / _(10)_ rosa. / _(11)_ morado. / _(12)_ rojo. / _(13)_ blanco. / _(14)_ amarillo. **What's your favorite color?** ¿Cuál es _su (Fam: tu)_ color favorito? **My favorite color is _(name)_.** Mi color favorito es el ___.

colorful adj colorido m, -da f, pintoresco m, -ca f

column n _(newspapers)_ columna f **penpal** ~ columna de intercambio de correspondencia **personal ad** ~ columna de anuncios personales

comb n peine m

combination n _(1. combining; 2. of a lock)_ combinación f **I forgot the combination.** Olvidé la combinación.

combine vt combinar _(1)_ **I'm / _(2)_ We're combining business with pleasure.** _(1)_ Estoy / _(2)_ Estamos combinando el negocio con el placer.

come vi venir; ir; llegar **Are you coming?** ¿Vas a llegar? **I'm (not) coming.** (No) Voy a llegar. **We're (not) coming.** (No) Vamos a llegar. **Is _(1)_ he / _(2)_ she coming?** ¿Va a llegar _(1)_ él _(2)_ ella? **_(1)_ He / _(2)_ She is (not) coming.** _(1)_ Él / _(2)_ ella (no) va a llegar. **Are they coming?** ¿Van a llegar? **They are (not) coming.** (No) Van a llegar. **Can you come?** ¿Puede usted (Fam: Puedes) venir? _(1)_ **I'd / _(2)_ We'd love to come.** _(1)_ Me / _(2)_ Nos encantaría ir. **Can I come (with you)?** ¿Puedo ir _(con usted [Fam: contigo])_? **Yes, you can come (with me).** Sí, _usted puede (Fam: tú [1,2] puedes)_ venir (conmigo). **No, you can't come (with me).** No, _usted no puede (Fam: no puedes)_ venir (conmigo). **I'll come with you.** Yo iré _con usted (Fam: contigo)_. **Would it be possible for you to come _(1)_ with me? / _(2)_ ([_3_] here... / [_4_] to my hotel...) after work?** ¿Sería posible que _viniera usted (Fam: vinieras) (1)_ conmigo? / _(2)_ ([_3_] aquí... / [_4_] a mi hotel...) después del trabajo? **Come with me to my _(1)_ apartment. / _(2)_ hotel. / _(3)_ house. / _(4)_ place. / _(5)_ room.** Ven conmigo a mi _(1)_ apartamento. / _(2)_ hotel. / _(3)_ casa. / _(4)_ hogar. / _(5)_ cuarto. **I'd love to have you come with me.** Me encantaría que vinieras conmigo. **We'd love to have you come with us.** Nos encantaría que vinieras con nosotros. **What time will you come?** A

qué hora *viene usted* (*Fam: vienes?*)? **I'll come at** *(time)*. Yo vengo a las
___. **What time** *(1)* **shall** */ (2)* **should I come?** ¿A qué hora *(1)* vengo */ (2)*
debo venir? **Come at** *(time)*. Ven a las ___. **I'll come (here) again** *(1)* **this
year.** */ (2)* **next year.** */ (3)* **in** *(month)*. Yo vendré (aquí) otra vez *(1)* este
año. */ (2)* el año que viene. */ (3)* en___. **Come (a little) closer.** Ven (un
poco) más cerca. **Come (here) to me.** Ven (aquí) conmigo. **Come on!**
¡Vamos! **Come over to** *(1)* **my** */ (2)* **our table.** *Venga usted* (*Fam: Vente*)
a *(1)* mi */ (2)* nuestra mesa. *(1)* **I'll** */ (2)* **We'll come over (to your place)**
(3) **at about** *(time)*. */ (4)* **right away.** *(1)* Vendré */ (2)* Vendremos (a *su
[Fam: tu]* casa) *(3)* aproximadamente a las ___. */ (4)* de inmediato.
- ★ **come back** *idiom* regresar *(1)* **I** */ (2)* **We want to come back here.**
  (1) Quiero */ (2)* Queremos regresar aquí.
- ★ **come in** *idiom* entrar *(1)* **Can** */ (2)* **Could I come in?** *(1)* ¿Puedo */ (2)*
  ¿Podría entrar? **Please come in.** Por favor entre. *(1,2)* **Come in!**
  (1) ¡Pase usted! */ (2)* ¡Entre usted!

comedian, -ienne *n* comediante *m&f*

comedy *n* comedia *f*

comfortable *adj* cómodo *m*, -da *f*, a gusto **Are you comfortable?** ¿Está
usted (Fam: ¿Estás) a gusto? *(1)* **I'm** */ (2)* **We're (quite) comfortable.** *(1)*
Estoy */ (2)* Estamos (bastante) a gusto. **I don't feel comfortable with
that.** No me siento a gusto con eso.

comical *adj* cómico *m*, -ca *f*

comment *n* comentario *m* **catty** ~ comentario malicioso **sarcastic** ~
comentario sarcástico **witty** ~ comentario ingenioso **I didn't understand
your (last) comment.** No entendí *su (Fam: tu)* (último) comentario.

commitment *n* compromiso *m* **lasting** ~ compromiso duradero **lifelong** ~
compromiso de por vida **make a** ~ asumir un compromiso **What I want
most of all in a relationship is commitment.** Lo que más quiero en una
relación es que haya compromiso. **I'm not ready to make a commitment.** No estoy listo *(-ta)* para asumir un compromiso.

common *adj* común *m&f* ~ **sense** sentido común **We have common interests.** Tenemos intereses en común.

common *n* común *m* **You and I have a lot in common.** *Usted (Fam: Tú)* y
yo tenemos mucho en común.

communicate *vi* comunicarse, entenderse **You and I communicate well together.** Tú y yo nos entendemos bien. **We don't seem to be communicat-
ing very well.** Parece que no nos estamos entendiendo muy bien. **It's
important to be able to communicate together.** Es importante que
podamos comunicarnos.

communication *n* comunicación *f*

Spanish "c" before "e" and "i" is pronounced like "s".

community *n (neighborhood)* comunidad *f*

companion *n* compañero *m*, -ra *f* ; acompañante *m & f* **constant ~** acompañante permanente **travel ~** compañero *(-ra)* de viaje **You're such a good companion (for me).** Eres muy buena compañía (para mí). **You're the kind of companion I've always dreamed of.** Tú eres la clase de compañía con la que siempre he soñado.

companionship *n* compañía *f* **I enjoy your companionship.** Disfruto mucho *su (Fam: tu)* compañía.

company *n* 1. *(companionship)* compañía *f*; 2. *(firm)* compañía *f*; 3. *(guests)* visita *f* **I love your company.** Me encanta tu compañía. **I (really) enjoy your company.** (De veras) gozo con *su (Fam: tu)* compañía. *(1)* **I've /** *(2)* **We've really enjoyed your company.** Verdaderamente *(1)* he / *(2)* hemos disfrutado *su (Fam: tu)* compañía. **Two is company, three is a crowd.** Dos son compañía, tres son multitud.

compare *vi* comparar **Nobody can compare to you.** Nadie se te puede comparar.

comparison *n* comparación *f* **There's no comparison.** No hay comparación.

compass *n* brújula *f* **If you have a compass, bring it.** Si tienes una brújula, tráela.

compassion *n* compasión *f* **If you have any shred of compassion, you'll let me see you tonight.** Si *tiene usted (Fam: tienes)* un poquito de compasión, me *dejará verla f (Fam: dejarás verte)* esta noche.

compassionate *adj* compasivo *m*, -va *f* **To show you how compassionate I am, I'm going to let you** *(1)* **carry my suitcase. /** *(2)* **go in first. /** *(3)* **kiss me (again).** Para mostrarte lo compasivo *(-va)* que soy, voy a dejar que *(1)* cargues mi maleta. / *(2)* tú vayas primero. / *(3)* me beses (otra vez).

compatible *adj* compatible *m&f* **You and I are** *(1)* **really /** *(2)* **so compatible together.** Tú y yo somos *(1)* de veras / *(2)* tan compatibles.

compete *vi* competir **We're going to compete for** *(what)*. Vamos a competir por ___.

competition *n* competencia *f*, concurso *m* **You have no competition (with me).** No tienes competencia (conmigo). **You're good competition.** *Es usted (Fam: Eres)* buena competencia.

complain *vi* quejarse *(1)* **I'm /** *(2)* **We're going to complain about it.** *(1)* Voy a quejarme... / *(2)* Vamos a quejarnos... por eso. **I'm not complaining.** No me estoy quejando.

complete *adj* completo *m*, -ta *f*, lleno *m*, -na *f*, pleno *m*, na *f* **You make my life complete.** Tú haces que mi vida sea plena.

completely *adv* completamente, por completo

complexion *n* cutis *m*, tez *f* **You have a lovely complexion.** *Tiene usted*

Numbers in Spanish are given on pages 411-412.

(Fam: Tienes) un cutis precioso.

complicated *adj* complicado *m*, -da *f* **It's a complicated situation.** Es una situación complicada.

compliment *n* halago *m*, cumplido *m* **Thank you for the (nice) compliment.** Gracias por ese cumplido (tan bonito). **That's the nicest compliment anyone has ever made to me.** Ese es el cumplido más bonito que me han hecho.

compose *vt* componer **I composed a poem for you.** Compuse un poema para tí.

compromise *vi* comprometerse **Let's compromise.** Vamos comprometiéndonos.

compromise *n* compromiso *m* **How about a compromise?** ¿Qué te parece si nos comprometemos?

computer *n* computadora *f* use a ~ usar una computadora **personal ~ (PC)** computadora personal **Where can I find a computer (for e-mail)?** ¿Dónde puedo encontrar una computadora (para un correo electrónico)? **Is there anywhere around here where we can use a computer?** ¿Hay algún lugar por aquí donde podamos usar una computadora?

conceited *adj* engreído *m*, -da *f*, presumido *m*, -da *f*

concentrate *vi* concentrarse **I can't concentrate on anything with you around.** No puedo concentrarme en nada cuando estás aquí.

concern *vt* concernir, importar **What does it concern?** ¿Qué importa? **It concerns...** Eso concierne… **As concerns me,...** En lo que a mí concierne...

concerned *adj (worried)* preocupado *m*, -da *f* *(1)* **I'm / *(2)* We're (very) concerned about it.** *(1)* Estoy (muy) preocupado *(-da)*… / *(2)* Estamos (muy) preocupados... por eso.

concert *n* concierto *m* **classical music** ~ concierto de música clásica **rock** ~ concierto de rock **I love concerts.** Me encantan los conciertos.

condition *n* 1. *(state)* estado *m*, condiciones *fpl* ; 2. *(provision)* condición *f* ; 3. *(physical)* estado *m*, condiciones *fpl* **It's in *(1)* bad / *(2)* excellent / *(3)* good condition.** Está en *(1)* malas / *(2)* excelentes / *(3)* buenas condiciones. **Okay, on one condition...** Está bien, con una condición… **You're in (very) good condition.** Estás en (muy) buena forma. **I try to keep in condition.** Trato de mantenerme en forma.

condom *n* condón *m*

condo(minium) *n* condominio *m*

cone *n* cono *m* **ice cream** ~ cono de helado

confess *vi* confesar **Confess! You're dying to kiss me.** ¡Confiesa! Te mueres por besarme.

confession *n* confesión *f* **I have a (small) confession to make. (I'm crazy**

Spanish "h" is always silent.

about you.) Tengo que hacer una (pequeña) confesión. (Estoy loco *[-ca]* por ti.)

confide *vi* confiar **Can I confide in you?** ¿Puedo confiar en *usted (Fam: ti)?* **You can always confide in me.** Puedes confiar siempre en mí.

confidence *n* confianza *f*, seguridad *f* **You have to have more confidence in yourself.** Tienes que tener más confianza en ti.

confident *adj* confiado *m*, -da *f*, con confianza **I feel confident** *(1)* **I** / *(2)* **we can do it.** Me siento con la confianza de que *(1)* puedo / *(2)* podemos hacerlo.

confirm *vt* confirmar *(1)* **I** / *(2)* **We have to confirm** *(3)* **my** / *(4)* **our flight.** *(1)* Tengo / *(2)* Tenemos que confirmar *(3)* mi / *(4)* nuestro vuelo.

confirmation *n* confirmación *f* ~ **number** número de confirmación **I have the confirmation (right here).** Yo tengo la confirmación (justo aquí).

confuse *vt* confundir, desconcertar **Am I confusing** *(1,2)* **you?** *(1)* ¿Lo *m* / *(2)* ¿La *f (Fam: Te)* estoy desconcertando? **You're confusing me.** *Usted me está (Fam: Me estás)* confundiendo. **You confused me.** *Usted me confundió (Fam: Me confundiste).* **I'm sorry if I** *(1,2)* **confused you.** Siento *(1)* haberlo *m* / *(2)* haberla *f (Fam: haberte)* confundido.

confused *adj* confundido *m*, -da *f* **become / get** ~ confundirse; desconcertarse **Are you confused?** ¿Está *usted (Fam: ¿Estás)* confundido *(-da)?* **I'm confused.** Estoy confundido *(-da).* **You look confused.** *Usted parece estar (Fam: Parece que estás)* desconcertado *(-da).*

confusing *adj* confuso *m*, -sa *f* **It's confusing, isn't it?** Eso está confuso. ¿Verdad?

congratulate *vt* felicitar *(1)* **I** / *(2)* **We congratulate you (on your [3] gradu-ation / [4] promotion / [5] success).** Lo *(Fam: Te) (1)* felicito / *(2)* felici-tamos (por *su [Fam: tu] (3)* graduación / *(4)* promoción / *(5)* éxito).

congratulation *n* felicitación *f* **Congratulations!** ¡Felicitaciones!

conjugate *vt* conjugar **Excuse me, could you tell me how to conjugate this verb (in the [1] future / [2] past / [3] present tense)?** *Disculpe (Fam: Disculpa),* ¿podría *usted (Fam: ¿podrías)* decirme cómo conjugar este verbo (en tiempo *[1]* futuro / *[2]* pasado / *[3]* presente)?

connect *vt* conectar **Where can I connect this?** ¿Dónde puedo conectar esto?

connection *n* conexión *f*

connoisseur *n* conocedor *m,* -dora *f* **I'm no connoisseur of wine, but this is great.** No soy un *(a)* conocedor *(-dora)* de vinos, pero este está fabuloso.

conscience *n* conciencia *f* **clear** ~ conciencia limpia **guilty** ~ **conciencia** culpable **My conscience is bothering me.** Me remuerde la conciencia. **Your conscience is bothering you, right?** Te remuerde la conciencia,

Questions about the metric system? See page 417.

¿verdad?

conscientious *adj* concienzudo *m*, -da *f*, esmerado *m*, -da *f*

consent *n* consentimiento *m* ~ **to get married** consentimiento para casarse **father's** ~ consentimiento del padre **give** ~ dar el consentimiento **mother's** ~ consentimiento de la madre **parents'** ~ consentimiento de los padres

consequently *adv* en consecuencia

conservative *adj* conservador *m*, -ra *f*

consider *vt* considerar, pensar **Please consider it.** Por favor, considéralo. *(1)* **I'll** / *(2)* **We'll certainly consider it.** Con toda seguridad lo *(1)* voy / *(2)* vamos a considerar.

considerable *adj* considerable *m&f*

considerate *adj* considerado *m*, -da *f* **You're very considerate.** Es usted *(Fam: Eres)* muy considerado *(-da)*. **That** *(1)* **is** / *(1)* **was very considerate of you.** Eso *(1)* es / *(2)* fue muy considerado de *su (Fam: tu)* parte.

consolation *n* consolación *f*, consuelo *m* ~ **prize** premio de consolación **As a consolation, I'd like to** *(1,2)* **invite you to dinner.** En consolación, me gustaría *(1)* invitarlo *m* / *(2)* invitarla *f (Fam: invitarte)* a cenar.

constant *adj* constante *m&f*

constantly *adv* constantemente **I think about you constantly.** Pienso en ti constantemente.

consulate *n* consulado *m (See terms under* **embassy** *for countries.)*

contact *vt* ponerse en contacto **How can I contact you?** ¿Cómo puedo ponerme en contacto *con usted (Fam: contigo?)*? **You can contact** *(1)* **me** / *(2)* **us at this** *(3)* **address.** / *(4)* **hotel.** / *(5)* **number.** *Puede usted ponerse (Fam: Puedes ponerte)* en contacto *(1)* conmigo / *(2)* con nosotros en este *(3)* domicilio. / *(4)* hotel. / *(5)* número.

contest *n* concurso *m* **Let's have a contest.** Vamos haciendo un concurso.

continue *vt* continuar, seguir **I want to continue our** *(1)* **conversation.** / *(2)* **discussion. (When can we meet again?)** Quiero seguir nuestra *(1)* conversación. / *(2)* plática. (¿Cuándo nos volvemos a ver?)

continuous *adj* continuo *m*, -nua *f*

continuously *adv* continuamente, sin interrupción

convenient *adj* conveniente *m&f*

conversation *n* conversación *f* **heart-to-heart** ~ conversación de corazón a corazón **interesting** ~ conversación interesante **nice** ~ conversación agradable **pleasant** ~ conversación placentera **I enjoyed our conversation together.** Disfruté mucho nuestra conversación.

convert *vt* convertir, transformar, cambiar *(1)* **I** / *(2)* **We need to convert some money.** *(1)* Necesito / *(2)* Necesitamos cambiar dinero.

convey *vt* enviar **Please convey** *(1)* **my** / *(2)* **our regards to your** *(3)* **fam-**

The letter "ñ" sounds like the "ny" in "canyon".

ily. / *(4)* **parents.** Por favor *envíe (Fam: envía) (1)* mis / *(2)* nuestros saludos a *(3)* su *(Fam: tu)* familia. / *(4)* sus *(Fam: tus)* padres.

cook *vt* cocinar **You cook very well.** Cocinas muy bien. **I like to cook.** Me gusta cocinar.

cook *n* cocinero *m*, -ra *f* **You're a (very) good cook.** Eres (muy) buen*(a)* cocinero *(-ra)*. **I'm (not) a good cook.** (No) Soy buen*(a)* cocinero *(-ra)*.

cool *adj* 1. *(not warm)* fresco *m*, -ca *f*; frío *m*, fría *f* 2. *(slang: nice, good)* bien, agradable *m&f*, chulo *m*, -la *f*; *(great, wonderful)* fenomenal *m&f*, fabuloso *m*, -sa *f*; 3. *(slang: stylish, trendy; smart-looking, chic)* en la onda; bonito *m*, -ta *f*; 4. *(calm, composed)* tranquilo *m*, la *f*, en calma ~ **music** música en la onda ~ **shirt** camisa bonita **You look very cool and fresh (in that outfit).** *Se ve usted (Fam: Te ves)* muy sereno *(-na)* y fresco *(-ca)* (con ese atuendo). **You seem so cool toward me.** Pareces muy frío *(fría)* conmigo. **That's a cool surfboard you've got.** Esa tabla de surf que tienes está chula. **Stay cool.** *(Don't get excited.)* Mantén la calma.

cool-looking *adj (slang: nice looking)* bonito *m*, -ta *f*, chulo *m*, -la *f* ~ **shirt** camisa chula **That's a cool-looking surfboard you've got.** Esa tabla de surf está chula.

cooperate *vi* cooperar *(1)* **I'm** / *(2)* **We're willing to cooperate.** *(1)* Estoy dispuesto... / *(2)* Estamos dispuestos... a cooperar.

cope *vi* soportar, aguantar **I don't know how you cope with it.** No sé cómo lo *soporta usted (Fam: sorportas.)*. **I can't cope with this.** No puedo soportarlo.

copier *n* copiadora *f*

copy *vt* copiar **Where can I copy this?** ¿Dónde puedo copiar esto?

copy *n* copia *f* ~ **shop** tienda *f* de copias **make a** ~ hacer una copia *(1)* **I** / *(2)* **We need** *(3)* **a copy** / *(4)* **copies of this.** *(1)* Necesito / *(2)* Necesitamos *(3)* una copia... / *(4)* copias... de esto.

corkscrew *n* tirabuzón *m*, sacacorchos *m*

corner *n* esquina *f* **Wait for** *(1)* **me** / *(2)* **us on the corner.** *(1)* Espéreme usted *(Fam: Espérame)* / *(2)* Espérenos usted *(Fam: Espéranos)* en la esquina. *(1)* **I'll** / *(2)* **We'll meet** *(3,4)* **you on the corner.** *(1)* Nos vemos / *(2)* Nos vemos en la esquina.

correct *adj* correcto *m*, -ta *f* **Is** *(1)* **this** / *(2)* **that correct?** ¿Es *(1)* esto / *(2)* eso correcto? **It's (not) correct.** (No) Es correcto.

correct *vt* corregir **Please correct my mistakes.** Por favor, *corrija usted (Fam: corrige)* mis errores.

correctly *adv* correctamente; bien **Do I say it correctly?** ¿Lo digo bien?

correspond *vi* corresponder, cartearse **I'd like to correspond with you (after I return home).** Me gustaría cartearme contigo (después de que regrese

Meet Mexicans online!
See pages 428-430 for websites.

a casa). **We can correspond by e-mail.** Podemos mantener correspondencia por correo electrónico.

correspondence *n* correspondencia *f* **carry on a ~** mantener correspondencia **start a ~** comenzar a mantener correspondencia

cosmic *adj* cósmico *m*, -ca *f* **~ feelings** sentimientos *m, pl* cósmicos

cosmos *n* cosmos *m*

cost *vt* costar **How much does it cost?** ¿Cuánto cuesta? **How much does (1) this / (2) that it cost?** ¿Cuánto cuesta (1) esto? / (2) eso? **It costs** *(price)*. Cuesta __. **How much do they cost?** ¿Cuánto cuestan? **How much do (1) these / (2) those cost?** ¿Cuánto cuestan (1) éstos? / (2) esos? **They cost** *(price)*. Cuestan __. **How much did it cost?** ¿Cuánto costó? **It cost** *(price)*. Costó __. **How much did they cost?** ¿Cuánto costaron? **They cost** *(price)*. Costaron __.

cost *n* costo *m* **high ~ of living** alto costo de vida **Spare no cost!** ¡No repares en costo!

Costa Rican *adj* costarricense *m&f* ★ *n* costarricense *m&f*, tico *m*, -ca *f (fam.)*

costume *n* disfraz *m* **Do I have to wear a costume?** ¿Tengo que ponerme un disfraz? **Do we have to wear costumes?** ¿Tenemos que ponernos disfraces?

cotton *adj* de algodón ★ *n* algodón *m*

couch *n* sofá *m*, diván *m* **~ potato** teleadicto *(-ta)*

could *aux v* poder **Could you?** ¿Podría usted (Fam:¿Podrías?)? **(1) I / (2) We could(n't).** (No) (1) Podría. / (2) Podríamos. **If you could.** Si usted pudiera (Fam: tú pudieras).

count *vi* contar **~ on** contar con **To me, that counts a lot.** Para mí, eso cuenta mucho. **You can (always) count on me.** Tú puedes (siempre) contar conmigo.

country *n* 1. *(nation)* país *m* ; 2. *(rural area)* campo *m* **In (1) my / (2) our / (3) your country...** En (1) mi / (2) nuestro / (3) su (Fam: tu) país… **Do you live in the city or the country?** ¿Vive usted (Fam: Vives) en la ciudad o en el campo? **(1) I / (2) We live in the country.** (1) Vivo / (2) Vivimos en el campo.

couple *n* pareja *f*, par *m* **happy ~** pareja feliz **married ~** pareja de casados; matrimonio **nice ~** bonita pareja **perfect ~** pareja perfecta **You and I make the perfect couple.** Tú y yo somos la pareja perfecta.

courage *n* valor *m* **You have a lot of courage.** Tiene usted (Fam: Tú tienes) mucho valor.

course *n* 1. *(golf)* campo *m* ; 2. *(educ)* curso *m* **golf ~** campo de golf **Of course.** Por supuesto. **What courses are you taking?** ¿Qué cursos estás

Spanish "o" is pronounced like "o" in "note"

tomando? *(1)* **I'm taking... /** *(2)* **I took... a course in** *(subject)*. *(1)* Estoy tomando... / *(2)* Tomé… un curso en ___.

court *n* 1. *(tennis)* cancha *f*; 2. tribunal *m* **go to** ~ acudir a los tribunales **tennis** ~ cancha de tenis

courteous *adj* cortés *m & f* **That's very courteous of you.** Eso es muy cortés de su parte.

cousin *n* primo *m*, -ma *f*

cover *vt* cubrir *(1)* **I want to... /** *(2)* **I'm going to... cover you with kisses.** *(1)* Quiero... / *(2)* Voy a…cubrirte de besos.

cow *n* vaca *f*

coward *n* cobarde *m&f* **Don't be a coward.** No seas cobarde.

cowboy *n* vaquero *m*

coyote *n* coyote *m*

cozy *adj* acogedor *m*, -dora *f* **You have a cozy apartment.** *Tiene usted (Fam: Tienes)* un departamento muy acogedor. **It's so cozy in your arms.** Es tan reconfortante estar en tus brazos.

crab(s) *n (pl)* cangrejo(s) *m (pl)*

crabbing *n (catching crabs)* cazar cangrejos **go** ~ ir a la caza de cangrejos

craft *n* oficio *m*, artesanía *f* **arts and** ~**s** artes y oficios **I like to do various crafts.** Me gusta hacer diversas artesanías.

craftsman *n* artesano *m*

craftswoman *n* artesana *f*

crave *vt* ansiar, desear **I crave affection.** Ansío mucho cariño.

crazy *adj* loco *m*, -ca *f*, chiflado *m*, -da *f* **act** ~ hacer locuras **You're a crazy** *(1)* **girl. /** *(2)* **guy.** Tú eres *(1)* una chica loca. / *(2)* un tipo loco. **Am I crazy?** ¿Estoy loco *(-ca)*? **That's crazy.** Es una locura. **I'm crazy about you.** Estoy loco *(-ca)* por ti. **You drive me (absolutely) crazy.** Me vuelves (totalmente) loco *(-ca)*.

cream *n (milk; lotion)* crema *f*

creamy *adj* cremoso *m*, -sa *f*

creamy-smooth *adj* suave *m&f* como la crema

create *vt* crear; formar ~ **a disturbance** crear un alboroto ~ **a family** formar una familia

creative *adj* creativo *m*, -va *f* **You're very creative.** *Es usted (Fam: Eres)* muy creativo *(-va)*.

creature *n* criatura *f* **You're the most beautiful creature I've ever met.** Eres la criatura más bella que he conocido jamás.

crippled *adj* inválido *m*, -da *f*, lisiado *m*, -da *f*, tullido *m*, -da *f*

credit card *n* tarjeta *f* de crédito

crime *n* delito *m*

Numbers in parentheses always signal choices.

criminal *n* delincuente *m&f*

critical *adj* crítico *m*, -ca *f*

criticism *n* crítica *f* **fair** ~ crítica justa **unfair** ~ crítica injusta

criticize *vt* criticar **I'm not criticizing you.** No te estoy criticando. **I don't mean to criticize.** No pretendo criticar.

cross-country *adj, adv* a campo traviesa **run** ~ correr a campo traviesa

crossroads *n* cruce *m*

crowd *n* muchedumbre *f*, gentío *m*

crowded *adj* abarrotado *m*, -da *f*, lleno *(-na)* de gente

crude *adj* 1. *(rude, vulgar)* grosero *m*, -ra *f*; 2. *(coarse)* tosco *m*, -ca *f*

cruel *adj* cruel *m&f* **You're so cruel (to me).** Eres tan cruel (conmigo). **Don't be so cruel to me.** No seas tan cruel conmigo.

cruise *vi* navegar, hacer un crucero

cruise *n* crucero *m* **I'm not** ~ **ship** crucero (embarcación) **ocean** ~ crucero transoceánico **river** ~ crucero fluvial **Would you like to go on a cruise with me?** ¿Le gustaría a usted (Fam: ¿Te gustaría) tomar un crucero conmigo? **Let's go on a cruise!** ¡Vámonos en un crucero!

crummy *adj* miserable *m&f*

crutches *n, pl* muletas *fpl*

cry *vi* llorar **Why are you crying?** ¿Por qué lloras? **Please don't cry.** Por favor, no llores.

cuddle *vi* acurrucarse, amartelarse, apapacharse **I want (so much) to cuddle up with you.** Deseo (tanto) acurrucarme contigo.

cuddlesome, cuddly *adj* amoroso *m*, -sa *f*, delicioso *m*, -sa *f*, adorable *m&f* **You're so (warm and) cuddly.** Eres tan (cálida y) delicioso *(-sa)*.

cuisine *n* cocina *f* **excellent** ~ excelente cocina **exotic** ~ cocina exótica **haute** ~ alta cocina **superb** ~ cocina espléndida

cultivated *adj* cultivado *m*, -da *f*, culto *m*, -ta *f*

cultural *adj* cultural *m&f* ~ **wonders** maravillas culturales

culture *n* cultura *f* **fascinating** ~ cultura fascinante **Mexican** ~ cultura mexicana

cup *n* taza *f*

Cupid *n* Cupido *m*

curiosity *n* curiosidad *f* **You have aroused my curiosity.** Usted ha (Fam: Has) despertado mi curiosidad. **«Curiosity killed a cat.»** «La curiosidad mató al gato.»

curious *adj* curioso *m*, -sa *f* **I'm curious. Where did you study English?** Seré curioso *(-sa)*. ¿Dónde estudió usted (Fam: estudiaste) inglés?

curl up *idiom* acurrucarse **I want to curl up with you (** *[1]* **in bed. /** *[2]* **on the sofa.)** Quiero acurrucarme contigo (en *[1]* la cama. / *[2]* el sofá.)

Spanish "a" is mostly like "a" in "mama".

currency *n* moneda *f*, divisa *f* **exchange** *(1,2)* ~ cambiar *(1)* moneda / *(2)* divisa

current *adj* actual *m&f*, vigente *m&f*, en curso

current *n (1. water; 2. electricity)* corriente *f* **strong** ~ corriente fuerte

currently *adv* actualmente, por lo común

curvaceous *adj* curvilíneo *m*, -nea *f*, escultural *m&f*

curve *n* curva *f* **delicate** ~s curvas delicadas **graceful** ~s curvas graciosas **soft feminine** ~s suaves curvas femeninas **supple** ~s curvas gráciles **You have such beautiful curves**. Tienes unas curvas tan hermosas.

curvy *adj* curvilíneo *m*, -nea *f* ~ **figure** figura curvilínea

custom *n* costumbre *f*, tradición *f* **Mexican** ~ costumbre mexicana **old** ~ vieja costumbre **I want to learn more about your customs.** Quiero conocer mejor tus costumbres. **Is that a custom in your country?** ¿Es esa alguna costumbre de tu país? **It's (not) a custom in** *(1)* **my** / *(2)* **our country.** (No) Es una costumbre de *(1)* mi / *(2)* nuestro país.

customs *n, pl* aduana *f* **go through** ~ pasar por la aduana

cut *vt* cortar **I cut myself.** Yo me corto. **Cut the cards.** Corta la baraja.

cute *adj* simpático *m*, -ca *f*, lindo *m*, -da *f*, bonito *m*, -ta *f*, mono *m*, -na *f* **kind of** ~ en cierto modo simpático *(-ca)* **You have a cute face.** Tienes una cara bonita. **What a cute** *(1)* **mouth** / *(2)* **nose you have.** Qué *(1)* boca / *(2)* nariz tan mona tienes. **You're just as cute as can be.** Eres lo más lindo que hay.

cycle *n (process)* ciclo *m*

cycling *n* ciclismo *m*

cynical *adj* cínico *m*, -ca *f* **You shouldn't be so cynical (about love).** No debes de ser tan cínico *(-ca)* (en el amor).

Articles: m = el, f = la, mpl = los, fpl = las

D

daffy *adj* chiflado *m*, -da *f*, loco *m*, -ca *f*, imbécil *m&f*

damage *n* daño *m* *(1)* **Is** / *(2)* **Was there any damage?** *(1)* ¿Hay / *(2)* ¿Hubo algún daño? **There** *(1)* **is** / *(2)* **was some damage**. *(1)* Hay / *(2)* Hubo algun daño. **There** *(1)* **is** / *(2)* **was no damage**. No *(1)* hay / *(2)* hubo daño.

damaged *adj* dañado *m*, -da *f* **Is it damaged?** ¿Está dañado *(-da)*? **It's (not) damaged**. (No) Está dañado *(-da)*.

dance *vt & vi* bailar ~ **fast** bailar rápido ~ **slow** bailar despacio ~ **(the) tango** bailar (el) tango ~ **a waltz** bailar un vals **place to** ~ lugar para bailar **Do you like to dance?** ¿Le *(Fam:* ¿*Te)* gusta bailar? **I** *(1)* **like** / *(2)* **love to dance**. Me *(1)* gusta / *(2)* encanta bailar. **Would you care to dance?** ¿Le *(Fam:*¿*Te)* gustaría bailar? **Let's dance**. Vamos a bailar. **You dance** *(1)* **very well.** / *(2)* **beautifully**. Usted baila *(Fam: Tú bailas)* *(1)* muy bien. / *(2)* hermoso. **I don't know how to dance**. Yo no sé bailar. **I'll teach you how to dance**. Yo le *(Fam: te)* enseñaré a bailar.

dance *n* baile *m* ~ **band** orquesta *f* de baile ~ **hall** salón *m* de baile **every** ~ cada baile **next** ~ el siguiente baile **May I have this dance?** ¿Me *concede usted (Fam: concedes)* este baile? **They're having a dance at** *(place)*. **(Would you like to go?)** Van a haber un baile en ___ (¿*Le [Fam: ¿Te]* gustaría ir?) **There's a big dance (tonight) at** *(place)*. Hay un gran baile (esta noche) en ___.

dancer *n* bailador *m*, -dora *f* **You're a good dancer**. Usted es *(Fam: Tú eres)* un*(a)* buen *(-na)* bailador *(-dora)*. **You're a marvelous dancer.** Usted es *(Fam: Tú eres)* un*(a)* bailador *(-dora)* maravilloso *(-sa)*. **I'm not a very good dancer**. Yo no soy muy buen *(-na)* bailador *(-dora)*.

dancing *n* baile *m* *(See phrases under* **go, like** *and* **love**.*)*

danger *n* peligro *m*

dangerous *adj* peligroso *m*, -sa *f*

Spanish "z" is pronounced like "s" in "safe".

dare *vt* retar, desafiar, atreverse **I dare** *(1,2)* **you (to do it).** *(1) Lo m / (2) La f (Fam: Te)* reto (a que lo *haga [Fam: hagas]*). **How dare you!** ¡Cómo *se atreve (Fam: te atreves)*!

dark *adj* oscuro *m,* -ra *f* **It's too dark**. Está demasiado oscuro *(-ra)*.

darling *n* querido *m,* -da *f,* tesoro *m* **little ~** tesorito **precious ~** preciosidad *f* **You're my darling**. Eres mi querido *(-da)*.

dart(s) *n (pl)* dardo(s) *m (pl)* **play ~s** jugar a los dardos

dartboard *n* diana *f*

date *n* 1. *(of the month)* fecha *f* ; compromiso *m* ; 2. *(appointment)* cita *f* **wedding ~** fecha de la boda **go on a ~ together** ir juntos a una cita **What's the date today?** ¿Cuál es la fecha de hoy? **The date today is** *(date)*. La fecha de hoy es ___. **It's a date!** ¡Es una cita! **It's out of date.** Está pasado de moda.

daughter *n* hija *f* **older ~** hija mayor **oldest ~** la mayor de las hijas **middle ~** hija de en medio *(1,2)* **younger ~** hija *(1)* pequeña / *(2)* menor **youngest ~** la menor de las hijas *(1)* **I** / *(2)* **We have** *(3)* **a daughter** / *(4)* **two daughters**. *(1)* Yo tengo... / *(2)* Nosotros tenemos... *(3)* una hija. / *(4)* dos hijas. **This is** *(1)* **my** / *(2)* **our daughter** *(name)*. Esta es *(1)* mi / *(2)* nuestra hija ___. **How old is your (** *[1]* **older** / *[2]* **younger) daughter?** ¿Qué edad tiene *su (Fam: tu)* hija (*[1]* mayor / *[2]* menor)? *(1)* **My** / *(2)* **Our (** *[3]* **older** / *[4]* **younger) daughter is** *(number)* **years old.** *(1)* Mi / *(2)* Nuestra hija (*[3]* mayor / *[4]* menor) tiene __ años. **This is a picture of** *(1)* **my** / *(2)* **our daughter(s).** Esta es una foto de *(1)* mi(s) / *(2)* nuestra(s) hija(s).

daughter-in-law *n* nuera *f*

day *n* día *m* **all ~** todo el día **any ~** cualquier día **beautiful ~** día hermoso **~ after ~** día tras día **~ after tomorrow** pasado mañana **~ and night** día y noche **~ before yesterday** antier, anteayer, antes de ayer **~ off** día libre **during the ~** durante el día **each ~** cada día **every ~** todos los días **for a ~** por un día **for** *(1)* **two** / *(2)* **three** / *(3)* **four** / *(4)* **five** / *(5)* **six~s** por *(1)* dos / *(2)* tres / *(3)* cuatro / *(5)* cinco / *(6)* seis días **in a ~** *(after)* dentro de un día **in** *(1)* **a** / *(2)* **one ~** *(within)* en *(1,2)* un día **in** *(1)* **two** / *(2)* **three** / *(3)* **four ~s** 1. *(within)* en *(1)* dos / *(2)* tres / *(3)* cuatro días; 2. *(after)* *(1)* dentro de dos / *(2)* tres / *(3)* cuatro días; **New Year's ~** Año Nuevo **nice ~** buen día **(on) any ~** (en) cualquier día **once a ~** una vez al día **one of these ~s** uno de estos días **perfect ~** día perfecto **rainy ~** día lluvioso **sunny ~** día asoleado **the next ~** al día siguiente **the other ~** el otro día **the same ~** el mismo día **Valentine's Day** día de los enamorados **warm ~** día tibio **wedding ~** el día de la boda **the whole ~** el día entero **wonderful ~** día hermoso **(On) What day?** ¿(En) Qué día? **Have a** *(1)* **nice** / *(2)* **great day**. Que

---

A tilde ~ in terms stands for the main entry word.

tenga (Fam: tengas) (un) *(1)* buen / *(2)* gran día. **Can you take the day off?** *¿Puede usted (Fam: ¿Puedes)* tomar el día libre? **I can(not) take the day off.** (No) Puedo tomar el día libre. **What are your days off?** ¿Cuáles días estás libre?

daydream *vi* soñar despierto *m*, -ta *f* **I hope I'm not just daydreaming.** Espero no estar soñando despierto.

daydream *n* ensoñacion *f*, fantasía *f*, **beautiful** ~ bella ensoñacion

daylight *n* luz *f* de día **in broad** ~ a plena luz del día

daytime *n* diurno *m*, día *m* **in the** ~ durante el día, de día

dazzling *adj* deslumbrante *m&f* ~ **smile** sonrisa *f* deslumbrante

dead *adj* muerto *m*, -ta *f*, difunto *m*, -ta *f* ~ **end** callejón *m* sin salida **My** *(1)* **mother** / *(2)* **father is dead.** Mi *(1)* madre / *(2)* padre va murió. **My parents are dead.** Mis padres va murieron. **The engine is dead.** El motor no enciende. **The line is dead.** El telefono está cortado. **This place is dead. Let's go someplace else.** El ambiente de este lugar está muerto, vamos a otro lado. **I'm dead tired.** Estoy muerto *(-ta)* de cansancio.

deadhead *n* aburrido *m*, -da *f*, lelo *m*, -la *f* **Don't be a** *(1,2)* **deadhead.** No seas aguado *(-da)*.

deaf *adj* sordo *m*, -da *f* **I'm deaf in my** *(1)* **left** / *(2)* **right ear.** Estoy sordo *(-da)* del oído *(1)* izquierdo. / *(2)* derecho.

deal *vt (cards)* repartir, dar **It's your turn to deal.** Te toca repartir. **Deal 5 cards to each person.** Reparte cinco cartas a cada persona.

deal *vi* tratar, encargarse, abordar **I'll deal with it.** Yo me encargo. **I don't know how to deal with it.** No sé cómo abordarlo. **You have a lot to deal with.** *Usted tiene (Fam: Tú tienes)* mucho de qué *encargarse (Fam: encargarte)*.

deal *n* 1. *(arrangement, transaction)* trato *m* ; 2. *(cards)* mano *m* **It's your deal.** *Le (Fam: Te)* toca repartir. **That sounds like a good deal.** Eso parece es un buen trato. **What a bum deal!** ¡Qué mala onda! **It's a deal!** ¡Trato hecho!

dear *adj* querido *m*, -da *f (1,2)* **You are so dear to me.** Te aprecio mucho. **Dear Maria...** Querida María... **Dear Jose...** Querido José...

debt *n* deuda *f (1)* **I'm** / *(2)* **We're in your debt.** *(1)* Estoy / *(2)* Estamos en deuda *con usted (Fam: contigo)*.

deceit *n* engaño *m* **I can't stand deceit.** No soporto el engaño.

deceive *vt* engañar **I would never deceive** *(1,2)* **you.** Nunca *(1)* lo *m* / *(2)* la *f (Fam: te)* engañaría.

December *n* diciembre *m* **in** ~ en diciembre **on** ~ **first** el primero de diciembre

decent *adj* decente *m&f*

decide *vi* decidir ~ **right away** decidir al momento **just (now)** ~ decidir

---

*Spanish "ch" is pronounced like ours
(e.g., "cheese," "charge").*

exactamente (ahora) **suddenly** ~ decidir de repente **Have you decided?** ¿Ya *decidió usted (Fam: decidiste)*? **What have you decided?** ¿Qué *ha decidido usted (Fam: has decidido)*? *(1)* **I** / *(2)* **We haven't decided.** No *(1)* he / *(2)* hemos decidido. *(1)* **I've** / *(2)* **We've decided** *(3)* **to do it.** / *(4)* **to go (home).** / *(5)* **not to go.** / *(6)* **to stay (longer).** / *(7)* **to wait.** / *(8)* **to leave** (*[9]* **tomorrow** / *[10]* **on** *(day)*.) *(1)* He / *(2)* Hemos decidido *(3)* hacerlo. / *(4)* *[1]* irme / *[2]* irnos (a casa). / *(5)* no ir. / *(6)* *[1]* quedarme / *[2]* quedarnos (más tiempo). / *(7)* esperar. / *(8)* *[1]* irme / *[2]* irnos (*[9]* mañana / *[10]* el).

decision *n* decisión *f* **What is your decision?** ¿Cuál es *su (Fam: tu)* decisión? **I've come to a decision.** He llegado a una decisión. **Let** *(1)* **me** / *(2)* **us know what your decision is.** *(1)* Déjeme (Fam: Déjame) / *(2)* Déjenos *(Fam: Déjanos)* saber cuál es *su (Fam: tu)* decisión.

deck *n (ship)* cubierta *f* **Let's go out on deck.** Salgamos a cubierta.

decorated *pp* decorado *m*, -da *f* **It's (very)** *(1)* **beautifully** / *(2)* **nicely decorated.** Está decorado *(-da)* (muy) *(1)* hermosamente. / *(2)* primorosamente.

decoration *n* decoración *f* **Christmas** ~s decoración navideña **party** ~s decoraciones festivas **What beautiful decorations!** ¡Qué decoraciones tan hermosas!

deep *adj* profundo *m*, -da *f (1,2)* ~ **in thought** *(1)* absorto *(-ta)* / *(2)* embebido *(-da)* en sus pensamientos ~ **subject** tema *m* profundo ~ **thoughts** pensamientos *mpl* profundos **How deep is it?** ¿Qué tan profundo es? **The water is deep** *(1)* **here.** / *(2)* **there.** El agua es profunda *(1)* aquí. / *(2)* allá.

deeply *adv* profundamente **feel** ~ sentir profundamente **think** ~ pensar profundamente **I love you deeply.** Te amo profundamente.

definite *adj* definido *m*, -da *f*

definitely *adv* definitivamente

definition *n* definición *f*

degree *n* 1. *(temperature)* grado *m* ; 2. *(university)* grado académico ~s **Centigrade** grados centígrados ~s **Fahrenheit** grados Fahrenheit **What's your degree in?** ¿De qué es *su (Fam: tu)* grado académico? *(1)* **I have...** / *(2)* **I want to get... a(n)** (*[3]* **BA** / *[4]* **BS** / *[5]* **MA** / *[6]* **MS) degree in** *(field)*. *(1)* Tengo... / *(2)* Quiero obtener... un grado de (*[3]* licenciatura en arte / *[4]* licenciatura en ciencias / *[5]* maestría en arte / *[6]* maestría en ciencias) en ____.

dejected *adj* abatido *m*, -da *f*, desanimado *m*, -da *f* **You look so dejected. What's the matter?** *Se ve usted (Fam: Te ves)* muy desanimado *(-da)*. ¿Qué sucede?

delay *n* demora *f (1)* **I'm** / *(2)* **We're sorry for the delay.** *(1)* Lamento / *(2)* Lamentamos la demora.

Spanish "i" is mostly "ee", but can also be shorter, like "i" in "sit," when together with other vowels.

delay *vt* demorar *(1)* I / *(2)* **We may be delayed. (Please wait.)** Es posible que *(1)* me demore. / *(2)* nos demoremos. (Por favor espere.) *(1)* **I was** / *(2)* **We were delayed by** *(what)*. *(1)* Me demoré... / *(2)* Nos demoramos.. por ___.

deliberate *adj* deliberado *m*, -da *f*, adrede *m&f* **That was deliberate!** ¡Eso fue adrede! **It wasn't deliberate**. No fue adrede.

deliberately *adv* deliberadamente, adrede, a propósito **You did that delib erately!** ¡Lo hiciste adrede!

delicate *adj (features)* delicado *m*, -da *f*

delicious *adj* delicioso *m*, -sa *f* **This is delicious!** ¡Está delicioso *(-sa)* **That was delicious!** ¡Estuvo delicioso *(-sa)*!

delight *n* deleite *m*, delicia *f*, encanto *m* **You're a cornucopia of delight** Eres un manantial de delicias.

delighted *past part* encantado *m*, -da *f*, contento *m*, -ta *f (1)* **I'd** / *(2)* **We'd be delighted.** *(1)* Estaría encantado *(-da)*. / *(2)* Estaríamos encantados *(-das) (1)* **I'm** / *(2)* **We're delighted to see you.** *(1)* Estoy encantado *(-da)*... / *(2)* Estamos encantados *(-das)*... de *verle a usted (Fam: verte)*.

delightful *adj* delicioso *m*, -sa *f*, encantador *m*, -dora *f*, muy agradable *m & f (1)* **I** / *(2)* **We had a delightful time.** *(1)* Pasé / *(2)* Pasamos un rato muy agradable.

delirious *adj* delirante *m&f*, loco *m*, -ca *f* **If I seem delirious, it's because I'm so happy.** Si parezco loco *(-ca)* es porque estoy muy feliz.

deliver *vt* entregar **Could you deliver this to** *(1)* **her?** / *(2)* **him?** / *(3)* **them?** ¿Podría usted entregarle esto a *(1)* ella? / *(2)* él ? / *(3)* ellos?

democracy *n* democracia *f* ★ **democratic** *adj* democrático *m*, -ca *f*

demonstrate *vt* demostrar, mostrar **Let me demonstrate**. *Déjeme (Fam: Déjame)* demostrarlo. **Perhaps you could demonstrate (for [1] me / [2] us).** Quizás *podría usted (Fam: podrías)* probarlo (por *[1]* mí / *[2]* nosotros.)

depart *vi* salir, partir, irse **What time will the** *(1)* **bus** / *(2)* **train** / *(3)* **flight depart?** ¿A qué hora sale el *(1)* camión? / *(2)* tren? / *(3)* vuelo? **The** *(1)* **bus** / *(2)* **train** / *(3)* **flight will depart at** *(time)*. El *(1)* camión / *(2)* tren / *(3)* vuelo sale a las ___. **When do you depart?** ¿Cuándo *se va usted (Fam: te vas)*? *(1)* **I** / *(2)* **We depart** *(3)* **today.** / *(4)* **tomorrow.** / *(5)* **two days from now.** / *(6)* **next week.** *(1)* Me voy... / *(2)* Nos vamos... *(3)* hoy. / *(4)* mañana. / *(5)* dentro de dos días. / *(6)* la próxima semana.

department store *n* tienda *f* departamental

departure *n* partida *f*, salida *f* ~ **time** hora *f* de la salida

depend (on) *vi* depender (de), contar (con) **You can (always) depend on me**. *Usted puede (Fam: Tú puede)* (siempre) contar conmigo. **It depends**

Help us improve our book!
Send us the feedback form on page 431.

on *(1)* **you.** / *(2)* **my work schedule.** / *(3)* **the weather.** Depende *(1)* de usted *(Fam: ti).* / *(2)* de mi horario de trabajo. / *(3)* del clima.

dependable *adj* confiable *m&f*, digno *(-na)* de confianza

depressed *adj* deprimido *m*, -da *f* **Try not to feel (so) depressed (about it).** *Trate (Fam: Trata)* de no *deprimirse (Fam: deprimirte)* (tanto) deprimido *(-da)* (por eso). **I feel depressed.** Me siento deprimido *(-da)*.

depressing *adj* deprimente *m&f*

describe *vt* describir **Can you describe it?** ¿*Puede usted (Fam: Puedes)* describirlo? **It's hard for me to describe (in Spanish).** Me cuesta trabajo describirlo (en Español). **I can't describe it.** No puedo describirlo. **No language can describe my feelings (for you).** No hay palabras para describir lo que siento (por *usted [Fam: ti]*).

description *n* descripción *f* **beyond** ~ indescriptible **Your description of it sounds** *(1)* **beautiful.** / *(2)* **exciting.** / *(3)* **like fun.** / *(4)* **lovely.** / *(5)* **nice.** / *(6)* **terrible.** La descripción que *usted da (Fam: tú das)* suena *(1)* hermosa. / *(2)* emocionante. / *(3)* divertida. / *(4)* encantadora. / *(5)* agradable. / *(6)* terrible.

desert *n* desierto *m*

deserve *vt* merecer **You deserve a lot better.** *Usted se merece (Fam: Te mereces)* algo mucho mejor.

desirable *adj* desable *m&f* **I've never met anyone as desirable as you.** Nunca conocí a nadie tan deseable como *usted (Fam: tú).*

desire *vt* desear **What do you desire in life?** ¿Qué es lo que *desea usted (Fam: deseas)* en la vida? **What I desire the most in life is** *(what)*. Lo que más deseo en la vida es ___. **I desire only** *(1,2)* **you.** Sólo *(1)* lo *m* / *(2)* la *f (Fam: te)* deseo a *usted (Fam: ti).*

desire *n* deseo *m* **You fill me with desire.** *Usted me llena (Fam: Tú me llenas)* de deseos.

desperate *adj* desesperado *m*, -da *f* **I'm desperate.** Estoy desesperado *(-da)*.

desperately *adv* desesperadamente **I love** *(1,2)* **you desperately.** *(1)* Lo *m* / *(2)* La *f (Fam: Te)* amo desesperadamente.

destination *n* destino *m*

destined *pp* destinado *m*, -da *f* **We were destined for each other.** Estamos destinados el uno para el otro.

destiny *n* destino *m*

destroy *vt* destruir *(1)* **It** / *(2)* **Everything was destroyed.** *(1)* Se... / *(2)* Todo se... destruyó.

detail *n* detalle *m* **Tell me** *(1)* **in detail.** / *(2)* **all the details.** *Cuénteme (Fam: Cuéntame) (1)* con detalle. / *(2)* todos los detalles.

detector *n* detector *m* **metal** ~ detector de metales

Spanish "j" is pronounced like "h".

determined *adj* resuelto *m*, -ta *f* **I'm determined to do it.** Estoy resuelto *(-ta)* a hacerlo.

devil *n* díablo *m* **silver-tongued** ~ labioso *m*, -sa *f* **You little devil!** ¡Eres un diablillo! **What a devil you are!** ¡Eres como el diablo!

devote *vt* dedicarse, consagrarse ~ **all my energies** consagrar todas mis energías ~ **my life** consagrar mi vida ~ **my time** dedicar mi tiempo **I want to devote all my time to you.** Quiero dedicar todo mi tiempo a *su (Fam. tu)* persona.

devoted *adj* devoto *m*, -ta *f* ~ **husband** esposo *m* devoto ~ **wife** esposa devota

devotion *n* devoción *f*

devout *adj* devoto *m*, -ta *f* **I'm a devout** *(1)* **Catholic** / *(2)* **Christian** *(3)(religion)*. Soy un*(a)* *(1)* católico *(-ca)* / *(2)* cristiano *(-na)* / *(3)* ___ devoto *(-ta)*.

dialect *n* dialecto *m*

diamond *n* 1. *(gem)* diamante *m* ; 2. *pl (card suit)* diamantes *mpl (1,2)* **Meeting you is like finding a diamond on a gravel road.** *(1)* Conocerlo *m* / *(2)* Conocerla *f (Fam: Conocerte)* es como encontrar un diamante en un camino pedregoso.

diaper *n* pañal *m* **change** ~**s** cambiar pañales

diarrhea *n* diarrea *f* **medicine for** ~ antidiarreico *m*

diary *n* díario *m* **keep a** ~ llevar un diario

dice *n, pl* dados *mpl* **throw the** ~ tirar los dados

dictionary *n* diccionario *m*

die *vi* morir, fallecer **My** *(1)* **father** / *(2)* **mother** / *(3)* **parents died** *(4)* **in** *(year)*. / *(5)* **when I was** *(age)*. Mi *(1)* padre / *(2)* madre falleció... / *(3)* Mis padres fallecieron... *(4)* en ___ / *(5)* cuando yo tenía ___. *(1)* **He** / *(2,* **She died (in** *[year]*). *(1)* Él / *(2)* Ella falleció (en ___). **You are the flower that never dies.** Tú eres la flor que nunca muere.

differ *vi* no estar de acuerdo **I beg to differ with you.** Lamento no estar de acuerdo *con usted (Fam: contigo)*.

difference *n* diferencia *f* **age** ~ diferencia de edad **big** ~ gran diferencia ~ **of opinion** diferencia de opinión **main** ~ principal diferencia **only** ~ la única diferencia **small** ~ pequeña diferencia **time** ~ diferencia de tiempo **tremendous** ~ tremenda diferencia **What's the difference?** ¿Cuál es la diferencia? **It doesn't make any difference.** Eso no hace ninguna diferencia.

different *adj* diferente *m&f* **I've got a different idea.** Tengo una idea diferente. **Would you like something different?** ¿Le *(Fam: Te)* gustaría algo diferente? **You're different than other** *(1)* **men** / *(2)* **women I've**

---

*Familiar "tu" forms in parentheses can replace
italicized polite forms.*

met. **(And I like the difference.)** *Usted es (Fam: Eres)* diferente a otros
(1) hombres / *(2)* mujeres que he conocido. (Y me gusta la diferencia.)
differently *adv* diferentemente, de manera diferente, de otro modo
difficult *adj* difícil *m&f* **Is it difficult?** ¿Es difícil? **It is(n't) (very) difficult.**
(No) Es (muy) difícil. **Was it difficult?** ¿Fue difícil? **It was(n't) (very)
difficult.** (No) Fue (muy) difícil. **Will it be difficult?** ¿Será difícil? **It
will (not) be (very) difficult.** (No) Será (muy) difícil.
difficulty *n* dificultad *f* **The difficulty is (that)...** La dificultad es (que)...
dignified *adj* digno *m*, -na *f*
diminish *vi* reducir, disminuir
dimple *n* hoyuelo *m* **You have a cute dimple** *(1)* **here.** / *(2)* **on your chin.** /
(3) **when you smile.** Tienes un hoyuelo gracioso *(1)* aquí. / *(2)* en tu barbilla.
/ *(3)* cuando sonríes.
dine *vi* cenar **I like to dine out.** Me gusta cenar fuera. **Shall we dine out
tonight?** ¿Cenamos fuera esta noche?
dinner *n* cena *f* **candlelight** ~ cena a la luz de las velas ~ **by candlelight** cena
a la luz de las velas *(1)* **I'd** / *(2)* **We'd like to** *(3,4)* **invite you to...** / *(5)*
Let's have... / *(6)* **Let's go to...** **dinner (together)** *(7)* **this afternoon.** / *(8)*
this evening. / *(9)* **tomorrow (evening).** / *(10)* **on Friday** / *(11)* **Saturday**
/ *(12)* **Sunday** *(13)* **afternoon.** / *(14)* **evening.** *(1)* Me / *(2)* Nos gustaría
(3) invitarlo *m* / *(4)* invitarla *f (Fam: invitarte)* a... / *(5)* Vayamos a... / *(6)*
Vamos a... cenar (juntos) *(7)* esta tarde. / *(8)* esta noche. / *(9)* mañana (por
la noche). / *(10)* el viernes / *(11)* el sábado / *(12)* el domingo *(13)* por la
tarde. / *(14)* por la noche. **Would you like to go (with** *[1]* **me** / *[2]* **us) to
dinner?** ¿Le *(Fam: Te)* gustaría ir (*[4]* conmigo / *[5]* con nosotros) a
cenar? **Where's a good place to have dinner?** ¿Dónde hay un buen lugar
para cenar? **I know a** *(1)* **good** / *(2)* **great** / *(3)* **wonderful place where we
can have dinner.** Yo conozco un *(1)* buen / *(2)* estupendo / *(3)* hermoso
lugar donde podemos cenar. **Let's go eat dinner (together).** Vayamos a
cenar (juntos). **That was a** *(1)* **good** / *(2)* **great** / *(3)* **wonderful dinner.**
Esa fue una *(1)* buena / *(2)* estupenda / *(3)* hermosa cena.
diploma *n* diploma *m*
direction *n* 1. *(course)* dirección *f* ; 2. *pl (instructions)* instrucciones *fpl*
Which direction is it? ¿En qué dirección es? **Could you give me directions to** *(place)*? ¿Podría usted *(Fam: ¿Podrías)* darme instrucciones para
___ ?
dirty 1. *(unclean)* sucio *m*, -cia *f*; 2. *(foul, obscene)* grosero *m*, -ra *f*, obsceno
m, -na *f*; 3. *(low, mean)* canalla *m&f* ~ **language** lenguaje *m* soez ~ **mind**
mente *f* cochina ~ **mouth** malhablado *m*, -da *f* ~ **story** cuento *m* colorado
~ **trick** mala pasada ~ **words** leperadas *fpl*

Spanish "x" is always like "ks", as in our word "taxi"

disability *n* discapacidad *f*, invalidez *f*

disabled *adj* discapacitado *m*, -da *f* **partially** ~ parcialmente discapacitado
(*-da*)

disadvantage *n* desventaja *f* **You have me at a disadvantage.** *Usted me
tiene (Fam: Me tienes) en desventaja.*

disagree *vi* disentir, no estar de acuerdo *(1,2)* **I disagree (with you).** *(1)
Estoy en desacuerdo... / (2) No estoy de acuerdo... (con usted [Fam:
contigo]).* **I'm afraid I have to disagree.** Me temo que tengo que disentir

disappear *vi* desaparecer **Suddenly you disappeared.** *Usted se desapareció
(Fam: te desapareciste) de repente.*

disappoint *vt* decepcionar, desilusionar **I'm sorry** I *(1,2)* **disappointed you.**
Lamento *(1) desilusionarlo m / (2) desilusionarla f (Fam: desilusionarte).*
I *(1)* **realize / *(2)* know that I've disappointed** *(3,4)* **you (and I beg you
to forgive me).** *(1) Me doy de que... / (2) Sé que... (3) lo m / (4) la f (Fam:
te) he decepcionado (y le [Fam: te] pido que me perdone [Fam: perdones]).*
You disappointed me (terribly). *Usted me decepcionó (Fam: Me
decepcionaste) (mucho).* **Please don't disappoint me.** *Por favor, no me
decepcione (Fam: decepciones).*

disappointed *adj* decepcionado *m*, -da *f* **I'm ([1] terribly / [2] very) disappointed.** Estoy *([1] terriblemente / [2] muy) decepcionado (-da).* **We're
([1] really / [2] terribly) disappointed.** Estamos *([1] verdaderamente /
[2] terriblemente) decepcionados (-das).*

disappointing *adj* decepcionante *m&f*

disappointment *n* decepción *f*, desilusión *f* **big** ~ gran desilusión **terrible** ~
decepción terrible **tremendous** ~ tremenda decepción

disaster *n* desastre *m*

disc *n* disco *m* **compact** ~ **(CD)** disco compacto, compact-disc (CD)

discard *vt (cards: throw away)* descartar **Discard a card.** Descarta
un naipe.

discharge *vt (mil.)* destituir, relevar **I was discharged from the** *(1)* **Air Force
/ *(2)* Army / *(3)* Navy in (*year*).** Me relevaron *(1)* de la fuerza aérea / *(2)*
del ejército / *(3)* de la marina en ___.

disco(theque) *n* disco(teca) *f*

discount *n* descuento *m* **Is there any discount for** *(1)* **children? / *(2)* handicapped? / *(3)* seniors? / *(4)* students?** ¿Hay descuento para *(1)* ninos? /
(2) personas incapacitadas? / *(3)* pensionados? / estudiantes?

discouraged *adj* desanimado *m*, -da *f* **Don't be discouraged.** No *se desanime
(Fam: te desanimes).*

discover *vt* descubrir *(1)* **I've / *(2)* We've discovered a great little restaurant.** *(1) Descubrí / (2) Descubrimos un restaurantito fenomenal.*

---

*Stress rule # 2: The next-to-last syllable is stressed
in words ending in "n", "s" or a vowel.*

discreet *adj* discreto *m*, -ta *f* **I'll be (very) discreet.** Seré (muy) discreto *(-ta)*. **We have to be discreet.** Tenemos que ser discretos *(-tas)*.

discretion *n* discreción *f* **I need your (total) discretion (in this).** Necesito *su (Fam: tu)* discreción (total) (en esto).

discriminate *vi* discriminar **It's wrong to discriminate (against people of other *[1]* nationalities / *[2]* races / *[3]* religions).** Es un error discriminar (a personas de otras *[1]* nacionalidades / *[2]* razas / *[3]* religiones).

discrimination *n* discriminación *f* **That's discrimination (and it's wrong).** Eso es discriminación (y está mal).

discuss *vt* platicar, deliberar **There's something I want to discuss with you.** Hay algo que quiero platicar *con usted (Fam: contigo)*. **Could we discuss it in private?** ¿Podríamos platicarlo en privado?

disease *n* enfermedad *f*

disgrace *n* desgracia *f*

disgraceful *adj* deshonroso *m*, -sa *f*, vergonzoso *m*, -sa *f* **That's (utterly) disgraceful.** Eso es (altamente) deshonroso.

disgusted *adj* asqueado *m*, -da *f*, hastiado *m*, -da *f* **I'm disgusted with *(what)*.** Estoy hastiado *(-da)* de ___.

disgusting *adj* desagradable *m&f*, repugnante *m&f*, odioso *m*, -sa *f* **That's disgusting!** ¡Qué repugnante!

dish *n* 1. *(plate)* plato *m* ; 2. *pl (collectively)* platos *mpl* ; 3. *(cooked food)* platillo *m* **What's your favorite dish?** ¿Cuál es *su (Fam: tu)* platillo favorito? **My favorite dish is *(name)*.** Mi platillo favorito es ___.

dishonest *adj* deshonesto *m*, -ta *f*, fraudulento *m*, -ta *f*

disk *n (comp.)* disco *m*

disoriented *adj* desorientado *m*, -da *f* **I feel (a little) disoriented.** Me siento (un poco) desorientado.

display *n* exhibición *f*, despliegue *m*, demostración *f* **fireworks ~** despliegue de fuegos artificiales

dispose *vi (of)* desechar **Where can I dispose of this?** ¿En dónde puedo desechar esto?

disposition *n* carácter *m* **happy-go-lucky ~** de carácter despreocupado, **nice ~** de carácter agradable **sweet ~** de carácter dulce **I like your cheerful disposition.** Me gusta *su (Fam: tu)* carácter alegre.

distance *n* distancia *f* **Is it in walking distance?** ¿Está a una distancia como para ir a pie? **It's in walking distance.** Está a una distancia como para ir a pie.

distant *adj* distante *m&f* **~ relative** pariente lejano *(-na)*

disturb *vt* perturbar, molestar *(1)* **I'm /** *(2)* **We're sorry to *(3,4)* disturb you.** *(1)* Lamento / *(2)* Lamentamos *(3) perturbarlo m /* *(4) perturbarla f*

Stress rule # 3: Syllables with accent marks have the stress there.

(Fam: perturbarte). **I hope** *(1)* **I'm** / *(2)* **we're not** *(3,4)* **disturbing you.** Espero que no *(1)* esté / *(2)* estemos *(3) perturbándolo m* / *(4) perturbándola f (Fam: perturbándote).* **I don't want to** *(3,4)* **disturb you.** No quiero *(3) perturbarlo m* / *(4) perturbarla f (Fam: perturbarte).*

dive *vi* zambullirse, saltar al agua

diving *n* buceo *m*, zambullida *f* **scuba** ~ bucear (con escafandra), submarinismo *m*

divine *adj* divino *m*, -na *f*

divorce *n* divorcio *m* **ask** *(1)* **her** / *(2)* **him for a** ~ pídele el divorcio *(1,2) (No her or him in Sp.)* ~ **decree** sentencia *f* de divorcio **file for a** ~ presentar una demanda de divorcio **get a** ~ obtener el divorcio **go through a** ~ pasar por el divorcio **I plan to get a divorce (from** *[1]* **her** / *[2]* **him).** Planeo obtener el divorcio *([1,2] [No her or him in Sp.]).* **Have you filed for a divorce yet?** ¿Ya *presentó usted (Fam: presentaste)* la demanda de divorcio? **I've already filed for a divorce.** Ya presenté la demanda de divorcio. **How long will the divorce take?** ¿Cuánto tiempo se va a llevar el divorcio? **The divorce will (probably) take (about) three months.** (Probablemente) El divorcio se llevará (aproximadamente) tres meses.

divorced *adj* divorciado *m*, -da *f* **I'm divorced.** Estoy divorciado *(-da).* **How long have you been divorced?** ¿Cuánto tiempo *lleva usted (Fam: llevas)* divorciado *(-da)?* **I've been divorced for** *(number)* **years.** Llevo divorciado *(-da)* __ años. **Why did you get divorced?** ¿Por qué *se divorció usted (Fam: te divorciaste)?* **I got divorced because...** Me divorcié porque…

dizzy *adj* mareado *m*, -da *f* **I feel dizzy.** Me siento mareado *(-da).*

do *vt* hacer **How're you doing?** ¿Cómo te está yendo? **What do you do?** *(job / profession / work) (Answer:* **I'm a** *[job title].)* Qué *hace usted (Fam: haces tú?)?* (Yo soy ___.) **What are you doing?** ¿Qué estás haciendo? **I'm not doing anything.** No estoy haciendo nada. **Will you do it?** ¿Lo *va usted (Fam: vas)* a hacer? *(1)* **I** / *(2)* **We will (not) do it.** (No) Lo *(1)* voy / *(2)* vamos a hacer. **What are you going to do?** ¿Qué *va usted (Fam: vas.)* a hacer? **Did you do it?** ¿Lo *hizo usted (Fam: hiciste tú?)?* *(1)* **I** / *(2)* **We did (didn't do) it.** *(1)* Yo (no) lo hice. / *(2)* Nosotros (no) lo hicimos. **What did** *(1)* **you** / *(2)* **he** / *(3)* **she** / *(4)* **they do (then)?** ¿Qué *(1)* hiciste / *(2)* hizo él / *(3)* hizo ella / *(4)* hicieron ellos (entonces)? **How did** *(1)* **you** / *(2)* **he** / *(3)* **she** / *(4)* **they do it?** ¿Cómo lo *(1)* hiciste / *(2)* hizo él / *(3)* hizo ella / *(4)* hicieron ellos? **Why did** *(1)* **you** / *(2)* **he** / *(3)* **she** / *(4)* **they do that?** ¿Por qué *(1)* hiciste / *(2)* hizo él / *(3)* hizo ella / *(4)* hicieron ellos eso? *(1)* **I** / *(2)* **We** / *(3)* **He** / *(4)* **She** / *(5)* **They did it because...** *(1)* Lo hice / *(2)* Lo hicimos / *(3)* Él lo hizo / *(4)* Ella lo hizo / *(5)* Ellos lo hicieron porque… **You shouldn't have done that.** No *debió usted (Fam: debiste)*

Some Spanish words have accented and unaccented forms to differentiate their meanings (e.g., el = the, él = he).

haber hecho eso. **What are you doing** *(1)* **this evening?** / *(2)* **tomorrow**
([3] morning? / *[4]* **afternoon?** / *[5]* **evening?)?** / *(6)* **on Friday?** ¿Qué
va usted (Fam: vas) a hacer *(1)* esta noche? / *(2)* mañana *([3]* por la mañana?
/ *[4]* por la tarde? / *[5]* por la noche?)? / *(6)* el viernes? **What would you
like to do?** ¿Qué te gustaría hacer? **I don't want to do it.** No quiero
hacerlo. **Don't!** ¡No! **Tell me what to do.** Dime qué hacer. **You don't
know what you do to me.** Tú no sabes lo que me haces. **What do you like
to do in your spare time?** *(For answers, see under* **like**.*)* ¿Qué *le (Fam:
te)* gusta hacer en *su (Fam: tu)* tiempo libre? **What sort of things do you
like to do?** *(For answers, see under* **like**.*)* ¿Qué clase de cosas *le (Fam:
te)* gusta hacer?

dock *vt & vi* atracar, fondear

dock *n* muelle *m*

doctor *n* doctor *m*, -tora *f* **Call a doctor.** Llame a un doctor. **You'd better
see a doctor.** Será mejor que *vea usted (Fam: veas)* a un doctor. **I need to
see a doctor.** Necesito ver a un doctor. **Is there a doctor around here?**
¿Hay algún doctor por aquí?

doctorate *n* doctorado *m*

document *n* documento *m* **necessary** ~s documentos necesarios

dog *n* perro *m* **I have a dog.** Tengo un perro. **What's the dog's name?**
¿Cómo se llama el perro? **The dog's name is** *(name)*. El perro se llama
___. *(1)* **I'm** / *(2)* **You're** / *(3)* **He's a lucky dog.** *(1)* Soy... / *(2)* Usted es...
(Fam: Eres...) / *(3)* Él es... un tipo con suerte.

doll *n* muñeca *f* **I collect dolls.** Colecciono muñecas.

dolphin *n* delfín *m*

domineering *adj* dominante *m&f*

domino *n* dominó *m* **Do you know how to play dominos?** ¿Sabe usted
(Fam: ¿Sabes) jugar al dominó?

doomed *adj* perdido *m*, -da *f*, condenado *m*, -da *f*

door *n* puerta *f* **next** ~ al otro lado, la puerta que sigue **out of** ~s en el
exterior, afuera, al aire libre

dork *n (slang: s.o. who acts weird / stupid)* tonto *m*, -ta *f*, baboso *m*, -sa *f*

dorky *adj (slang: weird)* tontamente *m&f*, a lo baboso

dorm(itory) *n* dormitorio *m*

double *adj* doble *m&f* ~ **bed** cama *f* doble ~ **room** cuarto *m* doble

doubt *vt* dudar ~ **very much** dudar demasiado **begin to** ~ comenzar a dudar
I doubt it. Lo dudo.

doubt *n* duda *f* **be in** ~ estar en duda **beyond any** ~ fuera de duda **have** ~s
tener dudas **no** ~ sin duda **serious** ~s serias dudas **slightest** ~ la menor
duda **without a** ~ sin duda **I don't want you to have any doubts (about**

---

*Spanish "g" is pronounced like "h" in front of "e" and "i".
In front of other vowels it sounds like our "g" in "gun".*

me). No quiero que *usted tenga (Fam: tú tengas)* ninguna duda (de mi).

doubtful *adj* dudoso *m*, -sa *f* **It's very doubtful.** Es muy dudoso.

down *adv* abajo **come ~** bajar **fall ~** caer **lie ~** acostarse **sit ~** sentarse **Come down to the** *(1)* **lobby.** / *(2)* **lounge.** Baja al *(1)* vestíbulo. / *(2)* salón. **Do you want to lie down?** ¿Quiere usted acostarse *(Fam: Quieres acostarte)*? **Please sit down.** *Siéntese usted (Fam: Siéntate)* por favor. **Let's sit down over there.** Vamos a sentarnos allá.

down *prep* abajo **~ the stairs** abajo, escaleras abajo

down *adj (sad, depressed)* triste *m&f*, deprimido *m*, -da *f* **I feel kind of down.** Me siento algo triste. **Why are you so down (in the dumps)?** ¿Por qué tan triste (y de capa caída)?

downhill *adv* de bajada

downstream *adv* río abajo

down-to-earth *adj* práctico *m*, -ca *f*, realista *m&f*

downtown *adv* centro *m* **Let's go downtown.** Vamos al centro.

doze *vi* dormitar **I dozed off.** Me adormecí.

drain *n* caño *m* **It all went down the drain.** Todo se fue por el caño.

drama *n* drama *m*

draw *vt* 1. *(illustrate)* dibujar; 2. *(cards: take)* sacar, tomar **You draw very well.** *Usted dibuja (Fam: Tú dibujas)* muy bien. **I like to draw.** Me gusta dibujar. **Draw a card.** Saca un naipe.

drawer *n* cajón *m*

drawing *n (illustration)* dibujo *m*

dread *vt* temer, sentir horror **I dread** *(1,2)* **leaving you.** / *(3)* **saying goodbye.** Me horroriza *(1)* dejarlo *m* / *(2)* dejarla *f (Fam: dejarte)*. / *(3)* despedirme.

dreadful *adj* horrible *m&f*, espantoso *m*, -sa *f*, asombroso *m*, -sa *f*

dream *vi* soñar **I've always dreamt of meeting someone like you.** Siempre soñé encontrar a alguien como *usted (Fam: tú)*. **I often dreamt about coming here.** Muchas veces soñé venir aquí. **Surely I must be dreaming**. De seguro estoy soñando.

dream *n* sueño *m* **bad ~** pesadilla *f* **beautiful ~** sueño hermoso **happy ~** sueño feliz **my ~ come true** mi sueño hecho realidad **pipe ~** sueño en el aire **strange ~** sueño extraño **wonderful ~** sueño maravilloso **My (big) dream is to...**Mi (gran) sueño es... **You are my dream come true.** *Usted es (Fam: Tú eres)* mi sueño hecho realidad. **I know where I met you – in (all of) my dreams.** Yo sé dónde *lo (Fam: te)* conocí – en (todos) mis sueños. *(1)* **Love with you is a beautiful dream.** El amor contigo es un sueño hermoso. **I hope this isn't (just) a dream.** Espero que esto no sea (sólo) un sueño. **I've been walking around in a dream.** He andado con la cabeza en las nubes. **If this is a dream, I don't want to wake up.** Si esto

---

English-Spanish and Spanish-English glossaries of food and drink are on pages 420-427.

es un sueño, no quiero despertar. **In your dreams!** ¡Ni lo sueñes!

dreamer *n* soñador *m*, -dora *f* **beautiful ~** hermoso *(-sa)* soñador *(-dora)* **hopeless ~** soñador *(-dora)* sin esperanza.

dreamy *adj* soñador *m*, -dora *f*, lánguido *m*, -da *f* **~ face** cara ensoñadora

dreary *adj* aburrido *m*, -da *f* **It's so dreary around here.** Esto está muy aburrido.

dress *vi* vestir **You dress very (1) well. / (2) nicely.** *Usted viste (Fam: Vistes)* muy *(1)* bien. / *(2)* bonito.

dress *n* vestido *m* **What a lovely dress!** ¡Qué vestido tan encantador! **That's a (very) beautiful dress.** Ese es un vestido (muy) hermoso. **You look beautiful in any dress you wear.** *Usted se ve (Fam: Te ves)* hermosa en cualquier vestido que se ponga *(Fam: te pongas)*.

drink *vt* beber, tomar **Do you drink?** ¿*Toma usted (Fam: Tomas)*? **I don't drink (alcohol).** Yo no tomo (alcohol). **I drink (1) a little. / (2) very little. / (3) very seldom. / (4) occasionally. / (5) sometimes. / (6) socially.** Tomo *(1)* un poco. / *(2)* muy poco. / *(3)* muy esporádicamente. / *(4)* ocasionalmente. / *(5)* a veces. / *(6)* socialmente. **I drink a beer (1) occasionally. / (2) every now and then.** Tomo una cerveza *(1)* ocasionalmente. / *(2)* de vez en cuando. **I (1,2) quit drinking (a long time ago).** Me *(1)* privé / *(2)* dejé de tomar (hace mucho tiempo). **Would you like to have something (cold) to drink?** ¿*Le (Fam: Te)* gustaría tomar algo (frío)? **I'll get us something (cold) to drink.** Voy a conseguir algo (frío) para tomar. **Do you drink (1) beer? / (2) rum? / (3) wine?** ¿*Toma usted (Fam: Tomas)* *(1)* cerveza? / *(2)* ron? / *(3)* vino?

drink *n* bebida *f*, copa *f* **soft ~** refresco *m* **Would you like to have a drink (with me)?** ¿*Le (Fam: Te)* gustaría *tomarse (Fam: tomarte)* una copa (conmigo)? **Let me (1) get (buy) / (2) buy you a drink.** *Déjeme (Fam: Déjame) (1,2) invitarle (Fam: invitararte)* una copa. **(1) I'll fix... / (2) Let me fix... you a drink.** *(1)* Yo *le (Fam: te)* preparo… / *(2)* *Déjeme prepararle (Fam: Déjame prepararte)*... una copa. **Let's have a drink (together).** Vamos a tomar una copa (juntos). **What's your favorite drink?** ¿Cuál es *su (Fam: tu)* bebida favorita? **My favorite drink is _(name)_.** Mi bebida favorita es ___.

drinker *n* bebedor *m*, -dora *f* **non-drinker** abstemio *m*, -mia *f* **I'm a (1) coffee / (2) tea drinker.** Soy un*(a)* bebedor *(-dora)* de *(1)* café. / *(2)* té.

drive *vt* 1. *(operate a veh.)* manejar; 2. *(transport)* llevar; 3. *(make)* volver **(1) I / (2) We can (3,4) drive you there.** *(1)* Puedo / *(2)* Podemos *(3)* llevarlo *m* / *(4)* llevarla *f (Fam: llevarte)*. **C'mon, I'll drive (1,2) you there.** Vamos, yo *(1)* lo *m* / *(2)* la *f (Fam: te)* llevo. **C'mon, we'll drive**

you there. Vamos, nosotros *(1)* lo m / *(2)* la f *(Fam: te)* llevamos. **You drive me (absolutely) crazy.** *Usted me vuelve (Fam: Tú me vuelves)* (completamente) loco *(-ca).*

drive *vi* 1. *(operate a veh.)* manejar; 2. *(go)* ir en carro **Do you know how to drive?** ¿Sabe usted *(Fam: ¿Sabes)* manejar (carro)? **I can drive.** Sí sé manejar. **I can't drive.** No sé manejar. **Let's drive over there.** Vamos a ir en carro allá.

drive *n* 1. *(pleasure trip)* paseo en carro; 2. *(automot.)* tracción f **4-wheel ~** tracción a las cuatro ruedas. **Do we need 4-wheel drive?** ¿Necesitamos tracción a las cuatro ruedas? **Would you like to go for a drive?** ¿Le *(Fam: ¿Te)* gustaría ir a dar un paseo en carro? **Let's go for a drive**. Vayamos a pasear en carro.

driver *n* chofer *m* **Let's hire a driver.** Contratemos un chofer.

drugs *n, pl* drogas f, pl **I don't use drugs.** Yo no uso drogas.

drunk *adj* borracho *m*, -cha f, tomado *m*, -da f **be ~** estar borracho *(-cha)*, estar tomado *(-da)* **get ~** emborracharse **I don't want to get drunk.** No quiero emborracharme. **I think you're drunk.** Creo que *usted está (Fam: estás)* borracho *(-cha)*. **You must be drunk.** Debe *estar usted (Fam: Debes estar)* borracho *(-cha)*. **You're too drunk to drive.** *Usted está (Fam: Tú estás)* demasiado borracho *(-cha)* como para manejar.

dry *adj* seco *m*, -ca f

dry *vt* secar **Let me** *(1,2)* **dry you off.** Déjeme *(1) secarlo m / (2) secarla f (Fam: Déjame secarte)*. **I have to dry my hair.** Tengo que secarme el cabello.

dull *adj (boring)* aburrido *m*, -da f, hastiado *m*, -da f

dumb *adj* tonto *m*, -ta f, mudo *m*, -da f

dummy *n (bantering, affectionate)* estúpido *m*, -da f, imbécil *m&f.*

dune *n* duna f **sand ~** duna de arena **Let's go sit in the sand dunes.** Vamos a sentarnos en las dunas.

during *prep* durante **~** *(1)* **my /** *(2)* **our flight** durante *(1)* mi / *(2)* nuestro vuelo **~** *(1)* **my /** *(2)* **our stay** durante *(1)* mi / *(2)* nuestra estancia **~** *(1)* **my /** *(2)* **our trip** durante *(1)* mi / *(2)* nuestro viaje **~** *(1)* **my /** *(2)* **our visit** durante *(1)* mi / *(2)* nuestra visita **~ the war** durante la guerra.

duty *n* cargo *m*, deber *m*, servicio *m*, guardia f **off ~** franco, no estar en servicio **on ~** en servicio

A slash always means "or".

E

each *adj* cada uno *m&f* ~ **of us** cada uno de nosotros ~ **of you** cada uno de ustedes ~ **other** cada uno ~ **person** cada persona ~ **time** cada vez

eager *adj* ansioso *m*, -sa *f*, deseoso *m*, -sa *f*

eagerly *adv* ansiosamente **I look forward eagerly to** *(1,2)* **seeing you again.** Espero ansiosamente *(1) verlo m / (2) verla f* de nuevo.

ear *n* oreja *f* **big ~s** orejas grandes **both ~s** ambas orejas **left ~** oreja izquierda **little ~** orejita **pierced ~s** orejas perforadas **play it by ~** tocar de oído **right ~** oreja derecha **I have a bad** *(1)* **left /** *(2)* **right ear.** Yo tengo la oreja *(1)* izquierda / *(2)* derecha mala. *(1,2)* **Oh, (you have) such a cute little ear!** ¡Oh, *(1)* tú tienes una orejita curiosa! / *(2)* ¡Oh, qué orejita tan curiosa! **I want to talk privately with your ear for a moment.** Quiero platicar con tu oreja en privado un momento.

early *adj* temprano *m*, -na *f* **earlier** más temprano

early *adv* temprano **Come as early as possible.** *Venga (Fam: Ven)* tan temprano como *le (Fam: te)* sea posible. **We should try to be there early.** Debemos de tratar de estar temprano. **I always get up early.** Siempre me levanto temprano.

earn *vt* ganar **How much do you earn (a** *[1]* **month /** *[2]* **year)?** ¿Cuánto *gana usted (Fam: ganas)* (*[1]* al mes / *[2]* al año)? **I earn** *(amount)* **(a** *[1]* **month /** *[2]* **year).** Gano ___ (*[1]* al mes / *[2]* al año).

earphones *n, pl* audífonos *m, pl*

earring *n* arete *m* **What** *(1)* **beautiful /** *(2)* **fascinating earrings!** ¡Qué aretes tan *(1)* hermosos! / *(2)* fascinantes!

earth *n* tierra *f* **on the face of the ~** en la faz de la tierra **salt of the ~** la sal de la tierra

earthquake *n* terremoto *m*

ease *n* serenidad *f*, tranquilidad *f* **I feel so at ease with you.** Siento tanta tranquilidad *con usted (Fam: contigo)*. **You make me feel so at ease.**

Spanish "v" is pronounced like a soft "b".

Usted hace (Fam: Tú haces) que me sienta con tanta tranquilidad. **Let me put your mind at ease.** *Déjeme (Fam: Déjame)* poner *su (Fam: tu)* mente en tranquilidad.

easily *adv* fácilmente **We can make it easily.** *(get there)* Puedes llegar fácilmente. *(1)* **I** / *(2)* **We can do it easily.** *(1)* Puedo / *(2)* Podemos hacerlo fácilmente.

east *n* este *m*

easy *adj* fácil *m&f*, sencillo *m*, -la *f*, agradable *m&f* ~ **climb** *(mountain climbing)* escalada fácil ~ **hike** caminata fácil ~ **trail** sendero fácil, pista fácil **That's (very) easy.** Eso es (muy) fácil. **Swimming is easy. I'll show you.** Nadar es sencillo. Te mostraré. **That's easier said than done.** Es más fácil decirlo que hacerlo. **It's so easy to talk with you.** Es tan fácil platicar *con usted (Fam: contigo).* **I'm easy to get along with.** Es fácil llevarse bien conmigo. **You're (very) easy to get along with.** Es (muy) fácil llevarse bien *con usted (Fam: contigo).* **Take it easy.** *Tómelo (Fam: Tómalo)* con calma. **Easy come, easy go.** Así como viene se va.

easygoing *adj* despreocupado *m*, -da *f* **I'm an easygoing person. (You'll see.)** Soy una persona despreocupada. (Verás.) **I'd say you're** *(1)* **quite** / *(2)* **very easygoing.** Yo diría que *usted es (Fam: tú eres)* una persona *(1)* algo / *(2)* muy despreocupada. **You have an easygoing nature.** *Usted es (Fam: Tú eres)* de naturaleza despreocupada.

eat *vt* comer ~ **breakfast** desayunar ~ **dinner** cenar (noche) ~ **lunch** comer (medio día) ~ **supper** merendar (noche) **Let's get something to eat.** Vamos por algo de comer. **Would you like something to eat?** *¿Le (Fam: ¿Te)* gustaría comer algo? **Where's a good place to eat** *(1)* **dinner?** / *(2)* **supper?** ¿En dónde hay un buen lugar para *(1)* cenar? / *(2)* merendar?

eavesdrop *vi* escuchar furtivamente, escuchar en secreto **I didn't mean to eavesdrop.** No quise escuchar.

eccentric *adj* excéntrico *m*, -ca *f*

ecology *n* ecología *f*

economic *adj* económico *m*, -ca *f* ~ **situation** situación económica

economy *n* economía *f*

ecstasy *n* éxtasis *m*, embeleso *m*, arrebato *m* **cosmic** ~ embeleso cósmico

educated *adj* educado *m*, -da *f* **college** ~ académico *m*, -ca *f* **well** ~ bien educado *(-da)*

education *n* educación *f* **college** ~ educación académica **higher** ~ educación superior **high school** ~ educación preparatoria **musical** ~ educación musical **university** ~ educación universitaria **I have a college education.** Tengo educación académica. **Where did you get your education?** ¿En dónde *recibió usted su (Fam: recibiste tu)* educación?

Time expressions are given on page 413.

effect *n* efecto *m* **devastating** ~ efecto devastador **good** ~ buen efecto **great** ~ gran efecto **has an** ~ tiene efecto **magical** ~ efecto mágico **no** ~ sin efecto **positive** ~ efecto positivo **powerful** ~ efecto poderoso **profound** ~ efecto profundo **tremendous** ~ efecto tremendo **very little** ~ muy poco efecto **What was the effect of that?** ¿Cuál fue el efecto de eso? **Did it have any effect?** ¿Tuvo algún efecto? **You have an effect on my heart that no amount of words can describe.** *Usted produce (Fam: Tú produces)* un efecto indescriptible en mi corazón. **You have a very powerful effect on me, do you know that?** *Usted produce (Fam: Tú produces)* un efecto poderoso en mi. ¿Lo *sabía (Fam: sabías)*?

effective *adj* efectivo *m*, -va *f*

effervescent *adj* efervescente *m&f* ~ **personality** personalidad efervescente

efficient *adj* eficiente *m&f*

effort *n* esfuerzo *m*, empeño *m* **great** ~ gran empeño **make every (possible)** ~ poner todo el empeño (que sea posible) **no** ~ sin esfuerzo **special** ~ empeño especial

ego *n* ego *m* **be on an** ~ **trip** satisfacer el ego **You have a (really) big ego.** (Verdaderamente) *usted tiene (Fam: tú tienes)* un ego elevado.

egoistic *adj* egoístamente *m&f*

either *adj* cualquiera *m&f* ~ **one** cualquiera **You can have either one.** *Usted puede quedarse (Fam: Puedes quedarte)* con cualquiera. **Either way is okay with me.** De cualquier manera estoy de acuerdo.

either (not either) *adv* tampoco **I don't smoke either.** Tampoco fumo. **I don't want to either.** Yo tampoco quiero.

either *pron* alguno **Do either of you have change for this?** ¿Alguno de ustedes tiene cambio de este?

elated *adj* entusiasmado *m*, -da *f*, exaltado *m*, -da *f* **You don't know how elated I am to run into** *(1,2)* **you again.** No *sabe usted (Fam: sabes tú)* lo entusiasmado *(-da)* que estoy por volver a *(1) encontrarlo m / (2) encontrarla f (Fam: encontrarte)*.

elbow *n* codo *m*

elderly *adj* persona mayor

electric *adj* eléctrico *m*, -ca *f* ~ **outlet** toma eléctrica **Your** *(1)* ...**touch is...** / *(2)* ...**kisses are... electric.** *(1)* Tu tacto es electrizante. / *(2)* Tus besos son electrizantes.

electricity *n* electricidad *f* **The electricity is off.** La electricidad está desconectada. **I love the magic electricity of your** *(1)* **lips.** / *(2)* **touch.** Me encanta la electricidad mágica de *(1)* tus labios. / *(2)* tu tacto.

elegant *adj* elegante *m&f* **You look (absolutely) elegant.** *Usted se ve (Fam: Te ves)* (totalmente) elegante.

Spanish "qu" is pronounced like "k".

elixir *n* elixir *m* **Your bright spirit is an elixir to my soul.** Tu espíritu brillante es el elixir de mi alma.

elope *vi* fugarse **Let's elope!** !Fuguémonos!

else *adj* 1. *(different)* diferente *m & f*; 2. *(additional)* otro más **What else do you need?** ¿Qué más *necesita usted (Fam: necesitas)*? **Who else will be there?** ¿Quién más estará allí? **Is there someone else?** ¿Hay alguien más? **There is no one else (I swear).** No hay nadie más (lo juro). **No one else could ever take your place.** Nadie más pudo tomado tu lugar jamás.

else *adv* más, diferente **Where else can we go?** ¿Adónde más podemos ir? **Let's go somewhere else.** Vamos a un lugar diferente.

e-mail *vt* escribir (un correo electrónico) **I'll e-mail you.** Yo *le (Fam: te)* escribo un correo. **E-mail me (at this address).** *Escríbame (Fam: Escríbeme)* un correo (a esta dirección).

e-mail *n* correo *m* electrónico **I'll send you an e-mail.** Yo *le (Fam: te)* enviaré un correo electrónico. **Send me an e-mail (at this address).** *Envíeme (Fam: Envíame)* un correo electrónico (a esta dirección). **What's your e-mail address?** ¿Cuál es *su (Fam: tu)* dirección de correo electrónico? **My e-mail address is...** Mi dirección de correo electrónico es... **I want to check my e-mail.** Quiero revisar mi correo electrónico.

embarrass *vt* avergonzar **I'm sorry I embarrassed *(1,2)* you.** Lamento *(1)* haberlo *m / (2)* haberla *f (Fam: haberte)* avergonzado.

embarrassed *adj* evergonzado *m*, -da *f* **I *(1)* am / *(2)* was (*[3]* really / *[4]* so / *[5]* terribly) embarrassed.** *(1)* Estoy / *(2)* Estaba (*[3]* verdaderamente / *[4]* tan / *[5]* terriblemente) avergonzado *(-da)*. **There's nothing to be embarrassed about.** No hay nada de qué avergonzarse. **What's there to be embarrassed about?** ¿De qué hay que avergonzarse?

embarrassing *adj* vergonzoso *m*, -sa *f* **~ situation** situación vergonzosa **This is (very) embarrassing.** Esto es (muy) vergonzoso.

embarrassment *n* vergüenza *f* **I'm sorry for the embarrassment that I've caused you.** Lamento la vergüenza que *le (Fam: te)* hice pasar.

embassy *n* embajada *f* **American ~** Embajada de los Estados Unidos **Australian ~** Embajada de Australia **British ~** Embajada de la Gran Bretaña **Canadian ~** Embajada de Canadá **Irish ~** Embajada de Irlanda **Japanese ~** Embajada del Japón **New Zealand ~** Embajada de Nueva Zelanda **Could you please tell me where the *(country)* embassy is?** ¿*Podría usted (Fam: ¿Podrías)* decirme dónde se encuentra la embajada de ___?

embrace *vt* abrazar **tenderly ~** abrazar con ternura **tightly ~** abrazar con fuerza **I believe in embracing life.** Creo en el apego a la vida.

embrace *n* abrazo *m* **sweet ~** abrazo dulce **tender ~** abrazo tierno **warm ~** abrazo amistoso **I want to lose myself in your embraces.** Quiero perderme

---

Words in parentheses (not italicized) are optional.

en tus abrazos.

embroider *vt* bordar

embroidery *n* bordado *m* **I like to do embroidery.** Me gusta hacer bordados.

emerald *adj (color)* verde esmeralda *m&f* ★ *n (gem)* esmeralda *f*

emergency *n* emergencia *f* **It's an emergency.** Es una emergencia. **In case of an emergency, call me at this number.** En caso de emergencia, llámame a este número.

emigrate *vi* emigrar **Do you (really) want to emigrate?** ¿(De verdad) *Quiere usted (Fam: Quieres)* emigrar? **Why do you want to emigrate?** ¿Por qué *quiere usted (Fam: quieres tú)* emigrar? **Where do you want to emigrate?** ¿Adónde *quiere usted (Fam: quieres)* emigrar?

emotion *n* emoción *f* **arouse** ~**s** levanta emociones **conflicting** ~**s** emociones conflictivas **floodgate of** ~**s** inundación de emociones **mixed** ~**s** mezcla de emociones **powerful** ~**s** emociones poderosas **whirlpool of** ~**s** remolino de emociones **I'm not very good at hiding my emotions.** No soy muy bueno para ocultar mis emociones. **It's hard for me to express my emotions.** Me es difícil expresar mis emociones. **You shouldn't hide your emotions so. You need to open up.** *Usted no debe de (Fam: Tú no debes de)* ocultar tus emociones así. *Usted necesita abrirse (Fam: Necesitas abrirte).*

emotional *adj* emocional *m&f*, emotivo *m*, -va *f* ~ **turmoil** torbellino emocional ~ **upheaval** levantamiento emocional **I'm very emotional.** Soy muy emotivo *(-va).*

empathic *adj* comprensivo *m*, -va *f*, considerado *m*, -da *f*

empathize *vi* comprender, considerar

empathy *n* empatía *f*

employed *adj* empleado *m*, -da *f* **Where are you employed?** ¿En dónde *está usted (Fam: estás)* empleado *(-da)*? **I'm employed (*[1]* fulltime / *[2]* part-time) at *(place)* (as a *[job]*).** Estoy empleado *(-da)* (de *[1]* tiempo completo / *[2]* medio tiempo) en ___ (como ___).

employee *n* empleado *m*, -da *f*

employer *n* empleador *m*, -dora *f*, patrón *m*, -trona *f* **former** ~ patrón *(-trona)* anterior **present** ~ patrón *(-trona)* actual

employment *n* empleo *m* ~ **ad(s)** anuncio(s) de empleo **fulltime** ~ empleo de tiempo completo **part-time** ~ empleo de medio tiempo **I'm looking for employment (as a *[job]*).** Busco empleo (como ___).

emptiness *n* vacío *m* **Until I met you I knew only loneliness and emptiness.** Hasta que te conocí sólo supe de soledad y vacío.

empty *adj* vacío *m*, -cia *f* ~ **head** cabeza vacía ~ **life** vida vacía **My life was**

A single Spanish "r" should be lightly trilled; double "r" ("rr") should be strongly trilled.

so empty until I met you. Mi vida estaba tan vacía hasta que te conocí. **My life would be empty without you.** Mi vida estaría vacía sin ti.

enchant *vt* encantar **You enchant me with your** *(1)* **beautiful smile.** / *(2)* **beautiful eyes.** / *(3)* **blithe spirit.** *Usted me encanta (Fam: Me encantas)* con *(1) su (Fam: tu)* hermosa sonrisa. / *(2) sus (Fam: tus)* ojos hermosos. / *(3) su (Fam: tu)* espíritu alegre.

enchanted *adj* encandado *m*, -da *f* **I am (completely) enchanted by your (radiant) beauty.** Estoy (totalmente) encantado con *su (Fam: tu)* belleza (radiante).

enchanting *adj* encantador *m*, -dora *f* **You have the most enchanting** *(1)* **face** / *(2)* **eyes I've ever seen.** *Usted tiene (Fam: Tienes)* *(1)* la cara más encantadora... / *(2)* los ojos más encantadores... que haya visto jamás.

encourage *vt* estimular, alentar

encouragement *n* estimulación *f*, aliento *m* **Thank you for your encouragement.** Gracias por el aliento que *usted me da (Fam: tú me das)*.

encouraging *adj* estimulante *m&f*, alentador *m&f*

end *vt* terminar, dar por terminado *(1,2)* **I want to end this.** *(1)* Quiero dar esto por terminado. / *(2)* Quiero terminar con esto. **I think we should end our relationship.** Creo que debemos de terminar con nuestra relación.

end *vi* terminar **When does it end?** ¿Cuándo termina? **It ends** *(1)* **at** *(time)*. / **on** *(day / date)*. Termina *(1)* a las ___. / *(2)* el ___. **I don't want these (wonderful) moments (with you) to ever end.** No quiero que terminen jamás estos momentos (maravillosos) (contigo).

end *n* final *m* **at the ~ (of)** al final (de) **dead ~** calle cerrada **in the ~** al final **no ~** sin final **rear ~** *(buttocks)* trasero *m* **without ~** sin final

endearment *n* caricia f, cariño *m* **term of ~** expresión de cariño

endless *adj* interminable *m&f*

endlessly *adv* interminablemente

energetic *adj* vigoroso *m*, -sa *f*, de mucha energia **You're really energetic.** Verdaderamente *es usted (Fam: eres)* vigoroso *(-sa)*.

energy *n* energía *f*, vigor *m* **high ~** alta eneregía **positive ~** energía positiva **You (really) have a lot of energy.** (Verdaderamente) *Tiene usted (Fam: Tienes)* mucha energía.

engage *vi (in an activity)* dedicarse **What kind of activities do you engage in (at school)?** ¿A qué tipo de actividades *se dedica (Fam: te dedicas)* (en la escuela)? **I engage in** *(1)* **environmental activism.** / *(2)* **outdoor activities.** / *(3)* **political activities.** / *(4)* **sports.** Me dedico *(1)* al activismo del medio ambiente. / *(2)* a actividades externas. / *(3)* a actividades políticas. / *(4)* a los deportes.

engaged *adj* comprometido *m*, -da *f* **~ to be married** comprometido *(-da)*

Familiar "tu" forms in parentheses can replace italicized polite forms.

en matrimonio **get ~ (to be married)** comprometerse **Are you engaged?** *¿Está usted (Fam: Estás)* comprometido *(-da)*? **I'm engaged.** Estoy comprometido *(-da)*. **We're engaged.** Estamos comprometidos. **We were engaged.** Estuvimos comprometidos.

engagement *n* compromiso *m* **We broke off our engagement.** Rompimos nuestro compromiso.

England *n* Inglaterra **from ~** desde Inglaterra **in ~** en Inglaterra **to ~** hacia Inglaterra

English *adj* inglés *m&f*

English *n (language)* inglés **speak ~** hablar inglés **Do you speak English?** ¿Hablas inglés? **Does anyone here speak English?** ¿Hay alguien que hable inglés por aquí? **I speak only English (, but I smile in any language).** Sólo hablo inglés (, pero sonrío en cualquier idioma).

Englishman *n* inglés *m*

Englishwoman *n* inglesa *f*

enjoy *vt* disfrutar **~ oneself** divertirse **Are you enjoying your *(1)* stay / *(2)* trip / *(3)* vacation / *(4)* visit (here)?** *¿Está usted (Fam: Estás)* disfrutando *su (Fam: tu) (1)* estancia / *(2)* viaje / *(3)* vacación / *(4)* visita (en este lugar)? ***(1)* I'm / *(2)* We're enjoying *(3)* my / *(4)* our *(5)* stay / *(6)* trip / *(7)* vacation / *(8)* visit (here) (very much).** *(1)* Estoy / *(2)* Estamos disfrutando (mucho) *(3)* mi / *(4)* nuestra *(5)* estancia / *(6)* viaje / *(7)* vacación / *(8)* visita (en este lugar). ***(1)* I / *(2)* We enjoy *(3)* the beach. / *(4)* camping. / *(5)* concerts. / *(6)* opera. / *(7)* the outdoors. / *(8)* sightseeing. / *(9)* the theater. / *(10)* traveling.** *(1)* Disfruto / *(2)* Disfrutamos de *(3)* la playa. / *(4)* el campamento. / *(5)* los conciertos. / *(6)* la ópera. / *(7)* el exterior. / *(8)* visitar lugares de interés. / *(9)* el teatro. / *(10)* viajar. **I (really) enjoy *(1)* ...being (together)... / *(2)* ...talking... / *(3)* ...doing things... with you.** (Verdaderamente) Disfruto *(1)* ...estar (juntos)... / *(2)* ...platicar... / *(3)* ...de hacer cosas... *con usted (Fam: contigo)*. **I (really) enjoy listening to your stories.** (Verdaderamente) Disfruto escuchar *sus (Fam: tus)* cuentos. ***(1)* I / *(2)* We enjoyed myself (*[3]* very much / *[4]* tremendously).** *(1)* Me divertí... / *(2)* Nos divertimos... (*[1]* mucho / *[2]* tremendamente). ***(1)* I / *(2)* We (really) enjoyed it.** (Verdaderamente) Lo *(1)* disfruté. / *(2)* disfrutamos.

enjoyable *adj* divertido *m&f (1)* **I / *(2)* We had a very enjoyable time.** *(1)* Pasé / *(2)* Pasamos un rato muy divertido. **That sounds very enjoyable.** Eso suena muy divertido.

enlighten *vt* ilustrar, instruir **Perhaps you could enlighten *(1)* me / *(2)* us about *(subject)*.** Quizás pudiera usted *(1)* ilustrarme / *(2)* ilustrarnos con respecto a ___. **You've enlightened *(1)* me / *(2)* us a great deal about**

Spanish "ll" is pronounced like "y" in "yes".

(subject). Usted *(1)* me / *(2)* nos ha ilustrado muchísimo con respecto a ___.

enlightening *adj* ilustrativo *m*, -va *f* **That** *(1)* **is** / *(2)* **was very enlightening.** Eso *(1)* es / *(2)* fue muy ilustrativo.

enlist *vi* alistar, reclutar **I enlisted in the** *(1)* **Air Force** / *(2)* **Army** / *(3)* **Navy** / *(4)* **Marine Corps (for** *[number]* **years).** Me recluté en *(1)* la fuerza aérea / *(2)* el ejército / *(3)* la marina / *(4)* la infantería de marina (por ___ años).

enlisted man *n (mil.)* soldado *m*

enlisted woman *n (mil.)* soldado *f*

enormous *adj* enorme *m&f*

enormously *adv* enormemente

enough *adj & adv* suficiente, bastante ~ **money** suficiente dinero ~ **time** tiempo suficiente **more than** ~ más que suficiente **not** ~ no es suficiente **old** ~ bastante antiguo *(-gua)* **Is that enough?** ¿Es suficiente? **It's (not) enough.** (No) Es suficiente. **Is there enough room?** ¿Hay suficiente espacio? **There's (not) enough room.** (No) Hay suficiente espacio. **Do you have enough time?** ¿Tiene usted *(Fam: Tienes)* suficiente tiempo? *(1)* **I** / *(2)* **We (don't) have enough time.** (No) *(1)* Tengo / *(2)* Tenemos tiempo suficiente. **I can never get enough of you.** Nunca puedo tener suficiente de tu persona.

enrich *vt* enriquecer **You enrich my life (more and more every day).** *Usted enriquece (Fam: Tú enriqueces)* mi vida (cada día más).

enroll *vi* inscribirse **I plan to enroll in the university (next fall).** Planeo inscribirme en la universidad (para el próximo otoño).

enter *vt* 1. *(go in)* entrar; 2. *(enroll, join)* ingresar **Where do we enter?** ¿Adónde ingresamos? **I entered the service in** *(year)*. Ingresé al servicio en ___. *(1)* **I'm** / *(2)* **He's** / *(3)* **She's going to enter** *(name of university)* **in the fall.** *(1)* Voy / *(2)* Él va / *(3)* Ella va a ingresar a la universidad de ___ en el otoño. **It never entered my mind.** Nunca me he metido a mi mente.

enterprising *adj* emprendedor *m*, -dora *f* **You're very enterprising.** Eres muy emprendedora.

entertain *vt* entretener **Thank you for entertaining** *(1)* **me.** / *(2)* **us.** Gracias por *(1)* entretenerme. / *(2)* entretenernos.

entertainment *n* diversión *f* **What do you do for entertainment?** ¿Qué *hace usted (Fam: haces tú)* para *divertirse (Fam: divertirte)*? **What kind of entertainment do you like?** ¿Qué tipo de diversión *le (Fam: te)* gusta? **What's for entertainment around here?** ¿Que hay para divertirse por aquí?

enthusiasm *n* entusiasmo *m* **boundless** ~ entusiasmo sin límites **great** ~

Common occupations are listed on pages 415-416.

gran entusiasmo **much** ~ mucho entusiasmo **show** ~ muestra entusiasmo **I admire your enthusiasm.** Admiro *su (Fam: tu)* entusiasmo. *(1,2)* **You don't seem to have much enthusiasm for it.** Eso no parece *(1) entusiasmarlo m* / *(2) entusiasmarla f (Fam: entusiasmarte)* mucho. **Hey, show a little more enthusiasm!** ¡Ea! ¡Muestra un poco más de entusiasmo!

enthusiastic *adj* entusiasmado *m & f* ~ **about life** entusiasmado por la vida **I'm really enthusiastic about** *(1)* **going there.** / *(2)* **seeing it.** / *(3)* **the trip.** / *(4)* **visiting it.** Verdaderamente estoy entusiasmado por *(1)* ir allí. / *(2)* verlo. / *(3)* el viaje. / *(4)* visitarlo. **You (don't) sound very enthusiastic (about it).** Usted *(no) suena (Fam: [No] Suenas)* muy entusiasmado *(-da)* (por eso). `

entice *vt* persuadir **Could I possibly entice** *(1,2)* **you to** *(3)* **go there with me?** / *(4)* **go to dinner with me?** / *(5)* **go on vacation with me?** / *(6)* **spend a couple of weeks here with me?** ¿Acaso podría *(1) persuadirlo m* / *(2) persuadirla f (Fam: persuadirte)* de *(3)* ir allí conmigo? / *(4)* ir a cenar conmigo? / *(5)* ir de vacaciones conmigo? / *(6)* pasar un par de semanas conmigo aquí?

enticing *adj* persuasivo *m*, -va *f*

entire *adj* completo *m*, -ta *f* ~ **month** mes completo, todo el mes ~ **time** tiempo completo ~ **week** semana completa **my** ~ **life** mi vida completa **I want to spend the entire time with you.** Quiero pasar el tiempo completo contigo.

entirely *adv* completamente **It's entirely up to you.** Es decisión *suya (Fam: tuya)* completamente. **You're entirely right.** Estás completamente bien.

entrance *n* entrada *f (1)* **I'll** / *(2)* **We'll wait for** *(3,4)* **you by the entrance.** *(3)* Lo *m* / *(4)* La *f (Fam: Te) (1)* esperaré / *(2)* esperaremos a la entrada.

entranced *adj* absorto *m*, -ta *f* **I'm completely entranced by your loveliness.** Estoy completamente absorto por *su (Fam: tu)* exquisitez.

entrancing *adj* absorbente ~ **eyes** ojos absorbentes ~ **smile** sonrisa absorbente

entrepreneur *n* empresario *m*, -ria *f*

entry *n* 1. *(entrance)* entrada *f*, ingreso *m* ; 2. *(signing up)* registro *m* ~ **in a contest** registro en un concurso ~ **into the country** entrada al país ~ **permit** permiso de ingreso ~ **visa** visa de ingreso

envelope *n* sobre *m*

envious *adj* envidioso *m*, -sa *f* **You're just envious.** Sólo eres envidioso *(-sa)*.

environment *n* medio *m* ambiente **destroy the** ~ destruir el medio ambiente **protect the** ~ proteger el medio ambiente **We need to do more to safe-**

Spanish "y" is "ee" when alone or at the end of words.

guard the environment. Es necesario que hagamos más por salvaguardar el medio ambiente.

environmental *adj* ambientalista *m&f* ~ **disaster** desastre ambientalista ~ **issues** asuntos ambientalistas ~ **problem** problema ambientalista

envision *vt* predecir, visualizar **What do you envision?** ¿Qué *predice usted (Fam: predices)*? **I envision …** Predigo …

envy *vt* envidiar **I** (*[1]* **don't** / *[2]* **really) envy** *(3,4)* **you.** (*[1]* No / *[2]* Verdaderamente) *(3) Lo m* / *(4) La f (Fam: Te)* envidio.

epidemic *n* epidemia *f*

equal *adj* igual *m&f* ~ **chance** igual oportunidad ~ **pay for** ~ **work** pago igual por un trabajo igual ~ **rights** derechos iguales **All people are equal.** Todas las personas son iguales.

equal *vt* igualar **Nine plus eight equals seventeen.** Nueve más ocho es igual a diecisiete. **No one can equal you.** Nadie puede igualarte.

equally *adv* igualmente ~ **well** igualmente bien **We'll divide this equally.** Dividiremos esto en partes iguales.

equipment *n* equipo *m* **camping** ~ equipo de campamento **mountain climbing** ~ equipo para ascenso de montañas **photographic** ~ equipo fotográfico **scuba diving** ~ equipo de buceo **sports** ~ equipo deportivo **Do you have all your equipment?** ¿Tiene usted (*Fam: ¿Tienes*) todo *su (Fam: tu)* equipo? **Check your equipment.** *Verifique (Fam: Verifica) su (Fam: tu)* equipo.

equivalent *n* equivalente *m* **What's the equivalent in Spanish?** ¿Cuál es el equivalente en español? **The equivalent in English is** *(what)*. El equivalente en inglés es ___.

eraser *n* borrador *m*

erotic *adj* erótico *m&f* ~ **book** libro erótico ~ **fantasies** fantasias eróticas ~ **movie** película erótica ~ **photos** fotos eróticas ~ **thoughts** pensamientos eróticos

errand *n* mandado *m*, mensaje *m (1)* **I** / *(2)* **We have some errands to run. (Come with** *[3]* **me.** / *[4]* **us.)** *(1)* Tengo / *(2)* Tenemos algunos mensajes que enviar. (*Venga [Fam: Ven] [3]* conmigo. / *[4]* con nosotros.)

error *n* error *m* **There's an error here.** Aquí hay un error.

escape *vi* escapar **Can we escape together for a** *(1)* **few hours?** / *(2)* **few days?** / *(3)* **weekend?** / *(4)* **while?** ¿Podemos escaparnos juntos por *(1)* unas cuantas horas? / *(2)* unos cuantos días? / *(3)* un fin de semana? / *(4)* un rato? **I used to work, but I escaped.** Solía trabajar, pero me escapé.

escort *vt* escoltar *(1)* **I'll** / *(2)* **We'll escort** *(3,4)* **you (to** *[5]* **your car.** / *[6]* **your hotel.** / *[7]* **your house.** / *[8]* **the station).** *(3) Lo m* / *(4) La f (1)* escoltaré / *(2)* escoltaremos (a *[5]* su carro. / *[6]* su hotel. / *[7]* su casa. / *[8]*

Feminine forms of words in phrases
are usually given in parentheses (italicized).

la estación.).

ESP *abbrev* = **extrasensory perception** PES = percepción *f* extrasensorial **You must have ESP. I was just thinking about** *(1)* **calling you.** / *(2)* **the same thing.** / *(3)* **you.** Tú debes tener percepción extrasensorial. Exactamente estaba pensando en *(1)* llamarte. / *(2)* lo mismo. / *(3)* ti.

especially *adv* especialmente **This is especially for you.** Esto es especialmente para *usted (Fam: ti)*. **I especially wanted to tell you that...** Especialmente quería *decirle (Fam: decirte)* que...

espresso *n* expreso *m*

essence *n* esencia *f* **You are the essence of** *(1)* **beauty.** / *(2)* **loveliness.** Eres la esencia *(1)* de la belleza. / *(2)* del encanto.

essential *adj* esencial *m&f* **It's essential that I get it (back)** *(1)* **today.** / *(2)* **tomorrow.** Es esencial que lo tenga (de vuelta) el día de *(1)* hoy. / *(2)* mañana.

establish *vt* establecer ~ **a business** establecer un negocio

esteem *n* estima *f* **I hold** *(1,2)* **you in very high esteem.** *(1)* Lo *m* / *(2)* La *f (Fam: Te)* tengo en muy alta estima.

estimate *n* estimación *f* **Can you give** *(1)* **me** / *(2)* **us an estimate (of the cost)?** ¿Puede usted *(1)* darme / *(2)* darnos una estimación (del costo)? **That's just an estimate.** Eso es solo una estimación.

et cetera etcétera

eternal *adj* eterno *m*, -na *f* ~ **love** amor eterno

eternally *adv* eternamente **I am eternally yours.** Soy tuya eternamente.

eternity *n* eternidad *f* **It seemed like an eternity.** Parecía una eternidad. **Each** *(1)* **minute** / *(2)* **hour** / *(3)* **day that we're apart seems like an eternity.** Cada *(1)* minuto / *(2)* hora / *(3)* día que estamos separados parece una eternidad.

ethereal *adj* etéreo *m*, -rea *f* ~ **beauty** belleza etérea

ethical *adj* ético *m*, -ca *f*

ethics *n* ética *f*

ethnic *adj* étnico *m*, -ca *f* ~ **food** comida étnica ~ **group** grupo étnico

etiquette *n* etiqueta *f* **What's the proper etiquette?** ¿Cuál es la etiqueta adecuada?

euphoria *n* euforia *f* **sensual** ~ euforia sensual

Europe *n* Europa *f* **from** ~ desde Europa **in** ~ en Europa **to** ~ hacia Europa

European *adj* européo *m*, -péa *f*

evade *vt* evadir **You're evading the question.** *Está usted (Fam: Estás)* evadiendo la pregunta.

evasive *adj* evasivo *m*, -va *f* ~ **answer** respuesta evasiva

even *adj* igual *m&f*, parejo *m*, -ja *f* **get** ~ desquitarse **The score is even.** El

---

Spanish "c" before "e" and "i" is pronounced like "s"

resultado es parejo. **Now we're even.** Ahora estamos parejos *(-jas)*.

even *adv* aún ~ **if** aún si ~ **though** aún cuando

evening *n* noche *f* **beautiful** ~ noche hermosa **every** ~ todas las noches **in the** ~ en la noche **memorable** ~ noche memorable **pleasant** ~ noche agradable **Saturday** ~ sabado en la noche **the whole** ~ toda la noche **this** ~ esta noche **tomorrow** ~ mañana en la noche **unforgettable** ~ noche inolvidable **yesterday** ~ ayer en la noche **Good evening!** *(early)* ¡Buenas tardes!; *(later)*¡Buenas noches! **What a** *(1)* **beautiful** / *(2)* **lovely** / *(3)* **nice** / *(4)* **wonderful evening!** ¡Que *(1)* hermosa / *(2)* amorosa / *(3)* buena / *(4)* maravillosa noche! **I love evenings like this.** Amo noches como esta. **I'll never forget this evening.** Nunca olvidaré esta noche.

event *n* evento *m* **cultural** ~s eventos culturales **in the** ~ **that** en el evento de que **musical** ~ evento musical **sporting** ~ evento deportivo

even-tempered *adj* calmado *m*, -da *f*, sereno *m*, -na *f*, tranquilo *m*, -la *f*

eventually *adv* finalmente, a la larga

ever *adv* alguna vez, siempre, jamás **Have you ever been there?** *¿Ha estado usted (Fam: Has estado) allí alguna vez?* **Have you ever seen the movie (name)?** *¿Ha visto usted (Fam: Has visto) alguna vez la película ___?* **Have you ever heard the song (name)?** *¿Ha oído usted (Fam: Has oído) alguna vez la canción ___?* **You're the nicest person I've ever met.** *Usted es (Fam: Eres) la persona más agradable que jamás haya conocido.* **I don't ever want to lose** *(1,2)* **you.** No quiero *(1) perderlo m* / *(2) perderla f (Fam: perderte)* jamás. **Thank you ever so much.** Sumamente agradecido.

everlasting *adj* perdurable *m&f* ~ **love** amor perdurable

every *adj* cada *m&f*, todo m, -da *f* ~ **day** a diario ~ **hour** a toda hora ~ **minute** en todo minuto ~ **night** cada noche ~ **time** cada vez **I want to see you every chance I get.** Quiero verte en toda oportunidad que se presente.

everybody *pron* todos

everyone *pron* todos

everyplace *adv* en todo lugar

everything *pron* todo **Is that everything?** ¿Eso es todo? **That's everything.** Eso es todo. **Tell me everything (about it).** *Dígame (Fam: Dime)* todo (lo relacionado con eso). **You are my everything.** *Usted es (Fam: Tú eres)* mi todo.

everywhere *adv* en todos lados **I want to go everywhere with you.** Quiero ir a todos lados contigo.

evidently *adv* evidentemente

evil *adj* malvado *m*, -da *f*, maligno *m*, -na *f* ~ **spirits** espíritus malignos

exact *n* exacto *m*, -ta *f*

exactly *adv* exactamente

Numbers in Spanish are given on pages 411-412.

exaggerate *vt & vi* exagerar **I'm (not) exaggerating.** (No) Estoy exagerando.

exaggeration *n* exageración *f* **That's no exaggeration.** Esa no es una exageración.

exam(ination) *n* examen *m* **final ~** examen final **physical ~** examen físico

examine *vt* examinar **Let me examine your eye.** *Déjeme (Fam: Déjame)* examinar *su (Fam: tu)* ojo.

example *n* ejemplo *m* **for ~** por ejemplo **Can you give me an example?** *¿Puede usted (Fam: Puedes)* darme un ejemplo? **A(n) (good) example is** *(what)*. Un buen ejemplo es ___. **Let me give you an example.** *Déjeme darle (Fam: Déjame darte)* un ejemplo.

exasperating *adj* exasperante *m&f*

ex-boyfriend *n* ex-novio *m*

excellent *adj* excelente *m&f*

except *prep* excepto, salvo **~ Saturday and Sunday** excepto sábado y domingo **~ weekends** excepto los fines de semana **There's no one except you.** No hay nadie excepto *usted (Fam: tú)*. **I can't think about anything except you.** No puedo pensar en nada excepto en *usted (Fam: ti)*.

except *conj* salvo **I won't do anything, except talk with you.** No haré nada, salvo platicar *con usted (Fam: contigo)*.

exception *n* excepción *f* **I'm making an exception for you.** Estoy haciendo una excepción *con usted (Fam: contigo)*.

exceptional *adj* excepcional *m&f* **You have an exceptional** *(1)* **figure.** / *(2)* **physique.** *Usted tiene (Fam: Tienes) (1)* una figura / *(2)* un físico excepcional. **You have exceptional talent.** *Usted tiene (Fam: Tienes)* un talento excepcional.

exceptionally *adv* excepcionalmente **You're exceptionally beautiful.** *Usted es (Fam: Eres)* excepcionalmente hermosa. **You** *(1)* **paint** / *(2)* **play exceptionally well.** *(1) Usted pinta (Fam: Pintas)* / *(2) Usted juega (Fam: Juegas)* excepcionalmente bien.

excessive *adj* excesivo *m*, -va *f*

exchange *vt* intercambiar; cambiar **Let's exchange.** Vamos a intercambiar. **Where can I exchange money?** En dónde puedo cambiar dinero?

excite *vt* emocionar **The idea excites me.** La idea me emociona.

excited *adj* emocionado *m*, -da *f* **Are you excited (about it)?** *¿Está usted (Fam: Estás)* emocionado *(-da)* (por eso)? **I can imagine that you're excited (about it).** Puedo imaginar que *usted está (Fam: tú estás)* emocionado *(-da)* (por eso). **I'm (so) excited (about it).** Estoy (tan) emocionado *(-da)* (por eso). **Don't get excited.** No te emociones. **You make me feel (strangely) excited.** Me haces sentir (raramente)

Spanish "h" is always silent.

emocionado *(-da)*.

excitement *n* emoción *f* **That's too much excitement for** *(1)* **me.** / *(2)* **us.** Eso es demasiada emoción para *(1)* mi. / *(2)* nosotros. **What do you do for excitement around here?** ¿Qué hacen por aquí para tener emoción? **I feel such excitement when you** *(1)* **do that.** / *(2)* **get close to me.** / *(3)* **kiss me.** / *(4)* **touch me.** Siento tanta emoción cuando tú *(1)* haces eso. / *(2)* te me acercas. / *(3)* me besas. / *(4)* me tocas.

exciting *adj* emocionante *m&f* *(1)* **This** / *(2)* **That is exciting.** *(1)* Esto / *(2)* Eso es emocionante.

excursion *n* excursión *f* **Would you like to go on an excursion (with** *[1]* **me** / *[2]* **us)?** ¿Le *(Fam: te)* gustaría ir de excursión (*[1]* conmigo / *[2]* con nosotros)?

excuse *vt* disculpar **Excuse me.** Discúlpame. **Excuse me?** *(When one has not heard or understood.)* ¿Cómo dijo, disculpe? **Please excuse** *(1)* **me.** / *(2)* **us.** Por favor *(1)* discúlpame. / *(2)* discúlpanos.

excuse *n* excusa *f* **flimsy** ~ excusa fútil **good** ~ buena excusa **lame** ~ excusa frívola **poor** ~ excusa pobre **I have an excuse.** Tengo una excusa. **I have no excuse.** No tengo excusa. **There's no excuse.** No hay excusa. **I don't want to hear your excuses.** No quiero oír tus excusas.

exercise *vi* hacer ejercicio **I exercise** *(1)* **everyday.** / *(2)* **regularly.** Yo hago ejercicio *(1)* diariamente. / *(2)* con regularidad.

exercise *n* ejercicio *m* **do ~s** hacer ejercicios ~ **equipment** equipo para ejercicio ~ **room** salón de ejercicio

ex-girlfriend *n* ex-novia *f*

exhausted *adj* exhausto *m*, -ta *f*, extenuado *m*, -da *f* **Aren't you exhausted?** ¿No *está usted (Fam: estás)* exhausto *(-ta)*? **You must be exhausted.** *Usted debe (Fam: debes)* estar exhausto *(-ta)*. **I'm (totally) exhausted.** Estoy (totalmente) exhausto *(-ta)*.

exhausting *adj* exhaustivo *m*, -va *f*

exhibit *n* muestra *f* **art** ~ muestra de arte

exhibition *n* exhibición *f*

exhibitionist *n* exhibicionista *m&f*

exhilarating *adj* estimulante *m&f*, regocijante *m&f*, deleitantes *m&f* **Your kisses are exhilarating.** *Sus (Fam: Tus)* besos son deleitantes.

exhilaration *n* regocijo *m*, deleite *m* **I feel such exhilaration being with you.** Siento tal deleite cuando estoy *con usted (Fam: contigo)*.

ex-husband *n* ex-marido *m*

exist *vi* existir **How did I exist without you?** ¿Cómo existí sin ti?

existence *n* existencia *f* **lonely** ~ existencia aislada **solitary** ~ existencia solitaria.

Questions about the metric system? See page 417.

exit *n* salida *f (1)* **I'll** / *(2)* **We'll wait for** *(3,4)* **you by the exit.** *(1)* Yo *(3)* lo *m* / *(4)* la *f (Fam: te)* esperaré… / *(2)* Nosotros *(3)* lo *m* / *(4)* la *f (Fam: te)* esperaremos… a la salida.

ex-love *n* ex-amor *m*

ex-lover *n* ex-amante *m&f*

ex-military *n* ex-militar *m*

exorbitant *adj* exorbitante *m&f*

exotic *adj* exótico *m*, -ca *f* **You have such exotic eyes.** *Usted tiene (Fam: Tienes)* unos ojos tan exóticos.

expect *vt* esperar **When can** *(1)* **I** / *(2)* **we expect** *(3,4)* **you?** ¿Cuándo *(1)* puedo / *(2)* podemos *(3)* esperarlo *m* / *(4)* esperarla *f (Fam: esperarte)*? **What time do they expect** *(1,2)* **you home?** ¿A qué hora *(1)* lo *m* / *(2)* la *f (Fam: te)* esperan en casa? **I'm expecting.** *(pregnant)* Estoy esperando.

expense *n* gasto *m* **Spare no expense!** ¡No repares en gastos!

expensive *adj* costoso *m*, -sa *f (1)* **It's** / *(2)* **That's** (*[3]* **rather** / *[4]* **too** / *[5]* **terribly** / *[6]* **very) expensive.** *(1)* Es / *(2)* Eso es (*[3]* algo / *[4]* demasiado / *[5]* terriblemente / *[6]* muy) costoso. *(1)* **It's** / *(2)* **That's not** (*[3]* **so** / *[4]* **too** / *[5]* **very) expensive.** *(1)* No es… / *(2)* Eso no es… (*[3]* tan / *[4]* demasiado / *[5]* muy) costoso.

experience *vt* experimentar **I've never experienced so much** *(1)* **excitement.** / *(2)* **fun.** / *(3)* **happiness.** Nunca he experimentado tanta *(1)* emoción. / *(2)* diversión. / *(3)* felicidad.

experience *n* 1.*(accumulated knowledge / practice)* experiencia *f*; 2. *(occurrence)* experiencia *f* **bizarre** ~ extravagante experiencia **funny** ~ 1. *(amusing)* experiencia divertida; 2. *(odd)* experiencia rara **great** ~ 1.*(accumulated knowledge / practice)* gran experiencia; 2. *(occurrence)* gran experiencia **job** ~ experiencia laboral **life** ~ experiencia de vida **my** ~ mi experiencia **new** ~ nueva experiencia **once-in-a-lifetime** ~ experiencia de una vez en la vida **personal** ~ experiencia personal **similar** ~ expeciencia similar **strange** ~ extraña experiencia **terrifying** ~ experiencia aterradora **wonderful** ~ experiencia maravillosa **work** ~ experiencia laboral **How much experience have you had (as a** *[job]*)**?** ¿Cuánta experiencia *ha tenido usted (Fam: has tenido)* (como ___)? **I've had** *(number)* **years of experience (as a** *[job]*)**.** He tenido ___ años de experiencia (como ___). **It was a very embarrassing experience.** Fue una experiencia muy vergonzosa.

experienced *adj* experimentado *m*, -da *f* **You seem to be (very) experienced.** Parece que *está usted (Fam: tú estás)* (muy) experimentado *(-da)*. **I'm not very experienced.** No soy muy experimentado *(-da)*.

experiment *vi* experimentar **We can experiment together.** Podemos experimentar juntos. **Let's experiment.** Vamos a experimentar.

The letter "ñ" sounds like the "ny" in "canyon".

expert *n* experto *m*

expire *vi* vencer **My visa expires on** *(date)*. Mi visa vence el ___ .

explain *vt* explicar **Could you explain this for me?** ¿*Podría usted (Fam: Podrías)* explicarme esto? **Please let me explain.** Por favor, *déjeme (Fam: déjame)* explicar. **I can explain (everything).** Yo puedo explicar (todo). **I'll try to explain (this) to you.** Trataré de *explicarle (Fam: explicarte)* (esto). **I'll explain the game to you.** Yo *le (Fam: te)* explico el juego.

explanation *n* explicación *f* **I owe you an explanation.** *Le (Fam: te)* debo una explicación.

explore *vt* explorar **I like to explore new places. Do you?** Me gusta explorar nuevos lugares. ¿Y a *usted (Fam: ti)*? **Let's go explore the city (together).** Vamos a explorar la ciudad (juntos). **I want to explore the universe with you.** Quiero explorar el universo *con usted (Fam: contigo)*.

express *vt* expresar **You express yourself very well.** Te expresas muy bien. **I wish I could express my feelings as well as you do.** Deseo poder expresar mis sentimientos tan bien como *usted (Fam: tú)*. **Words alone cannot express how I** *(1)* **feel about you.** / *(2)* **love you.** Las palabras solas no pueden expresar *(1)* lo que siento por *usted (Fam: ti)*. / *(2)* cuánto te amo.

expression *n* expresión *f* **blank** ~ expresión en blanco **funny** ~ 1. *(amusing)* expresión divertida; 2. *(odd)* expresión rara **idiomatic** ~ expresión idiomática **puzzled** ~ expresión de desconcierto **slang** ~ expresión vernácula **surprised** ~ expresión de sorpresa **worried** ~ expresión de preocupación **This gift is just a small expression of** *(2)* **my** / *(3)* **our gratitude (to you).** Este regalo solo es una pequeña expresión de *(1)* mi / *(2)* nuestra gratitud (hacia *usted [Fam: ti]*).

expressive *adj* expresivo *m*, -va *f* **You have such** *(1)* **an expressive face.** / *(2)* **expressive eyes.** *Usted tiene (Fam: Tienes)* *(1)* una cara tan expresiva. / *(2)* unos ojos tan expresivos.

exquisite *adj* exquisito *m*, -ta *f* **I'm captivated by your exquisite beauty.** Estoy cautivado por *su (Fam: tu)* exquisita hermosura.

extend *vt* prorrogar ~ **my visa** prorrogar mi visa

extension *n* prórroga *f* **visa** ~ prórroga de visa.

extensively *adv* extensamente *(1)* **I've** / *(2)* **We've traveled extensively (in Europe).** *(1)* He / *(2)* Hemos viajado extensamente (por Europa).

extent *n* alcance **To what extent?** ¿A qué alcance?

extra *adj* extra *m&f* **Do you have any extra** *(1)* **batteries?** / *(2)* **film?** ¿*Tiene usted (Fam: Tienes)* *(1)* algunas baterías extra? / *(2)* alguna película extra? **It's extra. You can have it.** Es extra. Puedes quedártelo. **Please take extra care with it.** Por favor, ten cuidado extra con eso.

Meet Mexicans online!
See pages 428-430 for websites.

extraordinarily *adv* extraordinariamente **You're extraordinarily beautiful.** *Usted es (Fam: Eres)* extraordinariamente hermosa.

extraordinary *adj* extraordinario *m*, -ria *f* **That's (really) extraordinary.** Eso es (verdaderamente) extraordinario.

extravagance *n* extravagancia *f* **What's life without an extravagance or two?** Qué es la vida sin una o dos extravagancias?

extravagant *adj* extravagante *m&f* **You shouldn't be so extravagant. (But, then, I'm worth it.)** No debes de ser tan extravagante. (Pero, luego, lo valgo.) **So, I'm extravagant. But you're worth it.** Así que, soy extravagante. Pero lo vales.

extreme *adj* extrremo *m*, -ma *f*

extreme *n* extremo *m* **Please, don't go to extremes.** Por favor, no *se vaya (Fam: te vayas)* a los extremos. **You go from one extreme to the other.** *Usted se va (Fam: Tú te vas)* de un extremo al otro.

extremely *adv* extremadamente **You've made me extremely happy.** *Usted me ha (Fam: Tú me has)* hecho extremadamente feliz. **That's extremely (1) generous / (2) kind /(3) nice of you.** Eso es extremadamente *(1)* generoso / *(2)* amable / *(3)* gentil de *su (Fam: tu)* parte.

extrovert *n* extrovertido *m*, -da *f* **I guess I'm something of an extrovert.** Creo que soy algo extrovertido *(-da)*.

exuberant *adj* exuberante *m & f*

ex-wife *n* ex-esposa *f*

eye *n* ojo **almond(-shaped)** ~s ojos almendrados **beautiful** ~s ojos hermosos **bedroom** ~s ojos sensuales **bewitching** ~s ojos hechizantes **big** *(1)* **blue /** *(2)* **brown** ~s grandes ojos *(1)* azules / *(2)* cafés **black** ~ ojo morado **blue** ~s ojos azules **both** ~s ambos ojos **bright** ~s ojos vivos **brown** ~s ojos cafés **closed** ~s ojos cerrados **dark** ~s ojos oscuros **enchanting** ~s ojos encantadores **exotic** ~s ojos exóticos **expressive** ~s ojos expresivos **friendly** ~s ojos amistosos **green** ~s ojos verdes **hazel** ~s ojos de azul avellana **intelligent** ~s ojos inteligentes **intriguing** ~s ojos intrigantes **kind(ly)** ~s ojos amables **laughing** ~s ojos risueños **left** ~ ojo izquierdo **light brown** ~s ojos café claro **lively** ~s ojos vivarachos **lovely** ~s ojos encantadores **my** ~s mis ojos **open** ~s ojos abiertos **pale blue** ~s ojos de azul pálido **right** ~ ojo derecho **sad** ~s ojos tristes **sexy** ~s ojos sensuales **sharp** ~s ojos de lince **sleepy** ~s ojos somnolientos **smiling** ~s ojos sonrientes **solemn** ~s ojos solemnes **sparkling** ~s ojos chispeantes **starry** ~s ojos estrellados **tired** ~s ojos cansados **violet-blue** ~s ojos de azul violeta **your** ~s *sus (Fam: tus)* ojos **Close your eyes.** *Cierre sus (Fam: Cierra tus)* ojos. **Look me in the eye.** *Míreme (Fam: Mírame)* a los ojos. **You have such beautiful eyes.** *Usted tiene (Fam: Tienes)* unos ojos tan hermosos. **Here's to your**

Spanish "o" is pronounced like "o" in "note".

beautiful (*[1]* blue / *[2]* dark) eyes. *(toast)* Brindo por *sus (Fam: tus)* ojos (*[1]* azules / *[2]* oscuros). **When I look into your eyes, I see the stars.** Cuando veo *sus (Fam: tus)* ojos, veo las estrellas. **You have the most enchanting eyes I've ever seen.** *Usted tiene (Fam: Tienes)* los ojos más encantadores que haya visto jamás. **Your eyes radiate such warmth.** *Sus (Fam: Tus)* ojos irradian tanto calor. **I could never forget your eyes.** Nunca podría olvidar *sus (Fam: tus)* ojos. **The best artist in the world could not do justice to your eyes.** Ni el mejor artista del mundo podría hacer justicia a *sus (Fam: tus)* ojos. **Your beautiful eyes melt my heart.** *Sus (Fam: Tus)* hermosos ojos derriten mi corazón. **It's such a thrill to gaze into your eyes.** Es tan emocionante mirar *sus (Fam: tus)* ojos. **I only have eyes for you.** Solo tengo ojos para *usted (Fam: ti)*. **Your smile caught my eye.** *Su (Fam: tu)* sonrisa atrajo mi mirada. **I had my eye on you since the first moment I saw you.** Tenía mis ojos puestos en *usted (Fam: ti)* desde el primer momento que *(1)* lo m / *(2)* la f *(Fam: te)* vi. **I lost my *(1)* left / *(2)* right eye in *(3)* the (Vietnam) war. / *(4)* an accident.** Perdí mi ojo *(1)* izquierdo / *(2)* derecho en *(3)* la guerra (de Vietnam). / *(4)* un accidente.

eyebrow *n* ceja *f* **beautiful ~s** hermosas cejas

eye-catching *adj* que atrapan las miradas

eyeful *n* visión *f* **You're quite an eyeful.** *Usted es (Fam: Eres)* una visión totalmente.

eyeglasses *n, pl* lentes *mpl*

eyelash(es) *n (pl)* pestaña(s) *f (pl)* **beautiful ~es** hermosas pestañas **false ~es** pestañas postizas **long ~es** largas pestañas

eyelid *n* párpado *m*

eyesight *n* vista *f* **good ~** buena vista **perfect ~** vista perfecta **poor ~** vista pobre **weak ~** vista débil

---

Numbers in parentheses always signal choices.

F

fabulous *adj* fabuloso *m*, -sa *f*

face *n* cara *f*, rostro *m*   **angelic** ~ rostro angelical **baby** ~ cara de bebé **cute** ~ cara mona **expressive** ~ cara expresiva **familiar** ~ cara conocida **friendly** ~ rostro amistoso **handsome** ~ cara bien parecida **happy** ~ cara feliz **intelligent** ~ rostro inteligente **nice** ~ 1. *(attractive)* cara bonita; 2. *(pleasant)* cara agradable **poker** ~ cara de palo **pretty** ~ cara bonita **smiling** ~ rostro sonriente **What a** *(1)* **cute /** *(2)* **beautiful /** *(3)* **lovely face (you have)!** ¡Qué cara tan *(1)* mona / *(2)* hermosa / *(3)* encantadora (tienes)! **You have the** *(1)* **cutest /** *(2)* **loveliest /** *(3)* **most beautiful /** *(4)* **most enchanting face I've ever seen**. *Usted tiene (Fam: Tú tienes)* la cara más *(1)* mona / *(2)* encantadora / *(3)* hermosa / *(4)* fascinante que haya visto jamás. **When I look at you, I see the face of an angel**. Cuando te miro, veo la cara de un ángel.

facilities *n, pl* instalaciones *fpl*   ~ **for the handicapped** instalaciones para discapacitados

fact *n* hecho *m* **as a matter of** ~ por cierto **in** ~ de hecho **plain** ~ hecho puro **simple** ~ hecho simple **Is that a fact?** ¿Es cierto eso? **That's a fact**. Es un hecho.

faculty *n* facultad *f* **university** ~ facultad universitaria **I'm a member of the faculty (at** *[university]*)**.** Soy miembro de la facultad (en la universidad de ___).

fail *vt* reprobar **I failed the exam**. Reprobé el examen. **What happens if you fail the exam?** ¿Qué sucede si *usted reprueba (Fam: repruebas)* el examen?

fail *vi* fallar, fracasar **If that fails,** *(1)* **I /** *(2)* **we will call you**. Si eso falla, *(1)* le *(Fam: te)* llamaré / *(2)* llamaremos. **Why did your marriage fail?** ¿Por qué fracasó *su (Fam: tu)* matrimonio? **My marriage failed because...** Mi matrimonio fracasó porque…

Spanish "a" is mostly like "a" in "mama".

failure *n* falla *f*; fracaso *m* **The whole thing was a failure (from the start).** Fue todo un fracaso (desde el principio).

faint *vi* desmayarse **I think I'm going to faint! You're on time!** ¡Creo que me voy a desmayar! ¡Llegaste a tiempo!

fair *adj* 1. *(honest, even-handed)* honrado *m*, -da *f*, justo *m*, -ta *f*; 2. *(fairhaired)* rubio *m*, -bia *f*, guero *m*, -ra *f* ~ **person** *(even-handed)* persona *f* justa ~ **question** pregunta *f* justa ~ **share** parte *f* justa ~ **skin** piel *f* blanca **No fair!** ¡No es justo! **That's fair, right?** Eso es justo, ¿no? **That's (not) fair.** Eso (no) es justo. **C'mon, be fair.** Vamos, sé justo.

fair *adv* justo **play** ~ juego limpio **You're not playing fair.** No estás jugando limpio.

fair *n* feria *f* **book** ~ feria del libro **trade** ~ feria comercial **Would you like to go to the fair (with *[1]* me / *[2]* us)?** ¿Le *(Fam: ¿Te)* gustaría ir a la feria (*[1]* conmigo / *[2]* con nosotros)?

fairly *adv (rather)* bastante

fairness *n* justicia *f* **in all** ~ con toda justicia

fairy *n* hada *f* ~ **godmother** hada madrina

fairytale *n* cuento *m* de hadas

faith *n* fe *f* **Have faith (in me).** Ten fe (en mí). **I have faith in you.** Tengo fe en ti. **Have you no faith (in me) at all?** ¿Qué no tienes nada de fe (en mi)?

faithful *adj* fiel **I will always be faithful to you.** Siempre le *(Fam: te)* sere fiel.

fake *adj* falso *m*, -sa *f*

fake(r) *n* farsante *m&f* **You big fake(r)!** ¡Qué farsante eres!

fall *vi* caer **Be careful you don't fall.** Ten cuidado de no caer. **Snow is falling.** Está cayendo nieve.

★ **fall apart** *idiom* desbaratarse, deshacerse

★ **fall down** *idiom* caerse **I fell down.** Me caí. **It's going to fall down.** Eso se va a caer.

★ **fall for** *idiom (be taken in)* caer en la trampa **I fell for it hook, line and sinker.** Caí en la trampa con todo y zapatos.

★ **fall in love** *idiom* enamorarse **I'm falling in love with you.** Me estoy enamorando de ti. **I've fallen in love with you.** Me he enamorado de ti. **The moment I saw you, I fell head over heels in love with you.** Al momento que te vi, me volví loco *(-ca)* por ti.

★ **fall over** *idiom* caerse **It's going to fall over.** Es se va a caer.

fall *n (autumn)* otoño *m* **in the** ~ en el otoño **last** ~ el otoño pasado **next** ~ el siguiente otoño

false *adj* falso *m*, -sa *f*; *(teeth)* postizo *m*, -za *f* ~ **alarm** falsa alarma ~ **idea** idea falsa ~ **impression** falsa impresión ~ **teeth** dientes postizos

---

Articles: m = el, f = la, mpl = los, fpl = las

familiar *adj* familiar *m&f*, conocido *m*, -da *f* **You look so familiar. I'm sure I've** *(1)* **seen** / *(2)* **met** *(3,4)* **you before.** Usted me parece conocido *(-da)*. Estoy seguro *(-ra)* de que *(3)* lo *m* / *(4)* la *f* *(1)* ...he visto... / *(2)* ...conocí... con anterioridad.

family *n* familia *f* **big ~** gran familia **broken ~** familia desunida **build a ~** formar una familia **close-knit ~** familia unida **extended ~** familia extendida **~ life** vida *f* familiar **~ member** miembro *m* de la familia **~ name** apellido *m* **happy ~** familia feliz **in a ~ way** esperando familia **make a ~** formar una familia **middle-class ~** familia de clase media **my ~** mi familia **no ~** sin familia **our ~** nuestra familia **poor ~** familia pobre **small ~** familia pequeña **start a ~** iniciar una familia **support a ~** mantener una familia **well-to-do ~** familia acomodada **working ~** familia trabajadora **your ~** su *(Fam: tu)* familia **I dream of building a family.** Sueño con formar una familia.

family-minded *adj* delicado *(-da)* a la familia

family-oriented *adj* amante *m&f* de la vida familiar

fan *n (enthusiast)* fanático *m*, -ca *f* **I'm a** *(1)* **baseball** / *(2)* **basketball** / *(3)* **football** / *(4)* **hockey** / *(5)* **soccer** / *(6)* **sports fan.** Soy fanático *(-ca)* ...del *(1)* béisbol. / *(2)* baloncesto. / *(3)* fútbol americano. / *(4)* hockey. / *(5)* fútbol. / *(6)* ...de los deportes.

fancy *adj* 1. *(high-class)* de lujo; chic; *(stylish)* estilizado *m*, -da *f*; 2. *(intricate)* complicado *m*, -da *f* **~ design** diseño *m* complicado **~ dress** disfraz *m* **~ hairdo** peinado *m* estilizado **~ hotel** hotel *m* de lujo **~ restaurant** restaurante *m* de lujo

fanny *n (slang: buttocks)* nalgas *fpl*, trasero *m*

fantasize *vi* fantasear, soñar despierto *(-ta)*

fantastic *adj* fantástico *m*, -ca *f*; maravilloso *m*, -sa *f*, de maravilla **You are (absolutely) fantastic!** ¡Eres (una verdadera) maravilla! **That was (absolutely) fantastic!** ¡Eso estuvo (de verdad) maravilloso! *(1)* **I** / *(2)* **We had a fantastic time.** *(1)* Pasé / *(2)* Pasamos un rato fantástico.

fantasy *n* fantasía *f* **You are all my fantasies come true.** Tú eres mi fantasía hecha realidad. **You are every** *(1)* **man's** / *(2)* **woman's fantasy.** Tú eres la fantasía de *(1)* todo hombre. / *(2)* toda mujer. **Tell me one of your fantasies. (And I'll tell you one of mine.)** Cuéntame una de tus fantasías. (Y te cuento una de las mías.)

far *adj* lejos **How far is it (from here)?** ¿Qué tan lejos está (de aquí)? **It's not (very) far.** No está (muy) lejos. **It's (very) far.** Es (muy) lejos. **Is your** *(1)* **house** / *(2)* **hotel far from here?** ¿Está su *(Fam: tu)* *(1)* casa / *(2)* hotel lejos de aqui? **You're going too far.** Usted se está *(Fam: Te estás)* yendo demasiado lejos.

Spanish "z" is pronounced like "s" in "safe"

far *adv* lejos **so ~** hasta ahora **Do you live far from here?** ¿*Vive usted (Fam: ¿Vives)* lejos de aquí?

fare *n* tarifa *f* **How much is the fare?** ¿Cuánto es la tarifa? **The fare is** *(amount).* La tarifa es de __.

farewell *n* despedida *f* **It's time to say farewell.** Es hora de darnos la despedida. **I hate farewells.** Odio las despedidas. **Farewell!** ¡Que te vaya bien!

farm *n* granja *f*, rancho *m* **Do you live on a farm?** ¿*Vive usted (Fam: ¿Vives)* en un rancho? *(1)* **I** / *(2)* **We live on a farm.** *(1)* Vivo / *(2)* Vivimos en un rancho.

farsighted *adj* clarividente *m&f*; hipermétrope *m&f*

farther *adj & adv* más distante, mas lejos, a mayor distancia

fascinate *vt* fascinar **You fascinate me (no end).** Me fascinas (absolutamente).

fascinating *adj* fascinante *m & f* **That's fascinating.** Eso es fascinante. **That's a fascinating** *(1)* **necklace.** / *(2)* **ring.** Ese es un *(1)* collar / *(2)* anillo fascinante. **What a fascinating story!** ¡Qué historia tan fascinante!

fashion *n* moda *f* **hip ~** moda del momento; moda de onda **in ~** a la moda **latest ~** última moda **new ~** nueva moda **out of ~** fuera de moda **You really have a flair for fashion.** Verdaderamente *tiene usted (Fam: tienes)* estilo para la moda.

fashionable *adj* a la moda

fast *adj* rápido *m*, -da *f* **What's the fastest way to get there?** ¿Cuál es el modo más rápido de llegar allá? **You're a fast worker.** Trabajas rápido. *(1)* **My** / *(2)* **Your watch...** / *(3)* **That clock... is fast.** *(1)* Mi / *(2)* su *(Fam: tu)* reloj … / *(3)* Ese reloj... se adelanta.

fast *adv* rápido **How fast can you do it?** ¿Qué tan rápido *puede (Fam: puedes)* hacerlo? **You're talking too fast for me.** *Usted está (Fam: Estás)* hablando demasiado rápido para mí. **Don't drive so fast.** No manejes tan rápido. **Promise me you won't drive too fast.** Prométeme que no vas a demasiado rápido. **You move pretty fast for an old** *(1)* **lady.** / *(2)* **man.** Camina usted bastante rápido para ser *(1)* una señora… *(2)* un hombre… mayor.

fasten *vt* sujetar; atar; amarrar **Can you fasten this for me?** ¿*Puede usted (Fam: Puedes)* sujetarme esto? **Let me fasten that for you.** *Déjeme (Fam: Déjame)* sujetarle *(Fam: sujetarte)* eso por *usted (Fam: ti).*

fat *adj* gordo *m*, -da *f*

fate *n* destino *m* **I believe that Fate brought us together (and I'm so grateful).** Creo que el destino nos juntó (y estoy tan agradecido).

father *n* padre **This is my father** *(name).* Este es mi padre __. **This is a picture of my father.** Esta es una foto de mi padre. **My father lives in**

A tilde ~ in terms stands for the main entry word.

(place). Mi padre vive en ___. **I live with my father.** Yo vivo con mi padre. **My father has passed away.** Mi padre ya murió.

father-in-law *n* suegro *m*

fattening *adj* engordador *m*, -dora *f* **Kisses are not fattening. You can have as many as you want.** Los besos no te engordan. Puedes tener todos los que quieras.

fault *n* falta *f*, culpa *f*, defecto *m* **It's (not)** *(1)* **my /** *(2)* **your fault.** (No) Es *(1)* mi / *(2)* su *(Fam: tu)* culpa. **It was (not)** *(1)* **my /** *(2)* **your fault.** (No) Fue *(1)* mi / *(2)* su *(Fam: tu)* culpa. **I have a lot of faults, but I hope you can overlook them.** Tengo muchos defectos, pero espero que *usted pueda (Fam: puedas)* disculparlos.

faux pas *n* metida *f* de pata **social** ~ desatino *m* social

favor *n* favor *m* **Could you (please) do** *(1)* **me /** *(2)* **us a (***[3]* **small /** *[4]* **big) favor?** ¿Podría usted *(Fam: Podrías)* *(1)* hacerme / *(2)* hacernos un *([3]* pequeño / *[4]* gran) favor? **Thanks for the favor.** Gracias por el favor.

favorable *adj* favorable *m&f*

favorite *adj* favorito *m*, -ta *f* ~ **season** temporada *f* favorita **What's your favorite** *(1)* **color? /** *(2)* **dish?** ¿Cuál es *su (Fam: tu)* *(1)* color / *(2)* platillo favorito? **What's your favorite** *(1)* **drink? /** *(2)* **flower? /** *(3)* **song?** ¿Cuál es *su (Fam: tu)* *(1)* bebida / *(2)* flor / *(3)* canción favorita? **Who's your favorite** *(1)* **(movie) actor? /** *(2)* **(male) singer?** ¿Quién es *su (Fam: tu)* *(1)* actor (de cine) / *(2)* cantante favorito? **Who's your favorite** *(1)* **(movie) actress? /** *(2)* **(female) singer?** ¿Quién es *su (Fam: tu)* *(1)* actriz (de cine) / *(2)* cantante favorita? **My favorite** *(person / thing)* **is** *(name)***.** Mi ___ favorito *(-ta)* es ___.

fax *n* fax *m* ~ **machine** máquina *f* de fax **send a** ~ enviar un fax

fear *n* temor *m* **There's no need for fear.** No hay por qué temer.

feast *vi* darse un banquete **I want to feast (night and day) on your lips.** Quiero darme un banquete (noche y día) con tus labios.

feast *n* banquete *m* ; festín *m*

features *n, pl (face)* rasgos *mpl*, facciones *fpl* **delicate** ~**s** facciones delicadas **fine** ~**s** facciones finas **lovely** ~**s** facciones encantadoras

February *n* febrero *m* **in** ~ en febrero **on** ~ **first** el primero de febrero

fed up *idiom* harto *m*, -ta *f* **be** ~ estar harto *(-ta)*

fee *n* precio *m* ; tarifa *f* ; honorarios *mpl* ; cuota *f* **admission / entrance** ~ (precio de) entrada *f* **no** ~ sin cuota **rental** ~ tarifa por alquiler **small** ~ cuota pequeña **How much is the fee?** ¿Cuánto es la cuota?

feed *vt* alimentar ~ **the baby** alimentar al bebé ~ **the cat** alimentar al gato ~ **the dog** alimentar al perro ~ **the ducks** alimentar a los patos ~ **the pigeons** alimentar a los pichones **You're feeding me a line.** Me estás dando por mi

---

*Spanish "ch" is pronounced like ours
(e.g., "cheese," "charge").*

lado.

feel *vt* sentir **I like to feel your hand in mine.** Me gusta sentir tu mano en la mía. **I feel so much love for you.** Siento tanto amor por ti.

feel *vi* sentir ~ **like** tener ganas, deseos ~ **the same** sentir lo mismo **How do you feel?** ¿Cómo *se siente usted (Fam: te sientes)?* **I feel** *(1)* **okay.** / *(2)* **fine.** / *(3)* **great.** / *(4)* **sick.** / *(5)* **terrible.** / *(6)* **dizzy.** Me siento *(1)* bien. / *(2)* muy bien. / *(3)* excelente. / *(4)* enfermo. / *(5)* mal. / *(6)* mareado. **I feel (much) better.** Me siento (mucho) mejor. **I don't feel (so) good.** No me siento (muy) bien. **I feel like I've known you all my life.** Siento como que te conozco de toda la vida. **I haven't felt so** *(1)* **good** / *(2)* **happy in years.** No me he sentido tan *(1)* bien / *(2)* feliz en años. **I've never felt this way about anyone (before).** Nunca (antes) me sentiasí con nadie. **I love the way you make me feel.** Me encanta la manera en que me haces sentir. **You make me feel** *(1)* **alive (again).** / *(2)* **so happy.** / *(3)* **wonderful.** / *(4)* **young (again).** Me haces sentir *(1)* con vida (de nuevo). / *(2)* tan feliz. / *(3)* maravillosamente. / *(4)* joven (de nuevo). **I feel** *(1)* **bad** / *(2)* **terrible about what I said.** Me siento *(1)* mal / *(2)* pésimamente por lo que dije. **I don't feel like** *(1)* **it.** / *(2)* **going.** *(1)* No tengo ganas. / *(2)* No tengo ganas de ir. **How do you feel about** *(1)* **the tax laws.** / *(2)* *(other issue)*. ¿Qué *piensa (Fam: piensas)* de *(1)* las leyes fiscales? / *(2)* ___? **I feel that...** Siento que...

feeling *n* sentimiento *m* **arouse** ~**s** despertar sentimientos **beautiful** ~**s** sentimientos hermosos **deep** ~**s** sentimientos profundos **experience** ~**s** experimentar sensaciones **express** *(1)* **my** / *(2)* **your** ~**s** expresar *(1)* mis / *(2)* sus *(Fam: tus)* sentimientos **funny** ~ *(odd)* rara sensación **good** ~ buen sentimiento **hurt** *(1)* **my** / *(2)* **your** ~**s** lastimar *(1)* mis / *(2)* sus *(Fam: tus)* sentimientos **nice** ~ sensación agradable **strange** ~ sensación extraña **strong** ~**s** sentimientos fuertes **such** ~**s** tales sentimientos **wonderful** ~ sentimiento maravilloso **I can't hold back my feelings any longer.** Ya no puedo reprimir mis sentimientos. **I've never had such feelings before.** Nunca antes tuve tales sentimientos. **You've awoken such wonderful feelings in me.** Me has despertado sentimientos tan maravillosos. **I want you to share your feelings with me.** Quiero que compartas conmigo tus sentimientos. **You shouldn't keep your feelings bottled up inside you.** No debes guardar tus sentimientos sólo para ti. **I wish I could express my feelings as well as you do.** Ojalá pudiera expresar mis sentimientos tan bien como tú. **I'm (very) sorry that I hurt your feelings.** Lamento (mucho) haber herido *sus (Fam: tus)* sentimientos. **I didn't mean to hurt your feelings.** No quise herir *sus (Fam: tus)* sentimientos.

fellow *adj:* ~ **countryman** compatriota *m* ~ **countrywoman** compatriota *f*

Stress rule #1: The last syllable is stressed if the word ends in a consonant (except "n" and "s").

~ **human being** congénere *m&f* ~ **traveler** compañero *(-ra)* de viaje
~ **worker** compañero *(-ra)* de trabajo

fellow *n* individuo *m*, tipo *m* **nice** ~ tipo simpatico **Who's that fellow (over there)?** ¿Quién es ese individuo (que está allá)?

female *adj* femenina *f*, -no *m* ★ *n* 1. *woman)* mujer *f*; 2. *(biol., zool.)* hembra *f*

feminine *adj* femenina *f*, -no *m* ~ **charms** encantos femeninos

feminist *n* feminista *f*

ferry *n* trasbordador *m* **We can go across on the ferry**. Podemos cruzar en el trasbordador.

fervent *adj* ferviente *m&f*

fervently *adv* fervientemente

festival *n* festival *m* **autumn** ~ festival de otoño **Christmas** ~ festival navideño **summer** ~ festival de verano **wine** ~ festival del vino **Would you like to go the festival with** *(1)* **me** / *(2)* **us** *(3)* **today?** / *(4)* **this evening?** / *(5)* **tomorrow?** / *(6)* **on** *(day)*? ¿Le (Fam: ¿Te) gustaría ir al festival *(1)* conmigo / *(2)* con nosotros *(3)* hoy? / *(4)* esta noche? / *(5)* mañana? / *(6)* el ___? **Come with** *(1)* **me** / *(2)* **us to the festival!** ¡Ven *(1)* conmigo / *(2)* con nosotros al festival!

fever *n* fiebre *f* **You (don't) have a fever**. (No) *Tiene (Fam: Tienes)* fiebre.

few *n* cuantos *mpl*, cuantas *fpl* **a** ~ **days** unos cuantos días **a** ~ **hours** unas cuantas horas **a** ~ **minutes** unos cuantos minutos **a** ~ **months** unos cuantos meses **a** ~ **people** unas cuantas personas **a** ~ **weeks** unas cuantas semanas **a** ~ **years** unos cuantos años **quite a** ~ unos cuantos

fiancé *n* prometido *m*, novio *m* **This is my fiancé** *(name)*. Este es mi prometido ___ . **This is a picture of my fiancé**. Esta es una foto de mi novia.

fiancée *n* prometida *f*, novia *f* **This is my fiancée** *(name)*. Esta es mi prometida ___. **This is a picture of my fiancée**. Esta es una foto de mi prometida.

fickle *adj* voluble *m&f*, -sa; caprichoso *m*, -sa *f*

fiction *n* ficción *f*

field *n* campo *m* ~ **of computers** campo de computadoras ~ **of electronics** campo de la electrónica **interesting** ~ *(of work)* campo interesante **playing** ~ campo de juego **play the** ~ andar *(un hombre)* con una y con otra *(mujer)* **soccer** ~ campo de fútbol **What field do you work in?** ¿Cuál es *su (Fam: tu)* campo de trabajo?

fierce *adj* feroz *m&f*

fight *vi* 1. *(physically)* pelear; 2. *(argue)* pelearse; 3. *(war)* combatir **Did you fight in the war?** ¿Combatió usted (Fam: ¿Combatiste) en la guerra? **I fought (in the war) in** *(place)*. Combatí (en la guerra) en ___. **Let's not fight**. No peleemos. **I don't want to fight**. No quiero pelear.

Spanish "i" is mostly "ee", but can also be shorter, like "i" in "sit," when together with other vowels.

fight *n* 1. *(physical)* pelea *f* ; 2. *(argument)* pleito *m* **big** ~ *(argument)* gran pleito

figure *n* figura *f* **curvaceous** ~ figura curvilínea **girlish** ~ figura de niña **good** ~ buena figura **great** ~ gran figura **hourglass** ~ figura de reloj de arena **lovely** ~ figura encantadora **nice** ~ bonita figura **shapely** ~ figura moldeada **slender** ~ figura delgada **terrific** ~ figura tremenda **your** ~ *su (Fam: tu)* figura **You have a** *(1)* **beautiful** / *(2)* **gorgeous figure.** *Usted tiene (Fam: Tú tienes)* una figura *(1)* hermosa / *(2)* despampanante.

figure out *vt* entender, resolver **Have you figured out where you're going to go?** ¿Ya *resolvió usted (Fam: resolviste)* adónde vas a ir? *(1)* **I** / *(2)* **We haven't figured out yet.** Aún no me *(1)* resuelvo. / *(2)* resolvemos. **I can't figure this out. Can you help me?** No puedo entender esto. ¿*Puede usted (Fam:¿Puedes)* ayudarme? **It's hard to figure you out.** Es difícil entenderte.

fill *vt* llenar **The** *(1)* **hotel** / *(2)* **restaurant is all filled up.** El *(1)* hotel / *(2)* restaurante está completamente lleno. **I'll fill it up (with gas).** Lo voy a llenar (con gasolina). **Fill it up.** Llénelo. **Be sure to fill up your** *(1)* **canteen.** / *(2)* **water bottle.** *Asegúrese (Fam: Asegúrate)* de llenar *su (Fam: tu)* *(1)* cantimplora. / *(2)* botella de agua. **You fill me with delight.** Me llenas de deleite. **You fill my heart with love.** Me llenas de amor el corazón.

★ **fill out** *(forms)* llenar **Could you help me fill out this form?** ¿*Podría usted (Fam: ¿Podrías)* ayudarme a llenar esta forma?

film *n* película *f* ; *(roll)* rollo *m* **black-and-white** ~ película en blanco y negro **color** ~ película a colores ~ **for prints** película para impresiones ~ **for slides** película para diapositivas *(1)* **I'm** / *(2)* **We're out of** *(3,4)* **film.** *(1)* Me quedé... / *(2)* Nos quedamos... sin *(3)* rollo / *(4)* película. *(1)* **I** / *(2)* **We have to get more film for the camera.** *(1)* Tengo / *(2)* Tenemos que conseguir más película para la cámara. **Where can** *(1)* **I** / *(2)* **we get some more film?** ¿Dónde *(1)* puedo / *(2)* podemos conseguir más película?

filter *n* filtro *m* **water** ~ filtro de agua

filthy *adj* mugroso *m*, -sa *f*

final *adj* final *m&f* ~ **exams** exámenes finales **What** *(1)* **is** / *(2)* **was the final score?** ¿Cuál *(1)* es / *(2)* fue el resultado final? **The final score** *(1)* **is** / *(2)* **was** *(score)*. El resultado final *(1)* es / *(2)* fue ___.

finally *adv* por fin; al fin; finalmente **I finally found you.** Por fin te encontré. **You finally made it.** *(arrived)* Al fin la hiciste.

finances *n, pl* finanzas *fpl* **How are your finances?** ¿Cómo están tus finanzas? *(1)* **My** / *(2)* **Our finances are** *(3)* **...not so good...** / *(4)* **...a bit strained... right now.** *(1)* Mis / *(2)* Nuestras finanzas *(3)* ...no son tan buenas... / *(4)*

Help us improve our book!
Send us the feedback form on page 431.

...están un poco apretadas... por el momento.

financial *adj* financiero *m*, -ra *f* ~ **difficulty** dificultad *f* financiera ~ **situation** situación *f* financiera

find *vt* encontrar, hallar ~ **happiness** encontrar la felicidad **I'll try to find** *(what)*. Trataré de encontrar __. **Did you find it?** ¿Lo *encontró (Fam: encontraste)*? *(1)* **I** / *(2)* **We found it.** Lo *(1)* encontré. / *(2)* encontramos. *(1)* **I** / *(2)* **We didn't find it.** No lo *(1)* encontré. / *(2)* encontramos. *(1)* **I** / *(2)* **We need to find a** *(3)* **hotel.** / *(4)* **room.** *(1)* Necesito / *(2)* Necesitamos encontrar *(3)* un hotel. / *(4)* una habitación. **I'm so happy that I found you (in this world).** Estoy tan feliz de encontrarte (en este mundo).

★ **find out** *idiom* averiguar **Let** *(1)* **me** / *(2)* **us know what you find out.** *(1)* Déjeme *(Fam: Déjame)* / *(2)* Déjenos *(Fam: Déjanos)* saber qué *averiguó (Fam: averiguaste)*. **Could you find out for** *(1)* **me?** / *(2)* **us?** ¿Podría usted *(Fam: ¿Podrías)* averiguar por *(1)* mí? / *(2)* nosotros? **What did you find out?** ¿Qué *averiguó (Fam: averiguaste)?* **I found out that...** Averigüé que...

fine *adj* bello *m*, -lla *f*; bien *m&f*; buen *m*, bueno *m*, -na *f*; fino *m*, -na *f* ~ **arts** bellas artes ~ **day** buen día ~ **person** fina persona **Fine, thank you. (And how are you?)** Bien, gracias. (¿Y cómo *está usted [Fam: estás tú]*?) **That's fine.** Está bien. **I feel fine.** Me siento bien. **I know a fine restaurant.** Conozco un buen restaurante.

finger *n* dedo *m* **index** ~ dedo índice **little** ~ dedo meñique **little** ~**s** dedos pequeños, deditos **long** ~**s** dedos largos **lovely** ~**s** dedos encantadores **middle** ~ dedo medio, dedo cordial **ring** ~ dedo anular **slender** ~**s** dedos delgados *(1)* **He** / *(2)* **She has a finger in every pie.** *(1)* Él / *(2)* Ella mete la nariz en todos lados. **The touch of your fingers is like fire.** El toque de tus dedos es como fuego.

fingernail(s) *n (pl)* uña(s) *f (pl)* ~ **clipper** cortaúñas *fpl* ~ **file** lima *f* para las uñas ~ **polish** esmalte *m* (de uñas) **long** ~**s** uñas largas **What beautiful fingernails (you have)!** ¡Qué uñas tan hermosas *(tiene usted [Fam: tienes])*!

finish *vi* acabar **What time does it finish?** ¿A qué hora se acaba? **It finishes at** *(time)*. Se acaba a las __.

finished *adj* acabado *m*, -da *f*, terminado *m*, -da *f* **Are you finished?** ¿Ya *acabó usted (Fam: acabaste)*? *(1)* **I'm** / *(2)* **We're (not) finished.** (No) *(1)* He / *(2)* Hemos acabado.

fin(s) *n (pl)* aleta(s) *f (pl)*

fire *n* fuego *m*, incendio *m* ~ **alarm** alarma *f* de incendios ~ **department** departamento *m* de incendios ~ **escape** escalera *f* de incendios ~ **extinguisher** extintor *m* de incendios **kiss of** ~ beso *m* de fuego **put out the** ~

Spanish "j" is pronounced like "h".

(campfire) apagar la hoguera **sit around the ~** *(campfire)* sentarse alrededor de la hoguera **start a ~** *(campfire)* encender la hoguera **Fire!** ¡Fuego! **Your beauty sets my heart on fire.** Tu belleza hace arder mi corazón.

fireball *n (slang:very lively person)* ser un bólido

firewood *n* leña *f*

fireworks *n, pl* fuegos artificiales **~ display** exhibición *f* de fuegos artificiales **shoot off ~** lanzar fuegos artificiales

firm *adj* firme *m&f*

firm *n (company)* firma *f*

first *adj* primero *m*, -ra *f* **~ aid** *n* primeros auxilios **~ aid kit** equipo *m* de primeros auxilios **~ class** primera clase **~ moment** primer momento **~ name** primer nombre **~ time** primera vez **give ~ aid** dar primeros auxilios **Do you have a first aid kit?** ¿Tiene usted *(Fam: Tienes)* un equipo de primeros auxilios? **Get a first aid kit.** Consigue un equipo de primeros auxilios.

first *adv (for the first time)* primero

first *n* principio *m* **at ~** al principio **~ of all** antes que nada

fish *vi* pescar **Do you like to fish?** ¿Le *(Fam: ¿Te)* gusta pescar? **Where's a good place to fish?** ¿Dónde hay un buen lugar para pescar? **Is it okay to fish here?** ¿Está bien si pesco aquí?

fish *n* pez *m*, pescado *m* **catch a ~** atrapar un pez **~ net** red *f* de pesca

fishhook *n* anzuelo *m*

fishing *adj* de pesca **~ gear** equipo *f* de pesca **~ guide** guía de pesca **~ line** línea de pesca **~ pole** caña *f* de pesca **~ rod** caña *f* de pescar **~ tackle** aparejos *m, pl* de pesca, equipo *m* de pesca

fishing *n* pesca *f* **deep-sea ~** pesca de altura **float ~** pesca de flote **fly ~** pesca con mosca **freshwater ~** pesca de agua dulce **go ~** ir de pesca **saltwater ~** pesca de agua salada **sport ~** pesca deportiva **Would you like to go fishing (with *[1]* me / *[2]* us)?** ¿Le *(Fam: ¿Te)* gustaría ir de pesca (*[1]* conmigo / *[2]* con nosotros)?

fit *adj (healthy)* saludable *m&f*, en forma, sano *m*, -na *f* **You look very fit.** Se ve *(Fam: Te ves)* muy saludable. **I try to *(1)* keep / *(2)* stay fit.** Trato de *(1)* mantenerme / *(2)* estar en forma.

fit *vt* quedar **How does it fit (you)?** ¿Cómo te queda? **How do they fit (you)?** ¿Cómo te quedan? **It fits you *(1)* perfectly. / *(2)* (very) well. / *(3)* beautifully.** Te queda *(1)* perfectamente. / *(2)* (muy) bien. / *(3)* hermoso. **They fit you *(1)* perfectly. / *(2)* (very) well. / *(3)* beautifully.** Te quedan *(1)* perfectamente. / *(2)* (muy) bien. / *(3)* hermosos.

fit *vi* quedar *(1)* **It fits... / *(1)* They fit... *(3)* beautifully. / *(4)* perfectly / *(5)* (very) well.** Me *(1)* queda / *(2)* quedan *(3)* bellamente. / *(4)* perfectamente / *(5)* (muy) bien. **It doesn't fit.** No me queda. **They don't fit.** No me

Familiar "tu" forms in parentheses can replace italicized polite forms.

quedan.

fitness *n* salud *f* ; (buena) condición *f* física ~ **center** gimnasio *m* ~ **club** gimnasio *m* **physical** ~ buen estado físico ~ **room** gimnasio *m*

fix *vt* 1. *(prepare)* preparar; 2. *(repair)* arreglar ~ **a** *(1,2)* **drink** preparar una *(1)* bebida / *(2)* copa ~ **a sandwich** preparar un sandwich ~ **breakfast** preparar el desayuno ~ **dinner** preparar la cena ~ **lunch** preparar la comida **Can you fix this (for** *[1]* **me /** *[2]* **us)?** ¿Puede usted (Fam: ¿Puedes) arreglar esto (por *[1]* mi / *[2]* nosotros)? **I'll fix it (for you).** Yo *se (Fam: te)* lo arreglo. **Where can I get this fixed?** ¿Dónde me pueden arreglar esto? **How long will it take to fix it?** ¿Cuánto tiempo se lleva arreglarlo? **They can't fix it.** No pueden arreglarlo.

fixated *adj* obsesionado *m*, -da *f* **I'm not a person who is fixated on making money**. No soy una persona que se obsesiona por hacer dinero.

flash (attachment) *n* flash *m*, luz *f* instantánea

flashlight *n* linterna *f*

flat *adj* plano *m*, -na *f*; ponchado *m*, -da *f* ~ **tire** llanta *f* ponchada **Can you help me change a flat tire?** ¿Puede usted (Fam: ¿Puedes) ayudarme a cambiar una llanta ponchada?

flatter *vt* halagar; adular **You flatter me.** *Usted me halaga (Fam: Tú me halagas.).*

flattery *n* halago *m* ; adulación *f* **That's not (just) flattery. It's the truth.** No es (solo) un halago. Es la verdad.

flavor *n* sabor *m* **What flavor (of ice cream) do you** *(1)* **like? /** *(2)* **want?** ¿De qué sabor *(1)* le (Fam: te) gusta… / *(2)* quiere (Fam: quieres)… (su [Fam: tu] helado)?

flea *n* pulga *f* *(1)* **He /** *(2)* **She** *(pet)* **has fleas.** *(1)* Él / *(2)* Ella tiene pulgas. **Is there a flea market in town?** ¿Hay algún mercado de segunda en la ciudad?

flexible *adj* 1. *(bendable)* flexible *m&f*; 2. *(schedules, plans)* flexible *(1)* **My /** *(2)* **Our plans are flexible.** *(1)* Mis / *(2)* Nuestros planes son flexibles.

flight *n* vuelo *m* **free** ~ *(recreation)* vuelo libre **What time does your flight depart?** ¿A que hora sale *su (Fam: tu)* vuelo? *(1)* **My /** *(2)* **Our flight departs at** *(time)*. *(1)* Mi / *(2)* Nuestro vuelo sale a las __ .

flipper(s) *n (pl)* aleta(s) *f (pl)*

flirt *vi* coquetear **In case you haven't noticed, I'm flirting with you.** En caso de que no lo hayas notado, te estoy coqueteando.

flirt *n (woman)* coqueta; *(man)* coqueto

flirtatious *adj* coqueto *m*, -ta *f* **be** ~ ser coqueto *(-ta)*

float *n (fishing)* boya *f*

floor *n* piso *m*, suelo *m* ~ **show** espectáculo *m* de cabaret *(1)* **I /** *(2)* **We can**

Spanish "e" is pronounced like English "e" in "get"

sleep (in *[3]* my / *[4]* our sleeping bag[s]) on the floor. *(1)* Yo puedo…
/ *(2)* Nosotros podemos… dormir en el suelo (en *[3]* mi / *[4]* nuestras
bolsa[s] de dormir) en el piso.

florist *n* florista *m&f* **Is there a florist around here?** ¿Hay algún florista
por aquí?

flower *n* flor *f* **beautiful ~** flor hermosa **bouquet of ~s** ramillete *m* de flores
bring ~s traer flores **favorite ~** flor favorita **give ~s** dar flores **I brought
you some flowers.** Te traje unas flores. **Thank you for the flower(s).**
Gracias por la(s) flor(es). **Here's a flower for your hair.** Ten una flor para
tu cabello. **You're the most beautiful flower there is.** Tú eres la flor más
hermosa que existe.

flu *n* gripa *f* **I think I have the flu.** Creo que tengo gripa.

fluent *adj* fluido *m*, -da *f* **~ English** inglés fluido **~ Spanish** español fluido

fluently *adv* fluidez, fluidamente **I (don't) speak it fluently.** (No) Lo hablo
fluidez. **I can read it fluently.** Lo puedo leer con fluidez.

flustered *adj* nervioso *m*, -sa *f*, aturdido *m*, -da *f* **I was a little flustered.**
Estaba un poco nervioso *(-sa)*.

fly *vt (airplane)* pilotar **~ a kite** volar un papalote

fly *vi* volar **Can we fly to *(place)*?** ¿Podemos volar a __? **Let's fly to *(place)*.**
Vamos volando a __. **How much does it cost to fly to *(place)*?** ¿Cuánto
cuesta volar a __?

fly *n* 1. *(insect)* mosca; 2. *(pants)* cierre *m* **Your fly is unzipped.** Tienes
abierto el cierre.

fog *n* bruma *f*

foggy *adj* brumoso *m*, -sa *f*

folk *adj* folklórico *m*, -ca *f*, tradicional *m&f* **~ music** música folklórica **~
song** canción *f* tradicional

folks *n, pl* 1. *(people)* gente *f*; 2. *(parents)* papás *mpl* **my ~** mis papás, mis
viejos **your ~** *sus (Fam: tus)* papás

follow *vt* seguir **Follow me.** Sígueme. **I'll follow *(1,2)* you.** Yo *(1)* lo *m* / *(2)*
la *f (Fam: te)* sigo. **We'll follow *(1,2)* you.** Nosotros *(1)* lo *m* / *(2)* la *f
(Fam: te)* seguimos. **Stop following me.** Deje *(Fam: Deja)* de seguirme.

fond *adj* encariñado *m*, -da *f* **be ~ of** *(like)* encariñarse con **I'm fond of you,
but I don't love you.** Estoy encariñado contigo, pero no te amo.

food *n* comida *f* **What kind of food do you like?** ¿Qué clase de comida *le
(Fam: te)* gusta? **How about some food?** ¿Qué te parece si comemos? *(1)*
Let's buy… / *(2)* We need to buy… some food. *(1)* Vamos a comprar… /
(2) Necesitamos comprar… comida.

fool *vt* engañar **You're forty? You could have fooled me.** ¿Tiene usted *(Fam:
¿Tienes)* cuarenta? *Pudo (Fam: Pudiste)* haberme engañado. **You fooled**

---

*Stress rule # 2: The next-to-last syllable is stressed
in words ending in "n", "s" or a vowel.*

(1) **me.** / *(2)* **us.** *(1)* Me / *(2)* Nos *engañó usted (Fam: engañaste).*
★ **fool around** *idiom* 1. *(play)* payasear; *(kid around)* bromear; *(act
    foolish)* tontear; 2. *(philander)* andar de mujeriego; 3. *(engage in
    petting)* acariciarse **I'm not the kind of person who fools around.**
    (philanders) Yo no soy del tipo de personas que se la pasa flirteando.
fool *n* tonto *m*, -ta *f* **I've been a (big) fool.** He sido un*(a)* (gran) tonto *(-ta)*.
    Do you take me for a fool? ¿Crees que soy tonto? **I'm not a fool.** No soy
    tonto *(-ta)*. **Oh, you sweet fool, how could you think such a thing?** Oh,
    qué tontín. ¿Cómo pudiste pensar eso?
foolish *adj* idiota *m&f* **I** *(1)* **feel** / *(2)* **felt (**[3] **rather** / [4] **really** / [5] **so** /
    [6] **very) foolish.** Me *(1)* siento / *(2)* sentí (*[3]* algo / *[4]* verdaderamente
    / *[5]* tan / *[6]* muy) idiota. **Forgive me for being so foolish.** Perdóname
    por ser tan idiota. **I hope you don't think I'm foolish.** Espero que no
    piense usted (Fam: pienses) que soy idiota.
foot *n* pie *m* **bare feet** descalzo *m*, -za *f* **get cold feet** acobardarse, echarse
    para atrás **left ~** pie izquierdo **pretty feet** pies bonitos **right ~** pie derecho
    You're cute in your bare feet. Te ves mona descalza. **Your feet must be
    cold. Let me massage them.** Tus pies deben estar fríos. Déjame darles un
    masaje. **I lost my** *(1)* **right** / *(2)* **left foot in** *(3)* **the (Vietnam) war.** / *(4)* **an
    accident.** Perdí mi pie *(1)* derecho / *(2)* izquierdo en *(3)* la guerra (de
    Vietnam). / *(4)* un accidente. **I'm afraid we got off on the wrong foot.**
    Me temo que empezamos con mal pie.
football *n (American)* fútbol *m* americano
for *prep* para, por **This is for you.** Este es para *usted (Fam: ti).* **What's this
    for?** ¿Para qué es esto? *(1)* **I'll** / *(2)* **We'll be there for three days.** *(1)*
    Estaré / *(2)* Estaremos allí por tres días. **Thanks for your** *(1)* **advice.** / *(2)*
    help. Gracias por *su (Fam: tu)* *(1)* consejo / *(2)* ayuda.
forbidden *adj* prohibido *m*, -da *f* **It's forbidden** *(1)* **to smoke (here).** / *(2)* **to
    take pictures (**[3] **here** / [4] **there).** Está prohibido *(1)* fumar (aquí). / *(2)*
    tomar fotos (*[3]* aquí / *[4]* allí).
force *vt* forzar **I don't want to** *(1,2)* **force you to do something you don't
    want to do.** No quiero *(1) forzarlo m* / *(2) forzarla f (Fam: forzarte)* a
    hacer algo que *usted no quiere (Fam: tú no quieres)* hacer. **Please don't
    try to force me.** Por favor, no *trate usted (Fam: trates)* de forzarme.
forecast *n* pronóstico *m* **What's the weather forecast for** *(1)* **today?** / *(2)*
    tomorrow? ¿Cuál es el pronóstico del clima para *(1)* hoy? / *(2)* mañana?
    It's supposed to be *(1)* **cloudy.** / *(2)* **cool.** / *(3)* **cold.** / *(4)* **foggy.** / *(5)* **hot.**
    / *(6)* **nice.** / *(7)* **rainy.** / *(8)* **snowy.** / *(9)* **sunny.** / *(10)* **warm.** / *(11)* **windy.**
    Se supone que estará *(1)* nublado. / *(2)* fresco. / *(3)* frío. / *(4)* brumoso. /
    (5) caliente. / *(6)* agradable. / *(7)* lluvioso. / *(8)* nevando. / *(9)* soleado. /

Spanish "x" is always like "ks", as in our word "taxi".

(10) templado. / *(11)* con viento.

forehead *n* frente *f*

foreign *adj* extranjero *m*, -ra *f*

foreigner *n* extranjero *m*, -ra *f* **I'm a foreigner.** Soy extranjero *(-ra)*. **We're foreigners.** Somos extranjeros *(-ras)*.

forest *n* bosque *m* **Let's go** *(1)* **hike** / *(2)* **walk in the forest.** Vamos a *(1)* hacer una excursión... / *(2)* caminar... al bosque.

forever *adv* para siempre, por siempre **I will remember** *(1)* **this** / *(2)* **you forever.** *(1)* Recordaré esto... / *(2)* Te recordaré... por siempre. **I want this to be forever.** Quiero que esto sea para siempre.

forget *vt* olvidar **I'm sorry, I forgot (your** *[1]* **name.** / *[2]* **phone number.** / *[3]* **address.).** Lo lamento, olvidé *(su (Fam: tu) [1]* nombre. / *[2]* número de teléfono. / *[3]* dirección.). **Don't forget.** No lo *olvide usted (Fam: olvides)*. **Don't forget me.** No me *olvide usted (Fam: olvides)*. **I don't want you to forget me.** No quiero que me *olvide usted (Fam: olvides)*. **I could never** *(1,2)* **forget you.** Nunca podría *(1)* olvidarlo *m* / *(2)* olvidarla *f (Fam: olvidarte)*. **You make me forget everything else** *(1)* **around me.** / *(2)* **in the world.** Me haces olvidar todo lo demás *(1)* a mi alrededor. / *(2)* en el mundo.

forgetful *adj* olvidadizo *m*, -za *f* **I'm getting forgetful in my old age.** Me estoy volviendo olvidadizo con la edad.

forgive *vt* perdonar **I beg you to forgive me.** *Le (Fam: Te)* ruego que me *perdone (Fam: perdones)*. **Please forgive** *(1)* **me.** / *(2)* **us.** Por favor, *(1)* perdóname. / *(2)* perdónanos. **Do you forgive me?** ¿Me *perdona usted (Fam: Perdonas)*? **I forgive** *(1,2)* **you.** *(1)* Lo *m* / *(2)* La *f (Fam: Te)* perdono.

forgiveness *n* perdón *m* **I beg your forgiveness.** Ruego *su (Fam: tu)* perdón.

form *n* 1. *(figure)* forma *f*; 2. *(document)* formulario *m*

formal *adj* formal ~ **attire** atuendo *m* formal **Do we have to be so formal? Can I call you by "tú"** ? ¿Tenemos que ser tan formales? ¿Puedo hablarle de tú?

former *adj* anterior *m&f*

formerly *adv* con anterioridad

fortunate *adj* afortunado *m*, -da *f* **How fortunate (to** *[1,2]* **run into you here)!** ¡Qué afortunado (de *[1]* encontrarlo *m*, *[2]* encontrarla *f [Fam: encontrarte]* aquí)! **I feel so fortunate to** *(1,2)* **have met you.** Me siento tan afortunado de *(1)* haberlo *m* / *(2)* haberla *f (Fam: haberte)* conocido.

fortunately *adv* afortunadamente, por fortuna

fortune *n* 1. *(fate)* fortuna *f*, suerte *f*; 2. *(much money)* fortuna *f* **tell** *(1)* **my**

Stress rule # 3: Syllables with accent marks have the stress there.

/ (2) **your** ~ decir *(1)* mi / *(2) su (Fam: tu)* suerte **Fortune really smiled at me when I met you.** La fortuna me sonrió de verdad cuando te conocí. **Give me your hand. I'll tell your fortune.** Dame *su (Fam: tu)* mano. *Le (Fam: Te)* diré *su (Fam: tu)* suerte. **This cost a fortune, but I'm giving it to you.** Esto cuesta una fortuna, pero te lo estoy dando.

forward *adj (overly familiar)* atrevido *m*, -da *f* **I hope you won't think it forward of me.** Espero que no *piense usted (Fam: pienses)* que soy atrevido *(-da)*.

forward *adv* adelante **Do you want to go forward or back?** *¿Quiere usted (Fam: ¿Quieres)* ir adelante o atrás? **Let's keep going forward.** Sigamos avanzando.

forward *vt* enviar, remitir **They'll forward my mail to me.** Me van a remitir mi correo.

foster *adj* de crianza, adoptivo *m*, -va *f* ~ **brother** hermano *m* de crianza ~ **daughter** hija *f* de crianza ~ **father** padre *m* de crianza ~ **mother** madre *f* de crianza ~ **parents** padres de crianza ~ **sister** hermana *f* de crianza ~ **son** hijo *m* de crianza

fountain *n* fuenta *f*

fragile *adj* frágil *m&f*

fragrance *n (1. aroma; 2. perfume)* fragancia *f* **haunting** ~ fragancia evocadora **intoxicating** ~ fragancia embriagante **nice** ~ fragancia agradable **soft** ~ suave fragancia **sweet** ~ fragancia dulce **The delicate fragrance that you wear intoxicates me.** Me embriaga el delicado perfume que *usa (Fam: usas)*. **I love the delicate fragrance of your hair.** Me encanta la delicada fragancia de tu cabello.

fragrant *adj* fragante *m&f* **Your hair is so fragrant.** Tu cabello es tan fragante.

frank *adj* franco *m*, -ca *f* **I'll be frank with you.** *Le (Fam: Te)* seré franco *(-ca)*. **Please be frank.** Por favor, *sea usted (Fam: sé)* franco *(-ca)*.

frankly *adv* francamente

fraternity *n (fraternal organization)* fraternidad *f* **I (1) belong / (2) belonged to a fraternity at the university.** *(1)* Pertenezco / *(2)* Pertenecí a la fraternidad de la universidad.

freak (out) *vi (slang: get real nervous; get scared; lose self-control)* desquiciarse, descontrolarse

freckle *n* peca *f* **I like your freckles.** Me gustan tus pecas.

free *adj* 1. *(at liberty)* libre *m&f*; 2. *(without cost)* gratis *m&f*, gratuito *m*, -ta *f* **for** ~ gratis ~ **country** país libre ~ **of charge** gratis, sin costo ~ **spirit** espíritu libre **You're free to do what you want to do.** Eres libre de hacer lo que quieras. **It's free.** *(1)* **We** / *(2)* **You don't have to pay anything.** Es

Spanish pronunciation rules are on pages 407-408.

gratis. *(1)* Nosotros no tenemos... / *(2)* Ustedes no tienen... que pagar nada. *(1)* **He** / *(2)* **She did it for free.** *(1)* Él / *(2)* Ella lo hizo gratis. *(1)* **He** / *(2)* **She will do it for free.** *(1)* Él / *(2)* Ella lo hará gratis.

freedom *n* libertad *f* **I love my freedom.** Me gusta mi libertad.

freeload *vi* gorronear, aprovecharse algo a costa de otros **Let** *(1)* **me** / *(2)* **us buy something.** *(3)* **I** / *(4)* **We don't want to freeload.** *(1)* Déjame / *(2)* Déjanos comprar algo. *(3)* No quiero ser aprovechado *(-da)*. / *(4)* No queremos ser aprovechados.

freeloader *n* aprovechado *m*, -da *f*

freeze *vi* congelar **You must be freezing.** Debe usted *(Fam: Debes)* estar congelándote. **I'm freezing.** Me estoy congelando.

frequent *adj* frecuente *m&f*

frequently *adv* frecuentemente, con frecuencia

fresh *adj* 1. *(not old; untired)* fresco *m*, -ca *f*; 2. *(slang: cheeky)* descarado *m*, -da *f* **You look very cool and fresh in that outfit.** Se ve usted *(Fam: Te ves)* muy fresco *(-ca)* con ese atuendo.

friend *n* amigo *m*, -ga *f* **a bunch of** *(1)* **my** / *(2)* **our** / *(3)* **your ~s** un grupo de *(1)* mis / *(2)* nuestros *(-tras)* / *(3)* sus amigos *(-gas)* **a couple of ~s of** *(1)* **mine** / *(2)* **ours** un par de amigos *(-gas)* *(1)* míos *(mías)* / *(2)* nuestros *(-tras)* **a ~ of** *(1)* **mine** / *(2)* **ours** / *(3)* **yours** un*(a)* amigo *(-ga)* *(1)* mío *(mía)* / *(2)* nuestro *(-tra)* / *(3)* de ustedes **close ~(s)** amigo(s) *(-ga[s])* íntimo(s) *(-ma[s])* **one of** *(1)* **my** / *(2)* **our** / *(3)* **your ~s** uno *(una)* de *(1)* mis / *(2)* nuestros *(-tras)* / *(3)* sus *(Fam: tus)* amigos *(-gas)* **some ~s of** *(1)* **mine** / *(2)* **ours** / *(3)* **yours** algunos *(-nas)* amigos *(-gas)* *(1)* míos *(mías)* / *(2)* nuestros *(-tras)* / *(3)* de ustedes **I'd like you to meet a friend of** *(1)* **mine.** / *(2)* **ours.** Me gustaría que conocieras a un*(a)* amigo *(-ga)* *(1)* mío *(mía)* / *(2)* nuestro *(-tra)*. **Who's your friend?** ¿Quién es su *(Fam: tu)* amigo *(-ga)*? **Introduce** *(1)* **me** / *(2)* **us to your** *(3)* **friend.** / *(4)* **friends.** *(1)* Presénteme *(Fam: Preséntame)* / *(2)* Preséntanos a *(3)* su *(Fam: tu)* amigo *(-ga)*. / *(4)* sus *(Fam: tus)* amigos *(-gas)*. **You'll make a lot of friends (, I'm sure).** Tú vas a hacer muchos *(-chas)* amigos *(-gas)* (, estoy seguro *[-ra]*). **Bring** *(1)* **a friend.** / *(2)* **a few friends.** / *(3)* **some friends.** Traiga *(Fam: Trae)* *(1)* un*(a)* amigo *(-ga)*. *(2)* unos *(unas)* cuantos *(-tas)* amigos *(-gas)*. / *(3)* algunos *(-nas)* amigos *(-gas)*. **Some friends of** *(1)* **mine** / *(2)* **ours** *(3)* **will be there.** / *(4)* **are coming along.** / *(5)* **will join us.** Unos *(Unas)* amigos *(-gas)* *(1)* míos *(mías)* / *(2)* nuestros *(-tras)* *(3)* estarán allá. / *(4)* van a venir. / *(5)* se reunirán con nosotros *(-tras)*.

friendliness *n* amistad *f*

friendly *adj* amigable *m&f*, amistoso *m*, -sa *f* **~ personality** personalidad *f* amistosa

---

> *Some Spanish words have accented & unaccented forms to differentiate their meanings (e.g., el = the, él = he).*

frighten *vt* asustar **I'm sorry if I** *(1,2)* **frightened you.** Lamento *(1)* haberlo m / *(2)* haberla f *(Fam: haberte)* asustado. **I didn't mean to** *(1,2)* **frighten you.** No quise *(1)* asustarlo m / *(2)* asustarla f *(Fam: asustarte)*.

frigid *adj* frígido m, -da f

frisbee n disco m **throw a** ~ lanzar un disco

frisky *adj* travieso m, -sa f, juguetón m, -tona f **You're a frisky one, aren't you?** Eres travieso *(-sa)*. ¿verdad?

frolic n juerga f **Let's go out for some fun and frolic together.** Salgamos de juerga a divertirnos juntos.

from *prep* de; desde ~ **head to toe** de pies a cabeza ~ **here** desde aquí ~ **there** desde allí ~ **time to time** de vez en cuando **It's open from 9 to 6.** Está abierto de nueve a seis. **Where are you from?** De dónde *viene usted (Fam: vienes)*? **I'm from** *(place)*. Yo soy de __ .

front n frente f *1)* **I'll** / *(2)* **We'll meet** *(3,4)* **you in front of the station.** *(3)* Lo m / *(4)* La f *(Fam: Te)* *(1)* veo / *(2)* vemos frente a la estación.

frost n escarcha f

frown *vi* fruncir el ceño **Why are you frowning?** ¿Por qué *frunce usted (Fam: frunces)* el ceño?

frozen *adj* congelado m, -da f *(1)* **My** / *(2)* **Your** *(3)* **feet** / *(4)* **hands are frozen!** *(1)* ¡Tengo / *(2)* ¡Tienes *(3)* los pies congelados! / *(4)* las manos congeladas!

frugal *adj* frugal m&f

fruit n fruta f

frustrated *adj* frustrado m, -da f **feel** ~ sentirse frustrado **get** ~ frustrarse

frustrating *adj* frustrante m&f **It's so frustrating!** ¡Es tan frustrante!

frustration n frustración f

full *adj* lleno m, -na f; pleno m, -na f; completo m, -ta f ~ **figure** figura f regordeta ~ **moon** luna f llena **The** *(1)* **bus** / *(2)* **hotel is full.** El *(1)* camión / *(2)* hotel está lleno. **No more for me. I'm full.** No más para mí. Estoy lleno *(-na)*. **My heart is full of love for you.** Mi corazón está lleno de amor por ti. **Give** *(1)* **me** / *(2)* **us a full report.** *(1)* Dame / *(2)* Danos un informe completo.

full-time *adv* tiempo m completo **Do you work full-time or part-time?** ¿Trabaja usted *(Fam: ¿Trabajas)* tiempo completo o medio tiempo?

fun *adj* de diversión

fun n diversión f **have** ~ divertirse **You're (a lot of) fun (to be around).** Andar contigo es bien divertido. **You're more fun than a barrel of monkeys.** Eres más divertido *(-da)* que un barril lleno de monos. **It will be (a lot of) fun.** Va a ser (super) divertido. **We can have (a lot of) fun together.** Juntos nos vamos a divertir (muchísimo). **That was (a lot of) fun.**

Spanish "g" is like "h" in front of "e" and "i".
In front of other vowels it's like our "g" in "gun".

Eso fue (super) divertido. *(1)* **I** / *(2)* **We had a lot of fun.** *(1)* Me he... / *(2)* Nos hemos... divertido un montón. **I've never had so much fun (with anyone).** Nunca me había divertido tanto (con nadie).

funeral *n* funeral *m*

funky *adj (slang)* 1. *(out of the ordinary)* extravagante *m & f*; *(daring, kind of wild)* estrafalario *m*, -ria *f*; 2. *(music)* funky ~ **fun** diversión estrambótica **I like your funky** *(1)* **dress.** / *(2)* **hat.** Me gusta tu estrambótico *(1)* vestido. / *(2)* sombrero.

fun-loving *adj* amante *m&f* de la diversión

funny *adj* 1. *(amusing)* chitoso *m*, -sa *f*; 2. *(odd)* raro *m*, -ra *f*; 3. *(improper)* fuera de lugar **That's (not) funny.** *(amusing)* Eso (no) es chistoso. **That's funny, it was here just minute ago.** *(odd)* Qué raro, estaba aquí hace un minuto. **Don't try** *(1,2)* **anything funny.** *(improper)* No intentes *(1)* ninguna cosa fuera de lugar. / *(2)* hacer nada inadecuado.

furious *adj* furioso *m*, -sa *f*

furnished *adj* amueblado *m*, -da *f* ~ **apartment** departamento amueblado

furniture *n* muebles *m, pl*

further *comp adj* más allá; más lejoj; más

fussy *adj* melindroso *m*, -sa *f* **Don't be so fussy.** No seas tan melindroso *(-sa)*. *(1)* **I'm** / *(2)* **We're not fussy about such things.** *(1)* No soy melindroso *(-sa)*... / *(2)* No somos melindrosos *(-sas)*... con esas cosas.

future *adj* futuro *m*, -ra *f* ~ **plans** planes *m, pl* a futuro

future *n* futuro **dream of the** ~ *(vi)* soñar en el futuro **great** ~ gran futuro **happy** ~ feliz futuro **in the** ~ en lo futuro; en el futuro **in the near** ~ en el futuro cercano **our** ~ nuestro futuro **wonderful** ~ futuro maravilloso **What are your plans for the future?** ¿Cuáles son *sus (Fam: tus)* planes para el futuro? **In the future I** *(1)* **plan** / *(2)* **want to...** En el futuro *(1)* planeo / *(2)* quiero... *(1)* **I** / *(2)* **We want to come here again in the future.** *(1)* Yo quiero... / *(2)* Nosotros queremos... venir aquí otra vez en el futuro. **You must come visit** *(1)* **me** / *(2)* **us in the future.** *Usted debe (Fam: Debes)* venir a *(1)* visitarme / *(2)* visitarnos en el futuro.

English-Spanish and Spanish-English glossaries of food and drink are on pages 420-427.

G

gal *n* muchacha *f*

gallery *n* galería *f* **art** ~ galería de arte **shooting** ~ tiro *m* al blanco

gamble *vi* 1. *(bet)* apostar; 2. *(risk)* arriesgarse **Do you like to gamble?** ¿Le *(Fam: Te)* gusta apostar? *(1)* I / *(2)* **We like to gamble.** *(1)* Me / *(2)* Nos gusta apostar. *(1)* I / *(2)* **We don't gamble.** *(1)* Yo no apuesto. / *(2)* Nosotros no apostamos.

gambling *n* juego *m* de azar ~ **casino** casino *m* de juegos

game *n* juego *m* **baseball** ~ juego de béisbol **basketball** ~ juego de baloncesto **board** ~ juego de mesa **card** ~ juego de cartas **computer** ~**s** juegos de computación **football** ~ *(American)* juego de futbol americano *(For soccer, see* **match.***)* **Would you like to go to a** *(type of sport)* **game (with me)?** ¿Le *(Fam: Te)* gustaría ir (conmigo) a un juego de __?

garage *n* taller **service** ~ taller de servicio

garden *n* jardín *m* **botanical** ~ jardín botánico **flower** ~ jardín de flores

gardening *n* jardinería *f*

gas *n* 1. *(gaseous)* gas *m* ; 2. *(gasoline)* gasolina *f* ~ **station** gasolinera *f* ~ **stove** estufa *f* de gas **propane** ~ gas propano *(1)* I / *(2)* **We need to get gas(oline).** *(1)* Necesito / *(2)* Necesitamos gasolina. **Where's a gas station?** ¿Dónde hay una gasolinera? **Where can I fill this with propane gas?** ¿Dónde puedo llenar esto con gas propano?

gather *vt* recoger ~ **firewood** recoger leña

gay *adj* 1. *(merry)* alegre *m&f* ; 2. *(homosexual)* homosexual *m&f*, de gays

gay *n (homosexual)* homosexual *m&f*, gay *m*

Gemini *(May 21 - Jun. 21)* Géminis

general *adj* general *m&f* **in** ~ en general

generally *adv* generalmente; por lo general

generosity *n* generosidad *f* *(1)* I / *(2)* **We appreciate your generosity.** *(1)* Aprecio / *(2)* Apreciamos su generosidad.

A phrasebook makes a great gift!
Use the order form on page 432.

generous *adj* generoso *m*, -sa *f* **You're very generous.** *Usted es (Fam: Tú eres)* muy generoso *(-sa)*. **That's very generous of you.** Eso es generoso de *su (Fam: tu)* parte.

genius *n* 1. *(person)* genio *m&f*; 2. *(quality)* genialidad *f* **sheer ~** pura genialidad **Only a genius like** *(1)* **me /** *(2)* **you could have thought of something like that.** Sólo un genio como *(1)* yo / *(2)* tú podría haber pensado en algo así.

genre *n* género *m* **I like music of** *(1)* **all /** *(2)* **most genres.** Me gusta la música de *(1)* todos / *(2)* la mayoría de los géneros.

gentle *adj* 1. *(soft)* suave *m&f*; 2. *(tender)* tierno *m*, -na *f*; 3. *(kind)* gentil *m&f*; 4. *(mild, calm; light)* apacible *m&f* **~ lover** amante *m&f* tierno *m*, -na *f*; **You're very gentle.** *Usted es (Fam: Tú eres)* muy gentil. **I love your gentle touch.** Me gusta tu suave tacto.

gentleman *n* caballero *m* **~ of the old school** caballero de la vieja escuela. **perfect ~** perfecto caballero **I promise to behave like a gentleman.** *Le (Fam: Te)* prometo portarme como un caballero.

genuine *adj* genuino *m*, -na *f*, verdadero *m*, -ra *f*, auténtico *m*, -ca *f*

gentleness *n* suavidad *f*, delicadeza *f*, gentileza *f*

gently *adv* suavemente, delicadamente, con suavidad

gesture *n* gesto *m* **That was a very** *(1)* **nice /** *(2)* **thoughtful gesture.** Ese fue un gesto muy *(1)* bonito. / *(2)* considerado.

get *vt* 1. *(obtain; achieve)* conseguir; 2. *(bring, fetch)* traer **Can I get you** *(1)* **a (cold) drink? /** *(2)* **a cup of coffee? /** *(3)* **something?** ¿Puedo traerle *(Fam. traerte)* *(1)* una bebida (fría)? / *(2)* una taza de café? / *(3)* algo? **I'll get you a** *(1)* **coke. /** *(2)* **lemonade. /** *(3)* **sandwich. /** *(4)* **piece of cake.** *Le (Fam. Te)* voy a traer *(1)* una coca. / *(2)* una limonada. / *(3)* un sándwich. / *(4)* un pedazo de pastel. **Did you get** *(1)* **it /** *(2)* **them?** *(1)* ¿Lo / *(2)* ¿Los conseguiste? *(1)* **I /** *(2)* **We got** *(3)* **it. /** *(4)* **them.** *(3)* Lo / *(4)* Los *(1)* conseguí. / *(2)* conseguimos. **Where can** *(1)* **I /** *(2)* **we get** *(3)* **batteries? /** *(4)* **film? /** *(5)* **stamps? /** *(6)* **tickets?** ¿Dónde *(1)* puedo / *(2)* podemos conseguir *(3)* pilas? / *(4)* película? / *(5)* timbres? / *(6)* boletos? *(1,2)* **Do you get it?** *(understand)* *(1)* ¿Lo entiende usted *(Fam: entiendes)*? / *(2*)¿Agarras la onda? **I (don't) get it.** *(understand)* (No) Lo entiendo.

get *vi* 1. *(arrive)* llegar; 2. *(become)* ponerse; hacerse **When did you get here?** ¿Cuándo *llegó usted (Fam: llegaste)* aquí? *(1)* **I /** *(2)* **We got here** *(3)* **yesterday. /** *(4)* **day before yesterday. /** *(5)* **3 days ago. /** *(6)* **last week.** *(1)* Llegué / *(2)* Llegamos aquí *(3)* ayer. / *(4)* anteayer. / *(5)* hace tres días. / *(6)* la semana pasada. **How do** *(1)* **I /** *(2)* **we get to** *(place)*? ¿Cómo *(1)* llego / *(2)* llegamos a __? **Can** *(1)* **I /** *(2)* **we get there by car?** ¿*(1)* Puedo *(2)* Podemos llegar allá en carro? **It's getting** *(1)* **cold. /** *(2)* **dark.**

A slash always means "or".

Se está poniendo *(1)* frío. / *(2)* oscuro. **You're getting good at this.** *Usted se está (Fam: Te estás) haciendo bueno (-na) en esto. (game)* **You're getting better.** *Usted se está (Fam: Te estás) poniendo mejor.* **Are you getting tired?** *¿Se está (Fam: Te estás) cansando?* **I'm getting tired.** *Me estoy cansando.*

★ **get along** *idiom* llevarse bien **You and I get along so well together.** Tú y yo juntos nos llevamos tan bien.

★ **get back** *idiom* volver **When I get back, I'll *(1)* call / *(2)* e-mail / *(3)* write you.** Cuando vuelva, *le (Fam: te)* *(1)* llamo. / *(2)* mando un correo electrónico. / *(3)* escribo. **When we get back, we'll *(1)* call / *(2)* e-mail / *(3)* write you.** Cuando volvamos, *le (Fam: te)* *(1)* llamamos. / *(2)* mandamos un correo electrónico. / *(3)* escribimos.

★ **get off** *idiom* 1. *(exit)* bajarse; 2. *(work: finish; take off)* salir (del trabajo) **Where *(1,2)* are you getting off?** *¿En dónde (1) se va (Fam: te vas) (2) se van a bajar?* *(1)* **I'm / *(2)* We're getting off at *(place)*.** *(1)* Me voy... / *(2)* Nos vamos... a bajar en __. **Which stop should *(1)* I / *(2)* we get off at?** *¿En qué parada (1)* debo de bajarme? / *(2)* debemos de bajarnos? **I'll get off with you. (Is that okay?)** Yo me bajo *con usted (Fam: contigo).* (*¿Está bien?*) **What time do you get off work?** *¿A qué hora sale usted (Fam: sales) del trabajo?* **I get off work at *(time)*.** Salgo del trabajo a las __. **I'll / *(2)* We'll meet you after you get off work.** *(1)* Me reuniré... / *(2)* Nos reuniremos... *con usted (Fam: contigo)* después de que *salga (Fam: salgas)* del trabajo. **Would it be possible to meet you after you get off work?** *¿Sería posible que nos reuniéramos con usted (Fam: contigo)* después de que *salga usted (Fam: salgas)* del trabajo? **Would it be possible for you to get *(1)* two / *(2)* three days / *(3)* a week / *(4)* two / *(5)* three weeks off?** *¿Sería posible que se saliera usted (Fam: te salieras)* del trabajo por *(1)* dos / *(2)* tres días? / *(3)* una semana? / *(4)* dos / *(5)* tres semanas?

★ **get on** *idiom (board)* subirse **Which car should *(1)* I / *(2)* we get on?** *(train)* *¿A cuál carro (1)* debo subirme? / *(2)* debemos subirnos?

★ **get together** *idiom* reunirse; juntarse **When can we get together?** *¿Cuándo nos podemos reunir?* **I want to get together with you again *(1)* soon. / *(2)* as soon as possible.** Quiero reunirme de nuevo con usted *(1)* pronto. / *(2)* lo más pronto posible. **Let's get together *(1)* after breakfast. / *(2)* this afternoon. / *(3)* this evening. / *(4)* tomorrow *(5)* morning. / *(6)* afternoon. / *(7)* evening.** Veámonos *(1)* después del desayuno / *(2)* esta tarde. / *(3)* esta noche. / *(4)* mañana en la *(5)* mañana / *(6)* tarde. / *(7)* noche. **Let's**

Spanish "v" is pronounced like a soft "b".

get together tomorrow for *(1)* **coffee.** / *(2)* **lunch.** / *(3)* **dinner.** / *(4)* **a drink.** Vamos reuniéndonos mañana para *(1)* un café. / *(2)* comer. / *(3)* cenar. / *(4)* un trago.

get-together *n* reunión *f* **social** ~ reunión social

ghost *n* fantasma *f* **Do you believe in ghosts?** ¿*Cree usted (Fam: Crees tú)* en fantasmas? **Have you ever seen a ghost?** ¿Alguna vez *ha visto usted (Fam: has visto)* algún fantasma?

giddy *adj* mareado *m*, -da *f*, aturdido *m*, -da *f* **make** ~ dar mareo **I feel a little giddy.** Me siento un poco mareado *(-da)*.

gift *n* don *m*, regalo *m* **birthday** ~ regalo de cumpleaños **Christmas** ~ regalo de Navidad **New Year's** ~ regalo de Año Nuevo **small** ~ regalo pequeño, regalito **wedding** ~ regalo de bodas **Thank you for the (***[1]* **beautiful /** *[2]* **lovely /** *[3]* **nice /** *[4]* **wonderful) gift.** Gracias por el *([1]* hermoso / *[2]* encantador / *[3]* bonito / *[4]* maravilloso) regalo. **This is a (small) gift for you.** Este es un (pequeño) regalo para *usted (Fam: ti).* **I'm sorry, I can't accept the gift.** Lo lamento, no puedo aceptar el regalo. **Having you in my life is the most wonderful gift that God could give me.** Tenerte en mi vida es el regalo más maravilloso que Dios pudo darme.

giggle *vi* reír **What are you giggling about?** ¿De qué te estás riendo?

girl *n (child)* niña *f*, chiquilla *f*; *(older)* chica *f*, muchacha *f* **attractive** ~ chica atractiva **bashful** ~ *(child)* chiquilla penosa; *(older)* chica retraída **beautiful** ~ chica hermosa **cute** ~ *(child)* chiquilla mona; *(older)* chica mona ~ **of my dreams** la chica de mis sueños **good** ~ *(child)* chiquilla buena **good-looking** ~ chica bien parecida **little** ~ chiquilla **naughty** ~ *(child)* chiquilla traviesa **nice** ~ *(child)* chiquilla simpática; *(older)* chica agradable **pretty** ~ *(child)* chiquilla linda; *(older)* chica bonita **quiet** ~ *(child)* chiquilla tranquila; *(older)* chica callada **shy** ~ *(child)* chiquilla tímida; *(older)* chica tímida **smart** ~ *(child)* chiquilla lista; *(older)* chica lista **sweet** ~ *(child)* chiquilla dulce; *(older)* chica dulce *(1)* **I /** *(2)* **We have** *(3)* **a girl.** / *(4)* **two girls.** *(1)* Tengo / *(2)* Tenemos *(3)* una niña. / *(4)* dos niñas.

girlfriend *n* novia *f* **ex-girlfriend** ex-novia **former** ~ novia anterior **previous** ~ novia anterior **This is my girlfriend** *(name).* Esta es mi novia ___. **Do you have a girlfriend?** ¿*Tiene usted (Fam: Tienes)* novia? **I (don't) have a girlfriend.** Yo (no) tengo novia. **I have a lot of friends, but no girlfriend.** Yo tengo muchas amigas, pero novia no.

give *vt* dar **Please give** *(1)* **me /** *(2)* **us...** Por favor *(1)* deme *(Fam: dame)...* / *(2)* denos *(Fam: danos)...* **Who did you give it to?** ¿A quién se lo *dio usted (Fam: diste)?* **I gave it to** *(person).* Se lo di a ___. **Who should I give it to?** ¿A quién debo dárselo? **I'll give it to** *(name).* Se lo daré a ___.

Time expressions are given on page 413.

Could you give me your *(1)* **address?** / *(2)* **phone number?** ¿Podría usted darme su *(1)* dirección? / *(2)* número de teléfono? **Here, let me give you my** *(1)* **address.** / *(2)* **phone number.** *Tenga, déjeme darle (Fam: Ten, déjame darte)* mi *(1)* dirección. / *(2)* número de teléfono. *(1)* **I** / *(2)* **We want to give you** *(3)* **this.** / *(4)* **this small present (for your birthday).** *(1)* Quiero / *(2)* Queremos darte *(3)* esto. / *(4)* este regalito (por tu cumpleaños). **I wish I could give you as much happiness as you've given me.** Ojalá pudiera darte tanta felicidad como la que tú me has dado. **You've given** *(1)* **me** / *(2)* **us so much.** *(3)* **I** / *(4)* **We really appreciate it.** *Usted (Fam: Tú)* *(1)* me / *(2)* nos ha *(Fam: has)* dado tanto. De verdad lo *(3)* aprecio. / *(4)* apreciamos.

★ **give up** *idiom* rendirse **I don't give up easily.** No me rindo fácilmente. **Don't give up. Keep trying.** No *se rinda (Fam: te rindas)*. Siga *(Fam: Sigue)* tratando.

glad *adj* contento *m*, -ta *f*, alegre *m&f* **I'm very glad to meet you.** Encantado *(-da)* de conocerlo *(-la)*. **I'm glad** *(1)* **I** *(2,3)* **met you.** / *(4)* **you came.** Me alegra *(1)* ...*(2)* haberlo *m* / *(3)* haberla *f* *(Fam: haberte)* conocido. / *(4)* que *haya (Fam: hayas)* venido. *(1)* **I'd** / *(2)* **We'd be glad to.** *(1)* Me / *(2)* Nos encantaría.

gladly *adv* con gusto

glamorous *adj* glamoroso *m*, -sa *f* **You look very glamorous (in that).** *Se ve usted (Fam: Te ves)* muy glamoroso *(-sa)* (con eso).

glass *n* 1. *(material)* vidrio *m* ; 2. *(drinking)* vaso *m* ; copa *f* **blown** ~ vidrio *m* soplado **stained** ~ vidrio de colores **magnifying** ~ lupa *f* **I do stained glass.** Yo hago vidrio de colores.

glassblower *n* soplador *m*, -dora *f* de vidrio

glasses *n, pl* lentes *m, pl* **reading** ~ lentes para leer

gloomy *adj* deprimido *m*, -da *f* **Why (are you) so gloomy?** ¿Por qué (estás) tan deprimido *(-da)*?

glove *n* guante *m* **pair of** ~**s** un par de guantes **Is this your glove?** ¿Es este *su (Fam: tu)* guante?

go *vi* ir **Go!** *(encouragement to team or player)* ¡Vamos! **Way to go!** *(Good performance!)* ¡Muy bien! **Where are you going?** ¿A dónde *va usted (Fam: vas)*? **I'm going** *(1)* **home.** / *(2)* **to work.** / *(3)* **to school.** / *(4)* **to the store.** / *(5)* **to my friend's house.** / *(6)* **shopping.** Voy *(1)* a la casa. / *(2)* al trabajo. / *(3)* a la escuela. / *(4)* a la tienda. / *(5)* a la casa de mi amigo *(-ga)*. / *(6)* de compras. **Where are you going next?** ¿Adónde vas a ir enseguida? **Next** *(1)* **I'm** / *(2)* **we're going to** *(place)*. Enseguida *(1)* voy / *(2)* vamos a ir a __. **Can you go (there) (with me)?** ¿Puede usted *(Fam: Puedes)* ir (allá) (conmigo)? **Would you like to go (there) with** *(1)* **me?** / *(2)* **us?** ¿Te

---

Spanish "qu" is pronounced like "k".

gustaría ir (allá) *(1)* conmigo? / *(2)* con nosotros? **I can(not) go (with you).** Yo (no) puedo ir *(con usted [Fam: contigo])*. **Can I go (with you)?** ¿Puedo ir *(con usted [Fam: contigo])*? **You can(not) go (with me).** *Usted (Fam: Tú)* (no) puede *(Fam: puedes)* ir (conmigo). **Let's go to *(1)* my / *(2)* your *(3)* apartment. / *(4)* hotel. / *(5)* house. / *(6)* place. / *(7)* room.** Vamos a *(1)* mi / *(2)* tu *(3)* apartamento. / *(4)* hotel. / *(5)* casa. / *(6)* lugar. / *(7)* cuarto. **Let's go eat dinner (together).** Vamos a cenar (juntos). **What time do you have to go?** ¿A qué hora *se tiene (Fam: te tienes)* que ir? *(1)* **I** / *(2)* **We have to go at** *(time)*. *(1)* Yo me tengo... / *(2)* Nosotros nos tenemos... que ir a las __. **Where do you want to go?** A dónde *quiere usted (Fam: quieres)* ir? *(1)* **I** / *(1)* **We want to go to** *(place)*. *(1)* Quiero / *(1)* Queremos ir a __. **I (don't) want to go.** Yo (no) quiero ir. **I (don't) want you to go.** Yo (no) quiero que *usted se vaya (Fam: tú te vayas)*. **Do you (really) have to go?** ¿(De verdad) *tiene usted (Fam: tienes)* que ir? **I wish you didn't have to go.** Ojalá que no *tenga usted (Fam: tengas)* que ir. *(1)* **I** / *(2)* **We must go.** *(1)* Debo irme. / *(2)* Debemos irnos. **Please go.** Por favor vete. **Please don't go.** Por favor no te vayas. *(1)* **I** / *(2)* **We will (not) go (there).** (No) *(1)* Iré / *(2)* Iremos (allá). *(1)* **I'm** / *(2)* **We're (not) going to go (there).** (No) *(1)* Voy / *(2)* Vamos a ir (allá). **I don't feel like going.** No tengo ganas de ir. *(1)* **When** / *(2)* **Where did** *(3)* **he** / *(4)* **she** / *(5)* **they** / *(6)* **you go?** ¿(1) Cuándo / *(2)* Adónde *(3)* fue él? / *(4)* fue ella? / *(5)* fueron ellos? / *(6)* fueron ustedes? *(1)* **I** / *(2)* **We** / *(3)* **He** / *(4)* **She** / *(5)* **They went** *(6)* **to** *(place)*. / *(7)* **there in** *(month / year)*. *(1)* Fui / *(2)* Fuimos / *(3)* Él fue / *(4)* Ella fue / *(5)* Ellos fueron *(6)* a __. / *(7)* allá en __. **Would you like to go (to a** *[1]* **ballet** / *[2]* **concert** / *[3]* **dance** / *[4]* **festival** / *[5]* **movie** / *[6]* **party** / *[7]* **play) (with me)?** ¿*Le (Fam: ¿Te)* gustaría ir (*[1]* a un ballet / *[2]* a un concierto / *[3]* a un baile / *[4]* a un festival / *[5]* al cine / *[6]* a una fiesta / *[7]* a una obra de teatro) (conmigo)? **Let's go (to a** *[1]* **ballet** / *[2]* **concert** / *[3]* **dance** / *[4]* **festival** / *[5]* **movie** / *[6]* **party** / *[7]* **play).** Vayamos (*[1]* a un ballet / *[2]* a un concierto / *[3]* a un baile / *[4]* a un festival / *[5]* al cine / *[6]* a una fiesta / *[7]* a una obra de teatro). **Would you like to go** *(1)* **biking?** / *(2)* **camping?** / *(3)* **hiking?** / *(4)* **ice-skating?** / *(5)* **rollerblading?** / *(6)* **shopping?** / *(7)* **sightseeing?** / *(8)* **skiing?** / *(9)* **swimming (with me)?** ¿*Le (Fam: ¿Te)* gustaría ir *(1)* a andar en bicicleta? / *(2)* a acampar? / *(3)* de caminata? / *(4)* a patinar sobre hielo? / *(5)* a patinar? / *(6)* de compras? / *(7)* a pasear? / *(8)* a esquiar? / *(9)* a nadar (conmigo)? **Let's go...** *(See choices above)* Vámonos... **Would you like to go for a walk?** ¿*Le (Fam: ¿Te)* gustaría ir a caminar? **Let's go for a walk.** Vayamos a caminar. **Would you like to go on a picnic?** ¿*Le (Fam: ¿Te)* gustaría ir de picnic? **Let's go on a**

Words in parentheses (not italicized) are optional.

picnic. Vámonos de picnic. **Do you like to go** *(1)* **biking?** / *(2)* **dancing?**
/ *(3)* **camping?** / *(4)* **hiking?** / *(5)* **rollerblading?** / *(6)* **sightseeing?** / *(7)*
skiing? / *(8)* **surfing?** / *(9)* **swimming?** / *(10)* **for (long) walks?** / *(11)* **on
picnics?** ¿Le *(Fam: ¿Te)* gusta ir *(1)* a andar en bicicleta? / *(2)* a bailar? /
(3) a acampar? / *(4)* de excursión? / *(5)* a patinar sobre hielo? / *(6)* a
pasear? / *(7)* a esquiar? / *(8)* de surfing? / *(9)* a nadar? / *(10)* a dar (largas)
caminatas? / *(11)* a un picnic? *(1)* **I** / *(2)* **We like to go....** *(See choices
above)* *(1)* Me / *(2)* Nos gusta ir.... **How's it going?** ¿Cómo va? **Don't be
so inhibited. Let yourself go.** No te inhibas tanto. Déjate ir. **Let me go.**
Déjame ir. **Let go of** *(1)* **me!** / *(2)* **my arm!** *(1)* ¡Suéltame! / *(2)*¡Suelta mi
brazo!

★ **go all the way** *idiom (have sex with)* llegar a todo, tener relaciones
    sexuales **I don't want to go all the way with you. (At least, not
    yet.)** No quiero llegar a todo contigo.(Al menos, todavía no.) **I
    don't think it's a good idea to go all the way with someone be-
    fore marriage.** No creo que sea buena idea tener relaciones sexu-
    ales antes del matrimonio.

★ **go away** *idiom* vete **Go away!** ¡Vete! **Please don't go away.** Por
    favor, no te vayas.

★ **go back** *idiom* regresar **Let's go back to the hotel.** Regresemos al
    hotel.

★ **go in** *idiom* entrar

★ **go in for** *idiom* interesarse; participar **What sort of** *(1)* **hobbies** / *(2)*
    ports do you go in for? ¿Qué tipo de *(1)* pasatiempos / *(2)* deportes
    le (Fam: te) interesan? **I don't go in for such things.** No me intere-
    san esas cosas.

★ **go on** *idiom* 1. *(continue)* continuar; 2. *(happen)* suceder **Please go
    on (with your story).** Por favor, *continúe (Fam: continúa)* (con
    su [Fam: tu] cuento). **What's going on?** ¿Qué sucede?

★ **go out** *idiom* salir **I'd like (very much) to go out with you (some-
    time). How about** *(1)* **this evening?** / *(2)* **tomorrow (evening)?** /
    (3) **next Saturday?** / *(4)* **in five minutes?** Me gustaría (muchísimo)
    salir con usted (alguna vez). ¿Qué le parece *(1)* esta noche? / *(2)*
    mañana (por la noche)? / *(3)* el próximo sábado? / *(4)* dentro de
    cinco minutos? **(How) would you like to go out to dinner with
    me** *(1)* **this evening?** / *(2)* **tomorrow (evening)?** / *(3)* **next Satur-
    day?** ¿Le *(Fam: ¿Te)* gustaría salir a cenar conmigo *(1)* esta noche?
    / *(2)* mañana (por la noche)? / *(3)* el próximo sábado? **Let's (you
    and I) go out to dinner** *(1)* **this evening.** / *(2)* **tomorrow (even-
    ing).** / *(3)* **next Saturday.** Salgamos a cenar (tú y yo) *(1)* esta

---

A single Spanish "r" should be lightly trilled;
double "r" ("rr") should be strongly trilled.

noche. / *(2)* mañana (por la noche). / *(3)* el próximo sábado.

★ **go too far** *idiom* ir demasiado lejos **This has gone too far.** Esto ha ido demasiado lejos. **I don't want to go too far.** No quiero ir demasiado lejos.

★ **go up** *idiom* subir **Prices keep going up.** Los precios siguen subiendo.

go *n* intento *m* **give it a ~** haz un intento **give it another ~** haz otro intento **I'll give it a go.** Haré el intento. **Let's give it a go.** Hagamos el intento.

goal *n* 1. *(aim, objective)* meta *f*; objetivo *m*; 2. *(soccer: net)* portería *f*; 3. *(scored point)* gol *m* **Who kicked the goal?** ¿Quién metió el gol?

goalie *n* portero *m*, arquero *m*

God; god *n* 1. *(God)* Dios *m*; 2. *(other)* dios *m* **nectar of the ~s** néctar de los dioses **Do you believe in God?** ¿Cree usted *(Fam: Crees)* en Dios? **I (don't) believe in God.** (No) Creo en Dios. **I'm grateful to God for bringing us together.** Le doy gracias a Dios por habernos juntado. **Thank God!** ¡Gracias a Dios! **Good God!** ¡Dios Santo! **My God!** ¡Dios mío!

goddess *n* diosa *f* **You are my goddess of love.** Tú eres mi diosa del amor.

gold *adj* dorado *m*, -da *f*, de oro **~ ring** anillo *m* de oro

gold *n* oro *m* **It's made of gold.** Es de oro.

golden *adj* dorado *m*, -da *f* **~ hair** cabello *m* dorado

golf *n* golf *m* *(See also phrases under* **like, love** *and* **play***.)* **~ ball(s)** pelota(s) *f (pl)* de golf **~ club(s)** palo(s) *m (pl)* de golf **~ course** campo *m* de golf **~ score** anotación *f* de golf **miniature ~** minigolf, golfito *m* **miniature ~ course** campo de minigolf **How about a round of golf?** ¿Qué *le (Fam: te)* parece una ronda de golf?

golfer *n* golfista *m&f* **avid ~** golfista apasionado *(-da)*

golfing *n* golf *m*

good *adj* bien *m&f*, bueno *m*, -na *f* **Good!** ¡Bien! **Good morning!** ¡Buenos días! **Good afternoon!** ¡Buenas tardes! **Good evening!** *(early)* ¡Buenas tardes!; *(later)* ¡Buenas noches! **Good night!** Buenas noches. **That *(1)* is / *(2)* was very good of you.** Eso *(1)* es / *(2)* fue muy bueno de *su (Fam: tu)* parte.

Goodbye! ¡Adiós!

goodhearted *adj* de buen corazón

good-looking *adj* bien parecido *m*, -da *f*, bonita *f*, actractivo *m*

good-natured *adj* bondadoso *m*, -sa *f* **I've never known anyone as good-natured as you.** Nunca conocí a nadie tan bondadoso *(-sa)* como tú.

Goodnight! ¡Buenas noches!

goofy *adj* tonto *m*, -ta *f* **~ girl** muchacha *f* tonta **~ guy** tipo *m* tonto

gorgeous *adj* espléndido *m*, -da *f*, despampanante *m&f*

gospel *n* evangelio *m*

Familiar "tu" forms in parentheses can replace italicized polite forms.

Gothic, gothic *adj* gótico *m*, -ca *f*

gourmet *n* gastrónomo *m*, -ma *f* ~ **cook** cocinero gastrónomo

government *n* gobierno *m* **I work for the government.** Trabajo para el gobierno.

gown *n* vestido *m* **beautiful** ~ vestido hermoso **bridal** ~ vestido de novia **cocktail** ~ vestido de cóctel **evening** ~ vestido de noche **wedding** ~ vestido de boda

grab *vt* agarrar; coger **Grab the line!** ¡Agarra la cuerda! **I'd like to grab you and kiss you right now.** Me gustaría tomarte y besarte en este momento.

graceful *adj* gracioso *m*, -sa *f* ~ **dancer** bailarina *f* graciosa

gracefully *adv* graciosamente, con gracia **move** ~ moverse con gracia

grade *n* 1. *(year in school)* grado; 2. *(school mark)* calificación ~ **point average (GPA)** puntos de calificación promedio **What grade are you in?** ¿En qué grado vas? **What grade is (1) he / (2) she in?** ¿En qué grado está *(1)* él? / *(2)* ella? *(1)* **He / *(2)* She is in the *(number)* grade.** *(1)* Él / *(2)* Ella está en el __ grado. **What kind of grades do you get?** ¿Qué clase de calificaciones obtienes? **My grades are *(1)* good. / *(2)* okay. / *(3)* so-so.** Mis calificaciones *(1)* son buenas. / *(2)* están bien. / *(3)* están más o menos.

gradually *adv* gradualmente

graduate *vi* graduarse **What university did you graduate from?** En qué universidad *se graduó usted (Fam: te graduaste)*? **I graduated from *(name of university)*.** Me gradué en la universidad de __. **When did you graduate?** ¿Cuándo *se graduó usted (Fam: te graduaste)*? **I graduated *(1)* this year. / *(2)* last year. / *(3)* in *(year)*.** Me gradué *(1)* este año. / *(2)* el año pasado. / *(3)* en __ . **When will you graduate?** ¿Cuándo *se va (Fam. te vas)* a graduar? **I'll graduate *(1)* this year. / *(2)* next year. / *(3)* in *(year)*.** Me voy a graduar *(1)* este año. / *(2)* el año que entra. / *(3)* en __. **What are you going to do after you graduate?** ¿Qué *va usted (Fam: vas)* a hacer después de que *se gradúe (Fam: te gradúes)*? **After I graduate, I'm going to...** Después de que me gradúe, voy a ...

graduation *n* graduación *f* **after** ~ después de la graduación

grammar *n* gramática *f* **I don't understand the grammar.** No entiendo la gramática. **Could you explain the grammar of this to me?** ¿Podría usted *(Fam: Podrías)* explicarme la gramática de esto?

grandchild *n* nieto *m*, nieta *f*

grandchildren *n, pl* nietos *m & both, pl*, nietas *fpl*

granddaughter *n* nieta *f*

grandfather *n* abuelo *m*

grandmother *n* abuela *f*

grandparents *n, pl* abuelos *m & both, pl*

Spanish "ll" is pronounced like "y" in "yes".

grandson *n* nieto *m*

grass *n* pasto *m* **Let's lie (over there) in the grass.** Vamos a acostarnos (allí) en el pasto.

grateful *adj* agradecido *m*, -da *f (1)* **I'm / (2) We're very grateful to you.** *(1)* Estoy muy agradecido *(-da)...* / *(2)* Estamos muy agradecidos *(-das)...* con usted *(Fam: contigo).*

gratitude *n* gratitud *f* **I want to show you my gratitude.** Quiero *expresarle (Fam: expresarte)* mi gratitud. **We want to show you our gratitude.** Queremos *expresarle (Fam: expresarte)* nuestra gratitud.

grave *n* sepultura *f*, tumba *f*

gray *adj* gris *m&f* ~ **hair** cana *f*

great *adj* 1. *(large)* gran *m & f*, grande *m & f*; 2. *(terrific; magnificent)* fenomenal *m & f*, magnífico *m*, -ca *f* **Great!** ¡Magnífico! **That's great.** Eso es fenomenal. **That was (absolutely) great.** Eso fue (absolutamente) fenomenal. *(1)* **I / (2) We had a great time.** *(1)* Pasé / *(2)* Pasamos un rato fenomenal. **We can have a great time together.** Juntos podemos pasar un rato fenomenal. **You look great!** ¡Te ves fenomenal!

great *adv* magníficamente, estupendamente **You played great.** Tocaste magníficamente.

greedy *adj* codicioso *m*, -sa *f*; *(avid, eager)* ávido *m*, -da *f* **Don't be greedy.** No seas codiciosa *(-so).* **I'm greedy about your kisses.** Estoy ávido *(-da)* de tus besos.

green *adj* verde *m&f*

greet *vt* saludar ~ **warmly** saludar afectuosamente

greeting *n* saludo *m* **Greetings!** ¡Buenas!

gregarious *adj* sociable *m&f*

grey *adj* gris *m&f (1,2)* ~ **day** día *m (1)* triste / *(2)* gris

grin *vi* sonreír **What are you grinning about?** ¿De qué te sonríes?

grin *n* sonrisa *f* **big** ~ gran sonrisa **Wipe that silly grin off your face!** ¡Quítate de la cara esa sonrisa idiota!

grocery store *n* tienda *f* de abarrotes **Is there a grocery story around here?** ¿Hay alguna tienda de abarrotes por aquí?

groom *n* novio *m*

grouchy *adj* gruñón *m*, -ñona *f* **Don't be so grouchy.** No seas tan gruñón *(-ñona).*

ground *n* suelo *m* **sleep on the** ~ dormir en el suelo

group *n* grupo *m* **Which group (1) ...am I... / (2) ...are we... / (3) ...are you... in?** ¿En qué grupo *(1)* estoy? / *(2)* estamos? / *(3)* está usted *(Fam: estás)*? **Can (1) I / (2) we join your group?** *(1)* ¿Puedo unirme... / *(2)* ¿Podemos unirnos... a su grupo? **You can join our group.** Usted puede

Common occupatons are listed on pages 415-416.

unirse a nuestro grupo.

grow *vi* crecer **I grew up** *(1)* **in** *(city).* / *(2)* **on a farm.** Creci *(1)* en ___ . / *(2)* en una granja. **My love for you grows more and more every day.** Mi amor por ti crece cada día más y más.

grumpy *adj* enojón *m*, -ona *f*, gruñón *m*, -ona *f* **You're awfully grumpy today.** Estás terriblemente enojón *(-ona)* el día de hoy.

guard *vt* guardar **Can you guard this for me (for a few minutes)?** ¿Puede usted guardarme esto (unos minutos)? *(1)* **I'll** / *(2)* **We'll guard it for you.** *(1)* Yo se *(Fam: te)* lo guardo. / *(2)* Nosotros se *(Fam: te)* lo guardamos.

Guatemalan *adj* guatemalteco *m*, -ca *f*

Guatemalan *n* guatemalteco *m*, -ca *f*

guess *vi* adivinar; suponer; imaginar **Guess** *(1)* **who.** / *(2)* **what.** Adivina *(1)* quién. / *(2)* qué. **Can you guess how old I am?** ¿Puede usted *(Fam: Puedes)* adivinar cuántos años tengo? **I would guess that you're about** *(age).* Imagino que *tiene (Fam: tienes)* aproximadamente __ . **I guess...** *(suppose)* Supongo...

guess *n:* **Take a guess!** ¡A ver si adivinas! **I'm going to take a wild guess.** Voy a decir lo primero que se me venga a la cabeza. **You get three guesses.** Tienes tres oportunidades para adivinar. **It was a lucky guess.** Adiviné de chiripa.

guest *n* invitado *m*, -da *f (1)* **I** / *(2)* **We want you to be** *(3)* **my** / *(4)* **our guest(s).** *(1)* Yo quiero... / *(2)* Nosotros queremos... que usted(es) sea(n) *(3)* mi(s) / *(4)* nuestro(s) *(-tra[s])* invitado(s) *(-da[s]).* **Be my guest.** Estás invitado *(-da).* **You're** *(1)* **my** / *(2)* **our guest.** *Usted es (Fam: Tú eres)* *(1)* mi / *(2)* nuestro *(-tra)* invitado *(-da).* **You're** *(1)* **my** / *(2)* **our guests.** *(2)* Ustedes son *(1)* mis / *(2)* nuestros *(-tras)* invitados *(-das).*

guesthouse *n* casa *f* de huéspedes

guide *vt* guiar **Can you guide** *(1)* **me?** / *(2)* **us?** ¿Puede usted *(1)* guiarme? / *(2)* guiarnos? **Thank you for guiding** *(1)* **me.** / *(2)* **us.** Gracias por *(1)* guiarme. / *(2)* guiarnos.

guide *n vt* 1. *(person)* guía *m&f* ; 2. *(book)* guía **tourist** ~ guía de turismo **You can be** *(1)* **my** / *(2)* **our guide.** *Usted puede (Fam: Tú puedes)* ser *(1)* mi / *(2)* nuestro *(-tra)* guía. **I'll be your guide.** Yo seré *su (Fam: tu)* guía. **Excuse me, do you know where I could find a guide?** Disculpe, ¿sabe dónde puedo encontrar un guía? **I need a guide around this city. Are you available?** Necesito un guía para la ciudad. ¿Está usted disponible? **I'd like to get a guide to show me around the art museum. Do you know where I could find one?** Me gustaría conseguir un guía para que me muestre el mueso de arte. ¿Sabe usted dónde podría encontrar uno?

guided *adj* guiado *m*, -da *f* ~ **tour** visita guiada

Spanish "y" is "ee" when alone or at the end of words.

guilty *adj* culpable *m&f* **You have a guilty look on your face.** Tienes cara de culpa. *(1)* **I** / *(2)* **We feel so guilty about it.** *(1)* Yo me siento tan culpable por eso. / *(2)* Nosotros nos sentimos tan culpables por eso.

guitar *n* guitarra *f (See phrases under* **know how, like, love** *and* **play**.*)* **Could you teach me how to play the guitar?** *¿Podría usted (Fam: Podrías)* enseñarme a tocar la guitarra? **Where can I** *(1)* **get my guitar fixed?** / *(2)* **get a new guitar string?** ¿Dónde *(1)* pueden arreglar mi guitarra? / *(2)* puedo conseguir una cuerda nueva para guitarra?

gullible *adj* crédulo *m*, -la *f* **You must think I'm awfully gullible.** Has de estar pensando que soy muy crédulo *(-la)*.

gum *n* goma *f* **chew** ~ masticar chicle **chewing** ~ chicle *m*, goma de mascar

gun *n* pistola *f* **I hate guns.** Odio las pistolas.

guy *n* tipo *m* **decent** ~ tipo decente **friendly** ~ tipo amigable **good-looking** ~ tipo bien parecido **handsome** ~ tipo guapo **lucky** ~ tipo con suerte **nice** ~ tipo agradable

gym(nasium) *n* gimnasio *m* **Let's go to the gym and work out.** Vamos al gimnasio a hacer ejercicio.

gymnast *n* gimnasta *m&f*

gymnastics *n* gimnasia *f*

gypsy *adj* gitano *m*, -na *f* **I have a gypsy heart. I love to travel and enjoy life.** Tengo corazón de gitano, me gusta viajar y gozar la vida.

gypsy *n* gitano *m*, -na *f* **There's a little bit of gypsy in my soul.** Hay un poco de gitano en mi alma.

H

habit *n* hábito *m* **bad** ~ mal hábito **good** ~ buen hábito

habitat *n* hábitat *m* **wildlife** ~ hábitat natural

hair *n* cabello *m* **auburn** ~ cabello castaño rojizo **black** ~ cabello negro **blonde** ~ cabello rubio **brown** ~ cabello castaño **brunette** ~ cabello castaño oscuro *(1,2)* **curly** ~ cabello *(1)* rizado / *(2)* ondulado *(Fam: chino)* **dark** ~ cabello oscuro **golden** ~ cabello dorado **grey** ~ cabello cano **long** ~ cabello largo **nice** ~ cabello bonito **red** ~ cabello rojo **short** ~ cabello corto **You have (such) beautiful hair.** *Usted tiene (Fam: Tienes)* el cabello (tan) hermoso. **What** *(1)* **beautiful** / *(2)* **gorgeous** / *(3)* **lovely hair (you have)!** ¡Qué cabello *(1)* hermoso / *(2)* espléndido / *(3)* lindo (tienes)! **Your hair looks** *(1)* **beautiful** / *(2)* **nice** / *(3)* **pretty (that way).** *Su (Fam: Tu)* cabello se ve *(1)* hermoso / *(2)* bonito / *(3)* gracioso (así). **I like the way you wear your hair.** Me gusta como *usted se peina (Fam: te peinas)*.

hairbrush *n* cepillo *m* (del pelo)

hairdo *n* peinado *m* **That's a** *(1)* **beautiful** / *(2)* **lovely hairdo (you have).** Ese peinado (suyo *[Fam: tuyo]*) es *(1)* hermoso. / *(2)* encantador.

hairy *adj* velludo *m*, -da *f*

half *n* medio *m*, mitad *f* **Take half.** *Tome (Fam: Toma)* la mitad. **You can have half.** *Usted puede (Fam: Tú puedes)* tomar la mitad.

halfway *adv* a medio camino **We're halfway there.** Estamos a medio camino de ese lugar.

hall *n* 1. *(corridor)* pasillo *m*, corredor *m* ; 2. *(billiards)* salón **concert** ~ sala de conciertos **pool** ~ salón de billar

Halloween *n* Víspera *f* de Todos los Santos, Día de Muertos

hammer *n* martillo *m*,

hammock *n* hamaca *f*

hand *n* mano *m* **beautiful** ~s manos hermosas **big** ~s manos grandes **both** ~s ambas manos **gentle** ~s manos delicadas ~ **in** ~ de la mano **hold** ~s

---

Spanish "c" before "e" and "i" is pronounced like "s".

tomarse de las manos **hold your ~ (in mine)** tomar tu mano (en la mía) **left ~** mano izquierda **little ~** manita; mano pequeña **lovely ~s** manos lindas **made by ~** hecho *(-cha)* a mano **make by ~** hacer a mano **right ~** mano derecha **shake ~s** saludarse de mano **slender ~s** manos delgadas **small ~s** manos pequeñas **soft ~s** manos suaves **strong ~s** manos fuertes **Hands off!** ¡Quita las manos! **Can you give me a hand?** *¿Puede usted (Fam: Puedes)* darme una mano? **Give me your hand.** *Deme su (Fam: Dame tu)* mano. **I like to walk hand in hand with you.** Me gusta caminar contigo de la mano. **I love the feel of your hand in mine.** Me encanta sentir tu mano en la mía. **You have such masterful hands.** Tienes unas manos tan hábiles. **I love the feel of your hands.** Me encanta sentir tus manos. **I lost my** *(1)* **left** / *(2)* **right hand** *(3)* **in the (Vietnam) war.** / *(4)* **an accident.** Perdí mi mano *(1)* izquierda / *(2)* derecha *(3)* en la guerra (de Vietnam). / *(4)* en un accidente.

handbag *n* bolsa *f*

handball *n* balonmano *m* **play ~** jugar balonmano

handicap *n* 1. *(disability)* impedimento *m* desventaja *f*; 2. *(golf)* hándicap *m*, desventaja *f* **I have a handicap.** Llevo desventaja.

handicapped *adj* discapacitado *m*, -da *f*, impedido *m*, -da *f* **~ person** persona *m&f* discapacitada

handicraft *n* artesanía *f* **I do various handicrafts.** Hago diversas artesanías.

handkerchief *n* pañuelo *m*

handle *vt (situation)* manejar **Can you handle it?** *¿Puede usted (Fam: ¿Puedes)* manejarlo? **I can handle it.** Puedo manejarlo. **I can't handle** *(1)* **it.** / *(2)* **the situation.** No puedo *(1)* manejarlo. / *(2)* manejar la situación. **Let me handle it.** Déjame manejarlo.

handmade *adj* hecho *m*, -cha *f* a mano

handsome *adj* bien parecido *m*, atractivo *m*, guapo *m* **You're** *(1)* **quite** / *(2)* **very handsome.** *Usted es (Fam: Tú eres)* *(1)* bastante / *(2)* muy bien parecido. **Who's the most handsome guy you know - and why am I?** ¿Quién es el tipo más guapo que conoces - y por qué soy yo?

handstand *n* parada *f* de manos **Can you do a handstand?** ¿Puedes pararte de manos? **I'll do a handstand for you.** Voy a hacer una parada de manos para ti.

handy *adj* hábil *m&f*, habilidoso *m*, -sa *f* *(1)* **I'm** / *(2)* **He's handy around the house.** *(1)* Soy... / *(2)* Él es ...habilidoso en la casa.

handyman *n* hombre habilidoso *m*

hang *vi* colgar, pender

★ **hang around** *idiom* quedarse en un lugar **Do you mind if I hang around?** ¿Te importa si me quedo por aquí?

Numbers in Spanish are given on pages 411-412.

★ **hang on** *idiom* estar pendiente, esperar **Hang on!** ¡Estate pendiente!, ¡Espera!
★ **hang onto** *idiom* aferrarse a algo; quedarse con alguien *(1)* **I'm going to...** / *(2)* **I want to... hang onto you.** *(1)* Voy a... / *(2)* Quiero... quedarme contigo.
★ **hang out** *idiom* 1. *(lounge around in malls, coffee shops, etc.)* vagar, deambular; 2. *(spend time with)* pasar el rato **My friends and I hang out in the mall.** Mis amigos y yo deambulamos por el centro comercial. **I like to hang out with my friends.** Me gusta pasar el rato con mis amigos.
★ **hang up** *vi idiom (telephone)* colgar **Why did you hang up?** ¿Por qué colgaste? **Don't hang up!** ¡No cuelgues!
hang-glide *vi* volar con ala delta
hang glider *n* ala *f* delta *(1)* **motor** / *(2)* **powered ~** *(1,2)* trike *m*, ala *f* delta con motor
hang gliding *n* (vuelo con) ala *f* delta
hangover *n* cruda *f*, resaca *f* **Do you have a hangover?** ¿Tienes una cruda? **I have a hangover.** Tengo una cruda. **I know just the thing for a hangover.** Yo sé exactamente lo que se necesita para una cruda.
hangup *n (inhibition)* inhibición *f* **I don't have any hangups (whatsoever).** Yo no tengo inhibiciones (de ninguna clase).
happen *vi* suceder **What happened?** ¿Qué sucedió? *(1)* **I** / *(2)* **We don't know what happened.** *(1)* No sé / *(2)* sabemos lo que sucedió. **Tell** *(1)* **me** / *(2)* **us what happened.** *(1)* Dígame (Fam: Dime) / *(2)* Díganos (Fam: Dinos) qué sucedió. **I'll tell you what happened.** Le (Fam: Te) diré lo que sucedió. **How did it happen?** ¿Cómo sucedió? **You won't believe what happened.** No *va usted (Fam: vas)* a creer lo que sucedió. **Something (*[1]* awful / *[2]* bad / *[3]* good / *[4]* great / *[5]* terrible / *[6]* wonderful) happened.** Sucedió algo (*[1]* atroz / *[2]* malo / *[3]* bueno / *[4]* fenomenal / *[5]* terrible / *[6]* maravilloso). **If something happens,** *(1)* **I'll** / *(2)* **we'll let you know.** Si algo sucede, *se (Fam: te)* lo *(1)* haré / *(2)* haremos saber. **Let's see what happens.** Veamos qué sucede. **It will never happen again.** Nunca volverá a suceder.
happiness *n* felicidad *f* **a little ~** un poco de felicidad **a lot of ~** mucha felicidad **complete ~** felicidad total **experience ~** experimentar felicidad **feel (such) ~** sentir (tal) felicidad **find ~** encontrar la felicidad **genuine ~** felicidad genuina **great ~** gran felicidad **infinite ~** felicidad infinita **moment of ~** momento *m* de felicidad **much ~** mucha felicidad **my ~** mi felicidad **our ~** nuestra felicidad **search for ~** búsqueda de la felicidad **such ~** tal felicidad **tremendous ~** tremenda felicidad **your ~** *su (Fam: tu)*

Spanish "h" is always silent.

felicidad **You bring me so much happiness.** Me traes tanta felicidad. **Happiness for me is being together with you.** La felicidad para mí es estar contigo. **My heart overflows with happiness.** Mi corazón rebosa de felicidad.

happy *adj* feliz *m&f* **I'm (**[1] **so /** [2] **very) happy.** Soy (*[1]* tan / *[2]* muy) feliz. **I feel happy.** Me siento feliz. **You look happy.** *Usted se ve (Fam: Te ves)* feliz. **I want you to be happy.** Quiero que *usted sea (Fam: seas)* feliz. **I want to (1,2) make you happy.** Quiero *(1) hacerlo m / (2) hacerla f (Fam: hacerte)* feliz. **You make me (very) happy.** *Usted me hace (Fam: Tú me haces)* (muy) feliz. **You've made me very happy.** *Usted me ha hecho (Fam: Tú me has hecho)* muy feliz. **If you're happy, I'm happy.** Si tú estás feliz, yo estoy feliz. **I'll do anything to make you happy.** Haré lo que sea por hacerte feliz.

happy-go-lucky *adj* despreocupado *m*, -da *f* **I like your happy-go-lucky disposition.** Me gusta tu carácter despreocupado. **You're really a happy-go-lucky person.** Eres una persona de verdad despreocupada.

harbor *n* puerto *m*

hard *adj* 1. *(firm, solid)* duro *m*, -ra *f*; 2. *(difficult)* difícil *m&f* ~ **body** cuerpo firme **That's (really) hard.** *(difficult)* Eso es (de verdad) difícil. **It's not hard. I'll show you.** No es difícil. *Se (Fam: Te)* lo mostraré.

hard *adv (conscientiously, strenuously)* mucho, duro, duramente **study** ~ estudiar mucho **work** ~ trabajar mucho

hardheaded *adj* testarudo *m*, -da *f* **Don't be so hardheaded.** No seas tan testarudo *(-da)*.

hard-hearted *adj* insensible *m&f* **You are so hard-hearted (to me).** Eres tan insensible (conmigo). **Why are you so hard-hearted (to me).** ¿Por qué eres tan insensible conmigo?

hardly *adv* apenas; casi no **I can hardly (1) keep up with you. / (2) stay awake.** Apenas puedo mantenerme *(1)* a la par contigo. / *(2)* despierto.

hardworking *adj* trabajador *m*, -dora *f*

harem *n* harén *m* **How many girls are there in your harem?** ¿Cuántas chicas hay en tu harén?

harmless *adj* inofensivo *m*, -va *f*

harmonica *n* armónica *f*

harmonious *adj* armonioso *m*, -sa *f* ~ **relationship** relación armoniosa **You (1) girls / (2) guys are really harmonious.** *(singing)* Ustedes *(1)* chicas / *(2)* chicos verdaderamente tienen armonía.

harmony *n* armonía *f* **complete** ~ armonía total **perfect** ~ perfecta armonía **I think harmony in a relationship is very important.** Opino que en una relación la armonía es muy importante. **I feel such harmony with you.**

Questions about the metric system? See page 417.

Siento tanta armonía contigo.

harness *n* arnés *m* **paragliding** ~ arnés para parapente

hasty *adj* precipitado *m*, -da *f* **That was a hasty remark. I'm sorry.** Ese fue un comentario precipitado. Lo siento. **I shouldn't have been so hasty.** No debí haber sido tan precipitado *(-da)*.

hat *n* sombrero *m* **beautiful** ~ sombrero hermoso **sun** ~ sombrero para el sol **You'd better wear a hat. The sun is very hot.** Será mejor que *se ponga (Fam: te pongas)* un sombrero. El sol está muy caliente. **You look great in that hat.** *Se ve (Fam: Te ves)* fenomenal con ese sombrero.

hatchet *n* hacha *f*, hachuela *f*

hate *vt* odiar, detestar **I hate** *(1)* **back-stabbing.** / *(2)* **bigots.** / *(3)* **deceit.** / *(4)* **discrimination.** / *(5)* **dishonesty.** / *(6)* **liars.** / *(7)* **small-mindedness.** / *(8)* **thieves.** Detesto *(1)* las puñaladas por la espalda. / *(2)* a los extremistas. / *(3)* el engaño. / *(4)* la discriminación. / *(5)* la falta de honradez. / *(6)* a la gente que miente. / *(7)* la estrechez mental. / *(8)* a los ladrones. **I hate** *(1)* **it** / *(2)* **them, too.** Yo también *(1)* lo / *(2)* los detesto. **I hate** *(1)* **to leave you.** / *(2)* **for you to leave.** Odio *(1)* dejarte. / *(2)* que te vayas. **Please don't hate me.** Por favor no me odies. **Do you hate me (so much)?** ¿Me odias (tanto)? **I (don't) hate you.** (No) Te odio.

haunt *vt* rondar, perseguir; inquietar **Your beautiful face haunts my mind day and night.** Tu hermosa cara ronda mi mente noche y día. **The fragrance of your perfume will haunt me forever.** La fragancia de tu perfume me perseguirá por siempre.

haunted *adj* embrujado *m*, -da *f* **They say that** *(1)* **castle** / *(2)* **house** / *(3)* **place is haunted. (Let's go see.)** Dicen que *(1)* ese castillo... / *(2)* esa casa... / *(3)* ese lugar... está embrujado. (Vamos a ver.)

have *vt* 1. *(possess)* tener; 2. *(partake; drink)* tomar ~ **a baby** tener un bebé ~ **breakfast** tomar el desayuno; desayunar ~ **a cup of coffee** tomar una taza de café ~ **dinner** tomar la cena; cenar ~ **a dream** tener un sueño; soñar ~ **a good time** tener un buen momento ~ **lunch** tomar la comida (a mediodía); comer ~ **something to drink** tomar algo de beber; beber ~ **something to eat** tomar algo de comer; comer ~ **supper** tomar la merienda; merendar **What'll you have?** ¿Qué *va a tomar usted (Fam: vas a tomar)*? **Could** *(1)* **I** / *(2)* **we have** *(thing)*? *(1)*¿Me / *(2)*¿Nos podría dar __? *(1)* **I'd** / *(2)* **We'd like to have...** *(1)* Me / *(2)* Nos gustaría tomar... **Do you have** *(1)* **an apartment or a house?** / *(2)* **any aspirin?** / *(3)* **a car?** / *(4)* **a cassette player?** / *(5)* **a CD player?** / *(6)* **a cell phone?** / *(7)* **children?** / *(8)* **a computer?** / *(9)* **a dictionary?** / *(10)* **enough money?** / *(11)* **a map?** / *(12)* **a telephone?** / *(13)* **time?** / *(14)* **a VCR? (Short replies: Yes, I do.** / **No, I don't)** ¿Tiene usted (Fam: ¿Tienes) *(1)* departamento o casa? / *(2)* una

Questions about the metric system? See page 417.

aspirina? / *(3)* carro? / *(4)* reproductora de cintas? / *(5)* reproductor de discos compactos? / *(6)* teléfono celular? / *(7)* hijos? / *(8)* computadora? / *(9)* un diccionario? / *(10)* suficiente dinero? / *(11)* un mapa? / *(12)* teléfono? / *(13)* tiempo? / *(14)* reproductora de cintas de vídeo? (Sí tengo. / No tengo.) **I have** *(1)* **an apartment.** / *(2)* **a house.** / *(3)* **a daughter.** / *(4)* **a son.** / *(5)* **two** / *(6)* **three** / *(7)* **four children.** / *(8)* **some aspirin.** Tengo *(1)* departamento. / *(2)* casa. / *(3)* una hija. / *(4)* un hijo. / *(5)* dos / *(6)* tres / *(7)* cuatro hijos. / *(8)* unas aspirinas. **I (don't) have** *(1)* **a car.** / *(2)* **a cassette player.** / *(3)* **a CD player.** / *(4)* **a cell phone.** / *(5)* **a computer.** / *(6)* **a dictionary.** / *(7)* **enough money.** / *(8)* **a map.** / *(9)* **a telephone.** / *(10)* **time.** / *(11)* **a VCR.** (No) Tengo *(1)* carro. / *(2)* reproductora de cintas. / *(3)* reproductora de discos compactos. / *(4)* teléfono celular. / *(5)* computadora. / *(6)* un diccionario. *(7)* suficiente dinero. / *(8)* un mapa. / *(9)* teléfono. / *(10)* tiempo. / *(11)* reproductora de cintas de vídeo. **I don't have any** *(1)* **aspirin.** / *(2)* **children.** No tengo *(1)* aspirinas. / *(2)* hijos.

have to *aux v* tener que **Do you (really) have to go?** ¿(De verdad) Tienes que ir?*(1)* **I** / *(2)* **We have to** *(3)* **go** / *(4)* **leave.** *(1)* Tengo / *(2)* Tenemos que *(3)* ir. / *(4)* salir. *(1)* **I** / *(2)* **We don't have to go.** No *(1)* tengo / *(2)* tenemos que ir. **Where do** *(1)* **I** / *(2)* **we** / *(3)* **you have to go?** ¿Adónde *(1)* tengo / *(2)* tenemos / *(3)* *tiene usted (Fam: tienes)* que ir? *(1)* **I** / *(2)* **We have to go to** *(place).* *(1)* Tengo / *(2)* Tenemos que ir a ___. **What do** *(1)* **I** / *(2)* **we** / *(3)* **you have to do?** ¿Qué *(1)* tengo / *(2)* tenemos / *(3)* *tiene usted (Fam: tienes)* que hacer? *(1)* **I** / *(2)* **We have to** ___. *(1)* Tengo / *(2)* Tenemos que ___.

hawk *n* halcón *m*

hay fever *n* fiebre *f* del heno

he *pron* él *m*

head *n* cabeza *f* **clear ~** cabeza despejada **empty ~** cabeza hueca **from ~ to toe** de pies a cabeza **good ~** *(smart)* buena cabeza **hard ~** cabeza dura **~ over heels** andar de cabeza **You set my head to whirling.** Me pones la cabeza como un torbellino. **You go to my head like wine.** Te me subes a la cabeza como el vino. **I've fallen head over heels in love with you.** Me he enamorado locamente de ti. **I want to cover you with kisses from head to toe.** Quiero cubrirte de besos de pies a cabeza. *(1)* **Beer** / *(2)* **Wine always goes to my head.** *(1)* La cerveza / *(2)* El vino siempre se me sube a la cabeza. **I lost my head. I'm sorry.** Perdí la cabeza. Lo siento.

headache *n* dolor *m* de cabeza **I have a (bad) headache.** Tengo un (terrible) dolor de cabeza.

headcase *n (slang) (mentally abnormal person)* lelo *m*, -la *f*

headstrong *adj* obstinado *m*, -da *f*, voluntarioso *m*, -sa *f*

health *n* salud *f* **~ problem** problema *f* de salud *(1)* **I'm** / *(2)* **He's** / *(3)* **She's**

in *(4)* **excellent** / *(5)* **good** / *(6)* **perfect** / *(7)* **poor health.** *(1)* Tengo... / *(2)* Él / *(3)* Ella tiene... una salud *(4)* excelente. / *(5)* buena. / *(6)* perfecta. / *(7)* pobre. **Good health is the most important thing.** La buena salud es lo más importante.

health-conscious *adj* consciente *m&f* de la salud

healthy *adj* saludable *m&f* ~ **food** comida saludable ~ **lifestyle** estilo de vida saludable

hear *vt* oír **Can you hear me?** ¿Puedes oírme? **I can(not) hear you.** (No) Puedo oírte. **Did you hear what I said?** ¿Oíste lo que dije? **I heard you.** Te oí. **I'm sorry, I didn't hear you.** Lo siento, no te oí.

hearing *n* oído *m* ~ **aid** audífono *m* **I'm hard of hearing.** Soy duro *(-ra)* de oído. **I have bad hearing.** Tengo mal oído.

heart *n* 1. *(body)* corazón *m* ; 2. *pl (card suit)* corazones *mpl* **big** ~ gran corazón **break** *(1)* **my** / *(2)* **your** ~ romper *(1)* mi / *(2)* tu corazón **broken** ~ corazón roto **by** ~ de memoria **cold** ~ corazón frío **deep in my** ~ muy dentro de mi corazón **faithful** ~ corazón fiel **from the bottom of my** ~ desde el fondo de mi corazón **gentle** ~ corazón tierno **give** *(1)* **my** / *(2)* **your** ~ **to** *(3)* **you** / *(4)* **me** *(1)* darte mi corazón / *(2)* darme tu corazón **good** ~ de buen corazón ~ **attack** ataque *m* al corazón ~ **failure** falla *f* en el corazón ~ **of gold** corazón de oro ~ **of stone** corazón de piedra ~ **surgery** cirugía *f* de corazón ~ **to** ~ de corazón a corazón **kind** ~ corazón amable **loving** ~ carazón cariñoso **open** ~ corazón abierto **open** *(1)* **my** / *(2)* **your** ~ abrir *(1)* mi / *(2)* tu corazón **pour out** *(1)* **my** / *(2)* **your** ~ volcar *(1)* mi / *(2)* tu corazón **soft** ~ corazón amable **touch** *(1)* **my** / *(2)* **your** ~ tocar *(1)* mi / *(2)* su *(Fam: tu)* corazón **warm** ~ corazón cálido **warm my** ~ conforta mi corazón **win** *(1)* **my** / *(2)* **your** ~ ganar *(1)* mi / *(2)* su *(Fam: tu)* corazón **with all my** ~ con todo mi corazón **Thank you from the bottom of my heart.** Te agradezco desde el fondo de mi corazón. **You have such a** *(1)* **good** / *(2)* **kind heart.** Usted tiene *(Fam: Tienes)* un corazón tan *(1)* bueno. / *(2)* amable. **It (really)** *(1)* **warms** / *(2)* **warmed my heart.** Eso (de verdad) *(1)* conforta / *(2)* confortó mi corazón. **I love you with all my heart.** Te amo con todo mi corazón. **My heart is full of love for you.** Mi corazón está lleno de amor por ti. **You make my heart** *(1)* **do flip flops.** / *(2)* **sing (with joy).** Haces que mi corazón *(1)* dé vuelcos. / *(2)* cante (de alegría). **You've found the key to my heart.** Has encontrado la llave de mi corazón. **Your beautiful eyes have set my heart afire.** Tus bellos ojos han hecho arder mi corazón. **No one will ever take your place in my heart.** Nadie ocupará jamás tu lugar en mi corazón. **My heart belongs to you.** Mi cora-zón te pertenece. **I want to fill your heart with boundless love.** Quiero llenar tu corazón con infinito amor. **I want to sit and talk**

The letter "ñ" sounds like the "ny" in "canyon".

with you heart to heart. Quiero sentarme a platicar contigo de corazón a corazón. **I cross my heart.** Te lo juro. **My heart is so heavy right now.** Mi corazón está tan lleno de pesar en este momento.

heartache *n* dolor *m* en el corazón **I feel such (terrible) heartache.** Siento un (terrible) dolor en el corazón. **You don't know the heartache that I feel.** Tú no sabes el dolor que siento en el corazón.

heartbroken *adj* con el corazón roto **I'm heartbroken.** Tengo el corazón roto.

heartless *adj* desalmado *m*, -da *f* ~ **swine** cerdo desalmado **How could you be so (cruel and) heartless?** ¿Cómo pudiste ser tan (cruel y) desalmado *(-da)?* **You're really heartless (do you know that?).** De verdad eres desalmado *(-da)* (¿sabías?)

heartsick *adj* descorazonado *m*, -da *f* *(1)* **I'm** / *(2)* **We're heartsick about it.** *(1)* Estoy descorazonado *(-da)...* / *(2)* Estamos descorazonados *(-das)...* por eso.

heat *n* calor *m* **The heat is getting me down.** El calor me está agotando.

heaven *n* cielo *m* **absolute** ~ cielo absoluto **for** ~**'s sake** en nombre del cielo ~ **on earth** el cielo en la tierra **in** ~ en el cielo **in seventh** ~ en el séptimo cielo **This is heaven!** ¡Esto es el cielo! **I feel like I'm in heaven.** Me siento como en el cielo. **Good heavens!** ¡Santos cielos! **Thank heavens!** ¡Gracias al cielo!

heavenly *adj (divine)* divino *m*, -na *f*, celestial *m&f* **That** *(1)* **is** / *(2)* **was (absolutely) heavenly!** ¡Eso *(1)* es / *(2)* fue (absolutamente) divino! **It's so heavenly to** *(1)* **be in your arms.** / *(2)* **kiss you.** Es tan divino *(1)* estar en tus brazos. / *(2)* besarte.

heavy *adj* pesado *m*, -da *f* **It's (not) heavy.** (No) Es pesado *(-da).* **That must be heavy. Let me help you.** Eso debe estar pesado. Déjame ayudarte. **My heart is heavy.** Mi corazón está apesadumbrado. **That's heavy.** *(sad, tragic, terrible)* Eso es atroz.

hedonist *n* hedonista *m&f*

hedonistic *adj* hedonista *m&f*

height *n* altura *f*, estatura *f*

hell *n* infierno *m* **That must have been hell for you.** Eso debe haber sido el infierno para *usted (Fam: ti).* *(1)* **I** / *(2)* **We went through hell.** *(1)* Pasé / *(2)* Pasamos por un infierno. **What a hell it was.** Qué infierno fue eso. **Go to hell!** ¡Vete al infierno!

Hello! *interj* ¡Hola!

helmet *n* casco *m* **bicycle** ~ casco para bicicleta **motorcycle** ~ casco para moto **rollerblading** ~ casco para patinaje (en línea)

help *vt* ayudar *(1,2)* **Help!** *(1)*¡Auxilio! / *(2)* ¡Socorro! **Perhaps you could**

Numbers in parentheses always signal choices.

help *(1)* **me.** / *(2)* **us.** Quizás usted pudiera *(1)* ayudarme. / *(2)* ayudarnos.
Could you (please) help *(1)* **me?** / *(2)* **us?** ¿Podría usted *(1)* ayudarme /
(2) ayudarnos (por favor)? *(1)* **I want...** / *(2)* **I'd like...** **to** *(3,4)* **help you.**
(1) Quiero… / *(2)* Me gustaría... *(3)* ayudarlo *m* / *(4)* ayudarla *f (Fam:*
ayudarte). **Can I** *(1,2)* **help you?** ¿Puedo *(1)* ayudarlo *m* / *(2)* ayudarla *f*
(Fam: ayudarte)? **Tell me how I can help (**[*1,2*] **you).** Dígame *(Fam:*
Dime) **cómo puedo** ayudar (*[1]* ayudarlo *m* / *[2]* ayudarla *f [Fam:*
ayudarte]). **Let me** *(1,2)* **help you.** Déjeme *(Fam: Déjame)* *(1)* ayudarlo
m / *(2)* ayudarla *f (Fam: ayudarte)*. *(1)* **I** / *(2)* **We can** *(3,4)* **help you.** *(1)*
Yo puedo... / *(2)* Nosotros podemos... *(3)* ayudarlo *m* / *(4)* ayudarla *f*
(Fam: ayudarte). *(1)* **I** / *(2)* **We will help** *(3,4)* **you.** *(1)* Yo / *(2)* Nosotros
(3) lo *m* / *(4)* la *f (Fam: te)* *(1)* ayudaré. / *(2)* ayudaremos. *(1)* **I** / *(2)* **We**
can't *(3,4)* **help you.** No *(1)* puedo / *(2)* podemos *(3)* ayudarlo *m* / *(4)*
ayudarla *f (Fam: ayudarte)*. **I can't help myself.** No puedo evitarlo.
help *n* ayuda *f* **I appreciate your help (very much).** Agradeceré (mucho) *su*
(Fam: tu) ayuda. **I need your help.** Necesito de *su (Fam: tu)* ayuda. **If you**
need any help, let *(1)* **me** / *(2)* **us know.** Si *necesita usted (Fam: necesitas)*
ayuda *(1)* me / *(2)* nos *avisa (Fam: avisas)*.
helpful *adj* servicial *m&f* ; *(kind)* amable *m&f* **You've been very helpful.**
Usted ha (Fam: Tú has) sido muy amable.
helpless *adj* indefenso *m*, -sa *f*
here *adv* aquí; acá *(1)* **Stay** / *(2)* **Wait here.** *(1)* Quédate / *(2)* Espérate aquí.
Come here. Ven acá. **Here it is!** ¡Aquí está! **Here you are.** 1. *(Please*
take.) Aquí *tiene usted (Fam: tienes)*. 2. *(This is where you are.)* Helo aquí.
3. *(You have come.)* Aquí *está usted (Fam: estás)*. **Here's to** *(1)* **our**
friendship. / *(2)* **your beautiful eyes.** *(toast)* Esta es por *(1)* nuestra
amistad. / *(2)* tus bellos ojos.
hero *n* héroe *m* **You are my hero.** Tú eres mi héroe.
herpes *n* herpes *m*
heterosexual *n* heterosexual *m&f*
Hey! *interj* ¡Epa! ¡Ey!
Hi! *interj* ¡Hola!
hiccups *n, pl* hipo *m* **I'll show you how to stop the hiccups. First, put your**
mouth against mine... Te mostraré cómo detener el hipo. Primero, pon tu
boca contra la mía...
hickey *n* chupete *m* **Don't give me a hickey.** No me hagas un chupete.
hide *vt* esconder, ocultar **Hide** *(1,2)* **it** / *(3,4)* **them in** *(place)*. *(1)* Escóndelo
m / *(2)* Escóndela *f* / *(3)* Escóndelos *m, pl* / *(4)* Escóndelas *f, pl* en ___.
Where did you hide it? ¿Dónde lo escondiste? **You're hiding some-**
thing from me. Me estás ocultando algo. **I would never hide anything**

Spanish "a" is mostly like "a" in "mama".

from you. Nunca te ocultaría nada. **You can't hide the fact that you're crazy about me.** No puedes ocultar el hecho de que estás loco *(-ca)* por mí.

hide *vi* ocultar, esconder

high *adj* alto *m*, -ta *f*; elevado *m*, -da *f* ~ **income** ingresos *m, pl* elevados ~ **jump** salto *m* de altura ~ **level** alto nivel ~ **pay** pago *m* elevado ~ **school** escuela *f* superior ~ **speed** alta velocidad *f* **The price is too high.** El precio es demasiado alto. **Prices are very high.** Los precios están muy altos. **You're in high spirits today.** *Usted está (Fam:Estás)* de buen ánimo el día de hoy.

highway *n* carretera *f*

hike *vi* ir de caminata *(See also phrases under* **like** *and* **love***.)*

hike *n* caminata *f* **go on a (***[1]* **long /** *[2]* **overnight)** ~ ir a una caminata (*[1]* larga / *[2]* por la noche)

hiking *n* excursión *f (See phrases under* **go, like** *and* **love***.)*

hill *n* cerro *m*, colina *f* **go down the** ~ bajar la colina **go up the** ~ subir la colina **top of the** ~ en la cumbre de la colina

hint *vi* insinuar **What are you hinting at?** ¿Qué insinúas?

hint *n* indirecta *f* **gentle** ~ leve indirecta **subtle** ~ indirecta sutil **Give me a hint.** Dame una pista. **I can take a hint.** Yo sí capto las indirectas.

hip *adj (slang)* 1. *(knowing the latest trends)* en la onda; 2. *(following the latest trends)* del momento ~ **fashion** moda del momento; moda de onda

hip *n* cadera *f* **slender ~s** caderas finas **You have lovely hips.** Tienes lindas caderas.

hire *vt* contratar **Let's hire a** *(1)* **guide. /** *(2)* **taxi.** Contratemos *(1)* un guía. / *(2)* un taxi. **How much would it cost to hire you for** *(1)* **two hours? /** *(2)* **a half day? /** *(3)* **the whole day?** *(taxi)* ¿Cuánto costaría contratarlo por *(1)* dos horas? / *(2)* medio día? / *(3)* todo el día?

historic(al) *adj* histórico *m*, -ca *f*

history *n* historia *f*

hit *vt* pegar, golpear **You have to hit it like this.** *(tennis)* Tienes que pegarle así. **Don't hit me!** ¡No me pegues!

★ **hit it off** *idiom (get along well together)* llevarse bien **You and I just seemed to hit it off together from the very start.** Desde el principio se notó que tú y yo nos llevamos bien. **I'm glad we hit it off so well with each other.** Me alegra que nos llevemos tan bien. **It's wonderful the way we hit it off together.** Es maravilloso lo bien que nos llevamos.

★ **hit on** *(slang: flirt with)* coquetear **Was he hitting on you?** ¿Te estaba coqueteando? **He was hitting on me.** Me estaba coqueteando.

Spanish "z" is pronounced like "s" in "safe".

hoarse *adj* ronco *m*, -ca *f* **Your voice sounds hoarse.** Tu voz suena ronca.

hoax *n* broma *f* **It was all a (big) hoax.** Todo fue una (gran) broma.

hobby *n* pasatiempo *m* **fascinating ~** pasatiempo fascinante **interesting ~** pasatiempo interesante **What kind of hobbies (and interests) do you have?** ¿Qué clase de pasatiempos (e intereses) *tiene usted (Fam: tienes)*? **My hobbies are** *(what)*. Mis pasatiempos son ___.

hockey *n* hockey *m* **field ~** hockey sobre hierba **ice ~** hockey sobre hielo

hocus-pocus *n* galimatías *m*, abracadabra *f*

hold *vt* sostener, sujetar; *(have)* tener **Could you please hold this (for me)?** ¿*Podría usted (Fam: Podrías)* sostener esto (por mí)? **Let me hold that for you.** *Déjeme (Fam: Déjame) sostenerle (Fam: sostenerte)* eso. **Hold my hand.** Sujeta mi mano. **I** *(1)* **love** / *(2)* **want to hold you** *(3)* **in my arms.** / *(4)* **close to me.** *(1)* Me encanta / *(2)* quiero tenerte *(3)* en mis brazos. / *(4)* cerca de mí. **Hold it!** *(Wait!)* ¡Espera!

hole *n* orificio *m*, hoyo *m* ; *(golf)* hoyo *m*

holiday *n* día *m* festivo; festividad *f* **official ~** día festivo oficial **religious ~** festividad religiosa **unofficial ~** día festivo no oficial **What holiday is it?** ¿Qué festividad es?

holy *adj* santo *m*, -ta *f*, sagrado *m*, -da *f* **Holy Scripture** Las Sagradas Escrituras

home *n* casa, hogar **at ~** en casa **cozy ~** hogar acogedor **get ~** llegar a casa **go ~** ir a casa **leave ~** salir de casa **mobile ~** casa rodante **stay ~** quedarse en casa **trailer ~** casa en remolque **Where's your home?** ¿En dónde está *su (Fam: tu)* casa? *(1)* **My** / *(2)* **Our home is in** *(city / state).* *(1)* Mi / *(2)* Nuestra casa está en ___. **What time do you (usually) get home?** ¿A qué hora *llega usted (Fam: llegas)* a casa (normalmente)? **Can I** *(1,2)* **escort** / *(3,4)* **walk you home?** ¿Puedo *(1)* escoltarlo *m* / *(2)* escoltarla *f (Fam: escoltarte)* / *(3)* encaminarlo *m* / *(4)* encaminarla *f (Fam: encaminarte)* a *su (Fam: tu)* casa? **You have a nice home.** *Usted tiene (Fam: Tienes)* una casa agradable. **Is** *(name)* **at home?** ¿Se encuentra ___ en casa? **When will** *(1)* **he** / *(2)* **she be home?** ¿A qué hora llega *(1)* él / *(2)* ella a casa? **There's no place like home.** No hay nada como estar en casa.

homebody *n* persona *f* hogareña

homely *adj (plain, ugly)* sin gracia, feo *m*, fea *f*

homemade *adj* hecho *m (-cha)* en casa, de fabricación casera

homemaker *n* ama *f* de casa

homesick *adj* nostálgico *m*, -ca *f (1)* **I'm** / *(2)* **We're a little homesick.** *(1)* Me siento un poco nostálgico *(-ca)*. / *(2)* Nos sentimos un poco nostálgicos *(-cas)*. *(1)* **I'm** / *(2)* **We're not homesick.** *(1)* Yo no me siento nostálgico *(-ca)*. / *(2)* Nosotros no nos sentimos nostálgicos *(-cas)*. **Sometimes I get homesick.** A veces me pongo nostálgico.

Articles: m = el, f = la, mpl = los, fpl = las

homosexual *n* homosexual *m&f*

Honduran *adj* hondureño *m*, -ña *f* ★ *n* hondureño *m*, -ña *f*

honest *adj* honrado *m*, -da *f*, honesto *m*, -ta *f*; *(frank)* franco *m*, -ca *f* **brutally** ~ brutalmente franco *(-ca)* **Honest?** ¿En serio? **Honest!** ¡En serio! **Please be honest (with me).** Por favor, sé franco *(-ca)* conmigo. **I'll be (completely) honest with you.** Le *(Fam: Te)* seré (completamente) franco *(-ca)*. **To be honest...** Para ser franco *(-ca)*...

honestly *adv* honestamente; *(frankly)* francamente; *(sincerely)* sinceramente **I honestly (don't) think…** Sinceramente (no) creo... **Tell me honestly.** Dime, francamente.

honesty *n* honestidad *f* **I give total honesty and I expect total honesty.** Doy total honestidad y espero total honestidad. **Honesty is very important in a relationship.** La honestidad es muy importante en una relación.

honey *n* 1. *(sweet substance)* miel *f*; 2. *(darling)* cariño *m&f* **Your lips taste like honey.** Tus labios saben a miel. **Oh, Honey, I love you!** ¡Oh, cariño *(-ña)*! ¡Te amo!

honeymoon *n* luna de miel **We're on our honeymoon.** Estamos en nuestra luna de miel. **Where would you like to go** *(1)* **for /** *(2)* **on a honeymoon?** ¿Adónde te gustaría ir *(1)* de luna de miel? / *(2)* en nuestra luna de miel?

honor *n* honor *m* *(1)* **I /** *(2)* **We would consider it an honor.** Lo *(1)* consideraría / *(2)* consideraríamos un honor. **I give you my word of honor.** Le *(Fam: Te)* doy mi palabra de honor.

hook *n* *(fishing)* anzuelo *m*

hoola hoop *n* aro *m*, hula-hula *m*

hope *vi* esperar **I hope so.** Así lo espero. **I hope not.** Espero que no. **I hope (that)** *(1)* **I can see** *(2,3)* **you** *([4]* **again /** *[5]* **tonight /** *[6]* **tomorrow). /** *(7)* **we can see each other soon. /** *(8)* **you have a good time.** Espero que *(1)* pueda *(2)* verlo / *(3)* verla *f (Fam: verte)* *([4])* de nuevo / *[5]* esta noche / *[6]* mañana). / *(7)* que podamos vernos pronto. / *(8)* que lo *pase usted* *(Fam: pases)* bien. **You're all I could ever hope for.** Eres todo lo que pude haber esperado.

hope *n* esperanza *f* **all my** ~**s** todas mis esperanzas **any** ~ cualquier esperanza **cling to the** ~ aferrarse a la esperanza **faint** ~ leve esperanza **fervent** ~ ferviente esperanza **give me** ~ dame esperanzas **great** ~ gran esperanza **last** ~ la última esperanza **live in the** ~ **(that)** vivir con la esperanza (de que) **lose** ~ perder las esperanzas **my** ~ espero que **no** ~ **(at all)** no hay esperanza (de plano) **not lose** ~ no perder la esperanza **only** ~ la única esperanza **slightest** ~ la más leve esperanza **strong** ~ esperanza firme **Is there any hope that I can** *(1,2)* **see you** *(3)* **again? /** *(4)* **tonight? /** *(5)* **tomorrow?** ¿Hay alguna esperanza de poder *(1)* verlo *m* / *(2)* verla *f (Fam:*

A tilde ~ *in terms stands for the main entry word.*

verte) (3) de nuevo? / *(4)* esta noche? / *(5)* mañana? **That's my greatest hope.** Esa es mi mayor esperanza. **You are the cynosure of all my hopes (and dreams).** Tú eres el centro de todas mis esperanzas (y sueños).

hopeful *adj* esperanzado *m,* -da *f* ; *(optimistic)* optimista *m&f* **I'm hopeful that I can come back *(1)* soon.** / *(2)* **in *(month)*.** / *(3)* **next year.** Estoy ilusionado *(-da)* de poder regresar *(1)* pronto. / *(2)* en __. / *(3)* el año que entra.

hopefully *adv* con optimismo

hopeless *adj* caso *m* perdido, ,sin esperanzas **You're hopeless!** ¡Eres un caso perdido! **I know it's hopeless, but I love you.** Sé que no tengo esperanzas, pero te amo.

hopscotch *n* bebeleche *m* **play** ~ jugar bebeleche

horizon *n* horizonte *m* **We can explore new horizons together.** Juntos podemos explorar nuevos horizontes.

horoscope *n* horóscopo *m* **Do you believe in horoscopes?** ¿Cree usted *(Fam: Crees)* en los horóscopos? **I (don't) believe in horoscopes.** (No) Creo en los horóscopos. **According to your horoscope, you're going to meet a *(1)* beautiful stranger.** / *(2)* **handsome stranger.** Según su *(Fam: tu)* horóscopo, usted va *(Fam: tú vas)* a conocer a *(1)* una extranjera hermosa / *(2)* un extranjero atractivo.

horrible *adj* horrible *m&f* **Oh, how horrible!** ¡Oh, qué horrible!

horse *n* caballo *m* **Do you like to ride horses?** ¿Le *(Fam: Te)* gusta montar a caballo? *(1)* **I** / *(2)* **We like to ride horses.** *(1)* Me / *(2)* Nos gusta montar a caballo.

horse around *idiom (play around)* bromear; matar el tiempo

horseback *n (also on* ~*)* a caballo **ride** ~ montar a caballo

horseback riding *n* montar a caballo, cabalgata *f* **go** ~ ir a montar a caballo **Where can we go horseback riding?** ¿Adónde podemos ir a montar a caballo?

hospital *n* hospital *m*

hospitality *n* hospitalidad *f* **friendly** ~ cálida hospitalidad **wonderful** ~ hospitalidad maravillosa **Thank you very much for your kind hospitality.** Mucho le *(Fam: te)* agradezco su *(Fam: tu)* amable hospitalidad.

host *n* anfitrión *m* **You've been a wonderful host.** Tú has sido un anfitrión maravilloso.

hostel *n* albergue *m,* residencia *f* **elder** ~ residencia para personas mayores **youth** ~ albergue juvenil *(1)* **I'm** / *(2)* **We're staying in a youth hostel.** *(1)* Me estoy... / *(2)* Nos estamos... quedando en un albergue juvenil.

hostess *n* anfitriona *f* **You've been a wonderful hostess.** Tú has sido una anfitriona maravillosa.

---

*Spanish "ch" is pronounced like ours
(e.g., "cheese," "charge").*

hot *adj* caliente *m&f* ~ **chocolate** chocolate *m* caliente **It's too hot.** *(weather)* Hace demasiado calor. **You make me hot.** Tú me pones caliente.

hotel *n* hotel *m (See also phrases under* **come** *and* **go.**) **big** ~ gran hotel **book a room at a** ~ reservar una habitación en un hotel **cheap** ~ hotel barato **expensive** ~ hotel caro **fancy** ~ hotel de lujo **good** ~ buen hotel **nice** ~ hotel agradable **quiet** ~ hotel tranquilo **reasonable** ~ hotel con precios justos **small** ~ hotel pequeño; hotelito **Let's** *(1)* **find /** *(2)* **get a hotel.** Vamos a *(1)* buscar / *(2)* conseguir un hotel. **What hotel are you staying at?** ¿En qué hotel *se está usted (Fam: te estás)* quedando? **I'm staying at the Hotel** *(name)*. Me estoy quedando en el Hotel ___ .

hour *n* hora *f* **a couple of** ~s un par de horas **a few** ~s unas cuantas horas **for an** ~ por una hora **for** ~s **on end** por horas sin fin **half an** ~ media hora **in an** ~ en una hora **many** ~s muchas horas **several** ~s varias horas

house *n* casa *f (See also phrases under* **come, go** *and* **home.**) **big** ~ casa *f* grande **medium-size** ~ casa mediana **new** ~ casa nueva **nice** ~ casa bonita **old** ~ casa vieja **one-story** ~ casa de un piso **small** ~ casita **two-story** ~ casa de dos pisos

housewife *n* ama *f* de casa

how *adv* cómo ~ **about** qué te parece **How are you?** ¿Cómo *está usted (Fam: estás)*? **How're you doing?** ¿Cómo *le (Fam: te)* está yendo? **How's it going?** ¿Cómo va? **How do you do?** ¿Cómo le va? **How come?** ¿Cómo es eso? **How much (** *[1]* **is it? /** *[2]* **are they?)?** ¿Cuánto (*[1]* cuesta? / *[2]* cuestan?)? **How many?** ¿Cuántos? **How far (is it) (from here)?** ¿Qué tan lejos (está) (desde aquí)? **How often?** ¿Con qué frecuencia? **How long (does it take)?** ¿Cuánto tiempo (se toma)? **How do I get to** *(place)*? ¿Cómo llego a___? **How about** *(1)* **her? /** *(2)* **him? /** *(3)* **them? /** *(4)* **you?** ¿Y *(1)* ella? / *(2)* él? / *(3)* ellos? / *(4)* usted (Fam: tú)?

however *conj* sin embargo

hug *vt* abrazar **It's so nice to hug you.** Se siente tan bonito abrazarte.

hug *n* abrazo *m* **Give me a hug.** Dame un abrazo.

huggable *adj* abrazable *m&f* **Mmm! You're so huggable!** ¡Mmm! ¡Eres tan abrazable!

hum *vt* tararear **Can you hum it?** ¿Puedes tararearla? **I can hum it.** Yo puedo tararearla.

human *adj* humano *m*, -na *f* ~ **being** ser *m* humano ~ **nature** naturaleza *f* humana ~ **race** raza *f* humana

humane *adj* humanitario *m*, -ria *f*

humble *adj* humilde *m&f* **Please accept my humble apologies.** Por favor, acepta mis humildes disculpas.

Stress rule #1: The last syllable is stressed if the word ends in a consonant (except "n" and "s").

humbly *adv* humildemente; con humildad **I humbly apologize.** Con humildad me disculpo. **I humbly beg your forgiveness.** Con humildad ruego *su (Fam: tu)* perdón. **I humbly beseech you.** Le *(Fam: Te)* imploro con humildad.

humdrum *adj* rutinario *m*, -ria *f*, aburrido *m*, -da *f*, monótono *m*, -na *f*

humiliated *adj* humillado *m*, -da *f* **I've never felt so humiliated.** Nunca me había sentido tan humillado *(-da)*.

humiliating *adj* humillante *m&f* **It's (absolutely) humiliating.** Eso es (absolutamente) humillante.

hummingbird *n* colibrí *m* **You're my flower and I'm your hummingbird.** Tú eres mi flor y yo soy tu colibrí.

humor *n* humor *m* **good sense of** ~ buen sentido del humor **great sense of** ~ gran sentido del humor **impish sense of** ~ pícaro sentido del humor **irreverent sense of** ~ irreverente sentido del humor **keen sense of** ~ agudo sentido del humor **lively sense of** ~ vivaz sentido del humor **marvelous sense of** ~ maravilloso sentido del humor **quirky sense of** ~ extravagante sentido del humor **tremendous sense of** ~ tremendo sentido del humor **wry sense of** ~ sardónico sentido del humor **I love your sense of humor.** Me encanta *su (Fam: tu)* sentido del humor. **You have a caustic sense of humor.** Tienes un cáustico sentido del humor.

humorless *adj* sin sentido del humor; *(dull)* desabrido *m*, -da *f*

humorous *adj* humorístico *m*, -ca *f*, gracioso *m*, -sa *f*

hungry *adj* hambriento *m*, -ta *f* **get** ~ tener hambre **Are you hungry?** ¿Tiene usted *(Fam: Tienes)* hambre? *(1)* **I'm** / *(2)* **We're** (*[3]* **rather** / *[4]* **really) hungry.** *(1)* Tengo / *(2)* Tenemos (*[3]* bastante / *[4]* verdadera) hambre.

hunt *vt* cazar ~ **deer** cazar venados ~ **ducks** cazar patos ~ **rabbits** cazar conejos

hunt *vi* buscar ~ **for a job** buscar un empleo ~ **for treasure** buscar tesoros ~ **for waterfowl** buscar acuática *(1)* **I'm** / *(2)* **We're hunting for** *(3)* **an apartment.** / *(4)* **a room.** *(1)* Estoy / *(2)* Estamos buscando *(3)* un departamento. / *(4)* una habitación. **Let's hunt for** *(1)* **a coffee shop.** / *(2)* **a restaurant.** / *(3)* **some ice cream.** Busquemos *(1)* una cafetería. / *(2)* un restaurante. / *(3)* un helado.

hunting *n* caza *f*, cacería *f* **go** ~ ir de cacería **treasure** ~ buscar tesoros

Hurray! ¡Viva!

hurry *vi* apresurarse **Hurry (up)!** ¡Apresúrate! **We'd better hurry. (We're going to be late.)** Mejor nos apresuramos. (Vamos a llegar tarde.) **There's no need to hurry.** No hay necesidad de apresurarse.

hurry *n* prisa *f* **Are you in a hurry?** ¿Tienes prisa? *(1)* **I'm** / *(2)* **We're in a hurry.** *(1)* Tengo / *(2)* Tenemos prisa. **Don't be in such a hurry.** No

---

Spanish "i" is mostly "ee", but can also be shorter, like "i" in "sit," when together with other vowels.

tengas tanta prisa. **What's the hurry?** ¿Cuál es la prisa?

hurt *vt* lastimar; herir **Did you hurt yourself?** *¿Se lastimó (Te lastimaste)?* **I didn't mean to hurt** *(1)* **you.** / *(2)* **your feelings.** No quise *(1)* lastimarte. / *(2)* herir tus sentimientos. **Please forgive me if I hurt** *(1)* **you.** / *(2)* **your feelings.** Por favor perdóname si *(1)* te lastimé. / *(2)* herí tus sentimientos.

hurt *vi* doler **Does it hurt?** ¿Duele? **Where does it hurt?** ¿Dónde duele? **It hurts (here).** Duele (aquí). **It only hurts when I smile.** Sólo me duele cuando sonrío.

husband *n* esposo *m* **Do you have a husband?** *¿Tiene usted (Fam: Tienes)* esposo? **I (don't) have a husband** (No) Tengo esposo. **This is my husband** *(name)*. Este es mi esposo ___. **This is a picture of my husband.** Esta es una foto de mi esposo. **Your husband is very good-looking.** *(photo)* Su *(Fam: Tu)* esposo es muy bien parecido. **My husband passed away (in** *[year]***).** Mi esposo falleció (en __).

husky *adj* ronco *m*, -ca *f*

hut *n* cabaña *f*

hypnotic *adj* hipnótico *m*, -ca *f* **There's something (very) hypnotic about you.** Hay algo (muy) hipnótico en *usted (Fam: ti).*

hypnotize *vt* hipnotizar **You hypnotize me with your** *(1)* **beautiful** / *(2)* **exotic** / *(3)* **dark eyes.** *Usted me hipnotiza (Fam: Me hipnotizas)* con *sus (Fam: tus)* ojos *(1)* hermosos. / *(2)* exóticos. / *(3)* oscuros.

hypocrite *n* hipócrita *m&f*

hypocritical *adj* hipócrita *m&f* **be ~** ser hipócrita

hysterical *adj* histérico *m*, -ca *f* **Don't get hysterical.** No te pongas histérico *(-ca).*

Help us improve our book!
Send us the feedback form on page 431.

I

ice *n* hielo *m* **bowl of ~ cream** bola de nieve **cup of ~ cream** tasa de nieve **~ cream** helado *m* ; *(sorbet)* nieve *f* **~ cream bar** barra de la helada **~ cream cone** cono de helado **~ cream shop** heladería; *(sorbet)* nievería **~ cream vendor** dendedor de helado **~ cubes** cubos *m, pl* de hielo **~ machine** máquina *f* de hielo **Do you like ice cream?** ¿Quieres una helado? **Let's get some ice cream.** Vamos a comprar helado. **What flavor of ice cream do you like?** ¿Qué sabor de helado te gusta? **I'm glad you broke the ice.** Me alegra que *usted rompiera (Fam: rompieras)* el hielo.

ice-skate *vi* patinar sobre hielo *(See also phrases under* **like** *and* **love***.)*

ice-skates *n, pl* patines *mpl* de hielo

ice-skating *n* patinaje *m* sobre hielo *(See phrases under* **go, like** *and* **love***.)* **~ rink** pista *f* de hielo

ID = identification *n* documento *m* de identificación

idea *n* idea *f* **bad ~** mala idea **brilliant ~** idea brillante **clever ~** idea inteligente **crazy ~** idea loca **different ~** idea diferente **funny ~** *(amusing)* idea chistosa **general ~** idea general **goofy ~** idea tonta **not a bad ~** no es mala idea **original ~** idea original **rough ~** *(approximate)* idea aproximada **smart ~** idea inteligente **super ~** idea fabulosa **terrific ~** idea sensacional **weird ~** idea rara **wonderful ~** idea maravillosa **That's a** *(1)* **good /** *(2)* **great /** *(3)* **marvelous idea.** Esa es una *(1)* buena idea. / *(2)* gran idea. / *(3)* idea maravillosa. **I have an idea.** Tengo una idea. **I have no idea.** No tengo idea. **I'm always open to new ideas.** Estoy siempre abierto a nuevas ideas. **I haven't the slightest idea.** No tengo la menor idea. **Please don't get the wrong idea (about me).** Por favor, no se hagan una idea equivocada (de mí). **Somebody may get the wrong idea.** Alguien pudiera hacerse una idea equivocada.

ideal *adj* ideal *m & f* **That would be ideal.** Eso sería ideal. **Everything was ideal.** Todo estuvo ideal. **It was such an ideal evening together.** Estar

---

Spanish "j" is pronounced like "h".

juntos fue una velada ideal. **You are ideal for me.** Tú eres ideal para mí.

idealist *n* idealista *m&f*

idealistic *adj* idealista *m&f*

idealize *vt* idealizar **You idealize me too much.** Me idealizas demasiado.

identical *adj* idéntico *m*, -ca *f* ~ **twins** gemelos *(-las)* idénticos *(-cas)*

identification *n* identificación *f*

idiom *n* expresión *f* idiomática

idiosyncracy *n* idiosincracia *f*; manía *f* **It's one of my idiosyncracies.** Es una de mis manías.

idiot *n* idiota *m & f* **absolute** ~ idiota total **complete** ~ idiota por completo

idiotic *adj* idiota *m & f* **That's the most idiotic thing I ever heard.** Eso es lo más idiota que he oído.

idle *adj* perezoso *m*, -sa *f*

idolize *vt* idolatrar **I idolize you.** Te idolatro.

idyllic *adj* idílico *m*, -ca *f* **This time together with you is idyllic.** Este momento contigo es idílico.

if *conj* si

ignorant *adj* ignorante *m&f*

ignore *vt* ignorar **Just ignore** *(1)* **him.** / *(2)* **her.** / *(3)* **them.** Sólo *(1)* ignóralo. / *(2)* ignórala. / *(3)* ignóralos.

ill *adj* enfermo *m*, -ma *f* **be** ~ estar enfermo *(-ma)* **be** ~ **at ease** estar incómodo *(-da)* **feel** ~ **at ease** sentirse turbado *(-da)*, sentirse incómodo *(-da)*

illegal *adj* ilegal *m&f*

illness *n* enfermedad *f*

illusion *n* ilusión *f* **Have I shattered all your illusions about** *(1)* **men?** / *(2)* **women?** ¿He roto todas tus ilusiones acerca de *(1)* los hombres? / *(2)* las mujeres?

imagine *vt* imaginar **Imagine that.** *Imagínese usted (Fam: Imagínate)* eso. **That's hard to imagine.** Es difícil imaginarlo. **I imagine that must be very hard for you.** Imagino que debe ser muy difícil para *usted (Fam: ti).* **I can't imagine being with anyone else (but you).** No me puedo imaginar con ninguna otra persona (sino contigo). **You can't even imagine how much I love you.** No puedes imaginar siquiera cuánto te amo.

imagination *n* imaginación *f* **active** ~ imaginación activa **arouse my** ~ **despertar** mi imaginación **excite my** ~ excitar mi imaginación **fertile** ~ imaginación fértil **great** ~ gran imaginación **lively** ~ vívida imaginación **my** ~ mi imaginación **rich** ~ rica imaginación **wild** ~ imaginación delirante **your** ~ *su (Fam: tu)* imaginación **It's all in your imagination.** Es pura imaginación tuya. **My imagination is running wild.** Mi imaginación se está alocando.

---

*Familiar "tu" forms in parentheses can replace
italicized polite forms.*

imaginative *adj* imaginativo *m*, -va *f*
imbecile *n* imbécil *m&f*
imitate *vt* imitar
immature *adj* inmaduro *m*, -ra *f*
immediately *adv* inmediatamente, de inmediato
immense *adj* inmenso *m*, -sa *f*
immigrant *n* inmigrante *m&f*
immigrate *vi* inmigrar
immoral *adj* inmoral *m&f*
imp *n* diablillo *m*, -lla *f* **You're a mischievous little imp!** Eres un*(a)* diablillo *(-lla)* travieso *(-sa)*.
impatient *adj* impaciente *m&f* **Don't be impatient.** No seas impaciente.
impersonate *vt* imitar, remedar
impersonation *n* imitación **Let me give you my impersonation of Donald Duck.** Déjame hacerte mi imitación del Pato Donald.
impetuous *adj* impetuoso *m*, -sa *f*
implore *vt* implorar **fervently** ~ implorar con fervor **I implore you.** *Se (Fam: Te)* lo imploro.
imply *vt* dar a entender, insinuar **I didn't mean to imply that...** No quise insinuar que...
impolite *adj* descortés *m&f* **That was very impolite (of me).** Eso fue muy descortidle *adj*és (de mi parte).
importance *n* importancia *f*
important *adj* importante *m&f* **It's (not) (very) important.** (No) Es (muy) importante.
impossible *adj* imposible *m & f* **It's impossible** *(1)* **not to love you.** / *(2)* **to stay away from you.** / *(3)* **to stop looking at you.** Es imposible *(1)* no amarte. / *(2)* estar lejos de ti. / *(3)* dejar de mirarte.
impress *vt* impresionar
impression *n* impresión *f* **bad** ~ mala impresión **big** ~ gran impresión **deep** ~ impresión profunda **different** ~ impresión diferente **false** ~ falsa impresión **favorable** ~ impresión favorable **first** ~ primera impresión **give** *(1)* **me /** *(2)* **you the** ~ *(1)* darme / *(2)* darle *(Fam: darte)* la impresión **good** ~ buena impresión **make an** ~ causar una impresión **nice** ~ bonita impresión **overall** ~ impresión general **wrong** ~ impresión equivocada **your** ~ su *(Fam: tu)* impresión **I hope you** *(1)* **don't /** *(2)* **won't get the wrong impression (about me).** Espero que no *(1)* se haga usted *(Fam: te hagas)* / *(2)* se hará usted *(Fam: te harás)* una impresión equivocada (de mí). **I'm sorry if I gave you the wrong impression.** Lamento si *le (Fam: te)* di una impresión equivocada.

Spanish "e" is pronounced like English "e" in "get"

improper *adj (impolite)* incorrecto *m*, -ta *f*; *(inappropriate)* inadecuado *m*, -da *f*

improve *vt* mejorar **Can you help me improve my Spanish?** *¿Puede usted (Fam:¿Puedes)* ayudarme a mejorar mi español?

improve *vi* mejorar **You're improving already.** Ya estás mejorando.

impudent *adj* insolente *m&f*, descarado *m*, -da *f*

impulse *n* impulso *m* **sudden** ~ impulso repentino **I have an overpowering impulse to kiss you.** Tengo un impulso irresistible de besarte. **I couldn't resist the impulse.** No pude resistir el impulso.

impulsive *adj* impulsivo *m*, -va *f* **You shouldn't be so impulsive.** No debieras ser tan impulsivo *(-va)*. **It was an impulsive thing to do.** Eso que hiciste fue muy impulsivo.

inappropriate *adj* inadecuado *m*, -da *f* **That was inappropriate.** Eso fue inadecuado.

incapable *adj* incapaz *m&f*

incense *n* incienso *m*

incessantly *adv* incesantemente, sin cesar

incident *n* incidente *m* **unfortunate** ~ incidente desafortunado

incidentally *adv* incidentalmente

include *vt* incluir **Does that include** *(1)* **me?** / *(2)* **us?** ¿Eso *(1)* me / *(2)* nos incluye? **That includes** *(1,2)* **you.** Eso *(1)* lo *m* / *(2)* la *f (Fam: te)* incluye. **What does the tour include?** ¿Qué incluye el recorrido? **The tour includes...** El recorrido incluye...

income *n* ingresos *mpl* **above-average** ~ ingresos por arriba del promedio **good** ~ buenos ingresos **high** ~ ingresos elevados **modest** ~ ingresos modestos **monthly** ~ ingresos mensuales **small** ~ pocos ingresos **steady** ~ ingresos estables **What is your yearly income?** ¿Cuáles son *sus (Fam: tus)* ingresos anuales? **My yearly income is** *(amount)*. Mis ingresos anuales son ___.

incomparable *adj* incomparable *m&f*

incompatible *adj* incompatible *m&f* **We were incompatible.** Nosotros éramos incompatibles.

inconvenience *vt* incomodar *(1)* **I** / *(2)* **We don't want to inconvenience you.** No *(1)* quiero / *(2)* queremos incomodarte.

inconvenient *adj* inconveniente *m&f* **Would that be inconvenient for you?** ¿Eso sería inconveniente para *usted (Fam: ti)*?

incorrect *adj* incorrecto *m*, -ta *f*

increase *vi* aumentar, crecer *(1)* **The population...** / *(2)* **Unemployment... is increasing.** El desempleo va en aumento. **Prices are increasing.** Los precios van en aumento.

Stress rule # 2: The next-to-last syllable is stress in words ending in "n", "s" or a vowel.

incredible *adj* increíble *m&f* **You are (absolutely) incredible.** Eres (absolutamente) increíble.

incredibly *adv* increíblemente

indecent *adj* indecente *m&f*

indeed *adv* en efecto, en verdad

indefinitely *adv* indefinidamente

independence *n* independencia *f*

independent *adj* independiente *m&f* **I like to be independent.** Me gusta ser independiente.

indescribable *adj* indescriptible *m&f*

indifferent *adj* indiferente *m&f*

indigestion *n* indigestión *f*

indiscreet *adj* indiscreto *m*, -ta *f*

individual *n* individuo *m* -dua *f*

indoors *adv* en el interior, dentro, adentro, en casa

industrious *adj* diligente *m&f*, laborioso *m*, -sa *f*

industry *n* industria *f*

inedible *adj* no comestible *m&f*

inevitable *adj* inevitable *m&f*

inevitably *adv* inevitablemente

inexcusable *adj* imperdonable *m&f*

inexpensive *adj* barato *m*, -ta *f*

inexperience *n* inexperiencia *f*

inexperienced *adj* inexperto *m*, -ta *f*

infant *n* infante *m&f*, niñito *m*, -ta *f*

infatuated *adj* encaprichado *m*, -da *f*, **become** ~ encapricharse **You're just infatuated with me.** Nomás estás encaprichado *(-da)* conmigo. **I'm not just infatuated with you. I love you.** No estoy nomás encaprichado *(-da)* contigo. Yo te amo.

infatuation *n* encaprichamiento *m* **mere** ~ mero encaprichamiento **You don't really love me. It's just infatuation.** Tú no me amas de verdad. Es puro encaprichamiento.

infidelity *n* infidelidad *f* **I can't stand infidelity.** No soporto la infidelidad.

infinite *adj* infinito *m*, -ta *f*

infinitely *adv* infinitamente

infinitive *n* infinitivo *m*

infinity *n* infinidad *f*

inflatable *adj* inflable *m&f*

inflate *vt* inflar **Let me inflate it for you.** Permíteme inflarlo por ti.

inflation *n* inflación *f*

Spanish "x" is always like "ks", as in our word "taxi".

influence *vt* influir **What influenced you to** *(1)* **become a** *(member of a profession)*? / *(2)* **do that?** ¿Qué influyó en *usted (Fam: ti)* para *(1)* que *se hiciera (Fam: te hicieras* ___? / *(2)* hacer eso?

influence *n* influencia *f* **great ~** gran influencia **have an ~** tener una influencia **tremendous ~** tremenda influencia

inform *vt* informar, avisar **Please inform** *(1)* **me.** / *(2)* **us.** Por favor, *(1)* avíseme *(Fam: avísame).* / *(2)* avísenos *(Fam: avísanos).* *(1)* **I'll** / *(2)* **We'll inform you.** *(1)* Yo le *(Fam: te)* aviso / *(2)* Nosotros le *(Fam: te)* avisamos. **Thanks for informing** *(1)* **me.** / *(2)* **us.** Gracias por *(1)* avisarme. / *(2)* avisarnos.

informal *adj* informal *m&f* **~ attire** ropa informal **~ dinner** cena informal **~ party** fiesta informal

information *n* información *f* **Thanks for the information.** Gracias por la información. **Could you get the information for** *(1)* **me?** / *(2)* **us?** ¿Podría usted *(Fam: ¿Podrías)* *(1)* conseguirme... / *(2)* conseguirnos... la información ? *(1)* **I'll** / *(2)* **We'll get the information for you.** *(1)* Yo le *(Fam: te)* consigo... / *(2)* Nosotros le *(Fam: te)* conseguimos... la información . *(1)* **I** / *(2)* **We couldn't get the information.** *(1)* Yo no pude... / *(2)* Nosotros no pudimos... conseguir la información.

informed *adj* informado *m*, -da *f* **be ~** estar informado *(-da)* **You're very well informed.** *Usted está (Fam: Estás)* muy bien informado *(-da)*.

ingenious *adj* ingenioso *m*, -sa *f*

ingenuity *n* ingenuidad *f*

inhibit *vt* inhibir

inhibited *adj* inhibido *m*, -da *f* **Don't be so inhibited. Let yourself go.** No seas tan inhibido *(-da)*. Déjate ir. **You should try to be less inhibited.** Trata de ser menos inhibido *(-da)*.

inhibition *n* inhibición *f* **I'm going to help you get rid of all your inhibitions.** Voy a ayudarte a que te liberes de todas tus inhibiciones. **You've got to learn how to overcome your inhibitions.** Tienes que aprender a superar tus inhibiciones. **Just let (all) your inhibitions go.** Sólo deja ir (todas) tus inhibiciones. **I have no inhibitions (at all).** Yo no tengo inhibiciones (para nada).

inhumane *adj* inhumano *m*, -na *f*

initiative *n* iniciativa *f* **take the ~** tomar la iniciativa

initials *n, pl* iniciales *fpl*

injure *vt* herir, lesionar, lastimar

injured *adj* herido *m*, -da *f*, lesionado *m*, -da *f*, lastimado *m*, -da *f* **Were you injured (in the accident)?** ¿Se lastimó usted *(Fam: ¿Te lastimaste)* (en el accidente)? **How were you injured?** ¿Cómo fue que *se lesionó usted*

Stress rule # 3: Syllables with accent marks have the stress there.

(Fam: te lesionaste)?

injury *n* lesión *f*, herida *f*

inn *n* posada *f* **Is there an inn around here that we can stay at?** ¿Hay alguna posada por aquí donde nos podamos quedar?

innocence *n* inocencia *f* **bewitching** ~ inocencia encantadora **You beguile me with your wide-eyed innocence.** Me cautivas con tu cándida inocencia.

innocent *adj* inocente *m & f* **You have such an innocent look.** *Usted tiene (Fam: Tú tienes)* una apariencia tan inocente.

inquire *vi* preguntar **I'll inquire at the** *(1)* **desk.** / *(2)* **office.** Voy a preguntar en *(1)* el mostrador. / *(2)* la oficina.

inquisitive *adj* inquisitivo *m*, -va *f* **Am I being overly inquisitive?** ¿Soy demasiado inquisitivo *(-va)*? **You're quite inquisitive.** *Usted es (Fam: Tú Eres)* bastante inquisitivo *(-va)*.

insane *adj* demencial *m&f*, demente *m&f*, loco *m*, -ca *f* **This is totally insane.** Esto es totalmente demencial. **You must be insane!** ¡Debes estar loco *(-ca)*!

insanely *adv* locamente *(1)* **He** / *(2)* **She is insanely jealous.** *(1)* Él está loco de celos. / *(2)* Ella está loca de celos.

insanity *n* demencia *f*, locura *f*

insatiable *adj* insaciable *m&f* **I have to warn you, I'm insatiable.** Tengo que advertirte, soy insaciable. **If I seem insatiable, it's your fault.** Si parezco insaciable, es tu culpa.

inscription *n* inscripción *f*

insecure *adj* inseguro *m*, -ra *f*

insensitive *adj* insensible *m&f*

inside *prep* dentro de

inside *adv* dentro, adentro

inside *n* interior ~ **out** al revés

insincere *adj* insicero *m*, -ra *f*

insist *vi* insistir *(1)* **I** / *(2)* **We insist (that you come with** *[3]* **me** / *[4]* **us).** *(1)* Insisto / *(2)* Insistimos (en que *usted venga [Fam: vengas] [3]* conmigo / *[4]* con nosotros.)

inspiration *n* inspiración *f* **You're a real inspiration to me.** *Usted es (Fam: Tú eres)* una verdadera inspiración para mí.

inspire *vt* inspirar **I need someone like you to inspire me.** Necesito a alguien como *usted (Fam: tú)* para inspirarme. **You possess the kind of beauty that inspires** *(1)* **masterpieces of art .** / *(2)* **great paintings.** / *(3)* **poetry.** *Usted tiene (Fam: Tú tienes)* la clase de belleza que inspira *(1)* grandes obras de arte. / *(2)* .grandes pinturas. / *(3)* poesía.

inspiring *adj* inspirador *m*, -dora *f*

Spanish pronunciation rules are on pages 407-408.

instance *n* caso *m* **for** ~ por ejemplo

instant *adj* instantáneo *m*, -nea *f*, inmediato *m*, -ta *f* ~ **attraction** atracción inmediata ~ **rapport** afinidad inmediata

instantly *adv* instantáneamente, de inmediato, al instante

instead *adv* en cambio ~ **of** en lugar de

instinct *n* instinto *m* **My instincts told me you would be right for me. And they were right.** Mis instintos me decían que tú estarías bien para mí. Y tenían razón.

instinctive *adj* instintivo *m*, -va *f*

instinctively *adv* instintivamente, por instinto

institute *n* instituto *m*

instruct *vt* enseñar, instruir **I'd be glad to instruct you.** Con gusto *le (Fam: te)* enseño. **Could you instruct (1) me? / (2) us?** ¿Podría usted (Fam: ¿Podrías tú) (1) enseñarme? / (2) enseñarnos?

instruction *n* 1. *(instructing)* instrucción *f*, orientación *f*; 2. *pl (directions)* instrucciones *f, pl* **Thanks for the instruction.** Gracias por la orientación.

instructor *n* instructor *m*, -tora *f*, profesor *m*, -sora *f* **You're a good instructor.** Usted es (Fam: Tú eres) un*(a)* buen *(-na)* profesor *(-ra)*.

insult *vt* insultar **I didn't mean to (1,2) insult you.** No quise *(1) insultarlo m / (2) insultarla f (Fam: insultarte)*. **I'm sorry if I insulted (1,2) you.** Si *(1) lo m / (2) la f (Fam: te)* insulté, lo lamento. **You have insulted me.** Usted me ha (Fam: Me has) insultado.

insult *n* insulto *m* **That's an insult.** Eso es un insulto.

insurance *n* seguro *m* **car** ~ seguro de automóviles **collision** ~ *(car)* seguro de colisiones *or* seguro de choques **full** ~ **coverage** *(car)* seguro automovilístico con cobertura total **health** ~ seguro de salud **medical** ~ seguro médico **liability** ~ *(car)* seguro automovilístico contra daños a terceros **life** ~ seguro de vida

integrity *n* integridad *f*

intellect *n* intelecto *m* **I truly admire your intellect. (And your legs.)** De verdad admiro *su (Fam: tu)* intelecto. (Y *sus [Fam: tus]* piernas.)

intellectual *adj* intelectual *m&f*

intellectual *n* intelectual *m&f*

intellectually *adv* intelectualmente **We bond so well intellectually.** Nos acoplamos tan bien intelectualmente.

intelligence *n* inteligencia *f*

intelligent *adj* inteligente *m&f*

intend *vi* pretender **What do you intend to do?** ¿Qué *pretende usted (Fam: pretendes)* hacer? **(1) I / (2) We intend to (3) do it. / (4) go there. / (5) leave soon.** *(1)* Pretendo / *(2)* Pretendemos *(3)* hacerlo. / *(4)* ir allá. / *(5)*

Some Spanish words have accented and unaccented forms to differentiate their meanings (e.g., el = the, él = he).

irnos pronto. *(1)* **I** / *(2)* **We intended to *(3,4)* call you.** *(1)* Pretendía / *(2)* Pretendíamos *(3) llamarlo m* / *(4) llamarla f (Fam: llamarte)*.

intense *adj* intenso *m*, -sa *f*

intensely *adv* intensamente

intention *n* intención *f (1)* **My** / *(2)* **Our intention is...** *(1)* Mi / *(2)*Nuestra intención es... **I have no intention of losing you.** No tengo intención de perderte. **My intentions are honorable, I assure you.** Mis intenciones son honestas, te lo aseguro. **The road to hell is paved with good intentions.** El camino al infierno está lleno de buenas intenciones.

intentional *adj* intencional, adrede **That was (not)** *(1,2)* **intentional.** Eso (no) fue *(1)* intencional. / *(2)* adrede.

intentionally *adv* adrede, a propósito, intencionalmente **You did that intentionally.** Tú lo hiciste a propósito. **I didn't do it intentionally.** No lo hice a propósito. **I would never intentionally hurt you.** Nunca intentaría lastimarte.

intercourse *n* relaciones *fpl*, coito *m* **have ~** tener relaciones **sexual ~** relaciones sexuales **I don't want to have intercourse with you.** No quiero tener relaciones contigo. **I've never had intercourse with anyone.** Nunca he tenido relaciones con nadie.

interest *vt* interesar **What sort of things interest you?** ¿Qué clase de cosas *le (Fam: te)* interesan? **Does that interest you (at all)?** ¿Eso *le (Fam: te)* interesa (en serio)? **That interests me (very much).** Eso me interesa (muchísimo). **That doesn't interest me (at all).** Eso no me interesa (para nada). **You interest me (very much).** *Usted me interesa (Fam: Tú me interesas)* (muchísimo).

interest *n* interés *m* **arouse my ~** despertar mi interés **artistic ~s** intereses artísticos **common ~s** intereses comunes **genuine ~** genuino interés **great ~** gran interés **have ~** tener interés **intense ~** agudo interés **keen ~** sumo interés **literary ~s** intereses literarios **lively ~** vivo interés **my ~s** mis intereses **no ~** sin interés **particular ~** interés particular **personal ~s** intereses personales **romantic ~** interés romántico **similar ~s** intereses similares **varied ~s** intereses variados **What kind of (hobbies and) interests do you have?** ¿Qué clase de (pasatiempos e) intereses *tiene usted (Fam: tienes)*? **Tell** *(1)* **me** / *(2)* **us about your interests.** *(1)* Cuénteme *(Fam: Cuéntame)* / *(2)* Cuéntenos *(Fam: Cuéntanos)* de *sus (Fam: tus)* intereses.

interested *adj* interesado *m*, -da *f* **What kind of things are you interested in?** ¿En qué clase de cosas *está usted (Fam: estás)* interesado *(-da)*? **Are you interested in _(subject)_?** ¿*Está usted (Fam:¿Estás)* interesado *(-da)* en ___? **I'm (not) interested in _(subject)_.** Yo (no) estoy interesado *(-da)*

Spanish "g" is like "h" in front of "e" and "i".
In front of other vowels it's like our "g" in "gun".

en ___.

interesting *adj* interesante *m&f* **That's (very) interesting.** Eso es (muy) interesante.

international *adj* internacional *m&f*

interpret *vt* interpretar **Is there somebody (here) who could interpret (for *[1]* me / *[2]* us)?** ¿Hay (aquí) alguien que pudiera *[1] servirme [2]servirnos* de intérprete? **Could you possibly interpret for *(1)* me? / *(2)* us?** ¿Podría usted (Fam: ¿Podrías) tal vez hacer de intérprete para *(1)* mí? / *(2)* nosotros? **You interpret very well.** Usted hace (Fam: Tú haces) muy buenas interpretaciones.

interpreter *n* intérprete *m&f* **Where can *(1)* I / *(2)* we get an interpreter?** ¿Dónde *(1)* puedo / *(2)* podemos conseguir un intérprete?

interrupt *vt* interrumpir *(1)* **I'm / *(2)* We're sorry to *(3,4)* interrupt you.** *(1)* Lamento / *(2)* Lamentamos *(3) interrumpirlo m / (4) interrumpirla f (Fam: interrumpirte).*

intimacy *n* intimidad *f* **It's so wonderful to share intimacy with you.** Es tan maravilloso compartir la intimidad contigo.

intimate *adj* íntimo *m*, -ma *f*

intimately *adv* íntimamente

intoxicated *adj* embriagado *m*, -da *f*, intoxicado *m*, -da *f (1)* **He / *(2)* She is intoxicated.** *(1)* Él está embriagado. / *(2)* Ella está embriagada.

intoxicating *adj* embriagante *m&f* **The smell of your hair is intoxicating.** El olor de tu cabello es embriagante.

intrigue *vt* intrigar **You (really) intrigue me.** Usted (de verdad) *me intriga (Fam: Tú me intrigas).* **Your beautiful *(1)* blue / *(2)* dark / *(3)* green eyes intrigue me endlessly.** Sus (Fam: Tus) bellos ojos *(1)* azules / *(2)* oscuros / *(3)* verdes me intrigan infinitamente.

intriguing *adj* interesante *m&f*, fascinante *m&f*; enigmático *m*, -ca *f* **I find that very intriguing.** Encuentro eso muy enigmático. **You have an intriguing way of *(1)* looking at me. / *(2)* moving your eyes. / *(3)* speaking.** Tiene usted (Fam: Tienes) un modo misterioso de *(1)* mirarme. / *(2)* mover los ojos. / *(3)* hablar.

introduce *vt* presentar *(1)* **Let me... / *(2)* I want to... introduce you to my *(3)* wife. / *(4)* girlfriend. / *(5)* fiancée. / *(6)* mother. / *(7)* daughter. / *(8)* sister. / *(9)* husband. / *(10)* boyfriend. / *(11)* fiancé. / *(12)* father. / *(13)* son. / *(14)* brother. / *(15)* friend. / *(16)* friends. / *(17)* parents. / *(18)* children.** *(1) Permítame (Fam: Permíteme)… / (2)* Quiero… *presentarle (Fam: presentarte)* a mi(s) *(3)* esposa. / *(4)* novia. / *(5)* prometida. / *(6)* madre. / *(7)* hija. / *(8)* hermana. / *(9)* esposo. / *(10)* novio. / *(11)* prometido. / *(12)* padre. / *(13)* hijo. / *(14)* hermano. / *(15)* amigo (-ga). / *(16)* amigos (-

---

English-Spanish and Spanish-English glossaries of food and drink are on pages 420-427.

gas). / *(17)* padres. / *(18)* hijos *(-jas)*. **We haven't been introduced. My name is** *(name)*. No nos han presentado. Mi nombre es ___. **I'm glad we were introduced.** Me alegra que nos hayan presentado.

intrude *vi* importunar, inmiscuirse, interferir **I'm sorry to intrude.** Lamento interferir.

intuition *n* intuición *f* **feminine ~** intuición femenina **keen ~** intuición aguda **woman's ~** intuición de mujer **It's my woman's intuition.** Es mi intuición de mujer.

intuitive *adj* intuitivo *m*, -va *f*

intuitively *adv* intuitivamente, por intuición **I knew intuitively that you were the one for me.** Supe intuitivamente que tú eras la persona para mí.

invigorating *adj* estimulante *m&f* *(1)* **Your company... /** *(2)* **This air... is invigorating.** *(1)* Su *(Fam: Tu)* compañía… / *(2)* Este aire… es estimulante.

invitation *n* invitación *f* **Thank you for your invitation (to dinner).** Gracias por *su (Fam: tu)* invitación a cenar. *(1)* **I /** *(2)* **We accept your invitation.** *(1)* Yo acepto... / *(2)* Nosotros aceptamos… *su (Fam: tu)* invitación. **I'm sorry,** *(1)* **I /** *(2)* **we can't accept your invitation.** Lo siento, *(1)* no puedo... / *(2)* no podemos... aceptar *su (Fam: tu)* invitación. *(1)* **I /** *(2)* **We appreciate your invitation (, but** *[1]* **I /** *[2]* **we have other plans for that day).** *(1)* Aprecio / *(2)* Apreciamos *su (Fam: tu)* invitación (, pero *[1]* tengo / *[2]* tenemos otros planes para ese día).

invite *vt* invitar *(1)* **I'd /** *(2)* **We'd like to invite** *(3,4)* **you to** *(5)* **...dinner...** / *(6)* **...a birthday party...** / *(7)* **...a party /** *(8)* **concert /** *(9)* **ballet /** *(10)* **dance /** *(11)* **play /** *(12)* **movie...** / *(13)* **...my home...** / *(14)* **...meet my parents...** / *(15)* **...meet** *(16)* **my /** *(17)* **our family...** *(18)* **this afternoon.** / *(19)* **this evening.** / *(20)* **tomorrow (evening).** / *(21)* **on Friday /** *(22)* **Saturday /** *(23)* **Sunday (** *[24]* **afternoon /** *[25]* **evening).** *(1)* Me gustaría... / *(2)* Nos gustaría ... *(3)* invitarlo *m* / *(4)* invitarla *f (Fam: invitarte)* / *(5)* ...a cenar... / *(6)* ...a una fiesta de cumpleaños... / *(7)* ...a una fiesta... / *(8)* ...a un concierto... / *(9)* ...al ballet... / *(10)* ...a bailar... / *(11)* ...a una obra de teatro... / *(12)* ...al cine... / *(13)* ...a mi casa... / *(14)* ...a conocer a mis padres... / *(15)* ...a conocer a / *(16)* mi / *(17)* nuestra familia... / *(18)* esta tarde / *(19)* esta noche. / *(20)* mañana (al anochecer). / *(21)* el viernes / *(22)* el sábado / *(23)* el domingo *([24]* por la tarde / *[25]* al anochecer). **As a small token of my appreciation, I'd like to invite you to dinner.** En señal de mi aprecio, me gustaría invitarte a cenar. **Thank you for inviting** *(1)* **me /** *(2)* **us (to dinner).** Gracias por *(1)* invitarme / *(2)* invitarnos (a cenar).

inviting *adj* incitante *m&f* **Your lips are so inviting.** Tus labios son tan incitantes.

involve *vt* consistir, implicar **What does it involve?** ¿Y eso qué implica?

What does your job involve? ¿En qué consiste *su (Fam: tu)* trabajo?
involved *adj* involucrado *m*, -da *f* **Are you (romantically) involved with anyone?** ¿Está usted (Fam: ¿Estás) involucrado *(-da)* (románticamente) con alguien? **I'm not (romantically) involved with anyone.** No estoy involucrado (-da) (románticamente) con nadie. **I'm involved with someone.** Estoy involucrado *(-da)* con alguien.
Irishman *n* irlandés *m*
Irishwoman *n* irlandesa *f*
iron *vt (press)* planchar **I have to iron some clothes.** Tengo que planchar una ropa.
ironic *adj* irónico *m*, -ca *f*
irony *n* ironía *f*
irrelevant *adj* irrelevante *m&f*
irresistible *adj* irresistible *m & f* **You are (absolutely) irresistible.** Eres (absolutamente) irresistible.
irresponsible *adj* irresponsable *m&f*
irreverent *adj* irreverente *m&f*
irritate *vt* irritar **That irritates me.** Eso me irrita.
irritated *adj* irritado *m*, -da *f*, molesto *m*, -ta *f* **be ~** estar irritado *(-da)* **get ~** irritarse **I hope you're not irritated with me.** Espero que no estés molesto *(-ta)* conmigo.
irritating *adj* irritante *m&f*
island *n* isla *f*
issue *n* 1. *(problem)* problema *f*; 2. *(matter)* asunto *m* **It's not a big issue.** No es un gran problema.

A slash always means "or".

J

jack *n* 1. *(cards)* sota *f* ; 2. *(car)* gato *m*
jacket *n* chaqueta *f*, saco *m* **life ~** chaleco *m* salvavidas
jackpot *n* premio *m* gordo **hit the ~** sacarse el premio gordo
Jacuzzi *n* jacuzzi *m*
jade *n* jade *m*
jail *n* cárcel *f* **go to ~** ir a la cárcel
jam *n* 1. *(tough situation)* aprieto *m* ; 2. *(congestion)* embotellamiento *m* **be in a ~** estar en un aprieto **traffic ~** embotellamiento de tráfico **get out of a ~** salirse de un aprieto **I wonder if you could help me. I'm in a jam.** Me pregunto si podrías ayudarme, estoy en un aprieto.
January *n* enero *m* **in ~** en enero **on ~ first** el primero de enero
jasmine *n* jazmín *m*
jealous *adj* celoso *m*, -sa *f* **be ~** estar celoso *(-sa)* **get ~** ponerse celoso *(-sa)* **insanely ~** estar delirante de celos. **madly ~** estar loco *(-ca)* de celos **wildly ~** tener unos celos salvajes **Are you jealous (of** *[1]* **him /** *[2]* **her)?** ¿Tienes celos (de *[1]* él / *[2]* ella)? **I'm (not) jealous.** (No) estoy celoso *(-sa)*. **Are you a jealous person?** ¿Eres una persona celosa? **I'm (not) a jealous person.** (No) Soy una persona celosa. **You make me jealous.** Me pones celoso *(-sa)*. **You never have to be jealous about me.** Nunca tienes que sentir celos de mí.
jealousy *n* celos *m, pl*, envidia *f* **feel pangs of ~** sentir punzadas de envidia, sentir un ataque de celos **I feel such (fierce) jealousy anytime you look at someone else.** Siento unos celos (feroces) cada vez que miras a otra persona. **You're blinded by jealousy.** Estás ciego *(-ga)* de la envidia. **There's no reason for such jealousy.** No hay motivo para tal envidia.
jeans *n, pl* pantalón *m or* pantalones *m, pl* de mezclilla **You look** *(1)* **good /** *(2)* **great in jeans.** Te ves *(1)* bien / *(2)* sensacional con pantalón de mezclilla.

Spanish "v" is pronounced like a soft "b".

jellyfish *n* medusa *f,* aguamala *f*

jerk *n (slang)* 1. *(despicable or obnoxious person)* pendejo *m,* -ja *f (vulg)*; 2. *(foolish person)* idiota *m&f* **stupid** ~ estúpido *m,* -da *f*

jet lag *n* desfase *m* horario, jet-lag *m (1)* **I have...** / *(2)* **I'm suffering from...** *(3,4)* **jet lag.** *(1,2)* Estoy agotado *(-da)* por el *(3)* desfase horario. / *(4)* jet-lag. *(1)* **You have...** / *(2)* **You're suffering from... jet lag.** *(1,2)* Usted está agotado *(-da)* por el *(3)* desfase horario. / *(4)* jet-lag.

jet ski *n* moto *m* acuática

jetty *n* 1. *(breakwater)* espigón *m,* malecón *m* ; 2. *(for landing)* desembarcadero *m*

Jew *n* judío *m*

jewelry *n* joyas *f, pl,* alhajas *f, pl* ~ **shop** joyería *f* **You have the kind of beauty that makes all jewelry seem trivial.** *Usted tiene (Fam: Tú tienes)* la clase de belleza que hace que todas las joyas luzcan triviales.

Jewess *n* judía *f*

Jewish *adj* judío *m,* -día *f*

Jezebel *n* Jezabel *f,* mala pécora, mala mujer

jilt *vt* plantar; dejar plantado *m,* -da *f (1)* **He** / *(2)* **She jilted me.** *(1)* Él me dejó plantada. / *(2)* Ella me dejó plantado.

job *n* trabajo *m,* empleo *m* **dead-end** ~ empleo sin futuro **full-time** ~ trabajo de tiempo completo **part-time** ~ trabajo de medio tiempo **stable** ~ empleo fijo **steady** ~ empleo estable **I have a good job.** Tengo un buen trabajo. **I have a** *(1)* **full-time** / *(2)* **part-time job.** Tengo un trabajo de *(1)* tiempo completo. / *(2)* medio tiempo. **I don't have a job right now.** No tengo trabajo por el momento.

jog *vi* trotar **Do you like to jog?** ¿Le *(Fam: ¿Te)* gusta trotar? **I jog** *(1)* **everyday.** / *(2)* **regularly.** Salgo a trotar *(1)* todos los días. / *(2)* con regularidad.

jogging *n* trotar **Let's go jogging (together) (tomorrow).** Vámonos a trotar (juntos) (mañana).

join *vt* acompañar **May** *(1)* **I** / *(2)* **we** *(3,4)* **join you?** *(1)* ¿Puedo / *(2)* ¿Podemos *(3)* acompañarlo *m* / *(4)* acompañarla *f*? **Please join** *(1)* **me.** / *(2)* **us.** Por favor *(1)* acompáñeme. / *(2)* acompáñenos. **Won't you join** *(1)* **me** / *(2)* **us (for** *[3]* **coffee?** / *[4]* **a drink?** / *[5]* **breakfast?** / *[6]* **lunch?** / *[7]* **dinner?)** ¿No *(1)* me *acompaña usted (Fam. acompañas)* / *(2)* nos *acompaña usted (Fam: acompañas)* (*[3]* a un café? / *[4]* a una copa? / *[5]* a desayunar? / *[6]* a comer? / *[7]* a cenar?)? **Thank you,** *(1)* **I'd** / *(2)* **we'd love to** *(3,4)* **join you.** Gracias, *(1)* me / *(2)* nos encantaría *(3)* acompañarlo *m* / *(4)* acompañarla *f (1)* **I'll** / *(2)* **we'll join** *(3,4)* **you later.** *(3)* Lo *m* / *(4)* La *f (Fam: Te) (1)* acompaño / *(2)* acompañamos más tarde.

Time expressions are given on page 413.

joke *vi* bromear **Are you joking (or are you serious)?** *¿Está usted (Fam:¿Estás)* bromeando (o es en serio)? **I'm (not) joking.** (No) Estoy bromeando.

joke *n* broma *f,* chiste *m* **It's (just) a joke.** (Sólo) Es una broma. **I was making a joke.** Estaba haciendo una broma. **I'll tell you a joke.** Te voy a contar un chiste. **Do you know any good jokes?** ¿Te sabes algún chiste bueno?

joker *n* 1.*(person)* bromista *m&f*; 2. *(cards)* comodín *m*

jolly *adj* alegre *m&f,* jovial *m&f*

journey *n* viaje *m* **I'm glad we're taking this journey together.** Me alegra que hagamos juntos este viaje.

jovial *adj* jovial *m&f* **You're certainly a jovial type.** Eres de verdad un tipo jovial.

joy *n* alegría *f,* júbilo *m,* gozo *m,* gusto *m* **be full of** ~ estar lleno *(-na)* de júbilo **dance with** ~ bailar de gusto **experience** ~ experimentar júbilo **feel** ~ sentir júbilo **feeling of** ~ sentimiento de alegría **fill with** ~ llenarse de júbilo **find** ~ hallar gozo **great** ~ gran júbilo **greatest** ~ el mayor gusto **infinite** ~ gozo infinito **kaleidoscope of** ~ calidoscopio de júbilo **jump with** ~ saltar de alegría **only** ~ puro gusto **pure** ~ puro gozo **radiate** ~ irradiar júbilo **share** ~ compartir el júbilo **such** ~ tal júbilo **tremendous** ~ júbilo tremendo **what** ~ qué dicha **You fill my heart with joy.** Me llenas el corazón de júbilo. **You're a constant joy to me.** Eres una dicha constante para mí. **You're a joy to be around.** *Usted es (Fam. Tú eres)* la alegría del lugar. **I've never known so much joy (with anyone).** Nunca he conocido tanta alegría (con nadie). **Thank you for bringing so much joy into my life.** Gracias por traer tanta alegría a mi vida.

joyful *adj* feliz *m&f,* alegre *m&f*

joyous *adj* alegre *m&f,* feliz *m&f*

jubilant *adj* jubiloso *m,* -sa *f,* dichoso *m,* -sa *f* **be** ~ estar radiante *m&f* de júbilo **I feel absolutely jubilant.** Me siento plenamente dichoso *(-sa)*.

jubilation *n* júbilo *m,* regocijo *m* **What jubilation I feel!** ¡Qué regocijo siento!

jubilee *n* jubileo *m*

judge *vt* juzgar **I'm not one to judge others.** No soy quien para juzgar a los demás.

judgement *n* sentencia *f,* juicio *m* **cast** ~ emitir un juicio **pass** ~ aprobar una sentencia **You seem like a person of good judgement.** Pareces ser una persona de buen juicio.

judo *n* judo *m* **Could you teach me judo?** ¿Podrías enseñarme judo?

juggle *vt* malabarear, hacer malabarismos

Spanish "qu" is pronounced like "k".

juggler *n* malabarista *m&f*

juice *n* jugo *m*

July *n* julio *m* **in** ~ en julio **on** ~ **first** el primero de julio

jump *vi* saltar ~ **with joy** saltar de alegría

jump *n (skydiving)* salto *m*

June *n* junio *m* **in** ~ en junio **on** ~ **first** el primero de junio

junk *n* 1. *(trash)* basura *f*; 2. *(stuff, things)* trastos *mpl*

just *adv* 1. *(only)* sólo; 2. *(exactly)* justo; exactamente; 3. *(barely)* apenas; 4. *(at the moment)* en este momento ~ **about** aproximadamente **I'm just curious.** Sólo tengo curiosidad. **You're just the person who can help me.** Tú eres justo la persona que me puede ayudar. *(1)* **I** / *(2)* **We just made it.** Apenas *(1)* la hice / *(2)* la hicimos. *(1)* **I was...** / *(2)* **We were... just** *(3)* **going to** *(4,5)* **call you.** / *(6)* **leaving.** Justo en este momento *(1)* iba / *(2)* íbamos *(3)* a *(4)* *llamarlo m* / *(5)* *llamarla f (Fam. llamarte)*. / *(6)* a salir. **Just a minute!** ¡Un momento, por favor!

Words in parentheses (not italicized) are optional.

K

kaleidoscope *n* caleidoscopio *m* ~ **of ecstasy** caleidoscopio de éxtasis ~ **of joy** calidoscopio de alegría

karaoke *n* karaoke *m*

karate *n* karate *m* ~ **chop** golpe *m* de karate

karma *n* karma *m* **good** ~ buen karma

kayak *vi* remar en kayak

kayak *n* kayak *m*

kayaking *n* remar en kayak **sea** ~ kayak *m* de mar **Have you ever gone kayaking?** ¿Alguna vez has ido a remar en kayak? **I enjoy kayaking.** Me gusta remar en kayak.

keen *adj* 1. *(sharp, acute)* agudo *m*, -da *f*; 2. *(ardent)* vehemente *m&f* ~ **eyesight** vista *f* aguda ~ **interest** interés *m* vehemente

keep *vt* 1. *(retain)* quedarse; 2. *(hold; store)* guardar; 3. *(maintain)* mantener **You can keep it.** *Usted puede (Fam: Puedes) quedárselo (Fam. quedártelo).* **Please keep it.** Por favor *quédeselo (Fam. quédatelo).* **Can you keep my (1) backpack / (2) suitcase while I'm gone?** ¿*Puede usted (Fam: ¿Puedes)* guardar mi *(1)* mochila / *(2)* maleta mientras estoy fuera? **I can hardly keep my eyes open.** Apenas puedo mantener los ojos abiertos. **I would never keep anything from you.** Nunca me quedaría secretos con tuyo. **Where do you keep your cups?** ¿Dónde guardas tus tazas?

keep (on) *vi (continue)* continuar, seguir **If I'm not there, please keep trying.** Si no estoy ahí, por favor sigan intentando.

keepsake *n* recuerdo *m (1)* **This / (2) Here is a small keepsake (of our trip) for you.** *(1)* Este es... / *(2)* Aquí hay para ti un pequeño recuerdo (de nuestro viaje).

key *n* llave *f* **apartment** ~ llave del departamento **car** ~ llave del carro **house** ~ llave de la casa **room** ~ llave del cuarto *(1)* **I / (2) We lost (3) my / (4) our key.** *(1)* Perdí / *(2)* Perdimos *(3)* mi / *(4)* nuestra llave. **You have**

A single Spanish "r" should be lightly trilled;
double "r" ("rr") should be strongly trilled.

found the key to my heart. Tú has encontrado la llave de mi corazón.

kick *vt* reprochar **I kick myself for not** *(1)* **calling** / *(2)* **telling you sooner.** / *(3)* **remembering.** Me reprocho por no *(1)* ...haberte llamado... / *(2)* ...habértelo dicho... antes. / *(3)* recordado.

kick *n (slang) (enjoyment*; *pl: fun) (Use verb:)* divertirse; deleitearse *(See examples)* **I get a kick out of watching you do that.** Me divierto al verte hacer eso. **I get my kicks from water skiing.** Me divierto haciendo esquí acuático.

kid *vt* bromear, tomar el pelo, engañar **Are you kidding (me)?** *¿Está usted (Fam: ¿Estás)* bromeando (conmigo) *or* tomándome el pelo? *(1)* **I'm...** / *(2)* **I was... just kidding (you).** *(1)* Estoy / *(2)* Estaba nomás bromeando *(con usted [Fam: contigo]).* *(1)* **I'm...** / *(2)* **I was... not kidding (you).** No *(1)* estoy / *(2)* estaba bromeando *(con usted [Fam: contigo]).*

kid *n (child)* niño *m*, niña *f*, chiquillo *m*, -lla *f*, escuincle *m*, -cla *f* **I love kids.** Me encantan los niños. **I'm just a kid at heart.** Soy un*(a)* niño *(-ña)* de corazón.

kill *vt* matar *(1)* **He** / *(2)* **She was...** / *(3)* **They were... killed in** *(4)* **a(n) (car) accident.** / *(5)* **earthquake.** / *(6)* **fire.** / *(7)* **flood.** / *(8)* **the war.** *(1)* Él / *(2)* Ella murió... / *(3)* Ellos murieron... en *(4)* un accidente (automovilístico). / *(5)* un terremoto. / *(6)* un incendio. / *(7)* una inundación. / *(8)* la guerra. **I don't believe in killing things.** No soy partidario *(-ria)* de matar nada.

kind *adj* amable *m&f*, gentil *m&f* **You're a kind man.** Usted es *(Fam: Tú eres)* un hombre amable. **You're a kind** *(1)* **woman.** / *(2)* **person.** Usted es *(Fam: Tú eres)* una *(1)* mujer / *(2)* persona amable. **That** *(1)* **is** / *(2)* **was very kind of you.** Eso *(1)* es / *(2)* fue muy amable de su *(Fam: tu)* parte. **You are (so) kind (to me).** Usted es *(Fam: Tú eres)* (tan) amable (conmigo). **You were (so) kind (to me).** Fue usted *(Fam: Fuiste)* (tan) amable (conmigo). **The years have been very kind to you.** Los años han sido muy generosos *con usted (Fam: contigo).*

kind *n* clase *f*, tipo *m* **any ~ of** cualquier clase de **different ~s (of things)** diferentes clases (de cosas) **other ~s (of things)** otra clase (de cosas) **some ~ of** alguna clase de **that ~** esa clase **this ~** esta clase **what ~ of** qué clase de **What kind do you** *(1)* **have?** / *(2)* **like?** / *(3)* **need?** / *(4)* **want?** ¿De qué clase *(1)* tiene usted *(Fam. tienes)*? / *(2)* le *(Fam: te)* gusta? / *(3)* necesita usted *(Fam. necesitas)*? / *(4)* quiere usted *(quieres)*? **What kind of** *(1)* **camera** / *(2)* **dog** / *(3)* **music tapes do you have?** ¿Qué clase de *(1)* cámara / *(2)* perro / *(3)* cintas de música tiene usted *(Fam: tienes)*? **What kind of wine is that?** ¿Qué clase de vino es ese? **I like** *(1)* **this** / *(2)* **that kind of** *(3)* **beer.** / *(4)* **bread.** / *(5)* **food.** / *(6)* **music.** / *(7)* **wine.** Me gusta *(1)* esta / *(2)* esa clase de *(3)* cerveza. / *(4)* pan. / *(5)* comida. / *(6)* música.

---

*Familiar "tu" forms in parentheses can replace
italicized polite forms.*

/ *(7)* vino. **I'm not that kind of** *(1)* **girl.** / *(2)* **woman.** / *(3)* **guy.** / *(4)* **man.** / *(5)* **person.** Yo no soy esa clase de *(1)* muchacha. / *(2)* mujer. / *(3)* tipo. / *(4)* hombre. / *(5)* persona. **You're one of a kind.** Usted es *(Fam: Eres)* único *(-ca)* en su *(Fam: tu)* clase.

kind-hearted *adj* de buen corazón **You are such a kind-hearted person.** Usted es *(Fam: Tú eres)* una persona de tan buen corazón.

kindness *n* amabilidad *f,* bondad *f* ; *(generosity)* generosidad *f* **Thank you for your kindness.** Gracias por su *(Fam: tu)* amabilidad. *(1)* **I** / *(2)* **We appreciate your kindness (very much).** *(1)* Aprecio / *(2)* Apreciamos (mucho) su *(Fam: tu)* generosidad. **You've shown** *(1)* **me** / *(2)* **us so much kindness.** Usted *(Fam: Tú)(1)* me / *(2)* nos has dado muestras de tanta generosidad.

king *n* rey *m* **I'm king of the world!** ¡Soy el rey del mundo!

kinky *n (slang) (perverted)* pervertidillo *m,* -lla *f*

kiss *vt* besar ~ **again** besar de nuevo ~ **all over** besar todo ~ **a thousand times** besar mil veces ~ **endlessly** besar interminablemente ~ **everything** besar todo ~ **everywhere** besar por todas partes ~ **gently** besar con ternura ~ **goodnight** 1. *(bedtime)* dar el beso de buenas noches; 2. *(parting)* dar el beso de despedida ~ **here** besar aquí ~ **lovingly** besar con amor ~ **me** besarme ~ **on the cheek** besar en la mejilla ~ **on the lips** besar en los labios ~ **on the mouth** besar en la boca ~ **on the neck** besar en el cuello ~ **over and over** besar una y otra vez ~ **tenderly** besar con ternura ~ **there** besar allí ~ **with feeling** besar con sentimiento ~ **you** besarte ~ **your lips** besar tus labios **Kiss me (***[1]* **again.** / *[2]* **here.** / *[3]* **all over.** / *[4]* **with feeling.)** Bésame (*[1]* otra vez. / *[2]* aquí. / *[3]* por todas partes. / *[4]* con sentimiento.). **I want (so much) to kiss you.** Quiero besarte (tanto). **I want to kiss you so much I can hardly stand it.** Quiero besarte tanto que apenas me puedo contener. **I love to kiss you.** Me encanta besarte. **I love the way you kiss.** Me encanta tu modo de besar. **I don't want to stop kissing you.** No quiero dejar de besarte. **No one ever kissed me like that.** Nadie me había besado así jamás. **I've been aching to kiss you since the first** *(1)* **moment** / *(2)* **time I** *(3)* **met** / *(4)* **saw you.** He estado sufriendo por besarte desde *(1)* …el primer momento… / *(2)* …la primera vez… que te *(3)* conocí. / *(4)* vi.

kiss *n* beso *m* **adoring** ~**(es)** beso(s) de adoración **burning** ~**(es)** beso(s) ardiente(s) **cover you with** ~**es** cubrirte de besos **French** ~ beso francés **gentle** ~**(es)** beso(s) suave(s) **give** *(1)* **me** / *(2)* **you a** ~ *(1)* darme / *(2)* darte un beso **goodbye** ~ beso de despedida **goodnight** ~ beso de buenas noches **long** ~ beso largo **loving** ~**(es)** beso(s) de amor **many** ~**es** muchos besos **need your** ~**es** necesitar tus besos **nice** ~ beso bonito **passionate** ~**(es)**

Spanish "ll" is pronounced like "y" in "yes".

beso(s) apasionado(s) **slow ~(es)** beso(s) lento(s) **soft ~(es)** beso(s) suave(s) **steal a ~** robar un beso **sweet ~(es)** beso(s) dulce(s) **tender ~(es)** beso(s) tierno(s) **wet ~** beso húmedo **Give me a kiss.** Dame un beso. **What a *(1)* beautiful / *(2)* heavenly / *(3)* wonderful kiss.** Qué beso *(1)* hermoso. / *(2)* divino. / *(3)* maravilloso. **That was a perfect kiss.** Ese fue un beso perfecto. **I love your kisses.** Me encantan tus besos. **I'm (hopelessly) addicted to your kisses.** Soy (irremediablemente)adicto *(-ta)* a tus besos. **Don't be stingy with your kisses.** No escatimes tus besos.

kissable *adj* besable *m&f***You're so kissable!** ¡Eres tan besable! **Your mouth looks so kissable.** Tu boca se ve tan besable. **You've got the most kissable mouth in the world.** Tienes la boca más besable del mundo. **Are you as kissable as you look?** ¿Eres tan besable como pareces?

kisser *n* besador *m*, -dora *f* **You're a *(1)* fantastic / *(2)* great kisser.** Eres un*(a)* besador *(-dora) (1)* fantástico *(-ca)* / *(2)* fenomenal.

kissing *n* besar **Your lips were made for kissing.** Tus labios están hechos para besar.

kit *n* equipo *m* **first aid ~** equipo de primeros auxilios. **Do you have a first aid kit?** ¿Tienes un equipo de primeros auxilios? **Get a first aid kit.** Consigue un equipo de primeros auxilios.

kitchen *n* cocina *f* **You're a wizard in the kitchen.** *Usted es (Fam: Eres)* un*(a)* mago *(-ga)* en la cocina.

kite *n* papalote *m*, cometa *f* **Do you like to fly kites?** ¿Te gusta volar papalotes?

kitesurfing *n* kitesurf *m*

kitten *n* gatito *m*, -ta *f*

knee *n* rodilla *f* **bad ~** rodilla mala **left ~** rodilla izquierda **right ~** rodilla derecha **smooth ~s** rodillas suaves

knife *n* cuchillo *m*

knock *vi* tocar **Knock *(1)* like this. / *(2)* three times.** Toca *(1)* así. / *(2)* tres veces.

know *vt* 1. *(have knowledge of)* saber; 2. *(be acquainted with)* conocer **Do you know *(1)* her? / *(2)* him? / *(3)* them?** *(1)* ¿La / *(2)* ¿Lo / *(3)* ¿Los conoce usted (Fam: conoces)*? **Do you know *(1)* the way? / *(2)* what time it is? / *(3)* where the post office is?** ¿Sabe usted (Fam: ¿Sabes) *(1)* el camino? / *(5)* qué hora es? / *(6)* dónde está la oficina de correos? **I know.** Sí sé. **I don't know.** No sé. **I'd like (very much) (to get) to know you better.** Me gustaría (muchísimo) (llegar a) *(1) conocerlo m /* *(2) conocerla f (Fam. conocerte)* mejor. **I want to take it slow and get to *(1,2)* know you (better).** Quiero irme despacio y llegar a *(1) conocerlo m* / *(2) conocerla f (Fam: conocerte)* (mejor). **You don't know what you do**

Common occupations are listed on pages 415-416.

to me. No sabes lo que me haces. **I feel like I've known you** *(1)* **for a long (long) time.** / *(2)* **all my life.** Siento como si te conociera *(1)* desde hace (mucho) tiempo. / *(2)* de toda mi vida. **I've never known anyone** *(1)* **who's as much fun as your are.** / *(2)* **as** *(3)* **sweet** / *(4)* **nice** / *(5)* **charming** / *(6)* **affectionate** / *(7)* **loving as you are.** Nunca conocí a nadie *(1)* que fuera tan divertido *(-da)* como tú. / *(2)* tan *(3)* dulce / *(4)* agradable / *(5)* encantador *(-ra)* / *(6)* afectuoso *(-sa)* / *(7)* cariñoso *(-sa)* como tú. **The more I know you, the more I love you.** Cuanto más te conozco, más te amo.

★ **know how** *idiom* saber **Do you know how to** *(1)* **drive?** / *(2)* **play chess?** / *(3)* **play a guitar?** / *(4)* **play the piano?** / *(5)* **swim?** / *(6)* **use a computer?** ¿Sabe usted *(Fam: Sabes tú)* *(1)* manejar? / *(2)* jugar ajedrez? / *(3)* tocar guitarra? / *(4)* tocar el piano? / *(5)* nadar? / *(6)* usar una computadora? **I know how.** Sí sé. **I don't know how.** No sé.

knowledge *n* conocimiento *m* **You (certainly) have a lot of knowledge on the subject.** (Verdaderamente) *Tiene usted (Fam: Tienes tú)* mucho conocimiento en la materia.

kook *n (slang: screwball, crazy guy)* chiflado *m*, -da *f*

Spanish "y" is "ee" when alone or at the end of words.

L

lackluster *adj (uninspiring)* deslucido *m*, -da *f*

lady *n* dama *f* *(See also* **female, girl** *and* **woman***)* **dragon** ~ mata-hari **fun** ~ dama alegre **nice** ~ dama agradable **Here's a small gift for my special lady.** Este es un regalito para mi dama especial.

ladylove *n* bienamada *f*

lag *vi* rezagarse **Don't lag behind.** No *se (Fam. te)* rezagues.

lagoon *n* laguna *f*

laid back *adj (slang) (easy-going)* despreocupado *m*, -da *f*

lamb *n* cordero *m*, –ra *f*, borrego *m*, -ga *f*

lamp *n* lámpara *f*

land *vi* aterrizar **We're going to land (soon). (Could you give me your phone number?)** (Pronto) vamos a aterrizar. (¿*Podría usted [Fam. ¿Podrías]* darme *su [Fam. tu]* número de teléfono?)

land *n* tierra *f*

landscape *n* paisaje *m* **Isn't this a beautiful landscape?** ¿No es un paisaje bonito?

language *n* idioma *m*, lenguaje *m* **bad** ~ malas palabras **body** ~ lenguaje corporal **foreign** ~ idioma extranjero **obscene** ~ lenguaje obsceno **What (other) languages do you speak?** ¿Qué (otros) idiomas *habla usted (Fam: hablas)*? **I speak** *(1)* **two /** *(2)* **three /** *(3)* **four /** *(4)* **five languages.** Hablo *(1)* dos / *(2)* tres / *(3)* cuatro / *(4)* cinco idiomas. **The languages I speak are Spanish, French, German and English.** Los idiomas que hablo son español, francés, alemán e inglés. **I don't speak any (***[1]* **foreign /** *[2]* **other) languages.** Yo no hablo ningún (*[1]* idioma extranjero / *[2]* otro) idioma. **No language can describe my feelings (for you).** Ningún idioma puede describir lo que siento (por ti).

lap *n* 1. *(on legs)* regazo *m* ; 2. *(circuit)* vuelta *f* **swim** ~s dar vueltas a nado **Come sit on my lap.** Ven y siéntate en mi regazo. **Let's run four laps**

---

*Feminine forms of words in phrases
are usually given in parentheses (italicized).*

around the field. Vamos corriendo cuatro vueltas alrededor del campo.
Let's swim a few laps in the pool. Nademos unas cuantas vueltas en la
piscina.

lapis-lazuli *n* lapislázuli *m*, azul *m* ultramarino

laptop *n (computer)* laptop *f*

large *adj* grande *m&f*

lashes *n, pl (eyelashes)* pestañas *fpl* **false** ~ pestañas postizas **long** ~ pestañas
largas **thick** ~ pestañas gruesas

last *adj* último *m*, -ma *f* ~ **but not least** por último pero no por menos
importante ~ **chance** la última oportunidad ~ **name** apellido ~ **time** la vez
pasada **next to** ~ penúltimo *(-ma)*; casi al último **What time is the last** *(1)*
bus? */ (2)* **train?** ¿A qué hora sale el último *(1)* camión? */ (2)* tren? **This is**
our last chance. Esta es nuestra última oportunidad. **This is the last time.**
Esta es la última vez.

last *vi* durar, perdurar **I want this to last forever.** Quiero que esto perdure
por siempre. **I hope our love will last forever.** Espero que tu amor perdure
por siempre. **The marriage lasted only three years.** El matrimonio duró
sólo tres años.

last *n* fin *m*; lo último **at** ~ al fin **at long** ~ por fin **That's the last of** *(1)* **it.** */*
(2) **my** */ (3)* **our money.** Eso es lo último que queda de *(1)* esto. */ (2)* mi */*
(3) nuestro dinero.

late *adj* tarde *adv* **be** ~ estar retrasado; llegar tarde **I'm sorry I'm late.**
Lamento llegar tarde. **We're sorry we're late.** Lamentamos llegar tarde.
(1) **I'm** */ (2)* **We're going to be a little bit late.** *(1)* Voy */ (2)* Vamos a
llegar un poco tarde. **Don't be late.** No llegues tarde. **You're late. What**
happened? Llegaste tarde. ¿Qué pasó? **Better late than never.** Mejor
tarde que nunca.

late *adv* tarde **arrive** ~ llegar tarde **get up** ~ levantarse tarde *(1)* **I'm** */ (2)*
We're going to get there a little bit late. *(1)* Voy */ (2)* Vamos a llegar un
poco tarde. *(1)* **I** */ (2)* **We got up late.** *(1)* Me levanté */ (2)* Nos levantamos
tarde.

lately *adv* últimamente, recientemente

later *adv* más tarde, después *(1)* **I'll** */ (2)* **We'll** *(3)* **call** */ (4)* **see** *(5,6)* **you**
later. *(5)* Lo m */ (6)* La f *(Fam: Te) (1,3)* llamaré */ (2,3)* llamaremos */ (1,4)*
veré */ (2,4)* veremos más tarde.

latest *adj* lo último *m*, el último *m*, la última *f* **What's the latest?** ¿Cuál es
la última novedad? **Have you heard the latest?** ¿Ya oíste la última?

laugh *vi* reír **Okay, what are** *(1,2)* **you laughing about?** Bueno, ¿de qué *(1)*
(Fam:) te estás... */ (2) (Pl:)* se están... riendo? *(1)* **I'm** */ (2)* **We're laugh-**
ing about *(what)*. *(1)* Me estoy... */ (2)* Nos estamos... riendo de ___. **Who**

Spanish "c" before "e" and "i" is pronounced like "s".

gave you permission to laugh? ¿Quién *le (Fam. te)* dio permiso de reír? **I like to hear you laugh.** Me gusta oírle *(Fam: oírte)* reír.

laugh *n* risa *f* **You have a** *(1)* **nice /** *(2)* **sexy laugh**. Usted tiene *(Fam: Tú tienes)* una risa *(1)* agradable. / *(2)* sensual.

laughter *n* risa *f* **What's all the laughter about?** ¿A qué se debe la risa? **Laughter is contagious, isn't it?** La risa es contagiosa ¿verdad?

launch *vt (boat)* botar; *(canoe)* lanzar

lavender *n* lavanda *f*

laundry 1. *(clothes)* ropa de lavar *f*; 2. *(shop)* lavandería *f*

lavish *adj* abundante *m&f*

lavish *vt* derrochar **I'm going to lavish love and affection on you**. Voy a derrochar amor y cariño por ti.

law *n* derecho *m* ; ley *f* **adoption** ~ leyes de adopción **against the** ~ contra la ley **immigration** ~ leyes de inmigración **Mexican** ~ leyes mexicanas **obey the** ~ obedecer las leyes **I don't want to break the law.** No quiero infringir la ley.

lawyer *n* abogado *m*, -da *f* **divorce** ~ abogado *(-da)* de divorcios

lay *vt* colocar, poner **Can I lay it** *(1)* **here? /** *(2)* **there?** ¿Puedo ponerlo *(1)* aquí? / *(2)* allá? **Lay it** *(1)* **here. /** *(2)* **there.** Ponlo *(1)* aquí. / *(2)* acá. **Lay your head on my shoulder.** Pon tu cabeza en mi hombro. **You're the most beautiful** *(1)* **girl /** *(2)* **woman I ever laid eyes on**. Tú eres la *(1)* muchacha / *(2)* mujer más hermosa en que haya puesto yo mis ojos. **If you lay one hand on me, I'll call the police.** Si me pones una mano encima, llamo a la policía. **I was laid off from my job.** Me suspendieron del trabajo.

lazy *adj* perezoso *m*, -sa *f*, flojo *m*, -ja *f* **You're a lazy critter.** Eres un bicho perezoso. **Don't be so lazy.** No seas tan flojo *(-ja)*. **If I wasn't so lazy, I'd go to sleep.** Si no fuera yo tan flojo *(-ja)*, me iría a dormir.

lead *vt* 1. *(direct)* dirigir; 2. *(take)* llevar **Who's going to lead?** ¿Quién va a dirigir? **I'll lead.** Yo dirijo. **Lead the way!** ¡Dirige el camino! **Where are you leading us?** ¿Adónde nos *lleva usted (Fam: llevas?)*? **Are you leading me astray?** ¿Me estás llevando por mal camino? **I know your leading me astray and I love it.** Sé que me llevas por mal camino, y me encanta.

lead *vi* ganar **Who's leading?** *(game)* ¿Quién va ganando? *(1)* **I'm /** *(2)* **He's / *(3)* **She's /** *(4)* **They're /** *(5)* **We're leading (by ten points).** *(1)* Yo voy / *(2)* Él va / *(3)* Ella va / *(4)* Ellos van / *(5)* Nosotros vamos ganando (por diez puntos).

lead *n* delantera *f* *(1)* **I'm /** *(2)* **We're going to let you take the lead.** *(1)* Voy / *(2)* Vamos a dejar que *usted tome (Fam: tú tomes)* la delantera.

leader *n* líder *m*, lideresa *f* **exalted** ~ líder eminente **glorious** ~ líder glorioso

Numbers in Spanish are given on pages 411-412.

noble ~ líder noble

leaf *n* hoja *f* **I love it when the leaves** *(1)* **begin to fall.** / *(2)* **change color.** Me encanta cuando las hojas *(1)* comienzan a caer. / *(2)* cambian de color.

lean *vi* apoyarse **You can lean on my shoulder.** *Puede usted apoyarse (Fam. Puedes apoyarte) en mi hombro.*

learn *vt* aprender ~ **the hard way** aprender de los propios errores **Where did you learn** *(1)* **English?** / *(2)* **Spanish?** ¿Dónde *aprendió usted (Fam: aprendiste) (1)* inglés? / *(2)* español? **I learned it** *(1)* **at home.** / *(2)* **in college.** Lo aprendí en *(1)* casa. / *(2)* la escuela. *(1)* **I'm trying...** / *(2)* **I want... to learn (more) Spanish.** *(1)* Estoy tratando de... / *(2)* Quiero... aprender (más) español. **I'll help you learn English.** Yo *le (Fam: te)* ayudo a aprender inglés. **It's not hard to learn.** No es difícil de aprender. **A person like you can learn it easily.** Una persona como *usted (Fam. tú)* puede aprenderlo con facilidad.

★ **learn about** *idiom (find out)* enterarse, saber de

learner *n* aprendiz *m&f* *(1)* **I'm** / *(2)* **You're a fast learner.** *(1)* Yo aprendo... / *(2) Usted aprende (Fam: Tú aprendes)...* rápido.

least *adv* lo mínimo; lo último; el de menor, el menos ~ **important** el de menor importancia ~ **of all** menos que nada

least *n* lo último *m*, la última *f*; al / lo menos **at** ~ al menos **That's the least of my worries.** Esa es la última de mis preocupaciones. **The least you could have done was** *(1)* **call me.** / *(2)* **tell me.** / *(3)* **let me know.** Lo menos que pudiste haber hecho era *(1)* llamarme. / *(2)* decirme. / *(3)* contarme. **At least we met and had a few days together.** Al fin nos conocimos y pasamos juntos unos cuantos días. **I don't care if you're late. At least you came.** No importa si llegas tarde. Al menos viniste.

leather *adj* de piel ★ *n* piel *f*

leave *vt* dejar **Did I leave my** *(1)* **camera** / *(2)* **passport** / *(3)* **purse here?** ¿Dejé aquí mi *(1)* cámara? / *(2)* pasaporte? / *(3)* monedero? **Leave me alone!** *¡Déjeme (Fam: ¡Déjame)* en paz!

leave *vi* salir, irse **When are you leaving?** ¿Cuándo *sale usted (Fam: sales?)*? *(1)* **I 'm** / *(2)* **We're leaving** *(3)* **today.** / *(4)* **tomorrow.** *(1)* Salgo / *(2)* Salimos *(3)* hoy. / *(4)* mañana. **Please leave.** Por favor vete. **Please don't leave.** Por favor no te vayas. **I don't want to leave.** No quiero irme. **I don't want you to leave.** No quiero que *se vaya (Fam: te vayas).*

lecher *n* libertino *m*, -na *f*, lujurioso *m*, -sa *f*

lecherous *adj* libidinoso *m*, -sa *f*, lascivo *m*, -va *f*

leer *vi* mirar con lascivia **Stop leering at me.** Deja de mirarme con lascivia.

left *adj* izquierdo *m*, -da *f* ~ **foot** pie izquierdo ~ **hand** mano izquierda ~ **side** lado izquierdo

---

Spanish "h" is always silent.

left *n* izquierda *f* **It's on the left**. Es a la izquierda.

left-handed *adj* zurdo *m*, -da *f* **I'm left-handed.** Soy zurdo *(-da)*.

left out *idiom* relegado *m*, -da *f*; dejado *m*, -da *f*; abandonado *m*, -da *f* **I felt (rather) left out.** Me sentí (bastante) relegado *(-da)*.

leg *n* pierna *f* **bare ~s** piernas desnudas (sin medias) **bow ~s** piernas arqueadas **left ~** pierna izquierda **little ~s** piernitas **long ~s** piernas largas **muscular ~s** piernas musculosas **my ~s** mis piernas **pretty ~s** piernas bonitas **right ~** pierna derecha **slender ~s** piernas esbeltas **smooth ~s** piernas tersas **your ~s** sus *(Fam: tus)* piernas **You have** *(1)* **beautiful /** *(2)* **fantastic /** *(3)* **gorgeous /** *(4)* **sexy legs.** Tú tienes piernas *(1)* hermosas. / *(2)* fantásticas. / *(3)* despampanantes. / *(4)* sensuales. **You've got the** *(1)* **best /** *(2)* **most beautiful /** *(3)* **nicest /** *(4)* **sexiest legs I've ever seen.** Tú tienes las piernas *(1)* mejores / *(2)* más hermosas / *(3)* más bonitas / *(4)* más sensuales que yo he visto. **I lost my (**[1]** left /** [2] **right) leg in** *(3)* **an accident. /** *(4)* **the (Vietnam) war.** Perdí mi pierna (*[1]* derecha / *[2]* izquierda) en *(3)* un accidente. / *(4)* la guerra (de Vietnam).

legal *adj* legal *m&f* **Is that legal?** ¿Es eso legal?

legally *adv* legalmente **We're legally separated.** Estamos legalmente separados. **We're still legally married, but we live apart.** Aún estamos legalmente casados, pero vivimos separados.

legible *adj* legible *m&f* **Your handwriting is almost legible.** Tu escritura es casi ilegible.

leisure *n* ocio *m*, tiempo *m* libre

leisurely *adj* de placer, placentero *m*, -ra *f* **~ journey** viaje de placer **~ vacation** vacaciones *fpl* placenteras **~ visit** visita *f* placentera *(1)* **I'm /** *(2)* **We're just taking a leisurely** *(3)* **trip /** *(4)* **vacation.** *(1)* Yo sólo estoy... / *(2)* Nosotros sólo estamos... tomando *(3)* un viaje... / *(4)* unas vacaciones... de placer.

lend *vt* prestar **Could you lend me some money?** ¿Podrías prestarme dinero? **Sure,** *(1)* **I'd /** *(1)* **we'd be glad to lend you some money. How much do you need?** Claro, *(1)* me / *(2)* nos dará gusto prestarte dinero. ¿Cuánto necesitas? *(1)* **I'm /** *(2)* **We're sorry,** *(3)* **I'm /** *(4)* **we're not able to lend you the money.** *(1)* Lo lamento / *(2)* Lo lamentamos, no *(3)* puedo / *(4)* podemos prestarte el dinero. **Here's the money you lent** *(1)* **me. /** *(2)* **us.** Aquí está el dinero que *(1)* me / *(2)* nos prestaste.

lens *n* lente *m* **contact ~es** lentes de contacto **I wear contact lenses.** Yo uso lentes de contacto. **I** *(1)* **dropped /** *(2)* **lost my contact lens.** *(1)* Se me cayó... / *(2)* Perdí... mi lente de contacto.

Leo *(Jul. 23 - Aug. 22)* Leo

lesbian *n* lesbiana *f*

Questions about the metric system? See page 417.

less *adj* menos *m&f*

less *adv* menos **I couldn't care less.** No podría importarme menos. **I love you more than yesterday and less than tomorrow.** Te amo más que ayer y menos que mañana.

less *n* menos *m* **more or** ~ más o menos **I'll be back in less than fifteen minutes.** Regreso en menos de quince minutos.

lesson *n* lección *f*; clase *f* **bitter** ~ amarga lección **hard** ~ lección dura **I take** *(1)* **music** / *(2)* **Spanish** / *(3)* **tennis lessons.** Tomo clases de *(1)* música. / *(2)* español. / *(3)* tenis. **Could you give** *(1)* **me** / *(2)* **us lessons in Spanish?** ¿Podría usted (Fam. ¿Podrías) *(1)* darme / *(2)* darnos clases de español? **I could give you lessons in English.** Yo podría *darle (Fam. darte)* clases de inglés. **I want to give you a lesson in lip magic.** Quiero darte una lección de magia labial. **Let that be a lesson to you.** Que eso te sirva de lección.

let *vt* dejar ~ **go** dejar ir **Let's go!** ¡Vámonos! **Let's** *(1)* **dance.** / *(2)* **get something to eat.** / *(3)* **have a cup of coffee.** / *(4)* **play** *(game).* / *(5)* **sit down.** Vayamos *(1)* a bailar. / *(2)* a conseguir algo de comer. / *(3)* a tomar un café. / *(4)* a jugar ___. / *(5)* a sentarnos. **Let me** *(1)* **see.** / *(2)* **think.** Déjame *(1)* ver. / *(2)* pensar. **Please, let me pay (for this one).** Por favor, déjame pagar (ésta). **Let me know, okay?** Me avisas, ¿sí? **I'll let you know.** Yo te aviso. **I never want to let you go.** No quiero dejarte ir nunca. **Don't ever let me go.** Nunca me dejes ir.

let down *idiom* decepcionar **I'll never let you down.** Nunca te voy a decepcionar. **You let me down.** Tú me decepcionas.

letter *n* carta *f* **answer** *(1)* **my** / *(2)* **your** ~ contestar *(1)* mi / *(2)* su *(Fam: tu)* carta **forward the** ~ despachar la carta **get** *(1)* **my** / *(2)* **your** ~ llegar *(1)* mi / *(2)* su *(Fam: tu)* carta **in** *(1)* **my** / *(2)* **your** ~ en *(1)* mi / *(2)* su *(Fam: tu)* carta **mail the** ~ enviar la carta por correo **read** *(1)* **my** / *(2)* **your** ~ leer *(1)* mi / *(2)* su *(Fam: tu)* carta **receive** *(1)* **my** / *(2)* **your** ~ recibir *(1)* mi / *(2)* su *(Fam: tu)* carta **send a** ~ enviar una carta **translate** *(1)* **my** / *(2)* **your** ~ traducir *(1)* mi / *(2)* su *(Fam: tu)* carta **You said in your letter that...** Usted decía (Fam: Tú decías) en *su (Fam: tu)* carta que... **I wrote you a letter. Did you get it?** *Le (Fam: Te)* escribí una carta. ¿*Le (Fam: ¿Te)* llegó? **I got your letter.** Me llegó *su (Fam: tu)* carta. **I didn't get your letter (yet).** No me llegó *su (Fam: tu)* carta (todavía). **Thanks a lot for your letter.** Muchas gracias por *su (Fam: tu)* carta. **I was real happy to get your letter.** Me dio mucho gusto recibir *su (Fam: tu)* carta. **I'll write you a letter (as soon as I get back).** Te voy a escribir una carta (en cuanto llegue). **I'll send you a letter by e-mail.** *Le (Fam: Te)* voy a enviar una carta por correo electrónico. **Write me a letter (by e-mail).** Escríbeme

---

The letter "ñ" sounds like the "ny" in "canyon".

una carta (por correo electrónico).

levelheaded *adj* sensato *m*, -ta *f*

levity *n* ligereza *f*; frivolidad *f* **I'm prone to frequent levity.** Suelo ser dado *(-da)* a la ligereza.

lewd *adj* libinidoso *m*, -sa *f* ~ **remark** comentario *m* libinidoso

liable *adj (likely)* inclinado *m*, -da *f* a, ser dado *m* a **I'd better write it down. I'm liable to forget.** Mejor lo escribo. Soy muy dado *(dada)* a olvidar.

liberal *adj* liberal *m&f* **politically** ~ liberal en política

liberty *n* libertad *f* **take** ~**ies** tomarse libertades **take the** ~ tomarse la libertad

Libra *(Sep. 23 - Oct. 22)* Libra

library *n* biblioteca *f*

license *n* licencia *f*, permiso *m* **driver's** ~ licencia de conducir **fishing** ~ permiso de pesca **hunting** ~ permiso de caza **marriage** ~ licencia de matrimonio **Where do we apply for a marriage license?** ¿Dónde se solicita una licencia de matrimonio?

lick *vt* lamer

lie *vi* acostarse ~ **down** acostarse **I'm going to lie down.** Me voy a acostar. **Why don't you lie down?** ¿Por qué no te acuestas? **Let's go lie by the pool.** Vamos a echarnos junto a la alberca. **I want to lie with you in my arms.** Quiero acostarme contigo en mis brazos.

lie *vi (not tell the truth)* mentir **You're lying (to me).** (Me) Estás mintiendo. **I'm not lying (to you).** No (te) estoy mintiendo. **I would never lie to you.** Nunca te mentiría **Please don't lie to me.** Por favor no me mientas.

lie *n* mentira *f* **big** ~ gran mentira **tell a** ~ decir una mentira

life *n* vida *f* **active** ~ vida activa **all** *(1)* **my** / *(2)* **your** ~ toda *(1)* mi / *(2)* su *(Fam: tu)* vida **bachelor** ~ vida de soltero *(-ra)* **boring** ~ vida aburrida **brighten my** ~ iluminar mi vida **build a** ~ construir una vida **busy** ~ vida ocupada **carefree** ~ vida despreocupada **change** *(1)* **my** / *(2)* **your** ~ cambiar *(1)* mi / *(2)* su *(Fam: tu)* vida **city** ~ vida citadina **come into** *(1)* **my** / *(2)* **your** ~ venir a *(1)* mi / *(2)* su *(Fam: tu)* vida **comfortable** ~ vida cómoda **country** ~ vida campestre **cultural** ~ vida cultural **easy** ~ vida fácil **empty** ~ vida vacía **enjoy** ~ **(to the fullest)** gozar la vida (al máximo) **exciting** ~ vida emocionante **family** ~ vida familiar **full of** ~ lleno *(-na)* de vida **gypsy** ~ vida de gitano **happy** ~ vida feliz **hard** ~ vida difícil **hectic** ~ vida agitada **lead a (normal)** ~ llevar una vida (normal) ~ **of the party** el alma de la fiesta ~ **together** vida en común **live a comfortable** ~ tener una vida cómoda **lonely** ~ vida solitaria **long** ~ larga vida **lose** *(1)* **her** / *(2)* **his** ~ perder *(1,2)* su vida **love** ~ vida amorosa **love of my** ~ amor de mi vida **make my** ~ **complete** llenar mi vida **married** ~ vida matrimonial **military**

~ vida militar **miserable** ~ vida miserable **my** ~ mi vida **new** ~ nueva vida **outlook on** ~ posición en la vida **part of my** ~ parte de mi vida **peaceful** ~ vida apacible **personal** ~ vida personal **put** *(1)* **my** / *(2)* **your** ~ **in order** poner *(1)* mi / *(2)* su *(Fam: tu)* vida en orden **satisfied with** ~ satisfecho *(-cha)* con la vida **sex** ~ vida sexual **share our lives together** compartir nuestras vidas en unión **single** ~ vida de soltero*(-ra)* **social** ~ vida social **solitary** ~ vida solitaria **spend (all)** *(1)* **my** / *(2)* **your** ~ pasar (toda) *(1)* mi / *(2)* su *(Fam. tu)* vida **start a new** ~ comenzar una nueva vida **void in my** ~ vacío en mi vida **your** ~ su *(Fam: tu)* vida **You have a(n)** *(1)* **busy** / *(2)* **interesting life**. *Usted tiene (Fam: Tú tienes)* una vida *(1)* ocupada / *(2)* interesante. **What is your ambition in life?** ¿Cuál es *su (Fam: tu)* ambición en la vida? **What do you want in life?** ¿Qué *quiere usted (Fam: quieres)* de la vida? *(1)* **I want to hear...** / *(2)* **Tell me... the story of your life.** *(1)* Quiero escuchar... / *(2) Cuénteme (Fam: Cuéntame)*… la historia de *su (Fam. tu)* vida. **I lead** *(1)* **...a rather quiet...** / *(2)* **...an ordinary... life**. Llevo una vida *(1)* ...bastante sosegada / *(2)* ...común y corriente. **I have a busy life**. Llevo una vida muy ocupada. **My social life is (not) very active.** Mi vida social (no) es muy activa. **I'm so happy that you're in my life.** Estoy muy feliz de tenerte en mi vida. **You have changed my life (forever).** Has cambiado mi vida (para siempre). **You make my life complete.** Tú llenas mi vida. **You brighten my life with your sweet smile and loving ways.** Tú iluminas mi vida con tu dulce sonrisa y tus modos cariñosos. **Where have you been all my life?** ¿Dónde has estado toda mi vida? **You fill my life with love.** Tú llenas mi vida de amor. **Life is** *(1)* **beautiful.** / *(2)* **short.** La vida es *(1)* bella. / *(2)* breve. **I believe in** *(1)* **enjoying life.** / *(2)* **taking life one day at a time.** Creo en *(1)* disfrutar la vida. / *(2)* tomar la vida día por día.

lifeguard *n* salvavidas *m* **Is there a lifeguard on duty?** ¿Hay algún salvavidas de turno?

lifestyle *n* estilo de vida *m* **active** ~ estilo de vida activo **casual** ~ estilo de vida informal **fun** ~ estilo de vida divertido **healthy** ~ estilo de vida saludable

lifetime *n* curso de la vida *f* **whole** ~ la vida entera

lift *vt* levantar ~ **weights** levantar pesas

light *adj* 1. *(not heavy)* ligero *m*, -ra *f*, liviano *m*, -na *f*; 2. *(delicate, slight)* leve *m&f*; 3. *(soft)* suave *m&f*

light *vt* encender ~ **up** iluminar **You light up my (whole) life.** Tú iluminas (toda) mi vida. **You have a smile that would light up a city.** *Su (Fam: Tu)* sonrisa podría iluminar una ciudad.

light *n* luz *f* **city** ~s luces de la ciudad **dim** ~s luces tenues **Turn out the**

Spanish "o" is pronounced like "o" in "note".

light. Apaga la luz.

lightheaded *adj* atolondrado *m*, -da *f*, aturdido *m*, -da *f*, mareado *m*, -da *f* **I feel a little lightheaded.** Me siento un poco aturdido *(-da)*.

lightly *adv* 1. *(slightly)* levemente, ligeramente; poco; 2. *(gently)* ligeramente, suavemente

lightning *n* rayo *m*, relámpago *m* **The first time I** *(1)* **saw /** *(2)* **kissed you, it was like being hit by lightning.** La primera vez que te *(1)* vi / *(2)* besé, fue como si me golpeara un rayo.

likable *adj* agradable *m&f*, simpático *m*, -ca *f*

like *vt* 1. *(be fond of)* gustar; 2. *(want)* querer **Do you like to** *(1)* **bike (***or* **go biking)? /** *(2)* **dance (***or* **go dancing)? /** *(3)* **go camping? /** *(4)* **go sightseeing? /** *(5)* **go for (long) walks? /** *(6)* **go on picnics? /** *(7)* **hike (***or* **go hiking)? /** *(8)* **iceskate (***or* **go ice-skating)? /** *(9)* **listen to music? /** *(10)* **play badminton? /** *(11)* **play baseball? /** *(12)* **play basketball? /** *(13)* **play board games? /** *(14)* **play cards? /** *(15)* **play football? /** *(16)* **play golf? /** *(17)* **play soccer? /** *(18)* **play tennis? /** *(19)* **play the guitar? /** *(20)* **play the piano? /** *(21)* **play volleyball? /** *(22)* **read? /** *(23)* **rollerblade (***or* **go rollerblading)? /** *(24)* **run? /** *(25)* **ski (***or* **go skiing)? /** *(26)* **swim (***or* **go swimming)? /** *(27)* **travel? /** *(28)* **watch ballet? /** *(29)* **watch movies? /** *(30)* **watch sports? /** *(31)* **watch videos? /** *(32)* **watch TV?** ¿Le *(Fam:* ¿*Te)* gusta *(1)* andar en bicicleta? / *(2)* ir a bailar? / *(3)* ir a acampar? / *(4)* ir de paseo? / *(5)* dar (largas) caminatas? / *(6)* ir de picnic? / *(7)* ir de caminata? / *(8)* patinar sobre hielo? / *(9)* escuchar música? / *(10)* jugar bádminton? / *(11)* jugar béisbol? / *(12)* jugar baloncesto? / *(13)* jugar juegos de mesa? / *(14)* jugar cartas? / *(15)* jugar fútbol americano? / *(16)* jugar golf? / *(17)* jugar fútbol soccer? / *(18)* jugar tenis? / *(19)* tocar guitarra? / *(20)* tocar piano? / *(21)* jugar voleibol? / *(22)* leer? / *(23)* patinar? / *(24)* correr? / *(25)* esquiar? / *(26)* nadar? / *(27)* viajar? / *(28)* ver ballet? / *(29)* ver películas? / *(30)* ver deportes? / *(31)* ver videos? / *(32)* ver televisión? **I (don't) like to...** *(See choices above)* A mí (no) me gusta... **Do you like** *(1)* **it? /** *(2)* **them?** ¿Le *(Fam:* ¿*Te)* *(1)* gusta / *(2)* gustan? **I (don't) like** *(1)* **it. /** *(2)* **them.** A mí (no) me *(1)* gusta / *(2)* gustan. **What would you like (for your birthday)?** ¿Que te gustaría para tu cumpleaños? **What kind of music do you like?** ¿Qué clase de música le*(Fam: te)* gusta? **I like** *(type of music)*. A mí me gusta ___. **I like your** *(1)* **blouse. /** *(2)* **dress. /** *(3)* **face. /** *(4)* **hair. /** *(5)* **outfit. /** *(6)* **personality.** *(7)* **shirt. /** *(8)* **smile. /** *(9)* **suit. /** *(10)* **sweater. /** *(11)* **tie.** Me gusta *su (Fam: tu)* *(1)* blusa. / *(2)* vestido. / *(3)* cara. / *(4)* pelo. / *(5)* atuendo. / *(6)* personalidad. / *(7)* camisa. / *(8)* sonrisa. / *(9)* traje. / *(10)* suéter. / *(11)* corbata. **I like your eyes.** Me gustan *sus (Fam: tus)* ojos. **I like you (a lot).** Me gustas (mucho). **I don't like you.**

Numbers in parentheses always signal choices.

No me gustas. **I like you, but I don't love you.** Me gustas, pero no te amo.

likely *adv* probable **It's likely to rain.** Es probable que llueva. **It's not likely.** No es probable.

like-minded *adj* del mismo parecer; de ideas afines

lilac *n* lila *f*

lily *n* lirio *m*, azucena *f*

limit *n* límite *m* **speed ~** límite de velocidad **Watch the speed limit.** Vigila el límite de velocidad. **That's off limits.** Eso está en zona prohibida.

limousine *n* limosina *f* **Where can** *(1)* **I /** *(2)* **we rent a limousine?** ¿Dónde *(1)* puedo / *(2)* podemos rentar una limosina?

line *n* 1. *(qeue)* fila *f*; 2. *(tel.)* línea *f*; 3. *(fishing)* sedal *m*; 4. *(area of work)* campo *m*; línea *f* **long ~** larga fila **We have to stand in line.** Tenemos que ponernos en fila. **We'd better get in line.** Será mejor que hagamos cola. **There's a long line (for tickets).** Hay una larga fila (para los boletos). **Excuse me, are you in line?** Disculpe, ¿está usted en la fila? **I'm (not) in line.** Yo (no) estoy en fila. **What is this line for?** ¿Para qué es esta fila? **This is the line for** *(what)*. Esta es la fila para ___. **The line is busy.** *(tel.)* La línea está ocupada. **What line of work are you in?** ¿Cuál es *su (Fam: tu)* línea de trabajo? **You're feeding me a line.** Me estás dando por mi lado.

linen *n* ropa *f* blanca **bed ~** ropa de cama

liner *n* *(ship)* trasatlántico *m* **cruise ~** crucero *m*

linger *vi* *(tarry)* quedarse, entretenerse **Let's just linger around here for a while.** Quedémonos por aquí un rato.

lingerie *n* lencería *f* **silk ~** lencería de seda

linguist *n* lingüista *m&f* **I'm not much of a linguist.** No soy muy buen(a) lingüista.

lip *n* labio *m* **read ~s** leer los labios **chapped ~s** labios partidos **full ~s** labios llenos **honey-sweet ~s** labios dulces como la miel **inviting ~s** labios incitantes **kissable ~s** labios besables **lower ~** labio inferior **magic(al) ~s** labios mágicos **perfect ~s** labios perfectos **pierced ~** labios perforados **red ~s** labios rojos **scarlet ~s** labios rojo escarlata **soft ~s** labios suaves **sweet ~s** labios dulces **tantalizing ~s** labios tentadores **tender ~s** labios tiernos **upper ~** labio superior **warm ~s** labios cálidos **Your lips are absolutely** *(1)* **fantastic. /** *(2)* **heavenly. /** *(3)* **incredible. /** *(4)* **wonderful.** Tus labios son absolutamente (1) fantásticos. / (2) divinos. / (3) increíbles. / (4) maravillosos. **You have such (soft,) beautiful (, kissable) lips.** Tienes unos labios tan (suaves,) hermosos (, besables). **You have perfect lips.** Tus labios son perfectos. **You have lips that were made for kissing.** Tus

---

Spanish "a" is mostly like "a" in "mama".

labios fueron hechos para besar. **Your lips look so** *(1)* **inviting.** / *(2)* **soft.** / *(3)* **sweet.** / *(4)* **tempting.** Tus labios se ven tan *(1)* atrayentes. / *(2)* suaves. / *(3)* dulces. / *(4)* tentadores. **I love the sweet taste of your lips.** Me encanta el dulce sabor de tus labios. **I'm a lip reader and I love reading yours.** Yo sé leer los labios y me encanta leer los tuyos. **My lips are sealed.** Mis labios están sellados.

lipstick *n* lápiz *m* labial *m*

liquid *n* líquido *m* **How about some liquid refreshments?** ¿Qué tal si nos refrescamos con un líquido?

liquor *n* licor *m* **hard ~** licor *m* fuerte **No hard liquor for me, please.** Nada de licor fuerte para mí, por favor.

lissome *adj* grácil *m&f*

list *n* lista *f* **waiting ~** lista de espera **I'll put our names on the waiting list.** Voy a poner nuestros nombres en la lista de espera. *(1)* **I'm** / *(2)* **We're on the waiting list.** *(1)* Estoy / *(2)* Estamos en la lista de espera. **You'd better put your** *(1)* **name** / *(2)* **names on the waiting list.** Será mejor que *(1)* ...pongas tu nombre... / *(2)* ...pongan sus nombres... en la lista de espera. **You're on my black list.** Estás en mi lista negra.

listen *vi* escuchar *(See also phrases under* **go,** **like** *and* **love***.)* **Listen to** *(1)* **me.** / *(2)* **this.** *(1)* Escúchame. / *(2)* Escucha esto. **Are you listening (to me)?** ¿Me estás escuchando? **I'm listening.** Estoy escuchando. **I'm sorry, I wasn't listening.** Lo siento, no estaba escuchando. **Have you ever listened to** *(kind of music)***?** ¿Alguna vez *ha escuchado usted (Fam: has escuchado)* a ___? **What kind of music do you like to listen to?** ¿Qué tipo de música *le (Fam: te)* gusta escuchar? **I love listening to** *(1)* **music.** / *(2)* **your stories.** Me encanta escuchar *(1)* música. / *(2)* tus cuentos.

listener *n* oyente *m&f* **I'm a good listener.** Yo soy buen(a) oyente.

liter *n* *(= 1.06 qts)* litro *m*

literally *adv* literalmente **Do you mean that literally?** ¿Eso lo *dice (Fam: dices)* literalmente? **I (don't) mean it literally.** (No) lo digo literalmente.

literary *adj* literario *m,* -ria *f*

literature *n* literatura *f*

little *adj* 1. *(small size)* pequeño *m,* -ña *f*; 2. *(small amount)* poco *m,* -ca *f* **~ chance** poca oportunidad **~ hope** poca esperanza **~ person** personita **~ time** poco tiempo

little *adv* poco

little *n* poco *m* **a ~ (bit)** un poco **~ by ~** poco a poco **I'm a little (bit) disappointed.** Estoy un poco decepcionado *(-da)*.

live *vi* vivir **~ a boring life** llevar una vida aburrida **~ a carefree life** llevar una vida despreocupada **~ alone** vivir a solas **~ a lonely life** llevar una

---

Articles: m = el,　f = la,　mpl = los,　fpl = las

vida solitaria ~ **a long time** vivir mucho tiempo ~ **and let** ~ vivir y dejar vivir ~ **an interesting life** llevar una vida interesante ~ **a solitary life** llevar una vida solitaria ~ **comfortably** vivir con comodidad ~ **happily ever after** vivir feliz por siempre ~ **in harmony** vivir en armonía ~ **it up** darse la gran vida, darse gusto ~ **like a monk** vivir como un monje ~ **on a pension** vivir de una pensión ~ **on my salary** vivir de mi salario ~ **quietly** llevar una vida tranquila ~ **simply** llevar una vida sencilla ~ **together (with** *[1]* **me /** *[2]* **you)** vivir en unión (*[1]* conmigo / *[2]* contigo) **Where do you live?** ¿En dónde *vive usted (Fam: vives)*? *(1)* **I /** *(2)* **We live in** *(city).* *(1)* Vivo / *(2)* Vivimos en ___. *(1)* **I /** *(2)* **We used to live in** *(city).* *(1)* Solía / *(2)* Solíamos vivir en ___. **How far away (from here) do you live?** ¿Qué tan lejos *vive (Fam: vives)* (de aquí)? **Do you live alone or with your parents?** ¿*Vive usted (Fam: ¿Vives)* solo *(-la)* o con *sus (Fam. tus)* padres? **I live** *(1)* **alone. /** *(2)* **with my** *(3)* **children. /** *(4)* **daughter. /** *(5)* **son. /** *(6)* **parents. /** *(7)* **father. /** *(8)* **mother.** Vivo *(1)* solo *(-la).* / *(2)* con mi(s) *(3)* hijos. / *(4)* hija. / *(5)* hijo. / *(6)* padres. / *(7)* padre. / *(8)* madre. **Does** *(name)* **live here?** ¿Vive aquí___? **I'd like to live here (with you).** Me gustaría vivir aquí (contigo). **You've given me something to live for.** Tú me has dado motivos para vivir. **I believe two people should try to live in balance.** Creo que dos personas deben procurar vivir en equilibrio. **You only live once.** Sólo se vive una vez.

livelihood *n* subsistencia *f,* medios *mpl* de vida

lively *adj* animado *m* –da *f,* vivaz *m&f,* vivaracho *m,* -cha *f,* alegre *m&f* **We certainly had a lively time.** Sin duda pasamos un rato alegre. **You're a lively little** *(1)* **devil. /** *(2)* **imp. /** *(3)* **soul.** Tú eres un pequeño *(-ña)* *(1)* diablo vivaracho. / *(2)* travieso vivaracho. / *(3)* alma vivaracha.

liven (up) *vt* animar **You liven up any occasion.** Tú animas toda ocasión.

living *n* vida *f* **earn a** ~ ganarse la vida **standard of** ~ estándar de vida **way of** ~ modo de vida **You exude a genuine joy for living.** *Usted irradia (Fam: Tú irradias)* una genuina alegría de vivir.

lizard *n* lagarto *m* **wall** ~ lagartija *f*

load *n* carga *f* ~**s of time** mucho tiempo **That's quite a load you have there. Can I help you** *(1,2)* **carry it?** *Tiene usted (Fam: Tienes)* allí bastante que cargar. ¿Puedo *(1)* ayudarlo *m* / *(2)* ayudarla *f (Fam. ayudarte)* a llevarlo? **No hurry. We have loads of time.** No hay prisa. Tenemos mucho tiempo.

loaded *adj (slang) (drunk)* borracho *m,* -cha *f,* cuete *m & f (Mex. slang)* **get** ~ emborracharse, ponerse cuete

loaf *vi* holgazanear, flojear **Let's just loaf around (today).** Vamos nomás a flojear (hoy). **I seldom loaf (around).** Pocas veces flojeo.

loan *vt (See* **lend***)* prestar

Spanish "z" is pronounced like "s" in "safe".

loan *n* préstamo *m*

lobby *n* sala *f* de espera, vestíbulo *m* **hotel ~** vestíbulo del hotel

lobe *n* lóbulo *m* **ear ~s** lóbulos de la oreja

lobster *n* langosta *f*

local *adj* local *m&f* **~ call** *(tel.)* llamada local **~ dialect** dialecto local **~ time** hora local

locale *n* localidad *f,* escenario *m*

locate *vt* localizar *(1)* **I'm /** *(2)* **We're trying to locate** *(place)*. *(1)* Estoy / *(2)* Estamos tratando de localizar ____.

location *n* sitio *m* **What a** *(1)* **beautiful /** *(2)* **nice location!** ¡Qué sitio tan *(1)* hermoso! / *(2)* bonito! **This is going to be the location of my next movie.** Este va a ser el sitio de mi próxima película.

lock *vt* cerrar con llave **Lock the door.** Cierra la puerta con llave. **Don't lock the door.** No cierres la puerta con llave. **Did you lock it?** ¿Lo *cerró usted (Fam: cerraste)* con llave? **I (didn't) lock(ed) it**. Yo (no) lo cerré con llave.

lock *n* 1. *(doors, etc)* cerradura *f*; 2. *(hair)* mechón *m* **I'd love to have a lock of your hair to carry around with me.** Me encantaría tener un mechón de tu cabello para llevarlo conmigo.

locket *n* relicario *m* ; guardapelo *m*

lodge *n* hotel *m*; posada *f* **There's a nice lodge we can stay in.** Hay un hotel bonito donde podemos quedarnos.

log *n* leño *m* **I slept like a log.** Dormí como un leño.

logic *n* lógica *f* **fuzzy ~** lógica enredada **That's (absolutely) marvelous logic.** Esa es una lógica (absolutamente) maravillosa. **Logic would tell you that...** La lógica les diría que... **Let's not get confused by logic.** No nos confundamos con la lógica.

logical *adj* lógico *m*, -ca *f* **The logical thing to do would be...** Lo lógico sería que hiciéramos...

loneliness *n* soledad *f* **terrible ~** soledad terrible **unbearable ~** soledad insoportable **I've had an awful lot of loneliness in my life.** He pasado una soledad tremenda en mi vida. **You've banished all my loneliness.** Tú has desvanecido toda mi soledad. **I want to make you forget your loneliness of the past.** Quiero hacerte olvidar la soledad que has pasado.

lonely *adj (solitary)* solitario *m*, -ria *f*; *(lonesome)* solo *m*, -la *f*; *(sad)* triste *m&f* **feel** *(1,2)* **~** sentirse *(1)* solo *(-la)* / *(2)* triste **lead a** *(1,2)* **~ life** llevar una vida *(1)* solitaria / *(2)* triste **I get (a little)** *(1,2)* **lonely sometimes.** A veces me siento (un poco) *(1)* solo *(-la)*. / *(2)* triste. **I'll be (very) lonely without you.** Estaré (muy) *(1)* solo *(-la)* / *(2)* triste sin ti. **Before I met you, I was always (terribly)** *(1,2)* **lonely.** Antes de conocerte, siempre

---

A tilde ~ in terms stands for the main entry word.

estuve (tremendamente) *(1)* solo *(-la)*. / *(2)* triste. **I'm going to be with you all the time and you'll never be** *(1,2)* **lonely again.** Voy a estar contigo todo el tiempo y nunca más volverás a sentirte *(1)* solo *(-la)*. / *(2)* triste.

lonesome *adj* solo *m*, -la *f*, triste *m&f*

long *adj* 1. *(length, distance)* largo *m*, –ga *f*; 2. *(time)* largo *m*, –ga *f* **as ~ as** 1. *(for as much time)* mientras que, en tanto que; 2. *(inasmuch as)* puesto que; 3. *(provided that)* siempre y cuando ~ *(1,2)* **time** largo *(1)* rato / *(2)* tiempo ~ **trip** viaje *m* largo ~ **walk** caminata *f* larga ~ **way** camino *m* largo *(1)* **I** / *(2)* **We waited a long time for** *(3,4)* **you.** *(3)* Lo *m* / *(4)* La *f (Fam: Te)* *(1)* esperé / *(2)* esperamos largo rato. **It's a rather long way (from here).** Es un camino algo largo (desde aquí). **I like to take long walks.** Me gusta dar largas caminatas. **Let's take a long walk together.** Vayamos a dar una larga caminata. **So long!** ¡Hasta luego!

long *adv* mucho tiempo **How long will you stay here?** ¿Cuánto tiempo te vas a quedar aquí? **Will you be staying long?** ¿Se va *(Fam: ¿Te vas)* a quedar mucho tiempo? *(1)* **I** / *(2)* **We won't be staying for long.** No *(1)* me voy / *(2)* nos vamos a quedar mucho tiempo. **How long will it take (to get there)?** ¿Cuánto tiempo nos tomará (llegar allá)? **It won't take long.** No tomará mucho tiempo. **Did you wait long?** ¿Esperó usted *(Fam: ¿Esperaste)* mucho?

long *vi* estar deseando ~ **to see** estar deseando ver

★ **long for** *idiom* añorar, anhelar

longing *n* anhelo *m*, deseo *m* **I have such an intense longing for you.** Tengo un anhelo tan intenso por ti.

long-winded *adj* denso *m*, -sa *f*, prolijo *m*, -ja *f*, interminable *m&f*

look *vi* 1. *(use vision)* mirar, ver; 2. *(appear, seem)* verse ~ **around** mirar ~ **like** parecerse **Look (at** *[1]* **that /** *[2]* **this)!** ¡Mira (*[1]* eso / *[2]* esto)! **Let's go look around the** *(1)* **market. /** *(2)* **town. /** *(3)* **waterfront.** Vamos a ver (1) el mercado. / (2) el pueblo. / (3) los muelles. **Let's go out (tonight) and look at the stars together.** Salgamos juntos (esta noche) y miremos las estrellas. **I love to look at you.** Me encanta mirarte. **When you look at me, I forget everything else in the world.** Cuando me miras, me olvido de todo lo demás en el mundo. **I like the way you look at me.** Me gusta tu modo de mirarme. **It looks like a (real) nice day, doesn't it?** Parece un día (de veras) bonito. ¿Verdad? **You look** *(1)* **beautiful. /** *(2)* **fantastic. /** *(3)* **gorgeous. /** *(4)* **great. /** *(5)* **terrific.** Usted se ve *(Fam: Te ves)* *(1)* hermosa. / *(2)* fantástica. / *(3)* despampanante. / *(4)* fenomenal. / *(5)* sensacional. **You look** *(1)* **sad. /** *(2)* **unhappy. What's the matter?** Se ve usted *(Fam: Te ves)* *(1)* triste. / *(2)* desdichado *(-da)*. ¿Qué pasa?

---

*Spanish "ch" is pronounced like ours
(e.g., "cheese," "charge").*

★ **look after** *idiom* cuidar **Who looks after your** *(1)* **children** / *(2)* **daughter** / *(3)* **son (while you're at work)?** ¿Quién cuida a *(1) sus (Fam: tus)* hijos / *(2) su (Fam: tu)* hija / *(3) su (Fam: tu)* hijo (mientras *usted está [Fam: estás]* en el trabajo)?

★ **look for** *idiom* buscar **What are you looking for?** ¿Qué *está usted (Fam: estás)* buscando? **I'm looking for** *(1)* **my ticket.** / *(2) (thing)*. Estoy buscando *(1)* mi boleto. / *(2)* ___. **Who are you looking for? (Me, I hope.)** ¿A quién *busca usted (Fam: buscas tú)*? (A mí, espero). **I've been looking for you all my life.** He estado buscándote toda mi vida.

★ **look forward** to *idiom* esperar, tener deseos de *(1)* **I** / *(2)* **We look forward to** *(3,4)* **seeing you again.** *(1)* Espero / *(2)* Esperamos *(3) verlo m* / *(4) verla f (Fam: verte)* de nuevo.

★ **look out** *idiom (be alert)* cuidado **Look out!** ¡Cuidado!

★ **look up** *idiom (find in a dictionary)* buscar

look *n* 1. *(glance)* mirada *f*; 2. *pl (appearance)* apariencia *f*; 3. *(expression)* expresión *f* **have a** ~ mirar; dar un vistazo **take a** ~ mirar, dar un vistazo **Can I take a look (at it)?** ¿Puedo mirar(lo)? **Here, have a look.** Ven, mira. **A good heart means more to me than good looks.** Para mí un buen corazón significa más que la buena apariencia. **You have a puzzled look on your face. Why?** Se te ve una expresión de desconcierto. ¿Por qué?

loony *adj (slang)* lunático *m*, -ca *f*, chiflado *m*, -da *f*

loopy *adj (slang: goofy, kind of crazy)* chiflado *m*, -da *f*, deschavetado *m*, -da *f*

loose *adj* 1. *(not tight)* suelto *m*, -ta *f*, flojo *m*, -ja *f*; 2. *(loose-fitting)* amplio *m*, -plia *f*, holgado *m*, -da *f*, flojo *m*, -ja *f*; 3. *(not securely in place)* flojo *m*, -ja *f*, suelto *m*, -ta *f*; 4. *(dissolute)* libertino *m*, -na *f*, disoluto *m*, -ta *f* ~ **morals** moral *f* licenciosa ~ **tooth** diente flojo *(1,2)* ~ **translation** traducción *(1)* aproximada / *(2)* libre **Your pack straps are too loose.** Las cintas de tu mochila están demasiado flojas. **The button on your coat is loose.** El botón de tu abrigo está por caerse. **I'm** *(1,2)* **at loose ends.** Estoy sin *(1)* derrotero. / *(2)* rumbo.

loose *adv (free, unrestrained)* libre; *(off, untied)* suelto **come** ~ desprenderse, soltarse **get** ~ soltarse **let** ~ soltar *(1)* **My** / *(2)* **Our** / *(3)* **Somebody's dog got loose.** *(1)* Mi perro... / *(2)* Nuestro perro... / *(3)* El perro de alguien... se soltó. **The thing came loose.** Esa cosa se desprendió. **This** *(1)* **button** / *(2)* **stake is coming loose.** Este *(1)* botón / *(2)* palo está por caerse. **I don't want to let you loose.** No quiero soltarte.

loosen *vt* aflojar **Can you loosen this for me?** ¿Puedes aflojarme esto?

loosen up *vi (slang: relax)* relajarse **You need to loosen up a bit.** Necesitas

---

Stress rule #1: The last syllable is stressed if the word ends in a consonant (except "n" and "s").

relajarte un poco.

lopsided *adj* desigual *m&f* ~ **score** puntuación muy desigual

loquacious *adj* locuaz *m&f* **Forgive me for being so loquacious.** Perdóname por ser tan locuaz.

lord *n* señor *m* **Good Lord!** ¡Dios mío!, ¡Dios bendito! **Lord, have mercy!** ¡Señor, ten misericordia!

lose *vt* perder, extraviar **What did you lose?** ¿Qué *perdió usted (Fam: perdiste)*? **I lost** *(1)* **my ticket.** / *(2)* *(thing)*. Perdí *(1)* mi boleto. / *(2)* ___. **I'm afraid I've lost my way.** Me temo que me extravié. **We seem to have lost our way.** Parece que nos extraviamos. **I hope you won't lose patience with me. (I'm a slow learner.)** Espero que no *pierda usted (Fam: pierdas)* la paciencia conmigo. (Soy lento *(-ta)* para aprender.) **I'm sorry I lost my temper.** Lamento haber perdido los estribos. **I don't ever want to lose you.** No quiero perderte nunca. **Have you lost your mind?** ¿Has perdido la cabeza? **I lost my** *(1)* **husband /** *(2)* **wife** *(3)* **last year. /** *(4)* **in** *(year)*. Perdí a mi *(1)* esposo / *(2)* esposa *(3)* el año pasado. / *(4)* en ___. *(1)* **I /** *(2)* **We /** *(3)* **They /** *(4)* **You lost.** *(games)* *(1)* Yo perdí. / *(2)* Nosotros perdimos. / *(3)* Ellos perdieron. / *(4)* *Usted perdió (Fam: Tú perdiste)*. **How much (money) did you lose?** *(gambling)* ¿Cuánto (dinero) perdió *usted (Fam: perdiste)*?

loser *n* perdedor *m*, -dora *f* **The loser has to buy** *(1)* **dinner /** *(2)* **drinks /** *(3)* **ice cream for everyone.** Quien pierda tiene que pagar *(1)* la cena / *(2)* las bebidas / *(3)* helados para todos.

loss *n* pérdida *f* **That makes three wins and two losses for us.** Eso es tres ganados y dos pérdidas para nosotros. **It was a great loss for** *(1)* **me. /** *(2)* **us.** Fue una gran pérdida para *(1)* mí. / *(2)* nosotros. **I'm at a loss for words.** Me faltan las palabras.

lost *adj* perdido *m*, -da *f* **be** ~ estar perdido *(-da)* **get** ~ perderse *(1)* **I'm /** *(2)* **We're lost.** *(1)* Estoy perdido *(-da)*. / *(2)* Estamos perdidos *(-das)*. **I'm sorry** *(1)* **I'm /** *(2)* **we're late.** *(3)* **I /** *(4)* **We got lost.** *(1)* Lamento / *(2)* Lamentamos llegar tarde. / *(3)* Me perdí. / *(4)* Nos perdimos. **I'd be lost without you.** Estaría perdido *(-da)* sin ti. **I want to make up for lost time.** Quiero compensar el tiempo perdido.

lot *n* 1. *(much)* mucho *m*, -cha *f*; *(many)* muchos *m pl*, -chas *fpl*; 2. *(plot of land)* lote *m* **a** ~ un montón *m (colloq.)*, mucho *(-cha)*; muchos *(-chas)* ~**s of** montones *mpl* de, mucho *(-cha)*; muchos *(-chas)* **parking** ~ estacionamiento **We have** *(1)* **a lot /** *(2)* **lots of time.** Tenemos *(1)* un montón *(2)* montones de tiempo. **I want to give you** *(1)* **a lot /** *(2)* **lots of love.** Quiero darte *(1,2)* mucho amor. **There are lots of reasons.** Hay muchas razones.

Spanish "i" is mostly "ee", but can also be shorter, like "i" in "sit," when together with other vowels.

lotion *n* loción *f* **suntan ~** loción bronceadora **Let me spread the lotion on your back.** Déjame untarte loción en la espalda.

lottery *n* lotería *f* **~ ticket** billete *m* de lotería **I feel like someone who has just won the world's biggest lottery.** Me siento como si me acabara de ganar la lotería más grande del mundo.

loud *adj* fuerte *m&f*, alto *m*, -ta *f*; *(shrill)* estridente *m&f* **~ music** música estridente **Please, not so loud.** Por favor, no tan fuerte. **I'm not a fan of loud music.** No soy fanático de la música estridente. **Is that too loud for you?** ¿Eso es demasiado fuerte para *usted (Fam: ti?)*? **It's (not) too loud.** (No) Es demasiado fuerte. **Could you please speak louder?** ¿Por favor, *podría usted (Fam: podrías)* hablar en voz más alta?

loudly *adv* fuerte; *(in high voice)* en voz alta

lounge *vi* haraganear, flojear *(1)* **I'm /** *(2)* **We're just going to lounge around (today).** (Hoy) Solamente *(1)* voy / *(2)* vamos a haraganear. **Let's just lounge around for a while.** Vamos haraganeando un rato. **Oh, it's wonderful to lounge around with you like this.** Oh, es maravilloso haraganear así contigo.

lounge *n* salón *m* **Let's have a drink in the lounge.** Vamos a tomarnos una copa en el salón.

lousy *adj (terrible)* malo *m*, -la *f*, malísimo *m*, -ma *f*, pésimo *m*, -ma *f*; asqueroso *m*, -sa *f* **What a lousy break.** Qué mala pata *(Fam)*. **What lousy weather.** Qué pésimo clima.

lovable *adj* adorable *m&f* **What a sweet, lovable person you are.** Qué persona tan dulce y adorable eres.

love *vt* querer, amar; *(like)* gustar **I love to** *(1)* **bike** (*or* **go biking**). / *(2)* **dance** (*or* **go dancing**). / *(3)* **go camping.** / *(4)* **go sightseeing.** / *(5)* **go for (long) walks.** / *(6)* **go on picnics.** / *(7)* **hike** (*or* **go hiking**). / *(8)* **ice-skate** (*or* **go ice-skating**). / *(9)* **listen to music.** / *(10)* **play badminton.** /*(11)* **play baseball.** / *(12)* **play basketball.** / *(13)* **play board games.** / *(14)* **play cards.** / *(15)* **play football.** / *(16)* **play golf.** / *(17)* **play soccer.** / *(18)* **play tennis.** / *(19)* **play the guitar.** / *(20)* **play the piano.** / *(21)* **play volleyball.** / *(22)* **read.** /*(23)* **rollerblade** (*or* **go rollerblading**). / *(24)* **run.** / *(25)* **ski** (*or* **go skiing**). / *(26)* **swim** (*or* **go swimming**). / *(27)* **travel.** / *(28)* **watch ballet.** / *(29)* **watch movies.** / *(30)* **watch sports.** / *(31)* **watch videos.** / *(32)* **watch TV.** Me encanta *(1)* andar en bicicleta. / *(2)* bailar. / *(3)* acampar. / *(4)* ir de paseo. / *(5)* ir a caminar. / *(6)* ir de picnic. / *(7)* ir de caminata. / *(8)* patinar sobre hielo. / *(9)* escuchar música. / *(10)* jugar bádminton. / *(11)* jugar béisbol. / *(12)* jugar baloncesto. / *(13)* jugar juegos de mesa. /*(14)* jugar a las cartas. / *(15)* jugar fútbol americano. / *(16)* jugar golf. / *(17)* jugar fútbol soccer. / *(18)* jugar tenis. / *(19)* tocar

Help us improve our book!
Send us the feedback form on page 431.

guitarra. / *(20)* tocar piano. / *(21)* jugar voleibol. / *(22)* leer. / *(23)* patinar. / *(24)* correr. / *(25)* esquiar. / *(26)* nadar. / *(27)* viajar. / *(28)* ver el ballet. / *(29)* ver películas. / *(30)* ver deportes. / *(31)* ver videos. / *(32)* ver televisión. **I'd love to** *(1)* **get together with you again.** / *(2)* **go (with you).** / *(3)* **have dinner with you.** / *(4)* **see you again** Me gustaría *(1)* volver contigo otra vez. / *(2)* ir (contigo). / *(3)* cenar contigo. / *(4)* verte otra vez. **I love you (very much).** Te amo (mucho). **I love you with all my heart.** Te amo con todo mi corazón. **I love everything about you.** Amo todo lo tuyo. **I will do everything to prove that I love you.** Yo haré todo para probar que te amo.

love *n* amor *m* **be in** ~ estar enamorado *(-da)* **fall in** ~ enamorarse **make** ~ hacer el amor **I'm in love with you.** Yo estoy enamorado *(-da)* de ti. **I think I'm falling in love with you.** Yo creo que me estoy enamorando de ti. **I'm head over heels in love with you.** Me traes loco *(-ca)* de amor. **I want (so much) to make love with you.** Tengo (muchas) ganas de hacer el amor contigo.

lovebirds *n, pl* tórtolos *mpl*, enamorados *mpl*

lovebite *n* mordisco *m* de amor

lovefest *n* festín *m* de amor

love-kitten *n* gatito *m*, -ta *f*, amoroso *m*, -sa *f*

loveliness *n* hermosura *f*, belleza *f* **breathtaking** ~ belleza pasmosa **essence of** ~ esencia *f* de la belleza **exquisite** ~ belleza exquisita **radiant** ~ belleza radiante **You have a loveliness that time can never diminish.** *Tiene usted (Fam: Tú tienes)* una belleza que el tiempo no puede marchitar. **You are the epitome of loveliness.** *Es usted (Fam: Eres)* el epítome de la belleza. **Your face is a paragon of loveliness.** Tu cara es un modelo de belleza. **I'm completely captivated by your (vivacity and) loveliness.** Estoy totalmente cautivado por *su (Fam: tu)* (vivacidad y por *su [Fam: tu]*) belleza.

lovely *adj* bello *m*, -lla *f*, hermoso *m*, -sa *f*, precioso *m*, -sa *f* **absolutely** ~ absolutamente bella **exceptionally** ~ excepcionalmente bella **indescribably** ~ indescriptiblemente bella ~ **beyond words** bella más allá de las palabras **very** ~ muy bella **That's a lovely** *(1)* **blouse.** / *(2)* **skirt.** Es una *(1)* blusa / *(2)* falda hermosa. **That's a lovely** *(1)* **coat.** / *(2)* **dress.** / *(3)* **jacket.** / *(4)* **sweater.** Es un *(1)* vestido / *(2)* abrigo / *(3)* saco / *(4)* suéter hermoso. **You are incredibly lovely.** Eres increíblemente bella. **I can't believe how lovely you are.** No puedo creer lo bella que eres.

lovemaking *n* cópula *f*, relaciones sexuales *fpl*

lover *n* 1. *(partner in love)* amante *m&f*; 2. *(enthusiast)* amante *m&f* **beach** ~ amante de la playa **book** ~ amante de los libros **cat** ~ amante de los gatos

---

Spanish "j" is pronounced like "h".

dog ~ amante de los perros **fantastic** ~ amante fantástico *(-ca)* **former** ~ ex-amante **horse** ~ amante de los caballos **ideal** ~ amante ideal **imaginative** ~ amante imaginativo *(-va)* **incredible** ~ amante increíble **innovative** ~ amante con inventiva **music** ~ amante de la música **nature** ~ amante de la naturaleza **outdoor(s)** ~ amante del aire libre **sun** ~ amante del sol **terrific** ~ amante tremendo *(-da)* **travel** ~ amante de los viajes **wonderful** ~ amante maravilloso *(sa)* **You're the most wonderful lover anyone ever had**. Tú eres el *(la)* amante más maravilloso *(-sa)* que nadie haya tenido. **You're the lover of my dreams.** Tú eres el *(la)* amante de mis sueños. **I want you to be my wife, my friend and my lover.** Quiero que seas mi esposa, mi amiga y mi amante.

love-sick *adj* enfermo *(-ma)* de amor, perdidamente enamorado *(-da)*

lovey-dovey *adj (slang)* excesivamente amoroso *(-sa)*, encimoso *m*, -sa *f*

loving *adj* encantador *m*, -dora *f* **You're the most loving woman I've ever met.** Tú eres la mujer más encantadora que he conocido. **You're the most loving man I've ever met.** Tú eres el hombre más encantador que he conocido.

loving *n* amar *f* **You were made for loving.** Tú fuiste hecha para el amor.

lovingly *adv* amorosamente, afectuosamente, cariñosamente

low *adj* bajo *m*, -ja *f* ~ **prices** precios *mpl* bajos ~ **salary** salario *m* bajo ~ **score** un marcador *m* bajo ~ **tide** marea *f* baja

low *adv* abajo, debajo **Could you turn it low? Thanks.** ¿Podrías ponerlo más bajo? Gracias. **We're getting low on gas.** Se nos está acabando la gasolina.

lower *adj* inferior *m&f (1,2)* ~ **berth** litera *f* *(1)* inferior / *(2)* baja ~ **deck** cubierta *f* inferior

low-fat *adj* bajo *m*, -ja *f* en grasa

low-paying *adj* de poca paga ~ **job** trabajo de poca paga

loyal *adj* leal *m&f*

loyalty *n* lealtad *f* **Loyalty is what really counts in a relationship.** En una relación lo que de veras cuenta es la lealtad.

lubricate *vt* lubricar **The car needs to be lubricated.** El carro necesita lubricación.

luck *n* suerte *f* **bad** ~ mala suerte **bum** ~ perra suerte **fantastic** ~ suerte fantástica **good** ~ buena suerte **incredible** ~ suerte increíble **lousy** ~ pinche suerte **Good luck!** ¡Buena suerte! **I wish you** *(1)* **(lots of) luck.** / *(2)* **all the luck in the world.** Te deseo *(1)* (mucha) suerte. / *(2)* toda la suerte del mundo. **What tremendous good luck it was to meet you.** Qué suerte tan tremenda haberte conocido. **Talk about luck! Wow!** ¡Hablando de suerte! ¡Guau! **Don't push your luck.** No fuerces la suerte.

Familiar "tu" forms in parentheses can replace italicized polite forms.

luckily *adv* afortunadamente; por suerte; por fortuna

lucky *adj* afortunado *m*, -da *f* ; *(Fam)* suertero *m*, -ra *f* **incredibly ~** increíblemente afortunado *(-da)* **~ dog** perro suertero **unbelievably ~** increíblemente afortunado *(-da)* **You're the luckiest person I ever saw.** Tú eres la persona más afortunada que yo he visto. **I can't believe how lucky you are.** No puedo creer lo afortunado *(-da)* que eres. **How lucky can you get?** Más suerte, ya no se puede. **I'm so lucky to have found you (in this world).** Soy tan afortunado *(-da)* por haberte encontrado (en este mundo).

ludicrous *adj* ridículo *m*, -la *f*, absurdo *m*, -da *f*

luggage *n* equipaje *m* **Can I help you with your luggage?** ¿Puedo *(1) ayudarlo m / (2) ayudarla f (Fam: ayudarte)* con *su (Fam: tu)* equipaje? **Is this your luggage?** ¿Es este *su (Fam: tu)* equipaje? **Where's your luggage?** ¿En dónde está *su (Fam: tu)* equipaje? *(1)* **My /** *(2)* **Our luggage is** *(3)* **over there. /** *(4)* **in the** *(place / vehicle).* *(1)* Mi / *(2)* Nuestro equipaje está *(3)* allá. / *(4)* en ___. *(1)* **I /** *(2)* **We have to get** *(3)* **my /** *(4)* **our luggage.** *(1)* Tengo / *(2)* Tenemos que recoger *(3)* mi / *(4)* nuestro equipaje.

lunatic *n* lunático *m*, -ca *f*, loco *m*, -ca *f*

lunch *n* comida *f* **Would you like to have lunch (with** *[1]* **me /** *[2]* **us)?** ¿*Le (Fam: ¿Te)* gustaría comer (*[1]* conmigo / *[2]* con nosotros)? **Let's go have lunch (together).** Vamos a comer (juntos).

lure *vt* seducir, atraer **You have my permission to lure me anywhere.** Tienes mi permiso para seducirme donde sea.

lure *n (fishing)* cebo *m* artificial, señuelo *m*

luxurious *adj* lujoso *m*, -sa *f*, de lujo

luxury *n* lujo *m* **This is pure luxury.** Esto es puro lujo.

lyrics *n, pl* letra *f* **Teach** *(1)* **me /** *(2)* **us the lyrics.** *(1)* Enséñame / *(2)* Enséñanos la letra.

Spanish "e" is pronounced like English "e" in "get"

M

MA *abbrev* = **Master of Arts degree** grado de maestría en artes o en humanidades.

machine *n* máquina *f* **coke** ~ máquina expendedora de coca cola **ice** ~ máquina para hacer hielo **vending** ~ máquina expendedora **washing** ~ lavadora

macho *adj* macho *m*, -cha *f*

mad *adj* 1. *(crazy)* loco *m*, -ca *f*; 2. *(angry)* enojado *m*, -da *f* **be** ~ 1. *(crazy)* estar loco *m*, -ca *f*; 2. *(angry)* estar furioso *m*, -sa *f* **be** ~ **about** *(infatuated)* estar encaprichado *(-da)* con **get** ~ *(angry)* enojarse **Are you mad (at me)?** ¿Está usted *(Fam: ¿Estás)* enojado *(-da)* conmigo? **I'm (not) mad (at you).** (No) Estoy enojado *(-da)* (contigo). **I'm mad about you.** Estoy loco *(-ca)* por ti.

madly *adv* locamente, con locura, a lo loco **I'm madly in love with you.** Estoy locamente enamorado *(-da)* de ti.

madman *n* loco *m*, demente *m*, lunático *m*

madness *n* locura *f* **absolute** ~ locura total **sheer** ~ locura pura **This is (sheer) madness.** Esta es (pura) locura. **Some kind of madness came over me.** Me vino una especie de locura.

madwoman *n* loca *f*, demente *f*, lunática *f*

magazine *n* revista *f* **Could I take a look at your magazine?** ¿Puedo darle un vistazo a *su (Fam: tu)* revista? **Didn't I see (1,2) you on the cover of a magazine?** ¿No (1) lo *m* / (2) la *f* (Fam: te) he visto en la portada de una revista?

magic *n* magia *f* **heavenly** ~ magia celestial ~ **of your kisses** la magia de tus besos ~ **tricks** trucos de magia **natural** ~ magia natural **pure** ~ magia pura **soft** ~ magia suave **warm** ~ cálida magia **Let me show you some magic tricks.** *Déjeme enseñarle (Fam: Déjame enseñarte)* unos trucos de magia. **There's such magic in your smile.** Hay tal magia en *su (Fam: tu)* sonrisa. **The sweet magic of your kisses captivates my soul.** La dulce

---

Stress rule # 2: The next-to-last syllable is stress in words ending in "n", "s" or a vowel.

magia de tus besos me cautiva el alma. **Sometimes magic happens.** A veces la magia ocurre.

magic(al) *adj* mágico *m*, -ca *f* ~ **spell** hechizo *m*; encantamiento *m* ~ **wand** varita *f* mágica **You've cast a magical spell over me.** Me has hechizado. **What a magical night this is.** Qué noche tan mágica es esta. **You have a magical touch.** Tienes un toque mágico.

magician *n* mago *m*, -ga *f* **You're quite a magician.** *Usted es (Fam. Tú eres)* todo *(-da)* un*(a)* mago *(-ga)*.

magnet *n* imán *m*

magnetic *adj* magnético *m*, -ca *f* **You have such a magnetic attraction for me.** Ejerces tal atracción magnética sobre mí.

magnetism *n* magnetismo *m* **animal** ~ magnetismo animal **inner** ~ magnetismo interior **You have a magnetism that is irresistible.** Tienes un magnetismo irresistible.

magnificent *adj* magnífico *m*, -ca *f*; espléndido *m*, -da *f* ~ **sight** vista magnífica **You are magnificent.** *Usted es (Fam: Tú eres)* una persona magnífica. **That was magnificent!** ¡Eso fue magnífico!

magnificently *adv* magníficamente **You (1,2) played magnificently.** *Usted (1) (game) jugó (Fam: jugastes) / (2) (instrument) tocó (Fam: tocastes)* magníficamente.

magnifying glass *n* lente *m* de aumento, lupa *f*

maid *n* 1. *(young woman)* joven *f*; 2. *(worker)* mucama *f*, camarera *f* **become an old** ~ convertirse en una solterona ~ **of honor** dama *f* de honor **old** ~ solterona *f*

maiden *n* joven *f* soltera, doncella *f* **This, my fair maiden, is for you.** Esto, mi hermosa doncella, es para ti.

mail *vt* enviar por correo, mandar por correo **I'll mail it (1) to you. / (2) for you.** *(1)* Yo *se (Fam: te)* lo enviaré por correo. / *(2)* Yo lo enviaré por correo para *usted (Fam: ti)*. **I have to mail this.** Tengo que enviar esto por correo. **Where can I mail this?** ¿Dónde puedo enviar esto por correo?

mail *n* correo *m* **air** ~ correo aéreo **e-mail** correo electrónico **express** ~ correo exprés ~ **carrier** porteador de correo **registered** ~ correo registrado **surface** ~ correo por vía terrestre **voice** ~ correo de voz **Is there any mail for (1) me? / (2) us?** ¿Hay correo para *(1)* mí? / *(2)* nosotros? **I'll send it to you by (1) air / (2) express / (3) registered mail.** Yo *se (Fam. te)* lo envío por correo *(1)* aéreo. / *(2)* exprés. / *(3)* registrado. **I'll let you know by e-mail.** Yo *le (Fam: te)* aviso por correo electrónico.

mailbox *n* buzón *m* **Is there a mailbox around here?** ¿Hay algún buzón por aquí?

mailman *n* cartero *m*

Spanish "x" is always like "ks", as in our word "taxi".

main *adj* principal *m&f* ~ **course** platillo *m* principal ~ **highway** carretera *f* principal ~ **reason** motivo *or* razón principal ~ **thing** lo principal

mainly *adv* principalmente

mainsail *n* vela *f* mayor

majestic *adj* majestuoso *m*, -sa *f*

majesty *n* majestad *f* **Yes, Your Majesty!** ¡Sí, Su Majestad! **Right away, Your Majesty!** ¡Inmediatamente, Su Majestad!

major *adj* muy importante *m&f*, mayor *m&f* ; *(grave)* grave *m&f* ~ **eye contact** contacto visual a fondo ~ **mistake** error grave

major *n* 1. *(main course of study)* especialidad; 2. *(mil.)* mayor, comandante

majority *n* la mayoría *f*, la mayor parte *f*

make *vt* hacer ~ **friends** hacer amigos *or* hacer amistad ~ **love** hacer el amor **Did you make this (yourself)?** ¿Hizo usted (Fam: Hiciste) esto (usted [Fam: tú] mismo)? **I made it (myself).** Yo lo hice (Lo hice yo mismo). **I'll make you a sandwich.** Yo le (Fam: te) voy a hacer un sandwich. **How much do you make a** *(1)* **month /** *(2)* **year?** ¿Cuánto hace usted (Fam: haces) *(1)* al mes / *(2)* al año? **I make** *(amount)* **a** *(1)* **month /** *(2)* **year**. Hago ___ *(1)* al mes / *(2)* al año. **It doesn't make any difference.** Da lo mismo. **Do you think we'll make it?** *(reach / get there)* ¿Crees que la hagamos? *(1)* **I'll /** *(2)* **We'll make it.** *(reach / get there)* *(1)* Yo sí la haré. / *(2)* Nosotros sí la haremos. *(1)* **I /** *(2)* **We can't make it.** *(come / get there)* / *(1)* Yo no puedo llegar. / *(2)* Nosotros no podemos llegar. *(1)* **I /** *(2)* **You /** *(3)* **We made it!** *(reach / get there)* *(1)* ¡Sí la hice! / *(2)* ¡Sí la hizo usted (Fam. hiciste)! / *(3)* ¡Sí la hicimos! **You make me** *(1)* **so /** *(2)* **very happy.** Usted me hace (Fam: Tú me haces) *(1)* tan / *(2)* muy feliz. **You make me feel so good.** Usted me hace (Fam: Tú me haces) sentir tan bien. **I want (so much) to make love with you.** Deseo (tanto) hacer el amor contigo.

★ **make up** *idiom* 1. *(invent)* inventar; 2. *(assemble, prepare)* preparar; 3. *(cosmetics)* maquillarse

★ **make up for** *idiom* compensar **I want to make up to you for yesterday.** Quiero compensarte por lo de ayer.

makeup *n (cosmetics)* maquillaje *m* **I have to freshen my makeup.** Tengo que retocarme el maquillaje.

maladroit *adj* torpe *m&f*

male *adj* masculino *m*, -na *f* ~ **perspective** perspectiva *f* masculina

male *n* macho *m*, varón *m (See terms under* **boy**, **guy** *and* **man**)*

maleness *n* masculinidad *f*

malfunction *vi* fallar; funcionar mal

malicious *adj* malicioso *m*, -sa *f* **That was a malicious thing to say.** Eso

---

Stress rule # 3: Syllables with accent marks have the stress there.

que dijiste fue con malicia.

mall *n (shopping center)* centro *m* comercial **Let's go shopping at the mall.** Vamos de compras al centro comercial. **We could hang out at the mall.** Podríamos vagar por el centro comercial.

mama *n* mamá *f* **hot ~** mujer *f* sensual

man *n* hombre *m* **another ~** otro hombre **bad ~** mal hombre **best ~** *(wedding)* padrino **big ~** hombre grande **dirty old ~** viejo verde **elderly ~** hombre mayor **enlisted ~ (EM)** *(mil.)* hombre enlistado **family ~** hombre de familia **friendly ~** hombre amigable **good ~** buen hombre **good-looking ~** hombre bien parecido **handsome ~** hombre guapo **hard-working ~** hombre laborioso **intelligent ~** hombre inteligente **kind ~** hombre amable **lonely ~** hombre solitario **~ of experience** hombre experimentado **~ of means** hombre de recursos **married ~** hombre casado **nice ~** hombre agradable **old ~** hombre anciano **quiet ~** hombre tranquilo **real ~** hombre de verdad **single ~** hombre soltero **strong ~** hombre fuerte **young ~** hombre joven **You're the man** *(1)* **of my dreams.** / *(2)* **that I've been waiting for all my life.** Tú eres el hombre *(1)* de mis sueños. / *(2)* que he esperado toda mi vida. **You're the only man for me.** Tú eres el único hombre para mí. **I'm a one-woman man.** Soy hombre de una sola mujer.

manage *vt* administrar **I manage a (small)** *(1)* **business.** / *(2)* **company.** / *(3)* **restaurant.** / *(4)* **store.** Yo administro *(1)* un negocio (pequeño). / *(2)* una compañía (pequeña). / *(3)* un restaurante (pequeño). / *(4)* una tienda (pequeña).

manage *vi* lograr, arreglárselas, poder **I hope you can manage to come.** Espero que *usted logre (Fam: tú logres)* venir. **I'm glad you managed to come.** Me alegra que *usted haya (Fam: hayas)* podido venir. **I managed to** *(1)* **get away (early).** / *(2)* **get** *(3)* **it.** / *(4)* **them.** Me las arreglé para *(1)* salir (temprano). / *(2)* conseguirlo. / *(3)* conseguirlas.

manager *n* gerente *m&f*

maneuver *vt* 1. *(move)* maniobrar; 2. *(manipulate)* manipular, manejar **You maneuvered me into this.** Tú me metiste en esto.

maneuver *n* maniobra *f* **clever ~** maniobra inteligente **That was sure a slick maneuver.** Esa fue sin duda una diestra maniobra.

maniac *n* maniático *m*, -ca *f* **amateur ~** aprendiz *m&f* de maniático **professional ~** maniático profesional

manicure *n* manicura *f*

manipulate *vt* manipular **I don't believe in manipulating people.** Yo no creo en manipular a la gente.

manipulator *n* manipulador *m*, -dora *f*

mankind *n* humanidad *f*, género *m* humano

Spanish pronunciation rules are on pages 407-408.

manly *adj* varonil *m&f*

man-made *adj* artificial *m&f*, sintético *m*, -ca *f*

manner *n* 1. *(behavior)* modo *m*, manera *f*, comportamiento *m* ; *(attitude)* actitud *f*; 2. *pl (etiquette)* etiqueta *f*; 3. *(way)* modales *m pl* **aloof** ~ actitud distante **bad** ~s malos modales **cultured** ~s modales educados **gentle** ~ modales finos **good** ~s buenos modales **proper** ~ modales adecuados **refined** ~s modales refinados **That's not good manners.** Esos no son buenos modales. **Mind your manners.** Cuida tus modales.

mannerism *n* gesto *m*, manerismo *m* **nervous** ~ gesto *m* nervioso

mansion *n* mansión *f*

manufacture *vt* manufacturar, fabricar **What do they manufacture there?** ¿Qué es lo que fabrican ahí?

many *adj* mucho(s) *m (pl)*, -cha(s) *f (pl)* **as** ~ **as** tanto como ~ **people** mucha gente ~ **things** muchas cosas ~ **ways** muchas maneras **not** ~ no muchos *(chas)* **too** ~ demasiados *(-das)* **very** ~ muchísimos *(-mas)* **How many (are there)?** ¿Cuántos *(-tas)* (hay)?

map *n* mapa *m* **city** ~ mapa de la ciudad ~ **of the country** mapa del país **Could you show** *(1)* **me** / *(2)* **us on the map?** ¿Podría usted *(Fam: ¿Podrías) (1)* indicarme / *(2)* indicarnos en el mapa? **Could** *(1)* **I** / *(2)* **we look at your map?** ¿*(1)* Podría / *(2)* Podríamos mirar *su (Fam: tu)* mapa?

marathon *n* maratón *m* **I like to run in marathons.** Me gusta correr en maratones.

March *n* marzo *m* **in** ~ en marzo **on** ~ **first** el primero de marzo

marijuana *n* mariguana *f*, mota *m*

marina *n* puerto *m* deportivo

marine *n* marina *f* ~ **Corps** infantería de marina **merchant** ~ marina mercante **I'm in the Marine Corps.** Estoy en la infantería de marina. **I'm a** *(1)* **sergeant** / *(2)* **lieutenant** / *(3)* *(rank)* **in the Marine Corps.** Soy *(1)* sargento / *(2)* teniente / *(3)* ____ de la infantería de marina. **I served three years in the Marine Corps.** Presté servicio durante tres años en la infantería de marina.

mark *n (bruise, scar, etc)* marca *f* **black-and-blue** ~ marca azul y negra **kiss** ~ marca de un beso

market *n* mercado *m* **black** ~ mercado negro **fruit** ~ mercado de fruta **local** ~ mercado local **vegetable** ~ mercado de verduras

marlin *n* aguja *f*

marriage *n* matrimonio *m* **former** ~ matrimonio anterior **future** ~ futuro matrimonio **go into a** ~ tener un matrimonio **happy** ~ matrimonio feliz **harmonious** ~ matrimonio en armonía **loveless** ~ matrimonio sin amor **previous** ~ matrimonio anterior **strong** ~ matrimonio sólido **unhappy** ~

Some Spanish words have accented and unaccented forms to differentiate their meanings (e.g., el = the, él = he).

matrimonio infeliz **We have a good marriage.** Tenemos un buen matrimonio. **You and I will have a** *(1)* **beautiful** / *(2)* **wonderful marriage**. Tú y yo tendremos un matrimonio *(1)* hermoso. / *(2)* maravilloso. **Have you ever thought about marriage?** ¿Alguna vez *ha pensado usted (Fam: has pensado)* en el matrimonio? **I'm (not) ready for marriage.** (No) estoy listo *(-ta)* para el matrimonio. **I want to have a marriage full of love and harmony.** Quiero tener un matrimonio lleno de amor y armonía. **Marriage is not for me.** El matrimonio no es para mí.

married *adj* casado *m*, -da *f* **be ~** estar casado, *(-da)* **decide to get ~** decidir casarse **decide not to get ~** decidir no casarse **get ~** casarse **happily ~** felizmente casados **intend to get ~** pretender casarse **legally ~** legalmente casados **officially ~** oficialmente casados **plan to get ~** planear casarse **want to get ~** querer casarse **I think it would be wonderful to be married to you.** Creo que sería maravilloso estar casado *(-da)* contigo. **Let's get married.** Casémonos. **Where can we get married?** ¿Dónde nos podemos casar? **What do we have to do to get married?** ¿Qué tenemos que hacer para casarnos?

marry *vt* casarse **Will you marry me?** ¿Te casas conmigo? **I want to marry you.** Quiero casarme contigo. **Yes, I'll marry you.** Sí me caso contigo. **I don't want to marry you.** No quiero casarme contigo. **I'm sorry, I can't marry you.** Lo siento, no puedo casarme contigo.

marry *vi* casarse **~ for life** casarse para toda la vida **I believe a person should marry only for love.** Creo que una persona sólo por amor debe casarse.

marsh *n* pantano *m* ; *(coastal)* marisma *f*

marshmallow *n* malvavisco *m* **Let's roast marshmallows over the fire.** Vamos a tostar malvaviscos en el fuego.

martial arts *n, pl* artes *fpl* marciales

marvel *vi* maravillarse **I marvel at** *(1)* **the extent of your knowledge.** / *(2)* **your exceptional loveliness.** / *(3)* **your talent.** Me maravillo ante *(1)* la amplitud de *sus (Fam: tus)* conocimientos. / *(2)* su *(Fam: tu)* **e**xcepcional belleza. / *(3)* su *(Fam: tu)* talento.

marvelous *adj* maravilloso *m*, -sa *f* **How marvelous!** ¡Qué maravilla! **What a marvelous idea!** ¡Qué maravillosa idea! **That would be marvelous.** Eso sería maravilloso. **You have marvelous taste.** Tienes un gusto maravilloso. *(1)* **I** / *(2)* **We had a marvelous time.** *(1)* Pasé / *(2)* Pasamos un rato maravilloso.

marvelously *adv* maravillosamente, de maravilla

masculine *adj* masculino *m*, -na *f*

mask *n* máscara *f (1,2)* **wear a ~** *(1)* ponerse / *(2)* usar una máscara

---

Spanish "g" is like "h" in front of "e" and "i".
In front of other vowels it's like our "g" in "gun".

masquerade *n* mascarada *f*, farsa *f*, baile *m* de disfraces *m* ~ **party** fiesta *f* de disfraces

mass *n* 1. *(great amount)* masa *f* ; 2. *(Catholic)* misa *f*

massage *vt* masajear; dar masaje **Let me (gently) massage your** *(1)* **back.** / *(2)* **legs.** / *(3)* **neck.** / *(4)* **shoulders.** Déjame masajear (suavemente) *(1)* tu espalda. / *(2)* tus piernas. / *(3)* tu cuello. / *(4)* tus hombros.

massage *n* masaje *m* ~ **parlor** salón *m* de masajes **foot** ~ masaje de pies **full body** ~ masaje corporal **gentle** ~ masaje suave **give a** ~ dar un masaje **thorough** ~ masaje completo **Let me give you a real nice massage.** Déjame darte un masaje de veras bueno. **Would you like a massage?** ¿Le *(Fam: ¿Te)* gustaría un masaje?

masseur *n* masajista *m&f* ★ **masseuse** *n* masajista *m&f*

master *vt* dominar, aprender **I'm sure you could master** *(1)* **English** / *(2)* **it in no time.** Estoy seguro *(-ra)* de que *usted puede (Fam: tú puedes)* dominar *(1)* el inglés / *(2)* eso de inmediato. **You certainly mastered the game quickly.** *Dominó usted (Fam: dominaste)* ese juego de verdad muy rápido.

master *n* 1. *(expert)* maestro *m* ; 2. *(head)* señor *m*, amo *m*

masterful *adj* magistral *m&f*, potente *m&f*, diestro *m*, -tra *f*

masterpiece *n* obra *f* maestra **I love to look at the old masterpieces.** Me encanta mirar las antiguas obras maestras. **That's truly a masterpiece.** Eso es de verdad una obra maestra. **You possess the kind of beauty that inspires masterpieces of art.** *Usted posee (Fam: Tú posees)* la clase de belleza que inspira obras maestras del arte.

mastery *n* maestría *f*, dominio *m*, destreza *f* **You have a real mastery of the** *(1)* **game.** / *(2)* **sport.** *Usted tiene (Fam: Tienes)* un verdadero dominio *(1)* del juego. / *(2)* del deporte.

match *vt* 1. *(compare with, equal)* igualar, equiparar, comparar; 2. *(go with)* hacer juego; 3. *(correspond to)* ajustarse, corresponder ~ **up** *(introduce, bring together)* presentar **No one can match you (in any way).** Nadie se puede igualar contigo (de ninguna manera). **I know someone** *(1)* **I** / *(2)* **we could** *(3,4)* **match you up with.** Conozco a alguien con quien *(1)* pudiera / *(2)* pudiéramos *(3) presentarlo m* / *(4) presentarla f (Fam: presentarte)*.

match *n* 1. *(contest)* partido *m*, combate *m*, match *m* ; 2. *(suitable mate)* pareja *m&f*; 3. *(for lighting fire)* cerillo *m* **book of** ~**es** carterita *f* de cerillos **box of** ~**es** caja *f* de cerillos **boxing** ~ boxeo *m*, pelea *f* de box **ice hockey** ~ partido de hockey ~ **point** punto *m* para partido **soccer** ~ partido de fútbol **wrestling** ~ combate de lucha libre **Would you like to go to a** *(name of sport)* **match (with me)?** Le *(Fam: Te)* gustaría ir a un partido de ___ (conmigo)? **How about a couple matches of tennis?** ¿Qué tal unas

---

English-Spanish and Spanish-English glossaries of food and drink are on pages 420-427.

partidas de tenis? **You're a(n) perfect match for me.** *Usted es (Fam: Tú eres)* la pareja perfecta para mí. **Do you have any matches?** *¿Tiene usted (Fam: ¿Tienes)* cerillos? **Don't forget to bring matches.** No *se olvide (Fam: te olvides)* de traer cerillos.

matchmaker *n* casamentero *m*, -ra *f* **Are you a good matchmaker?** *¿Es usted (Fam: ¿Eres tú)* buena casamentero *(-ra)*?

matchmaking *n* hacer de casamentero *m (-ra) f* **My friend is all alone. How good are you at matchmaking?** Mi amigo *(-ga)* está muy solo *(-la)*. ¿Qué tal *es usted (Fam: eres)* como casamentero *(-ra)*?

mate *n* compañero *m*, -ra *f* **classmate** compañero *(-ra)* de clase **pillow ~** compañero *(-ra)* de cama **roommate** compañero *(-ra)* de habitación **You're a wonderful mate.** Tú eres un*(a)* compañero *(-ra)* maravilloso *(-sa)*.

material *n* material *m*

materialist *n* materialista *m & f* ★ **materialistic** *adj* materialista *m & f*

matrimony *n* matrimonio *m* **I'm not keen on matrimony.** No soy dado *(-da)* al matrimonio.

matter *vi* importar **It doesn't matter.** No importa. **Nothing matters except being with you.** Nada importa, excepto estar contigo.

matter *n (question, subject)* cuestión *f*, materia *f*; tema *m* ; *(affair)* asunto *m* **another ~** otro asunto **business ~s** asuntos de negocios **complicated ~** asunto complicado **confidential ~** asunto confidencial **delicate ~** cuestión delicada **different ~** cuestión diferente **financial ~s** cuestiones financieras **important ~** cuestión importante **no laughing ~** asunto serio **personal ~** asunto personal **private ~** asunto privado **serious ~** asunto serio **simple ~** cuestión simple **small ~** cuestión pequeña **urgent ~** asunto urgente *(1)* I / *(2)* **We have some (personal) matters to take care of.** *(1)* Tengo / *(2)* Tenemos unos asuntos (personales) que atender. **There's an** *(1)* **important /** *(2)* **urgent matter** *(3)* I / *(4)* **we have to take care of.** Hay un asunto *(1)* importante / *(2)* urgente que *(3)* tengo / *(4)* tenemos que atender. **What's the matter (with you)?** ¿Qué *(le [Fam: te])* pasa? **Tell me what the matter is.** *Dígame (Fam: Dime)* qué pasa. **Nothing is the matter.** No pasa nada. **I don't know what's the matter.** No sé qué pasa. **Something's the matter with** *(1)* **the engine. /** *(2)* **this.** Algo pasa con *(1)* el motor. / *(2)* esto. **As a matter of fact,** *(1)* **yes. /** *(2)* **no.** De hecho, *(1)* sí / *(2)* no. **No matter what I do, no matter where I go, I think of you.** No importa lo que haga, no importa a dónde vaya, yo pienso en ti.

mattress *n* colchón *m* **air ~** colchón *m* de aire **inflate the air ~** inflar el colchón *m* de aire **Do you have a pump for the air mattress?** ¿Tiene usted *(Fam: Tienes)* una bomba *f* para el colchón de aire?

mature *adj* maduro *m*, -ra *f* ; adulto *m*, -ta *f*

A phrasebook makes a great gift!
Use the order form on page 432..

maximum *n* máximo *m* **to the ~** al máximo

may *aux v* 1. *(permission)* poder; 2. *(possibility)* ser posible **May I (1) borrow your magazine? / (2) come in? / (3) have a look? / (4) join you?** ¿Puedo *(1)* tomar prestada *su (Fam: tu)* revista? / *(2)* entrar? / *(3)* mirar? / *(4)* unirme a *usted (Fam:. ti)*? *(1)* **I** / *(2)* **We may have to leave tomorrow.** Es posible que *(1)* tenga / *(2)* tengamos que salir mañana. **It may rain (1) today / (2) tomorrow.** Es posible que *(1)* llueva hoy / *(2)* mañana. **There may not be any more rooms.** Es posible que ya no haya habitaciones.

May *n* mayo *m* **in ~** en mayo **on ~ first** el primero de mayo

Mayan *adj* maya *m&f*

maybe *adv* quizás, tal vez *(1,2)* **Maybe I will and maybe I won't.** *(1)* Quizás sí y quizás no. / *(2)* Tal vez sí y tal vez no.

MBA *abbrev* = **Master of Business Administration** maestría *f* en administración de empresas

meadow *n* pradera *f* **I want to make a picnic with you in some nice meadow.** Quiero hacer contigo un día de campo en alguna pradera bonita.

meal *n* comida *f*

mean *adj* 1. *(bad, cruel)* malo *m*, -la *f*; 2. *(stingy)* tacaño *m*, -ña *f* **Don't be (so) mean (to me).** No seas (tan) malo *(-la)* conmigo. **Why are you so mean to me?** ¿Por qué eres tan malo *(-la)* conmigo? **That was a mean thing to do.** Eso que hiciste fue malo.

mean *vt* 1. *(have meaning)* significar, querer decir; 2. *(intend)* pretender; 3. *(have in mind)* querer decir; 4. *(say seriously)* decir en serio **What does (1) this / (2) that mean?** ¿Que significa *(1)* esto? / *(2)* eso? **Can you tell me what this means?** ¿Puedes decirme lo que significa esto? *(1)* **This /** *(2)* **That means...** *(1)* Esto / *(2)* Eso significa... **Do you understand what I mean?** ¿Entiendes lo que quiero decir? **I (don't) understand what you mean.** Yo (no) entiendo lo que quieres decir. **What do you mean?** ¿Qué quieres decir? **I mean...** Yo quiero decir... **Do you mean it?** ¿Lo dices en serio? **I (don't) mean it.** Yo (no) lo digo en serio.

meaning *n* significado *m*, acepción *f*, sentido *m* **double ~** doble sentido **give ~** dar sentido **great ~** gran significado **have ~** tener sentido **hidden ~** significado oculto **real ~** significado real **You give my life a whole new meaning.** Tú le das a mi vida todo un nuevo sentido. **You have taught me the true meaning of love.** Tú me has enseñado el verdadero significado del amor.

meaningful *adj (important, worthwhile)* significativo *m*, -va *f*, valioso *m*, -sa *f*, importante *m&f*

meaningless *adj* sin sentido

means *n, pl (way, method)* medios *mpl* **by all ~s** por supuesto **by ~s of** por

---

A slash always means "or".

medio *m* de **by no ~s** de ninguna manera

meantime *n* entretanto, mientras tanto   *m*   **in the ~** mientras tanto

meanwhile *adv* mientras tanto, entretanto

measly *adj* mísero *m*, -ra *f*, miserable *m&f*

measure *n* medida *f* **beyond ~** inconmensurable, sin medida **precautionary ~s** medidas *f, pl* de precaución **My love for you is beyond measure.** Mi amor por ti no tiene medida.

meat *n* carne *f (1)* **I** / *(2)* **We don't eat meat.** *(1)* Yo no como... / *(2)* Nosotros no comemos... carne.

mechanic *n* mecánico *m*, -ca *f*

mechanical *adj* mecánico *m*, -ca *f*, maquinal *m&f* **~ aptitude** aptitudes *fpl* mecánicas

mechanism *n* mecanismo *m*

medal *n* medalla *f* **You deserve a medal (for that).** Te mereces una medalla (por eso). **I hereby award you the medal for outstanding beauty.** Te premio, pues, con la medalla a la belleza sobresaliente.

medical *adj* médico *m*, -ca *f*, clínico *m*, -ca *f*

medicine *n* 1. *(field)* medicina *f*; 2. *(pharm.)* medicina *f*, medicamento *m*

mediocre *adj* mediocre *m&f*

meditate *vi* 1. *(dwell in thought)* meditar; 2. *(contemplate spiritually)* meditar **Are you meditating? About me?** ¿Estás meditando? ¿Acerca de mí?

meditation *n* 1. *(deep thought)* meditación *f*, reflexión *f* 2. *(spiritual contemplation)* meditación *f*, contemplación *f*

medium *adj* mediano *m*, -na *f* **~ build** de complexión *f* mediana **~ height** de estatura *f* mediana

meet *vt* 1. *(encounter)* encontrarse, verse; 2. *(become acquainted with)* conocerse **I don't believe I've met you. My name is** *(name)*. Yo no creo que nos conozcamos. Mi nombre es ___. **It's a (real) pleasure to** *(1,2)* **meet you.** Es un (gran) placer *(1)* conocerlo. / *(2)* conocerla. **I'm (very)** *(1)* **glad** / *(2)* **happy** / *(3)* **pleased to** *(4,5)* **meet you.** Estoy (muy) *(1)* contento *(-ta)* / (2) feliz / (3) complacido *(-da)* de *(4)* haberlo *m* / *(5)* haberla *f* conocido. **I was hoping I could meet you.** Estaba esperando *(1)* poder conocerlo *m*. / *(2)* conocerla *f*. **Where shall** *(1)* **I** / *(2)* **we meet** *(3,4)* **you?** ¿Dónde *(3)* lo *m* / *(4)* la *f (Fam: te)* *(1)* veré? / *(2)* veremos? *(1)* **I'll** / *(2)* **We'll meet** *(3,4)* **you** *(5)* **at the corner of** *(name)* **and** *(name)* **streets.** / *(6)* **in the hotel lobby.** / *(7)* **in front of the bus station.** / *(8)* **by the entrance to the Opera House.** / *(9)* **at the airport** / *(10)* **bus station** / *(11)* **train station.** / *(12)* **right here.** / *(13)* **right over there.** / *(14)* **at your place.** *(3)* Lo *m* / *(4)* La *f (Fam: te)* *(1)* veré / *(2)* veremos (5) en la esquina de la calle ___ y ___. / *(6)* en el vestíbulo del hotel. / *(7)* frente a la estación

Spanish "v" is pronounced like a soft "b".

de autobus. / *(8)* por la entrada de la Ópera. / *(9)* en el aeropuerto. / *(10)* en la terminal de autobuses. / *(11)* en la estación del tren. / *(12)* aquí. / *(13)* por allá. / *(14)* en *su (Fam: tu)* casa. **Meet** *(1)* **me** / *(2)* **us...** *(Same choices as above.)* *(1)* Encuéntreme *(Fam:* Encuéntrame)**...** / *(2)* Encuéntrenos *(Fam:* Encuéntranos)**....** **What time shall** *(1)* **I** / *(2)* **we meet you?** ¿A qué hora *(1)* ...me encuentro... / *(2)* ...nos encontramos... *con usted (Fam: contigo)*? **I'll meet** *(1,2)* **you at** *(time)*. Yo *(1)* lo m / *(2)* la f *(Fam: te)* veré a las___. **We'll meet** *(1,2)* **you at** *(time)*. Nosotros *(1)* lo m / *(2)* la f *(Fam: te)* veremos a las___. **Meet** *(1)* **me** / *(2)* **us at** *(time)*. *(1)* Encuéntrate conmigo / *(2)* con nosotros a las ___. **Would it be possible to** *(1,2)* **meet you** *(3)* **this afternoon?** / *(4)* **this evening?** / *(5)* **tonight?** / *(6)* **tomorrow** (*[7]* **morning** / *[8]* **afternoon** / *[9]* **evening)?** / *(10)* **after work?** / *(11)* **after you get off work?** ¿Sería posible *(1)* verlo m / *(2)* verla f *(Fam: verte)* *(3)* esta tarde? / *(4)* al anochecer? / *(5)* esta noche? / *(6)* mañana (*[7]* por la mañana? / *[8]* por la tarde? / *[9]* al anochecer?) / *(10)* después del trabajo? / *(11)* después de que *salga usted (Fam: salgas)* de trabajar? **From the first moment I** *(1)* **noticed** / *(2)* **saw you, I wanted to meet you.** Desde el primer momento que te *(1)* noté / *(2)* vi, yo quise conocerte.

meet *vi* 1. *(encounter)* encontrarse, verse; 2. *(become acquainted)* conocerse **I'm** (*[1]* **really** / *[2]* **very)** *(3)* **glad** / *(4)* **happy (that) we met.** Estoy (*[1]* de verdad *[2]* muy) *(3)* contento *(-ta)* / *(4)* alegre de que nos conocimos. **Haven't we met before?** ¿No nos hemos conocido antes? **Didn't we meet at** *(place)*? ¿Que no nos conocimos en ___ ? **We met at** *(place)*. Nos conocimos en ___. **Where shall we meet?** ¿Dónde nos vamos a ver? **Let's meet** *(1)* **at the corner of** *(name)* **and** *(name)* **streets.** / *(2)* **in the hotel lobby.** / *(3)* **in front of the bus station.** / *(4)* **by the entrance to the Opera House.** / *(5)* **at the airport** / *(6)* **bus station** / *(7)* **train station.** / *(8)* **right here.** / *(9)* **right over there.** / *(10)* **at your place.** Nos veremos *(1)* en la esquina de la calle ___ y ___. / *(2)* en el vestíbulo del hotel. / *(3)* frente a la estación de autobus. / *(4)* por la entrada de la Ópera. / *(5)* en el aeropuerto. / *(6)* en la terminal de autobuses. / *(7)* en la estación del tren. / *(8)* aquí. / *(9)* por allá. / *(10)* en *su (Fam: tu)* casa. **What time shall we meet?** ¿A qué hora nos vamos a ver? *(1)* **Let's meet...** / *(2)* **We'll meet... at** *(time)*. *(1,2)* Veámonos a las ___. **I hope we'll meet again soon.** Espero que pronto nos volvamos a ver. **I hope (very much) that you'll give me the opportunity to meet with you again.** (Mucho) Espero que me *dé usted (Fam: des)* la oportunidad de vernos otra vez. **When our eyes met, I knew I had to meet you.** Cuando nuestros ojos se encontraron, supe que tenía que conocerte.

meeting *n* reunión *f* **arrange a ~** concertar una reunión **attend a ~** asistir a

---

Time expressions are given on page 413.

una reunión **brief ~** reunión breve **business ~** reunión de negocios **cancel our ~** cancelar nuestra reunión **first ~** primera reunión **go to a ~** ir a una reunión **last ~** la última reunión **next ~** la próxima reunión **postpone our ~** posponer nuestra reunión **previous ~** reunión previa **I look forward to our meeting.** Espero con gusto que podamos reunirnos.

melancholic, melancholy *adj* melancólico *m*, -ca *f*

melancholy *n* melancolía *f*

mellow *adj* 1. *(person)* apacible *m&f*; 2. *(wine)* añejo *m*, -ja *f* **You seem like a mellow sort of person.** Pareces ser una persona apacible.

mellow *vi (person)* suavizar, moderar **I've** *(1,2)* **mellowed with age.** Me he *(1)* suavizado / *(2)* moderado con la edad.

melodic *adj* melodioso *m*, -sa *f* **Your** *(1)* **name** / *(2)* **voice has a melodic quality to it.** *Su (Fam. Tu) (1)* nombre / *(2)* voz tiene un timbre melodioso.

melody *n* melodía *f* **That's a** *(1)* **beautiful** / *(2)* **nice melody, isn't it?** Esa es una *(1)* hermosa / *(2)* bonita melodía ¿verdad?

melon *n* melón *m*

melt *vt* derretir **Your beautiful eyes melt my heart.** Tus hermosos ojos me derriten el corazón. **The sunshine of your love has melted away all of my loneliness.** La luz de tu amor ha derretido toda mi soledad.

melt *vi* derretir **All the ice has melted.** Todo el hielo se derritió. **Every time you look at me, I (just) melt.** Cada vez que me miras, (simplemente) me derrito.

member *n* miembro *m&f*, socio *m*, -cia *f* **become a ~** afiliarse, hacerse socio *(-cia)* **club ~** socio *(-cia)* del club **family ~** miembro de la familia **Members only.** Sólo para socios. **How do I become a member?** ¿Cómo hago para hacerme socio? **How do we become members?** ¿Cómo hacemos para hacernos socios?

membership *n* membresía *f* **apply for ~** solicitar membresía **~ application** solicitud de membresía **~ card** credencial *f* de socio *(-cia)* **~ fee** cuota *f* de membresía

memento *n* recuerdo *m* **Thank you for the memento.** Gracias por el recuerdo. **Here is a little memento that I want you to have.** He aquí un pequeño recuerdo que quiero que *usted tenga (Fam: tengas).* **I will always treasure this memento of the (wonderful) time we spent together.** Siempre atesoraré este recuerdo por el tiempo (maravilloso) que pasamos juntos.

memoirs *n, pl* memorias *fpl* **I plan to write my memoirs soon and you would be just the person to spice them up for me.** Pienso escribir pronto mis memorias y *usted sería (Fam: tú serías)* justo la persona que las haría más amenas.

memorable *adj* memorable *m&f*

Spanish "qu" is pronounced like "k".

memorial *n* monumento *m* **war** ~ monumento de guerra

memorize *vt* memorizar, aprender de memoria **Don't worry, I've already got it permanently memorized.** No te preocupes, ya lo tengo fijo en la memoria. **I memorized it in elementary school.** Me lo aprendí de memoria en la primaria.

memory *n* 1. *(ability)* memoria *f*; 2. *(recollection)* recuerdo *m (1,2)* **awaken ~ies** *(1)* despertar / *(2)* avivar recuerdos *m, pl* **bad ~ies** malos recuerdos **bitter ~ies** amargos recuerdos **bring back ~ies** traer recuerdos **childhood ~ies** recuerdos de infancia **distant ~ies** recuerdos remotos **fond ~ies** cariñosos recuerdos **good ~ies** buenos recuerdos **good ~** *(ability to remember)* buena memoria **happy ~ies** felices recuerdos **lousy ~** *(ability to remember)* pésima memoria **~ies of my youth** recuerdos de mi juventud **nice ~ies** bonitos recuerdos **painful ~ies** dolorosos recuerdos **poor ~** *(ability to remember)* escasa memoria **sad ~ies** recuerdos tristes **share ~ies** compartir los recuerdos **treasure the ~** atesorar los recuerdos *(1)* **these /** *(2)* **those ~ies** *(1)* estos / *(2)* esos recuerdos **vague ~ies** recuerdos vagos **warm ~ies** cálidos recuerdos **My memory fails me.** Me falla la memoria. **It slipped my memory.** Se me fue de la memoria. **I'm doing a test of my memory. What's your telephone number?** Estoy probando mi memoria. ¿Cuál es *su (Fam: tu)* número de teléfono? **I want to make beautiful memories with you.** Quiero tener recuerdos hermosos contigo. *(1)* **I /** *(2)* **We will always cherish the memories of these** *(3)* **beautiful /** *(4)* **wonderful times (together).** Siempre *(1)* apreciaré / *(2)* apreciaremos los recuerdos de estos momentos *(3)* hermosos / *(4)* maravillosos.

menage a trois *n Fr (3 people together in a love affair)* ménage a trois; arreglo de tres

mend *vt* arreglar, reparar, remendar **Could you mend this for me?** ¿Podría usted *(Fam. Podrías)* arreglarme esto? **Thank you for mending it for me.** Gracias por arreglármelo.

menstrual *adj* menstrual *m&f* ~ **period** período *m* menstrual

menstruate *vi* menstruar

mental *adj* mental *m&f* ~ **case** *(crazy person)* caso *m* psiquiátrico ~ **handicap** discapacidad *f* mental ~ **hospital** hospital *m* psiquiátrico ~ **illness** enfermedad *f* mental

mentality *n* mentalidad *f* **bizarre** ~ mentalidad insólita **different** ~ diferente mentalidad **strange** ~ mentalidad extraña

mentally *adv* mentalmente ~ **handicapped** mentalmente discapacitado *(-da)* ~ **ill** mentalmente enfermo ~ **unbalanced** mentalmente desequilibrado *(-da)*

mention *vt* mencionar, decir **Don't mention it.** No hay de qué. **You men-**

Words in parentheses (not italicized) are optional.

tioned it before. Lo *dijo usted (Fam: dijiste)* antes. **You mentioned that...** *Usted dijo (Fam: Tú dijiste)* que... **As I mentioned...** Como dije... **You never mentioned it.** Nunca lo *mencionó usted (Fam: mencionaste).* **Not to mention...** Ya no digamos ...

menu *n* menú *m* **What's on the menu?** ¿Qué hay en el menú?

merciful *adj* misericordioso *m*, -sa *f*

merciless *adj* despiadado *m*, -da *f* **You're merciless, aren't you?** Tú eres despiadado *(-da)* ¿verdad?

mercurial *adj* mercurial *m&f*, voluble *m&f* ~ **temper** de temperamento *m* voluble

mercy *n* clemencia *f*, piedad *f* **Have mercy on me.** Ten piedad de mí. **I beg for mercy.** Imploro clemencia. **I'm going to show no mercy.** No voy a tener clemencia. **Don't plead for mercy. It's useless.** No pidas clemencia. Es en vano.

mere *adj* mero *m*, -ra *f*, simple *m&f*; puro *m*, -ra *f*, sólo *m*, -la *f* ~ **curiosity** pura curiosidad **The price is a mere five thousand dollars.** El precio es de sólo cinco mil dólares.

merely *adv* simplemente, solamente, meramente, nada más

merit *n* mérito *m* **The idea has (a certain) merit.** La idea tiene (cierto) mérito.

mermaid *n* sirena *f*

merrily *adv* alegremente, con alegría **"Row, row, row your boat, Gently down the stream. Merrily, merrily, merrily. Life is but a dream."** "Rema, rema, rema tu bote. Suavemente río abajo. Con alegría, con alegría, con alegría. La vida no es más que un sueño."

merriment *n* alegría *f*, júbilo *m*, risas *fpl* **unabashed** ~ alegría desenfadada **It's time for some merriment.** Es hora de tener un poco de alegría.

merry *adj* alegre *m&f*, feliz *m&f*, divertido *m*, -da *f* **make** ~ divertirse **Merry Christmas!** ¡Feliz Navidad! **That was a** *(1,2)* **merry time.** Ese fue un *(1)* momento divertido. / *(2)* tiempo feliz. **I've never** *(1,2)* **had such a merry time.** Nunca había *(1)* tenido un momento tan divertido. / *(2)* pasado un rato tan alegre.

merry-go-round *n* carrusel *m*

mesmerize *vt* hipnotizar, cautivar, fascinar **I'm mesmerized by your** *(1)* **beauty.** / *(2)* **charm.** Estoy fascinado *(-da)* por *su (Fam: tu) (1)* belleza. / *(2)* encanto.

mess (up) *vt* estropear, desarreglar, desordenar **Don't mess up my stuff, okay?** No desordenes mis cosas. ¿De acuerdo? **It messed up** *(1)* **my** / *(2)* **our plans.** Eso estropeó (1) mis / (2) nuestros planes.

mess *n* 1. *(disorder)* desorden *m*, revoltijo *m* ; 2. *(difficulty)* dificultad *f*, lío

---

*A single Spanish "r" should be lightly trilled;
double "r" ("rr") should be strongly trilled.*

m, rollo *m* **I've made a (terrible) mess of things.** Hice un revoltijo de cosas (espantoso). *(1,2)* **What a mess!** *(1)* ¡Qué desorden! *(2)* ¡Qué lío! *(1,2)* **Everything is a mess.** *(1)* Todo está en desorden. *(2)* Todo es un revoltijo.

mess around *idiom* 1. *(play)* jugar, juguetear; *(kid around)* travesear, juguetear, bromear; *(be foolish)* vagar, entretenerse, tontear; 2. *(pet)* mimar, manosear, acariciarse; 3. *(philander)* flirtear, jugar con los sentimientos

mess with *(slang) (bother, annoy)* meterse en asuntos ajenos **Don't mess with** *(1)* **me.** / *(2)* **my girl.** No te metas *(1)* conmigo. / *(2)* con mi chica.

message *n* mensaje *m* **e-mail** ~ mensaje de correo electrónico **If** *(1)* **I'm** / *(2)* **we're not there, please leave a message.** Si no *(1)* estoy / *(2)* estamos allí, por favor *deje usted (Fam: deja)* un mensaje. **I left you a message.** *Le (Fam: Te)* dejé un mensaje. **Did you get** *(1)* **my** / *(2)* **our message?** *¿Recibió (Fam: ¿Recibiste)* *(1)* mi / *(2)* nuestro mensaje? *(1)* **I** / *(2)* **We (didn't get) got your message.** (No) *(1)* Recibí / *(2)* Recibimos *su (Fam: tu)* mensaje.

messy *adj* desordenado *m*, -da *f (1,2)* **I'm sorry it's so messy.** *(1)* Lamento que esté tan desordenado. / *(2)* Perdón por el desorden. **It's not messy at all. It looks great.** No está nada desordenado. Se ve fenomenal.

metal *adj* metálico *m*, -ca *f*, de metal

metal *n* metal *m* **heavy** ~ *(rock music)* rock pesado **made of** ~ hecho *(-cha)* de metal

metaphysical *adj* metafísico *m*, -ca *f* ★ **metaphysics** *n* metafísica *f*

meteor *n* meteoro *m* **Let's go out and watch the meteors in the sky.** Salgamos a ver los meteoros en el cielo.

meter *n (= 3.3 ft)* metro *m*

method *n* método *m* ~ **of birth control** método de control de natalidad **new** ~ método nuevo **traditional** ~ método tradicional **It's a** *(1)* **good** / *(2)* **great** / *(3)* **poor method.** Es un método *(1)* bueno. / *(2)* fenomenal. / *(3)* inadecuado. **Let's try a different method.** Probemos un método diferente.

meticulous *adj* meticuloso *m*, -sa *f*. minucioso *m*, -sa *f* ~ **housekeeper** ama de casa meticulosa

Mexican *adj* mexicano *m*, -na *f* ★ *n* mexicano *m*, -na *f*

microphone *n* micrófono *m*

mid 20's (30's, 40', etc) a mediados de los veinte (treinta, cuarenta, etc.) **I thought you were in your mid 20's.** Pensé que andabas por los veinticinco.

middle *adj* mediano *m*, -na *f*, medio *m*, -dia *f* ~ **age** de mediana edad ~ **finger** dedo medio, dedo del corazón ~ **name** segundo nombre

middle *n* centro *m*, medio *m*, mitad *f* **in the** ~ **of the street** en medio de la calle **You're the one in the middle (of the photo).** Tú eres el *(la)* que está en el centro (de la foto).

Familiar "tu" forms in parentheses can replace italicized polite forms.

middle-aged *adj* de mediana edad, de edad madura

middle-class *adj* de clase *f* media

mid-life *adj* madurez *f*, edad *f* madura, mitad *f* de la vida ~ **crisis** crisis de la edad madura

midget *n* enano *m*, -na *f*, diminuto *m*, -ta *f*

midnight *n* medianoche *f* **after** ~ después de medianoche **at** ~ a medianoche

miffed *adj* molesto *m*, -ta *f* **I hope you're not miffed (at me).** Espero que no estés molesto *(-ta)* conmigo.

might *aux v* pudiera; podría **I might do it.** Yo podría hacerlo. **You might be right.** *Usted pudiera (Fam: Pudieras)* tener razón. **You might have *(1)* called / *(2)* told me.** *Pudo usted (Fam. Pudiste)* haberme *(1)* llama-do. / *(2)* dicho. **I might have known.** Debí haberlo sabido.

mighty *adj* 1. *(powerful)* poderoso *m*, -sa *f*, potente *m&f*; 2. *(great, large)* grande *m&f*, enorme *m&f*

mighty *adv (very)* muy, mucho **That's mighty nice of you.** Eso es muy gentil de tu parte. **I'm getting mighty tired of this.** Esto me está cansando mucho.

mild *adj* 1. *(moderate)* moderado *m*, -da *f*; 2. *(not severe)* leve *m&f*, benigno *m*, -na *f*, *(not strong)* suave *m&f*, leve *m&f*; 3. *(gentle in na-ture)* afable *m&f*, dulce *m&f*, apacible *m&f* ~ **cold** resfrío *m* leve ~ **headache** dolor *m* de cabeza *f* leve ~ **weather** clima *m* benigno

mildly *adv* suavemente, con suavidad **to put it** ~ para decirlo con suavidad

mild-mannered *adj* de modales afables

mile *n (= 1.6 km)* milla *f*

military *adj* militar *m&f* ~ **rank** rango *m* militar ~ **service** servicio *m* militar **Do they have compulsory military service?** ¿Tienen servicio militar obligatorio?

military *n* militares *mpl*, fuerzas armadas *fpl* **How long were you in the military?** ¿Cuánto tiempo *estuvo usted (Fam: estuviste)* en las fuerzas armadas?

milk *n* leche *f* ~ **shake** batido *m* de leche, leche malteada

Milky Way *n* Vía Láctea *f*

millimeter *n (= 0.04 inches)* milímetro *m*

million *n* millón *m* **I want to give you a million kisses. And more tomor-row.** Quiero darte un millón de besos. Y mañana más.

millionaire *n* millonario *m*, -ria *f* **You make me feel like a millionaire.** *Usted me hace (Fam: Tú me haces)* sentir como si fuera millonario *(-ria)*.

mimic *vt* imitar, remedar

mind *vi (care, object)* importar **Would you mind, if I...?** *(Reply:* **No, go right ahead.***)* ¿Te importaría si yo...? *(Respuesta:* No, adelante.*)* **If you**

Spanish "ll" is pronounced like "y" in "yes".

don't mind ... Si no te importa... **I don't mind. (Go right ahead.).** No me importa. (Adelante.) **Never mind.** No importa.

mind *n* mente *f* **analytical** ~ mente analítica **blow my** ~ *(slang)* saltar la tapa f de los sesos *m, pl* **boggle the** ~ quedar pasmado *(-da)*; pasmar la mente **brilliant** ~ mente brillante **dirty** ~ mente sucia **drive you out of your** ~ sacarte de tus casillas **enrich the** ~ enriquecer la mente **exceptional** ~ mente excepcional **go out of** *(1)* **my** / *(2)* **your** ~ perder *(1)* mi / *(2)* tu juicio **great** ~ mente grandiosa **inquisitive** ~ mente inquisitiva *(1,2)* **keen** ~ mente *(1)* ágil / *(2)* aguda **lose one's** ~ perder el juicio **on my** ~ en mi juicio **open** ~ de mente abierta **practical** ~ mente práctica **quick** ~ mente ágil **state of** ~ estado *m* mental **strong** ~ mente fuerte **weak** ~ mente débil **with an open** ~ con mente abierta **You were on my mind all day.** *Usted estuvo (Fam: Estuviste)* en mi mente todo el día. **You fill my mind every moment of the day (and night).** Llenas mi mente en todo momento del día (y de la noche). *(1,2)* **Is there something on your mind?** *(1)* ¿*Usted tiene (Fam: ¿Tú tienes)* algo en mente? / *(2)* ¿Hay algo que te preocupa? **You drive me out of my mind.** Tú me sacas de quicio *m.* **Please don't change your mind.** Por favor, no *cambie usted (Fam: cambies)* de parecer. **Did you change your mind?** ¿*Cambió usted (Fam: ¿Cambiaste)* de parecer? **I changed my mind.** Cambié de parecer *m.* **We changed our minds.** Cambiamos de parecer. **Nothing will make me change my mind.** Nada me hará cambiar de parecer. *(1)* **I can't... /** *(2)* **I wish I could... read your mind.** *(1)* No puedo… / *(2)* Ojalá pudiera … leer *su (Fam: tu)* mente.

mind-boggling *adj* inconcebible *m&f*, alucinante *m&f*, pasmoso *m*, -sa *f*

mindless *adj* insensato *m*, -ta *f*, sin sentido, salvaje *m&f*

mind-set *n* modo *m* de pensar, estado *m* mental

mine *poss. pron* mío(s) *m(pl)*, mía(s) *f(pl)* **Is this yours or mine?** ¿Es esto tuyo o mío? **It's (not) mine.** (No) Es mío. **You're mine (and mine alone).** Tú eres mía (y solamente mía). **I want you always to be mine.** Quiero que siempre seas mía.

minimum *adj* mínimo *m*, -ma *f* ~ **age** edad *f* mínima ~ **salary** salario *m* mínimo ~ **wage** sueldo *m* mínimo

minimum *n* mínimo *m*, -ma *f* **at the (very)** ~ *(1)* al / *(2)* a lo mínimo

miniskirt *n* minifalda *f*

minister *n* ministro *m*, -tra *f*

minor *adj* menor *m&f*, de poca importancia

minor *n (underaged person)* menor *m&f* de edad

minority *n* minoría *f* **ethnic** ~ minoría étnica **racial** ~ minoría racial

minus *prep* menos, sin

minute *n* minuto *m* **any** ~ en cualquier minuto **fifteen ~s ago** hace quince

---

Common occupations are listed on pages 415-416.

minutos **five ~s ago** hace cinco minutos **for a ~** por un minuto **ten ~s ago** hace diez minutos *(1,2)* **Just a minute.** *(1)* Un momento. / *(2)* Sólo un minuto. **Wait a minute.** Espera un momento. **I'll just be a minute.** Será sólo un minuto.

miracle *n* milagro *m* **Now, for my next miracle...** Ahora, para mi próximo milagro... **What a miracle that you're not married!** ¡Qué milagro que no estés casado *(-da)*! **Your love is a miracle for me.** Tu amor es un milagro para mí.

miraculous *adj* milagroso *m*, -sa *f*, prodigioso *m*, -sa *f*, maravilloso *m*, -sa *f* **~ shot** *(golf, basketball, tennis, etc)* tiro *m* prodigioso

mirror *n* espejo *m* **You want to see the most beautiful woman in the world? Look in the mirror.** ¿Quiere usted *(Fam: ¿Quieres)* ver la mujer más hermosa del mundo? Mira el espejo.

mirth *n* regocijo *m*, alborozo *m*, alegría *f* **Okay, what's all this mirth about?** Bueno, ¿a qué se debe todo este regocijo?

miscarriage *n* aborto *m* espontáneo, fracaso *m* *(1,2)* **I had a miscarriage.** *(1)* Tuve un aborto espontáneo. / *(2)* Perdí un bebé.

miscellaneous *adj* diversos *mpl*, -sas *fpl* **~ adventures** aventuras *fpl* diversas **~ pleasures** placeres *mpl* diversos

mischief *n* malicia *f*, travesura *f*, diablura *f* **You're full of mischief, aren't you?** Estás lleno *(-na)* de malicia ¿verdad? **Stay out of mischief, okay?** No te metas en diabluras. ¿De acuerdo?

mischievous *adj* travieso *m*, -sa *f*, pícaro *m*, -ra *f*, malicioso *m*, -sa *f*; **You're a mischievous little imp!** ¡Eres un diablillo travieso!

miser *n* avaro *m*, -ra *f*, tacaño *m*, -ña *f*

miserable *adj* 1. *(unhappy)* desdichado *m*, -da *f*; *(wretched)* miserable *m&f*; *(heartbroken)* desconsolado *m*, -da *f*; *(sad)* triste *m&f*; 2. *(terrible)* pésimo *m*, -ma *f* **~ experience** experiencia *f* desdichada **~ place** lugar *m* miserable **~ time** tiempo *m* pésimo **You must have been miserable.** *Usted debe (Fam: Debes)* haber sido desdichado *(-da)*. **I'm (totally) miserable without you.** Sin ti soy (completamente) desdichado *(-da)*. **I'd be miserable without you.** Sería desdichado *(-da)* sin ti. **What miserable weather we're having.** Qué clima tan pésimo tenemos.

misery *n* desdicha *f* **sheer ~** desdicha total

misgiving *n* 1. *(apprehension)* recelo *m* ; 2. *(doubt)* duda *f* **I have misgivings (about this).** Tengo dudas (sobre esto). **I don't want you to have any misgivings (about this).** No quiero que *usted tenga (Fam:. tengas)* dudas (sobre esto).

mishap *n* percance *m*, contratiempo *m* *(1)* **I** / *(2)* **We had a little mishap.** *(1)* Tuve / *(2)* Tuvimos un pequeño contratiempo.

Spanish "y" is "ee" when alone or at the end of words.

misplace *vt (lose)* extraviar **I misplaced my** *(thing)*. Extravié mi ___.

miss *vt* 1. *(long for)* extrañar, añorar; 2. *(fail to meet)* faltar, perder; 3. *(be late for)* llegar tarde; 4. *(let slip by)* soltar; 5. *(not hit)* fallar **Did you miss me?** ¿Me extrañaste? **I missed you (a lot).** Te extrañé (muchísimo). **Will you miss me?** ¿Me vas a extrañar? **I'm going to miss you (a lot).** Voy a extrañarte (muchísimo). *(1)* **I** / *(2)* **We missed** *(3)* **my** / *(4)* **our flight.** *(1)* Perdí / *(2)* Perdimos *(3)* mi / *(4)* nuestro vuelo. *(1)* **I** / *(2)* **We missed the** *(3)* **bus.** / *(4)* **train.** *(1)* Perdí / *(2)* Perdimos el *(3)* camión. / *(4)* tren. **I'm sorry I missed your** *(1)* **birthday.** / *(2)* **party.** Lamento haber faltado a tu *(1)* cumpleaños. / *(2)* fiesta. **Oh, I missed!** *(didn't hit)* ¡Oh, fallé! **You missed!** *(didn't hit)* ¡Fallaste!

★ **miss** *idiom* perderse (la diversión) **You missed out on a great** *(1)* **concert.** / *(2)* **game.** Te perdiste de un gran *(1)* concierto. / *(2)* juego. **You missed out on a great** *(1)* **movie.** / *(2)* **party.** / *(3)* **play.** Te perdiste una gran *(1)* película. / *(2)* fiesta. / *(3)* obra.

miss *n (unmarried woman)* señorita *f*

mission *n (relig)* misión *f*

missionary *n* misionero *m*, -ra *f*

mist *n* bruma *f*

mistake *vt* confundir **I'm sorry, I mistook** *(1,2)* **you for someone else.** Perdón, *(1)* lo *m* / *(2)* la *f (Fam: te)* confundí con otra persona. **I think you're mistaking me for someone else.** Creo que *usted me confunde (Fam: me confundes)* con otra persona.

mistake *n* error *m* **big** ~ gran error **embarrassing** ~ un error bochornoso **little** ~ error pequeño **terrible** ~ error tremendo **I'm sorry, my mistake.** Perdón, fue error mío. **I'm sorry, I made a mistake.** Lo siento, cometí un error. **I think you've made a mistake.** Creo que *usted cometió (Fam: cometiste)* un error. **There's some mistake here.** Aquí hay un error. **There's no mistake about it.** No hay duda de ello. **No problem. Mistakes happen.** No hay problema. Los errores suceden.

mistaken *adj* incorrecto *m*, -ta *f*, equivocado *m*, -da *f* ~ **identity** identidad *f* equivocada **I believe you're mistaken.** Creo que *usted está (Fam: estás)* equivocado *(-da)*.

mister *n* señor *m*

mistletoe *n* muérdago *m* **If you stand under mistletoe, it means I can kiss you.** Si te detienes bajo un muérdago, significa que puedo besarte. **There's an old Welsh saying that if you put a sprig of mistletoe under your pillow, you'll dream of the man that will marry you.** Un viejo refrán galés dice que si pones una ramita de muérdago bajo tu almohada, soñarás con el hombre que se casará contigo.

Feminine forms of words in phrases
are usually given in parentheses (italicized).

misunderstand *vt* malinterpretar, entender mal, no comprender **I'm sorry, I misunderstood** *(1,2)* **you.** Perdón, no *(1)* lo m / *(2)* la f *(Fam:. te)* entendí. **Perhaps you misunderstood me.** Quizás no me *entendió usted (Fam: entendiste)*. **Please don't misunderstand me.** Por favor, no me *malentienda usted (Fam: malentiendas)*.

mix *vt* 1. *(combine)* mezclar, combinar; 2. *(make)* preparar ~ **business with pleasure** mezclar el negocio con el placer **I'll mix you a drink.** Le *(Fam: Te)* voy a preparar una copa.

   ★ **mix up** *idiom (confuse)* revolver; confundir **I think** *(1)* **I** / *(2)* **you mixed them up.** Creo que los *(1)* confundí / *(2)* confundió usted *(Fam: confundiste)*.

mixed up *adj* confuso *m*, -sa f, desorientado *m*, -da f, confundido *m*, -da f **be ~** estar confundido *(-da)* **get ~** confundirse, desorientarse **I'm** *(1,2)* **mixed up.** Estoy *(1)* confundido *(-da)*. / *(2)* desorientado *(-da)*. **We're** *(1,2)* **mixed up.** Estamos *(1)* confundidos. / *(2)* desorien-tados. **You've got me mixed up with someone else.** Usted me confundió *(Fam: Tú me confundiste)* con otra persona.

mixture *n* mezcla f, mixtura f

mix-up *n* lío *m*, confusión f **There was a mix-up (in the schedule).** Hubo una confusión (en el programa). **I'm sorry about the mix-up.** Lamento la confusión.

mocha *n* moca *m*, moka *m*

model *adj* 1. *(reproducted in small scale)* a escala; 2. *(exemplary)* modelo *m&f* **I make model** *(1)* **airplanes.** / *(2)* **cars.** / *(3)* **soldiers.** / *(4)* **trains.** Fabrico *(1)* aeroplanos / *(2)* carros / *(3)* soldados / *(4)* trenes a escala.

model *vi* modelar **Would you model for me?** ¿Modelaría usted *(Fam: ¿Modelarías)* para mí? **I'd love to have you model for me.** Me encantaría que *usted modelara (Fam: tú modelaras)* para mí.

model *n* 1. *(small reproduction)* modelo *m*, maqueta f; 2. *(standard)* modelo *m* ; 3. *(one who models)* modelo *m&f* ~ **of good behavior** modelo de buena conducta ~ **of patience** modelo de paciencia **I like to make models.** Me gusta fabricar modelos. **I think you would be a perfect model.** Creo que *usted sería (Fam: serías)* un*(a)* modelo perfecto *(-ta)*.

moderate *adj* moderado *m*, -da f, módico *m*, -ca f

moderately *adv* moderadamente, con moderación

moderation *n* moderación f **I drink in moderation.** Bebo con moderación.

modern *adj* moderno *m*, -na f ~ **way** modernamente, a lo moderno

modest *adj* modesto *m*, -ta f **You're too modest.** Eres demasiado modesto *(-ta)*.

modesty *n* modestia f **Such modesty!** ¡Qué modestia!

Spanish "c" before "e" and "i" is pronounced like "s".

mole *n (blemish)* lunar *m*

molehill *n* topera *f* **You're making a mountain out of a molehill.** Estás haciendo una montaña de un grano de arena.

mom *n colloq.* mamá *f*, mami *f*

moment *n* momento *m*, instante *m* **at any ~** en cualquier momento **at this ~** en este momento **beautiful ~** momento hermoso **for the ~** por el momento **happy ~s** momentos felices **magic(al) ~** momento mágico **precious ~** momento precioso **present ~** momento actual **right ~** momento justo **tense ~** momento de tensión **this ~** este momento **up to this ~** hasta este momento **Just a moment.** Un momento. **Can I talk with you alone for a moment?** ¿Puedo hablar un momento a solas *con usted (Fam: contigo)?* **I'll never forget these wonderful moments with you.** Nunca olvidaré estos momentos maravillosos contigo. **There's never a dull moment (with you).** Nunca hay un momento de aburrimiento *(con usted [Fam. contigo])*. **I haven't known a dull moment since I met (1,2) you.** No he tenido un solo momento de aburrimiento desde que *(1) lo m / (2) la f (Fam: te)* conocí.

momentarily *adv* momentáneamente, por el momento **It eludes me momentarily.** De momento se me escapa. **Excuse me. I'm momentarily (1) awestruck. / (2) dazzled.** Discúlpame. De momento estoy *(1)* apabullado *(-da). / (2)* deslumbrado *(-da)*.

monastery *n* monasterio *m*

money *n* dinero *m* **a lot of ~** mucho dinero **earn ~** ganar dinero **lose ~** perder dinero **make ~** hacer dinero **no ~** sin dinero **not much ~** no mucho dinero **play for ~** jugar por dinero **transfer ~** transferir dinero **wire ~** enviar dinero por telegrama **Do you have enough money?** ¿Tiene usted *(Fam:* ¿Tienes) suficiente dinero? *(1)* **I / (2) We (don't) have enough money.** (No) *(1)* Tengo / *(2)* Tenemos suficiente dinero. **Could you lend me some money (until...)?** ¿Podría usted *(Fam:* ¿Podrías) prestarme dinero (hasta …)? *(1)* **I / (2) We can lend you some money.** *(1)* Yo puedo... / *(2)* Nosotros podemos... *prestarle (Fam: prestarte)* dinero. **Where can (1) I / (2) we exchange money?** ¿Dónde *(1)* puedo / *(2)* podemos cambiar dinero? *(1)* **I / (2) We need to exchange money.** *(1)* Necesito / *(2)* Necesitamos cambiar dinero. **Money can't buy (1) happiness. / (2) love.** El dinero no puede comprar *(1)* la felicidad. / *(2)* el amor.

monk *n* monje *m* **live like a ~** vivir como un monje

monkey *n* mono *m*, -na *f*, mico *m*, -ca *f* **~ business** chanchullo *m*, truco *m*, diablura *f*

monotonous *adj* monótono *m*, -na *f*

monotony *n* monotonía *f* **relieve the ~** romper la monotonía

---

Numbers in Spanish are given on pages 411-412.

monster *n* monstruo *m*

month *n* mes *m* **all** ~ todo el mes **a** ~ **ago** hace un mes **a whole** ~ un mes completo **every** ~ todos los meses **for a (whole)** ~ por (todo) un mes **for** *(1)* **two** / *(2)* **three** / *(3)* **four** ~**s** por *(1)* dos / *(2)* tres / *(3)* cuatro meses **for** por *(1)* cinco / *(2)* seis meses **in** *(1)* **a** / *(2)* **one** ~ 1. *(within)* en *(1,2)* un mes; 2. *(after)* dentro de *(1,2)* un mes **in** *(1)* **two** / *(2)* **three** / *(3)* **four** / *(4)* **five** / *(5)* **six** ~**s** 1. *(within)* en *(1)* dos / *(2)* tres / *(3)* cuatro / *(4)* cinco / *(5)* seis meses; *(after)* dentro de *(1)* dos / *(2)* tres / *(3)* cuatro / *(4)* cinco / *(5)* seis meses; **last** ~ el último mes **next** ~ el mes próximo **once a** ~ una vez al mes **the whole** ~ el mes entero **this** ~ este mes **two** ~**s ago** hace dos meses

monthly *adj* mensual *m&f*, mensualmente, al mes ~ **salary** salario *m* mensual

monument *n* monumento *m*

mooch *vi (slang)* vivir de gorra, vagar

moocher *n (slang)* vago *m*, -ga *f*, gorrón *m*, -na *f*

mood *n* humor *m*, temperamento *m*, ánimo *m* **cheerful** ~ temperamento alegre **great** ~ gran humor **melancholy** ~ ánimo melancólico **playful** ~ ánimo juguetón **sad** ~ ánimo triste **somber** ~ humor sombrío **wonderful** ~ humor maravilloso **You're in a** *(1)* **bright** / *(2)* **good** / *(3)* **happy** / *(4)* **grouchy** / *(5)* **grumpy** / *(6)* **sour mood today.** *Usted está (Fam: Estás)* de un humor *(1)* muy animado / *(2)* bueno / *(3)* feliz / *(4)* rezongón / *(5)* gruñón / *(6)* amargo el día de hoy. **Your** *(1)* **cheery** / *(2)* **happy** / *(3)* **sunny mood is very infectious.** *Su (Fam: Tu)* humor *(1)* jovial / *(2)* feliz / *(3)* risueño es muy contagioso. **I'm sorry I was in such a** *(1)* **bad** / *(2)* **grouchy** / *(3)* **sour mood (yesterday).** Lamento haber *(1)* estado de mal humor / *(2)* de humor gruñón / *(3)* amargo (el día de ayer). **My mood always improves when you're around.** Mi humor siempre se mejora cuando *usted está (Fam: tú estás)* cerca. **I'm (really) not in the mood (***[1]* **for that.** / *[2]* **for games.** / *[3]* **for jokes.** / *[4]* **to do that.** / *[5]* **to go.** / *[6]* **to discuss it.).** (De veras) No estoy de humor (para *[1]* eso. / *[2]* juegos. / *[3]* bromas. / *[4]* hacer eso. / *[5]* ir. / *[6]* discutirlo.

moody *adj* malhumorado *m*, -da *f*, temperamental *m&f*

moon *n* luna *f* **full** ~ luna llena **half** ~ media luna

moonbeam *n* rayo *m* de luna

moonlight *n* luz *f* de luna **I want to** *(1)* **...dance with you...** / *(2)* **...kiss you... in the moonlight.** Quiero *(1)* ...bailar *con usted (Fam: contigo)*… / *(2)* ... besarte... a la luz de la luna.

moonlit *adj* iluminado *(-da)* por la luna

moon-struck *adj* 1. *(romantically sentimental)* soñador *m*, -dora *f*; 2. *(mad)* lunático *m*, -ca *f*

moped *n* bicimoto *f* **Let's rent a moped.** Vayamos a rentar una bicimoto.

Spanish "h" is always silent.

moral *adj* moral *m&f*

moral *n* 1. *pl (standards of conduct)* ética *f*, moral *f* ; 2. *(point, lesson)* moraleja *f* **old-fashioned** ~**s** moral anticuada **person of good** ~**s** persona de buena moral **person of loose** ~**s** persona de moral libertina **strong** ~**s** moral sólida **The moral of the story is, ...** La moraleja del cuento es ...

morale *n* moral *f*, estado *m* de ánimo **You're very good for my morale.** Eres muy bueno *(-na)* para mi estado de ánimo.

more *adj* más ~ **love** más amor ~ **money** más dinero ~ **opportunity** más oportunidad ~ **time** más tiempo **The more, the merrier.** Mientras más haya, mejor.

more *adv* más **any** ~ más ~ **and more** más y más ~ **or less** más o menos   **no** ~ nomás **You're more beautiful than she is.** *Usted es (Fam: Tú eres)* más hermosa que ella. **I love you more than I can say.** Te amo más que lo que puedo decir.

morning *n* mañana *f* **every** ~ cada mañana **in the** ~ por la mañana **this** ~ esta mañana **tomorrow** ~ mañana por la mañana **yesterday** ~ ayer por la mañana **Good morning!** ¡Buenos días!

mortgage *n* hipoteca *f (1)* **I** / *(2)* **We pay a monthly mortgage (of $[amount])** **on** *(3)* **my** / *(4)* **our house.** *(1)* Pago / *(2)* Pagamos una hipoteca mensual (de $___) sobre *(3)* mi / *(4)* nuestra casa.

mortifying *adj* mortificante *m&f* **This is mortifying.** Esto es mortificante.

mosquito *n* mosquito *m* ~ **bite** piquete *m* de mosquito ~ **repellent** repelente *m* de mosquitos **There are too many mosquitoes around here.** Hay demasiados mosquitos por aquí. **This will keep the mosquitoes off you.** Esto mantendrá a los mosquitos lejos de tí.

most *adj* la mayoría *f* ~ **people** la mayoría de la gente

most *adj* por demás, de lo más ~ **beautiful** por demás hermosa ~ **difficult** por demás difícil ~ **interesting** por demás interesante ~ **of all** más que nada **What I want most of all right now is** *(what)*. Lo que yo quiero ahora más que nada es ___. **What** *(1)* **I** / *(2)* **we need most of all is** *(what)*. Lo que *(1)* necesito / *(2)* necesitamos más que nada es ___. **You're the most beautiful woman I've ever met.** *Usted es (Fam: Tú eres)* la mujer más hermosa que he conocido.

most *n* la mayor parte *f* ~ **of my life** la mayor parte de mi vida ~ **of the time** la mayor parte del tiempo

mostly *adv* principalmente, en su mayor parte

motel *n* motel *m*

mother *n* madre *f* **foster** ~ madre *f* adoptiva

mother-in-law *n* suegra *f*

motherly *adj* maternal *m&f*

Questions about the metric system? See page 417.

motion *n* movimiento *m*, moción *f* **go through the ~s** hacer las cosas por no dejar ~ **sickness** náuseas *f pl*, mareo *m*

motivate *vt* motivar **I need someone like you to motivate me.** Necesito a alguien como *usted (Fam: tú)* para que me motive.

motive *n* motivo *m* **ulterior ~** motivo ulterior

motor *n* motor *m* **~ scooter** patín *m* motorizado **Something is wrong with the motor.** Algo anda mal con el motor. **The motor needs to be fixed.** El motor necesita reparación.

motorbike *n* motocicleta *f*

motorboat *n* bote *m* motorizado **Let's rent a motorboat.** Rentemos un bote motorizado. **Where can** *(1)* **I / (2) we rent a motorboat?** ¿Dónde *(1)* puedo / *(2)* podemos rentar un bote motorizado?

motorcycle *n* motocicleta *f*, moto *f* **Let's rent a motorcycle.** Rentemos una moto. **Would you like to ride with me on my motorcycle?** ¿Le *(Fam. Te)* gustaría pasear conmigo en mi moto? **I don't like motorcycles.** No me gustan las motos.

motorhome *n* casa *f* rodante (motorizada)

mountain *n* montaña *f* **climb a ~** escalar una montaña **hike in the ~s** caminar en las montañas **~ climber** montañista *m & f* **~ climbing** montañismo *m* **I love to climb mountains.** Me encanta escalar montañas. **Have you ever climbed mountains?** ¿Ha escalado usted *(Fam: ¿Has escalado)* montañas alguna vez? **I'll teach you mountain climbing.** Yo te enseño a escalar montañas.

mountainous *adj* montañoso *m*, -sa *f*

mouse *n* ratón *m* **You're quiet as a mouse.** Usted es *(Fam: Tú eres)* callado *(-da)* como un ratón.

mouth *n* boca *f* **big ~** boca grande **cute ~** boca linda **full ~** boca plena **little ~** boca chica **lovely ~** boca adorable **pretty ~** boca bonita **sensual ~** boca sensual **sexy ~** boca sexy **small ~** boca pequeña **soft ~** boca suave **sweet ~** boca dulce **tantalizing ~** boca provocativa *(1)* **Close / (2) Open your mouth.** *(1)* Cierra / *(2)* Abre la boca. **You have such a beautiful mouth.** *Usted tiene (Fam: Tienes)* una boca tan bonita. **What a wonderful mouth you have!** ¡Qué maravilla de boca tienes! **You took the words right out of my mouth.** *Usted me quitó (Fam: Me quitaste)* las palabras de la boca.

move *vt* 1. *(cause to move)* mover; 2. *(change places)* cambiar **Let me help you move that.** Déjame ayudarte a mover eso. **Why don't you move your stuff over here?** ¿Por qué no cambias tus cosas para allá?

move *vi* 1. *(make a motion)* moverse; 2. *(change places)* cambiarse; 3. *(home)* mudarse **Don't move!** ¡No te muevas! **Let's move over there.** Vayámonos para allá. **Let's move into the shade.** Pongámonos a la sombra. *(1)* **I / (2)**

The letter "ñ" sounds like the "ny" in "canyon".

We might move *(3)* **down here.** / *(4)* **to** *(city)*. Es posible que *(1)* me mude / *(2)* nos mudemos *(3)* aquí. / *(4)* a ___.

★ **move in** *idiom (a residence)* mudarse a; ocupar

★ **move out** *idiom (from a residence)* mudarse de; desocupar

movie *n* película *f* **action** ~ película de acción **adult** ~ película para adultos **animated** ~ película animada (caricaturas) **boring** ~ película aburrida **cartoon** ~ película de caricaturas **charming** ~ película fascinante **dumb** ~ película tonta **erotic** ~ película erótica **exciting** ~ película excitante **good** ~ buena película **great** ~ gran película **heart-warming** ~ película que llega al corazón **horror** ~ película de terror **lousy** ~ película pésima **full of suspense** película llena de suspenso **poor** ~ película mediocre **romantic** ~ película romántica **sci-fi** ~ película de ciencia-ficción **spy** ~ película de espionaje **terrific** ~ película magnífica **thrilling** ~ película de suspenso **weird** ~ película extraña **wonderful** ~ película maravillosa **Have you seen the movie** *(title)*? ¿Ya viste la película ___? **You should see (the movie)** *(title)*. Debes de ver (la película) ___. **A real good movie was** *(title)*. Una Buena película fue ___. **Are there any good movies around here that are in both English and Spanish?** ¿Hay películas buenas aquí que estén tanto en Inglés como en Español? **I have two tickets to this movie. Would you like to see it with me?** Tengo dos boletos para esta película. ¿Te gustaría verla conmigo?

moxie *n* 1. *(pluck; audacity)* coraje *m*, audacia *f*; 2. *(ingenuity)* ingenio *m*, ingeniosidad *f*

Mrs señora

MS *abbrev* = 1. **Master of Science degree** maestría *f* en ciencias exactas; 2. **multiple sclerosis** esclerosis *f* múltiple

much *adj* tanto **as** ~ **as** tanto como **(not)** ~ **money** (no) tanto dinero **(not)** ~ **time** (no) tanto tiempo **too** ~ demasiado *m*, -da *f* **very** ~ muchísimo **Not too much for me, please.** No tanto para mí, por favor. **That's (way) too much!** ¡Eso es muchísimo! *(1)* **I** / *(2)* **We don't have much time.** No *(1)* tengo / *(2)* tenemos tanto tiempo. **I don't have as much audacity as you do.** No tengo tanta audacia como *usted (Fam: tú).* **How much does it cost?** ¿Cuánto cuesta?

much *adv* tanto; mucho **not** ~ no tanto **too** ~ demasiado **very** ~ mucho **I love you very much.** Te amo muchísimo. **Nothing much.** No mucho.

mud *n* lodo *m* **There's too much mud.** Hay demasiado lodo.

muddy *adj* lodoso *m*, -sa *f* **It's too muddy.** Está demasiado lodoso.

muffler *n* mofle *m*, silenciador *m*

multilingual *adj* miltilingüe *m&f*

munch *vi* masticar, mascar **Would you care for something to munch on?**

¿Te gustaría algo para comer?

mundane *adj* mundano *m*, -na *f*

muscle *n* músculo *m*

muscular *adj* muscular *m&f*

museum *n* museo *m* art ~ museo de arte **history** ~ museo histórico **Excuse me, do you know where the art museum is?** Disculpe, ¿sabe usted dónde se encuentra el museo de arte?

mushy *adj* efusivo *m*, -va *f*, demasiado sentimental *m&f*, baboso *m*, -sa *f* **I hope I don't sound mushy.** Espero no sonar demasiado sentimental.

music *n* música *f (See also phrases under* **go, like** *and* **love***.)* **all kinds of** ~ toda clase de música **alternative** ~ música alternativa **blue-grass** ~ música de bluegrass **classical** ~ música clásica **country-western** ~ música country **enjoy** ~ disfrutar la música **folk** ~ música folklórica **good** ~ buena música **guitar** ~ música de guitarra **instrumental** ~ música instrumental **listen to** ~ escuchar música **loud** ~ música alta **New Age** ~ música de la nueva era **organ** ~ música de órgano **play** ~ tocar música **popular** ~ música popular **rock** ~ música rock **romantic** ~ música romántica **sentimental** ~ música sentimental **soft** ~ música suave **soul** ~ música soul **spiritual**~ música espiritual **what kind of** ~ qué clase de música **What's the best place here to listen to** *(type)* **music? (Would you like to go there with** *[1]* **me? /** *[2]* **us?** ¿Cuál es el mejor lugar aquí para escuchar música ___? (¿Te gustaría ir ahí *[1]* conmigo / *[2]* con nosotros? **What kind of music do you like?** ¿Qué clase de música le *(Fam: te)* gusta? **I (don't) like** *(type of)* **music.** (No) Me gusta la música ___. **Let's listen to some music.** Vamos a escuchar algo de música. **I'll put on some music.** Voy a poner algo de música. **That's** *(1)* **beautiful /** *(2)* **great /** *(3)* **nice /** *(4)* **wonderful music.** Esa es música. *(1)* hermosa. / *(2)* fenomenal. / *(3)* buena. / *(4)* maravillosa. **Do you know the words to the music?** ¿Se sabe usted *(Fam: Te sabes)* la letra de esa música? **Teach me the words to the music.** Enséñeme *(Fam: Enséñame)* la letra de esa música.

musical *adj* musical *m&f* ~ **ability** habilidad *f* musical ~ **instrument** instrumento *m* musical ~ **show** espectáculo *m* musical ~ **talent** talento *m* musical ~ **voice** voz *f* melodiosa **Do you play any musical instruments?** ¿Toca usted *(Fam: ¿Tocas)* algún instrumento musical?

musician *n* músico *m*, música *f*

musky *adj* almizcle *m&f*

must *v aux* 1. *(necessity)* tener que, deber; 2. *(strong possibility)* debe ~ **not** no debe *(1)* **I /** *(2)* **We (really) must go.** (De veras) *(1)* Tengo / *(2)* Tenemos que ir. **You really must** *(1)* **go there. /** *(2)* **read it. /** *(3)* **see it. /** *(4)* **try it.** En serio, tienes que *(1)* ir allá / *(2)* leerlo. / *(3)* verlo. / *(4)* intentarlo. **You**

Spanish "o" is pronounced like "o" in "note".

must come visit *(1)* **me.** / *(2)* **us.** Tienes que venir a *(1)* visitarme. / *(2)* visitarnos. **You must be out of your mind.** Debes estar loco *(-ca)*.

mustache *n* bigote *m* **handsome** ~ atractivo bigote

mutter *vi* murmurar **What are you muttering about?** ¿Qué estás murmurando?

mutual *adj* mutuo *m*, -tua *f* ~ **acquaintance** conocido *(-da)* mutuo *(-tua)* ~ **attraction** atracción *f* mutua ~ **friend** amigo *(-ga)* mutuo *(-tua)* ~ **respect** respeto *m* mutuo

my *poss. adj* mi *sing.*, mis *pl*

myself *pers. pron* 1. *(reflexively)* a mí mismo *m*, -ma *f*; 2. *(for emphasis)* yo solo *m*, -la *f*; yo mismo *m*, -ma *f* by ~ solo *m*, -la *f* *(1,2)* **I hurt myself.** *(1)* Yo solo *(-la)* me lastimé. / *(2)* Yo mismo *(-ma)* me lastimé. **I said to myself...** Me dije...

mysterious *adj* misterioso *m*, -sa *f* **You're a rather mysterious person.** *Usted es (Fam: Tú eres)* una persona bastante misteriosa.

mysteriously *adv* misteriosamente

mystery *n* misterio *m* **It's a mystery to me.** Es un misterio para mí.

mystical *adj* místico *m*,-ca *f*

mystify *vt* desconcertar **You (really) mystify me (at times).** (De veras) Me desconciertas (a veces).

mystique *n* mística *f* **feminine** ~ mística femenina

myth *n* mito *m*

Numbers in parentheses always signal choices.

N

nails *n, pl (fingernails)* uñas *fpl*
naive *adj* inocente *m&f*
naked *adj* desnudo *m,* -da *f* **completely** ~ completamente desnudo *(-da)* **run around** ~ andar desnudo *(-da)* **stark** ~ completamente desnudo *(-da)*
name *n* nombre *m* **cat's** ~ nombre del gato **daughter's** ~ nombre de la hija **dog's** ~ nombre del perro **family** ~ apellido *m* **first** ~ primer nombre **last** ~ apellido **maiden** ~ nombre de soltera **middle** ~ segundo nombre **my** ~ mi nombre ~ **of the restaurant** nombre del restaurante **son's** ~ nombre del hijo **your** ~ su *(Fam: tu)* nombre *(1,2)* **What's your name?** *(1)(full name:)*¿Cuál es su nombre completo? / *(2)(full or first:)* ¿Cómo se llama? *(1,2)* **My name is** *(name)*. *(1) (full name:)* Mi nombre es ___ . / *(2) (full or first:)* Me llamo ____ . **I'm sorry, I forgot your name.** Lo siento, olvidé *su (Fam: tu)* nombre. **How do you spell your name?** ¿Cómo se escribe *su (Fam: tu)* nombre?
nap *n* siesta *f (1)* **I'm /** *(2)* **We're going to take a nap.** *(1)* Voy / *(2)* Vamos a dormir una siesta. **Let's take a nap.** Vamos a dormir una siesta.
napkin *n* servilleta *f* **sanitary** ~**(s)** toalla(s) higiénica(s)
narrow *adj* estrecho *m,* -cha *f*
narrow-minded *adj* de mente estrecha
nasty *adj* 1. *(disgusting, vile)* repugnante *m&f*; 2. *(obscene)* obsceno *m,* -na *f*; 3. *(mean, ill-tempered)* grosero *m,* -ra *f* ~ **language** lenguaje obsceno ~ **remark** comentario grosero **words** palabras obscenas **That was nasty!** ¡Eso fue grosero!
nation *n* nación *f*
national *adj* nacional *m&f* ~ **anthem** himno nacional
native *adj* nativo *m,* -va *f* ~ **American** nativo *(-va)* americano *(-na)*
natural *adj* 1. *(from nature)* natural *m&f*; 2. *(normal)* natural *m&f* ~ **beauty** belleza f natural ~ **talent** talento *m* natural **It seems so natural**

Spanish "a" is mostly like "a" in "mama".

being with you. Me parece tan natural estar *con usted (Fam: contigo)*. **It feels so natural talking to you.** Se siente tan natural platicar *con usted (Fam: contigo)*.

naturally *adv* 1. *(in a natural way)* naturalmente, con naturalidad; 2. *(of course)* naturalmente **act** ~ actuar con naturalidad **behave** ~ comportarse con naturalidad

nature *n* 1. *(character)* naturaleza *f* ; 2. *(outdoors)* naturaleza *f* **artistic** ~ naturaleza artística **caring** ~ naturaleza bondadosa **cheerful** ~ naturaleza alegre **enjoy** ~ disfrutar de la naturaleza **friendly** ~ naturaleza amigable **gentle** ~ naturaleza gentil **impulsive** ~ naturaleza impulsiva **loving** ~ naturaleza cariñosa **quiet** ~ naturaleza tranquila **warm** ~ naturaleza cálida **The beauty of all this nature is fantastic.** La belleza de toda esta naturaleza es fantástica. *(1)* **I** / *(2)* **We enjoy nature.** *(1)* Yo disfruto... / *(2)* Nosotros disfrutamos ... de la naturaleza. **There is such (genuine) warmth in your nature.** Hay en *su (Fam: tu)* naturaleza tanta (genuina) calidez. **I have a very passionate nature.** Yo soy de naturaleza muy apasionada.

naughty *adj* 1. *(mischievous)* pícaro *m*, -ra *f* ; 2. *(risque)* atrevido *m*, -da *f* **Don't be naughty.** No seas atrevido *(-da)*. **That was a naughty thing to do.** Eso fue una cosa muy fea.

navy *n* marina *f* ~ **base** base de la marina **I'm in the Navy.** Estoy en la marina de guerra. **I'm a** *(1)* **Petty Officer** / *(2)* **an Ensign** / *(3)* *(rank)* **in the Navy.** Soy *(1)* suboficial de marina / *(2)* alférez / *(3)* ___ en la marina de guerra. **I served four years in the Navy.** Presté servicio en la marina de guerra durante cuatro años.

near *adj* cercano *m*, -na *f* **in the** ~ **future** en el futuro cercano ~ **miss** estar en un tris **Is it near here?** ¿Está cerca de aquí? **It's near here.** Está cerca de aquí. **Where's the nearest** *(1)* **bank?** / *(2)* **cash machine?** / *(3)* **gas station?** / *(4)* **internet café?** / *(5)* **pharmacy?** / *(6)* **shopping center?** / *(7)* **supermarket?** ¿Dónde está *(1)* ...el banco... / *(2)* ...el cajero automático... / *(3)* ...la estación de gasolina... / *(4)* ...el café de Internet... / *(5)* ...la farmacia... / *(6)* ...el centro comercial... / *(7)* ...el supermercado... más cercano *(-na)*? **When you're near me, I can't think straight.** Cuando estás cerca de mí, no puedo pensar bien. **I like it when you're near me.** Me gusta cuando estás cerca de mí.

near *adv* cerca **come** ~ **me** acércate a mí **Come sit near** *(1)* **me.** / *(2)* **us.** Siéntate cerca de *(1)* mí. / *(2)* nosotros.

nearby *adj* cercano *m*, -na *f*, en la cercanía, *(1)* **My** / *(2)* **Our hotel is nearby.** *(1)* Mi / *(2)* Nuestro hotel está cerca de aquí.

nearby *adv* en la cercanía

nearly *adv* casi, por poco **I nearly missed** *(1,2)* **meeting you.** Por poco no

---

Articles: m = el, f = la, mpl = los, fpl = las

lo m, la f (Fam: te) encuentro.

nearsighted *adj* miope *m&f*

neat *adj* 1. *(orderly, tidy) (person)* pulcro *m*, -cra *f*; *(appearance)* arreglado *m*, -da *f*; *(room)* ordenado *m*, -da *f*; *(clean)* limpio *m*, -pia *f*; 2. *(slang: great)* genial *m&f* ~ **and tidy** limpio y ordenado

neatly *adv* cuidadosamente, pulcramente

necessary *adj* necesario *m*, -ria *f* ~ **equipment** equipo *m* necesario ~ **evil** mal *m* necesario **if** ~ si es necesario **It's (not) necessary.** (No) Es necesario.

neck *vi (slang) (kiss)* besuquear

neck *n* 1. *(body)* cuello *m* ; 2. *(garment)* cuello *m* ~ **and** ~ a la par **delicate** ~ cuello delicado **graceful** ~ cuello gracioso **little** ~ cuello pequeño **long** ~ cuello largo **lovely** ~ cuello adorable **slender** ~ cuello delgado **This game is neck and neck.** Este juego es parejo. **What a pain in the neck!** ¡Qué molestia!

necklace *n* collar *m* **What a beautiful necklace!** ¡Qué collar tan bonito!

neckline *n* línea *f* del cuello

necktie *n* corbata *f* **You don't need a necktie.** No necesitas corbata. **You should probably wear a necktie.** Tal vez debieras ponerte una corbata.

nectar *n* néctar *m* ~ **of the gods** néctar de los dioses. **I love the sweet nectar of your kisses.** Adoro el dulce néctar de tus besos.

need *vt* necesitar **What do you need?** ¿Qué *necesita usted (Fam: necesitas)*? **What do I need?** ¿Qué necesito? *(1)* **I** / *(2)* **We** / *(3)* **You need** ___ . *(1)* Necesito ___ . / *(2)* Necesitamos ___ . / *(3)* *Necesita usted (Fam: Necesitas)* ___ . *(1)* **I** / *(2)* **We don't need it.** No lo *(1)* necesito. / *(2)* necesitamos. *(1)* **I** / *(2)* **We don't need anything** *(1)* No necesito / *(3)* necesitamos nada. **I need to** *(1,2)* **see you.** / *(3)* **talk to you.** / *(4)* **take care of some business (first).** Necesito *(1)* verlo *m* / *(2)* verla *f (Fam: verte).* / *(3)* hablar *con usted (Fam: contigo).* / *(4)* atender (primero) un asunto. **If you need help, let** *(1)* **me** / *(2)* **us know.** Si *necesita usted (Fam: necesitas)* ayuda, *(1)* avíseme *(Fam: avísame)* / *(2)* avísenos *(Fam: avísanos).* **All I need to make me happy is you.** Tú eres todo lo que necesito para ser feliz. **I need you (very much).** Te necesito (muchísimo).

needle *vt (taunt, tease)* fastidiar **I'm sorry, I don't mean to needle you (about that).** Lo siento, no quise fastidiarte (con eso).

needle *n* aguja *f* **It's like finding a needle in a haystack.** Es como hallar una aguja en un pajar. *(1)* **I'm** / *(2)* **We're on pins and needles.** *(1)* Estoy.... / *(2)* Estamos en ascuas.

negative *adj* negativo *m*, -va *f* ~ **attitude** actitud *f* negativa ~ **outlook** punto de vista negativo **Don't be so negative.** No seas tan negativo *(-va).*

negative *n (photo)* negativo *m*

Spanish "z" is pronounced like "s" in "safe".

neglect *vt* 1. *(not pay proper attention to)* desatender; 2. *(forget, fail to)* descuidar **I didn't mean to neglect you.** No quise desatenderte. **You've been neglecting me terribly.** Me has estado desatendiendo mucho.

neglected *adj* descuidado *m*, -da *f*

negligee *n* negligé *m*

neighbor(s) *n (pl)* vecino(s) *m(pl)*, -na(s) *f(pl)* **next-door** ~ el vecino *(la vecina)* de junto

neighborhood *n* vecindario *m*, barrio *m* **in** *(1)* **my** / *(2)* **our** / *(3)* **your** ~ en *(1)* mi / *(2)* nuestro / *(3)* su *(Fam: tu)* vecindario

neighboring *adj* adyacente *m&f*

neither *adj* ni ~ **one** ninguno *m*, -na *f*

neither *pron* ninguno *m*, -na *f* ~ **of us** ninguno de nosotros~ **of them** ninguno de ellos ~ **of you** ninguno de ustedes

nephew *n* sobrino *m*

nerd *n (slang)* 1. *(dim-wit)* naco *m*, -ca *f*; 2. *(very scholarly person; expert)* sabihondo *m*, -da *f*

nerve *n* 1. *(anat.)* nervio *m* ; 2. *(courage)* valor *m*; 3. *(audacity; impudence)* descaro *m* **It's getting on my nerves.** Me está poniendo de nervios. **You're a bundle of nerves. Take it easy.** Estás muy nervioso *(-sa)*. Tómalo con calma. **You really have a lot of nerve.** Mira que tienes descaro.

nervous *adj* nervioso *m*, -sa *f* ~ **breakdown** colapso *m* nervioso **be** ~ estar nervioso *(-sa)* **feel** ~ sentirse nervioso *(-sa)* **make** *(1)* **me** / *(2)* **you** ~ *(1)* ponerme / *(2)* ponerte nervioso *(-sa)* **Why are you so nervous?** ¿Por qué estás tan nervioso *(-sa)*? **Don't be (so) nervous.** No seas (tan) nervioso *(-sa)*. **I'm (not) nervous (about it).** (No) Estoy nervioso (por eso). **There's nothing to be nervous about.** No hay de qué ponerse nervioso *(-sa)*.

nestle *vi (cuddle)* acurrucar ~ **in my arms** acurrucarte en mis brazos

net *n* red *m* **fish** ~ nasa **tennis** ~ red de tenis **volleyball** ~ red de voleibol

neurotic *adj* neurótico *m*, -ca *f*

neutral *adj* neutral *m&f* ~ **opinion** opinion *f* neutral **I want to stay neutral in this.** Quiero permanecer neutral en esto.

never *adv* nunca ~ **again** nunca jamás **I've never** *(1)* **been here before.** / *(2)* **seen it.** Yo nunca antes *(1)* he estado aquí. / *(2)* lo he visto. **We've never** *(1)* **been here before.** / *(2)* **seen it.** Nosotros nunca antes *(1)* hemos estado aquí. / *(2)* lo hemos visto. **I never want to leave here.** Nunca me quiero ir de aquí. **I will never forget you.** Nunca te olvidaré. **I never met anyone like you.** Nunca conocí a nadie como *usted (Fam: tú)*. **Better late than never.** Mejor tarde que nunca. **Never mind**. No *se preocupe (Fam: te preocupes)*.

A tilde ~ in terms stands for the main entry word.

nevertheless *adv* sin embargo

new *adj* nuevo *m*, -va *f* **What's new?** ¿Qué hay de nuevo? **Happy New Year!** ¡Feliz Año Nuevo!

newcomer *n* recién llegado *m*, -da *f*

newlyweds *n, pl* recién casados *mpl*

news *n* noticias *f* **latest** ~ las últimas noticias **Have you heard the news?** ¿Ya oíste las noticias?

newspaper *n* periódico *m* **I saw your ad in the newspaper.** Vi *su (Fam: tu)* anuncio en el periódico. **I read in the newspaper that...** Leí en el periódico que...

next *adj* 1. *(next after preceding)* siguiente *m&f*; 2. *(next in time)* próximo *m*, -ma *f* ~ **door** la puerta de al lado ~ **month** el mes próximo ~ **stop** la próxima parada ~ **time** la próxima vez ~ **week** la semana próxima ~ **year** el año próximo *(1)* **I** / *(2)* **We get off at the next** *(3)* **station** / *(4)* **stop.** *(1)* Yo me bajo... / *(2)* Nosotros nos bajamos... en la próxima *(3)* estación / *(4)* parada. **Who's next?** ¿Quién sigue? **You're next.** Tú sigues. **Who lives next door?** ¿Quién vive en la puerta de al lado?

next *adv* luego, después **What happened next?** ¿Qué pasó después?

next to *phr prep* cerca de, junto a ~ **to last** penúltimo *(-ma)* **come sit next to me.** Siéntate junto a mí. **Would you like to sit next to the window?** *¿Le (Fam: Te)* gustaría *sentarse (Fam: sentarte)* junto a la ventana?

nibble *vt* mordisquear

Nicaraguan *adj* nicaragüense *m&f* ★ *n* nicaragüense *m&f*

nice *adj* 1. *(good, pleasant)* agradable *m&f*, afable *m&f*; 2. *(polite; gracious)* amable *m&f*, ; 3. *(friendly)* simpático *m*, -ca *f*; 4. *(attractive)* bonito *m*, -ta *f*; 5. *(well done)* bueno *m*, -na *f*, bien hecho *m*, -cha *f*; 6. *(respectable, decent)* buen *m*, buena *f* ~ **figure** bonita figura ~ **girl** *(respectable)* buena muchacha ~ **smile** sonrisa bonita ~ **trip** viaje agradable ~ **weather** clima agradable **How nice.** Qué agradable. **Be nice.** Sé amable. **That's very nice of you.** Es muy amable de tu parte. **That was very nice of you.** Eso fue muy amable de tu parte. *(1)* **I** / *(2)* **We had a very nice time.** *(1)* Pasé / *(2)* Pasamos un rato muy agradable. **That was a nice** *(1)* **play.** / *(2)* **shot.** *(1)* Esa fue una buena jugada. / *(2)* Ese fue un buen tiro. **I've never known anyone as nice.** Nunca conocí a nadie tan bueno *(-na)*.

nice-looking *adj* bien parecido *m*, -da *f*

nicely *adv* amablemente

nickname *n* apodo *m*

niece *n* sobrina *f*

night *n* noche *f* **all** ~ **long** toda la noche **at** ~ en la noche **beautiful** ~ noche hermosa **during the** ~ durante la noche **entire** ~ la noche entera **every** ~

---

*Spanish "ch" is pronounced like ours
(e.g., "cheese," "charge").*

cada noche **Friday** *(etc)* ~ el viernes por la noche *(etc.)* **lonely ~s** noches solitarias **long ~s** noches largas **last** ~ anoche **moonlit** ~ noche de luna **nice** ~ noche agradable ~ **after** ~ noche tras noche ~ **owl** ave *f* nocturna, noctámbulo *m*, -la *f* **quiet** ~ noche tranquila **sleepless** ~ noche de insomnio **starry** ~ noche estrellada **summer** ~ noche de verano **tomorrow** ~ mañana por la noche **warm** ~ noche tibia **the whole** ~ toda la noche **What a beautiful night.** Qué noche tan hermosa. **I'll never forget this night.** Nunca olvidaré esta noche. **The night is young (and you're so beautiful).** La noche es joven (y tú tan hermosa). **Good night!** ¡Buenas noches!

nightcap *n (colloq.) (drink before parting)* la del estribo **Would you care for a nightcap?** ¿Te tomas la del estribo? **How about a nightcap?** ¿Qué tal si nos tomamos la del estribo?

nightclub *n* club *m* nocturno

nightgown, nightie *n* camisón *m*

nightlife *n* vida *f* nocturna **Let's go check out the nightlife.** Vamos a ver la vida nocturna.

nightmare *n* pesadilla *f*

nighttime *n* la noche *f*

nipple *n* pezón *m*

no *adv* no

noble *adj* noble *m&f* ~ **gesture** gesto noble

nobody *pron* nadie **There's nobody there.** No hay nadie allí. **Nobody answers.** *(tel.)* Nadie contesta. **There's nobody (else) (in my life) except you.** No hay nadie (más) (en mi vida) excepto tú. **Nobody is looking.** Nadie está mirando. **Nobody will notice.** Nadie lo notará.

nocturnal *adj* nocturno *m*, -na *f* ~ **animal** animal nocturno

noise *n* ruido *m* **Did you hear that noise?** ¿Oíste ese ruido? **There's too much noise (here).** Hay mucho ruido (aquí).

noisy *adj* ruidoso *m*, -sa *f* **It's too noisy.** Es demasiado ruidoso.

nomad *n* nómada *m&f* **cultural** ~ nómada cultural **In my heart I'm a nomad.** Soy nómada de corazón.

nomadic *adj* nómada *m&f* ~ **life** vida nómada

nominate *vt* nombrar, nominar *(1)* **I** / *(2)* **We nominate you to** *(3)* **be the leader.** / *(4)* **do it.** / *(5)* **go first.** *(1)* Te nombro / *(2)* Te nombramos para *(3)* que seas líder. / *(4)* hacerlo. / *(5)* que vayas primero.

nonalcoholic *adj* no alcohólico *m*, -ca *f* **I'd like something nonalcoholic, please.** Quiero algo sin alcohol, por favor.

nonchalant *adj* despreocupado *m*, -da *f*

nonconformist *n* inconformista *m&f*

nondrinker *n* abstemio *m*, -mia *f*

Stress rule #1: The last syllable is stressed if the word ends in a consonant (except "n" and "s").

none *pron* ninguno *m*, -na *f* ~ **of it** ninguno *(-na)* de esos *(esas)* ~ **of them** ninguno *(-na)* de ellos *(ellas)* ~ **of us** ninguno *(-na)* de nosotros *(-tras)*

nonetheless *adv* no obstante, sin embargo

nonsense *n* disparate *m*, tontería *f* **utter** ~ disparate total **That's a lot of nonesense.** Eso es pura tontería.

nonsmoker *n* no fumador *m*, no fumadora *f*

nonstop *adj* directo *m*, -ta *f*, sin escalas ★ **nonstop** *adv* sin escalas

noon *n* mediodía *m* **around** ~ alrededor del mediodía **at** ~ a mediodía

no one *pron* nadie *m&f (See phrases under* **nobody***)*

normal *adj* normal *m&f* ~ **childhood** niñez normal **I know it's hard, but please try to be normal.** Sé que es difícil, pero por favor, trata de ser normal.

normally *adv* normalmente

north *n* norte *m* **in the** ~ en el norte **to the** ~ al norte

northeast *n* noreste *m*

northern *adj* norteño *m*, -ña *f*, nórdico *m*, -ca *f*

northwest *n* noroeste *m*

nose *n* nariz *f* **big** ~ nariz grande **button** ~ nariz chata **cute** ~ nariz linda **little** ~ naricita **long** ~ nariz larga **petite** ~ nariz pequeña **pretty** ~ nariz bonita **Roman** ~ nariz romana **short** ~ nariz corta **slender** ~ nariz afilada **small** ~ nariz pequeña **tip of your** ~ la punta de tu nariz **turned-up** ~ nariz respingada **I don't mean to poke my nose into your (personal) business.** No quiero meter mi nariz en *sus (Fam: tus)* asuntos (personales). **Forgive me for poking my nose into your (personal) business.** Perdóname por meter mi nariz en *sus (Fam: tus)* asuntos (personales).

nosebleed *n* hemorragia *f* nasal

nostalgic *adj* nostálgico *m*, -ca *f* **It makes me feel nostalgic.** Me hace sentir nostálgico *(-ca)*.

nosy *adj* metiche *m&f* **Don't be so nosy.** No seas tan metiche. **You're sure nosy.** De verdad eres metiche *(-sa)*. **I don't mean to be so nosy.** No quiero ser metiche.

not *adv* no **I'd rather not.** Mejor no. **Not at all.** Nada de eso.

note *n* nota *f*, mensaje *m* **brief** ~ nota breve **little** ~ notita **love** ~ mensaje de amor **short** ~ nota breve **sweet** ~ nota dulce **I** *(1)* **got /** *(2)* **found /** *(3)* **read your note.** Me *(1)* llegó / *(2)* encontré / *(3)* leí *su (Fam: tu)* mensaje. **We** *(1)* **got /** *(2)* **found /** *(3)* **read your note.** Nos *(1)* llegó / *(2)* encontramos / *(3)* leímos *su (Fam: tu)* mensaje. *(1)* **I /** *(2)* **We left you a note.** Le *(Fam: Te)* *(1)* dejé / *(2)* dejamos una nota. **Did you get** *(1)* **my /** *(2)* **our note?** ¿ Le *(Fam: Te)* llegó *(1)* mi / *(2)* nuestro mensaje?

notebook *n* cuaderno *m*

Spanish "i" is mostly "ee", but can also be shorter, like "i" in "sit," when together with other vowels.

nothing *n* nada *f* **sweet ~s** palabras *fpl* de amor **There's nothing** *(1)* **here** / *(2)* **there.** No hay nada *(1)* aquí / *(2)* allí. **There was nothing (there).** No había nada (allí). **There's nothing to worry about.** No hay de qué preocuparse. **There's nothing** *(1)* **I** / *(2)* **we** / *(3)* **you can do.** No hay nada que *(1)* ...yo pueda... / *(2)* ...nosotros podamos... / *(3)* ...ustedes puedan... hacer. **Nothing ventured, nothing gained.** El que no arriesga no gana.

notice *vt* fijarse, notar, ver **Did you notice the ...?** ¿Te fijaste en...? **I didn't notice it.** No me fijé. **I noticed you the minute you walked in.** Me fijé en ti desde que entraste. **From the moment I** *(1, 2)* **noticed** *(3,4)* **you, I wanted to** *(5,6)* **meet you.** Desde el momento en que *(3)* lo *m* / *(4)* la *f* *(Fam: te)* *(1)* / *(2)* vi, quise *(5)* conocerlo *m* / *(6)* conocerla *f (Fam: conocerte)*. **How could I not notice you? You're so beautiful.** ¿Cómo no te iba a notar? Eres tan guapa.

notice *n* aviso *m*

notion *n* idea *f*, noción *f* **You have the wrong notion about me.** *Usted tiene (Fam: Tú tienes)* una idea equivocada de mí. **What gave you that notion?** ¿De dónde sacas esa idea?

novel *adj* original *m&f*, novedoso *m*, -sa *f* **~ idea** idea *f* novedosa

novel *n* novela *f*

novelty *n* novedad *f*

November *n* noviembre *m* **in ~** en noviembre **on ~ first** *(etc)* el primero de noviembre *(etc.)*

now *adv* ahora **a week from ~** dentro de una semana **a year from ~** dentro de un año **by ~** por ahora **from ~ on** de ahora en adelante **~ and then** de vez en cuando **right ~** ahora mismo **two weeks from ~** dentro de dos semanas **until ~** hasta ahora **up till ~** hasta ahora

nowhere *adv* en ninguna parte **in the middle of ~** en medio de ninguna parte **~ near** en ningún lugar cercano **There's nowhere to sit.** No hay dónde sentarse. **We're getting nowhere.** No estamos llegando a ninguna parte .

nude *adj* desnudo *m*, -da *f* **completely ~** completamente desnudo *(-da)* **lie ~** acostarse desnudo *(-da)* **~ photo** foto al desnudo

nude *n* desnudo *m* **in the ~** al desnudo **pose in the ~** posar al desnudo

nudist *n* nudista *m&f* **~ colony** colonia nudista

nuisance *n* molestia *f*, fastidio *m* **What a nuisance!** ¡Qué molestia! **I don't mean to make a nuisance of myself.** No quiero ser una molestia.

numb *adj* 1. *(from cold)* entumido *m*, -da *f*; 2. *(emotionally)* aturdido *m*, -da *f* **My** *(1)* **feet** / *(2)* **hands are numb.** Mis *(1)* pies están entumidos. / *(2)* manos están entumidas.

number *n* número *m* **apartment ~** número de departamento **bus ~** número de autobús **fax ~** número de fax **find the ~** encontrar el número **flight ~**

número de vuelo **forget the** ~ olvidar el número **hotel (phone)** ~ número del hotel **house** ~ número de casa **know the** ~ saber el número **look up the** ~ buscar el número **lucky** ~ número de la suerte **not know the** ~ no saber el número **passport** ~ número de pasaporte **remember the** ~ recordar el número **room** ~ número de cuarto **route** ~ número de ruta **(tele)phone** ~ número de teléfono **train** ~ número de tren **write down the** ~ anotar el número **What's your (phone) number?** ¿Cuál es *su (Fam: tu)* número (de teléfono)? **Could you give me your phone number?** ¿*Podría usted (Fam: Podrías)* darme *su (Fam: tu)* número de teléfono? **My (phone) number is** *(number)*. Mi número (de teléfono) es ___. **Here's my (phone) number.** Aquí está mi número (de teléfono). **Write down the number.** Anota el número. **I'll write down my phone number for you.** *Le (Fam: Te)* anoto mi número de teléfono. **I (don't) know the number.** (No) Me sé el número. **Don't forget the number.** No *olvide usted (Fam: olvides)* el número. **I forgot the number.** Olvidé el número. **I'm sorry I didn't call. I lost your number.** Lamento no haber llamado. Perdí *su (Fam: tu)* número. **What's the number to call?** ¿A qué número hay que llamar?

numerous *adj* numeroso *m*, -sa *f*

nun *n* monja *f*

nurse *vt* amamantar ~ **the baby** amamantar al bebé **It's time for me to nurse the baby.** Ya es hora de que amamante al bebé.

nurse *n* niñera *f*, enfermera *f*

nut *n* 1. *(fruit)* nuez *f* ; 2. *(for a bolt)* tuerca *f* ; 3. *(slang) (crazy person)* chiflado *m*, -da *f*; 4. *(ardent enthusiast)* apasionado *m*, -da *f* **golf** ~ apasionado *(-da)* del golf **sports** ~ apasionado *(-da)* de los deportes **tennis** ~ apasionado *(-da)* del tenis

nutrition *n* nutrición *f* **good** ~ buena nutrición **healthy** ~ nutrición saludable

nuts *pred adj (slang) (crazy)* loco *m*, -ca *f* **drive** ~ volver loco a alguien **You drive me nuts!** ¡Me vuelves loco *(-ca)*! **You gotta be nuts!** ¡Tienes que estar loco *(-ca)*!

nutty *adj (slang) (crazy)* chiflado *m*, -da *f* **a little** ~ un poco chiflado *(-da)* ~ **as a fruitcake** más loco *(-ca)* que una cabra

nuzzle *vt* frotar con la nariz

nymph *n* ninfa *f*, crisálida *f*

Spanish "j" is pronounced like "h".

O

oar *n* remo *m*

obey *vt* obedecer

object *vi* objetar **I hope you won't object.** Espero que no tengas objeción.
Would you object if I...? ¿Tendrías objeción si yo...?

object *n* 1. *(thing)* objeto *m*; 2. *(goal)* objeto *m* **strange ~** objeto extraño
Unidentified Flying ~ (UFO) objeto volador no identificado (OVNI)
What's the object (of the game)? ¿Cuál es el objeto del juego? **The
object of the game is ...** El objeto del juego es ...

objection *n* objeción *f* **If you have no objection...** Si no *tiene usted (Fam:
tienes)* objeción...

objective *adj* objetivo *m*, -va *f*

obligated *adj* obligado *m*, -da *f* **I don't want you to feel obligated.** No
quiero que *se sienta (Fam: te sientas)* obligado *(-da)*.

obliging *adj* servicial *m&f*, atento *m*, -ta *f*

oblivion *n* olvido *m*

oblivious *adj* olvidadizo *m*, -za *f*, absorto *m*, -ta *f* **When I'm with you, I'm
oblivious to everything else.** Cuando estoy contigo, me olvido de todo lo
demás.

obnoxious *adj* odioso *m*, -sa *f*, detestable *m&f*

obscene *adj* obsceno *m*, -na *f*, indecente *m&f* **~ language** lenguaje *m* obsceno

observant *adj* observador *m*, -dora *f*, perspicaz *m&f* **You're very observant.** *Usted es (Fam: Tú eres)* muy observador *(-ra)*.

observation *n* observación *f* **have under ~** tener en observación

observe *vt* 1. *(watch)* observar; 2. *(celebrate)* celebrar **We can observe it
better from there.** Lo podemos observar mejor desde aquí. **What holidays do you observe?** ¿Cuáles son los días de fiesta que celebran? **We
observe (the holidays)...** Nosotros celebramos (la fiesta de)...

obsessed *adj* obsesionado *m*, -da *f*

---

*Familiar "tu" forms in parentheses can replace
italicized polite forms.*

obsession *n* obsesión *f*
obsolete *adj* obsoleto *m*, -ta *f*
obstacle *n* obstáculo *m*
obstinate *adj* obstinado *m*, -da *f*
obtain *vt* obtener **Where can** *(1)* **I /** *(2)* **we obtain tickets?** ¿Dónde *(1)* puedo / *(2)* podemos conseguir boletos? **Where did you obtain your education?** ¿En dónde *obtuvo usted (Fam: obtuviste) su (Fam: tu)* educación?
obvious *adj* obvio *m*, -via *f* **I'm a master at identifying the obvious.** Soy un as para identificar lo obvio.
obviously *adv* obviamente
occasion *n* ocasión *f*, suceso *m*, oportunidad *f* **happy ~** ocasión feliz **special ~** ocasión especial **What's the occasion?** ¿Qué se celebra?
occasional *adj* ocasional *m&f* **I take an occasional drink.** Me tomo una copa de vez en cuando.
occasionally *adv* ocasionalmente **We** *(1)* **...come here... /** *(2)* **...go there... occasionally.** Nosotros *(1)* venimos aquí... / *(2)* vamos allá... ocasionalmente.
occult *n* ocultismo *m* **I'm (very) interested in the occult.** Me interesa (mucho) el ocultismo.
occupation *n* ocupación *f* **What's your occupation?** ¿Cuál es *su (Fam: tu)* ocupación? **My occupation is** *(what)*. Mi ocupación es ___.
occupied *adj* ocupado *m*, -da *f* **It's occupied.** Está ocupado.
occupy *vt* ocupar **I occupy myself with** *(what)*. Me ocupo en ___.
occur *vi* 1. *(happen)* ocurrir; 2. *(come to mind)* ocurrir **It just occurred to me that...** Se me acaba de ocurrir que... **That never occurred to me.** Eso nunca me ocurrió.
ocean *n* océano *m*, mar *m* **I love to** *(1)* **play /** *(2)* **swim in the ocean.** Me encanta *(1)* jugar / *(2)* nadar en el mar.
October *n* octubre *m* **in ~** en octubre **on ~ first** el primero de octubre
octopus *n* pulpo *m* **You're like an octopus.** Eres como un pulpo.
odd *adj* 1. *(strange)* raro *m*, -ra *f*; 2. *(not even)* non **~ numbers** números *mpl* nones
oddball *(n) (slang) (strange person)* excéntrico *m*, -ca *f*, tipo *(-pa)* raro *(-ra)*
odds *n, pl* disparidades *fpl*, desigualdades *fpl*, posibilidades *fpl* **~ and ends** cachivaches *mpl*, retazos *mpl*, cosas *fpl* sueltas **What are the odds (of winning)?** ¿Cuáles son las posibilidades de ganar? **What kind of odds will you give me?** ¿Qué posibilidades me das? **The odds are that...** Las posibilidades son que...
odor *n* olor *m*

Spanish "e" is pronounced like English "e" in "get"

off *adj* libre *m&f* **day** ~ día libre **get** *(a day)* ~ tener un día libre **have** ~ tener el día libre **The computer is off.** La computadora está apagada. **What days do you have off?** ¿Qué días *tiene usted(Fam: tienes)* libres? **Are you off on Saturday?** ¿Estás libre el sábado? **Would it be possible for you to get** *(1)* **today /** *(2)* **tomorrow off?** ¿Sería posible que *tomara usted (Fam: tomaras) (1)* el día de hoy / *(2)* el día de mañana libre? **Would it be possible for you to get** *(1)* **two /** *(2)* **three days off?** ¿Sería posible que *tomara usted (Fam: tomaras) (1)* dos / *(2)* tres días libres? **Would it be possible for you to get** *(1)* **a week off? /** *(2)* **two /** *(3)* **three weeks off?** ¿Sería posible que *tomara usted (Fam: tomaras) (1)* una semana libre? / *(2)* dos / *(3)* tres semanas libres?

off *adv* lejos, fuera, por entero **come** ~ soltarse **fall** ~ caerse **get** ~ *(work)* terminar **get** ~ **early** terminar temprano **get** ~ **late** terminar tarde **jump** ~ saltar ~ **and on** ocasionalmente **take** ~ quitarse **turn** ~ apagar **Turn off the light.** Apaga la luz. **What time do you get off (work)?** ¿A qué hora *sale usted (Fam: sales)* (del trabajo)? **When you get off, call me.** Cuando *salga usted (Fam: salgas), llámeme (Fam: llámame)*.

off *prep* de, desde, a **be** ~ **duty** no estar en servicio **What time are you off work?** ¿A qué hora *sale usted (Fam: sales)* del trabajo?

offbeat *adj* poco convencional *m&f*, inusitado *m*, -da *f*

offend *vt* ofender **I didn't mean to** *(1,2)* **offend you.** No quise *(1) ofenderlo m* / *(2) ofenderla f (Fam: ofenderte)*. **I hope I didn't** *(1,2)* **offend you.** Espero no *(1) haberlo m* / *(2) haberla f (Fam: haberte)* ofendido. **I don't want to** *(1,2)* **offend you.** No quiero *(1) ofenderlo m* / *(2) ofenderla f (Fam: ofenderte)*. **I'm sorry if I offended** *(1,2)* **you.** Si *(1) lo m* / *(2) la f (Fam: te)* ofendí lo siento mucho.

offer *vt* ofrecer **It's very nice of you to offer it.** Muy amable de *su (Fam: tu)* parte ofrecerlo.

offer *n* oferta *f*, ofrecimiento *m* **Thank you for the offer.** Gracias por el ofrecimiento. **I'm afraid** *(1)* **I /** *(2)* **we can't accept your offer.** Me temo que no *(1)* puedo / *(2)* podemos aceptar tu ofrecimiento.

office *n* oficina *f* **box** ~ taquilla *f* **home** ~ oficina en casa **hotel** ~ oficina del hotel **manager's** ~ oficina del gerente ~ **clerk** oficinista *m&f* ~ **worker** oficinista *m&f* **private** ~ oficina privada **work in an** ~ trabajar en una oficina **Where is the office located?** ¿Dónde se encuentra la oficina? **Let's ask at the office.** Preguntemos en la oficina.

officer *n* 1. *(police)* policía *m&f*; 2. *(of an institution)* agente *m&f*, funcionario *m*, -ria *f*

official *adj* oficial *m&f*

official *n* funcionario *m*, -ria *f* **customs** ~ funcionario *(-ria)* de aduana **gov-**

Stress rule # 2: The next-to-last syllable is stress in words ending in "n", "s" or a vowel.

ernment ~ funcionario *(-ria)* de gobierno
officially *adv* oficialmente
off-the-wall *adj (slang) (unusual, goofy)* estrambótico *m*, -ca *f*, estrafalario *m*, -ria *f* ~ **idea** idea estrambótica ~ **remark** disparate *m*
often *adv* con frecuencia, a menudo **How often?** ¿Con qué frecuencia? **Do you** *(1)* ...**come here...** / *(2)* ...**go there... often?** ¿*(1) Viene usted (Fam: Vienes)* aquí... / *(2)* ¿*Va usted (Fam: Vas)* allá... con frecuencia? *(1)* **I** / *(2)* **We (don't)** *(3)* ...**come here...** / *(4)* ...**go there... often.** (No) *(1,3)* Vengo / *(2,3)* Venimos aquí... / *(1,4)* Voy / *(2,4)* Vamos ...allá... con frecuencia.
oil *n* 1. *(petroleum)* petróleo *m* ; 2. *(viscouse substance)* aceite *m* **massage** ~ aceite para masajes
ointment *n* ungüento *m*
O.K., okay *adj (well)* bien *m&f* ; *(not bad)* bien **Are you okay?** ¿*Está usted (Fam: Estás)* bien? **I'm okay.** Estoy bien. **I feel okay.** Me siento bien. **Is that okay?** ¿Está bien? **That's okay (with** *[1]* **me** / *[2]* **us).** Está bien (por *[1]* mí / *[2]* nosotros). **Would** *(1)* **Saturday** / *(2)* **Sunday** / *(3)* **tonight** / *(4)* **tomorrow be okay?** ¿Estaría bien *(1)* el sábado? / *(2)* el domingo? / *(3)* esta noche? / *(4)* mañana?
O.K., okay *adv (well)* bien; *(not bad)* bien, correcto **You did okay.** *Usted lo hizo (Fam: Lo hiciste)* bien. **I can** *(1)* **skate** / *(2)* **ski okay.** Yo *(1)* patino / *(2)* esquío bien.
O.K, okay *interj: (1-3)* **Okay.** *(1)* Está bien. / *(2)* Muy bien. / *(3)* Bueno.
old *adj* viejo *m*, -ja *f*, antiguo *m*, -gua *f* ~ **custom** costumbre antigua ~ **friend** viejo *(-ja)* amigo *(-ga)* ~ **job** empleo antiguo ~ **maid** solterona *(1,2)* **How old are you?** *(1)* ¿Qué edad *tiene usted (Fam: tienes)*? / *(2)* ¿Cuántos años *tiene usted(Fam: tienes)*? **I'm** *(1)* **twenty** / *(2)* *(number)* **years old.** Tengo *(1)* veinte / *(2)* ___ años. **How old is your** *(1)* **daughter?** / *(2)* **son?** ¿Qué edad tiene *su (Fam: tu)* *(1)* hija? / *(2)* hijo? **My** *(1)* **daughter** / *(2)* **son is** *(number)* **years old.** Mi *(1)* hijo / *(2)* hijo tiene ___ años. **How old do you think I am?** ¿Cuántos años crees que tengo? **You don't look that old.** No te ves de esa edad.
old-fashioned *adj* anticuado *m*, -da *f*
once *adv* 1. *(one time)* una vez; 2. *(on a previous occasion)* en una ocasión **for** ~ por una vez siquiera **just this** ~ sólo esta vez ~ **and for all** de una vez por todas ~ **before** una vez antes ~ **in a while** de vez en cuando ~ **more** una vez más ~ **or twice** una o dos veces *(1)* **I've** / *(2)* **We've been here once before.** *(1)* Ya *había* / *(2)* habíamos estado aquí una vez.
one *adj* un *m*, una *f* ~ **day** un día ~ **month** un mes ~ **person** una persona ~ **thing** una cosa ~ **time** una vez ~ **week** una semana
one *n (number)* uno *m* ~ **at a time** uno a la vez ~ **by** ~ uno a uno, uno por uno

---

Spanish "x" is always like "ks", as in our word "taxi".

one *pron:* un *m*, uno *m*, una *f* ~ **another** el uno al otro **that** ~ ése *m*, ésa *f* **this** ~ éste *m*, ésta *f* **Which one?** ¿Cuál? **The** *(1,2)* **ones over** *(3)* **here.** / *(4)* **there.** *(1,2)* Los que están por *(3)* aquí / *(4)* allá. **You are my one and only.** Tú eres el *(la)* único *(-ca)* en mi vida. **You're the one I've been waiting for.** Tú eres *el hombre [m] (la mujer [f])* que he estado esperando. **I think you've had one too many.** *(drinks)* Creo que has tomado demasiado.

one-sided *adj (games)* desigual *m&f*

online *adv (location)* en línea; *(onto)* a Internet **go** ~ conectarse a Internet

only *adj* único *m*, -ca *f* ~ **chance** única oportunidad ~ **person** única persona ~ **thing** única cosa ~ **time** única vez ~ **way** único camino **You are my one and only.** Tú eres el *(la)* único *(-ca)*. **You're the only** *(1)* **girl** / *(2)* **woman for me.** Tú eres la única *(1)* chica / *(2)* mujer para mí. **You're the only** *(1)* **guy** / *(2)* **man for me.** Tú eres el único *(1)* chico / *(2)* hombre para mí. **That's the only thing** *(1)* **I** / *(2)* **we** / *(3)* **you can do.** Esa es la única cosa que *(1)* puedo / *(2)* podemos hacer.

only *adv* solamente, sólo **I** *(1)* **love** / *(2)* **want only you.** Te *(1)* amo / *(2)* quiero sólo a ti. **I only wish you could go with me.** Sólo deseo que *pueda usted (Fam: puedas)* ir conmigo. **I only hope you'll forgive me.** Sólo espero que *pueda usted (Fam: puedas)* perdonarme.

open *adj* 1. *(not closed)* abierto *m*, -ta *f*; 2. *(free)* libre *m&f* ~ **air** *(outdoors)* al aire libre **Is it open (yet)?** ¿(Ya) Está abierto? **It's (not) open.** (No) Está abierto. **I like to be out in the open air.** Me gusta estar al aire libre.

open *vt* abrir **Open the door. (It's me.)** Abre la puerta. (Soy yo.) **Could you help me open this?** ¿Podría usted (Fam: Podrías) ayudarme a abrir esto? **Could you open this for me?** ¿Podría usted (Fam: Podrías) abrirme esto? **I want you to open your heart to me.** Quiero que me abras tu corazón.

open *vi* abrir **What time does it open?** ¿A qué hora se abre ? **It opens at** *(time)*. *Se abre a las ___.*

opener *n* abridor *m*, destapador *m* **bottle** ~ destapador de botellas **can** ~ abrelatas *m*

open-hearted *adj* 1. *(straightforward)* con el corazón abierto; 2. *(big-hearted, kind)* de gran corazón

openly *adv* abiertamente, libremente

open-minded *adj* 1. *(unprejudiced)* de mente abierta; 2. *(receptive)* receptivo *m*, -va *f*

opera *n* ópera *f*

operate *vt* 1. *(use, control)* funcionar; 2. *(manage)* administrar **How do you operate this?** ¿Cómo funciona esto? **Could you show me how to oper-**

---

*Stress rule # 3: Syllables with accent marks
have the stress there.*

ate this? ¿Me enseñas cómo funciona esto? **You operate it like this.** Esto funciona así. **I operate a small business.** Administro un pequeño negocio.

operate *vi (med.)* operar **They operated on me (last month).** Me operaron (el mes pasado).

operation *n (med.)* operación *f* **I had an operation.** Me operaron.

opinion *n* opinión *f* **What's your opinion about...?** ¿Qué *opina usted (Fam: opinas)* de...? *(1)* **I'm** / *(2)* **We're very interested in your opinion.** *(1)* Me ... / *(2)* Nos interesa mucho ... *su (Fam: tu)* opinión. **In my opinion,...** Yo opino que ...

opponent *n* rival *m&f* **You're a tough opponent.** Eres un *(una)* rival difícil.

opportunity *n* oportunidad *f* **first ~** primera oportunidad **get the ~** buscar la oportunidad **give me the ~** dame la oportunidad **good ~** buena oportunidad **great ~** gran oportunidad **have the ~** tener la oportunidad **last ~** la última oportunidad **miss the ~** perder la oportunidad **only ~** la única oportunidad **pass up the ~** pasar la oportunidad **take advantage of the ~** sacar ventaja de la oportunidad **take the ~** tomar la oportunidad **wonderful ~** oportunidad maravillosa **I hope you'll give me the opportunity to** *(1,2)* **see you again.** Espero que me *dé usted (Fam: des)* la oportunidad de *(1) verlo m* / *(2) verla f (Fam: verte)* de nuevo. **I want to** *(1,2)* **see you at every opportunity.** Quiero *(1) verlo m* / *(2) verla f (Fam: verte)* en toda oportunidad. *(1)* **I** / *(2)* **We wouldn't miss the opportunity for anything.** No *(1)* me perdería / *(2)* nos perderíamos por nada esa oportunidad.

opposite *adj* contrario *m*, -ria *f* **~ direction** dirección contraria **~ side(s)** lado(s) contrario(s)

opposite *n* lo opuesto *m*, al contrario *m* **Just the opposite.** Exactamente al contrario.

optimist *n* optimista *m&f* **incurable ~** optimista incorregible

optimistic *adj* optimista *m&f*

or *conj* 1. *(alternative)* o; 2. *(otherwise)* o **This one or that one?** ¿Esta o la otra? **Be good or I'll leave.** Te portas bien o me voy.

orange *adj* anaranjado *m*, -da *f*

orchestra *n* orquesta *f*

order *vt (place an order)* ordenar **Can I order you something?** ¿Puedo ordenar algo para *usted (Fam: ti)*? **What would you like to order?** ¿Qué *le (Fam: te)* gustaría ordenar? **Let's order...** Vamos ordenando…

order *n* 1. *(command)* orden *f*; 2. *(proper conditon)* en orden **give ~s** dar órdenes **in ~ to** a fin de que **Is everything in order?** ¿Está todo en orden? **Everything is in order.** Todo está en orden. **It's out of order.** Está fuera de servicio.

Spanish pronunciation rules are on pages 407-408.

ordinarily *adv* comúnmente, normalmente

ordinary *adj* común *m&f*, normal *m&f*, ordinario *m*, -ria *f*

organ *n (music)* órgano *m*

organization *n* organización *f*

organize *n* organizar *m* ~ **a contest** organizar un concurso ~ **a game** organizar un juego ~ **a party** organizar una fiesta ~ **a tournament** organizar un torneo

organized *adj* organizado *m*, -da *f*

orgy *n* orgía *f*

original *adj* original *m&f* **That's an original idea.** Es una idea original.

originally *adv* originalmente **Originally I'm from** *(place).* Soy originario *(-ria)* de ___.

ornament *n* ornamento *m*, adorno *m* **Christmas tree ~s** adornos del árbol de Navidad.

ornate *adj* ornamentado *m*, -da *f*

orphan *n* huérfano *m*, -na *f*

orphanage *n* orfelinato *m*, hospicio *m (1)* **I'm / (2) We're going to visit an orphanage.** *(1)* Voy / *(2)* Vamos a visitar un orfelinato.

other *adj* otro *m*, otra *f* **in ~ words** en otras palabras **in the ~ direction** en la otra dirección **no ~ man** ningún otro hombre **no ~ woman** ninguna otra mujer ~ **children** otros niños ~ **people** otras personas **some ~ time** en alguna otra ocasión **the ~ day** el otro día **the ~ one** el otro **the ~ way** 1. *(manner)* la otra manera; 2. *(road)* el otro camino **Perhaps some other time.** Quizás en otra ocasión.

other *n & pron* otro *m*, otra *f* **each ~** uno al otro **We can get to know each other better.** Podemos llegar a conocernos mejor. **Where are the others?** ¿Dónde están los demás? **The others left.** Los demás se fueron.

otherwise *adv (if not)* si no

ought *v aux* debería, debiera **The** *(1)* **bus / (2) train ought to be here soon.** El *(1)* autobús / *(2)* tren debería llegar pronto. **You ought to see it.** *Debería usted (Fam: Deberías)* verlo. *(1)* **I / (2) We ought to go.** *(1)* Debería / *(2)* Deberíamos ir.

our *poss adj* nuestro *m*, -tra *f* ~ **car** nuestro carro ~ **children** nuestros hijos ~ **hotel** nuestro hotel ~ **house** nuestra casa ~ **room** nuestra habitación / cuarto

ours *poss pron* de nosotros **a friend of ~** un*(a)* amigo *(-ga)* de nosotros *(-tras)* **friends of ~** amigos *(-gas)* de nosotros *(-tras)*

ourselves *pers pron* nosotros *(-tras)* mismos *(-mas)* **by ~** solos *(-las)*

outdoor *adj* al aire libre *adv* ~ **activities** actividades al aire libre

outdoors *n, pl (nature)* la naturaleza **I love the outdoors.** Me encanta la

---

Some Spanish words have accented and unaccented forms to differentiate their meanings (e.g., el = the, él = he).

naturaleza.

outfit *n* atuendo *m* **beautiful ~** bonito atuendo **cool ~** *(slang) (nice-looking)* un atuendo super **elegant ~** atuendo elegante **new ~** atuendo nuevo **What a lovely outfit!** ¡Qué atuendo tan encantador! **That's a (very) beautiful outfit.** Ese es un atuendo (muy) bonito.

outfox *vt* ser más listo **You outfoxed** *(1)* **me.** / *(2)* **us.** Fuiste más listo *(-ta)* que *(1)* yo. / *(2)* nosotros *(-tras)*.

outgoing *adj (extroverted)* sociable *m&f*, extrovertido *m*, -da *f*

outlook *n* apariencia *f*, perspectiva *f* **healthy ~** apariencia saludable **~ on life** perspectiva sobre la vida **positive ~** perspectiva positiva **similar ~** perspectiva similar **You and I have a similar outlook on life.** *Usted (Fam: Tú)* y yo tenemos una perspectiva similar sobre la vida. **I admire your positive outlook.** Admiro *su (Fam: tu)* perspectiva positiva.

out-of-date *adj* pasado *(-da)* de moda, anticuado *m*, -da *f*

outrage *n* ultraje *m*, atrocidad *f* **This is an outrage.** Esto es un ultraje.

outrageous *adj* atroz *m&f*, ultrajante *m&f*, escandaloso *m*, -sa *f* **~ price** precio escandaloso **~ remark** comentario ultrajante **You say the most outrageous things.** Tú dices las cosas más injuriosas.

outside *adv* afuera **Let's go outside.** Vamos afuera.

outsider *n* persona *m&f* de fuera, persona *m&f* ajena *m*

outskirts *n, pl* alrededores *mpl* **It's on the outskirts of town.** Es en los alrededores del pueblo.

outsmart *vt* ser más astuto *m*, -ta *f*

outstanding *adj (exceptional, marvelous)* excepcional *m&f*

over *adj (finished)* terminado *m*, -da *f*, acabado *m*, -da *f* **all ~** 1. *(everywhere)* por todos lados; 2. *(finished)* terminado *m*, -da *f*, acabado *m*, -da *f* **What time will it be over?** ¿A qué hora se termina? **It's all over between** *(1)* **her** / *(2)* **him and me.** Ya se acabó todo entre *(1)* ella / *(2)* él y yo.

overboard *adv (slang) (to extremes)* al extremo **go ~** *(overdo)* excederse, pasarse de la raya; *(try too hard)* intentar en serio; *(go to great lengths)* ir a fondo

overcoat *n* abrigo *m*, sobretodo *m*

overconfident *adj* demasiado confiado *m*, -da *f*

overdo *vt (carry too far)* excederse, exagerar

overdress *vi* vestir demasiado elegante

overdrink *vi* beber en exceso

overdue *adj* vencido *m*, -da *f*, retrasado *m*, -da *f*, demasiado *m*, -da *f* **I was overdue for a win.** Ya era hora de que yo ganara.

overeat *vi* comer en exceso

overexert *vt* esforzarse demasiado **~ myself** esforzarme demasiado **~ your-**

Spanish "g" is like "h" in front of "e" and "i".
In front of other vowels it's like our "g" in "gun".

self esforzarte demasiado **Don't overexert yourself.** No *se esfuerce (Fam: te esfuerces)* demasiado.

overhear *vt* oír por casualidad **I couldn't help but overhear what you said.** No pude evitar oír por casualidad lo que *usted dijo (Fam: dijiste).* **I overheard your conversation.** Por casualidad oí *su (Fam: tu)* conversación.

overjoyed *adj* encantado *m*, -da *f*, rebosante *m&f* de alegría **I'd be overjoyed.** Estaría encantado *(-da).*

overnight *adj* de noche ~ **stay** quedarse a pasar la noche

overnight *adv* toda la noche **stay** ~ quedarse a pasar la noche **Can you stay overnight?** ¿Puedes quedarte a pasar la noche?

overreact *vi* reaccionar en exceso

overseas *adv* en el extranjero **go** ~ ir al extranjero **live** ~ vivir en el extranjero

oversleep *vi* dormir en exceso **I overslept.** Me quedé dormido. **We overslept.** Nos quedamos dormidos.

overtired *adj* demasiado cansado *m*, -da *f*

overweight *adj* obeso *m*, -sa *f*, pasado *m*, -da *f* de peso *(1-3)* **I'm (a little) overweight.** *(1)* Estoy (un poco) obeso *(-sa)*. / *(2)* Estoy (un poco) pasado *(-da)* de peso. / *(3)* Tengo (un poco) de sobrepeso.

overwhelm *vt* abrumar, agobiar **Your beauty overwhelms me.** *Su (Fam: Tu)* belleza me abruma.

overwhelmed *adj* abrumado *m*, -da *f* **I'm (really) overwhelmed by** *(1)* **you.** / *(2)* **all of your attention.** Estoy (de verdad) abrumado por *(1)* tu. / *(2)* todas tus atenciones. *(1)* **I'm** / *(2)* **We're a bit overwhelmed by it all.** *(1)* Estoy un poco abrumado... / *(2)* Estamos un poco abrumados... por todo eso.

overwhelming *adj* abrumador *m*, -dora *f*, agobiante *m&f*

owe *vt* deber **How much do** *(1)* **I** / *(2)* **we owe you?** ¿Cuánto *le (Fam: te)* *(1)* debo / *(2)* debemos? **I owe you an apology.** *Le (Fam: Te)* debo una disculpa.

owl *n* búho *m*, tecolote *m* **night** ~ ave *f* nocturna, noctámbulo *m*, -la *f*

own *adj* propio *m*, -pia *f* **I saw it with my own eyes.** Lo vi con mis propios ojos. **To each his own.** A cada quien lo suyo.

own *vt* ser dueño *m*, -ña *f* **Do you own your apartment or rent it?** ¿*Es usted (Fam: Eres)* dueño *(-ña)* de *su (Fam: tu)* departamento o lo *renta (Fam: rentas)*? **I own a** *(1)* **condo(minium)** / *(2)* **home in** (*city*). Soy dueño *(-ña)* de *(1)* un condominio / *(2)* una casa en ___.

English-Spanish and Spanish-English glossaries of food and drink are on pages 420-427.

P

pack *vt* empacar **I have to pack my suitcase.** Tengo que hacer mi maleta. **We have to pack our suitcases.** Tenemos que hacer nuestras maletas.

pack *vi* empacar *(1)* **I / *(2)* We have to pack.** *(1)* Tengo / *(2)* Tenemos que empacar. **Can I help *(1,2)* you pack?** ¿Puedo *(1)* ayudarlo *m* / *(2)* ayudarla *f (Fam: ayudarte)* a empacar?

pack *n* 1. *(backpack)* mochila *f* ; 2. *(small package)* paquete *m* **heavy ~** mochila pesada **~ of cigarettes** paquete de cigarros **Put it in *(1)* my / *(2)* your pack.** Ponlo en *(1)* mi / *(2)* su *(Fam: tu)* mochila. **Your pack is too heavy.** Su *(Fam: Tu)* mochila está muy pesada.

package *n* paquete *m* **receive a ~** recibir un paquete **send a ~** mandar un paquete *(1)* **I / *(2)* We have to mail a package.** *(1)* Yo tengo / *(2)* Nosotros tenemos que mandar un paquete por correo.

packet *n* paquete *m*

pad *n* 1. *(cushion)* cojín *m* ; 2. *(of paper)* bloc *m* **elbow ~s *(rollerblading)*** coderas *fpl* **knee ~s *(rollerblading)*** rodilleras *fpl*

paddle *vi* remar **Let me paddle for a while.** Déjame remar un rato.

paddle *n (oar)* remo *m*

page *n* página *f* **next ~** página siguiente **previous ~** página anterior **web ~** página 'web'

pain *n* dolor *m* **~ in the neck** fastidio **sharp ~** dolor agudo **slight ~** dolor ligero **terrible ~** dolor terrible **Where's the pain?** ¿Dónde duele? **I've got a (sharp) pain right here.** Tengo un dolor (agudo) aquí.

painful *adj (physical)* doloroso *m*, -sa *f*

paint *vt* pintar **What kind of things do you paint?** ¿Qué cosas *pinta usted (Fam: pintas)*? **I like to paint *(1)* animals. / *(2)* flowers. / *(3)* landscapes. / *(4)* people.** Me gusta pintar *(1)* animales. / *(2)* flores. / *(3)* paisajes. / *(4)* gente.

paint *vi* pintar **I love to paint.** Me encanta pintar. **Do you paint in oil or**

A phrasebook makes a great gift!
Use the order form on page 432.

water colors? ¿*Pinta usted (Fam: Pintas)* al óleo o en acuarela? **You paint** *(1)* **beautifully.** / *(2)* **very well.** *Usted pinta (Fam: Pintas) (1)* bellamente. / *(2)* muy bien. **I wish I could paint so that I could capture your beauty on canvas.** Ojalá supiera yo pintar, para captar en un lienzo *su (Fam: tu)* belleza .

paint *n* pintura *f* **body ~** pintura corporal

painter *n* 1. *(artist)* pintor *m*, pintora *f* ; 2. *(worker)* pintor *m*, pintora *f* **favorite ~** pintor *(-ra)* favorito *(-ta)* **portrait ~** retratista *m&f* **Who are your favorite painters?** ¿Quiénes son sus pintores favoritos? **My favorite painters are** *(names)*. Mis pintores favoritos son ___ .

painting *n* 1. *(the art)* pintura *f* ; 2. *(picture)* pintura *f* **You possess the kind of beauty that inspires great paintings.** *Tiene usted (Fam: Tú tienes)* la clase de belleza que inspira grandes pinturas.

pair *n* par *m* **in ~s** por pares

pajamas *n, pl* piyama *f*

pal *n* amigo *m*, -ga *f*, cuate *m*, cuata *f* **true ~** amigo *(-ga)* de verdad

palace *n* palacio *m*

pal around *vi* andar de amigos *(1)* **He** / *(2)* **She is just someone I pal around with.** *(1)* Él / *(2)* Ella y yo somos cuates nada más.

pale *adj* pálido *m*, -da *f*

palm *n* palma *f*, mano *f* **I'll read your palm.** Te voy a leer la mano. **According to your palm, you're going to have 37 children.** Según las líneas de tu mano, vas a tener treinta y siete hijos. **Funny, that's what mine says, too.** Qué curioso, eso dice también la mía.

pamper *vt* consentir, mimar

panic *vi* asustarse **Take it easy. Don't panic.** Calma. No te asustes.

panorama *n* panorama *m* **What a** *(1)* **beautiful** / *(2)* **breath-taking panorama.** Qué *(1)* hermoso / *(2)* impresionante panorama.

panties *n, pl* pantaletas *fpl*

pants *n, pl* pantalones *mpl* **You should probably wear long pants.** Tal vez *le (Fam: te)* conviene usar pantalones largos.

pantyhose *n* pantimedias *fpl*

paper *n* 1. *(material)* papel *m* ; 2. *pl (documents)* documentos *mpl* ; 3. *(newspaper)* periódico *m* ; 4. *(written work)* texto *m* **piece of ~** un papel **term ~** composición de examen trimestral **toilet ~** papel de baño **wrapping ~** papel de envoltura

par *n (golf)* par *m* **over ~** sobre par **under ~** bajo par

parachute *n* paracaídas *m (also pl)*

parade *n* desfile *m* *(1)* **Where...** / *(2)* **What time... will the parade be?** *(1)* ¿Dónde... / *(2)* ¿A qué hora... será el desfile? **Let's go watch the parade.**

A slash always means "or".

Vamos a ver el desfile.

paradise *n* paraíso *m* **absolute** ~ paraíso total **beautiful** ~ paraíso hermoso
real ~ paraíso real **wonderful** ~ paraíso maravilloso **What a paradise!**
¡Qué paraíso! **This is my idea of paradise.** Para mí esto es el paraíso. **I
feel like a stranger in paradise.** Me siento como un extraño en el paraíso.

paraglider *n* parapente *m*

paragraph *n* párrafo *m*

paralyzed *adj* paralizado *m*, -da *f*

paramotor *n* paramotor *m*

paranoid *adj* paranoico *m*, -ca *f*

parasol *n* sombrilla *f*

parcel *n* paquete *m* *(1)* **I** / *(2)* **We need to mail a parcel.** *(1)* Necesito / *(2)*
Necesitamos enviar un paquete por correo.

pardon *vt* perdón **Pardon me.** Disculpe.

pardon *n* perdón *m* **(I) Beg your pardon?** *(Didn't hear)* ¿Cómo dijo, disculpe?
(Fam: Disculpa, cómo dijiste)? *(1,2)* **I beg your pardon.** *(Sorry)* *(1)* Perdón.
/ *(2)* Disculpe *(Fam: Disculpa)*.

parents *n, pl* padres *mpl* **both** ~s ambos padres **foster** ~s padres adoptivos
my ~s mis padres **your** ~s *sus (Fam: tus)* padres

park *vi* estacionarse **Where can we park?** ¿Dónde nos podemos estacionar?
Is it okay to park *(1)* **here?** / *(2)* **there?** ¿Está bien si me estaciono *(1)*
aquí? / *(2)* allá? **How much does it cost to park** *(1)* **here?** / *(2)* **there?**
¿Cuánto cuesta estacionarse *(1)* aquí? / *(2)* allá? **We can't park** *(1)* **here** /
(2) **there**. No podemos estacionarnos *(1)* aquí. / *(2)* allá.

park *n* parque *m* **amusement** ~ parque de diversiones **Let's go for a walk in
the park.** Vamos a caminar al parque. **Let's make a picnic in the park.**
Vamos a hacer un día de campo en el parque.

parka *n* abrigo (abrigo esquimal con capucha) *m*

parking *n* estacionamiento *m* ~ **garage** cochera *f* ~ **lot** lote *m* de
estacionamiento ~ **meter** estacionómetro *m* ~ **place** lugar *m* para
estacionarse

parlor *n* sala *f* **beauty** ~ salón *m* de belleza

part *vi* partir, separar **I guess it's time to part.** Creo que es hora de partir. **I
hate to part with you.** Odio separarme de ti.

part *n* 1. *(portion)* parte *f*; 2. *(role)* papel *m* **best** ~ la mejor parte **big** ~ gran
parte **easy** ~ parte fácil **first** ~ primera parte **for the most** ~ en su mayor
parte **hard** ~ parte difícil **important** ~ parte importante **last** ~ última parte
main ~ parte principal **my** ~ mi parte **other** ~ otra parte **small** ~ parte
pequeña **special** ~ parte especial **take** ~ tomar parte **worst** ~ peor parte
your ~ *su (Fam: tu)* parte **What part of the city do you live in?** ¿En qué

Spanish "v" is pronounced like a soft "b".

parte de la ciudad *vive usted (Fam: vives)*? **Would you like part of it?** *¿Le (Fam: Te)* gustaría tener parte de esto? **You can take part if you want to.** *Puede usted (Fam: Puedes)* tomar parte si *quiere (Fam: quieres)*.

partially *adv* parcialmente

participate *vi* participar

particular *adj* 1. *(special)* especial *m&f*; 2. *(specific)* determinado *m*, -da*f*; 3. *(discriminating)* selectivo *m*, -va *f* **Is there anywhere particular that you would like to go?** ¿Le *(Fam: Te)* gustaría ir a algún lugar en especial? **I'm particular about such things.** Soy selectivo *(-va)* con estas cosas.

particular *n* particular *m* **in ~** en particular **No one in particular.** Nadie en particular.

particularly *adv* particularmente

parting *n* despedida *f* **I can't stand the thought of parting from you.** No soporto la idea de despedirme de ti.

partly *adv* en parte **It's partly my fault.** En parte es culpa mía.

partner *n (companion, mate)* compañero *m*, -ra*f*; *(associate)* socio *m*, -cia*f* **business ~** socio *(-cia)* comercial **change ~s** cambiar de compañeros **dancing ~** compañero *(-ra)* de baile **find a** *(1,2)* **~** encontrar un*(a)* *(1)* compañero *(-ra)* / *(2)* socio *(-cia)* **great ~** gran compañero *(-ra)* **life ~** compañero *(-ra)* de vida *(1)* **look ~** *(1)* buscar / *(2)* buscar un*(a)* compañero *(-ra)* **search for a ~** *(1)* buscar / *(2)* buscar un*(a)* compañero *(-ra)* **snuggle ~** mi mero *(-ra)* cuate *(-ta)* **tennis ~** compañero *(-ra)* de tenis **wonderful ~** compañero *(-ra)* maravilloso *(-sa)* **workout ~** compañero *(-ra)* de ejercicio **yearn for a ~** anhelar un*(a)* compañero *(-ra)*

part-time *adj & adv* medio tiempo **I work part-time as a** *(job title)*. Trabajo medio tiempo como ___.

party *vi* divertirse, ir de fiesta **I like to party sometimes.** Me gusta ir de juerga de vez en cuando. **We can party all night.** Podemos festejar toda la noche. **I've given up partying.** Ya dejé la juerga.

party *n* 1. *(event)* fiesta *f*; 2. *(polit org)* partido *m* **anniversary ~** fiesta de aniversario **big ~** gran fiesta **birthday ~** fiesta de cumpleaños **costume ~** fiesta de disfraces **dinner ~** cena de fiesta **engagement ~** fiesta de compromiso **farewell ~** fiesta de despedida **give a ~** dar una fiesta **goodbye ~** fiesta de despedida **go to a ~** ir a una fiesta **graduation ~** fiesta de graduación **have a ~** tener una fiesta **impromptu ~** fiesta improvisada **life of the ~** el alma de la fiesta **~ pooper** aguafiestas *m&f* **political ~** partido político **promotion ~** fiesta de promoción **small ~** fiesta pequeña **throw a ~** dar una fiesta **wedding ~** fiesta de bodas **welcome ~** fiesta de bienvenida **wild ~** fiesta salvaje *(1)* **I'd** / *(2)* **We'd like to** *(3,4)* **invite you to a party** *(5)* **this afternoon.** / *(6)* **this evening.** / *(7)* **tomorrow (evening).** / *(8)* **on Friday** / *(9)* **Saturday** / *(10)* **Sunday** *(11)* **afternoon.** / *(12)* **evening.** *(1)*

Time expressions are given on page 413.

Me / (2) Nos gustaría (3) *invitarlo m* / (4) *invitarla f (Fam: invitarte)* a una fiesta (5) por la tarde. / (6) por la noche. / (7) mañana (en la noche). / 8) el viernes / (9) el sábado / (10) el domingo (11) por la tarde. / (12) por la noche. **Would you like to go (with [1] me / [2] us) to a party?** ¿Le *(Fam: ¿Te)* gustaría ir ([1] conmigo / [2] con nosotros) a una fiesta? (1) **I'm** / (2) **We're having a party** (3) **tonight.** / (4) **tomorrow. Would you like to come?** (1) Voy / (2) Vamos a tener una fiesta (3) esta noche. / (4) mañana. ¿Le *(Fam: ¿Te)* gustaría venir?

party pooper *n* aguafiestas *m&f*

pass *vt* 1. *(go by)* pasar; 2. *(hand)* pasar; 3. *(throw)* pasar; 4. *(succeed in a test)* pasar; 5. *(while away)* pasar **What (1) station / (2) street did we just pass?** ¿Qué (1) estación / (2) calle acabamos de pasar? **Could you please pass me the (1) butter? / (2) milk? / (3) sugar?** ¿Podrías pasarme (1) la mantequilla? / (2) la leche? / (3) el azúcar? **Pass the ball a lot.** Pasar mucho la bola. **Pass it (to me)!** ¡Pásala! (¡Pásamela!). **I'm sure you'll pass the exam.** Estoy seguro de que *usted pasará (Fam: tú pasarás)* el examen. **Congratulations on passing the exam!** Felicidades por pasar tu examen. **I know a good way to pass the time.** Conozco un buen modo de pasar el rato.

pass *vi (go by)* pasar
  ★ **pass away** *idiom (die)* fallecer **My (1) brother / (2) father / (3) husband / (4) mother / (5) sister / (6) wife passed away in (year).** Mi (1) hermano / (2) padre / (3) esposo / (4) madre / (5) hermana / (6) esposa falleció en ___.
  ★ **pass for** *idiom (be accepted as)* pasar por **You could easily pass for (1) twenty-five / (2) thirty.** Fácilmente *usted podría (Fam: tú podrías)* pasar por (1) veinticinco / (2) treinta.
  ★ **pass out** *idiom (lose consciousness)* desmayarse

pass *n* 1. *(between mountains)* paso *m* ; 2. *(permit)* pase *m* ; 3. *(advance)* proposición *f* ; 4. *(mil: leave)* permiso *m* **bus ~** paso del camión **make a ~ (at...)** hacer una proposición (a...)

passenger *n* pasajero *m*, -ra *f* **~ lounge** sala de pasajeros

passer-by *n* transeúnte *m&f*

passion *n* pasión *f* **great ~** gran pasión **love with a ~** *(verb)* amar con pasión **~ for art** pasión por el arte **~ for life** pasión por la vida **~ for music** pasión por la música **sea of ~** mar de pasiones **wild ~** pasión salvaje **with a ~** con pasión, apasionadamente **I love (1) football / (2) golf with a passion.** Soy apasionado *(-da)* (1) del fútbol / (2) del golf. (1) **Climbing / (2) Cycling is my passion.** (1) Escalar / (2) Andar en bicicleta es mi pasión. **I have a passion for arts and music.** El arte y la música son mi pasión. **I hate it**

Spanish "qu" is pronounced like "k".

with a passion. Lo aborrezco con toda el alma.

passionate *adj* apasionado *m*, -da *f* ~ **kiss** beso apasionado **You're so passionate.** Eres tan apasionado *(-da)*. *(1)* **You** / *(2)* **I have a very passionate nature.** *(1)* Eres / *(2)* Soy de naturaleza muy apasionada. **I'm passionate about painting.** Soy apasionado *(-da)* de la pintura.

passionately *adv* apasionadamente **I love you passionately.** Te amo apasionadamente.

passive *adj* 1. *(not active)* pasivo *m*, -va *f*; 2. *(gram.)* pasivo *m*, -va *f* ~ **voice** voz *f* pasiva

passport *n* pasaporte *m* ~ **number** número de pasaporte **I lost my passport.** Perdí mi pasaporte.

password *n* contraseña *f* **enter the** ~ *(comp)* introducir la contraseña **I forgot the password.** Olvidé la contraseña.

past *adj* pasado *m*, -da *f* ~ **tense** tiempo pasado **What is past is past.** Lo pasado pasado. **What's the past tense of** *(verb)*? ¿Cuál es el pasado de ___?

past *n* pasado *m* **in the** ~ en el pasado **I don't care about the past.** No me interesa el pasado. **That's all in the past.** Todo eso quedó en el pasado. **Everybody has a past.** Todo mundo tiene un pasado. **I'd prefer not to talk about the past.** Preferiría no hablar del pasado. **I'm going to make you forget about the past.** Voy a hacer que olvides el pasado.

pastime *n* pasatiempo *m* **What's your favorite pastime?** ¿Cuál es *su (Fam: tu)* pasatiempo favorito? **I guess my favorite pastime is** *(activity)*. Creo que mi pasatiempo favorito es ___. **That sounds like a** *(1)* **fun** / *(2)* **nice pastime.** Eso parece un pasatiempo *(1)* divertido. / *(2)* bonito.

pastor *n* pastor *m*

pastry *n* pastel *m* **Would you care for a pastry?** ¿ Le *(Fam: Te)* gustaría un pastelito?

patch *n (small piece of cloth)* parche *m* **I'll sew a patch on it (for you).** Le voy a poner un parche .

path *n* camino *m* ~ **of least resistance** el camino más fácil ~ **of life** camino de la vida **Which path should we take?** ¿Qué camino debemos tomar? **Let's take this path.** Tomemos este camino.

pathetic *adj* patético *m*, -ca *f*

patience *n* paciencia *f* **a lot of** ~ mucha paciencia **great** ~ gran paciencia **have** ~ tener paciencia **lose** ~ perder la paciencia **remarkable** ~ paciencia notable **take** ~ requiere paciencia **tremendous** ~ paciencia tremenda **You have a lot of patience.** *Tiene usted (Fam: Tú tienes)* mucha paciencia. **Please have patience with me.** Por favor, *tenga usted (Fam: ten)* paciencia conmigo. **It takes a lot of patience.** Se necesita mucha paciencia. **My**

patience is running out. Se me está acabando la paciencia.

patient *adj* paciente *m&f* **Please be patient with me.** Por favor, sé paciente conmigo. **Thank you for being so patient.** Gracias por ser tan paciente. **I'm very patient.** Soy muy paciente.

patient *n (med.)* paciente *m&f*

patio *n* patio *m* **on the ~** en el patio

pattern *n (design)* patrón *m*, diseño *m* **I (really) like that pattern.** (De verdad) me gusta el diseño. **What a *(1)* beautiful / *(2)* pretty pattern!** ¡Qué *(1)* hermoso / *(2)* bonito diseño!

pause *vi* detenerse, hacer una pausa **Let's pause for a bit, okay?** Hagamos una pausa. ¿Te parece?

pause *n* pausa *f*

pay *vt* poner; pagar **~ attention** poner atención **Did you pay the bill?** ¿Pagaste la cuenta? *(1)* **I / *(2)* We paid the bill (already).** (Ya) *(1)* Pagué / *(2)* Pagamos la cuenta. **Pay close attention.** Pon mucha atención. **You're not paying attention.** *No está usted (Fam: Tú no estás)* poniendo atención.

pay *vt* pagar **Please let *(1)* me / *(2)* us pay (for it).** Por favor, *(1)* déjeme *(Fam: déjame)* / *(2)* déjenos *(Fam: déjanos)* pagar (eso). *(1)* **I'll / *(2)* We'll pay for it.** *(1)* Yo lo pago. / *(2)* Nosotros lo pagamos. **It's *(1)* my / *(2)* our turn to pay.** *(1)* Me / *(2)* Nos toca pagar. **I paid (for it) (already).** (Ya) (Lo) Pagué ayer. **I didn't pay (for it).** Yo no (lo) pagué. **I didn't pay (for it) yet.** Todavía no (lo) pago.

peace *n* paz *f* **~ and quiet** paz y tranquilidad **There's such a sense of peace here.** Se siente tanta paz aquí. *(1)* **I / *(2)* We need some peace and quiet.** *(1)* Necesito / *(2)* Necesitamos paz y tranquilidad.

peaceful *adj* apacible *m&f* **It's so peaceful here.** Este lugar es tan apacible.

peach *n* durazno *m* **ripe ~** durazno maduro

peak *n* pico *m*, cumbre *f* **climb to the ~** escalar a la cumbre **mountain ~** cumbre de la montaña **~ of pleasure** la cumbre del placer **How high is the peak?** ¿Qué tan alta es la cumbre?

peanuts *n, pl* cacahuates *mpl*

pearl *adj* de perlas **~ earrings** aretes de perlas **~ necklace** collar de perlas

pearl *n* perla *f* **cultured ~s** perlas cultivados **string of ~s** sarta *f* de perlas

pecs, pectorals *n, pl* pectorales *mpl*

peculiar *adj (strange)* peculiar *m&f*

pedal *vi* pedalear **~ hard** pedalear duro **~ slowly** pedalear despacio

pedal *n* pedal *m*

peek *vi* fisgar, fisgonear **Don't peek!** ¡No fisgones! **I promise I won't peek. (Maybe.)** Te prometo que no voy a fisgonear. (Quizás.) **No fair! You peeked!** ¡No es justo! ¡Estuviste fisgando!

A single Spanish "r" should be lightly trilled;
double "r" ("rr") should be strongly trilled.

peel *vt (remove a peeling)* pelar

pen *n* pluma *f* **Could I borrow your pen?** ¿Me *presta su (Fam: prestas tu)* pluma?

penalize *vt* penalizar **I'm penalizing you eight kisses.** Te estoy penalizando con ocho besos.

penalty *n* multa *f* **You have to pay a penalty for that.** Tienes que pagar una multa por eso.

pencil *n* lápiz *m*

pendant *n* colgante *m&f*

peninsula *n* península *f*

penis *n* pene *m*

penpal *n* amigo *m*, -ga *f* por correspondencia ~ **magazine** revista *f* de amigos por correspondencia

pension *n* pensión *f* **government** ~ pensión gubernamental **live on a** ~ vivir de una pensión **military** ~ pensión militar **I get a (monthly) pension.** Me dan una pensión (mensual).

pensioner *n* pensionado *m*, -da *f*

people *n, pl* gente *f* **a few** ~ unas cuantas personas **a lot of** ~ mucha gente **friendly** ~ gente amigable **good** ~ buena gente **nice** ~ gente agradable **not many** ~ no mucha gente **some** ~ algunas personas

pepper *n* pimienta *f*

peppermint *n* menta *f*

percent *n* por ciento *m* **hundred** ~ cien por ciento

percentage *n* porcentaje *m* **big** ~ gran porcentaje **small** ~ pequeño porcentaje **What percentage?** ¿Qué porcentaje?

perceptive *adj* perceptivo *m*, -va *f* **You're very perceptive.** *Usted es (Fam: Tú eres)* muy perceptivo *(-va)*.

perfect *adj* perfecto *m*, -ta *f* ~ **body** cuerpo perfecto ~ **day** día perfecto ~ **fit** ajuste perfecto ~ **opportunity** oportunidad perfecta ~ **time** momento perfecto **Everything about you is perfect.** Todo lo tuyo es perfecto. **I'm not perfect. (But, oh, what a close call!)** No soy perfecto *(-ta)*. (Pero, casi casi!) **I don't expect you to be perfect.** No espero que seas perfecto *(-ta)*. **You look picture perfect in that dress.** Te ves perfecta para una foto con ese vestido.

perfection *n* perfección *f* **strive for** ~ empeñarse por la perfección **In your**

Familiar "tu" forms in parentheses can replace italicized polite forms.

beauty there is a perfection such as I've never seen before. Hay en tu belleza una perfección que jamás había visto .

perfectly *adv* perfectamente **You played perfectly.** *Usted jugó (Fam: Tú jugaste)* perfectamente. **It fits you perfectly.** *Le (Fam: Te)* queda perfectamente. **I think we're perfectly suited to one another.** Creo que nos acoplamos perfectamente .

perform *vt* 1. *(music)* tocar; 2. *(accomplish)* lograr ~ **a concert** tocar un concierto ~ **miracles** hacer milagros

performance *n* 1. *(rendition)* desempeño *m* ; 2. *(show)* representación *f* **first** ~ primera representación **give a** ~ representar **great** ~ gran representación **marvelous** ~ representación maravillosa **second** ~ segunda representación

performer *n* ejecutante *m&f*, actor *m*, actriz *f*

perfume *n* perfume *m* **bewitching** ~ perfume encantador. **bottle of** ~ frasco *m* de perfume **delicate** ~ perfume sutil **favorite** ~ perfume favorito **intoxicating** ~ perfume embriagador **I love your perfume.** Me encanta *su (Fam: tu)* perfume. **The fragrance of your perfume will haunt me for the rest of my life.** La fragancia de *su (Fam: tu)* perfume me seguirá por el resto de mi vida.

perhaps *adv* quizás

period *n* 1. *(time interval)* periodo *m* ; 2. *(menstrual period)* período *m* **waiting** ~ periodo de espera

permanent *adj* permanente *m&f* ~ **address** dirección *f* permanente ~ **relationship** relación *f* permanente

permanently *adv* permanentemente

permission *n* permiso *m* **get** ~ conseguir permiso **give** ~ dar permiso ~ **to get married** permiso para casarse **Whose permission do we need?** ¿A quién tenemos que pedir permiso?

permit *vt* permitir

permit *n* permiso *m* **business** ~ permiso comercial

perplexed *adj* perplejo *m*, -ja *f* **I'm a bit perplexed (about it all).** Estoy perplejo *(-ja)* (por todo eso).

persistence *n* persistencia *f* **Such persistence!** ¡Qué persistencia!

persistent *adj* persistente *m&f* **You're very persistent.** Eres muy persistente.

person *n* persona *f* **active** ~ persona activa **ambitious** ~ persona ambiciosa **carefree** ~ persona despreocupada **cheerful** ~ persona alegre **decent** ~ persona decente **different** ~ persona diferente **easy-going** ~ persona tranquila **friendly** ~ persona amigable **fun** ~ persona divertida **funny** ~ 1.

Spanish "ll" is pronounced like "y" in "yes".

(amusing) persona divertida; 2. *(odd)* persona extraña **funniest** ~ 1. *(most amusing)* la persona más divertida; 2. *(oddest)* la persona más rara **gentle** ~ persona gentil **good** ~ buena persona **good-hearted** ~ persona de buen corazón **good-natured** ~ persona bonachona **happy-go-lucky** ~ persona despreocupada **in** ~ en persona **intelligent** ~ persona inteligente **interesting** ~ persona interesante **kind** ~ persona amable **kind-hearted** ~ persona de buen corazón **lonely** ~ persona solitaria **lovable** ~ persona amorosa **nice** ~ persona agradable **night** ~ persona nocturna **quiet** ~ persona tranquila **remarkable** ~ persona sobresaliente **right** ~ persona correcta **shy** ~ persona tímida **simple** ~ persona sencilla **single** ~ persona soltera **spiritual** ~ persona espiritual **strange** ~ persona extraña **wonderful** ~ persona maravillosa **You seem like a** *(type of)* **person.** Parece que eres una persona ___. *(1)* **He /** *(2)* **She is a (very)** *(type of)* **person.** *(1)* Él / *(2)* Ella es una persona (muy) ___. **I'm that kind of person.** Yo soy ese tipo de persona. **You are the person** *(1)* **of my dreams. /** *(2)* **that I've been waiting for all my life.** Tú eres la persona *(1)* ...de mis sueños. / *(2)* ...que he estado esperando toda mi vida. **You're the** *(1)* **nicest /** *(2)* **sweetest person I've ever met.** Usted es *(Fam: Tú eres)* la persona más *(1)* agradable / *(2)* dulce que he conocido. **I have a lot of love to give to the right person.** Tengo mucho amor para darle a la persona correcta.

personal *adj* personal *m&f,* indiscreto *m,* -ta *f* **May I ask you a personal question? Are you** *(1)* **attached? /** *(2)* **married?** ¿Puedo *hacerle (Fam: hacerte)* una pregunta indiscreta? ¿*Está usted (Fam: Estás)* *(1)* comprometida *(-do)*? / *(2)* casado *(-da)*? **Am I being too personal?** ¿Estoy siendo indiscreto *(-ta)*? **That's (a little too) personal.** Eso es (un tanto) indiscreto.

personality *n* personalidad *f* **charming** ~ personalidad encantadora **cheerful** ~ personalidad alegre **great** ~ gran personalidad **marvelous** ~ personalidad maravillosa **quiet** ~ personalidad tranquila **radiant** ~ personalidad radiante **sunny** ~ personalidad alegre **terrific** ~ personalidad tremenda **vivacious** ~ personalidad vivaz **warm** ~ personalidad cariñosa **winning** ~ personalidad triunfante **wonderful** ~ personalidad maravillosa **You have a** *(1)* **beautiful /** *(2)* **nice /** *(3)* **sparkling personality.** Usted tiene *(Fam: Tú tienes)* una personalidad *(1)* bella. / *(2)* agradable. / *(3)* chispeante.

personally *adv* personalmente

personals *n pl (personal ads)* personales *f* **I read your ad in the personals.** Leí *su (Fam: tu)* anuncio en la sección de personales.

perspective *n* perspectiva *f* **different** ~ perspectiva diferente

perspire *vi* sudar

Common professions are listed on pages 415-416.

persuade *vt* convencer **You've persuaded me (, you silver-tongued devil).** Me has convencido (, mira que tienes labia). **Do you think you can persuade** *(1)* **her?** / *(2)* **him?** / *(3)* **them?** *¿Cree usted que pueda (Fam: Crees tú que puedas) (1)* convencerla? / *(2)* convencerlo? / *(3)* convencerlos *(-las)*?

persuasive *adj* convincente *m&f*

perverse *adj* perverso *m*, -sa *f*, maligno *m*, -na *f* **You get a perverse delight out of making me suffer, don't you?** Te encanta hacerme sufrir, ¿verdad?

pervert *n* pervertido *m*, -da *f* **What are you? Some kind of pervert?** ¿Y tú quién eres? ¿Alguna clase de pervertido?

perverted *adj* pervertido *m*, -da *f*

pessimist *n* pesimista *m&f*

pessimistic *adj* pesimista *m&f* **Don't be so pessimistic.** No seas tan pesimista.

pest *n (annoying person)* lata *f* **What a pest you are!** ¡Eres una lata!

pester *vt* molestar **I don't mean to** *(1,2)* **pester you.** No quiero ser una molestia para *usted (Fam: ti)*.

pet *vi (fondle)* acariciar, mimar

pet *n (animal)* mascota *f* **Do you have any pets?** ¿Tienes alguna mascota?

petal-soft *adj* suave *m&f* como pétalo

petite *adj* pequeño *m*, -ña *f* **You're so petite.** Eres tan menuda.

pharmacy *n* farmacia *f*

Ph.D. *abbrev* = **Philosophy Doctor (degree)** doctorado *m*

phenomenal *adj* fenomenal *m&f*

philander *vi* 1. *(flirt)* mujerear; 2. *(be unfaithful)* poner los cuernos **I'm not the kind that philanders.** No soy un mujeriego.

philanderer *n* mujeriego *m*

philately *n* filatelia *f*

philosopher *n* filósofo *m*, -fa *f* **amateur** ~ filósofo aficionado **part-time** ~ filósofo de medio tiempo

philosophical *adj* filosófico *m*, -ca *f*

philosophy *n* filosofía *f*

phone *vt (call)* telefonear *(See phrases under* **call***.)* **I'll phone you.** Yo te telefoneo.

phone *n* teléfono *m* **cellular** ~ teléfono celular ~ **number** número telefónico **public** ~ teléfono público **Can I use your phone?** ¿Puedo usar tu teléfono? **Is there a phone around here?** ¿Hay algún teléfono por aquí?

phonetic *adj* fonético *m*, -ca *f*

phony *adj* falso *m*, -sa *f*

phony *n* 1. *(deceptive person)* farsante *m&f*; 2. *(false thing)* falso *m*, falsa *f*

Spanish "y" is "ee" when alone or at the end of words.

photo   246   physical

photo *n* foto *m* **bad** ~ foto mala **black-and-white** ~ foto en blanco y negro
color ~ foto a color **current** ~ foto reciente **excellent** ~ foto excelente
family ~ foto familiar **good** ~ buena foto **graduation** ~ foto de graduación
great ~ gran foto **group** ~ foto de grupo **large** ~ foto grande **my** ~ mi foto
new ~ foto nueva **old** ~ foto vieja **only** ~ única foto **passport** ~ foto de
pasaporte **perfect** ~ foto perfecta ~ **of you** una foto de ti ~ **studio** foto de
estudio **poor** ~ foto mala **recent** ~ foto reciente **school** ~ foto escolar
small ~ foto pequeña **wedding** ~ foto de boda **your** ~ *su (Fam: tu)* foto
That's a *(1)* **beautiful /** *(2)* **great /** *(3)* **nice photo of you.** Esa es una foto
(1) linda / *(2)* fenomenal / *(3)* buena. **I like this photo (of you).** Me gusta
esta foto (de *suya [Fam: tuya]*). **This photo doesn't look like you.** Esta
foto no se parece a *usted (Fam: ti).* **Who's** *(1,2)* **that in the photo?** ¿Quién
es *(1)* ese *m /* *(2)* esa *f* en la foto? **This is a photo of my** *(1)* **brother. /** *(2)*
daughter. / *(3)* **family. /** *(4)* **father. /** *(5)* **fiancé. /** *(6)* **fiancee. /** *(7)*
husband. / *(8)* **mother. /** *(9)* **sister. /** *(10)* **son. /** *(11)* **wife.** Esta es una foto
de mi *(1)* hermano. / *(2)* hija. / *(3)* familia. / *(4)* papá. / *(5)* prometido. / *(6)*
prometida. / *(7)* esposo. / *(8)* mamá. / *(9)* hermana. / *(10)* hijo. / *(11)* esposa.
I want a photo of you. Quiero una foto *suya (Fam: tuya).* **Can I have a
photo of you?** Puedo tener una foto *suya (Fam: tuya)*? **You can have the
photo.** *Se puede usted (Fam: Te puedes)* quedar con la foto. **Can I keep
this photo?** ¿Me puedo quedar con esta foto? **Let me take a photo of
you.** *Déjeme tomarle (Fam: Déjame tomarte)* una foto. **Excuse me, could
you take a photo of us?** Disculpe, ¿nos puede tomar una foto? **Let's all
take a photo together.** Vamos a tomarnos una foto todos juntos.
photogenic *adj* fotogénico *m*, -ca *f* **I'm not very photogenic.** Soy no muy
fotogénico *(-ca)*.
photograph *vt* fotografiar **Would you mind if I photographed you?** ¿*Le
(Fam: Te)* importaría si *le (Fam: te)* tomo una foto?
photograph *n* fotografía *f (See photo)*
photographer *n* fotógrafo *m*, -fa *f* **You're a good photographer.** *Es usted
(Fam: Tú eres)* un *(-na)* buen *(-na)* fotógrafo *(-fa)* .
photographic *adj* fotográfico *m*, -ca *f* ~ **equipment** equipo fotográfico ~
memory memoria fotográfica
photography *n* fotografía *f* **I'm very interested in photography.** Estoy
muy interesado en la fotografía.
phrase *n* frase *f* ~ **book** libro *m* de frases **Can you teach me some phrases
in Spanish?** ¿*Puede usted (Fam: Puedes)* enseñarme algunas frases en
español?
physical *adj* físico *m*, -ca *f* ~ **ability** habilidad física ~ **education (P.E.)**
educación física ~ **examination** examen físico ~ **exercise** ejercicio físico ~

---

*Feminine forms of words in phrases
are usually given in parentheses (italicized).*

prowess destreza física

physically *adv* físicamente

physique *n* físico *m* **muscular ~** físico musculoso **perfect ~** físico perfecto
You have a *(1)* **great /** *(2)* **marvelous physique.** Tiene usted *(Fam: Tienes)*
(1) un gran físico / *(2)* un físico maravilloso. **An athlete would envy your
physique.** Un atleta *le (Fam: te)* envidiaría el físico.

pianist *n* pianista *m&f*

piano *n* piano *m (See phrases under* **know how, like, love** *and* **play.)** **Play
the piano for** *(1)* **me /** *(2)* **us.** Toque usted *(Fam: Toca)* el piano para *(1)*
mí / *(2)* nosotros. **You play the piano very well.** Usted toca *(Fam: Tú
tocas)* muy bien el piano.

pick *vt* 1. *(choose)* escoger ; 2. *(fruit)* pizcar, recoger **Pick a card, any card.**
Escoge una carta, cualquier carta. **Pick one.** Escoge una. **I'm glad you
picked me for your partner.** Me agrada que *usted me haya (Fam: tú me
hayas)* escogido como compañero *(-ra)*. **Let's pick some** *(1)* **berries /** *(2)*
plums. Vamos a recoger *(1)* unas bayas. / *(2)* unas ciruelas.

★ **pick up** *idiom* 1. *(get as a passenger)* recoger; 2. *(learn)* captar **Can** *(1)*
he / *(2)* **she /** *(3)* **they pick us up (at the** *[4]* **airport /** *[5]* **station)?**
¿Puede *(1)* él / *(2)* ella... / *(3)* ¿Pueden ellos... recogernos (en *[4]* el
aeropuerto / *[5]* la estación)? **Is somebody picking** *(1,2)* **you up (at
the** *[3]* **airport /** *[4]* **station)?** *(1)* ¿Lo m / *(2)* ¿La f *(Fam:¿Te)* va a
recoger alguien (en *[3]* el aeropuerto / *[4]* la estación)? **My friend
will pick us up (at the** *[1]* **airport /** *[2]* **station).** Mi amigo nos va
a recoger (en *[1]* el aeropuerto / *[2]* la estación). **May I pick you
up?** ¿Paso por *usted (Fam: ti)*? **What time shall** *(1)* **I /** *(2)* **we pick
you up?** ¿A qué hora *(1)* paso / *(2)* pasamos por ti? *(1)* **I'll /** *(2)*
We'll pick you up at *(time)*. *(1)* Yo te recojo... / *(2)* Nosotros te re-
cogemos... a las ___. **You pick it up very quickly.** *(learn)* Lo captó
usted *(Fam: Lo captaste)* muy rápido.

pick *n (choice)* selección *f* **Take your pick.** Haz tu selección.

pickup *n (truck)* camioneta *f*

picky *adj* quisquilloso *m*, -sa *f* **I'm picky about things like that.** Soy
quisquilloso *(-sa)* con esas cosas. **Don't be so picky.** No seas tan
quisquilloso *(-sa)*.

picnic *vi* hacer un día de campo **We can picnic** *(1)* **in the park. /** *(2)* **on the
beach.** Podemos hacer un día de campo en *(1)* el parque. / *(2)* la playa.

picnic *n* día *m* de campo, picnic *m (See phrases under* **go, like** *and* **love.)** **go
on a ~** ir de día de campo, ir de picnic **Let's make a picnic (**[1]** today /** [2]**
tomorrow /** [3]** on Saturday /** [4]** on Sunday).** Hagamos picnic (*[1]* hoy
/ *[2]* mañana / *[3]* el sábado / *[4]* el domingo).

Spanish "c" before "e" and "i" is pronounced like "s".

picture *n* 1. *(painting, drawing)* pintura *f* ; 2. *(photo)* foto(grafía) *f (See phrases under photo)* **take a ~** tomar una foto **take ~s** tomar fotos **I want to take a picture of you.** Quiero *tomarle (Fam: tomarte)* una foto. **Let me take a picture of you.** *Déjeme tomarle (Fam: Déjame tomarte)* una foto. **Could you take a picture of us?** *¿Podría usted (Fam: Podrías)* tomarnos una foto? **You're a picture of loveliness.** *Es usted (Fam: Eres)* la imagen de la belleza.

pie *n* pastel *m* **cutie** ~ preciosura *f* **sugar** ~ amorcito *m&f*

piece *n* 1. *(portion)* pedazo *m* ; 2. *(item)* artículo *m* ~ **of candy** pedazo de dulce ~ **of luggage** pieza *f* de equipaje ~ **of paper** una hoja de papel **Would you like a piece?** *¿Gusta (Fam: Gustas)* un pedazo?

pier *n* embarcadero *m*, muelle *m*

pierced *adj* perforado *m*, -da *f* ~ **ears** orejas *fpl* perforadas ~ **lip** labio *m* perforado ~ **tongue** lengua *f* perforada

pig *n* puerco *m*

pigeon-toed *adj* con los pies torcidos hacia adentro

piggyback *adv* a cuestas **You can ride piggyback on me.** Te puedo llevar a cuestas.

pigtail *n* trenza *f*, coleta *f*

pile *n* montón *m* ~ **of dirty clothes** montón de ropa *f* sucia

pill *n* píldora *f* **birth control ~s** píldoras anticonceptivas **Are you on the pill?** ¿Estás tomando la píldora? **I'm on the pill.** Estoy tomando la píldora.

pillow *n* almohada *f*

pimple *n* grano *m*, barro *m*

pin *vt* sujetar, prender **Pin it together (with this).** Sujétalo (con esto).

pin *n* alfiler *m* **safety** ~ alfiler de seguridad **You've got me on pins and needles.** *Me tiene usted (Fam: Me tienes)* en ascuas.

pinch *vt* pellizcar ★ *n* pellizco *m* **give a** ~ dar un pellizco

ping-pong *n* ping-pong *m (See also phrases under like, love and play.)*

pink *adj* rosa *f*, rosado *m*, -da *f*

pipe *n* 1. *(tube)* tubo *m* ; 2. *(smoking)* pipa *f* ~ **dream** sueño *m* guajiro

pirate *n* pirata *m*

Pisces *(Feb. 19 - Mar. 20)* Piscis

pistol *n* pistola *f*

pitch-dark *adj* oscuro *m*, -ra *f* como boca de lobo

pitiful *adj* lamentable *m&f*

pity *vt* tener lástima **I pity (1) her. / (2) him. / (3) them. / (4) you.** (1) Él / (2) Ella me da... / (3) Ellos me dan... / (4) Usted me da (Fam: Tú me das)... lástima.

pity *n* piedad *f*, lástima *f* **Have pity on me.** *Tenga (Fam: Ten)* piedad de mí.

Numbers in Spanish are given on pages 411-412.

It's a pity that you can't *(1)* **come.** / *(2)* **stay.** Es una lástima que *usted no pueda (Fam: tú no puedas)* *(1)* venir. / *(2) quedarse (Fam: quedarte).* **It's a pity that I can't** *(1)* **come.** / *(2)* **stay.** Es una lástima que yo no pueda *(1)* venir. / *(2)* quedarme.

pixie *n* duende *m*

pizza *n* pizza *f* **Let's go get a pizza.** Vamos por una pizza.

pizzazz *n* 1. *(style)* gracia *f*; 2. *(cheerfulness)* alegría *f*; 3. *(fire, ardor)* fuego *m*, pasión *f* **You really have a lot of pizzazz.** De verdad *tiene usted (Fam: tienes)* mucha pasión.

place *vt* poner ~ **an ad in the newspaper** poner un anuncio en el periódico

place *n* lugar *m (See also phrases under* come *and* go.*)* **bad** ~ mal lugar **beautiful** ~ lugar bonito ~ **to play** lugar para jugar ~ **to stay** lugar para quedarse **What place is this?** ¿Qué lugar es este? *(1)* **I** / *(2)* **We need to find a place to stay.** *(1)* Necesito / *(2)* Necesitamos un lugar donde quedarnos.

plain *adj* 1. *(simple)* simple *m&f*; 2. *(clear)* claro *m*, -ra *f*; 3. *(unattractive)* sin gracia **You're far from being plain. You're very good-looking.** *Usted dista (Fam: Tú distas)* mucho de ser simple. *Usted es (Fam: Tú eres)* muy guapo *(-pa).*

plan *vt* planear, pensar **What do you plan to do?** ¿Qué *piensa usted (Fam: piensas)* hacer? **Where do you plan to go?** ¿Adónde *planea usted (Fam: planeas)* ir? **I plan to...** Pienso … **We plan to...** Pensamos …

plan *n* plan *m* **change ~s** cambiar planes **good ~** buen plan **great ~** gran plan **make ~s** hacer planes **~s for the future** planes para el futuro **travel ~s** planes de viaje **vacation ~s** planes de vacaciones **wedding ~s** planes de boda **What are your plans?** ¿Cuáles son *sus (Fam: tus)* planes? **Do you have any plans?** ¿*Tiene usted (Fam: Tienes)* algún plan? *(1)* **I** / *(2)* **We don't have any plans.** *(1)* No tengo / *(2)* No tenemos planes. *(1)* **I** / *(2)* **We have changed** *(3)* **my** / *(4)* **our plans.** *(1)* He / *(2)* Hemos cambiado *(3)* mis / *(4)* nuestros planes.

plane *n (airplane)* avión *m*

planet *n* planeta *m*

plant *n* 1. *(vegetation)* planta *f*; 2. *(factory)* planta *f*

plastic *adj* plástico *m*, -ca *f* ★ *n* plástico *m*

plate *n (dish)* plato *m*

platform *n (train station)* andén *m* **Which platform will the train be on?** ¿En cuál andén va a estar el tren?

platonic *adj* platónico *m*, -ca *f* **I don't want just a platonic relationship.** No quiero nada más una relación platónica.

play 1. *(games, sports)* jugar; 2. *(musical instruments)* tocar **I** *(1)* **like** / *(2)*

Spanish "h" is always silent.

love to play *(3)* **badminton.** */(4)* **baseball.** */ (5)* **basketball.** */ (6)* **board games.** */ (7)* **cards.** */ (8)* **football.** */ (9)* **golf.** */ (10)* **ping-pong.** */ (11)* **soccer.** */ (12)* **tennis.** */ (13)* **volleyball.** *(1, 2)* Me gusta jugar *(3)* badminton. */ (4)* béisbol. */ (5)* baloncesto. */ (6)* juegos de mesa. */ (7)* a las cartas. */ (8)* futbol americano. */ (9)* golf. */ (10)* ping-pong. */ (11)* futbol. */ (12)* tenis. */ (13)* volibol. **I** *(1)* **like** */ (2)* **love to play the** *(3)* **guitar** */ (4)* **piano.** *(1, 2)* Me gusta tocar *(3)* guitarra. */ (4)* piano. **Do you know how to play...** *(See choices above)*? ¿Sabe usted *(Fam: Sabes)* jugar...? **I (don't) know how to play...** *(See choices above)*. Yo (no) sé jugar... **Do you know how to play a musical instrument?** ¿Toca usted *(Fam: Tocas)* algún instrumento musical? **Play (the** *[1]* **guitar** */ [2]* **piano) for me.** *Toque usted (Fam: Toca)* (*[1]* la guitarra */ [2]* el piano) para mí. *(1)* **Let's play...** */ (2)* **I'll teach you how to play...** *(3)* **badminton.** */ (4)* **cards.** */ (5)* **chess.** */ (6)* **golf.** */ (7)* **ping-pong.** */ (8)* **tennis.** *(1)* Vamos a jugar... */ (2)* *Le (Fam: Te)* voy a enseñar a jugar... *(3)* badminton. */ (4)* cartas. */ (5)* ajedrez. */ (6)* golf. */ (7)* ping-pong. */ (8)* tenis.

play *n* 1. *(recreation)* juego *m* ; 2. *(flirt)* conquista *f*; 3. *(drama)* obra *f* (teatral) **fair ~** juego limpio **make a ~ for** *(someone)* tratar de conquistar a ___ **watch a ~** ver una obra (teatral) **You made a great play.** *Hizo usted (Fam: Hiciste)* una gran jugada. **It's your play.** *(game)* Te toca. **It's a play on words.** Es un juego de palabras.

playboy *n* playboy *m*

player *n* jugador *m*, -dora *f* **CD ~** (reproductor *m* de) compact-disc *m*

playful *adj* juguetón *m*, -tona *f*, retozón *m*, -zona *f*

playground *n* campo *m* de juego

playoff *n* eliminatoria *f*, desempate *m* **We have to have a playoff.** Tenemos que jugar el desempate.

plaza *n* plaza *f*

pleasant *adj* agradable *m&f* **~ chat** plática agradable **~ day** día agradable **~ evening** noche agradable **~ time** momento agradable **~ trip** viaje agradable **~ visit** visita agradable **It's so pleasant here.** Este lugar es tan agradable. *(1)* **I** */ (2)* **We had a very pleasant time.** *(1)* Pasé */ (2)* Pasamos un rato muy agradable.

please *vt* complacer, gustar **Does it please you?** ¿Te gusta? **It pleases me (very much) (that you** *[1]* **came** */ [2]* **called).** Me complace (muchísimo) (que *haya usted [Fam: tú hayas] [1]* venido */ [2]* llamado). **I'm (very) easy to please.** Soy (muy) fácil de complacer. **Nothing would please me more.** Nada me gustaría más. **It would please me no end.** Me complacería infinitamente.

please *imperative* por favor

Questions about the metric system? See page 417.

pleasurable *adj* agradable *m&f*, grato *m*, -ta *f*

pleasure *vt* complacerse, deleitarse

pleasure *n* placer *m* **all kinds of** ~ todo tipo de placer **boundless** ~ placer sin límite **cosmic** ~ placer cósmico **derive** ~ tener placer **endless** ~ placer sin fin **feel** ~ sentir placer **find** ~ encontrar placer **genuine** ~ genuino placer **get** ~ tener placer **give** ~ dar placer **great** ~ gran placer **heights of** ~ clímax del placer **infinite** ~ placer infinito **particular** ~ placer especial **real** ~ verdadero placer **simple** ~**s (of life)** placeres sencillos (de la vida) **such** ~ tal placer **true** ~ placer verdadero **With pleasure.** Con gusto. **It was a (real) pleasure talking with you.** Hablar *con usted (Fam: contigo)* fue un (verdadero) placer. **It would be a pleasure.** Sería un placer. **What a pleasure to share this day with you.** Qué gusto compartir este día *con usted (Fam: contigo)*. **You give me so much pleasure.** Me das tanto placer.

pleased *adj* encantado *m*, -da *f (1,2)* **Pleased to meet you.** *(1)* Gusto de conocerlo *(-la)*. / *(2)* Mucho gusto.

pleasureful *adj* placentero *m*, -ra *f*

plentiful *adj* abundante *m&f*

plenty *n* bastante *m (1)* **I** / *(2)* **We have plenty of time.** *(1)* Tengo / *(2)* Tenemos bastante tiempo. **There's plenty.** Hay bastante.

pliers *n, pl* pinzas *fpl* **pair of** ~ par de pinzas

ploy *n* treta *f*, ardid *m*

plug *n* 1. *(stopper)* tapón *m* ; 2. *(elec.)* clavija *f* **ear** ~**s** tapones para los oídos **spark** ~ bujía *f*

plugged up *adj* enchufado *m*, -da *f*

plug in *idiom (elec.)* enchufar **Where can I plug this in?** ¿Dónde puedo enchufar esto? **Is it plugged in?** ¿Está enchufado?

plum *n* ciruela *f*

plumber *n* plomero *m*

plump *adj* rechoncho *m*, -cha *f* **pleasantly** ~ agradablemente rechoncho *(-cha)*

plural *n* plural *m* **What's the plural (of this word)?** ¿Cuál es el plural (de esta palabra)?

plus *prep* más

p.m. *abbrev* p.m. (pasado meridiano)

pocket *n* bolsillo *m*

pocketbook *n* libro *m* de bolsillo

pocketknife *n* navaja *f* de bolsillo

poem *n* poema *m* **I composed a poem for you.** Te compuse un poema.

poet *n* poeta *m&f* **You're quite a poet.** Eres todo un poeta.

The letter "ñ" sounds like the "ny" in "canyon".

poetic *adj* poético *m*, -ca *f*

poetry *n* poesía *f* **You bring out the poetry in my soul.** *Usted despierta (Fam: Tú despiertas) lo romántico que hay en mí.* **You make me want to compose poetry for you.** *Usted hace (Fam: Tú haces) que yo quiera escribir poesía para usted (Fam: ti).*

point *n* 1. *(sharp end)* punta *f*; 2. *(juncture)* punto *m*; 3. *(gist)* punto *m*; 4. *(purpose, sense)* punto *m*; 5. *(characteristic)* punto *m*; 6. *(scoring)* punto *m* **get the ~** *(understand)* agarrar el punto **good ~s** puntos buenos **good and bad ~s** puntos buenos y malos **make ~s** hacer puntos **make ~s (with)** *(gain favor)* hacer puntos (con) **~ of view** punto de vista **not get the ~** *(not understand)* no agarrar el punto **score ~s** anotar puntos **strong ~** punto fuerte **weak ~** punto débil *(1)* **This /** *(2)* **That is the starting point.** *(1)* Este / *(2)* Ese es el punto de partida. **What's the point (of it)?** ¿Cuál es el caso (de eso)? **The point is (that)...** El caso es (que)... **Come to the point.** Vamos al grano. **There's no point in arguing.** No tiene sentido discutir. **How many points do** *(1)* **we /** *(2)* **you have?** ¿Cuántos puntos *(1)* tenemos / *(2)* Tiene usted (Fam: tienes)? *(1)* **We /** *(2)* **You are** *(number)* **points** *(3)* **ahead /** *(4)* **behind.** *(1)* Llevamos / *(2)* Usted lleva (Fam: Llevas) ___ puntos *(3)* de ventaja. / *(4)* de desventaja.

pointless *adj* sin sentido

poison *n* veneno *m*

poisonous *adj* venenoso *m*, -sa *f*

poker *n* *(card game)* póquer *m*

pole *n* 1. *(upright stake)* poste *m*; 2. *(long stick)* palo *m* **fishing ~** caña *f* de pescar **ski** *(1,2)* **~s** *(1)* bastones *mpl* / *(2)* palos *mpl* de esquí

police *n* policía *m & f* **~ officer** policía *m&f* **~ station** estación *f* de policía **Call the police.** Llama a la policía. **I'll call the police.** Voy a llamar a la policía. **I called the police.** Llamé a la policía. **The police are coming.** Ahí viene la policía.

policeman *n* hombre *m* policía ★ **policewoman** *n* mujer *f* policía

polite *adj* cortés *m&f*

political *adj* político *m*, -ca *f* ★ **politics** *n* política *f*

pollution *n* contaminación *f*

polygamy *n* poligamia *f*

pompous *adj* pomposo *m*, -sa *f*

poncho *n* poncho *m*

pond *n* estanque *m*

pony *n* pony *m* **ride a ~** montar en pony

pool *n* 1. estanque *m*; 2. *(swimming)* piscina *f*, alberca *f*; 3. *(billiards)* billar *m* **~ table** mesa de billar **shoot ~** tiro de billar **swimming ~** piscina *f*,

Meet Mexicans online!
See pages 428-430 for websites.

alberca *f* **Let's go** *(1)* **lie** / *(2)* **sit by the pool.** Vamos a *(1)* echarnos / *(2)* sentarnos junto a la alberca.

poor *adj* 1. *(needy)* pobre *m&f;* 2. *(unfortunate)* pobre *m&f,* desafortunado *m,* -da *f;* 3. *(bad)* malo *m,* -la *f* ~ **game** mal juego ~ **(little) thing** pobrecito *m,* -ta *f* ~ **movie** película mala ~ **score** mal punto **You poor girl.** Pobre niña. **You poor guy.** Pobre tipo.

poorly *adv* mal **do** ~ hacerlo mal **play** ~ jugar mal

pop (music) *n* música *f* pop

popcorn *n* palomitas *fpl* de maíz **Do you like popcorn?** ¿Te gustan las palomitas de maíz? **Let's get some popcorn.** Vamos a comprar palomitas de maíz.

popular *adj* popular *m & f* ~ **song** canción popular

population *n* población *f* **What's the population of** *(city)*? ¿Cuál es la población de ___?

porcelain *adj* de porcelana ★ *n* porcelana *f*

pornographic *adj* pornográfico *m,* -ca *f* ~ **movie** película porno ~ **(web) site** sitio (de Internet) porno

pornography *n* pornografía *f*

port *n* *(seaport)* puerto *m*

portion 1. *(part)* porción *f;* 2. *(serving)* porción *f*

portrait *n* retrato *m* ~ **painter** retratista *m&f* **Let** *(1)* **her** / *(2)* **him paint your portrait.** *(1)* Deje (Fam: Deja) / *(2)* que *le (Fam: te)* haga un retrato. **Let's go have a portrait made.** Vamos a que nos hagan un retrato.

pose *vi* posar ~ **in the nude** posar al desnudo **Would you pose for me?** ¿Posaría usted (Fam: Posarías) para mí?

position *n* *(1. posture; 2. situation; 3. job)* posición *f* **What's your position in the company?** ¿Cuál es *su (Fam: tu)* posición en la compañía?

positive *adj* positivo *m,* -va *f* ~ **mental attitude** actitud mental positiva ~ **outlook** perspectiva positiva **I like your positive attitude.** Me gusta tu actitud positiva.

possessive *adj* posesivo *m,* -va *f*

possibility *n* posibilidad *f* **endless** ~**ies** posibilidades infinitas **Is there any possibility that you could** *(1)* **get off (work) tomorrow?** / *(2)* **go with** *(3)* **me?** / *(4)* **us?** ¿Hay alguna posibilidad de que *(1)* salga usted (Fam: salgas)* (del trabajo) mañana? / *(2)* ir *(3)* conmigo? / *(4)* con nosotros? **There's a possibility.** Hay una posibilidad. **There's no possibility.** No es posible .

possible *adj* posible *m&f* **Would it be possible to** *(1,2)* **see** / *(3)* **meet you** *(4)* **this afternoon** / *(5)* **this evening?** / *(6)* **tomorrow** (*[7]* **morning** / *[8]* **afternoon** / *[9]* **evening)?** / *(10)* **after you get off work?** ¿Sería posible

---

Spanish "o" is pronounced like "o" in "note".

(1) verlo m / (2) verla f (Fam: verte) / (3) reunirme con usted (Fam: contigo) (4) esta tarde? */ (5)* esta noche? */ (6)* mañana (por la *[7]* mañana / *[8]* tarde / *[9]* noche)? */ (10)* después del trabajo? **Would it be possible for you** *(1)* **to go** */ (2)* **come with me?** */ (3)* **to come (** *[4]* **here)** */ (* *[5]* **to my hotel) after work?** */ (6)* **to call me?** */ (7)* **to stay (with me) overnight?** ¿Sería posible que *(1) usted fuera (Fam: fueras) / (2) usted viniera (Fam: vinieras)* conmigo? */ (3) usted viniera (Fam: vinieras)* (*[4]* aquí / *[5]* a mi hotel) después del trabajo? */ (6) usted me llamara (me llamaras)?* */ (7) usted se quedara (Fam: tú te quedaras)* (conmigo) esta noche? **Would it be possible for you to** *(1)* **get** */ (2)* **take** *(3)* **today** */ (4)* **tomorrow off?** */ (5)* **a week off?** */ (6)* **two** */ (7)* **three days off?** */ (8)* **two** */ (9)* **three weeks off?** */ (10)* **a vacation (while I'm here)?** ¿Sería posible que *(1) usted se saliera (Fam: te salieras) / (2) usted se tomara (Fam: te tomaras)* el día libre *(3)* hoy? */ (4)* mañana? */ (5)* una semana libre? */ (6)* dos / *(7)* tres días libres? / *(8)* dos / *(9)* tres semanas libres? / *(10)* vacaciones (mientras estoy aquí)? **Would it be possible to** *(1)* **stay at your** *(2)* **house?** */ (3)* **apartment?** */ (4,5)* **visit you?** */ (6)* **stay for another** *(7)* **day?** */ (8)* **week?** */ (9)* **fix it (** *[10]* **today** / *[11]* **soon** / *[121]* **by tomorrow)?** ¿Sería posible *(1)* quedarnos en *su (Fam: tu)* (2) casa? */ (3)* departamento? */ (4) visitarlo m / (5) visitarla f (Fam: visitarte)?* */ (6)* ...quedarme *(7)* otro día? */ (8)* otra semana? */ (9)* arreglarlo (*[10]* hoy / *[11]* pronto / *[12]* para mañana)? **I'm afraid it's not possible.** Me temo que no es posible.

possibly *adv* posiblemente

postage *n* franqueo *m* **How much would the postage be for this (to *(place)*?** ¿Cuánto costaría el franqueo de esto (hacia ___)?

postcard *n* postal *f* *(1)* **I'll** */ (2)* **We'll send you a postcard.** *(1)* Le *(Fam: Te)* mando ... */ (2)* Le *(Fam: Te)* mandamos... una postal. **Send me a post-card, okay?** Me *manda (Fam: mandas)* una postal. ¿Sí?

poster *n* afiche *m* **What does that poster say?** ¿Qué dice ese afiche?

posterior *n (buttocks)* trasero *m* **shapely ~** trasero bien formado

post office *n* oficina *f* de correos

postpone *vt* posponer **The** *(1)* **concert** */ (2)* **game** */ (3)* **meeting** */ (4)* **show has been postponed.** Se pospuso *(1)* el concierto. */ (2)* el juego. */ (3)* la reunión. */ (4)* el programa.

pot *n* 1. *(for cooking)* olla *f*; 2. *(slang: marijuana)* mota *f* **sex ~** *(slang: sexy woman)* chica muy sexy

potato *n* papa *f* **couch ~** teleadicto *m*, -ta *f*

potion *n* pócima *f* **love ~** pócima de amor

pottery *n* alfarería *f* **make ~** hacer alfarería

pour *vt* vaciar, vertir **~ out** *(1)* **my** */ (2)* **your feelings** volcar *(1)* mis / *(2) sus*

Numbers in parentheses always signal choices.

(Fam: tus) sentimientos

poverty *n* pobreza *f* **live in** ~ vivir en pobreza

powder *n* polvo *m* **body** ~ talco *m* **talcum** ~ talco *m*

power *n* 1. *(strength; might)* poder *m* ; 2. *(electricity)* luz *f*, energía *f* eléctrica **intellectual** ~ poder intelectual **psychic** ~ poder psíquico **seductive** ~ poder seductor **You have such power over my senses.** Tienes tal poder sobre mis sentidos. **The power is out.** Se fue la luz.

powerboat *n* lancha a motor

powerful *adj* poderoso *m*, -sa *f*, fuerte *m&f* **You're very powerful.** *Tiene usted (Fam: Tienes)* mucha fuerza .

powerless *adj* sin potencia

practical *adj* práctico *m*, -ca *f* ~ **advice** consejo práctico ~ **idea** idea práctica ~ **mind** mente práctica ~ **person** persona práctica

practice *vt* 1. *(drill oneself in)* ejercitarse, ejercer; 2. *(engage in)* practicar ~ **dancing** ensayar baile ~ **law** ejercer derecho ~ **medicine** ejercer medicina ~ **the piano** ensayar piano **You should practice what you preach.** *Usted debiera (Fam: Tú debieras)* poner en práctica lo que *predica (Fam: predicas)*. **I need to practice my Spanish. Will you help me?** Necesito practicar mi español. ¿Me *ayuda usted (Fam: ayudas)*?

practice *vi (drill oneself)* practicar **How often do you practice?** ¿Con qué frecuencia practicas? **I practice (almost) everyday.** Practico (casi) diario. **I practice** *(1)* **three** / *(2)* **five times a week.** Practico *(1)* tres / *(2)* cinco veces a la semana. *(1)* **I** / *(2)* **You need to practice (more).** *(1)* Necesito / *(2)* Necesitas practicar (más).

practice *n* práctica *f* **When do you have practice?** ¿Cuándo tienes práctica? **Practice makes perfect.** La práctica hace al maestro.

prank *n* broma *f* **play a** ~ **on** hacer una broma **No more pranks, please.** No más bromas, por favor.

pray *vi* rezar, rogar **fervently** ~ rezar con fervor *(1)* **I** / *(2)* **We will pray for you.** *(1)* Yo voy… / *(2)* Nosotros vamos… a rezar por *usted (Fam: ti)*. *(1)* **I** / *(2)* **We pray that everything will be alright.** *(1)* Yo rezo… / *(2)* Nosotros rezamos… por que todo salga bien. **I pray that you can** *(1)* **come.** / *(2)* **go.** / *(3)* **stay.** Ruego por que *usted pueda (Fam: puedas)* *(1)* venir. / *(2)* ir. / *(3)* quedarse *(Fam: quedarte)*. **I was praying that** *(1)* **I would see** *(2,3)* **you again.** / *(4)* **you would call.** / *(5)* **you would look my way.** Estaba deseando *(1)* …*(2)* volver a *verlo m* / *(3)* *verla f (Fam: verte)*. / *(4)* que *usted llamara (Fam: llamaras)*. / *(5)* que *usted volteara (Fam: voltearas)* a verme. **Let's pray together.** Vamos rezando juntos. *(1)* **I** / *(2)* **We pray** *(3)* **at mealtimes.** / *(4)* **often.** *(1)* Rezo / *(2)* Rezamos *(3)* a la hora de comer. / *(4)* con frecuencia. **Will you pray with me?** ¿*Reza usted (Fam:*

Spanish "a" is mostly like "a" in "mama".

Rezas) conmigo?

prayer *n* oración *f* **say a ~** decir una oración **You're the answer to my** *(1)* **prayer.** / *(2)* **prayers.** Tú eres la respuesta a *(1)* mi oración. / *(2)* mis oraciones.

precaution *n* precaución *f* **We have to take precautions.** Tenemos que tomar precauciones.

preceding *adj* anterior *m&f*

precious *adj* valioso *m*, -sa *f* **This is very precious to me.** Esto es muy valioso para mí. **It's incredible how precious you have become to me.** Es increíble cuán valioso *(-sa)* te has vuelto para mí. **You are so precious to me.** Eres tan valioso *(-sa)* para mí.

predicament *n* predicamento *m* *(1)* **I'm** / *(2)* **We're in a predicament.** *(1)* Estoy / *(2)* Estamos en un predicamento.

predict *vt* predecir **~ the future** predecir el futuro **What do you predict?** ¿Qué *predice usted (Fam: predices tú)*?

prefer *vt* preferir **Which do you prefer?** ¿Cuál prefieres? **I prefer** *(1)* *(item)*. / *(2)* **to go with you.** / *(3)* **not to say.** Prefiero *(1)* ___. / *(2)* ir *con usted (Fam: contigo)*. / *(3)* no decir.

preferably *adv* preferentemente

pregnancy *n* embarazo *m*

pregnant *adj* embarazada **get ~** embarazarse **I'm (not) pregnant.** (No) Estoy embarazada. **How many months pregnant are you?** ¿Cuántos meses de embarazo *tiene usted (Fam: tienes)*? **I don't want to get pregnant.** No quiero embarazarme.

prejudice *n* prejuicio *m* **Prejudice is wrong.** El prejuicio es malo.

prejudiced *adj* prejuicioso *m*, -sa *f* **I'm not prejudiced against anyone.** No tengo prejuicios contra nadie.

preparation *n* preparativo *m* **wedding ~s** preparativos de boda

prepare *vt* preparar **I'll prepare everything for the** *(1)* **party.** / *(2)* **picnic.** Yo voy a preparar todo para *(1)* la fiesta. / *(2)* el día de campo. **You've prepared everything so nicely.** *Usted ha (Fam: Tú has)* arreglado todo muy bonito. **Are you prepared (for the test)?** ¿*Está usted (Fam: Estás)* preparado (para la prueba)?

prescription *n* receta *f* *(1)* **I** / *(2)* **We have to get a prescription filled.** *(1)* Tengo que / *(2)* Tenemos que hacer que nos surtan una receta.

present *adj (current)* presente *m&f*, actual *m&f* **at the ~ moment** de momento **at the ~ time** por ahora **~ tense** *(gram.)* tiempo presente

present *n* 1. *(present time)* presente *m* ; 2. *(gift)* regalo *m* **at ~** por ahora **birthday ~** regalo de cumpleaños **Christmas ~** regalo de Navidad **give a ~** dar un regalo **live for the ~** vivir el presente **small ~** regalito

presently *adv (at present)* en el momento, actualmente

Articles: m = el, f = la, mpl = los, fpl = las

preserver *n*: **life ~** salvavidas *f*
president *n* presidente *m&f*
press *vt* 1. *(push)* apretar; 2. *(apply pressure against)* presionar; 3. *(clothes)* planchar
pressure *vt* presionar **Please don't pressure me.** Por favor no me presiones. **I'm not going to pressure you.** No voy a presionarte.
pressure *n* presión *f* **a lot of ~** mucha presión **high blood ~** alta presión sanguínea **under ~** bajo presión **I don't want to put (any) pressure on you.** No quiero presionarte (de ninguna manera).
prestige *n* prestigio *m*
presume *vt* suponer **I presume that...** Supongo que…
presumptuous *adj* presumido *m*, -da *f*, presuntuoso *m*, -sa *f*
pretend *vi* fingir **I'm not pretending.** No estoy fingiendo. **Let's pretend.** Vamos fingiendo.
pretty *adj* bonito *m*, -ta *f* **~ as a picture** bonita como una pintura **You're very pretty.** Eres muy bonita. **You have a very pretty smile.** *Tiene usted (Fam: Tú tienes)* una sonrisa muy linda. **What a pretty blouse!** ¡Qué blusa tan bonita!
pretty *adv (colloq.) (rather)* bastante
pretzel *n* rosquilla *f*, pretzel *m*
prevent *vt* detener **What's preventing you?** ¿Qué *lo (Fam: te)* detiene?
preview *n (movies)* avance *m*
previous *adj* previo *m*, -via *f*, anterior *m&f* **~ job** empleo *m* anterior **~ marriage** matrimonio *m* anterior **on a ~ occasion** en una ocasión *f* anterior
previously *adv* previamente, antes **Where did you (1) live / (2) work previously?** ¿Dónde *(1) vivía usted (Fam: vivías) / (2) trabajaba usted (Fam: trabajabas)* antes?
price *n* precio *m* **bargain ~** precio de oferta **cheap ~** precio barato **discount ~** precio de descuento **exorbitant ~** precio exorbitante **good ~** buen precio **high ~** precio alto **high ~s** precios altos **pay the ~** pagar el precio **~ list** lista de precios **~ tag** etiqueta de precio **reasonable ~** precio razonable **reduced ~** precio reducido **ticket ~** etiqueta de precio **What's the price?** ¿Qué precio tiene? **The price has gone up.** El precio ha subido. **The prices keep going up.** Los precios siguen subiendo.
priceless *adj* invaluable *m&f* **You're priceless.** Eres invaluable.
pride *n* orgullo *m* **great ~** gran orgullo **You can take a lot of pride in what you've accomplished.** Puedes estar muy orgulloso *(-sa)* por lo que has logrado. **I'm going to swallow my pride and beg you.** Voy a tragarme mi orgullo y te voy a rogar.
priest *n* cura *m*, sacerdote *m*

Spanish "z" is pronounced like "s" in "safe".

prim *adj* recatado *m*, -da *f*, formal *m&f* **You** *(1)* **look** / *(2)* **looked so prim in that outfit.** Te *(1)* ves / *(2)* veías muy formal con ese atuendo.

primarily *adv* primordialmente

primitive *adj* primitivo *m*, -va *f* **You bring out all of my primitive instincts.** Tú despiertas todos mis instintos primitivos.

prince *n* príncipe *m* ~ **charming** príncipe encantado

princess *n* princesa *f* **beautiful** ~ bella princesa **fairy tale** ~ princesa de cuento de hadas **Mexican** ~ princesa mexicana **my little** ~ mi princesita ~ **of my heart** princesa de mi corazón **spicy** ~ princesa pícara

principle *n* principio *m* **high** ~s de elevados principios **strong** ~s de principios sólidos **That's against my principles.** Eso va contra mis principios. **I'm no paragon of virtue, but I have my principles.** No soy un dechado de virtudes, pero tengo mis principios. **Have you no principles (at all)? (Great, neither do I.)** ¿Qué no tienes principios (del todo)? (Qué bien, yo tampoco.) **It's my principle never to drink before five o'clock. What time is it now?** Por principio nunca bebo antes de las cinco. ¿Qué hora es?

print *vt* imprimir ~ **out** imprimir

printer *n* 1. *(business)* imprenta *f*; 2. *(computers)* impresora *f*

prior to antes de **Prior to coming here...** Antes de venir aquí …

priority *n* prioridad *f* **first** ~ primera prioridad **high** ~ alta prioridad **number one** ~ la prioridad número uno **top** ~ la prioridad principal **That's my number one priority.** Esa es mi prioridad número uno.

privacy *n* privacidad *f* **find** ~ encontrar privacidad **have** ~ tener privacidad **We need some privacy.** Necesitamos un poco de privacidad.

private *adj* 1. *(personal)* privado *m*, -da *f*; 2. *(confidential)* privado *m*, -da *f* ~ **matter** asunto privado ~ **property** propiedad privada

prison *n* cárcel *f* **go to** ~ ir a la cárcel **put** *(someone)* **in** ~ meter *(a alguien)* a la cárcel

prisoner *n* preso *m*, -sa *f*, prisionero *m*, -ra *f* **take** ~ llevar preso *(-sa)* **I'm a prisoner of your** *(1)* **beauty.** / *(2)* **charm.** Soy prisionero de *su (Fam: tu)* *(1)* belleza. / *(2)* encanto. **Okay, this is it. All or nothing. I take no prisoners.** *(game)* Bueno, se acabó. Todo o nada. No tomo prisioneros.

private *n (privacy)* privado *m* **in** ~ en privado **Could we discuss it in private?** ¿Podríamos platicarlo en privado? **I want to talk with you (about it) in private.** Quiero platicar *con usted (Fam: contigo)* (de eso) en privado. **Is there someplace we can talk in private?** ¿Hay algún lugar donde podamos platicar en privado?

privately *adv* privadamente

privilege *n* privilegio *m* **One of the privileges of membership is...** Uno de los privilegios de la membresía es... **It's been a privilege talking with**

A tilde ~ in terms stands for the main entry word.

you. Ha sido un privilegio platicar *con usted (Fam: contigo)*.

prize *n* premio *m* **first ~** primer premio **grand ~** el gran premio **second ~** segundo premio **third ~** tercer premio **win a ~** ganar un premio **What's the prize?** ¿Cuál es el premio? **The prize is...** El premio es...

probably *adv* probablemente *(1)* **I** / *(2)* **We will probably go.** Probablemente *(1)* vaya / *(2)* vayamos. **Probably not.** Probablemente no.

problem *n* problema *m* **complicated ~** problema complicado **difficult ~** problema difícil **have a ~** tener un problema **main ~** problema principal **real ~** verdadero problema **run into a ~** meterse en problemas **serious ~** problema serio **slight ~** pequeño problema **small ~** problemita *(1)* **I** / *(2)* **We have a (small) problem.** *(1)* Tengo / *(2)* Tenemos un (pequeño) problema. **Is there a problem (about this)?** ¿Hay algún problema (con eso)? **There's a (*[1]* big / *[2]* small) problem.** Hay un (*[1]* gran / *[2]* pequeño) problema. **What's the problem?** ¿Cuál es el problema? **The problem is that...** El problema es que... **Please tell *(1)* me** / *(2)* **us what the problem is.** Por favor, *(1)* dime / *(2)* dinos cuál es el problema. **We'll solve this problem somehow.** De algún modo resolveremos este problema.

procedure *n* procedimiento *m* **What's the procedure?** ¿Cuál es el procedimiento? **I'll explain the procedure to you.** Yo *le (Fam: te)* explico el procedimiento.

process *n* proceso *m* **difficult ~** proceso difícil **long ~** largo proceso **long, drawn-out ~** proceso largo y complicado **time-consuming ~** proceso que demanda mucho tiempo **What does the process involve?** ¿Qué implica el proceso?

procrastinate *vi* postergar

procrastinator *n* desidioso *m*, -sa *f* **champion ~** campeón *(campeona)* de la desidia **expert ~** experto *(-ta)* en desidia **prodigious ~** prodigio de desidia

prodigious *adj* prodigioso *m*, -sa *f*

prodigy *n* prodigio *m* **child ~** niño prodigio

produce *vt* producir **They produce...** Producen...

producer *n (of goods)* productor *m*, -tora *f*

product *n* producto *m* **~ of your imagination** producto de tu imaginación

production *n* producción *f*

profane *adj* irreverente *m&f* **No profane language, please.** Sin lenguaje irreverente, por favor. **It's not necessary to be profane.** No hay necesidad de ser irreverente.

profanity *n* irreverencia *f* **Let's cut out the profanity, please.** Dejemos la irreverencia, por favor.

profession *n (occupation)* profesión *f* **What's your profession?** ¿Cuál es su profesión? **My profession is *(type)*** Mi profesión es ___. **That's a(n)** *(1)*

Spanish "ch" is pronounced like ours
(e.g., "cheese," "charge").

excellent / *(2)* **good** / *(3)* **great profession.** Esa es una profesión *(1)* excelente. / *(2)* buena. / *(3)* fenomenal.

professional *adj* profesional *m&f* ~ **beachcomber** vago *m* profesional ~ **gambler** apostador *m* profesional ~ **musician** músico *m* profesional ~ **player** jugador *m* profesional ~ **sports** deporte *m* profesional ~ **weirdo** chiflado *(-da)* profesional

professional *n* profesional *m&f*

professor *n* profesor *m*, -sora *f*

proficient *adj* competente *m&f* **You're quite proficient at this.** *Usted es (Fam: Tú eres)* bastante competente en esto.

profit *n* ganancia *f*

profitable *adj* lucrativo *m*, -va *f*, provechoso *m*, -sa *f*

profound *adj* profundo *m*, -da *f* ~ **gratitude** profunda gratitud ~ **sympathy** condolencia *f* profunda

program *n* 1. *(schedule of events)* programa *m* ; 2. *(TV or radio show)* programa *m* ; 3. *(software)* programa *m* **What's on the program (for** *[1]* **today** / *[2]* **tonight)?** ¿Qué hay en programa (*[1]* para hoy / *[2]* esta noche)? **According to the program...** Según el programa... *(1)* **I** / *(2)* **We** / *(3)* **You better get with the program.** *(slang)* Mejor *(1)* sigo / *(2)* seguimos / *(3)* sigues el programa. **There's a good program on TV (tonight).** Hay un buen programa en la tele (esta noche).

programmer *n (comp.)* programador *m*, -dora *f*

programming *n (comp.)* programación *f*

progress *n* progreso *m*, avance *m* **You're making (** *[1]* **good** / *[2]* **great** / *[3]* **outstanding) progress.** *Usted está (Fam: Tú estás)* haciendo *[1]* buenos / *[2]* grandes / *[3]* notables progresos. **I'm not making any progress.** No estoy progresando. / No estoy avanzando.

progressive *adj* progresivo *m*, -va *f*

prohibit *vt* prohibir **That's prohibited.** Está prohibido.

project *n* proyecto *m* **big** ~ gran proyecto **I like to work on home projects.** Me gusta trabajar en proyectos caseros.

prominent *adj* prominente *m&f*, destacado *m*, -da *f*

promiscuous *adj* promiscuo *m*, -cua *f* **I don't believe in being promiscuous.** No me gusta la promiscuidad.

promise *vt* prometer **Do you promise (me)?** ¿(Me) Lo *promete usted (Fam: prometes)*? *(1)* **I** / *(2)* **We (don't) promise (you).** (No) *(se (Fam: te))* lo *(1)* prometo / *(2)* prometemos. **Promise me.** *Prométamelo (Fam: Prométemelo).* **You promised. (Remember?)** *Usted lo prometió (Fam: Tú lo prometiste).* *(¿Se acuerda usted [Te acuerdas]?)*

promise *n* promesa *f* **break** *(1)* **my** / *(2)* **your** ~ romper *(1)* mi / *(2)* su *(Fam:*

Stress rule #1: The last syllable is stressed if the word ends in a consonant (except "n" and "s").

tu) promesa **empty** ~s promesas vacías **firm** ~ promesa firme **give** *(1)* **me** / *(2)* **you** *(3)* **my** / *(4)* **your** ~ *(1)* darme / *(2)* darte *(3)* mi / *(4) su (Fam: tu)* promesa **keep** *(1)* **my** / *(2)* **your** ~ mantener *(1)* mi / *(2) su (Fam: tu)* promesa **make good on** *(1)* **my** / *(2)* **your** ~ cumplir *(1)* mis / *(2) sus (Fam: tus)* promesas **solemn** ~ promesa solemne **That's a promise.** Es una promesa. **Don't forget your promise.** No olvides *su (Fam: tu)* promesa. **Did you forget your promise?** *¿Olvidó su (Fam: Olvidaste tu)* promesa? **Promises, promises.** Promesas, promesas.

promote *vt* promover **I recently got promoted (to** *[position]*). Recientemente me promovieron (a __).

promotion *n* promoción *f* **get a** ~ obtener una promoción

prompt *adj (without delay)* pronto *m*, -ta *f*

promptly *adv* con prontitud

pronounce *vt* pronunciar **How do you pronounce this?** ¿Cómo *pronuncia usted (Fam: pronuncias tú)* esto? **Excuse me, could you tell me how to pronounce this word?** *Disculpe (Fam: Disculpa), ¿podría usted (Fam: podrías)* decirme cómo pronunciar esta palabra?

pronunciation *n* pronunciación *f* **Can you help me with my pronunciation?** *¿Puede usted (Fam: Puedes)* ayudarme con mi pronunciación?

proof *n* prueba *f* **You'll have to give me some proof.** Tienes que darme una prueba. **More proof of my indomitable mastery of the game.** Más pruebas de mi dominio absoluto del juego.

proper *adj* 1. *(correct)* correcto *m*, -ta *f*; 2. *(appropriate)* apropiado *m*, -da *f* ~ **clothing** ropa *f* adecuada ~ **equipment** equipo *m* adecuado ~ **technique** técnica *f* adecuada **Let me show you the proper technique.** *Déjeme enseñarle (Fam: Déjame enseñarte)* la técnica adecuada.

properly *adv* bien, correctamente

property *n* propiedad *f* **government** ~ propiedad del gobierno **personal** ~ propiedad personal **private** ~ propiedad privada *(1)* **I** / *(2)* **We own some property there.** *(1)* Soy dueño… / *(2)* Somos dueños… de una propiedad allí. **Whose property is** *(1)* **this?** / *(2)* **that?** ¿De quién es *(1)* esta / *(2)* esa propiedad?

proportion *n* proporción *f* **You have nice proportions.** *Usted tiene (Fam: Tienes)* bonitas proporciones.

proposal *n* propuesta *f* **accept** *(1)* **my** / *(2)* **your** ~ aceptar *(1)* mi / *(2) su (Fam: tu)* propuesta **marriage** ~ propuesta de matrimonio

propose *vt* proponer **Are you proposing (marriage) to me?** ¿Me estás proponiendo (matrimonio)? **I'm proposing to you. Will you marry me?** Te estoy proponiendo. ¿Te casas conmigo? **I'm not proposing marriage.** No estoy proponiendo matrimonio.

Spanish "i" is mostly "ee", but can also be shorter, like "i" in "sit," when together with other vowels.

prose *n* prosa *f*

prospect *n* prospecto *m* **bright ~s** prospectos brillantes **good ~s** buenos prospectos **I look forward to the prospect.** Espero con gusto el prospecto.

prosperous *adj* próspero *m*, -ra *f*

prosthesis *n* prótesis *f* **I have a prosthesis.** Tengo una prótesis.

prostitute *n* prostituta *f*

protect *vt* proteger **Don't worry, I'll protect** *(1,2)* **you.** No *se preocupe (Fam: te preocupes).* Yo *(1)* lo *m* / *(2)* la *f (Fam: te)* protejo. **I'm not worried. I know you'll protect me.** No estoy preocupado *(-da).* Sé que tú me proteges. **This will protect your** *(1)* **ears.** / *(2)* **lips.** / *(3)* **skin.** Esto protege *(1)* los oídos. / *(2)* los labios. / *(3)* la piel.

protection *n* protección *f* **ear ~** protección para los oídos **It's (too)** *(1)* **dangerous** / *(2)* **risky without some kind of protection.** Sin protección es (demasiado) *(1)* peligroso. / *(2)* riesgoso .

protest *vi* protestar **I protest!** ¡Protesto! **It won't do you any good to protest.** No te va a servir que protestes.

protest *n* protesta *f* **big ~** gran protesta **public ~** protesta pública **What's the protest about?** ¿Por qué es la protesta? **I want you to know that I'm playing this game under protest.** Quiero que sepas que juego este partido bajo protesta. **That does it! I'm going to submit a formal protest to your government.** ¡Eso es! Voy a presentar una protesta formal ante tu gobierno.

Protestant *adj* protestante *m&f* ★ *n* protestante *m&f*

protester *n* protestante *m&f*

proud *adj* orgulloso *m*, -sa *f* **I'm sure you must be very proud of** *(1)* **her.** / *(2)* **him.** / *(3)* **them.** Estoy seguro *(-ra)* de que debes estar muy orgulloso de *(1)* ella / *(2)* él / *(3)* ellos. **I'm very proud of** *(1)* **her** / *(2)* **him** / *(3)* **them.** Estoy muy orgulloso de *(1)* ella. / *(2)* él. / *(3)* ellos. **I'm proud to** *(1)* **have you by my side.** / *(2)* **have you with me.** / *(3)* **go places with you.** / *(4)* **have a girlfriend as beautiful as you.** / *(5)* **have a boyfriend as handsome as you.** Estoy orgulloso *(-sa)* *(1)* de tenerte a mi lado. / *(2)* de tenerte conmigo. / *(3)* de salir contigo. / *(4)* de tener una novia tan hermosa como tú. / *(5)* de tener un novio tan guapo como tú. **Aren't you proud of me?** ¿No estás orgulloso de mí?

prove *vt* probar **Prove it!** ¡Pruébalo! **I'm going to prove to you that** *(1)* **I love you.** / *(2)* **I'm the greatest player that ever lived.** Voy a probarte que *(1)* te amo. / *(2)* soy el mejor jugador del mundo.

proverb *n* proverbio *m*

provide *vt* proporcionar, dar **What do they provide?** ¿Qué ofrecen? **What kind of services do they provide?** ¿Qué tipo de servicios proporcionan?

Help us improve our book!
Send us the feedback form on page 431.

Do they provide *(1)* **breakfast?** / *(2)* **lunch?** / *(3)* **dinner?** / *(4)* **meals?** / *(5)* **the equipment?** / *(6)* **transportation?** ¿Dan *(1)* desayuno? / *(2)* comida? / *(3)* alimentos? / *(4)* el equipo? / *(5)* transporte? **You have to provide your own** *(1)* **equipment.** / *(2)* **transportation.** *Usted se tiene (Fam: Te tienes)* que agenciar *su (Fam: tu)* propio *(1)* equipo. / *(2)* transporte. **Everything is provided (at no extra cost).** Todo se proporciona (sin costo adicional).

province *n* provincia *f* **I live in the province of** *(name)*. Vivo en la provincia de ___.

provincial *adj* provincial *m&f* ~ **capital** capital provincial

provisions *n, pl (food supplies)* provisiones *mpl* **You'll need provisions for** *(number)* **days.** *Usted va (Fam: Tú vas)* a necesitar provisiones para ___ días.

provocative *adj* provocativo *m*, -va *f*

prow *n (of a ship)* proa *f*

prowess *n (skill)* destreza *f*, pericia *f* **physical** ~ destreza física

prowler *n* merodeador *m*

prude *n* 1. *(puts on modest / proper airs)* mojigato *m*, -ta *f* ; 2. *(extremely modest / proper)* púdico *m*, -ca *f* **You're such a prude!** ¡Eres un(a) mojigato *(-ta)*! **Don't be such a prude.** No seas tan mojigato *(-ta)*.

prudent *adj* prudente *m&f* **That's the prudent thing to do.** Eso es lo prudente.

prudish *adj* 1. *(putting on modest / proper airs)* melindroso *m*, -sa *f* ; 2. *(extremely modest / proper)* recatado *m*, -da *f* **Don't be so prudish.** ¡No seas tan melindrosa! **That's a (rather) prudish attitude.** Esa es una actitud (algo) recatada.

pry *vi (snoop)* husmear, entrometerse **I'm sorry, I didn't mean to pry (into your personal life).** Lo siento, no quise entrometerme (en tu vida personal).

pseudonym *n* pseudónimo *m* **That's my pseudonym. Super** *(1,2)* **Man /** *(3)* **Woman.** Ese es mi pseudónimo. *(1)* Superhombre. / *(2)* Supermán. / *(3)* La Mujer Maravilla.

psyche *n* psique *f* **female** ~ psique femenina **male** ~ psique masculina **You have really invaded my psyche, do you know that?** Realmente has invadido mi mente. ¿Sabes?

psyched (up) *adj (slang: excited)* alocado *m*, -da *f*, **be** ~ *(slang) (be excited)* estar alocado, -da **I gotta warn you, I'm really psyched up for this game.** Te advierto que estoy realmente estoy alocado con este juego.

psychic *adj* psíquico *m*, -ca *f* **I will now demonstrate my psychic powers.** Ahora te voy a demostrar mis poderes psíquicos. **Now you have wit-**

Spanish "j" is pronounced like "h".

nessed my awesome psychic powers. Ahora has sido testigo de mis imponentes poderes psíquicos.

psycho *n (slang: crazy person)* loco *m*, -ca *f*

psychological *adj* psicológico *m*, -ca *f* ~ **imbalance** desequilibrio *m* psicológico **You have a psychological advantage - I'm crazy about you.** Tienes una ventaja psicológica. Estoy loco *(-ca)* por ti.

psychology *n* psicología *f*

public *adj* público *m*, -ca *f* ~ **telephone** teléfono *m* público

public *n* público *m* **in** ~ en público **kiss in** ~ besarse en público

publication *n (published work)* publicación *f*

publicity *n* publicidad *f* ~ **agent** agente *m&f* publicitario **I need you for my publicity agent.** Te necesito como mi agente publicitario.

publish *vt* publicar *(1)* **When** / *(2)* **Where was it published?** ¿*(1)* Cuándo / *(2)* Dónde se publicó?

publisher *n* editor *m*, -tora *f*

puck *n (hockey)* disco *m* (de goma)

pudgy *adj* rechoncho *m*, -cha *f* **I like pudgy** *(1)* **girls** / *(2)* **guys like you.** Me gustan *(1)* las chicas rechonchitas... / *(2)* los tipos rechonchitos... como tú.

pull *vt* jalar, atraer **Pull (this).** Jala (esto). **Your beautiful eyes pull me to you.** Tus bellos ojos me atraen mucho.

★ **pull down** *idiom (lower)* bajar **Pull down the shade.** Baja la persiana.

★ **pull in** *idiom (drive in)* meterse **Pull in to that** *(1)* **entrance-way.** / *(2)* **gas station.** / *(3)* **parking lot.** *Métase (Fam: Métete)* *(1)* a esa entrada. / *(2)* a la gasolinera. / *(3)* al estacionamiento.

★ **pull over** *idiom (drive to the side)* orillarse **Pull over** *(1)* **to the side.** / *(2)* **by that store.** *Oríllese (Fam: Oríllate)* *(1)* a un lado. / *(2)* junto a esa tienda.

★ **pull up** *idiom (bring over / closer)* jalar **Pull up a chair (and join us).** *Jale (Fam: Jala)* una silla (y *únase (Fam: únete)* a nosotros).

pulse *n* pulso *m* **Let me check your pulse.** Déjame tomarte el pulso. **Just as I thought - there is none.** Tal como pensé. No tienes.

pump *vt*: ~ **iron** *(slang: lift weights)* hacer pesas

pumpkin *n* calabaza *f*

pumpkinhead *n* cabeza *f* hueca

punch *vt* 1. *(hit)* golpear, ponchar; 2. *(press, e.g., a button)* apretar **I'm going to punch you in a minute.** Te voy a ponchar en un minuto. **Stop punching me! I'm not a punching bag.** Deja de golpearme. No soy un punching bag.

punch *n* 1. *(hit)* puñetazo *m* ; 2. *(beverage)* ponche *m* **fruit** ~ ponche de frutas ~ **bowl** tazón *m* de ponche ~ **in the nose** puñetazo en la nariz

---

Familiar "tu" forms in parentheses can replace italicized polite forms.

punctual *adj* puntual *m&f*

punish *vt* castigar **Why are you punishing me this way?** ¿Por qué me castigas así? **You deserve to be punished. Give me your foot.** Mereces que te castigue. Dame tu pie.

punishment *n* castigo *m* **As punishment, I'm cutting your allotment of kisses in half.** En castigo, te voy a recortar a la mitad tu ración de besos .

pupil *n* 1. *(young student)* alumno *m*, -na *f*; 2. *(of the eye)* pupila *f*

puppet *n* títere *m*

pup(py) *n* cachorrito *m* **I'm going to follow you around like a puppy.** Te voy a seguir como un cachorrito.

pure *adj* puro *m*, -ra *f*

purple *adj* morado *m*, -da *f*

purpose *n* propósito *m*, objeto *m* **immoral ~s** propósito inmoral **selfish ~s** propósitos egoístas **What's the purpose?** ¿Cuál es el objeto? **It has no purpose.** No tiene objeto.

purr *vi* ronronear **I want to teach you how to purr.** Te quiero enseñar a ronronear.

purse *n* monedero *m* **I lost my purse.** Perdí mi monedero.

pursue *vt* buscar **~ happiness** buscar la felicidad **~ romance** buscar el romance

pursuit *n* 1. *(chasing)* persecución *f* ; 2. *(activity)* actividad *f* **cultural ~s** actividades culturales **intellectual ~s** actividades intelectuales **leisure ~s** pasatiempos *m, pl* **I enjoy (various) cultural pursuits.** Me gustan (diversas) actividades culturales.

push *vt* 1. *(shove)* empujar; 2. *(press)* presionar **Push!** ¡Empuja! **Push it.** Empújalo. **Don't push!** ¡No empujes!

push off *(idiom) (boats)* desatracar **Push off!** ¡Lárgate!

put *vt* 1. *(lay)* poner; 2. *(set)* instalar; 3. *(place)* colocar **Where shall I put *(1,2)* it?** ¿Dónde *(1)* lo *m* / *(2)* la *f* pongo? **Put it over *(1)* here. / *(2)* there.** Ponlo *(1)* aquí. / *(2)* allí. **Can you put this in your *(1)* bag *(= sack)*? / *(2)* pack? / *(3)* pocket? / *(4)* purse? / *(5)* suitcase?** ¿Puedes poner esto en tu *(1)* bolsa? / *(2)* mochila? / *(3)* bolsillo? / *(4)* monedero? / *(5)* maletín? **Where did you put it?** ¿Dónde lo *puso usted (Fam: pusiste)*? **I put it *(1)* there. / *(2)* in my *(3)* pocket. / *(4)* purse. / *(5)* suitcase. / *(6)* wallet. / *(7)* in / *(7)* on the *(place)*.** Lo puse *(1)* allí. / *(2)* en mi *(3)* bolsillo. / *(4)* monedero. / *(5)* maleta. / *(6)* cartera. / *(7,8)* en ___. **Could you put this on the rack for me?** ¿Podría usted *(Fam: Podrías)* poner esto en el estante? **Put your head on my shoulder.** Pon tu cabeza en mi hombro. **I'm going to put an ad in the paper.** Voy a poner un anuncio en el periódico.

   ★ **put away** *idiom (return to proper place)* guardar **Okay, put away the**

Spanish "e" is pronounced like English "e" in "get"

gun, I'll *(1)* **come.** / *(2)* **do it.** / *(3)* **kiss you.** Bueno, guarda la pistola, voy a *(1)* venir. / *(2)* hacerlo. / *(3)* besarte.

★ **put down** *idiom* 1. *(lay down)* dejar; *(set down)* bajar; 2. *(belittle)* menospreciar **I didn't mean to** *(1,2)* **put you down, I'm sorry.** Perdón, no quise *(1) menospreciarlo m* / *(2) menospreciarla f (Fam: menospreciarte).*

★ **put off** *idiom (postpone)* posponer *(1)* **I'm** / *(2)* **We're going to put off** *(3)* **my** / *(4)* **our departure until** *(day/date).* *(1)* Voy / *(2)* Vamos a posponer *(3)* mi / *(4)* nuestra salida hasta ___.

★ **put on** *idiom* 1. *(clothing)* ponerse; 2. *(deceive, lie to)* engañar, mentir **You'd better put on a** *(1)* **coat.** / *(2)* **jacket.** / *(3)* **sweater. (It's [4] cold.** / **[5] getting cold.).** Será mejor que *se ponga (Fam: te pongas)* *(1)* un abrigo. / *(2)* una chaqueta. / *(3)* un suéter. (*[4]* Está haciendo frío. / *[5]* Se está poniendo frío.) **You'd better put on a hat.** Será mejor que *se ponga (Fam: te pongas)* un sombrero. **Why don't you put on something comfortable?** ¿Por qué no *se pone (Fam: te pones)* algo cómodo? **Let's put on our swimsuits.** Vamos a ponernos los trajes de baño. **You're putting me on.** Me estás tomando el pelo.

★ **put together** *idiom (assemble)* ensamblar *(1)* **I'll** / *(2)* **We'll help you put it together.** *(1)* Yo / *(2)* Nosotros *le (Fam: te)* ayudamos a ensamblarlo.

★ **put up** *idiom (erect)* levantar ~ **a tent** armar una casa de campaña

★ **put up with** *idiom (endure)* aguantar, soportar, tolerar **How do you put up with it?** ¿Cómo lo *soporta (Fam: soportas)*? **I couldn't put up with it (anymore).** No pude aguantarlo (más). **I don't know how you put up with it.** No sé cómo lo *tolera (Fam: toleras).*

putter *vi* talachar **I like to putter around the** *(1)* **garden.** / *(2)* **house.** / *(3)* **my workshop.** Me gusta talachar en *(1)* el jardín. / *(2)* la casa. / *(3)* mi taller.

puzzle *vt* desconcertar, confundir **You (really)** *(1,2)* **puzzle me (at times).** (Realmente) Me *(1)* desconciertas / *(2)* confundes (a veces).

puzzle *n* 1. *(mystery)* enigma *m* ; 2. *(toy)* rompecabezas *m* ; *(jigsaw)* rompecabezas *m*

puzzled *adj* desconcertado *m*, -da *f*, confundido *m*, -da *f* **I'm (really)** *(1,2)* **puzzled (by...).** (Realmente) Estoy *(1)* desconcertado *(-da)* / *(2)* confundido *(-da)* (con…)

Stress rule # 2: The next-to-last syllable is stress in words ending in "n", "s" or a vowel.

Q

quaint *adj* raro *m*, -ra *f*, peculiar *m & f*, curioso *m*, -sa *f*

quality *adj* *(of high quality)* de calidad; *(relationship)* serio *m*, -ria *f*

quality *n* *(characteristic)* cualidad *f*; *(feature)* cualidad *f* **exceptional ~ies** cualidades excepcionales **fine ~** de buena calidad **high ~** alta calidad **physical ~ies** cualidades físicas **similar ~ies** cualidades similares **You have so many** *(1)* **fine** / *(2)* **good** / *(3)* **nice** / *(4)* **marvelous qualities.** Tienes tantas cualidades *(1)* finas. / *(2)* buenas. / *(3)* agradables. / *(4)* maravillosas.

quarrel *vi* pelear **always ~** pelear siempre **often ~** pelear mucho **sometimes ~** pelear a veces **I don't want to quarrel (with you).** No quiero pelear *con usted (Fam: contigo).*

quarrel *n* pleito *m* **big ~** gran pleito **childish ~** pleito de chiquillos **have a (big) ~** tener un (gran) pleito **little ~** pequeña discusión **senseless ~** pleito sin sentido **start a ~** comenzar un pleito **I hate quarrels.** Odio los pleitos.

queen *n* reina *f* **beauty ~** reina hermosa **~ of love** reina del amor **~ of my heart** reina de mi corazón

question *n* pregunta *f* **a few ~s** unas cuantas preguntas **answer** *(1)* **my** / *(2)* **your ~** contestar *(1)* mi / *(2)* su *(Fam: tu)* pregunta **ask** *(1)* **me** / *(2)* **you a ~** *(1)* hacerme / *(2)* hacerte una pregunta **different ~** pregunta diferente **difficult ~** pregunta difícil **foolish ~** pregunta tonta **important ~** pregunta importante **main ~** pregunta principal **many ~s** muchas preguntas **next ~** la siguiente pregunta **only ~** la única pregunta **personal ~** pregunta personal **repeat your ~** repetir tu pregunta **several ~s** varias preguntas **simple ~** pregunta sencilla **strange ~** pregunta extraña **stupid ~** pregunta tonta **understand** *(1)* **my** / *(2)* **your ~** entender *(1)* mi / *(2)* su *(Fam: tu)* pregunta **Can I ask you a (personal) question?** ¿Puedo *hacerle (Fam: hacerte)* una pregunta (personal)? **That's out of the question.** Ni pensarlo.

queue *n* fila *f*, hilera *f*, cola *f*

quick *adj* rápido *m*, -da *f (1)* **I'm** / *(2)* **You're a quick learner.** *(1)* Aprendo

---

Spanish "x" is always like "ks", as in our word "taxi".

/ *(2) Aprende usted (Fam: Aprendes)* rápido. **Be quick about it.** Date prisa con eso. **You have to be quicker than that.** Tienes que ser más rápido *(-da)*.

quick *adv* rápido, pronto **Come quick!** ¡Ven rápido!

quickly *adv* rápidamente **You learn quickly.** Aprendes rápido.

quick-witted *adj* agudo *m*, -da *f*, con chispa *m&f*

quiet *adj* callado *m*, -da *f*, tranquilo *m*, -la *f* **You're a (rather) quiet person.** Eres una persona (bastante) callada. **Why are you so quiet?** ¿Por qué eres tan callado *(da)*? **It's nice and quiet here.** Aquí es agradable y tranquilo. **Quiet!** ¡Silencio! **Be quiet!** ¡Cállate!

quiet *n* tranquilidad *f*, silencio *m* **peace and** ~ paz y tranquilidad

quietly *adv* con tranquilidad, silenciosamente

quilt *n* edredón *m*, cobertor *m* **make ~s** hacer edredones

quirk *n (peculiar trait)* peculiaridad *f*, rareza *f* **I've got a quirk or two, I suppose.** Supongo que tengo mis rarezas.

quirky *adj (peculiar)* peculiar *m&f*

quit *vt* dejar, renunciar **I quit** *(1)* **drinking.** / *(2)* **smoking.** Dejé de *(1)* de tomar. / *(2)* fumar. **I quit my job.** Renuncié a mi trabajo. **That's all for me. I quit.** Se acabó. Renuncio. **Quit doing that, okay?** Deja de hacer eso, ¿sí?

quite *adv* 1. *(rather; very)* muy; 2. *(entirely)* totalmente ~ **a few** bastantes **You're quite beautiful.** Eres muy hermosa. **I'm not quite sure.** No estoy muy seguro *(-ra)*. **Not quite enough.** No es suficiente.

---

*Stress rule # 3: Syllables with accent marks
have the stress there.*

R

rabbi *n* rabino *m*

race *vt* jugar carreras **Come on, I'll race you.** Ven, te juego una carrera.

race *n* 1. *(contest)* carreras *fpl* ; 2. *(human type)* raza *f* **auto** ~ carrera de autos **bicycle** ~ carrera de bicicletas **car** ~ carrera de coches *mpl* **have a** ~ tener una carrera **horse** ~ carrera de caballos *mpl* **human** ~ raza humana ~ **against time** carrera contra el tiempo **run a** ~ echar una carrera **Let's go to a horse race.** Vamos a las carreras de caballos. **As concerns race, I'm color blind.** En cuestiones de raza, soy daltónico *(-ca)*. **I don't care what race a person is.** No me interesa la raza de las personas.

racetrack *n (horse racing)* hipódromo *m*

racing *n* carreras *fpl* **car** ~ carreras de coches **horse** ~ carreras de caballos

racist *adj* racista *m&f* ~ **comment** comentario *m* racista

racist *n* racista *m&f*

racket *n* 1. *(tennis)* raqueta *f*; 2. *(loud commotion)* escándalo *m* **What's all the racket?** ¿Qué es ese escándalo?

radiant *adj* radiante *m&f* ~ **beauty** belleza *f* radiante **You look radiant.** Te ves radiante.

radiate *vt* 1. *(emit)* irradiar; 2. *(manifest glowingly)* irradiar, rebosar **You radiate *(1)* beauty. / *(2)* vitality.** Tú irradias *(1)* belleza / *(2)* vitalidad. **Your *(1)* blue / *(2)* dark eyes radiate *(3)* affection. / *(4)* warmth.** Tus ojos *(1)* azules / *(2)* oscuros irradian *(3)* cariño. / *(4)* calidez.

radiator *n (autom)* radiador *m* **The radiator has a leak.** El radiador tiene una fuga.

radical *adj* radical *m&f*, extremo *m*, -ma *f* ~ **views** punto de vista radical

radio *n* radio *m* **on the** ~ en la radio *f* ~ **station** estación *f* de radio

raft *n* balsa *f* **inflatable** ~ balsa neumática

rafting *n* navegación *f* en balsa **go white water** ~ ir en balsa por los rápidos **white water** ~ navegar en balsa por los rápidos, descenso en ríos

---

Spanish pronunciation rules are on pages 407-408.

railroad *vt* endilgar

railroad *n* ferrocarril *m*

rain *vi* llover **What if it rains?** ¿Y si llueve? **If it rains, ...** Si llueve, … **I hope it doesn't rain.** Espero que no llueva. **The forecast says it's going to rain.** El pronóstico dice que va a llover.

rain *n* lluvia *f* **Let's dance in the rain.** Vamos a bailar bajo la lluvia.

rainbow *n* arcoiris *m* **I want to teach you how to ride rainbows.** Te quiero enseñar a montar en arcoiris. **I'm always chasing rainbows.** Yo siempre voy a la caza del arcoiris.

raincoat *n* gabardina *f* **Bring your raincoat.** Trae tu gabardina.

rainforest *n* selva (tropical)

rainy *adj* lluvioso *m*, -sa *f* ~ **day** día lluvioso

raise *vt* 1. *(lift up)* levantar; 2. *(children: rear)* educar; 3. *(animals: breed)* criar; 4. *(plants: cultivate)* cultivar **I raised two children.** Yo eduqué dos hijos. **I was raised (by my grandparents) in** *(place)*. Me educaron (mis abuelos) en ___. **We raise** *(1)* **cattle.** / *(2)* **chickens.** / *(3)* **hogs.** Criamos *(1)* ganado. / *(2)* pollos. / *(3)* cerdos.

rambunctious *adj* revoltoso *m*, -sa *f* **You sure are rambunctious.** De veras eres revoltoso *(-sa)*.

ramp *n* rampa *f* **boat** ~ rampa para botes

ranch *n* rancho *m* **cattle** ~ rancho ganadero

range *n* campo *m* **archery** ~ campo de tiro al arco **rifle** ~ campo de tiro con rifle **skeet (shooting)** ~ campo de tiro al platillo

rank *n* rango *m* **What's your rank?** ¿Cuál es *su (Fam: tu)* rango? **My rank is** *(rank)* . Mi rango es ___. **What rank were you?** ¿Qué rango *tenía usted (Fam: tenías)*? **I was a** *(rank)*. Yo tenía rango de ___.

rap *n (music)* rap *m*

rapid *adj* rápido *m*, -da *f*

rapids *n, pl* los rápidos *mpl* **go down the** ~ bajar por los rápidos

rappel *vi* descender en rappel ★ **rappeling** *n* rappel *m*

rapport *n* relación *f* de comunicación *f* **You and I have such good rapport.** Tú y yo nos entendemos tan bien.

rapture *n* éxtasis *m*, embeleso *m*

rapturous *adj* extasiado *m*, -da *f*, embelesado *m*, -da *f*

rare *adj* raro *m*, -ra *f* **It's so rare to meet someone like you.** Es tan raro encontrarse a alguien como tú.

rarely *adv* raramente *(1)* **I** / *(2)* **We rarely travel abroad.** Raramente *(1)* viajo / *(2)* viajamos al extranjero.

rascal *n (imp)* pillo *m*, pilla *f*

rat *n* rata *f*

Some Spanish words have accented and unaccented forms to differentiate their meanings (e.g., el = the, él = he).

rate *n* 1. *(currency exchange)* tasa *f*; 2. *(price)* tarifa *f*; 3. *(pace)* paso *m* **pulse** ~ pulsaciones *f, pl* ~ **of exchange** tasa de cambio **room ~s** tarifas de habitaciones **At any rate...** En todo caso...

rather *adv* 1. *(somewhat)* algo; *(quite)* bastante, muy; 2. *(sooner, preferably)* preferentemente, preferir *(verb)* **I'm rather tired.** Estoy muy cansado *(-da).* **It's rather *(1)* difficult. / *(2)* expensive. / *(3)* far. / *(4)* late.** Es bastante *(1)* difícil. / *(2)* caro. / *(3)* lejos. / *(4)* tarde. **What would you rather do?** ¿Qué *prefiere usted (Fam: prefieres)* hacer? **Would you rather *(1)* go / *(2)* leave?** ¿Preferiría usted *(Fam: ¿Preferirías) (1)* ir / *(2)* salir? ***(1)* I'd / *(2)* We'd rather *(3)* go / *(4)* wait.** *(1)* Preferiría / *(2)* Preferiríamos *(3)* ir / *(4)* esperar. **I'd rather spend time with you.** Prefiero pasar el tiempo *con usted (Fam: contigo).* **I'd rather not talk about it.** Prefiero no hablar de eso.

rational *n* racional *m&f*, razonable *m&f* **Let's be rational about this.** Seamos razonables en esto.

rattlesnake *n* serpiente *f* (de) cascabel

raunchy *adj (slang)* fachoso *m*, -sa *f*

ravishing *adj* deslumbrante *m&f* **You look (absolutely) ravishing (in that *[1]* dress / *[2]* outfit).** *Se ve usted (Fam: Te ves)* (absolutamente) deslumbrante (con ese *[1]* vestido / *[2]* atuendo.)

raw *adj (uncooked)* crudo *m*, -da *f*

reach *vt* 1. *(come / go to)* llegar; 2. *(contact)* ponerse en contacto **What time will we reach *(place)*?** ¿A qué hora llegamos a ___? **Is there some way I can reach you?** ¿Hay alguna manera de ponerme en contacto *con usted (Fam: contigo)*? **You can reach me at this number.** *Usted puede (Fam: Tú puedes)* contactarme en este número.

react *vi* reaccionar **How did *(1)* he / *(2)* she react to that?** ¿Cómo reaccionó *(1)* él / *(2)* ella ante eso?

reaction *n* reacción *f*

read *vt* leer *(See also phrases under* **like** *and* **love**.*)* **Have you ever read *(title)*?** ¿Ha leído usted *(Fam: ¿Has leído)* ___? **What kind of books do you like to read?** ¿Qué tipo de libros *le (Fam: te)* gusta leer? **I like to read *(genre)*.** Me gusta leer ___.

reader *n* lector *m*, -tora *f* **I'm an avid reader.** Soy un*(a)* lector *(-tora)* ávido *(-da).*

reading *n* lectura *f*

ready *adj* listo *m*, -ta *f*, preparado *m*, -da *f* **get ~** alistarse, arreglarse **Are you ready (to go)?** ¿Estás listo *(-ta)* (para salir)? **I'm (not) ready (to go).** (No) Estoy listo *(-ta)* (para salir). **We're (not) ready (to go).** (No) Estamos listos *(-tas)* (para salir). **Everything is ready.** Todo está listo. *(1)* **I / *(2)* We**

Spanish "g" is like "h" in front of "e" and "i".
In front of other vowels it's like our "g" in "gun".

have to get ready. *(1)* Yo tengo que prepararme. / *(2)* Nosotros tenemos que prepararnos. **You'd better get ready.** Será mejor que *usted se arregle (Fam: tú te arregles).* **Hurry up and get ready.** *Apúrese y arréglese (Fam: Apúrate y arréglate).* **I'll go get ready.** Voy a arreglarme. **We'll go get ready.** Vamos a arreglarnos. *(1)* **I'll** / *(2)* **We'll be ready in fifteen minutes.** *(1)* Estaré listo *(-ta)...* / *(2)* Estaremos listos... en quince minutos.

real *adj* real *m & f,* verdadero *m,* -ra *f* **in the ~ world** en la realidad **~ life** la vida real **Is it real?** ¿Es de verdad? **It's (not) real.** (No) Es de verdad. **Let's be real.** Seamos realistas. **Our love is the real thing.** Nuestro amor es verdadero.

real *adv* muy, verdaderamente **~ early** muy temprano **~ estate** bienes *mpl* raíces **~ estate agent** agente *m&f* de bienes raíces **~ late** muy tarde *(1)* **I'm** / *(2)* **We're having a real good time.** *(1)* Estoy / *(2)* Estamos pasando un rato muy agradable. *(1)* **I** / *(2)* **We had a real good time.** *(1)* Pasé / *(2)* Pasamos un rato muy agradable.

realist *n* realista *m&f* ★ **realistic** *adj* realista *m&f*

realistically *adv* de manera realista

reality *n* realidad *f* **become ~** hacerse realidad **cold ~** realidad pura **do a ~ check** volver a la realidad **face ~** enfrentar la realidad **in ~** en realidad, realmente

realize *vt* 1. *(become aware)* darse cuenta; *(know)* comprender; 2. *(fulfill, bring to life)* realizarse **be realized** estar realizado *m,* -da *f* **I realize that...** Me doy cuenta de que... **I just realized that...** Me acabo de dar cuenta de que... **I didn't realize that...** No me di cuenta de que... **All my dreams are realized.** Todos mis sueños se han cumplido.

really *adv (truly)* de verdad, de veras; *(very, extremely)* muy, en serio **Really?** ¿De verdad? / ¿En serio? **You are really beautiful.** *Es usted (Fam: Eres)* de veras bonita. **You're really nice.** *Es usted (Fam: Eres)* muy agradable. **I'm really tired.** Estoy muy cansado *(-da).* *(1)* **I** / *(2)* **We really had a good time.** *(1)Pasé...* / *(2)* Pasamos... un rato muy agradable. *(1)* **I** / *(2)* **We really enjoyed it.** De verdad lo *(1)* disfruté / *(2)* disfrutamos. **Do you really want to** *(1)* **go?** / *(2)* **leave?** / *(3)* **stay?** ¿De veras *quiere usted (Fam: quieres) (1)* ir? / *(2)* irse *(Fam: irte)*? / *(3)* quedarse *(Fam: quedarte)*?

rear *n* 1. *(back section)* parte *f* posterior; 2. *(colloq: buttocks)* sentaderas *fpl,* trasero *m* **~ end** *(colloq: buttocks)* trasero **Let's sit in the rear.** Vamos a sentarnos atrás.

reason *n* razón *f,* motivo *m* **another ~** otra razón / otro motivo **any ~** cualquier razón / cualquier motivo **be the ~** ser la razón / ser el motivo **come up with a good ~** alegar un buen motivo **different ~** un motivo diferente **different** *(1,2)* **~s** diferentes *(1)* razones / *(2)* motivos **for** *(1)*

English-Spanish and Spanish-English glossaries of food and drink are on pages 420-427.

this / *(2)* **that ~** por *(1)* este / *(2)* ese motivo. **good ~** bueno motivo, buena razón **know the ~** conocer el motivo / conocer la razón **main** *(1,2)* **~** *(1)* razón / *(2)* motivo principal **only ~** la única razón, el único motivo **personal** *(1,2)* **~s** *(1)* razones / *(2)* motivos personales **real ~** verdadera razón, motivo real **secret ~** motivo secreto **see the ~** ver la razón **simple ~** sencilla razón **think up a good ~** pensar en un buen motivo **true ~** la verdadera razón, el verdadero motivo **valid ~** razón válida **various ~s** diversos motivos **For what reason?** ¿Con qué motivo? **Tell me what the reason is.** *Dígame (Fam: Dime)* cuál es el motivo. **I'll tell you the reason.** *Le (Fam: Te)* voy a decir el motivo. **There are a lot of (good) reasons.** Hay muchas (buenas) razones. **That's no reason.** Eso no es motivo.

reasonable *adj* 1. *(agreeing with reason, sensible)* razonable *m&f*; 2. *(fair, appropriate)* razonable *m&f*, moderado *m*, -da *f*, aceptable *m&f* **~ price** precio razonable **Be reasonable.** Sé razonable. **That's (***[1]*** quite /** *[2]* **very) reasonable.** Eso es (*[1]* bastante / *[2]* muy) razonable.

reasonably *adv (fairly)* razonablemente **~ well** razonablemente bien

rebound *n* rebote *m*, repercusión *f*

recall *vt (remember)* recordar **clearly ~** recordar con claridad **suddenly ~** recordar de repente **vaguely ~** recordar vagamente **I seem to recall that you...** Me parece recordar que *usted (Fam: tú)*...

receipt *n* recibo *m*

receive *vt* recibir **Did you receive** *(1)* **my /** *(2)* **our** *(3)* **e-mail? /** *(4)* **letter? /** *(5)* **message?** ¿*Recibió usted (Fam: ¿Recibiste)* *(1)* mi / *(2)* nuestro *(3)* correo electrónico? / *(4)* carta? / *(5)* mensaje? *(1)* **I /** *(2)* **We (didn't) receive(d) your** *(3)* **e-mail. /** *(4)* **letter. /** *(5)* **message.** *(1)* Yo (no) recibí... / *(2)* Nosotros (no) recibimos... *su (Fam: tu)* *(3)* correo electrónico. / *(4)* carta. / *(5)* mensaje.

recent *adj* reciente *m&f* **in ~** *(1)* **days /** *(2)* **weeks /** *(3)* **months /** *(4)* **years** en *(1)* días / *(2)* semanas / *(3)* meses / *(4)* años recientes **~ trip** viaje reciente

recently *adv* recientemente, hace poco **until ~** hasta hace poco **I just recently** *(1)* **arrived here. /** *(2)* **got married. /** *(3)* **graduated from college.** Acabo de *(1)* llegar aquí. / *(2)* casarme. / *(3)* graduarme en la universidad. **We just recently** *(1)* **arrived here. /** *(2)* **got married.** Acabamos de *(1)* llegar aquí. / *(2)* casarnos.

reception *n* recepción *f* **cold ~** recepción fría **friendly ~** recepción amistosa **warm ~** recepción cálida **wedding ~** recepción de bodas

recharge *vt* recargar **I need to recharge** *(1)* **the battery. /** *(2)* **my cell phone.** Necesito recargar *(1)* la batería. / *(2)* mi celular

recipe *n* 1. *(cooking)* receta *f*; 2. *(plot)* plan *m* **~ for romance** planes de romance **Could you give me the recipe for it?** ¿*Podría usted (Fam: Po-*

A phrasebook makes a great gift!
Use the order form on page 432..

drías) darme la receta de eso? **I'll write down the recipe for you.** Yo *le (Fam: te)* voy a anotar la receta.

reciprocate *vt* corresponder, reciprocar *(1)* **I** / *(2)* **We want to reciprocate your** *(3)* **generosity.** / *(4)* **hospitality.** *(1)* Quiero ... / *(2)* Queremos corresponder a *su (Fam: tu)* *(3)* generosidad. / *(4)* hospitalidad.

recite *vt* recitar ~ **a poem** recitar un poema **Can you recite it for me?** ¿Puedes recitármelo? **I'll recite it for you.** Te lo recito.

reckless *adj* imprudente *m&f* ~ **driver** conductor imprudente **That's a reckless thing to do.** Eso es imprudente. **Don't be reckless.** No seas imprudente. **That would be very reckless.** Eso sería muy imprudente.

recklessly *adv* imprudentemente **Please don't drive recklessly.** Por favor, maneja con prudencia.

recluse *n* recluido *m,* -da *f,* solitario *m,* -ria *f*

recognize *vt* reconocer **Do you recognize me?** ¿Me *reconoce usted (Fam: reconoces)*? **I (almost) didn't recognize** *(1,2)* **you.** (Casi) No *(1)* lo *m* / *(2)* la *f (Fam: te)* reconocí.

recommend *vt* recomendar **What** *(1)* **hotel** / *(2)* **place** / *(3)* **restaurant** / *(4)* **store do you recommend?** ¿Qué *(1)* hotel *(2)* lugar / *(3)* restaurante / *(4)* tienda *recomienda usted (Fam: recomiendas)*? **I recommend...** Yo recomiendo...

recommendation *n* recomendación *f* **Thanks for your recommendation.** Gracias por tu recomendación.

reconsider *vi* reconsiderar, recapacitar **I hope you'll reconsider?** Espero que recapacites. **Please reconsider.** Por favor, recapacita.

record *vt (audio, video)* grabar **I want to record** *(1,2)* **you singing.** Quiero *(1)* grabarlo *m* / *(2)* grabarla *f (Fam: grabarte)* cantando.

record *n* 1. *(written)* registro *m,* antecedente *m;* 2. *(sports)* marca *f;* 3. *(phonograph)* disco *m* **birth** ~ registro de nacimiento **divorce** ~**s** registros de divorcio **educational** ~**s** registros educativos **employment** ~**s** registros de empleo **keep a** ~ llevar un registro **marriage** ~ registro de matrimonio **medical** ~**s** registros médicos **obtain** ~**s** conseguir los registros **police** ~ antecedentes penales ~ **player** tocadiscos **school** ~**s** registros escolares **set a** ~ imponer una marca **We need to get your** *(type)* **records.** *(written)* Necesitamos conseguir tus documentos. **I believe you've set a new world record.** Creo que *usted ha (Fam: tú has)* impuesto una nueva marca mundial. **I want to set the record straight.** Quiero ordenar el registro.

recorder *n* grabadora *f* **tape** ~ grabadora de cintas

recount *n* recuento *m* **I demand a recount.** Exijo un recuento.

recover *vi (regain health)* recuperarse **I hope you recover soon.** Espero que

---

A slash always means "or".

se recupere (Fam: te recuperes) muy pronto.

recreation *n* diversión *f* **time for** ~ tiempo para la diversión **What do you do for recreation?** ¿Qué *hace usted (Fam: haces)* en su *(Fam: tu)* tiempo libre?

recreational *adj* recreativo *m*, -va *f* ~ **activities** actividades recreativas ~ **director** director de actividades recreativas ~ **program** programa recreativo

recuperate *vi* recuperarse

recycle *vt* reciclar

recycling *n* reciclaje *m*

red *adj* rojo *m*, -ja *f* ~ **face** cara roja ~ **hair** pelirrojo *m*, -ja *f* ~ **light** semáforo *m* ~ **tape** papeleo *m* **Is my face getting red?** ¿Me estoy poniendo rojo *(-ja)*? **Your face is getting red.** *Se está usted (Fam: Te estás)* poniendo rojo *(-ja)*. **I really like your red hair.** Me gusta mucho *su (Fam: tu)* pelo rojo. **There's a lot of red tape to go through.** Hay que hacer mucho papeleo.

redhead *n* pelirrojo *m*, -ja *f*

reduce *vi (lose weight)* bajar de peso **I'm trying to reduce.** Estoy tratando de bajar de peso.

reel (in) *vt (fishing)* enrollar

reel *n (fishing)* carrete *m*

re-enlist *vi (mil.)* volver a enrolarse **I re-enlisted for** *(1)* **three** / *(2)* **six years.** Me volví a enrolar por *(1)* tres / *(2)* seis años. **I'm going to re-enlist.** Me voy a volver a enrolar.

re-evaluate *vt* reconsiderar

referee *vt & vi* arbitrar, hacer de árbitro **Could you referee for us?** ¿Nos *podría usted (Fam: podrías)* hacer de árbitro? **I'll referee for you.** Yo les hago de árbitro

referee *n* árbitro *m*

refill *vt* rellenar *(1)* **I** / *(2)* **We need to refill it.** *(1)* Necesito / *(2)* Necesitamos rellenarlo. **Where can** *(1)* **I** / *(2)* **we refill it?** ¿Dónde *(1)* puedo / *(2)* podemos rellenarlo?

reflection *n* reflejo *m*

reflex *n* reflejo *m* **You have good reflexes.** *Tiene usted (Fam: Tú tienes)* buenos reflejos. **Good reflexes (for an old man), huh?** Buenos reflejos (para ser viejo), ¿no?

refrain *vi* abstenerse **Please refrain from kissing my feet.** Por favor, abstente de besarme los pies.

refreshing *adj* refrescante *m&f* **Ah, how refreshing!** ¡Ah, qué refrescante! **That was refreshing.** Eso fue muy refrescante.

refreshments *n, pl (food, drink)* refrigerio *m* **How about some refresh-**

Spanish "v" is pronounced like a soft "b".

ments? ¿Qué tal un refrigerio?

refrigerator *n* refrigerador *m*

refugee *n* refugiado *m*, -da *f* **I'm a refugee from work.** Soy un refugiado (*-da*) del trabajo.

refund *n* reembolso *m* **ask for a** ~ pedir un reembolso **get a** ~ obtener un reembolso **I want a refund.** Quiero un reembolso.

refuse *vt* rehusar, rechazar **I refuse to do it.** Me rehúso a hacerlo. **How could I possibly refuse such an offer?** ¿Cómo podría rechazar tal oferta? *(1)* **I** / *(2)* **We** / *(3)* **He** / *(4)* **She** / *(5)* **They refused.** *(1)* Me rehusé. / *(2)* Nos rehusamos. / *(3)* Él se rehusó. / *(4)* Ella se rehusó. / *(5)* Ellos se rehusaron. **Why did you refuse?** ¿Por qué te rehusaste?

regard *vt (consider)* considerar **As regards...** En lo que se refiere a...

regards *n, pl (greetings)* saludos *m, pl* **Please give** *(1)* **my** / *(2)* **our regards to your** *(3)* **family.** / *(4)* **husband.** / *(5)* **parents.** / *(6)* **wife.** Por favor da *(1)* mis / *(2)* nuestros saludos a tu *(3)* familia. / *(4)* esposo. / *(5)* padres. / *(6)* esposa.

regardless (of) *adv* independientemente (de)

region *n* región *f*

register *vi (sign up)* registrarse ~ **at a hotel** registrarse en un hotel ~ **for school** inscribirse en la escuela

registered *adj (postal)* registrado *m*, -da *f* ~ **letter** carta *f* registrada ~ **mail** correo *m* registrado ~ **package** paquete *m* registrado **I'd like to send this by registered mail.** Quisiera enviar esto por correo registrado.

registry *(place of registration)* registro *m*

regret *vt* lamentar, arrepentirse de **I regret what I** *(1)* **did.** / *(2)* **said.** Me arrepiento de lo que *(1)* hice. / *(2)* dije. *(1)* **I** / *(2)* **We regret that** *(1)* **I** / *(2)* **we can't accept your invitation.** *(1)* Lamento / *(2)* Lamentamos no poder aceptar *su (Fam: tu)* invitación.

regret *n* arrepentimiento *m*, pesar *m* **I hope you don't** *(1,2)* **have any regrets.** Espero que no te *(1)* arrepientas. / *(2)* pese. **I** *(1,2)* **have no regrets.** No me *(1)* arrepiento / *(2)* pesa.

regrettable *adj* lamentable *m&f*

regular *adj* 1. *(recurring regularly)* frecuente *m&f*; 2. *(customary)* acostumbrado *m*, -da *f*, habitual *m&f*; 3. *(steady)* regular *m&f* ~ **customer** cliente *m&f* habitual ~ **schedule** programa *m* habitual ~ **time** acostumbrado ~ **visitor** visitante *m&f* frecuente

regularly *adv* regularmente, con regularidad **Do you come here regularly?** ¿Vienes aquí con frecuencia? **I exercise regularly.** Hago ejercicio con regularidad.

rehearsal *n* ensayo *m*

Time expressions are given on page 413.

rehearse *vt & vi* ensayar

reins *n, pl* riendas *fpl*

reincarnation *n* reencarnación *f* **Do you believe in reincarnation?** *¿Cree usted (Fam: ¿Crees tú) en la reencarnación?*

reject *vt* rechazar

rejected *adj* rechazado *m,* -da *f* **I feel rejected.** Me siento rechazado *(-da).*

rejoice *vi* alegrarse, regocijarse **My heart rejoices every time I see you.** Mi corazón se alegra cada vez que te veo. **This is cause for rejoicing.** Esta es causa de alegría.

rejoin *vt* reunir **I'll rejoin you in a little bit.** Vuelvo contigo en un momento.

related *adj (kindred)* pariente *m&f,* emparentado *m,* -da *f* **Are you related?** *¿Son parientes? / ¿Están emparentados?* **We're not related.** No somos parientes. / No estamos emparentados.

relations *n, pl* relaciones *fpl* **intimate ~s** relaciones íntimas **sexual ~s** relaciones sexuales

relationship *n* relación *f* **bad ~** mala relación **break (off) a ~** romper una relación **business ~** relación comercial **close ~** relación estrecha **crummy ~** pésima relación **develop a ~** cultivar una relación **empty ~** relación hueca **end the ~** terminar la relación **enter a ~** entrar en relación **friendly ~** relación amistosa **get out of the ~** salirse de la relación **good ~** buena relación **harmonious ~** relación armoniosa **jump into a ~** precipitarse a una relación **long-term ~** relación a largo plazo **make our ~ work** hacer que nuestra relación funcione **meaningful ~** relación significativa **normal ~** relación normal **one-sided ~** relación dispareja **physical ~** relación física **previous ~** relación previa **~ based on** *(1)* **honesty /** *(2)* **respect /** *(3)* **trust** relación basada en *(1)* la honestidad / *(2)* el respeto / *(3)* la confianza **ruin a ~** arruinar una relación **short ~** relación breve **stable ~** relación estable **start a ~** comenzar una relación **what kind of ~** qué clase de relación **Are you interested in a relationship?** *¿Le interesa a usted (Fam: ¿Te interesa)* tener una relación? **I'd like to have a** *(1)* **long-term /** *(2)* **solid relationship (with someone).** Me gustaría tener una relación *(1)* a largo plazo / *(2)* sólida (con alguien). **I'm (definitely) ready for a (long-term) relationship.** (Definitivamente) Estoy listo *(-ta)* para una relación (a largo plazo). **My previous relationship was** *(1)* **disappointing. /** *(2)* **terrible.** Mi relación anterior fue *(1)* frustrante. / *(2)* terrible. **It takes two to make a relationship work.** Se necesitan dos para que una relación funcione. **I hope we can deepen our relationship.** Espero que podamos profundizar nuestra relación. **We're going to have a** *(1)* **beautiful /** *(2)* **great /** *(3)* **wonderful relationship together.** Vamos a tener una relación *(1)* hermosa. / *(2)* buenísima. / *(3)* maravillosa. **You and I have a beautiful relation-**

Spanish "qu" is pronounced like "k".

ship, don't we? Tú y yo tenemos una relación bonita, ¿verdad? **I want to keep our relationship platonic.** Quiero que nuestra relación siga siendo platónica. **I don't want (just) a platonic relationship.** No quiero una relación (solamente) platónica.

relative *n* pariente *m&f* **close ~** pariente cercano *(-na)* **distant ~** pariente distante **~ by marriage** pariente político *(-ca)*

relatively *adv* relativamente

relax *vi* 1. *(release tension)* relajarse; 2. *(rest, take it easy)* relajarse **Relax. (You're so tense.)** Relájese *(Fam: Relájate)*. *(Usted está [Fam: Estás]* muy tenso *[-sa].)* **It's so nice to relax like this.** Es tan rico relajarse así. *(1)* **I'm /** *(2)* **We're just going to rest and relax.** Sólo *(1)* ...voy a descansar y a relajarme. / *(2)* ...vamos a descansar y a relajarnos. **Just relax. I'll be right back.** Tranquilo. Ya vuelvo.

relaxation *n* distracción *f* **a little bit of ~** un poco de distracción **rest and ~** descanso y distracción

reliable *adj* confiable *m&f*

relic *n (ancient momento)* reliquia *f*

relief *n* alivio *m* **What a relief!** ¡Qué alivio!

relieved *adj* aliviado *m*, -da *f* **feel ~** sentirse aliviado *(-da)* *(1)* **I'm /** *(2)* **We're so relieved that** *(3)* **you're okay. /** *(4)* **you made it.** *(1,2)* Qué alivio que *(3)* usted esté *(Fam: tú estés)* bien. / *(4)* la hayas hecho.

religion *n* religión *f* **What religion are you?** ¿Cuál es tu religión?

religious *adj* religioso *m*, -sa *f*

religiously *adv* religiosamente **I work out religiously everyday.** Hago ejercicio religiosamente todos los días.

relic *n* reliquia *f* **sacred ~** reliquia sagrada

relish *vt* gustar de; disfrutar *(1)* **I /** *(2)* **We relish the prospect.** *(1)* Me / *(2)* Nos gusta el prospecto. **I relish the time we spend together.** Disfruto el tiempo que pasamos juntos.

reluctant *adj* renuente *m&f* **Why are you so reluctant?** ¿Por qué *está usted (Fam: estás)* tan renuente?

rely *vi* confiar **Can I rely on** *(1)* **you? /** *(2)* **your discretion? /** *(3)* **your word?** ¿Puedo confiar en *(1) usted (Fam: ti)*? / *(2)* en *su (Fam: tu)* discreción? / *(3)* en *su (Fam: tu)* palabra? **You can rely on me a hundred percent.** *Puede usted (Fam: Tú puedes)* confiar en mí al cien por ciento.

remain *vi* continuar, seguir siendo, quedar **~ friends** seguir siendo amigos **Remain calm.** Quédese tranquilo *(-la)*. **There's a lot remaining to do.** Queda mucho por hacer.

remainder *n* resto *m* **You can have the remainder.** Puedes quedarte con el resto.

Words in parentheses (not italicized) are optional.

remaining *adj* restante *m&f*, sobrante *m&f*

remark *n* observación *f*, comentario *m* **catty** ~ comentario venenoso **make a** ~ hacer una observación / hacer un comentario **mean** ~ comentario malintencionado **rude** ~ comentario grosero **sarcastic** ~ comentario sarcástico **witty** ~ comentario ingenioso **That was a** *(1)* **dumb** / *(2)* **thoughtless remark that I made.** Eso que dije fue un comentario *(1)* tonto. / *(2)* desconsiderado.

remarkable *adj* admirable *m&f*, sorprendente *m&f* **You have remarkable skill.** Tienes una habilidad admirable.

remarried *adj* casado *(-da)* en segundas nupcias

remarry *vi* volver a casarse

remember *vt* recordar, acordarse **Do you remember?** ¿*Se acuerda usted (Fam: ¿Te acuerdas)*? **I remember.** Me acuerdo. **I don't remember.** No recuerdo. **I will always remember you.** Siempre *(1)* lo *m* / *(2)* la *f (Fam: te)* recordaré. **I will always remember** *(1)* **this.** / *(2)* **this time together with you.** / *(3)* **your kind hospitality.** Siempre recordaré *(1)* esto. / *(2)* este tiempo junto a *usted (Fam: ti)*. / *(3)* su *(Fam: tu)* amable hospitalidad. **How** *(1)* **nice** / *(2)* **sweet** / *(3)* **thoughtful of you to remember (my birthday).** Qué *(1)* gentil / *(2)* amable / *(3)* considerado *(-da)* que *se acordó usted (Fam: te acordaste)* (de mi cumpleaños).

remembrance *n (memento)* recuerdo *m* **Please keep this as a small remembrance (of our time together).** Por favor, guarda esto como un recuerdo (de nuestro tiempo juntos). **I'll keep this as a remembrance (of our time together).** Conservaré esto como recuerdo (de nuestro tiempo juntos).

remind *vt* recordar **You remind me of** *(person)*. *Usted me recuerda (Fam: Tú me recuerdas)* a ___. **That reminds me.** Eso me recuerda... **Please remind me.** Por favor, *recuérdemelo usted (Fam: recuérdamelo)*. **I'll remind you.** Yo *se (Fam: te)* lo recuerdo. **Thanks for reminding me.** Gracias por recordármelo. **Don't remind me.** No me lo recuerdes.

reminder *n* recordatorio *m* **gentle** ~ recordatorio amable **painful** ~ recordatorio doloroso **small** ~ pequeño recordatorio **Thanks for the reminder.** Gracias por el recordatorio.

reminisce *vi* rememorar

remodel *vt* remodelar **We remodeled our house.** Remodelamos nuestra casa.

remote *adj* 1. *(distant)* remoto *m*, -ta *f* ; *(secluded)* remoto *m*, -ta *f* ; 2. *(estranged)* distante *m & f* ~ **chance** remota oportunidad ~ **place** lugar remoto ~ **possibility** remota posibilidad ~ **village** poblado remoto **You seem so remote (lately).** Pareces tan distante (últimamente).

A single Spanish "r" should be lightly trilled;
double "r" ("rr") should be strongly trilled.

remove *vt* retirar, quitar **Please remove your** *(1)* **arm.** / *(2)* **hand.** Por favor retira tu *(1)* brazo. / *(2)* mano.

rendezvous *vi* reunirse, encontrarse **Where shall we rendezvous?** ¿Dónde nos vamos a encontrar? **Let's (all) rendezvous at** *(place)*. Vamos (todos) a encontrarnos en ___.

rendezvous *n* encuentro *m*, reunión *f* **secret** ~ encuentro secreto

renege *vi* *(fail to keep)* incumplir **Don't renege on your promise.** No incumplas tu promesa.

renew *vt* renovar **I have to renew my** *(1)* **passport.** / *(2)* **visa.** Tengo que renovar mi *(1)* pasaporte. / *(2)* visa.

rent *vt*: rentar **Do you own your apartment or rent it?** ¿Es usted *(Fam: ¿Eres)* dueño *(-ña)* del departamento o lo *renta (Fam: rentas)*? *(1)* **I** / *(2)* **We rent** *(3)* **my** / *(4)* **our apartment (for** *(amount)* **a month).** *(1)* Rento mi / *(2)* Rentamos nuestro departamento (en *(cantidad)* al mes). *(1)* **I'll rent...** / *(2)* **Let's rent...** / *(3)* **We can rent...** *(4)* **bicycles.** / *(5)* **a boat.** / *(6)* **a cabin.** / *(7)* **a canoe.** / *(8)* **a car.** / *(9)* **a motorcycle.** / *(10)* **skates.** / *(11)* **skis.** *(1)* Voy a rentar... / *(2)* Vamos rentando... / *(3)* Podemos rentar... / *(4)* bicicletas. / *(5)* un bote. / *(6)* una cabaña. / *(7)* una canoa. / *(8)* un coche. / *(9)* una moto. / *(10)* patines. / *(11)* esquís. **Where can we rent (a)** *(item)*? ¿Dónde podemos rentar ___? **What would it cost to rent (a)** *(item)*? ¿Cuánto cuesta rentar ___?

rent *n* renta *f* **for** ~ se renta **pay the** ~ pagar la renta **How much is your rent?** ¿De cuánto es tu renta? *(1)* **My** / *(2)* **Our rent is** *(amount)* **a month.** *(1)* Mi / *(2)* Nuestra renta es de ___ al mes.

rental *n* renta *f*, arrendamiento *m* **car** ~ **agency** agencia *f* de renta de autos ~ **agreement** contrato *m* de arrendamiento

repair *vt* reparar **Where can I get it repaired?** ¿Dónde pueden repararlo? **How soon can they repair it?** ¿Qué tan pronto pueden repararlo? **How much will it cost to repair it?** ¿Cuánto costaría repararlo?

repartee *n* 1. *(quick, witty reply)* respuesta *f*, réplica *f*; 2. *(adroitness & cleverness in reply)* réplica aguda

repay *vt* retribuir, corresponder *(1)* **I** / *(2)* **We want to repay you.** *(1)* Quiero / *(2)* Queremos *retribuirle (Fam: retribuirte)*. **How can I ever repay you?** ¿Cómo podría yo retribuirte?

repeat *vt* repetir **Please repeat (that).** Por favor repite (eso). **Could you (please) repeat (that)?** ¿*Podría usted (Fam: Podrías)* repetir (eso) (por favor)?

reply *vi* responder ~ **to an ad** responder a un anuncio

reply *n* respuesta *f* **fast** ~ respuesta rápida **immediate** ~ respuesta inmediata **in** ~ **to your ad** en respuesta a su anuncio **quick** ~ respuesta rápida **re-**

ceive *(1)* **my** / *(2)* **your** ~ recibir *(1)* mi / *(2)* tu respuesta **send a** ~ enviar una respuesta **short** ~ respuesta breve **write a** ~ escribir una respuesta **Please send me a reply as soon as possible.** Por favor, envíame respuesta lo más pronto posible. **Thanks for your reply.** Gracias por tu respuesta.

report *vt* reportar, dar parte **You should report it (to the** *[1]* **manager /** *[2]* **police).** Debes de reportarlo (*[1]* al gerente / *[2]* a la policía). **I'm going to report it (to the** *[1]* **manager /** *[2]* **police).** Voy a reportarlo (*[1]* al gerente / *[2]* a la policía).

report *n* informe, reporte *m*, parte *m* **make a** ~ hacer un informe **police** ~ parte policiaco ~ **card** boleta *f* de calificaciones **weather** ~ reporte del clima

repulsive *adj* repulsivo *m*, -va *f*

reputation *n* reputación *f*, fama *f* **bad** *(1,2)* ~ mala *(1)* reputación / *(2)* fama **good** *(1,2)* ~ buena *(1)* reputación / *(2)* fama **ruin** *(1)* **my** / *(2)* **your** ~ arruinar *(1)* mi / *(2)* su *(Fam: tu)* reputación **spoil** *(1)* **my** / *(2)* **your** ~ echar a perder *(1)* mi / *(2)* su *(Fam: tu)* reputación **I'm putting my reputation on the line.** Me estoy jugando mi reputación. **Please don't let my reputation as a master of the** *(1)* **game /** *(2)* **sport intimidate you.** Por favor, no dejes que te intimide mi fama de campeón *(campeona)* del *(1)* juego. / *(2)* deporte. **Yes,** *(1)* **I've /** *(2)* **we've heard of your reputation for forming harems.** Sí, *(1)* he *(2)* hemos sabido que tienes fama por tus harenes.

request *vt* pedir, solicitar ~ **a change** pedir un cambio ~ **a different flight** solicitar un vuelo diferente ~ **an extension (of stay)** solicitar una prórroga (de estancia) ~ **a song** pedir una canción ~ **a visa extension** solicitar una prórroga de la visa

request *n* solicitud *f*, pedido *m* **grant my** ~ acceder a mi solicitud **make a** ~ hacer una solicitud / hacer un pedido **urgent** ~ solicitud urgente / pedido urgente

require *vt* necesitar, requerir **What do they require?** ¿Qué necesitan?

requirement *n* necesidad *f*

reschedule *vt* reprogramar **The** *(1)* **concert /** *(2)* **event /** *(3)* **excursion /** *(4)* **flight /** *(5)* **game has been rescheduled.** Se ha reprogramado *(1)* el concierto. / *(2)* el evento. / *(3)* la excursión. / *(4)* el vuelo. / *(5)* el juego.

rescue *vt* rescatar **I beg you, rescue me from this life of luxury and mindless extravagance.** Te lo ruego, rescátame de esta vida de lujo y despilfarro .

rescue *n* rescate *m* **It looks like I've come to your rescue just in time. You're terminally bored.** Parece que llegué a tiempo para rescatarte. Estás mortalmente aburrido *(-da)*.

research *n* investigación *f* **do** ~ hacer una investigación **I'm doing research**

Spanish "ll" is pronounced like "y" in "yes".

on the bio-electricity of lips. **I was wondering if you'd care to partici-pate in a study.** Estoy haciendo una investigación sobre la bioelectricidad de los labios. Me preguntaba si te gustaría participar en un estudio.

researcher *n* investigador *m*, -dora *f*

resemblance *n* parecido *m* **You bear a striking resemblance to a** *(1)* **friend /** *(2)* **relative of mine.** *Usted tiene (Fam: Tienes)* un parecido asombroso con un*(a)* *(1)* amigo *(-ga)* / *(2)* pariente mío *(mía)*.

resent *vt* ofenderse **I resent that remark. (Even though it's true.)** Ese comentario me ofende . (Aunque sea verdad.)

reservation *n* reservación *f* **make a** ~ hacer una reservación **Do you have a reservation?** ¿Tiene usted reservación? *(1)* **I /** *(2)* **We have a reservation.** *(1)* Tengo / *(2)* Tenemos una reservación.

reserve *vt* reservar ~ **a compartment** *(trains)* reservar un compartimiento ~ **a (hotel) room** reservar una habitación (en un hotel) ~ **a** *(1)* **seat /** *(2)* **seats** reservar *(1)* un asiento / *(2)* asientos ~ **a table** reservar una mesa **I re-served** *(1)* **seats /** *(2)* **a table.** Reservé *(1)* asientos / *(2)* una mesa.

reserve *vt* reservar *(1)* **I'll /** *(2)* **We'll reserve** *(3)* **a (hotel) room. /** *(4)* **seats.** / *(5)* **a table.** *(1)* Voy a reservar / *(2)* Vamos a reservar *(3)* una habitación (en un hotel). / *(4)* asientos. / *(5)* una mesa.

reserved *adj* reservado *m*, -da *f* ~ **compartment** *(trains)* compartimiento reservado ~ **seat** asiento reservado **This** *(1)* **seat /** *(2)* **table is reserved.** *(1)* Este asiento está reservado. / *(2)* Esta mesa está reservada.

residence *n (home)* residencia *f*

resist *vt* resistir ~ **the temptation** resistir la tentación **I couldn't resist the temptation (of** *[1,2]* **calling you. /** *[3,4]* **making your acquaintance. /** *[5]* **talking with you.)** No pude resistir la tentación (de *[1]* llamarlo *m* / *[2]* llamarla *f (Fam: llamarte).* / *[3]* conocerlo *m* / *[4]* conocerla *f (Fam: conocerte).* / *[5]* platicar *con usted (Fam: contigo).*) **It's impossible to resist you.** Es imposible resistirse a *usted (Fam: ti).* **I (simply) cannot resist** *(1)* **you /** *(2)* **your loveliness.** (Simplemente) No pude resistirme *(1)* a *usted (Fam: ti).* / *(2)* a *su (Fam: tu)* encanto. **You can't resist it. You're going to fall in love with me.** No te puedes resistir. Te vas a enamorar de mí.

resistance *n* resistencia *f* **When you** *(1)* **kiss /** *(2)* **touch me, all my resis-tance drains out of me.** Cuando me *(1)* besas / *(2)* tocas, toda mi resistencia se desvanece.

resolute *adj* resuelto *m*, -ta *f*

resonant *adj* resonante *m&f*

resort *vi* recurrir **Resorting to your old underhanded tricks again, eh?** Conque recurriendo a tus viejas mañas, eh?

Common occupations are listed on pages 415-416.

resort *n* centro *m* turístico **beach** ~ centro turístico costero **health** ~ centro turístico de salud **ski** ~ estación de esquí **vacation** ~ centro turístico vacacional

respect *vt* respetar **I respect** *(1,2)* **you a lot.** *(1)* Lo *m* / *(2)* La *f (Fam: Te)* respeto mucho.

respect *n* respeto *m* **deep** ~ respeto profundo **gain** *(1)* **my** / *(2)* **your** ~ ganar *(1)* mi / *(2)* su *(Fam: tu)* respeto **greatest** ~ el mayor de los respetos **have** ~ tener respeto **infinite** ~ infinito respeto **lose** *(1)* **my** / *(2)* **your** ~ perder *(1)* mi / *(2)* su *(Fam: tu)* respeto **mutual** ~ respeto mutuo **tremendous** ~ respeto tremendo **I have great respect for** *(1)* **you.** / *(2)* **her.** / *(3)* **him.** / *(4)* **them.** Tengo gran respeto por *(1)* ti. / *(2)* ella. / *(3)* él. / *(4)* ellos. **I have new respect for your playing.** Tengo un nuevo respeto por *su (Fam: tu)* juego. **I** *(1)* **need** / *(2)* **want your respect.** *(1)* Necesito / *(2)* Quiero *su (Fam: tu)* respeto. **Love and respect are the foundation of a strong and lasting marriage.** El amor y el respeto son la base de un matrimonio sólido y duradero. **I don't get any respect.** *(jokingly)* Nadie me respeta.

respectable *adj* respetable *m&f* **I know you're a respectable girl, but I forgive you.** Yo sé que eres una chica respetable, pero te perdono.

resplendent *adj* resplandeciente *m&f* **You look resplendent in that** *(1)* **outfit.** / *(2)* **suit.** / *(3)* **dress.** *Usted se ve (Fam: Tú te ves)* resplandeciente con ese *(1)* atuendo. / *(2)* traje. / *(3)* vestido.

respond *vi* responder ~ **instinctively** responder instintivamente

response *n* respuesta *f* **emotional** ~ respuesta emocional **What kind of a response is that?** ¿Qué clase de respuesta es esa?

responsibility *n* responsabilidad *f* **accept** ~ aceptar la responsabilidad **big** ~ gran responsabilidad **heavy** ~ responsabilidad pesada **huge** ~ enorme responsabilidad **my** ~ mi responsabilidad **no** ~ sin responsabilidad **our** ~ nuestra responsabilidad **take (on)** ~ asumir la responsabilidad **their** ~ su responsabilidad **tremendous** ~ tremenda responsabilidad **whose** ~ cuya responsabilidad **your** ~ *su (Fam: tu)* responsabilidad

responsible *adj* responsable *m&f* **feel** ~ sentirse responsable

rest *vi* descansar **Do you want to rest?** ¿Quiere usted *(Fam: ¿Quieres)* descansar? **Let's rest (a little).** Vamos descansando (un rato). **I feel like resting.** Tengo ganas de descansar.

rest *n* 1. *(resting)* descanso *m* ; 2. *(remainder)* el resto *m* **a short** ~ un breve descanso **take a** ~ tomarse un descanso **the** ~ **of** *(1)* **my** / *(2)* **your life** el resto de *(1)* mi / *(2)* su *(Fam: tu)* vida **the** ~ **of the time** el resto del tiempo **I need some rest. (I've been working too hard.)** Necesito un descanso. (He estado trabajando muy duro.) **What do you do the rest of the time?** ¿Qué *hace usted (Fam: haces)* el resto del tiempo? **You can have the rest.**

Spanish "y" is "ee" when alone or at the end of words.

Puede quedarse (Fam: Puedes quedarte) con el resto.

restaurant *n* restaurante *m* **fancy** ~ restaurante elegante **vegetarian** ~ restaurante vegetriano **Do you know a good restaurant around here?** *¿Conoce usted (Fam: ¿Conoces tú)* algún buen restaurante por aquí? **Where's a good restaurant?** ¿Dónde hay un buen restaurante? **I know a good restaurant (on [name] street).** Conozco un buen restaurante (en la calle ___). **Would you like to go the the (name) restaurant?** *¿Le (Fam: ¿Te)* gustaría ir al restaurante ___? **Let's go to the (name) restaurant.** Vamos al restaurante ___. **Let's meet at the (name) restaurant.** Nos vemos en el restaurante ___.

restful *adj* tranquilo *m*, -la *f* **It's very restful here.** Este lugar es muy tranquilo .

restrain *vt* contenerse **Please restrain yourself.** Por favor, contente.

restroom *n* baño *m* **men's** ~ baño de los hombres **women's** ~ baño de las mujeres

result *n* resultado *m* **good** ~s buenos resultados **great** ~s grandes resultados **What was the result?** ¿Cuál fue el resultado? **Let me know the result, okay?** Me avisas el resultado. ¿sí?

resumé *n* curriculum vitae *m*

retire *vi* retirarse, jubilarse **I retired from the** *(1)* **Army.** / *(2)* **Air Force.** / *(3)* **Navy.** / *(4)* **Marine Corps.** Me jubilé *(1)* del ejército. / *(2)* de la fuerza aérea. / *(3)* de la marina. / *(4)* de la infantería de marina. **I retired from the government.** Me jubilé del gobierno. **I retired from my job (at [place]).** Me jubilé de mi trabajo (en ___). *(1)* **I'd** / *(2)* **We'd like to retire here in Mexico.** *(1)* Me gustaría jubilarme... *(2)* Nos gustaría jubilarnos... aquí en México.

retired *adj* jubilado *m*, -da *f* **I'm retired.** Estoy jubilado *(-da)*.

retiree *n* jubilado *m*, -da *f* **military** ~ jubilado *(-da)* del ejército

retirement *n* retiro *m*, jubilación *f* **I'm enjoying my retirement.** Estoy disfrutando de mi jubilación. **We're enjoying our retirement.** Estamos disfrutando de nuestra jubilación.

return *vt* devolver **I'll return it** *(1)* **in a few minutes.** / *(2)* **tomorrow.** Lo devuelvo *(1)* en unos minutos. / *(2)* mañana. **Please return it.** Por favor devuélvelo.

return *vi* regresar **When will you return?** ¿Cuándo *regresa usted (Fam: regresas)*? *(1)* **I'll** / *(2)* **We'll return (home)** *(3)* **tomorrow.** / *(4)* **the day after tomorrow.** / *(5)* **next week.** / *(6)* **on (day).** *(1)* Regreso / *(2)* Regresamos (a casa) *(3)* mañana. / *(4)* pasado mañana. / *(5)* la próxima semana. / *(6)* el ___.

reunion *n* reunión *f* **have a (big)** ~ tener una (gran) reunión

---

Feminine forms of words in phrases
are usually given in parentheses (italicized).

reveal *vt* 1. *(show; uncover)* revelar; 2. *(disclose)* revelar ~ **a secret** revelar un secreto ~ *(1)* **my** / *(2)* **your feelings** revelar *(1)* mis / *(2)* sus *(Fam: tus)* sentimientos

revel *vi* 1. *(enjoy, delight in)* deleitarse; 2. *(feast, carouse)* parrandear **I revel in the happiness I've found with you.** Me deleito en la felicidad que he encontrado contigo. **Let's go out and revel all night.** Salgamos a parrandear toda la noche.

revelry *n* parranda *f*

revenge *n* venganza *f*, revancha *f (1)* **I'm** / *(2)* **We're going to get revenge.** *(games) (1)* Voy / *(2)* Vamos por la revancha. **Revenge is** *(1)* **mine!** / *(2)* **ours!** / *(3)* **sweet!** ¡La venganza es *(1)* mía! / *(2)* nuestra! / *(3)* dulce!

reverent *adj* reverente *m&f* ~ **admiration** admiración reverente

reverently *adv* con reverencia, reverentemente **gaze** ~ mirar con reverencia

reverse *n* 1. *(backward motion)* reversa *f* ; 2. *(back side)* reverso *m* ; 3. *(opposite)* contrario *m*, revés *m* **go in** ~ ir en reversa **on the** ~ al contrario

reversible *adj* reversible *m&f* ~ **coat** abrigo *m* reversible

review *n (critique)* reseña *f*, crítica *f* **book** ~ reseña de un libro **movie** ~ reseña de una película **I read a review of it.** Leí una reseña de eso. **According to the review, ...** Según la reseña, ...

revisit *vt* volver a visitar

revolting *adj* repugnante *m&f*, ofensivo *m*, -va *f*

reward *vt* recompensar, retribuir, premiar **What can I do to reward you?** ¿Qué puedo hacer en retribución? **I know just the way to reward you.** Ya sé cómo voy a *retribuirle (Fam: retribuirte).* **Come here, let me reward you.** Ven aquí, déjame darte un premio.

reward *n* recompensa *f* **collect** *(1)* **my** / *(2)* **your** ~ cobrar *(1)* mi / *(2)* su *(Fam: tu)* recompensa **give a** ~ dar una recompensa **nice** ~ recompensa agradable **small** ~ pequeña recompensa **What would you like for a reward?** ¿Qué *le (Fam: te)* gustaría en recompensa? **Now I want to collect my reward.** Ahora quiero cobrar mi recompensa. **Here's your reward.** Aquí está *su (Fam: tu)* recompensa. **If you do that for me, I'll give you a nice reward.** Si *usted hace (Fam: tú haces)* eso por mí, *le (Fam: te)* daré una bonita recompensa.

rewind *vt* rebobinar

rhyme *vi* rimar **Every other line rhymes on the end.** Cada tercer renglón rima al final.

rhythm *n* ritmo *m*

rib *vt* tomar el pelo *(1)* **He** / *(2)* **She is always ribbing me about** *(subject)*. *(1)* Él / *(2)* Ella siempre me está tomando el pelo con ___ .

rib *n* costilla *f* **broken** ~ costilla rota

Spanish "c" before "e" and "i" is pronounced like "s".

ribbon *n* listón *m* **tie with a** ~ amarrar con un listón **I like the ribbon in your hair.** Me gusta el listón de *su (Fam: tu)* cabello.

rich *adj* rico *m*, -ca *f* **filthy** ~ asquerosamente rico *(-ca)* **get** ~ enriquecerse *(1)* **I'm** / *(2)* **We're not rich by any means.** *(1)* No soy rico *(-ca)* ... / *(2)* No somos ricos... de ninguna manera. **I don't care about being rich.** No me interesa ser rico *(-ca)*.

rid *pp*: **be** ~ **of** deshacerse de **get** ~ **of** librarse de **Are you trying to get rid of me?** ¿Está usted *(Fam: ¿Estás)* tratando de *librarse (Fam: librarte)* de mí? **I thought I got rid of you.** Pensé que ya me había librado de ti. **Help me get rid of this guy.** Ayúdame a librarme de este tipo.

riddance *n*: **Good riddance!** ¡En buena hora!

ride *vt* 1. *(accompany)* pasear; 2. *(buses, trains)* subirse; 3. *(horses)* montar **Do you ride the** *(1)* **bus** / *(2)* **subway** / *(3)* **train to** *(4)* **school** / *(5)* **work everyday?** ¿Diario *se va usted (Fam: Te vas)* *(1)* en camión / *(2)* en metro / *(3)* en tren *(4)* a la escuela / *(5)* al trabajo? **Have you ever ridden a horse?** ¿Ha montado usted *(Fam: ¿Has montado tú)* a caballo alguna vez?

ride *vi* **You can ride with** *(1)* **me.** / *(2)* **us.** Puede usted *(Fam: Tú puedes)* pasear *(1)* conmigo. / *(2)* con nosotros. **Would you like to ride with** *(1)* **me?** / *(2)* **us?** ¿Le *(Fam: ¿Te)* gustaría pasear *(1)* conmigo / *(2)* con nosotros? **Come ride with me.** Ven a pasearte conmigo en carro.

ride *n* 1. *(in a car)* aventón *m* ; 2. *(balloon)* vuelo **get a** ~ conseguir un aventón **give a** ~ dar un aventón **hot air balloon** ~ vuelo en globo aerostático **Would you like a ride?** ¿Quiere *(Fam: Quieres)* un aventón? **May I give you a ride home?** ¿Puedo darte un aventón a casa? **Come on, I'll give you a ride.** *Venga, yo le (Fam: Ven, te)* doy un aventón. **Could you give me a ride (to** *[place]***).** ¿Me *puede (Fam: puedes)* dar un aventón (a ___)? **Thanks for the ride.** Gracias por el aventón.

ridicule *vt* burlarse **It's not polite to ridicule old people (like me).** No es correcto burlarse de las personas ancianas (como yo).

ridiculous *adj* ridículo *m*, -la *f* **That's absolutely ridiculous!** ¡Eso es totalmente ridículo! **I've never heard anything so ridiculous.** Nunca oí nada tan ridículo. **Isn't that ridiculous?** ¿No es eso ridículo? **Don't be ridiculous!** ¡No seas ridículo *(-la)*! **I** *(1)* **feel** / *(2)* **felt (a little) ridiculous.** Me *(1)* siento / *(2)* sentí (un poco) ridículo *(-la)*.

riding *n (horseback riding)* cabalgata *f*, montar a caballo **horseback** ~ montar a caballo ~ **school** escuela de equitación

right *adj* 1. *(correct)* correcto *m*, -ta *f*; 2. *(suitable, fitting)* adecuado *m*, -da *f*; 3. *(opposite of left)* derecho *m*, -cha *f* **do the** ~ **thing** hacer lo correcto ~ **eye** ojo *m* derecho ~ **foot** pie *m* derecho ~ **hand** mano *f* derecha ~ **place** lugar *m* adecuado ~ **side** lado *m* derecho **Right!** ¡Correcto! **Is that right?** 1. *(Is*

Numbers in Spanish are given on pages 411-412.

that correct?) ¿Es eso correcto?; 2. *(Really?, Is that so?)* ¿De verdad? **That's (not) right.** Eso no es correcto. **Is this the right** *(1)* **bus** / *(2)* **train for** *(place)*? ¿Es este el *(1)* camión / *(2)* tren para ___? **You're the right person for me.** Tú eres la persona adecuada para mí. **You and I are so right for each other.** Tú y yo nos adecuamos tan bien..

right *adv* 1. *(direction)* a la derecha; 2. *(immediately)* de inmediato, inmediatamente; 3. *(correctly)* bien, correctamente **go ~** ir a la derecha **~ away** de inmediato **~ now** ahora **turn ~** dar vuelta a la derecha *(1)* **Go** / *(2)* **Turn right.** *(1)* Ve / *(2)* Da vuelta a la derecha. *(1)* **I'll** / *(2)* **We'll be right back.** *(1)* Regreso / *(2)* Regresamos de inmediato.

right *n* 1. *(just claim)* derecho *m* ; 2. *(right side)* derecha *f* **civil ~s** derechos civiles **equal ~s** derechos iguales **have the ~** tener derecho **not have the ~** no tener derecho **on the ~** sobre la derecha **to the ~** a la derecha **Keep to the right.** Mantente a la derecha. **Turn to the right.** Da vuelta a la derecha. **It's on the right.** Está a la derecha. **You have no right to say that.** *Usted no tiene (Fam: Tú no tienes)* derecho a decir eso.

ring *vt* sonar, tocar **Ring the** *(1)* **bell** / *(2)* **doorbell.** *(1)* Suena la campana. / *(2)* Toca el timbre.

ring *vi* sonar **Why are the bells ringing?** ¿Por qué están sonando las campanas? **The alarm clock didn't ring.** No sonó la alarma del reloj. **The phone rang for a long time.** El teléfono sonó por largo rato. **I was in the shower and didn't hear the phone ring.** Estaba en la regadera y no oí sonar el teléfono.

ring *n* anillo m, aro *m* **beautiful ~** anillo hermoso **bellybutton ~** anillo para el ombligo **class ~** anillo de graduación **diamond ~** anillo de diamantes **engagement ~** anillo de compromiso **exchange ~s** intercambio de anillos **friendship ~** anillo de amistad **give a ~** dar un anillo **gold ~** anillo de oro **lip ~** anillo para los labios **navel ~** anillo para el ombligo **ornate ~** anillo de adorno **silver ~** anillo de plata **simple ~** anillo simple **tongue ~** anillo para la lengua **wear a ~** usar un anillo **wedding ~** anillo de bodas **This ring is a symbol of our everlasting love.** Este anillo es símbolo de nuestro amor duradero. **I want to put a ring on your finger.** Quiero poner un anillo en tu dedo. **I saw the ring on your finger and I thought you were married.** Vi que *lleva (Fam: llevas)* un anillo en el dedo y pensé que *usted es (Fam: tú eres)* casado *(-da)*.

ringleader *n* cabecilla *m&f*

riot *n (slang) (someone extremely funny)* comiquísimo *m*, -ma *f* **You're a riot!** ¡Eres comiquísimo *(-ma)*!

ripe *adj* maduro *m*, -ra *f* **Are these ripe enough to eat?** ¿Ya están maduros *(-ras)* para comerse? **Your lips look so ripe for kissing.** Tienes los labios

---

Spanish "h" is always silent.

bien carnosos, como para besarlos.

rip off *(slang)* 1. *(swindle)* estafar: 2. *(steal)* robar

rip-off *n (swindle)* estafa *f*

riser *n*: **I'm an early riser.** Soy madrugador *(-dora)*. **We're early risers.** Somos madrugadores.

risk *vt* arriesgar **I'll risk it.** Lo voy a arriesgar. **I don't want to risk it.** No quiero arriesgarlo.

risk *n* riesgo *m* **It's a (big) risk.** Es un (gran) riesgo. **It's too much of a risk.** Es demasiado riesgo. **I'm willing to take the risk.** Estoy dispuesto *(-ta)* a correr el riesgo. **Don't worry, there's no risk.** No te preocupes, no hay riesgo. **The risk is that...** El riesgo es que…

risky *adj* riesgoso *m*, -sa *f* ~ **climb** subida riesgosa **Isn't that kind of risky?** ¿No es medio riesgoso *(-sa)*? **It's too risky.** Es demasiado riesgoso.

risque *adj* escabroso *m*, -sa *f*

ritual *n* rito *m* **It's (1) my / (2) our daily ritual.** Es *(1)* mi / *(2)* nuestro rito cotidiano.

rival *n* rival *m & f* **Believe me, you have no rivals in my life.** Créeme, en mi vida no tienes rivales.

river *n* río *m* **Let's walk along the river.** Vamos a caminar a la orilla del río. **Let's have a picnic by the river.** Hagamos un día de campo junto al río. **Is it okay to swim in this river?** ¿Se puede nadar en este río? **What's the name of this river?** ¿Cómo se llama este río?

road *n* camino *m*, carretera *f* **main** ~ carretera principal ~ **map** mapa de carreteras **Which road should I take?** ¿Cuál camino hay que tomar? **here does this road go to?** ¿Adónde va este camino? **Is this the road to** *(place)*? ¿Es este el camino a ___? **Could you show me the road on this map?** ¿Podría usted (Fam: ¿Podrías tú) mostrarme la carretera en este mapa? **What's the condition of the road?** ¿En qué condiciones está el camino? **Is the road passable by car?** ¿Se puede pasar el camino en carro? **Stay on this road.** Manténgase en este camino.

roadtrip *n* travesía *f* por tierra

roam *vi* vagar **Let's go roam around town.** Vamos a vagar por la ciudad. **We can roam around the countryside together.** Podemos vagar juntos por el campo.

rob *vt* robar *(1)* **I was... /** *(2)* **We were... robbed.** *(1)* Me / *(2)* Nos robaron.

robber *n* ladrón *m*, -drona *f*

robe *n (bathrobe)* bata *f*

robot *n* robot *m*

robust *adj* robusto *m*, -ta *f*

rock *n* 1. *(stone)* piedra *f*, roca *f*; 2. *(rock music)* rock *m* **head like a** ~ cabeza

---

Questions about the metric system? See page 417.

dura como piedra **muscles like** ~ músculos de piedra **on the ~s** 1. *(in dire difficulty)* arruinado *m*, -da *f*; 2. *(with ice)* en las rocas ~ **climbing** escalar rocas, escalada *f* **Have you ever tried rock climbing?** ¿Ha intentado usted *(Fam: Has intentado)* escalar rocas alguna vez? **I like to climb rocks.** Me gusta escalar rocas.

rocket *n* cohete *m*

rod *n (fishing)* caña *f* (de pescar) **fishing** ~ caña de pescar

rodeo *n* rodeo *m*

role *n* papel *m*, rol *m* **big** ~ gran papel **leading** ~ papel estelar **main** ~ papel principal **new** ~ nuevo papel **play the** ~ **of** hacer el papel de **This is a new role for me.** Este es un nuevo papel para mí. **He plays the role of a policeman.** Él hace el papel de un policía.

roll *vt* rodar, lanzar ~ **dice** lanzar los dados **We roll the dice to see who starts.** Lanzamos los dados para ver quien comienza.

roll *vi* rodar **Let's roll!** ¡Vámonos! **Heads will roll!** ¡Rodarán cabezas! **This ship rolls a lot, doesn't it?** Este barco se balancea mucho, ¿verdad?

roll *n (film)* rollo *m* ~ **of film** rollo de película

rollerblade *vi* patinar *(See also phrases under* **like** *and* **love***.)* **Do you know how to rollerblade?** ¿Sabes patinar? **Where's a good place to rollerblade around here?** ¿Dónde hay por aquí un buen lugar para patines en línea?

rollerblades *n, pl* patines *mpl* en línea **Do you have rollerblades?** ¿Tiene usted *(Fam: ¿Tienes tú)* patines con ruedas en línea? **I (don't) have rollerblades.** Yo (no) tengo patines. **Where can we rent rollerblades?** ¿Dónde podemos rentar unos patines (en línea)?

rollerblader *n* patinador *m*, -dora *f* **I'm a rollerblader.** Soy patinador *(-dora)*.

rollerblading *n* patinaje *m* en línea *(See phrases under* **go, like** *and* **love***.)*

roly-poly *adj* regordete *m*, -ta *f*

romance *n* romance *m* **look for** ~ en busca de romance **start a** ~ iniciar un romance **I'm not ready for romance.** No estoy preparado *m (-da)* para un romance. **The spirit of romance floats in the air.** Se sienten aires de romance.

romantic *adj* romántico *m*, -ca *f* **highly** ~ altamente romántico *(-ca)* **hopelessly** ~ romántico *(-ca)* perdido *(-da)* ~ **atmosphere** ambiente romántico ~ **dinner** cena romántica ~ **evening** noche romántica ~ **gesture** gesto romántico ~ **letter** carta romántica ~ **music** música romántica ~ **song** canción romántica ~ **soul** alma romántica ~ **time together** momento romántico juntos ~ **vacation** vacaciones románticas **How romantic!** ¡Qué

The letter "ñ" sounds like the "ny" in "canyon".

romántico! **This is such a romantic place.** Este es un lugar tan romántico.
You're very romantic. Eres muy romántico *(-ca)*. **I'm (very) romantic
at heart.** Soy (muy) romántico *(-ca)* de corazón. **That was a very romantic gesture.** Ese fue un gesto muy romántico.

romp *vi* retozar **We can romp around all day.** Podemos retozar todo el día.

roof *n* techo *m* **on the** ~ en el techo **Let's go up on the roof and dance
under the stars.** Vamos a subirnos al techo y a bailar bajo las estrellas.

room *n* 1. *(chamber)* sala *f*, salón *m*, cuarto *m*, habitación *f*; 2. *(space)* espacio
m (See also phrases under **come** *and* **go***.)* **book a** ~ reservar una habitación
exercise ~ sala de ejercicios **get a** ~ conseguir un cuarto **hotel** ~ habitación
de hotel **large** ~ habitación grande **nice** ~ habitación agradable **_ocean-
front** ~ habitación *f* con vista al mar **quiet** ~ habitación tranquila
rec(reation) ~ salón de recreo **reserve a** ~ reservar una habitación **~ for
one (person)** habitación para una (persona) **~ for two** habitación para dos
~ service servicio a las habitaciones **~ with a** *(1)* **balcony** / *(2)* **bathroom**
/ *(3)* **shower** habitación con *(1)* balcón / *(2)* baño / *(3)* regadera **What's
your room number?** ¿Cuál es el número de *su (Fam: tu)* cuarto? **My
room number is** *(number)*. El número de mi cuarto es__. **Is there room
for** *(1)* **my suitcase?** / *(2)* **one more person?** ¿Hay espacio para *(1)* mi
maleta? / *(2)* una persona más? **There's room for** *(1)* **three** / *(2)* **four
people.** Hay espacio para *(1)* tres / *(2)* cuatro personas. **There's no more
room.** Ya no hay espacio.

roommate *n* compañero *m*, -ra *f* de cuarto

rope *n* cuerda *f* **climbing** ~ cuerda de escalar **jump** ~ *vt* saltar la cuerda **jump
~** *n* cuerda de saltar

rose *n* rosa *f* **bouqet of** ~s un buqué de rosas **lovely** ~s lindas rosas **Such
beautiful roses! Thank you ever so much.** ¡Qué rosas tan hermosas!
Muchísimas gracias. **If I had the money, I would send you a dozen red
roses everyday.** Si tuviera dinero, diario *le (Fam: te)* enviaría una docena
de rosas. **You're as lovely as a rose.** *Usted es (Fam: Tú eres)* tan linda
como una rosa. **Was there ever a rose as beautiful as you?** ¿Hubo
alguna vez una rosa tan linda como *usted (Fam: tú)*?

rough *adj* 1. *(not smooth)* áspero *m*, -ra *f*; 2. *(choppy, turbulent)* agitado *m*, -
da *f*; 3. *(difficult)* difícil *m&f*; 4. *(harsh, violent)* violento *m*, -ta *f*; 5.
(approximate) aproximado *m*, -da *f* **have a** ~ **time** pasar un momento
difícil **have it** ~ tenerlo difícil **~ customer** un tipo peligroso **~ estimate** un
cálculo aproximado **~ flight** un vuelo turbulento **~ guy** un tipo violento **~
idea** una idea aproximada **~ life** una vida difícil **~ neighborhood** un
vecindario peligroso **~ sea** un mar agitado **~ time** un momento difícil
You've really had a rough time. Pasaste un momento de veras difícil.

That gives you a rough idea. Eso te da una idea aproximada. **Your face is rough.** Tienes la cara áspera. **No rough stuff!** ¡Nada de violencia!.

rough adv (violently) violentamente, bruscamente **You play too rough.** Tú juegas muy brusco. **Don't get rough with me.** No te pongas brusco conmigo.

rough it (slang) (live without conveniences) vivir sin comodidades **I love roughing it.** Me encanta vivir sin comodidades. **I'm not afraid to rough it.** No temo vivir sin comodidades.

roughly adv (approximately) aproximadamente

roulette n ruleta f **play ~** jugar a la ruleta **~ wheel** rueda f de la ruleta

round adj redondo m, -da f **~ robin** (competition) torneo m **~ trip** viaje m redondo **You're soft and round in all the right places.** Eres suave y redonda en todos los lugares adecuados. **How much is a round-trip ticket (to [place])?** ¿Cuánto cuesta un viaje redondo (a ___)?

round adv (around) giro m **go ~** dar un giro **Love is what makes the world go round.** El amor es lo que hace que el mundo gire.

round n (drinks) ronda f **How about another round?** ¿Qué tal otra ronda? **One more round!** ¡Otra ronda! **I'll buy the next round.** La próxima ronda la pago yo.

route n ruta f **bicycle ~** ruta para bicicletas **scenic ~** ruta pintoresca **Do you know the route?** ¿Conoce usted (Fam: Conoces) la ruta? **What's the** (1) **best /** (2) **shortest route?** ¿Cuál es (1) la mejor ruta / (2) la ruta más corta? **Can you show me the route on the map?** ¿Podría usted (Fam: ¿Podrías tú) mostrarme la ruta en el mapa? **I think the best route would be...** Creo que la mejor ruta sería...

routine n rutina f **daily ~** rutina cotidiana **same old ~** la misma rutina de siempre **stale ~** rutina fastidiosa **usual ~** rutina usual

row vt & vi remar **I'll row.** Yo voy a remar. **I'll let you row.** Te dejo remar.

row n fila f **back ~** fila de atrás **front ~** fila de adelante **in a ~** en una fila

rowboat n bote m de remos **rent a ~** rentar un bote de remos

rowdy adj peleonero m, -ra f **Let's not get rowdy.** No nos pongamos peleoneros.

royal adj real m&f, regio m, -gia f

royalty n realeza f, regalía f

rub vt 1. (massage) masajear, sobar; 2. (spread) frotar, refregar **~** (whom) **the wrong way** caerle mal a ___ (1) **I'll rub... /** (2) **Let me rub... your** (3) **back /** (4) **neck /** (5) **shoulders.** (1) Yo le f (Fam: te) doy... / (2) Déjeme darle (Fam: Déjame darte)... un masaje en ... (3) la espalda / (4) el cuello / (5) los hombros. **We can rub each other with soap.** Nos podemos jabonar el uno al otro. **Could you rub (suntan) lotion on my back?** ¿Me puede

---

Spanish "o" is pronounced like "o" in "note".

usted (Fam: (puedes) poner loción (bronceadora) en la espalda? *(1)* **I'll rub... / (2) Let me rub... suntan lotion on your back.** *(1)* Yo *le (Fam: te)* pongo... / (2) *Déjeme ponerle (Fam: Déjame ponerte)* ... loción bronceadora en la espalda. **There's no need to rub it in.** No hace falta que me lo refriegues en la nariz.

rub *vi* acariciar

rub *n* masaje *m* **back** ~ masaje en la espalda **I can give you a great back rub.** Yo *le (Fam: te)* puedo dar un delicioso masaje en la espalda. **How about I give you a back rub?** ¿Qué tal si *le (Fam: te)* doy un masaje en la espalda?

rubber *adj* de hule

rubber *n (slang: condom)* preservativo *m*

rubdown *n* masaje *m*, fricción *f*

rubenesque *adj* rollizo *m*, -za *f* ~ **figure.** figura rolliza

ruby *n* rubí *m*

rucksack *n* mochila *f*

rudder *n* timón *m*

rude *adj* grosero *m*, -ra *f* **I'm sorry I was so rude.** Lamento haber sido tan grosero *(-ra)*.

rug *n* alfombra *f*, tapete *m*

rugby *n* rugby *m*

ruin *vt* arruinar *(1)* **My / (2) Our plans are ruined.** Se arruinaron *(1)* mis / *(2)* nuestros planes . **This ruins (1) my / (2) our plans.** Esto arruina *(1)* mis / *(2)* nuestros planes. **I've ruined the evening. I'm sorry.** Arruiné la velada. Lo siento. **You've ruined everything.** *Usted ha (Fam: Tú has)* arruinado todo.

ruins *n, pl* ruinas *f, pl* **Aztec** ~ ruinas aztecas **Maya(n)** ~ ruinas mayas

rule *n* regla *f* **as a** ~ por regla general ~**s of the game** las reglas del juego **The rules are simple.** Las reglas son sencillas. **Rule number one: I always win.** Regla número uno. Ganar siempre. **I'll teach you the rules.** *Le (Fam: Te)* voy a enseñar las reglas. **Can you teach me the rules?** ¿Me *puede usted (Fam: puedes)* enseñar las reglas? **I believe in playing by the rules.** Yo creo que hay que jugar según las reglas. **That's against the rules.** Eso va contra las reglas. **The rule is that...** La regla es que...

rumor *n* rumor *m* **If you hear a rumor that I love you, it's true.** Si oyes decir que te amo, es verdad. **I heard a rumor (that...).** Se rumora que...

rump *n (colloq.) (buttocks)* cuadriles *m, pl*, nalgas *f, pl*

rumpled *adj* arrugado *m*, -da *f* **My clothes are all rumpled.** Mi ropa está toda arrugada.

run *vi* correr *(See also phrases under* **like** *and* **love***.)* **Let's run along the beach.** Vamos a correr por la playa. **How far do you (usually) run?** ¿Qué

Numbers in parentheses always signal choices.

tan lejos *corre usted (Fam: corres tú)* normalmente? **I (usually) run** *(1)*
two / *(2)* **three** / *(3)* **five** / *(4)* **ten kilometers (everyday).** (Normalmente)
Corro *(1)* dos / *(2)* tres / 83) cinco / *(4)* diez kilómetros (diarios). **Where's
a good place to run around here.** ¿Por aquí dónde hay un buen lugar para
correr?

★ **run away** *idiom* huir **Don't run away (from me) (again).** No huyas
(de mí) (otra vez).

★ **run out** *idiom (be used up)* acabarse, quedarse sin… **We're running
out of gas.** Se nos está acabando el gas. *(1)* **I'm** / *(2)* **We're running out of** *(3)* **money** / *(4)* **time.** *(1)* Me estoy / *(2)* Nos estamos
quedando sin *(3)* dinero / *(4)* tiempo.

run *n:* carrera *f* **go for a** ~ ir a correr **in the long** ~ a la larga **take a** ~ echarse
una carrera **ten-kilometer** ~ una carrera de diez kilómetros **Do you want
to go for a (short) run?** ¿Quieres ir a dar una carrera (corta)? **Let's take
a run.** Vamos a dar una carrera. **It will pay you dividends in the long
run.** Te pagará dividendos a la larga.

runner *n* corredor *m*, -dora *f* **long-distance** ~ corredor de larga distancia
marathon ~ corredor de maratón

running *n* de carrera, corriente

rural *adj* rural *m&f* ~ **area** área rural ~ **life** vida rural

rush *vt* apresurar **I don't think we should rush things.** No creo que de-
bamos apresurar las cosas.

rush *vi* apurarse *(1)* **I** / *(2)* **We have to rush.** *(1)* Tengo que apurarme. / *(2)*
Tenemos que apurarnos.

rush *vi* apresurarse **I'm sorry, I have to rush (off).** Lo siento mucho, tengo que
apurarme. **There's no need to rush.** No hay ninguna prisa.

rush *n* prisa *f* **in a** ~ de prisa **What's the rush?** ¿Cuál es la prisa? **There's
no rush.** No hay prisa. **Don't be in such a rush.** No te apresures tanto.

rusty *adj* olvidado *m*, -da *f* **My Spanish is very rusty.** Se me ha olvidado
mucho el español. **I studied Spanish in** *(1)* **high school** / *(2)* **college, but
it's very rusty now.** Yo estudié español en *(1)* la preparatoria / *(2)* la
universidad, pero ya se me olvidó.

RV *abbrev* = **recreational vehicle** casa *f* rodante, vehículo *m* recreacional
We do a lot of traveling in our RV. Viajamos mucho en nuestra casa
rodante.

Spanish "a" is mostly like "a" in "mama".

S

sack *n* 1. *(bag)* saco *m* ; 2. *(slang: bed)* cama *f* **I'm going to hit the sack.** Me voy a acostar.

sacred *adj* sagrado *m*, -da *f* ~ **duty** deber sagrado

sacrifice *vt* sacrificar ~ **everything** sacrificar todo ~ **nothing** no sacrificar nada

sacrifice *n* sacrificio *m* **big** ~ un gran sacrificio **great** ~ un sacrificio mayúsculo **make a** ~ hacer un sacrificio **tremendous** ~ un sacrificio tremendo **You're worth the sacrifice.** Tú bien vales el sacrificio.

sad *adj* triste *m&f* ~ **news** noticias tristes ~ **story** un cuento triste **You look (so) sad.** Usted se ve *(Fam: Te ves)* (tan) triste. **Why are you (so) sad?** ¿Por qué *está usted (Fam: estás)* (tan) triste? **I feel (so) sad (because we're parting).** Me siento triste (porque nos vamos). **You *(1)* make / *(2)* made me sad.** Usted *(Fam: Tú) (1)* me *pone (Fam: pones)* / *(2)* me *puso (Fam: pusiste)* triste.

sadden *vt* entristecer **That saddens me (very much).** Eso me entristece (muchísimo).

saddle *vt* ensillar **Could you saddle the horse for me?** ¿Podría usted *(Fam: Podrías)* ensillarme el caballo? **I'll saddle the horse.** Voy a ensillar el caballo.

saddle *n* silla *f* de montar

safari *n* safari *m* **go on a** ~ ir de safari

safe *adj* seguro *m*, -ra *f* ~ **and sound** sano y salvo ~ **area** área segura ~ **place** lugar seguro ~ **sex** sexo seguro **Is it safe?** ¿Es seguro? **It's (not) safe.** (No) Es seguro. *(1)* **Put** / *(2)* **Keep this in a safe place.** *(1)* Ponga *(Fam: Pon)* / *(2)* Guarde *(Fam: Guarda)* esto en un lugar seguro.

safely *adv* con seguridad / sin riesgo **Please drive safely.** Por favor, maneja con prudencia.

safety *n* seguridad *f* **rules of** ~ las reglas de seguridad ~ **pin** alfiler de seguridad

---

Articles: m = el, f = la, mpl = los, fpl = las

Wear this for safety. Ponte esto por seguridad. **Remember, safety at all times.** Recuerda, seguridad ante todo.

Sagittarius *(Nov. 22 - Dec. 21)* Sagitario

sail *vt* navegar **Do you know how to sail a sailboat?** *¿Sabe usted (Fam: Sabes)* navegar en bote de vela? **I (don't) know how to sail a sailboat.** (No) Sé navegar en bote de vela.

sail *vi* navegar, zarpar **When does the ship sail?** ¿Cuándo zarpa el barco? **It sails at** *(time)*. Zarpa a __. **Where is** *(1)* **this / (2) that ship sailing to?** ¿Adónde navega *(1)* este / *(2)* ese barco? **Where are you sailing to?** ¿Adónde *navega usted (Fam: navegas)*? **I'm / (2) We're going to sail to** *(place)*. *(1)* Voy / *(2)* Vamos a navegar a __. **Have you ever sailed on a sailboat before?** *¿Ha navegado usted (Fam: has navegado)* antes en bote de vela?

sail *n* vela *f* **windsurfing** ~ vela windsurf

sailboard *n* tabla *f* a vela

sailboat *n* bote *m* de vela **Let's rent a sailboat.** Vamos a rentar un bote de vela.

sailing *n* navegar **Would you like to go sailing?** *¿Le (Fam: Te)* gustaría ir a navegar? **Let's go sailing on the lake.** Vamos a navegar en el lago.

sailor *n* marinero *m*

sake *n*: **Do it for my sake, okay?** Hazlo por mí ¿sí? **I'll do it for your sake.** Lo voy a hacer por *usted (Fam: ti)*. **For Heaven's sake!** ¡Santo Cielo! **For goodness sake!** ¡Por Dios!

salary *n* salario *m* **high** ~ salario elevado **low** ~ salario bajo **How much is your salary?** ¿De cuánto es *su (Fam: tu)* salario? **My salary is** *(amount)* **per** *(1)* **week. / (2) month.** Mi salario es de ___ *(1)* a la semana. / *(2)* al mes.

sale *n* 1. *(selling)* venta *f*; 2. *(at reduced prices)* rebaja *f* **~s receipt** recibo de venta **~s tax** impuesto sobre la venta **Is this for sale?** ¿Se vende? **Are they for sale?** ¿Se venden? **Is it on sale?** ¿Está en rebaja? **Are they on sale?** ¿Están en rebaja? **They're having a (big) sale.** Están en (gran) rebaja.

salon *n* salón *m* **beauty** ~ salón de belleza

Salvadoran *adj* salvadoreño *m*, -ña *f* ★ *n* salvadoreño *m*, -ña *f*

same *adj* mismo *m*, -ma *f* **feel the** ~ sentir lo mismo **look the** ~ verse igual **not the** ~ no es lo mismo **the** ~ **age** la misma edad **the** ~ **day** el mismo día **the** ~ **old story** el mismo cuento de siempre **the** ~ **place** el mismo lugar **the** ~ **thing** la misma cosa **the** ~ **time** el mismo tiempo **the** ~ **way** la misma manera **I feel the same way.** Yo siento lo mismo.

sand *n* arena *f* **build a** ~ **castle** hacer un castillo de arena **I'm a person who loves sun, surf and sand.** Soy amante del sol, las olas y la arena.

Spanish "z" is pronounced like "s" in "safe".

sandals *n, pl* sandalias *fpl* **beach** ~s sandalias de playa

sandwich *n* sándwich *m* **make a** ~ hacer un sándwich **make some ~es** hacer unos sándwiches **Would you like a sandwich?** ¿*Quiere (Fam: Quieres)* un sándwich?

sane *adj* cuerdo m, -da *f* **It's no fun being sane.** Ser cuerdo *(-da)* no es divertido. **No one ever accused me of being sane.** Nunca nadie me acusó de ser cuerdo *(-da)*.

sanity *n* cordura *f* **If I had any sanity, it's gone now.** Si alguna cordura tuve, ya desapareció.

Santa Claus *n* Santa Claus, Santa Clos, San Nicolás

sarcasm *n* sarcasmo *m* **Do I detect a note of sarcasm?** ¿Es un sarcasmo?

sarcastic *adj* sarcástico m, -ca *f* **That was a sarcastic thing to say.** Eso que dijiste fue sarcástico. **Don't be so sarcastic.** No seas tan sarcástico *(-ca)*.

satire *n* sátira *f*

satisfactory *adj* satisfactorio m, -ria *f* ~ **progress** avance satisfactorio **The room is satisfactory.** La habitación es satisfactoria.

satisfied *adj* satisfecho m, -cha *f* ~ **with life** satisfecho *(-cha)* de la vida **Are you satisfied (with it)?** ¿Estás satisfecho *(-cha)* (con eso)? **I'm (not) satisfied (with it).** (No) Estoy satisfecho *(-cha)* (con eso). **We're (not) satisfied (with it).** (No) Estamos satisfechos *(-chas)* (con eso). **I'm sure you'll be satisfied with it.** Seguro que *estará usted (Fam: estarás)* satisfecho *(-cha)* con eso.

satisfy *vt* satisfacer **You can't satisfy everyone.** No puedes satisfacer a todos.

Saturday *n* sábado *m* **last** ~ el sábado pasado **next** ~ el próximo sábado **on** ~ el sábado

sauna *n* sauna *m*

save *vt* 1. *(rescue)* salvar; 2. *(not throw away)* guardar; 3. *(reserve, hold aside)* apartar, reservar; 4. *(conserve)* conservar; 5. *(spare)* ahorrar **Save me from this life of decadent wealth.** Sálvame de esta vida de riqueza decadente. **Save it. You might need it later.** *Guárdelo (Fam: Guárdalo)*, *podría (Fam: podrías)* necesitarlo después. **Save your** *(1)* **energy.** / *(2)* **strength.** *Reserve sus (Fam: Reserva tus) (1)* energías. / *(2)* fuerzas. **It'll save you** *(1)* **money.** / *(2)* **time.** / *(3)* **trouble.** *Le (Fam: Te)* ahorrará *(1)* dinero. / *(2)* tiempo. / *(3)* problemas. **Can you save** *(1)* **a seat for** *(2)* **me?** / *(3)* **us?** / *(4)* **my place in line?** / *(5)* **my seat?** ¿*Puede usted (Fam: Puedes)* *(1) ...(2)* apartarme / *(3)* apartarnos un asiento? / *(4)* apartarme lugar en la fila? / *(5)* apartarme asiento? *(1)* **I'll** / *(2)* **We'll save** *(3)* **a seat for you.** / *(4)* **your seat.** *(1)* Yo *le (Fam: te)* aparto... / *(2)* Nosotros *le (Fam: te)* apartamos... *(3)* un asiento. / *(4)* *su (Fam: tu)* asiento. **I'll save this as a momento of** *(1)* **our time together.** / *(1)* **our trip.** Guardaré esto en recuerdo

---

A tilde ~ in terms stands for the main entry word.

de *(1)* nuestros momentos juntos. / *(2)* nuestro viaje.

savor *vt* saborear **I want to savor the sweetness of your lips.** Quiero saborear la dulzura de tus labios.

saw *n* sierra *f*

say *vt* decir, hablar **What did you say?** ¿Que *dijo usted (Fam: dijiste)*? **I said….** Yo dije… **What did (1) he / (2) she say?** ¿Qué dijo *(1)* él? / *(2)* ella? *(1)* **He / (3) She said…** *(1)* Él / *(3)* Ella dijo… **What did they say?** ¿Qué dijeron? **They said…** Dijeron… **I didn't (1) hear / (2) understand what you said.** Yo no *(1)* oí / *(2)* entendí lo que *usted dijo (Fam: tú dijiste)*. **That's not what I said.** Eso no fue lo que dije. **You said…** Usted dijo *(Fam: Tú dijiste)*… **Please say yes.** Por favor, di que sí. **How do you say *(word)* in Spanish?** ¿Cómo se dice ___ en español? **In English we say *(what)*.** En inglés decimos ___.

scandal *n* escándalo *m* **Careful, you'll cause a scandal.** Cuidado, vas a hacer un escándalo.

scar *n* cicatriz *f*

scare *vt* asustar **Did I scare (1,2) you?** *(1)* ¿Lo *m* / *(2)* ¿La *f (Fam: ¿Te)* asusté? **You scared me.** Me asustó usted *(Fam: Me asustaste)*. **It scared me.** Me asustó.

scared *adj* asustado *m*, -da *f* **Are you scared?** ¿Está usted *(Fam: Estás)* asustado *(-da)*? **I'm (not) scared.** (No) Estoy asustado *(-da)*. **I was (really) scared.** Estaba (de veras) asustado *(-da)*.

scarcely *adv* apenas **I scarcely know you.** Apenas *(1)* lo *m* / *(2)* la *f (Fam: te)* conozco.

scarecrow *n* espantapájaros *m*

scarf *n* bufanda *f*

scary *adj* pavoroso *m*, -sa *f* ~ **experience** experiencia pavorosa **That was really scary.** Eso fue de veras pavoroso.

scatterbrain *n* cabeza *f* de chorlito

scenario *n* escenario *m* **worst-case** ~ el peor de los escenarios

scene *n* 1. *(place of occurrence)* escena *f*, escenario *m* ; 2. *(play, movie)* escena *f*; 3. *(uproar)* escena *f*; 4. *(picture)* escena *f*; 5. *(view)* paisaje *m* ; 6. *(mileu, culture)* ambiente *m* **bar** ~ ambiente de cantina **make a** ~ **in public** hacer una escena en público. **I don't care for the bar scene.** No me gusta andar en las cantinas. **The bar scene is a waste of time.** El ambiente de cantina es una pérdida de tiempo. **Please don't make a scene.** Por favor, no hagas una escena.

scenery *n* paisaje *m* **enjoy the** ~ disfruta del paisaje **The scenery is beautiful, isn't it?** Bonito paisaje ¿verdad? **I love the scenery (1) here. / (2) there.** Me encanta el paisaje de *(1)* aquí. / *(2)* allá. **What is the scenery**

Spanish "ch" is pronounced like ours
(e.g., "cheese," "charge").

like there? ¿Cómo es el paisaje allá?

scenic *adj* pintoresco *m*, -ca *f* ~ **area** un área pintoresca ~ **region** una región pintoresca ~ **route** una ruta panorámica ~ **wonders** maravillas pintorescas

scent *n* perfume *m*, aroma *m* **bewitching** ~ perfume hechizante **exotic** ~ perfume exótico **intoxicating** ~ aroma embriagador **lovely** ~ perfume delicioso ~ **of flowers** perfume floral ~ **of roses** aroma de rosas **soft** ~ aroma suave **sweet** ~ aroma dulce **I love the scent of your perfume.** Me encanta el aroma de *su (Fam: tu)* perfume.

schedule *n* programa *m*, horario *m* **according to the** ~ según el programa **bus** ~ horario del camión **check the** ~ checar el programa **flight** ~ horario de vuelo **on** ~ según el programa **train** ~ horario del tren **I'm going to find out what the schedule is.** Voy a averiguar cuál es el programa. **Let's go check the schedule.** Vamos a verificar el programa. **The schedule says...** El programa dice...

scheme *n (plot)* trama *f* **devious** ~ trama engañosa **What kind of scheme are you cooking up?** ¿Qué clase de trama estás maquinando?

schemer *n* intrigante *m&f*

schmooze *vi (slang: chatter)* chismear, cotorrear

scholarship *n* beca *f* **get a** ~ conseguir una beca **I got a scholarship.** Conseguí una beca .

school *n* escuela *f,* plantel *m* **art** ~ escuela de arte **elementary** ~ escuela elemental, primaria **high** ~ alta escuela **law** ~ escuela de derecho **middle** ~ escuela secundaria **music** ~ escuela de música ~ **of dance** escuela de danza ~ **of drama** escuela de teatro ~ **principal** director de escuela **teach** ~ enseñar en la escuela **technical** ~ escuela técnica **Do you go to school?** ¿Vas a la escuela? **What school do you go to?** ¿A cuál escuela vas? **I go to** *(name of school).* Voy a la___. **Do you like school?** ¿Te gusta la escuela? **When do you start school?** ¿Cuándo comienzas la escuela? **When is your school out?** ¿Cuándo termina tu escuela? *(1)* **I'm /** *(2)* **We're out of school for the summer.** *(1)* Salí / *(2)* Salimos de la escuela en verano.

schoolteacher *n* profesor *m (-sora f)* de escuela

science *n* ciencia *f*

scientific *adj* científico *m*, -ca *f*

scientist *n* científico *m*, -ca *f*

scintillating *adj* fulgurante *m&f* ~ **personality** personalidad fulgurante

scissors *n, pl* tijeras *fpl* **Do you have a pair of scissors?** ¿Tiene usted *(Fam: Tienes)* unas tijeras?

scooter *n* patineta *f* **motor** ~ motoneta *f* **Let's rent a motor scooter.** Vamos a rentar una motoneta. **Where can we rent a motor scooter?** ¿Dónde podemos rentar una motoneta?

Stress rule #1: The last syllable is stressed if the word ends in a consonant (except "n" and "s").

score *vt* anotar ~ **a goal** anotar un gol **How many points did you score?** ¿Cuántos puntos anotaste? *(1)* **I** / *(2)* **We scored** *(number)* **points.** *(1)* Anoté / *(2)* Anotamos ___ puntos.

score *vi* anotar **Yay!** *(1)* **We** / *(2)* **They scored! (Finally.)** ¡Bravo! *(1)* ¡Anotamos! / *(2)* ¡Anotaron! (Finalmente.)

score *n* marcador *m* **close** ~ marcador reñido **high** ~ marcador elevado **keep** ~ **llevar** el marcador **lopsided** ~ marcador a favor **low** ~ marcador bajo **What's the score?** ¿Cuál es el marcador? **The score is** *(score)*. El marcador es ___. **What was the (final) score?** ¿Cuál fue el marcador (final)? **The final score was** *(score)*. El marcador final fue ___. **The score is tied.** El marcador está empatado. **There's no score (yet).** (Aún) No hay marcador. **We** *(1)* **won** / *(2)* **lost by a score of** *(score)*. *(1)* Ganamos / *(2)* Perdimos por un marcador de ___. **They** *(1)* **won** / *(2)* **lost by a score of** *(score)*. *(1)* Ganaron / *(2)* Perdieron por un marcador de ___. **Do you want to keep score?** ¿Quiere usted (*Fam: Quieres*) llevar el marcador? **You keep score.** *Lleve usted (Fam: Tú lleva)* lleva el marcador. **I'll keep score.** Yo llevo el marcador.

scoreboard *n* tablero *m* del marcador

scorekeeper *n* persona *f* encargada del marcador

scoreless *adj* sin marcador **The game is scoreless.** El partido está sin marcador.

Scorpio *(Oct. 23 - Nov. 21)* Escorpión

scorpion *n* escorpión *m*

scoundrel *n* sinvergüenza *m&f* **Why, you scoundrel!** ¡Mira, qué sinvergüenza!

scout *vi (reconnoiter)* explorar **I'll go scout for a** *(1)* **hotel.** / *(2)* **travel agency.** Voy a explorar a ver si encuentro *(1)* un hotel. / *(2)* una agencia de viajes.

scrape up *(idiom) (money: find, amass)* reunir **I hope** *(1)* **I** / *(2)* **we can scrape up enough money.** Espero que *(1)* pueda / *(2)* podamos reunir suficiente dinero. **I don't know if I can scrape up that much.** No sé si pueda reunir tanto.

scratch *vt* raspar, rascar **Don't scratch it.** No lo raspes. **Can you scratch my back?** ¿Me puedes rascar la espalda?

scream *vi* gritar, clamar ~ **for mercy** clamar por misericordia **Stop screaming!** ¡Deja de gritar! **What are you screaming about?** ¿A qué viene esa grita? **It's not necessary to** *(1)* **scream.** / *(2)* **scream at me.** No es necesario *(1)* gritar. / *(2)* que me grites. **Sometimes I feel like I could scream.** A veces quisiera gritar.

scream *n* grito *m* **let out a** ~ dejar salir un grito

screen *n* 1. *(partition)* mampara *f*; 2. *(movies)* pantalla *f* **smoke** ~ cortina de

---

Spanish "i" is mostly "ee", but can also be shorter, like "i" in "sit," when together with other vowels.

humo

screw *n* tornillo *m* **I think** *(1)* **he** / *(2)* **she has got a screw loose.** Creo que a *(1)* él / *(2)* ella le falta un tornillo.

screwdriver *n* desarmador *m*

screw up *(slang: botch)* arruinar **Everything is screwed up.** Todo se arruinó. **My fault, I screwed up.** Culpa mía, yo lo arruiné.

screwball *n (crazy guy)* chiflado *m*, -da *f*

scrounge (up) *colloq* gorrear **I'll see if I can scrounge (up) a newspaper.** Voy a ver si me puedo gorrear un periódico.

scruffy *adj* fachoso *m*, -sa *f*

scrumptious *adj* delicioso *m*, -sa *f*, de rechupete ~ **meal** comida de rechupete **It looks scrumptious.** ¡Se ve de rechupete!

scuba *n* mascarilla *f* de buceo ~ **diving** bucear (con mascarilla) ~ **diving equipment** equipo de buceo (con mascarilla) ~ **diving lessons** lecciones de buceo (con mascarilla) ~ **mask** mascarilla de buzo ~ **suit** traje de buzo **I often go scuba diving.** Voy a bucear con frecuencia.

sculpture *n* escultura *f*

sea *n* mar *m* **on the** ~ en el mar ~ **breeze** brisa del mar ~ **wall** malecón *m* **smell of the** ~ el aroma del mar I **love the sea.** Me encanta el mar. **The sea has a strong attraction for me.** El mar me atrae mucho. **The sea is** *(1)* **beautiful** / *(2)* **calm** / *(3)* **choppy** / *(4)* **rough today.** El mar está *(1)* hermoso / *(2)* tranquilo / *(3)* picado / *(4)* fuerte hoy.

seacoast *n* costa *f* del mar

seafood *n* mariscos *mpl*

seagull *n* gaviota *f*

search *vi* buscar ~ **for love** buscar el amor **I've been searching for the right person.** He estado buscando la persona ideal. **I'm searching for a** *(1)* **better** / *(2)* **new job.** Estoy buscando un *(1)* mejor / *(2)* nuevo trabajo. **What kind of job are you searching for?** ¿Qué tipo de trabajo *busca usted (Fam: buscas)*?

seashell(s) *n* concha(s) *f(pl)* (de mar)

seashore *n* playa *f* **Let's go to the seashore.** Vamos a la playa. **I'd like to spend a few days at the seashore.** Me gustaría pasar unos días en la playa. **Let's rent a cabin by the seashore.** Vamos a rentar una cabaña en la playa.

seasick *adj* mareado *m*, -da *f* **get** ~ marearse **Take this and you won't get seasick.** Tómate esto y no te vas a marear.

seaside *adj* de la costa ★ *n* costa *f*

season *n* 1. *(quarter of the year)* estación *f*; 2. *(period of activity)* temporada *f* **baseball** ~ temporada de béisbol **basketball** ~ temporada de básquetbol

Help us improve our book!
Send us the feedback form on page 431.

football ~ 1. *(soccer)* temporada de fútbol; 2. *(American football)* temporada de fútbol americano **hunting** ~ temporada de caza **rainy** ~ temporada de lluvias **hurricane** ~ temporada de huracanes **What's your favorite season?** ¿Cuál es *su (Fam: tu)* estación favorita? *(1)* **Spring** / *(2)* **Summer** / *(3)* **Fall** / *(4)* **Winter is my favorite season.** *(1)* La primavera / *(2)* El verano / *(3)* El otoño / *(4)* El invierno es mi estación favorita.

seat *n* asiento *m* **back** ~ **(of a car)** asiento de atrás **front** ~ **(of a car)** asiento del frente **good** ~**s** buenos asientos **reserved** ~**s** asientos reservados **reserve** ~**s** reservar asientos ~**s near the front** asientos cerca del frente **You can have my seat.** *(bus, metro or streetcar)* Tome usted *(Fam: Toma)* mi asiento. **Is this seat taken?** ¿Está ocupado este asiento? **This seat is** *(1)* **occupied** / *(2)* **taken.** Este asiento *(1)* está ocupado. / *(2)* apartado. **Could you save** *(1)* **a seat for** *(2)* **me?** / *(3)* **us?** / *(4)* **my seat?** ¿Podría usted *(Fam: Podrías)* *(1)* guardarme / *(2)* guardarnos *(3)* un asiento? / *(4)* mi asiento? *(1)* **I'll** / *(2)* **We'll save** *(3)* **a seat for you.** / *(4)* **your seat.** *(1)* Yo le *(Fam: te)* guardo / *(2)* Nosotros le *(Fam: te)* guardamos *(3)* un asiento. / *(4)* su *(Fam: tu)* asiento. **There are no seats left.** Ya no hay asientos.

seatbelt *n* cinturón *m* de seguridad **Fasten your seatbelt.** *Abroche su (Fam: abrocha tu)* cinturón.

secluded *adj* apartado *m*, -da *f*, solitario *m*, -ria *f* ~ **beach** playa solitaria **find a** ~ **spot** encontrar un lugar solitario ~ **place** lugar solitario ~ **spot** sitio solitario

second *adj* segundo *m*, -da *f* ~ **chance** segunda oportunidad ~ **class** *(trains)* segunda clase ~ **nature** segunda naturaleza ~ **place** *(in competition)* segundo lugar ~ **prize** segundo premio ~ **thought** pensándolo bien ~ **wind** segundo aire **travel** ~ **class** viajar en segunda clase **I'm getting my second wind.** Estoy teniendo mi segundo aire. **On second thought, I think I'll wait.** Pensándolo bien, creo que voy a esperar. **I'm having second thoughts about this.** Estoy pensando mejor este asunto.

second *n* 1. *(1/60 of a minute)* segundo *m* ; 2. *(moment)* segundo *m*, momento *m* **Just a second!** ¡Un momento! **Wait a second!** ¡Espera un momento! **I'll be back in a second.** Regreso en un momento.

second-class *adj* de segunda clase ~ **car** *(trains)* carro de segunda clase ~ **citizen** ciudadano *(-na)* de segunda

secondly *adv* en segundo lugar

secrecy *n* secreto *m* **Why all the secrecy?** ¿Por qué tanto secreto?

secret *adj* secreto *m*, -ta *f* **keep** ~ guardar el secreto **I promise I'll keep it secret.** Prometo guardar el secreto.

secret *n* secreto *m* **deep dark** ~ un secreto muy bien guardado **deep** ~ un gran secreto **keep a** ~ guardar un secreto **my** ~ mi secreto **our** ~ nuestro

---

Spanish "j" is pronounced like "h".

secreto **reveal a ~** revelar un secreto **~s of love** secretos de amor **your ~** *su (Fam: tu)* secreto **I'll tell you a secret.** *Le (Fam: Te)* digo un secreto. **Your secret is safe with me. (Hey, Joe! Listen to this?)** Tu secreto está a salvo conmigo. (¡Oye, Joe, ven a oír esto!)

secretary *n* secretario *m*, -ria *f*

section *n* 1. *(part)* sección *f*; 2. *(of a newspaper, store, agency, etc)* sección *f*; 3. *(of a book)* sección *f* **personals ~** *(of a newspaper)* sección de personales

secure *adj* seguro *m*, -ra *f* **financially ~** con seguridad económica, financieramente seguro **~ area** área segura **~ storage** almacenaje seguro **Will it be secure (there)?** ¿Estará seguro (allí)? **It will be secure (there).** (Allí) Va a ser seguro. **I feel secure with you.** Me siento seguro *(-ra) con usted (Fam: contigo)*.

security *n* 1. *(safety)* seguridad; 2. *(guards)* seguridad; 3. *(material well-being)* seguridad **financial ~** seguridad económica **sense of ~** sentido de seguridad **They have good security.** Tienen buena seguridad. **Call security.** Llama a seguridad.

sedate *adj* tranquilo *m*, -la *f*

sedative *n* sedante *m*

sedentary *adj* sedentario *m*, -ria *f* **~ job** trabajo sedentario

seduce *vt* seducir **In case you haven't noticed, I'm trying to seduce *(1,2)* you.** Por si no *se ha (Fam: te has)* dado cuenta, estoy tratando de *(1) seducirlo m / (2) seducirla f (Fam: seducirte)*. **I give up, you've seduced me.** Me rindo, me has seducido.

seductive *adj* seductor *m*, -tora *f* **look ~** mirada seductora **You're very seductive, you know that?** *Es usted (Fam: Eres)* muy seductor *(-ra)*, ¿sabías?

see *vt* ver **~ each other** vernos **Can you *(1)* see? / *(2)* see it?** ¿*Puede usted (Fam: Puedes) (1)* ver? / *(2)* verlo? **I *(1)* can / *(2)* can't see (it).** *(1)* Sí puedo / *(2)* No puedo ver(lo). **Did you see *(1)* it? / *(2)* that?** *(1)* ¿Lo vió usted (Fam: viste)? / *(2)* ¿Vió usted (Fam: Viste) eso? **I *(1)* saw / *(2)* didn't see it.** *(1)* Sí... / *(2)* No… lo vi. **I *(1)* saw / *(2)* didn't see that.** *(1)* Sí... / *(4)* No… vi eso. **Would you like to see a movie?** ¿ *Le (Fam: Te)* gustaría ver una película? **Have you ever seen *(name of movie)*?** ¿Ya has visto ___ ? **I've seen it.** Ya la vi. **I haven't seen it.** No la he visto. **The moment I saw you, *(1)* I wanted to meet you. / *(2)* my heart did flip-flops.** Al momento que *(i) lo m, (ii) la f (Fam: te)* vi, *(1)* quise conocerte. / *(2)* me dio un vuelco el corazón. **I want (very much) to see *(1,2)* you** (again) (*[3]* soon / *[4]* tonight / *[5]* tomorrow). Tengo (muchos) deseos de volver a *(1)* verlo *m* / *(2)* verla *f (Fam: verte)* (*[3]* pronto / *[4]* esta noche / *[5]* mañana). **I want to see *(1,2)* you *(3)* often / *(4)* everyday. / *(5)* every**

Familiar "tu" forms in parentheses can replace italicized polite forms.

chance I get. Quiero *(1) verlo m / (2) verla f (Fam: verte) (3)* con frecuencia. / *(4)* diario. / *(5)* en toda oportunidad que se presente. **When can I see *(1,2)* you (again)?** ¿Cuándo puedo *(1) verlo m / (2) verla f (Fam: verte)* (otra vez)? **Would it be possible to see you *(1)* this afternoon? / *(2)* this evening? / *(3)* tonight? / *(4)* tomorrow (*[5]* morning / *[6]* afternoon / *[7]* evening)? / *(8)* after work? / *(9)* after you get off work?** ¿Sería posible *(1) verlo m / (2) verla f (Fam: verte) (1)* esta tarde? / *(2)* al anochecer? / *(3)* esta noche? / *(4)* mañana (*[5]* por la mañana / *[6]* por la tarde / *[7]* por la noche)? / *(8)* después del trabajo? / *(9)* después de que salgas de trabajar? **I can't wait *(1,2)* to see you again.** No me aguanto las ganas de volver a *(1) verlo m / (2) verla f (Fam:verte)*. **I don't want to see you anymore.** No quiero volver a verte. **I'll see what I can do.** Veré qué puedo hacer. **I see.** *(understand)* Ya veo. **See *(1, 2)* you *(3)* later. / *(4)* soon. / *(5)* tomorrow.** *(1,2)* Nos vemos *(3)* más tarde. / *(4)* pronto. / *(5)* mañana.

seed *n* semilla *f* **pumpkin ~s** semillas de calabaza **sunflower ~s** semillas de girasol

seek *vt* buscar **~ adventure** buscar una aventura **~ good times** buscar los buenos tiempos **~ love** buscar el amor

seem *vi* parecer, verse **You seem familiar.** Usted me parece *(Fam: Tú me pareces)* conocido *(-da).* **You seem so *(1)* melancholy. / *(2)* nervous. / *(3)* quiet. / *(4)* sad.** Se ve usted *(Fam: Te ves)* tan *(1)* melancólico *(-ca).* / *(2)* nervioso *(-sa).* / *(3)* callado *(-da).* / *(4)* triste. **You don't seem very *(1)* enthusiastic / *(2)* excited / *(3)* happy (about it).** No se ve usted *(te ves)* muy *(1)* entusiasmado *(-da)* / *(2)* emocionado *(-da)* / *(3)* feliz (por eso). **It seems like *(1)* spring / *(2)* summer, doesn't it?** Parece que es *(1)* primavera / *(2)* verano, ¿verdad? **Yeah, it seems like it.** Sí, así parece. **How does it seem to you?** ¿Qué *le (Fam: te)* parece? **It seems that...** Parece que...

seize *vt* agarrar, aprovechar **You have to seize the moment.** Tienes que aprovechar el momento. **I don't know what seized me.** No sé qué me agarró.

seldom *adv* raramente

selective *adj* selectivo *m*, -va *f*

self-centered *adj* egocéntrico *m*, -ca *f*

self-confidence *n* confianza *f* en sí mismo

self-confident *adj* seguro *m*, -ra *f* de sí

self-conscious *adj* cohibido *m*, -da *f*

self-control *n* dominio *m* de sí mismo **I have to watch my self-control around you.** Cuando estoy contigo tengo que controlarme.

self-critical *adj* autocrítico *m*, -ca *f*

Spanish "e" is pronounced like English "e" in "get"

self-defense *n* defensa *f* propia **It was self-defense.** Fue en defensa propia

self-destruction *n* autodestrucción

self-destructive *adj* autodestructivo *m*, -va *f*

self-employed *adj* por cuenta propia, autónomo *m*, -ma *f* **be ~** trabajar por cuenta propia

self-esteem *n* dignidad *f*, autoestima *f* **gain ~** aumentar la autoestima **lose ~** perder autoestima **low ~** poca autoestima **You've done a lot to boost my self-esteem.** *Usted ha hecho (Fam: Tú has hecho)* mucho para aumentar mi autoestima.

self-image *n* imagen *f* de sí mismo *(-ma)* **negative ~** imagen negativa de sí mismo *(-ma)* **positive ~** imagen positiva de sí mismo *(-ma)*

selfish *adj* egoísta *m & f* **~ interests** intereses egoístas **I have a selfish reason.** Tengo un motivo egoísta.

selfless *adj* desinteresado *m*, -da *f* **in a ~ way** de manera desinteresada

selflessly *adv* desinteresadamente

self-love *n* egolatría *f*

self-pity *n* autocompasión *f*, compasión *f* de sí mismo **wallow in ~** regodearse en la autocompasión

self-portrait *n* autorretrato *m*

self-reliant *adj* independiente *m&f*

self-respect *n* dignidad *f*, amor *m* propio **I would lose all my self respect. (But who needs it?)** Perdería toda mi dignidad. (Pero, ¿quién la necesita?)

self-restraint *n* dominio *m* de sí **Where's your self-restraint?** ¿Dónde está tu autodominio? **My self-restraint is restraining itself.** Mi autodominio se está autodominando.

self-righteous *adj* santurrón *m*, -rrona *f* **~ attitude** actitud *f* santurrona

self-sacrifice *n* abnegación *f* **You realize, this is a tremendous self-sacrifice.** Te das cuenta, esta es una abnegación tremenda.

self-satisfied *adj* orondo *m*, -da *f*

self-service *n* auto-servicio *m*

self-study *n* autodidacta *m&f* **I learned it through self-study.** En esto soy autodidacta.

self-sufficient *adj* independiente *m&f*

self-supporting *adj* independiente *m&f*

self-taught *adj* autodidacta *m&f* **~ cook** cocinero *(-ra)* autodidacta **~ lover** amante autodidacta **~ painter** pintor *(-tora)* autodidacta

self-torture *n* autoflagelación *f*

sell *vt* vender **What are *(1)* they / *(2)* you selling?** ¿Qué *(1)* venden / *(2)* vendes? **They're selling ___.** Venden ___. **What is *(1)* he / *(2)* she selling?** ¿Qué vende *(1)* él? / *(2)* ella? **What do they sell there?** ¿Qué venden

---

Stress rule # 2: The next-to-last syllable is stress in words ending in "n", "s" or a vowel.

allí? **Where do they sell ___?** ¿Dónde venden ____? **Will you sell it to me?** ¿Me lo *vende usted (Fam: vendes)?* **I'll sell it to you (for** *[price]***).** *Se (Fam: Te)* lo vendo (por ___).

semi-athletic *adj* medio atleta *m&f* **I'm semi-athletic.** Soy medio atleta.

seminar *n* seminario *m* **I'm going to attend a seminar.** Voy a asistir a un seminario.

send *vt* enviar, mandar *(1)* **I'll** / *(2)* **We'll send you** *(3)* **an e-mail.** / *(4)* **a postcard.** / *(5)* **some photos.** *Le (Fam: Te) (1)* voy / *(2)* vamos a mandar *(3)* un correo electrónico. / *(4)* una postal. / *(5)* unas fotos. **Please send** *(1)* **me** / *(2)* **us** *(3)* **an e-mail.** / *(4)* **a postcard.** / *(5)* **some photos.** Por favor *(1)* mándeme *(Fam: mándame)* / *(2)* mándenos *(Fam: mándanos) (3)* un correo electrónico. / *(4)* una postal. / *(5)* unas fotos.

senior *adj (older)* mayor *m&f*.

senior *n* 1. *(final-year student)* del último grado *m* ; 2. *(pensioner)* pensionado *m*, -da *f* ~ **in college** último grado en la universidad ~ **in high school** último grado en la preparatoria

sensation *n* sensación *f* **dizzy(ing)** ~ sensación de mareo **fantastic** ~ sensación fantástica **giddy** ~ sensación de mareo **incredible** ~ sensación increíble **overwhelming** ~ sensación apabullante **pleasant** ~ sensación placentera **powerful** ~ sensación poderosa **stream of** ~**s** caudal de sensaciones **tingling** ~ sensación de picazón **torrent of** ~**s** torrente de sensaciones **weird** ~ sensación extraña **wonderful** ~ sensación maravillosa

sensational *adj* sensacional *m&f* **What a sensational** *(1)* **performance!** / *(2)* **show!** ¡Qué *(1)* actuación / *(2)* función tan sensacional!

sense *vt* sentir, notar **I could sense that you were right for me.** Pude sentir que eras ideal para mí. **I sensed that you had feelings for me.** Noté que tenías sentimientos por mí. **I sense** *(1)* **a change in you.** / *(2)* **something is wrong.** Siento *(1)* un cambio en ti. / *(2)* que algo está mal.

sense *n* sentido *m* **come to** *(1)* **my** / *(2)* **your** ~**s** *(1, 2)* abrir los ojos **common** ~ sentido común **great** ~ **of humor** un gran sentido del humor **keen** ~ **of humor** un agudo sentido del humor **no** ~ **of humor** sin sentido del humor ~ **of adventure** sentido aventurero ~ **of direction** sentido de orientación ~ **of humor** sentido del humor **I love your sense of humor.** Me encanta *su (Fam:* tu*)* sentido del humor.

senseless *adj* sin sentido **It's senseless to waste so much time.** No tiene sentido perder tanto tiempo.

sensible *adj* sensato *m*, -ta *f* **Let's be sensible (about this).** Seamos sensatos (con esto). **That's a sensible** *(1)* **idea.** / *(2)* **plan. (I'm glad I thought of it.)** Esa es *(1)* una idea sensata. / *(2)* un plan sensato. (Qué bueno que se me ocurrió.)

Spanish "x" is always like "ks", as in our word "taxi".

sensitive *adj* sensible *m&f* ~ **spot** un punto sensible **I'm very sensitive about such things.** Soy muy sensible con esas cosas.

sensitivity *n* sensibilidad *f* **Hey! A little sensitivity, please.** ¡Oye! Un poco de sensibilidad, por favor.

sensual *adj* sensual *m&f* **deliciously** ~ deliciosamente sensual **excitingly** ~ sensualmente excitante **You make me feel so sensual.** Me haces sentir tan sensual. **You look wickedly sensual.** Te ves perversamente sensual.

sensuality *n* sensualidad *f* **Your beauty and sensuality take my breath away.** *Su (Fam: Tu)* belleza y sensualidad me dejan sin aliento. **I've never seen a mouth that expresses sensuality the way yours does.** Nunca había visto una boca que expresara tanta sensualidad .

sensuous *adj* sensual *m&f* **You are such a sensuous *(1)* woman. / *(2)* person.** Eres una *(1)* mujer / *(2)* persona tan sensual. **You are such a sensuous man.** Eres un hombre tan sensual.

sentence *n* 1. *(gram.)* oración *f*; 2. *(prison)* sentencia *f* **Is *(1)* this / *(2)* that sentence correct?** ¿Está correcta *(1)* esta *(2)* esa oración? **Was that sentence correct?** ¿Fue correcta esa oración? **Could you correct a sentence for me?** ¿Podría usted *(Fam: Podrías)* corregirme una oración?

sentiment *n* 1. *(feeling)* sentir *m*, sentimiento *m* ; 2. *(sentimentality)* sentimiento *m* **romantic** ~**s** sentimientos románticos **tender** ~**s** sentimientos tiernos **Those are my sentiments exactly.** Esos son exactamente mis sentimientos.

sentimental *adj* sentimental *m&f* **I'm a sentimental person.** Soy una persona sentimental.

separate *vi (part company)* separarse **We separated (*[1]*...several months... / *[2]* ...over a year... ago).** Nos separamos (hace *[1]* unos meses. / *[2]* más de un año.)

separated *adj* separado *m*, -da *f* *(1)* **My wife... / *(2)* My husband... and I are separated.** *(1)* Mi esposa... / *(2)* Mi esposo... y yo estamos separados. **How long have you been separated?** ¿Cuánto tiempo *lleva usted (Fam: llevas)* separado (-da)? **We've been separated for *(1)* several months. / *(2)* over a year.** Hemos estado separados por *(1)* varios meses. / *(2)* más de un año.

September *n* septiembre **in** ~ en septiembre **last** ~ en septiembre pasado **next** ~ el próximo septiembre **on** ~ **first** el primero de septiembre **since** ~ desde septiembre

serenade *vt* dar una serenata **Serenade us!** ¡Danos una serenata!

serenade *n* serenata *f* **Your voice in my ear is like a serenade of love.** Tu voz es como una serenata de amor para mis oídos.

serene *adj* sereno *m*, -na *f*, tranquilo *m*, -la *f* **What a wonderfully serene**

---

*Stress rule # 3: Syllables with accent marks
have the stress there.*

place. Qué lugar tan maravillosamente sereno.

series *n* serie *m* ~ **of games** serie de juegos

serious *adj* serio *m*, -ria *f* **Are you serious?** ¿En serio? **I'm (not) serious.** (No) Es en serio. **You couldn't be serious.** No puede ser en serio. **You look so serious.** Te ves tan serio *(-ria)*. **I'm getting (very) serious about you.** Estoy siendo (muy) sincero *(-ra)* contigo.

seriously *adv* con seriedad **I take** *(1)* ...**you...** / *(2)* ...**everything you say... seriously.** *(1)* Te tomo en serio. / *(2)* Tomo en serio todo lo que dices. **I mean it seriously.** Lo digo en serio.

servant *n* servidor *m*, -dora *f* **I'm your humble servant.** Yo soy tu humilde servidor *(-dora)*.

serve *vt* servir **Are they serving** *(1)* **breakfast** / *(2)* **lunch** / *(3)* **dinner yet?** ¿Ya están sirviendo *(1)* el desayuno? / *(2)* la comida? / *(3)* la cena? **They're serving** *(1)* **breakfast.** / *(2)* **lunch.** / *(3)* **dinner.** Están sirviendo *(1)* el desayuno. / *(2)* la comida. / *(3)* la cena. **How may I serve you, beautiful Lady?** ¿Cómo puedo servirla, hermosa dama?

serve *vi* prestar servicio **I served in the** *(1)* **Air Force** / *(2)* **Army** / *(3)* **Marine Corps** / *(4)* **Navy (for** *[5]* **two** / *[6]* **three** / *[7]* **four years).** Yo presté servicio en *(1)* la fuerza aérea / *(2)* el ejército / *(3)* la infantería de marina / *(4)* la marina de guerra (durante *[5]* dos / *[6]* tres / *[7]* cuatro años.)

serve *n (tennis)* servicio *m* **It's your serve.** Es *su (Fam: tu)* servicio.

service *n* 1. *(restaurants, hotels, etc)* servicio *m* ; 2. *(assistance)* servicio *m*; 3. *(military)* servicio *m* ; 4. *(religious)* oficio *m* ; 5. *(transp. / comm.)* servicio *m* **bus** ~ servicio de camiones **church** ~ oficio religioso **dating** ~ servicio de concertación de citas románticas **introduction** ~ servicio de presentación **military** ~ servicio militar **rail** ~ servicio de trenes ~ **charge** cargo por servicios ~ **station** estación de servicio **wedding** ~ ceremonia de boda **Were you in the military service?** ¿Estuviste en el servicio militar? **Is there** *(1)* **bus** / *(2)* **rail service there?** ¿Hay *(1)* camión / *(2)* tren a ese lugar?

session *n* sesión *f*

set *adj* 1. *(ready)* listo *m*, -ta *f*; 2. *(alarm clocks)* puesto *m*, -ta *f* **Are you all set (to go)?** ¿Están listos (para irnos)? *(1)* **I'm** / *(2)* **We're all set (to go).** *(1)* Estoy listo *(-ta)* (para ir). / *(2)* Estamos listos *(-tas)* (para ir). **Is the alarm set?** ¿Ya está puesta la alarma?

set *vt* 1. *(put, place)* poner, colocar; 2. *(time: appoint)* fijar; 3. *(establish)* establecer; 4. *(clocks, radios)* poner; 5. *(tables)* poner ~ **a date** fijar una cita **Where shall I set it?** ¿Dónde lo pongo? **Set it** *(1)* **here.** / *(2)* **there.** Ponlo *(1)* aquí. / *(2)* allá. **I think you've set a new world's record.** Creo

Spanish pronunciation rules are on pages 407-408.

que has establecido una nueva marca mundial. **Let's set a limit.** Pongamos
un límite. **Don't forget to set the alarm clock.** No olvides poner la alarma
del reloj. **I'll set the table.** Yo pongo la mesa.

set *vi (sun)* ponerse **Look, the sun is setting.** Mira, el sol se está poniendo.

set *n* 1. *(group of related things)* conjunto *m*, juego *m*; 2. *(TV)* aparato *m* ; 3.
(tennis) partida *f*, set *m* **chess** ~ juego de ajedrez ~ **of jewelry** juego de
alhajas ~ **of tools** juego de herramientas **TV** ~ una tele **Want to play a
couple sets of tennis?** ¿Quieres jugar una partida de tenis?

set off *idiom (detonate)* tronar ~ **firecrackers** tronar petardos ~ **fireworks**
quemar fuegos artificiales **They're going to set off fireworks.** Van a lanzar
fuegos artificiales.

set up *idiom* levantar, armar, montar ~ **a tent** armar una casa de campaña
~ **camp** levantar el campamento **Let's set up** *(1)* **camp...** / *(2)* **our tent...**
(3) **here.** / *(4)* **there.** Vamos a montar *(1)* el campamento… / *(2)* nuestra
casa de campaña… *(3)* aquí. / *(4)* allá.

setting *n (surroundings)* ambiente *m* **What a lovely setting.** Qué ambiente
tan bonito.

settle *vt* resolver, arreglar **Maybe** *(1)* **he** / *(2)* **she** / *(3)* **they can settle it.** Tal
vez *(1)* él pueda… / *(2)* ella pueda… / *(3)* ellos puedan… arreglarlo. **Let
me settle this.** Déjame arreglar esto. *(1)* **Everything** / *(2)* **The matter is
settled.** *(1)* Todo... / *(2)* El asunto... está arreglado.

settle *vi (take up residence)* establecerse **We settled in** *(city)* **in** *(date)*. Nos
establecimos en ___ en ___.

★ **settle down** *idiom* echar raíces **I'm (really) ready to settle down.**
Estoy (realmente) listo *(-ta)* para echar raíces.

settlement *n (small inhabited area)* asentamiento *m*

several *adj* varios *mpl*, -rias *fpl* ~ **days** varios días ~ **girls** varias muchachas
~ **guys** varios tipos ~ **hours** varias horas ~ **months** varios meses ~ **people**
varias personas ~ **times** varias veces ~ **ways** varias maneras ~ **weeks** varias
semanas ~ **years** varios años **sew** *vt* coser ~ **on a button** coser un botón
Could you sew this for me? ¿*Podría usted (Fam: Podrías)* coserme esto?
I'll sew it for you. Yo *se (Fam: te)* lo coso.

sewing *n* costura *f*

sex *n (activity)* sexo *m* **beautiful** ~ bello sexo **casual** ~ sexo promiscuo
fantastic ~ sexo fantástico **great** ~ sexo estupendo **have** ~ tener sexo
incredible ~ sexo increíble **oral** ~ sexo oral ~ **appeal** sex appeal, atractivo
sexual ~ **drive** impulso sexual ~ **fanatic** fanático sexual ~ **fiend** bestia
sexual **wonderful** ~ sexo maravilloso **I've never had sex with a** *(1)* **girl**
/ *(2)* **woman before.** Nunca había tenido sexo con una *(1)* muchacha. / *(2)*
mujer. **I've never had sex with a** *(1)* **boy** / *(2)* **man before.** Nunca había

---

*Some Spanish words have accented and unaccented forms to
differentiate their meanings (e.g., el = the, él = he).*

tenido sexo con un *(1)* muchacho. / *(2)* hombre. **I'm so ignorant about sex. You have to teach me.** Soy muy ignorante en asuntos de sexo. Tienes que enseñarme. **All you think about is sex.** Sólo en sexo piensas. **Sex is important, but it's not everything.** El sexo es importante, pero no lo es todo. **I'm not interested in just sex.** No me interesa sólo el sexo. **I don't want to have sex (with you).** No quiero tener sexo (contigo). **Sex with you is** *(1)* **incredible.** / *(2)* **wonderful.** El sexo contigo es *(1)* increíble. *(2)* maravilloso. **You have a lot of sex appeal.** Tienes mucho sex appeal.

sexual *adj* sexual *m&f* ~ **appetite** apetito sexual ~ **preference** preferencia sexual

sexuality *n* sexualidad *f*

sexy *adj* sexy *m&f,* sensual *m&f* **look** ~ mirada sexy ~ **figure** figura sexy ~ **legs** piernas sexy ~ **mouth** boca sensual **talk in a** ~ **way** hablar de un modo sexy **I've never met anyone as sexy and desirable as you.** Nunca había conocido a nadie tan sensual y deseable como tú.

shack *n* cabaña *f,* jacal *m*

shade *n* sombra *f* **Let's sit in the shade.** Vamos a sentarnos a la sombra.

shadow *n* sombra *f* **eye** ~ sombra para los ojos **There's too much shadow.** *(photog.)* Hay demasiada sombra.

shady *adj* sombreado *m,* -da *f* **Let's find a shady place.** Busquemos un lugar sombreado.

shaggy *adj* peludo *m,* -da *f*

shake *vt* 1. *(agitate)* agitar; 2. *(unnerve)* sacudir; *(stir feelings)* sacudir **Shake** *(1)* **it.** / *(2)* **them.** *(1)* Agítalo. / *(2)* Agítalos. **Your kiss really shook me.** Tu beso verdaderamente me sacudió.

shake up *idiom (unnerve; stir feelings)* conmocionar

shallow *adj* 1. *(water)* poco profundo *m,* -da *f*; 2. *(superficial)* superficial *m&f* ~ **mind** mente frívola **The lake is shallow.** El lago es poco profundo.

shame *n* vergüenza *f,* pena *f* **It's a shame that you can't go.** Es una pena que no puedas ir. **You put me to shame.** *(games)* Me pones en vergüenza. **Have you no shame?** ¿No tienes vergüenza? **Shame on you!** ¡Qué vergüenza! **What a shame!** ¡Qué vergüenza!

shameful *adj* vergonzoso *m,* -sa *f*

shameless *adj* insolente *m&f* **It was shameless of me.** Fue insolente de mi parte. **You are utterly shameless.** Eres perfectamente insolente.

shape *n* forma *f,* figura *f* **fantastic** ~ forma fantástica **good** ~ buena forma **great** ~ figura estupenda **hourglass** ~ figura de reloj de arena **lovely** ~ linda forma **nice** ~ forma bonita **slender** ~ figura esbelta **wonderful** ~ forma maravillosa **You have a beautiful shape.** *Tiene usted (Fam: Tienes)* una bella figura. **I try to keep in shape.** Trato de mantenerme en forma.

Spanish "g" is like "h" in front of "e" and "i".
In front of other vowels it's like our "g" in "gun".

You look like you're in good shape. Parece que *está usted (Fam: estás)* en buena forma. **I'm a little bit out of shape.** Estoy un poco fuera de forma.

shapely *adj* bien formado *m*, -da *f*

share *vt* compartir **Thank you for sharing** *(1)* **this** / *(2)* **that with** *(3)* **me.** / *(4)* **us.** Gracias por compartir *(1)* esto / *(2)* eso *(3)* conmigo. / *(4)* con nosotros. **It** *(1)* **is** / *(2)* **was very nice of you to share** *(3)* **this** / *(4)* **that with** *(5)* **me.** / *(6)* **us.** *(1)* Es / *(2)* Fue muy gentil de *su (Fam: tu)* parte compartir *(3)* esto / *(4)* eso / *(5)* conmigo. / *(6)* con nosotros. *(1)* **I'd** / *(2)* **We'd like to share this with you.** *(1)* Me / *(2)* Nos gustaría compartir esto *con usted (Fam: contigo)*. **May** *(1)* **I** / *(2)* **we share your table?** *(1)* ¿Puedo / *(2)* ¿Podemos compartir su mesa? **The time we share together is (so) precious to me.** El tiempo que pasamos juntos es (tan) precioso para mí. **I love the time we share together.** Me encanta el tiempo que pasamos juntos. **I want to share** *(1)* **...my whole vacation...** / *(2)* **...everything... with you.** Quiero compartir *(1)* ...todas mis vacaciones... / *(2)* ...todo... *con usted (Fam: contigo)*.

share *n* parte *f* **lion's ~** la mejor parte **There's a share for everybody.** Hay para todos. **I've had my share of** *(1)* **heartache.** / *(2)* **troubles.** Ya tuve mi parte de *(1)* penas de amor. / *(2)* tribulaciones.

shark *n* tiburón *m*

sharp *adj* 1. *(cutting)* filoso *m*, -sa *f*; 2. *(keen)* agudo *m*, -da *f*; 3. *(clever)* listo *m*, -ta *f*; 4. *(nicely dressed)* elegante *m&f* **~ tongue** lengua filosa **Careful, it's sharp.** Cuidado, está filoso. **You have sharp eyes.** *Tiene usted (Fam: Tienes)* buena vista. **You have a very sharp mind.** *Tiene usted (Fam: Tienes)* una mente muy ágil. **Hey, this kid is sharp!** ¡Uy, este muchacho *(-cha)* es bien listo! **You look sharp (in that** *[1]* **dress** / *[2]* **suit).** *Se ve usted (Fam: Te ves)* elegante (con ese *[1]* vestido / *[2]* traje).

shatter *vt* destrozar **You have shattered all my** *(1)* **dreams.** / *(2)* **illusions.** Has destrozado *(1)* todos mis sueños. / *(2)* todas mis ilusiones.

shave *vi* rasurarse **You need to shave.** Necesitas rasurarte. **I forgot to shave, I'm sorry.** Se me olvidó rasurarme, lo siento.

she-devil *n* diabla *f*

sheep *n* oveja *f* **I'm the black sheep of the family.** Soy la oveja negra de la familia.

sheer *adj* 1. *(see-through)* transparente *m&f*; 2. *(utter, absolute)* puro *m*, -ra *f* **~ gown** vestido transparente **~ pleasure** delicia pura *(1)* **Holding you in my arms ...** / *(2)* **Kissing you... is sheer heaven.** *(1)* Tenerte en mis brazos … / *(2)* Besarte ...es una pura delicia.

sheet *n* 1. *(for a bed)* sábana *f*; 2. *(paper, metal)* hoja *f* **~ of paper** hoja de

---

English-Spanish and Spanish-English glossaries of food and drink are on pages 420-427.

papel

shelter *n* refugio *m* **We need to find shelter.** Necesitamos hallar refugio. **Let's build a shelter.** Vamos a construir un refugio. **Let's take shelter over there.** Vamos a refugiarnos allá.

shift *n (work)* turno *m* **I work the** *(1)* **day /** *(2)* **evening /** *(3)* **night shift.** Yo trabajo en el turno *(1)* diurno. / *(2)* vespertino. / *(3)* nocturno.

shiftless *adj* inútil *m&f*, holgazán *m*, -zana *f* ~ **skunk** pinche *m* holgazán

shine *vi* brillar **I love to see your eyes shine (like this).** Me gusta ver que *le (Fam: te)* brillen (así) los ojos .

ship *vt (send)* enviar **I want to ship this back to** *(1)* **Britain. /** *(2)* **Canada. /** *(3)* **the States.** Quiero enviar esto a *(1)* Inglaterra. / *(2)* Canadá. / *(3)* los Estados Unidos.

ship *n* barco *m* **cruise ~** crucero *m* **When does the ship sail?** ¿Cuándo parte el barco? **The ship sails** *(1)* **at** *(time)* **/** *(2)* **on** *(day / date)*. El barco parte *(1)* a las ___ / *(2)* el ___. **What places does the ship sail to?** ¿A qué lugares navega el barco? **The ship sails to** *(place)* **(and** *[place]*). El barco navega a ___ (y ___).

shipping *adj* envío **How much are the shipping charges?** ¿Cuánto cuesta el envío?

shirt *n* camisa *f*

shiver *vi* temblar **You're shivering. You must be cold.** Está usted (Fam: Estás) temblando. *Debe (Fam: Debes)* tener frío.

shock *vt* conmocionar, horrorizarse, escandalizarse **I hope what I'm going to tell you doesn't shock** *(1,2)* **you.** Espero que no sea una conmoción lo que *le (Fam: te)* voy a decir. **Does that shock you?** ¿Le *(Fam: ¿Te)* escandaliza eso? **That doesn't shock me.** Eso no me escandaliza. **Did I shock you?** *(1)* ¿Lo *m* / *(2)* ¿La *f (Fam: ¿Te)* escandalicé? **You (didn't shock) shocked me.** *(1)* Usted *(Fam: Tú)* (no) me *escandalizó (Fam: escandalizaste)*. **Nothing shocks me.** Nada me escandaliza.

shock *n* conmoción, impresión **It was really a shock.** Fue una verdadera conmoción. **What a shock!** ¡Qué impresión!

shocked *adj* conmocionado *m*, -da *f* impactado *m*, -da *f* **Are you shocked?** ¿Está usted *(Fam: Estás)* impactado *(-da)*? **I'm (not) shocked.** (No) Estoy impactado *(-da)*. **I'm not easily shocked.** No me impacto fácilmente.

shocking *adj* espantoso *m*, -sa *f*, horrible *m&f* ~ **development** acontecimiento espantoso ~ **experience** experiencia espantosa ~ **news** noticias espantosas **Nothing is too shocking for me.** Nada es demasiado espantoso para mí. **Such shocking behavior!** ¡Qué horrible comportamiento!

shoe *n* zapato *m* **pair of ~s** un par de zapatos **Take your shoes off.** Quítate los zapatos.

> *A phrasebook makes a great gift!*
> *Use the order form on page 432.*

shoot *vt* 1. *(weapon: discharge)* disparar; 2. *(fire and hit)* disparar; 3. *(fire and kill)* disparar ~ **off fireworks** disparar los fuegos artificiales ~ **the breeze** cotorrear

shoot *vi (fire a weapon)* disparar **Would you like to go shoot at a shooting gallery?** ¿Le *(Fam: Te)* gustaría practicar tiro al blanco en una galería de tiro?

shooting *n* tiro *m* **skeet** ~ tiro al platillo

shop *vi* comprar **Do you want to go shopping?** ¿Quiere usted *(Fam:* ¿Quieres)* ir de compras? **Let's go shopping.** Vámonos de compras. **What do you want to shop for?** ¿Qué *quiere usted (Fam: quieres)* comprar? *(1)* **I** / *(2)* **We want to shop for** *(item)*. *(1)* Quiero / *(2)* Queremos comprar ___. **Where's a good place to shop for** *(item)*? ¿Dónde hay un buen lugar para comprar ___?

shop *n* 1. *(small store)* tienda *f*; 2. *(repairs)* taller *m* **antique** ~ tienda de antigüedades **barber** ~ peluquería *f* **beauty** ~ salón *m* de belleza **book** ~ librería *f* **candy** ~ dulcería *f* **coffee** ~ cafetería *f* **electronics** ~ tienda de productos electrónicos **flower** ~ florería *f* **gift** ~ tienda de regalos **jewelry** ~ joyería *f* **pastry** ~ confitería **repair** ~ taller de reparaciones **souvenir** ~ tienda de recuerdos **tea** ~ salón *m* de té **thrift** ~ tienda de descuento

shopping *adj* de compras ~ **bag** bolsa *f* de compras ~ **center** centro *m* comercial ~ **list** lista *f* de compras ~ **mall** centro *m* comercial

shopping *n* compras *fpl* **Where's the best place to go shopping?** ¿Cuál es el mejor lugar para ir de compras? **Would you like to go shopping (with [1] me / [2] us)?** ¿Le *(Fam:* ¿Te)* gustaría ir de compras ([1] conmigo / [2] con nosotros)? **Let's go shopping (together) (for [1] some clothes for you. / [2] something [3] nice / [4] pretty for you.).** Vamos (juntos) a comprarte ([1] ropa. / [2] algo [3] agradable / [4] bonito.)

shore *n* orilla *f* **the other** ~ la otra orilla

short *adj* 1. *(time or length)* breve *m&f,* corto *m,* -ta *f* ; 2. *(height)* bajo *m,* -ja *f* ~ **distance** distancia corta ~ **memory** mala memoria ~ **stay** estancia corta ~ **story** historia breve ~ **time** tiempo corto ~ **trip** viaje corto ~ **vacation** vacaciones cortas ~ **visit** visita breve ~ **walk** caminata corta **What's the shortest way (to** *[place]*)? ¿Cuál es el camino más corto (hacia ___). *(1)* **I'm /** *(2)* **We're taking a short vacation.** *(1)* Voy / *(2)* Vamos a tomar unas vacaciones cortas. *(1)* **I'm /** *(2)* **We're going on a short trip (to** *[place]*). *(1)* Voy / *(2)* Vamos a hacer un viaje corto (a ___). *(1)* **I'm /** *(2)* **We're only here for a short time.** *(1)* Estoy / *(2)* Estamos aquí por poco tiempo. **Life is short.** La vida es breve. *(1)* **I /** *(2)* **We have to cut** *(3)* **my / *(4)* our trip short.** *(1)* Tengo que acortar mi viaje. / *(2)* Tenemos que acortar nuestro viaje. **You're a short little thing.** Eres una cosita chiquita.

A slash always means "or".

To make a long story short... Para no alargar la historia … **My name is William, but people call me Bill for short.** Mi nombre es Guillermo, pero me dicen Guille. **Time is getting short.** El tiempo se está acortando. *(1)* **I'm /** *(2)* **We're a little short of** *(3)* **funds. /** *(4)* **money.** *(1)* Estoy un poco corto de / *(2)* Estamos un poco cortos de *(3)* fondos. / *(4)* dinero.

shortcoming *n* defecto *m* **No matter what your flaws and shortcomings are, I love you.** No importa cuáles sean tus fallas y defectos, yo te amo. **I hope you can block out my shortcomings.** Espero que puedas obviar mis defectos.

shortcut *n* atajo *m* **Do you know any shortcuts?** *¿Conoce usted (Fam: Conoces)* algún atajo? *(1)* **I /** *(2)* **We know a good shortcut** *(1)* Conozco / *(2)* Conocemos un buen atajo. **Let's take a shortcut.** Vamos tomando un atajo.

shortly *adv* en breve *(1)* **I'll /** *(2)* **We'll be there shortly.** *(1)* Estaré / *(2)* Estaremos ahí en breve.

shorts *n, pl* short *m,* **You look** *(1)* **fabulous /** *(2)* **great in shorts.** Se ve usted *(Fam: Te ves) (1)* fabuloso *(-sa) /* *(2)* fenomenal en short.

shot *n* 1. *(firearms)* disparo *m* ; 2. *(photo)* foto *f* ; 3. *(sports)* tiro *m* ; 4. *(innoculation)* inyección *f* ; 5. *(drink)* caballito *m* **Was that a shot?** ¿Eso fue un disparo? **It's a shot in the dark.** Es un disparo en la oscuridad. **This is a nice shot (of you).** Esta es una buena foto. **Good shot!** ¡Buen tiro! **You made a great shot.** Hiciste un buen tiro. **You're going to have to** *(1,2)* **get a typhus shot.** *Usted va (Fam: Tú vas)* a tener que ir a que *(1)* lo *m* / *(2)* la *f (Fam: te)* inyecten contra el tifus. **Pour me a shot of that.** Sírveme un caballito de eso.

should *v aux* debe de **What should** *(1)* **I /** *(2)* **we do?** ¿Qué *(1)* debo / *(2)* debemos hacer? **You (really) should** *(1)* **call her. /** *(2)* **call him. /** *(3)* **do it. /** *(4)* **get it checked. /** *(5)* **see a doctor. /** *(6)* **stay (longer).** (Realmente) *Usted debería (Fam: Deberías) (1)* llamarla. / *(2)* llamarlo. / *(3)* hacerlo. / *(4)* verificarlo. / *(5)* ver a un doctor. / *(6)* quedarte (un poco más). **I (really) should** *(1)* **change some money. /** *(2)* **find out. /** *(3)* **go (now). /** *(4)* **start packing.** (Realmente) Debo *(1)* cambiar dinero. / *(2)* saber. / *(3)* ir (ahora). / *(4)* comenzar a empacar.

shoulder *n* hombro *m* **~ blade** omóplato *m* **broad ~s** hombros amplios **lovely ~s** hombros lindos **powerful ~s** hombros poderosos **smooth ~s** hombros tersos **soft ~s** hombros suaves **sore ~** hombros adoloridos **I need your shoulder to lean on.** Necesito tu hombro para recargarme. **You can lean on my shoulder any time.** *Se puede usted (Fam: Te puedes)* recargar en mi hombro cuando *usted quiera (Fam: tú quieras)*. **You have a lot on your shoulders.** *Lleva usted (Fam: Llevas)* una gran carga sobre los

---

Spanish "v" is pronounced like a soft "b".

hombros. **Why are you giving me the cold shoulder?** ¿Por qué me estás volviendo la espalda?

shout *vi* gritar *(1)* **I** / *(2)* **We shouted, but you didn't hear** *(3)* **me.** / *(4)* **us.** *(1)* Grité / *(2)* Gritamos, pero *usted (Fam: tú)* no *(1)* me / *(2)* nos *oyó (Fam: oíste)*. **You don't have to shout.** No tienes que gritar.

shovel *vt* palear ~ **dirt on the fire** palear tierra sobre la fogata ~ **snow** palear nieve

shovel *n* pala *f* **camp(ing)** ~ pala de campismo **clam** ~ pala cerrada

show *vt* mostrar, demostrar, enseñar ~ **affection** demostrar afecto ~ **love** demostrar amor **Can you show** *(1)* **me** / *(2)* **us on the map?** ¿Puede usted *(Fam: ¿Puedes)* *(1)* mostrarme / *(2)* mostrarnos en el mapa? **I'll show you on the map.** Yo te muestro en el mapa. **Can you show me (how to do it)?** ¿Puede usted *(Fam: ¿Puedes)* enseñarme (cómo se hace)? **Let me show you (how to do it).** Déjeme enseñarle *(Fam: Déjame enseñarte)* (cómo se hace). **I'll show you (how to do it).** Yo le enseño *(Fam: te enseño)* (cómo se hace). *(1)* **Show me...** / *(2)* **I'll show you...** *(3)* **her** / *(4)* **his** / *(5)* **their** / *(6)* **your photo.** *(1)* Muéstreme *(Fam: Muéstrame)*... / *(2)* Yo *le (Fam: te)* muestro... la foto / *(3)* de ella / *(4)* de él / *(5)* de ellos / *(6)* tu foto. **Could you show** *(1)* **me** / *(2)* **us where it is?** ¿Podría usted *(Fam:¿Podrías)* *(1)* mostrarme / *(2)* mostrarnos dónde es? **I'll show you where it is.** Yo *le (Fam: te)* muestro dónde es. **I'd like to show you** *(place)*. Me gustaría mostrarle ___. **Could you show** *(1)* **me** / *(2)* **us around the city?** ¿Podría usted *(Fam: ¿Podrías)* *(1)* mostrarme / *(2)* mostrarnos la ciudad? **That was really nice of you to show** *(1)* **me** / *(2)* **us around the city.** Fue muy amable de tu parte *(1)* mostrarme / *(2)* mostrarnos la ciudad. **Could you show me how to play the guitar?** ¿Me puede enseñar a tocar la guitarra?

show *n* 1. *(demonstration)* demostración *f*; 2. *(performance)* espectáculo *m*; 3. *(exhibition)* exhibición *f* **magic** ~ espectáculo de magia **tickets to the** ~ boletos para el espectáculo **Did you enjoy the** *(1,2)* **show?** ¿Disfrutó usted *(Fam: Disfrutaste)* *(1)* el espectáculo? / *(2)* la exhibición? *(1)* **I** / *(2)* **We really enjoyed the** *(3,4)* **show.** (Realmente) *(1)* Disfruté / *(2)* Disfrutamos *(3)* el espectáculo. / *(4)* la exhibición.

shower *vt (with kisses)* cubrir, bañar **I'm going to shower you with kisses.** Te voy a cubrir de besos.

shower *n* regadera *f* **room with a** ~ habitación con regadera **take a** ~ **(together)** darse un regaderazo (juntos)

show off *idiom* presumir **You're just showing off.** Nomás estás presumiendo. **Stop showing off!** ¡Deja de presumir!

show-off *n* presumido *m*, -da *f* **What a big show-off you are.** Qué gran

Time expressions are given on page 413.

presumido eres.

show up *idiom (appear)* aparecer *(1)* I / *(2)* **We waited, but you didn't show up.** *(1)* Esperé / *(2)* Esperamos, pero *usted no se apareció (Fam: no te apareciste)*. **I was wondering if you were going to show up.** Me preguntaba si *usted se iba (Fam:* te ibas*)* a aparecer.

shrewd *adj* vivo *m*, -va *f*, sagaz *m&f* **You're a shrewd one.** Qué vivo *(-va)* eres. **That's a shrewd idea.** Esa es una idea sagaz.

shudder *vi* estremecerse **I shudder to think what might happen.** Me estremezco al pensar lo que podría suceder.

shuffle *vt* barajar **Shuffle the cards.** Baraja las cartas.

shut *adj* cerrado *m*, -da *f* **Is it shut?** ¿Está cerrado? **It's (not) shut.** (No) Está cerrado.

shut *vt* cerrar **Shut the** *(1)* **door.** / *(2)* **window.** *Cierre usted (Fam: Cierra) (1)* la puerta. / *(2)* la ventana.

shut up *(rude slang: be quiet)* callarse **Shut up!** ¡Cállate! **Why don't you shut up?** ¿Por qué no te callas?

shuttlecock *n (badminton)* gallito *m*

shy *adj* tímido *m*, -da *f* **I'm basically a shy person.** Básicamente soy una persona tímida. **Don't be (so) shy.** No *sea usted (Fam:* seas*)* (tan) tímido *(-da)*. **You don't have to be shy with me.** *Usted no tiene (Fam: Tú no tienes)* por qué ser tímido *(-da)* conmigo.

shyness *n* timidez *f* **I want to help you get over your shyness.** Quiero ayudarte a superar tu timidez.

sick *adj* 1. *(ill)* enfermo *m*, -ma *f*; 2. *(fed up)* harto *m*, -ta *f*; 3. *(deranged, insane)* desquiciado *m*, -da *f* **be ~** estar enfermo *(-ma)* **feel ~** sentirse enfermo *(-ma)* **get ~** marearse **Do you feel sick?** *¿Se siente usted (Fam: ¿Te sientes)* enfermo *(-ma)*? **I feel sick** Me siento enfermo *(-ma)*. **I hope you're not sick.** Espero que no *esté usted (Fam: estés)* enfermo *(-ma)*. **My** *(1)* **wife** / *(2)* **daughter is sick.** Mi *(1)* esposa / *(2)* hija está enferma. **My** *(1)* **husband** / *(2)* **son is sick.** Mi *(1)* esposo / *(2)* hijo está enfermo. **I'm sick (and tired) of** *(1)* **all this rain.** / *(2)* **waiting around.** Estoy harto *(-ta)* (y aburrido *-da)* de *(1)* toda esta lluvia. / *(2)* de esperar. **That is (really) sick.** Eso es (de veras) asqueroso.

sickness *n* enfermedad *f*

side *adj* lateral *m&f* **no ~ effects** sin efectos laterales **~ street** calle lateral

side *n* lado *m* **both ~s** ambos lados **choose ~s** *(sports)* elegir lados **left ~** lado izquierdo **on the flip ~** al lado contrario **our ~** *(sports)* de nuestro lado **right ~** lado derecho **~ by ~** lado a lado **~ of the road** a un lado del camino **the other ~** al otro lado **Whose side are you on?** ¿De qué lado estás? **I'm on your side.** Estoy de tu lado. **I see you have a** *(1)* **humorous**

Spanish "qu" is pronounced like "k".

/ *(2)* **ro-mantic side.** Veo que tienes tu lado *(1)* humoroso. / *(2)* romántico.
I want to go through life side by side with you. Quiero ir por la vida
lado a lado contigo.

sidewalk *n* acera *f*, banqueta *f*

sight *n* 1. *(vision)* vista *f*; 2. *(s.th. seen)* vista *f*, paisaje *m*; 3. *(scenic place)*
lugar *m* de interés **beautiful ~** hermosa vista / hermoso paisaje **catch ~ of**
avistar **magnificent ~** un paisaje magnífico **wonderful ~** un paisaje
maravilloso **Isn't that a sight!** ¡Qué paisaje! **I've never seen such a sight.**
Nunca había visto un paisaje así. **Let's go around the city and see the**
sights. Vamos a andar por la ciudad para ver los lugares de interés. **Just**
the sight of you fills me with *(1)* **excitement.** / *(2)* **joy.** El sólo verte me
llena de *(1)* emoción. / *(2)* alegría. **Out of sight, out of mind.** Ojos que no
ven, corazón que no siente.

sightseeing *n* paseo *m (See phrases under* **go, like** *and* **love***.)* **go ~** ir de
paseo **~ tour** un recorrido por los lugares de interés

sign *vt* firmar **Sign your name (here).** *Firme (Fam: Firma)* con *su (Fam: tu)*
nombre aquí. **You forgot to sign it.** Se *le (Fam: te)* olvidó firmarlo.

sign *n* 1. *(indication)* muestra *f*, señal *f*; 2. *(indicator, mark, symbol)* signo
m; 3. *(store, road, etc)* rótulo *m* **~(s) of affection** muestra(s) de afecto **~ of**
old age señal de vejez **zodiac ~** signo del zodiaco *(See various zodiac*
signs under **zodiac***)* **That's a** *(1)* **bad /** *(2)* **good sign.** Eso es *(1)* mala / *(2)*
buena señal. **That's a sign that you're madly in love with me.** Eso es
señal de que estás perdidamente enamorado *(-da)* de mí. **What does that**
sign say? ¿Qué dice ese rótulo?

signal *vt* hacer señas **I was trying to signal you.** Estaba tratando de hacerte
señas.

signal *n* señal *f*, seña *f* **Give me a signal. (Like this.)** *Hágame (Fam: Hazme)*
una seña. (Como esta.) **I'll give you a signal.** Yo *le (Fam: te)* hago una
seña. **My eyes were sending you love signals all evening. (Did you read**
them?) Mis ojos te estuvieron haciendo señales de amor toda la noche.
(¿Las viste?)

sign up *idiom* anotarse **Did you sign up (for the** *[1]* **program /** *[2]* **show /**
[3] **tour)?** ¿Se anotó *(Fam:* ¿*Te anotaste)* (para *[1]* el programa / *[2]* el
espectáculo / *[3]* el recorrido)? **Let's go sign up (for the** *[1]* **program /**
[2] **show /** *[3]* **tour).** Vamos anotándonos (para *[1]* el programa / *[2]* el
espectáculo / *[3]* el recorrido). *(1)* **I /** *(2)* **We signed up already.** *(1)* Ya me
anoté. / *(2)* Ya nos anotamos.

signature *n* firma *f*

silence *n* silencio *m* **awkward ~** un silencio incómodo **complete ~** silencio
absoluto **gloomy ~** silencio lúgubre **long ~** un largo silencio **total ~** silencio

---

Words in parentheses (not italicized) are optional.

total **Why the gloomy silence?** ¿Por qué tanto silencio? **I love the silence here.** Me encanta el silencio que hay aquí. **There is such serene silence here.** Hay aquí un silencio tan apacible. **Your silence speaks volumes.** Tu silencio es elocuente.

silent *adj* silencioso *m*, -sa *f* **Be silent!** ¡Estate en silencio! **You have to be very silent.** *(wildlife watching)* Tiene usted (Fam: Tienes) que ser muy silencioso *(-sa)*. **You're so silent. Why?** Usted es (Fam: Tú eres) muy silencioso *(-sa)*. ¿Por qué? **Oh, so now you're going to give me the silent treatment.** Ah, así que ahora vas a darme el tratamiento del silencio. **I'm saying a silent prayer.** Estoy rezando en silencio.

silently *adv* silenciosamente, en silencio **Move silently!** *(wildlife watching)* ¡Muévete en silencio!

silhouette *n* silueta *f*

silk *n* seda *f* **Your skin is as smooth as silk.** Tu piel es suave como la seda.

silky *adj* sedoso *m*, -sa *f*

silly *adj* tonto *m*, -ta *f* **act** ~ actuar tontamente **feel** ~ sentirse tonto **I (1) feel / (2) felt so silly.** (1) Me siento / (2) Me sentí tan tonto *(-ta)*. **Don't be silly.** No seas tonto *(-ta)*. **That was a silly thing to do.** Eso que hiciste fue muy tonto.

silver *adj* plateado *m*, -da *f*

silver *n* plata *f*

silver-tongued *adj* elocuente *m&f*, con pico de oro **You talked me into it, you silver-tongued devil, you.** Tú me convenciste, con tu pico de oro.

similar *adj* similar *m&f* **We have similar (1) interests. / (2) tastes.** Tenemos (1) intereses / (2) gustos similares.

similarity *n* similitud *f*, parecido *m*

simple *adj* fácil *m&f*, simple *m&f*, sencillo *m*, -lla *f* ~ **explanation** una simple explicación ~ **game** un juego sencillo ~ **life** una vida sencilla **It's (really) simple. (Try it.)** Es (de veras) fácil. (Inténtalo.) **There must be a simpler way.** Debe haber una manera más fácil.

simple-minded *adj* de mente sencilla

simpleton *n* simplón *m*, -plona *f*

simply *adv* con sencillez, simplemente **live** ~ vivir con sencillez **I simply can't.** Simplemente no puedo. **You simply must (1) come with (2) me. / (3) us. / (4) see it. / (5) try it.** Simplemente tienes que (1) venir (2) conmigo. / (3) con nosotros. / (4) verlo. / (5) intentarlo.

sin *vi* pecar **You realize, you have sinned terribly.** Te das cuenta, has pecado horriblemente.

sin *n* pecado *m* **It's an unforgivable sin.** Es un pecado imperdonable. **It's not a sin.** No es pecado. **Is it a sin for me to love you?** ¿Es pecado que yo

A single Spanish "r" should be lightly trilled; double "r" ("rr") should be strongly trilled.

te ame?

since *prep* desde ~ **1998** desde mil novecientos noventa y ocho ~ **last Saturday** desde el sábado pasado ~ **that time** desde ese momento ~ **then** desde entonces ~ **when?** ¿Desde cuándo? ~ **yesterday** desde ayer **The weather has been** *(1)* **great** / *(2)* **terrible since** *(3)* **I** / *(4)* **we arrived.** El clima ha estado *(1)* fantástico / *(2)* horrible desde que *(3)* llegué. / *(4)* llegamos. **I've loved you since the first moment I** *(1)* **met** / *(2)* **saw you.** Te amé desde el primer momento que te *(1)* conocí. / *(2)* vi.

sincere *adj* sincero m, -ra f ~ **apologies** disculpas sinceras ~ **condolences** sinceras condolencias **I'm sincere in everything I say (to you).** Soy sincero en todo lo que *(le (Fam: te)* digo. **My feelings for you are completely sincere.** Mis sentimientos hacia *usted (Fam: ti)* son completamente sinceros.

sincerely *adv* sinceramente *(1)* **I** / *(2)* **We sincerely hope that** *(3)* **everything goes okay.** / *(4)* **you can come.** / *(5)* **you succeed.** *(1)* Sinceramente espero que / *(2)* esperamos que *(3)* todo salga bien. / *(4)* pueda usted *(Fam: puedas)* venir. / *(5)* tenga usted *(Fam: tengas)* éxito. **I sincerely apologize.** Mis sinceras disculpas. **I mean it sincerely.** Lo digo sinceramente.

sinful *n* pecaminoso m, -sa f **Oh, this is so delicious it's sinful!** Oh, esto es tan delicioso que es pecado. **I'm having sinful thoughts about you.** Estoy teniendo malos pensamientos por ti.

sing *vt & vi* cantar **Let's sing (a song)!** ¡Vamos a cantar (una canción)! **Do you like to sing?** ¿Le *(Fam: ¿Te)* gusta cantar? **I** *(1)* **like** / *(2)* **love to sing.** Me *(1)* gusta / *(2)* encanta cantar. **You sing** *(1)* **beautifully.** / *(2)* **very well.** *Usted canta (Fam: Tú cantas) (1)*lindo. / *(2)* muy bien. **You make my heart sing (with joy).** *Usted hace (Fam: Tú haces)* que mi corazón cante (de alegría).

singer *n* cantante *m&f* **You're a (real) good singer.** Es usted *(Fam: Eres)* (muy) buen*(-a)* cantante.

singing *n* canto m

single *adj* soltero m, -ra f **every ~ time** en cada ocasión / todas las veces ~ **mother** madre soltera ~ **parent** padre soltero **stay ~** quedarse soltero **Are you single?** ¿Es usted *(Fam: ¿Eres)* soltero *(-ra)*? **I'm single.** Soy soltero *(-ra)*.

single-handed(ly) *adv* sin ayuda de nadie

single-minded *adj* decidido m, -da f

singular *n (gram.)* singular m **That's the plural. What's the singular?** Ese es el plural. ¿Cuál es el singular?

sinister *adj* siniestro m, -tra f **It sounds very sinister to me.** Me suena muy

---

*Familiar "tu" forms in parentheses can replace
italicized polite forms.*

siniestro.

sink *vi* 1. *(go down in the water)* hundirse; 2. *(heart: become dispirited)* caerse el alma **If it sinks, I'm counting on you to rescue me.** Si se hunde, cuento contigo para que me rescates. **My heart sank.** Se me cayó el alma al suelo.

sink in *idiom (become realized)* caer en cuenta **It finally sank in that...** Finalmente caí en cuenta de que... **It hasn't really sunk in yet.** Todavía no ha caído en cuenta..

sinker *n (fishing)* plomada *f*

sinner *n* pecador *m*, -dora *f*

sip *n* sorbo *m* **Take a sip.** Tome *(Fam: Toma)* un sorbo. **Can I have a sip?** ¿Puedo tomar un sorbo?

sir *n* 1. *(form of address)* señor *m* ; 2. *(mil.) (lieutenant)* teniente *m* ; *(captain)* capitán *m (etc, depending on rank)* **Yes, sir!** *(mil.)* ¡Sí, capitán! **Right away, sir!** ¡De inmediato, capitán!

siren *n* sirena *f*

sister *n* hermana *f* **half ~** media hermana **older ~** hermana mayor **oldest ~** la mayor de las hermanas **middle ~** la hermana de en medio **younger ~** hermana menor **youngest ~** la menor de las hermanas **This is my sister** *(name)*. Esta es mi hermana ____.

sister-in-law *n* 1. *(wife's sister)* cuñada *f*; 2. *(husband's sister)* cuñada *f*; 3. *(brother's wife)* cuñada *f* ; 4. *(spouse's brother's wife)* concuña *f*

sit *vi* sentarse **Is anyone sitting here?** ¿Está ocupado este asiento? **Do you mind if I sit (1) here? / (2) with you?** ¿Le *(Fam: Te)* importa si me siento *(1)* aquí? / *(2)* contigo? **Please sit down.** Por favor, *siéntese (Fam: siéntate)*. **You can sit (1) here. / (2) next to me. / (3) with me. / (4) at my table.** *Puede usted sentarse (Fam: Puedes sentarte) (1)* aquí. / *(2)* junto a mí. / *(3)* conmigo. / *(4)* a mi mesa. **Come sit (1) with me. / (2) at my table.** *Venga a sentarse (Fam: Ven a sentarte) (1)* conmigo. / *(2)* a mi mesa. **Let's sit (1) here. / (2) (over) there. / (3) by the pool. / (4) in the shade.** Vamos a sentarnos *(1)* aquí. / *(2)* (por) allá. *(3)* junto a la piscina *(4)* a la sombra.

sit around *idiom (sit idly)* sentado **I've just been sitting around, doing nothing.** He estado sentado *(-da)* sin hacer nada. **Let's do something besides sit around.** Vamos a hacer algo más que estar sentados. **I don't want to sit around all day.** No quiero quedarme sentado *(-da)* todo el día.

site *n* sitio *m* **archaeological ~** sitio arqueológico **Aztec ~** sitio azteca **Maya(n) ~** sitio maya **web ~** sitio de Internet

situated *adj* situado *m*, -da *f*, instalado *m*, -da *f (1)* I / *(2)* **We finally got**

Spanish "ll" is pronounced like "y" in "yes".

situated (in *[3]* **my /** *[4]* **our new apartment).** Finalmente *(1)* me instalé / *(2)* nos instalamos (en *[3]* mi / *[4]* nuestro nuevo departamento). **When we get situated, we'd like to have you come visit us.** Cuando nos instalemos, nos gustaría que *usted viniera (Fam: vinieras)* a visitarnos.

situation *n* situación *f* **awkward** ~ situación incómoda **complicated** ~ situación complicada **critical** ~ situación crítica **desperate** ~ situación desesperada **difficult** ~ situación difícil **embarrassing** ~ situación bochornosa **family** ~ situación familiar **financial** ~ situación financiera **funny** ~ 1. *(amusing)* situación chistosa; 2. *(strange)* situación rara **hopeless** ~ situación sin remedio **marital** ~ situación marital **money** ~ situación monetaria **nightmarish** ~ situación de pesadilla **sticky** ~ situación peliaguda **strange** ~ situación rara **terrible** ~ situación horrible **ticklish** ~ situación delicada **unpleasant** ~ situación desagradable **weird** ~ situación inverosímil **What's your situation like at home?** ¿Cómo es *su (Fam: tu)* situación en casa? **My situation at** *(1)* **home /** *(2)* **work is** *(what)*. Mi situación en *(1)* casa / *(2)* el trabajo es ___.

six-pack *n (6 cans of beer)* un seis de cerveza *f*

size *n* talla *f*, tamaño *m*, medida *f* **child's** ~ talla para niños **extra-large** ~ talla extra grande **large** ~ talla grande **medium** ~ talla mediana **pants** ~ talla de pantalones **petite** ~ talla extra-pequeña **right** ~ la talla exacta **ring** ~ medida del anillo **shoe** ~ medida del calzado **small** ~ talla pequeña **wrong** ~ talla equivocada **What's your** *(1)* **blouse /** *(2)* **dress size?** ¿Cuál es la talla de *su (Fam: tu)* *(1)* blusa? / *(2)* vestido? **What size do you wear?** ¿Qué talla *usa usted (Fam: usas)*? **The size is just right.** La talla es correcta. **It's the wrong size.** Es la talla equivocada.

skate *vi* 1. *(iceskate)* patinar sobre hielo; 2. *(rollerskate)* patinar sobre ruedas

skateboard *n* monopatín *m*, tabla *f* skateboard

skateboarding *n* deporte *m* del monopatín, skateboard *m*

skating *n* 1. *(iceskating)* patinaje *m* sobre hielo; 2. *(rollerskating)* patinaje *m* sobre ruedas **figure** ~ patinaje artístico **ice** ~ patinaje sobre hielo **inline** ~ *(rollerblading)* patinaje sobre ruedas en línea ~ **lessons** lecciones de patinaje ~ **rink** pista de patinaje

skeptical *adj* escéptico *m*, -ca *f* **I'm skeptical of that.** En eso soy escéptico *(-ca)*.

sketch *vt* esbozar, bosquejar **Can you sketch it for me?** ¿Me lo *puede usted (Fam: puedes)* esbozar? **I'll sketch it for you.** Yo *se (Fam: te)* lo esbozo.

sketch *n* esbozo *m*, bosquejo *m* **nice** ~ un bosquejo bonito **rough** ~ un bosquejo

ski *vi* esquiar *(See also phrases under* **like** *and* **love***.)* **Can you teach me to ski?** ¿*Puede usted (Fam: ¿Puedes)* enseñarme a esquiar? **I'll teach you**

Common occupations are listed on pages 415-416.

how to ski. Yo *le (Fam: te)* enseño a esquiar.

ski *n* esquí *m* **pair of ~s** un par de esquís **rent ~s** rentar esquís **~ binders** sujetadores *m, pl* para esquís **~ boots** botas *f, pl* para esquiar **~ course** pista *f* de esquí **~ lift** elevador *m* para esquiadores **~ lodge** salón *m* de esquí **~ poles** postes *m, pl* de esquí **~ resort** centro *m* de esquí **Do you have skis?** ¿Tiene usted *(Fam: ¿Tienes)* esquís? **Can we rent skis (there)?** ¿(Aquí) Podemos rentar esquís?

skier *n* esquiador *m*, -dora *f* **You're a good skier.** Es usted *(Fam: Eres)* un*(-a)* buen*(-a)* esquiador *(-dora)*. **I'm (not) a good skier.** (No) Soy un*(-a)* buen*(-a)* esquiador *(-dora)*.

skiing *n* esquiar *(See phrases under* **go, like** *and* **love**.*)* **cross-country ~** esquiar a campo traviesa **~ lessons** lecciones para esquiar *(1)* **I** / *(2)* **We want to take skiing lessons.** *(1)* Quiero / *(2)* Queremos tomar lecciones para esquiar.

skilift *n* telesquí *m*

skill *n* habilidad *f*, destreza *f* **acrobatic ~** destreza acrobática **good communication ~s** buenas dotes para la comunicación **social ~s** habilidades sociales **You have a lot of skill.** *Tiene usted (Fam: Tienes)* mucha habilidad. **That takes a lot of skill.** Eso requiere mucha habilidad.

skillful *adj* habilidoso *m*, -sa *f*, hábile *m & f*

skillfully *adv* con destreza, con habilidad **You play so skillfully!** ¡Usted juega *(Fam: ¡Tú juegas)* con mucha habilidad! **Skillfully done!** ¡Hecho con habilidad!

skimp *vi* economizar *(1)* **I** / *(2)* **We have to sort of skimp.** *(1)* Tengo / *(2)* Tenemos que economizar.

skimpy *adj (clothing)* ligero *(-ra)* de ropas

skin *n* piel *f* **baby soft ~** piel de bebé **clear ~** piel clara **copper(-toned) ~** piel cobriza **creamy ~** piel cremosa **dark ~** piel morena **delicate ~** piel delicada **ebony ~** piel de ébano **fair ~** piel clara **golden ~** piel dorada **ivory ~** piel marfileña **lovely ~** piel preciosa **pale ~** piel pálida **satin ~** piel satinada **sensitive ~** piel sensible **silky ~** piel sedosa **~ and bones** (piel y huesos) huesudo *(-da)* **~ like a(n)** *(1)* **apricot** / *(2)* **peach** piel de *(1)* melocotón *m* / *(2)* durazno *m* **snow-white ~** piel blanca como la nieve **soft ~** piel suave **tender ~** piel delicada **velvet(ty) ~** piel aterciopelada **You have such perfect skin.** *Tiene usted (Fam: Tienes)* una piel tan perfecta. **Your skin is soft as** *(1)* **velvet.** / *(2)* **a baby's.** / *(3)* **a kitten.** Tu piel es suave como *(1)* terciopelo. / *(2)* de bebé. / *(3)* como un gatito. **I love the feel of your skin.** Me encanta sentir tu piel. **I can't stay in the sun long. I have sen-sitive skin.** No puedo tomar mucho sol. Soy de piel sensible.

skinny *adj* flaco *m*, -ca *f*

Spanish "y" is "ee" when alone or at the end of words.

skinny-dipping *n (slang: swimming in the nude)* nadar en cueros **Let's go skinny-dipping!** ¡Vámonos a nadar en cueros!

skip *vt (pass up)* saltarse, prescindir **Why don't we skip the *(1)* party?** / *(2)* **program?** / *(3)* **show?** / *(4)* **tour?** ¿Por qué no nos saltamos *(1)* la fiesta? / *(2)* el programa? / *(3)* el espectáculo? / *(4)* el recorrido?

skirt *n* falda *f* **short ~** falda corta **That's a (very) beautiful skirt.** Esa es una falda (muy) bonita.

skunk *n* 1. *(animal)* zorrillo *m* ; 2. *(no-good person)* canalla *m&f*

sky *n* cielo *m* **blue ~** cielo azul **clear ~** cielo despejado **cloudy ~** cielo nublado **endless ~** cielo infinito **in the ~** en el cielo **night ~** cielo nocturno **out of a clear blue ~** de la nada **starry ~** cielo estrellado **summer ~** cielo estival **What a lovely sky!** ¡Qué precioso cielo! **I want to lie in the grass with you and gaze up at the sky.** Quiero acostarme en el pasto contigo y mirar el cielo. **Our love is like the sky - big and beautiful and forever.** Nuestro amor es como el cielo: grande y hermoso y para siempre. **I love you all the way up to the sky.** Te amo de aquí hasta el cielo.

skydive *vi* lanzarse en paracaídas

skydiving *n* paracaidismo *m*

slacks *n, pl* pantalones *mpl* **pair of ~** unos pantalones de deporte

slang *n* jerga *f*

slap *vt* dar una bofetada **I ought to slap your face.** Debería darte una bofetada.

slave *n* esclavo *m*, -va *f* **Do you need a slave? I want to volunteer.** ¿Necesitas un esclavo? Me ofrezco como voluntario. **I am (completely) *(1)* your slave.** / *(2)* **a slave to your beauty.** Soy *(1)* tu (rendido) esclavo . / *(2)* esclavo de tu belleza. **You have made me a slave of love.** Me has hecho esclavo de tu amor. **I'm not your slave.** Yo no soy tu esclavo.

sleazy *adj* 1. *(ethically low)* canalla *m&f* ; 2. *(unsightly, sloppy)* desaliñado *m*, -da *f*

sled *n* trineo *m*

sledding *n* montar en trineo **go ~** ir a montar en trineo

sleep *vi* dormir **I was sleeping.** Estaba dormido *(-da)*. **How did you sleep?** ¿Qué tal *durmió usted (Fam: dormiste)*? **Did you sleep well?** ¿*Durmió usted (Fam: ¿Dormiste)* bien? **I slept *(1)* well.** / *(2)* **poorly.** Dormí *(1)* bien. / *(2)* mal. **I *(1)* can't** / *(2)* **couldn't sleep.** No *(1)* puedo / *(2)* pude dormir. **You can sleep on my shoulder.** Puedes dormir en mi hombro. **You're so *(1)* adorable** / *(2)* **angelic** / *(3)* **beautiful** / *(4)* **lovely** / *(5)* **pretty when you're sleeping.** Eres tan *(1)* adorable / *(2)* angelical / *(3)* hermosa / *(4)* adorable / *(5)* bonita cuando estás dormida. **Sleep at my place tonight.** Duerme en mi casa esta noche. **I can't sleep with you.** No puedo dormir contigo. **We can(not) sleep together.** (No) Podemos dormir juntos.

sleep *n* sueño *m* **deep** ~ sueño profundo **sound** ~ sueño reparador **Sometimes I talk in my sleep.** A veces hablo en sueños. **I hope you don't walk in your sleep.** Espero que no seas sonámbulo *(-la)*.

sleepy *adj* somnoliento *m*, -ta *f* **be** ~ estar somnoliento *(-ta)* **get** ~ ponerse somnoliento *(-ta)*, dar sueño **Are you getting sleepy?** ¿Le *(Fam: ¿Te)* está dando sueño? **I'm getting sleepy.** Me está dando sueño.

sleepyhead *n* dormilón *m*, -lona *f*

slender *adj* delgado *m*, -da *f*

slide *vi* deslizarse, resbalarse

slide *n (playground, pool)* tobogán *m*, resbaladero *m* **water** ~ tobogán de agua

slight *adj* 1. *(not great)* menudo *m*, -da *f* ; 2. *(slim)* delgado *m*, -da *f* ~ **chance** una remota oportunidad

slightly *adv* apenas, ligeramente

slim *adj* delgado *m*, -da *f*

slinky *adj* ceñido *m*, -da *f*, ajustado *m*, -da *f* ~ **dress** vestido ceñido ~ **evening gown** vestido de noche ceñido

slip *vi (lose footing)* resbalarse **I slipped.** Me resbalé. **Be careful, don't slip.** *Tenga (Fam: Ten)* cuidado, no *se resbale (Fam: te resbales)*.

slip *n 1. (lapse)* lapsus *m*; 2. *(undergarment)* ropa *f* interior **That was a slip of the tongue.** Ese fue un lapsus.

slip on *idiom (put on)* ponerse **I'll slip on a sweater.** Me voy a poner un suéter.

slippers *n, pl* pantuflas *fpl*

slob *n (slang) (sloppy person)* zarrapastroso *m*, -sa *f*

slope *n* declive *m* **ski** ~ pista para esquiar

sloppiness *n* dejadez *f*

sloppy *adj* desaliñado *m*, -sa *f*, descuidado *m*, -da *f*

slothful *adj* holgazán *m*, -zana *f*

slovenly *adj* desaseado *m*, -da *f*, desaliñado *m* –da *f*

slow *adj* lento *m*, -ta *f* **in** ~ **motion** en cámara lenta ~ **kiss** beso prolongado

slow *adv* calma **I want to take it slow and get to know you (better).** Quiero llevarla con calma para conocerte (mejor).

slow down *idiom* despacio **Slow down!** ¡Despacio!

slowly *adv* despacio, lentamente **drive** ~ manejar despacio **move** ~ moverse despacio **walk** ~ caminar despacio **Please speak a little more slowly.** Por favor, *hable usted (Fam: habla)* un poco más despacio.

slowpoke *n* lento *(-ta)* como tortuga **I'm sorry I'm such a slowpoke.** Me apena ser lento *(-ta)* como una tortuga.

Spanish "c" before "e" and "i" is pronounced like "s".

sluggish *adj* amodorrado *m*, -da *f* **I feel kind of sluggish (today).** Me siento como amodorrado (hoy).

slums *n, pl* barriadas *fpl*, barrios *mpl* bajos

sly *adj* taimado *m*, -da *f* **on the** ~ a escondidas ~ **fox** zorro taimado **You're a sly one, aren't you?** Tú eres bien colmilludo *(-da)*, ¿verdad?

small *adj* chico *m*, -ca *f*, chiquito *m*, -ta *f*, pequeño *m*, -ña *f* ~ **body** cuerpecito *m*, cuerpo pequeño ~ **change** suelto *m* ~ **hands** manitas, manos chiquitas ~ **person** persona pequeña

small-minded *adj* de mente cerrada

smart *adj* 1. *(intelligent, clever, bright)* listo *m*, -ta *f*, brillante *m&f*; inteligente *m&f*; 2. *(stylish, elegant)* elegante *m&f* ~ **aleck** sabelotodo *m&f*

smell *vt* oler **Smell this.** Huele esto.

smell *vi* oler **That smells** *(1)* **delicious.** / *(2)* **great.** / *(3)* **heavenly.** / *(4)* **wonderful.** Eso huele *(1)* delicioso. / *(2)* riquísimo. / *(3)*divino. / *(4)* maravilloso. **Your hair smells nice.** Tu cabello huele rico.

smell *n* 1. *(general)* olor *m*; *(fragrance)* olor *m*; 2. *(unpleasant)* olor *m* **I love the smell of your hair.** Me encanta el olor de tu cabello.

smile *vi* sonreír ~ **back** devolver la sonrisa **Smile!** ¡Sonríe! **I like the way you smile.** Me gusta *su (Fam: tu)* sonrisa. **When you smile,** *(1)* **the whole world lights up.** / *(2)* **it's like another sun in the sky.** Cuando *usted sonríe (Fam: sonríes)*, *(1)* el mundo entero se ilumina. / *(2)* es como que hubiera otro sol en el cielo.

smile *n* sonrisa *f* **bewitching** ~ mágica sonrisa **bright** ~ sonrisa luminosa **captivating** ~ sonrisa cautivadora **cheerful** ~ sonrisa alegre **cute** ~ linda sonrisa **dazzling** ~ sonrisa deslumbrante **friendly** ~ sonrisa amistosa **gorgeous** ~ sonrisa preciosa **great** ~ gran sonrisa **happy** ~ sonrisa feliz **heart-melting** ~ sonrisa irresistible **lovely** ~ sonrisa encantadora **nice** ~ sonrisa agradable **pretty** ~ sonrisa bonita **sensual** ~ sonrisa sensual **sunny** ~ sonrisa luminosa **sweet** ~ sonrisa dulce **winning** ~ sonrisa victoriosa **You have such a beautiful smile.** *Usted tiene (Fam: Tú tienes)* una sonrisa tan bonita. **You have the most enchanting smile I've ever seen.** *Tiene usted (Fam: Tienes)* la sonrisa más encantadora que he visto. **I love the sunshine of your smile.** Me encanta lo luminoso de *su (Fam: tu)* sonrisa. **There's such magic in your smile.** Hay tanta magia en *su (Fam: tu)* sonrisa. **You have a smile** *(1)* **like a lighthouse by the sea.** / *(2)* **that would light up a city.** *Su (Fam: Tu)* sonrisa es *(1)* como un faro junto al mar. / *(2)* ilumina una ciudad. **Your beautiful smile caught my eye.** Me atrajo *su (Fam: Tu)* bella sonrisa. **When I saw your radiant smile, I was completely entranced.** Me quedé (completamente) alelado al ver tu radiante sonrisa. **I want to kiss your beautiful smile - and everything connected to it.**

Numbers in Spanish are given on pages 411-412.

Quiero besar tu hermosa sonrisa – y todo lo que venga con ella.

smirk *n* sonrisita *f* **Wipe that smirk off your face!** Quítate esa sonrisita.

smoke *vt* fumar **Do you smoke?** ¿Fumas? **I smoke.** Sí fumo. **I don't smoke.**
No fumo. **I'm glad you don't smoke.** Me alegra que *usted no fume (Fam:*
tú no fumes). Is it okay to smoke here? ¿Puedo fumar aquí?

smoker *n* fumador *m*, -dora *f* **ex-smoker** ex-fumador *m*, -dora *f* **heavy ~**
fumador *(-dora)* empedernido *(-da)* **light ~** poco fumador *(-dora)* **moderate**
~ fumador *(-dora)* moderado *(-da)*

smoking *n* fumar **No smoking in here.** Prohibido fumar.

smooth *adj* suave *m&f* **Your is so smooth.** Tu es tan suave. **Your** *(1)* **body**
/ (2) **hand** */ (3)* **skin is so smooth.** Tu *(1)* cuerpo */ (2)* mano */ (3)* piel es tan
suave. **Your** *(1)* **arms** */ (2)* **cheeks** */ (3)* **legs** */ (4)* **shoulders are so smooth.**
Tus *(1)* brazos */ (2)* mejillas */ (3)* piernas */ (4)* hombros son tan suaves.

smoothly *adv* suavemente, bien **I hope everything goes smoothly (for you).**
Espero que todo *le (Fam: te)* salga bien. **Everything went real smoothly.**
Todo salió super bien.

smooth-tongued *adj* con mucha labia

smug *adj* petulante *m&f* **Don't look so smug.** No seas tan petulante.

smuggle *vt* contrabandear **I want to smuggle you back to the States.** Quiero
llevarte de contrabando a los Estados Unidos.

snack *n* botana *f*, tentempié *m*, bocadito *m* **~ bar** bar *m*, cafetería *f* **How**
about a snack? ¿Qué tal un tentempié? **I'd like a snack. How about**
you? Se me antoja un tentempié. ¿Y a *usted (Fam: ti)?* **Let's get a snack.**
Vamos a buscar un tentempié. **Here's a small snack.** Toma un bocadito.
Is there someplace around here where we can get a snack? ¿Hay por
aquí algún lugar donde podamos botanear?

snag *n (problem, complication)* problema *m*, impedimento *m* **There's a snag.**
Hay un problema.

snail *n* caracol *m* **This thing moves like a snail.** Esto se mueve a paso de
tortuga.

snake *n* serpiente *f*, culebra *f* **Are there any (poisonous) snakes around** *(1)*
here? */ (2)* **there?** ¿Hay culebras (venenosas) por *(1)* aquí? */ (2)* ahí?

snakebite *n* mordedura *f* de serpiente

snap *vt (make a snapping sound)* chasquear **If you need me, just snap your**
fingers. Si *usted* me *necesita (Fam: necesitas)*, nomás *chasquee (Fam:*
chasqueas) los dedos.

snap *vi (speak sharply / angrily)* hablar con brusquedad **I didn't mean to**
snap at you. No quise hablarte con brusquedad.

snap *n (simple task)* cosa *f* fácil **Don't worry, it's a snap.** No te preocupes,
es cosa fácil.

Spanish "h" is always silent.

snapshot *n* foto *f* instantánea

snarl *vi* rezongar **You don't have to snarl at me.** No tienes que rezongarme.

sneak *vi* escurrirse, escabullirse ~ **around** vagar ~ **in(to)** meterse a escondidas
~ **out** salirse a escondidas ~ **up** escabullirse

sneakers *n, pl* zapatos *mpl* tenis

sneaky *adj* taimado *m*, -da *f* **That was a sneaky thing to do.** Eso fue muy
taimado.

sneeze *vi* estornudar **In America, when you sneeze, we say "Bless you!".**
What do you say? En los Estados Unidos, cuando estornudas, decimos
"¡Bless you!" ¿Qué dicen ustedes?

snob *n* esnob *m&f*

snoop *vi* curiosear ~ **around** curiosear

snore *vi* roncar **Do you snore?** ¿Roncas? **I snore (sometimes).** Ronco (a
veces). **I hope I don't keep you awake with my snoring.** Ojalá no te
despierten mis ronquidos. **You were snoring.** Estabas roncando.

snorkel *vi* nadar con esnórquel **Where can we snorkel?** ¿Dónde podemos
bucear con esnórquel?

snorkel *adj* para esnorquel ~ **fins** aletas para esnórquel ~ **gear** equipo para
esnórquel ~ **mask** careta para esnórquel

snorkeling *n* nadar con esnórquel **Have you ever gone snorkeling?** ¿Alguna
vez *ha (Fam: has)* nadado con esnórquel? **Let's go snorkeling.** Vamos a
nadar con esnórquel.

snow *vi* nevar **It's snowing!** Está nevando. **It's going to snow (tomorrow).**
(Mañana) Va a nevar .

snow *n* nieve *f*

snowboard *vi* deslizarse en tabla para la nieve

snowboard *n* tabla *f* para la nieve, tabla *f* snowboard

snowboarding *n* deslizarse en tabla para la nieve, snowboard *m* **go** ~ ir a
deslizarse en tabla para la nieve

snowman *n* muñeco *m* de nieve

snowmobile *n* motonieve *f*

snug *adj* cómodo *m*, -da *f* **It's so nice and snug like this.** Estar así es tan
agradable y cómodo.

snuggle (up) *vi* acurrucarse **I** *(1)* **love / *(2)* want to snuggle up with you.**
(1) Me encanta… / *(2)* Quiero… acurrucarme contigo. **It's so nice to**
snuggle up with you. Es tan rico acurrucarse contigo.

so *adv* 1. *(to an indicated extent)* tanto; *(to a high extent)* muy; 2. *(in that*
manner) así; 3. *(likewise)* también ~ **many** tantos, tantas ~ **much** tanto,
tanta **It's so far to** *(1)* **drive / *(2)* walk.** Es muy lejos para *(1)* ir en carro /
(2) ir a pie. **It's still so early.** Todavía es muy temprano. **Do you have to**

Questions about the metric system? See page 417.

leave so soon? ¿ *Se tiene usted (Fam: Te tienes)* que ir tan pronto? **You are so beautiful.** *Es usted (Eres)* tan bonita. **I'm so tired.** Estoy tan cansado *(-da)*. **I (don't) think so.** (No) Lo creo. **I hope so.** Espero que sí. **Is that so?** ¿Ah sí? **So far, so good.** Hasta aquí, muy bien. **So do** *(1)* **I** / *(2)* **we.** *(1)* Yo / *(2)* Nosotros también. **And so on.** Y así sucesivamente. **Please let me know, so that I can plan what to do.** Por favor *avíseme (Fam: avísame)*, para que podamos planear qué hacer. **So what?** ¿Y qué? **So long!** ¡Hasta luego!

soap *n* jabón *m* **bar of** ~ pastilla *f* de jabón **laundry** ~ jabón de lavar **Do you have any soap?** ¿*Tiene usted (Fam: ¿ Tienes)* jabón? **I'd love to rub soap all over you.** Me encantaría jabonarte toda.

sober *adj* sobrio *m*, -ria *f* **stay** ~ mantente sobrio

sober up *idiom* despejarse la borrachera **You have to sober up.** Te tienes que quitar la borrachera.

soccer *n* fútbol *m (See also phrases under* **like, love** *and* **play.***)* ~ **ball** pelota *f* de fútbol ~ **field** campo *m* de fútbol ~ **match** partido *m* de fútbol ~ **team** equipo de *m* fútbol

sociable *adj* sociable *m&f* **I was just trying to be sociable.** Sólo trataba de ser sociable. **Hey, c'mon, be a little more sociable!** ¡Oye, por favor, sé un poco más sociable!

social *adj* 1. *(about society)* social *m&f*; 2. *(about relationships)* social *m&f* ~ **behavior** conducta *f* social ~ **life** vida *f* social ~ **Security** Seguro *m* Social ~ **skills** habilidades *fpl* sociales ~ **visit** visita *f* social

socialize *vi* socializar **I like to socialize with friends.** Me gusta platicar con mis amigos.

socializing *n* socializar **I enjoy socializing with my friends.** Disfruto platicando con mis amigos.

sock *n* calcetín *m* **pair of** ~**s** par de calcetines **warm** ~**s** calcetines calientitos

sofa *n* sofá *m* **I can sleep on the sofa.** Yo puedo dormir en el sofá.

soft *adj* suave *m&f*, terso *m*, -sa *f* ~ **as silk** suave como la seda ~ **drink** refresco *m* ~ **heart** buen corazón *m* ~ **lips** labios *mpl* suaves ~ **touch** suave al tacto **velvety** ~ aterciopelado *m*, -da *f* **Your skin is soft as** *(1)* **velvet.** / *(2)* **a baby.** / *(3)* **a kitten.** Tu piel es suave como *(1)* terciopelo. / *(2)* de bebé. / *(3)* un gatito. **You're soft and round in all the right places.** Eres suave y redondita en todos los lugares adecuados. **I have a soft spot in my heart for** *(1)* **animals.** / *(2)* **cats.** / *(3)* **dogs.** Tengo debilidad por *(1)* los animales. / *(2)* los gatos. / *(3)* los perros.

soft-hearted *adj* de buen corazón

softly *adv* suavemente **I like it when you whisper softly in my ear.** Me gusta cuando me susurras suavemente al oído.

The letter "ñ" sounds like the "ny" in "canyon".

softness *n* suavidad *f* **wonderful ~** suavidad maravillosa **I love the sweet softness of your lips.** Me encanta la dulce suavidad de tus labios.

software *n* software *m*

softy *n (slang)* blandengue *m&f*

soiree *n (evening party)* velada *f*

sojourn *n (stay, visit)* estadía *f*, estancia *f* **brief ~** breve estancia

solace *n* solaz *m*, sosiego *m* **I will know no solace until I see** *(1,2)* **you again.** No voy a tener sosiego hasta que *(1) lo m / (2) la f (Fam: te)* vuelva a ver.

soldier *n* soldado *m&f*

solemn *adj* solemne *m&f* **You look so solemn.** *Parece usted (Fam: Pareces)* tan solemne.

solemnly *adv* solemnemente **I solemnly swear...** Juro solemnemente...

solid *adj* 1. *(strong, sturdy)* sólido *m*, -da *f* ; 2. *(upstanding)* sólido *m*, -da *f* **~ body** cuerpo macizo **~ citizen** ciudadano recto **~ relationship** relación seria **Solid bone and muscle (from the neck up).** Músculos y huesos sólidos (del cuello para arriba.)

solution *n* solución *f* **good ~** buena solución **quick ~** solución rápida **I've got solution (to the problem).** Tengo la solución (al problema.)

solve *vt* resolver **We'll solve the problem somehow.** De algún modo vamos a resolver el problema.

some *adj* 1. *(unspecified amount)* algo de; 2. *(a few)* algunos *m, pl*, algunas *f, pl* ; 3. *(certain ones)* unos *mpl*, unas *fpl* **~ apples** unas manzanas **~ cake** algo de pastel **~ candy** algo de dulce **~ coffee** algo de café **~ people** unas personas **~ places** unos lugares **~ pizza** algo de pizza **~ tickets** unos boletos **Some other time perhaps.** Quizás en otra ocasión.

some *pron* 1. *(certain ones)* unos, unas; 2. *(an amount)* algo **I went with some of my** *(1)* **friends.** / *(2)* **relatives.** Fui con unos *(1)* amigos. / *(2)* parientes. **Would you care for some?** ¿*Le (Fam: ¿Te)* gustaría tomar algo? **I already have some.** Ya tengo.

somebody *pron* alguien *m&f* **~ else** alguien más **somebody's** es de alguien

someday *pron* algún día

somehow *pron* de algún modo / de alguna manera *(1)* **I'll /** *(2)* **We'll manage somehow.** *(1)* Ya me las arreglaré / *(2)* Ya nos las arreglaremos de alguna manera. **Somehow I must see** *(1,2)* **you again.** Sea como sea, tengo que volver a *(1) verlo m / (2) verla f (Fam: verte)*.

someone *pron* alguien **~ else** alguien más **someone's** es de alguien *(1,2)* **Are you with someone?** *(1)* ¿Viene / *(2)* ¿Está usted con alguien? *(1,2)* **I'm with someone.** *(1)* Vengo / *(2)* Estoy con alguien.

something *pron* algo **~ else** algo más **Can I get you something?** ¿Puedo *traerle (Fam: traerte)* algo? **May I ask you something?** ¿Puedo *preguntarle (Fam: preguntarte)* algo? **Something is happening to my heart.** Algo le está pasando a mi corazón. **There's something about you.** Hay algo de *usted (Fam: ti)* que me atrae.

sometime *adv* en algún momento, alguna vez **Call me sometime (when you have a chance).** *Llámeme (Fam: Llámame)* en algún momento (cuando tengas chance.)

sometimes *adv* a veces

somewhat *adv* en cierto modo, una especie de, algo

somewhere *adv* en algún lugar ~ **else** en algún otro lugar

son *n* hijo *m* **older** ~ hijo mayor **oldest** ~ el mayor de los hijos **middle** ~ el hijo de en medio **younger** ~ hijo menor **youngest** ~ el menor de los hijos *(1)* **I** / *(2)* **We have** *(3)* **a son** /*(4)* **two sons.** *(1)* Yo tengo / *(2)* Nosotros tenemos *(3)* un hijo / *(4)* dos hijos. **This is** *(1)* **my** / *(2)* **our son** *(name).* Este es *(1)* mi / *(2)* nuestro hijo ___. **How old is your** (*[1]* **older** / *[2]* **younger) son?** ¿Cuántos años tiene *su (Fam: tu)* hijo (*[1]* mayor / *[2]* menor)? *(1)* **My** / *(2)* **Our** (*[3]* **older** / *[4]* **younger) son is** *(number)* **years old.** *(1)* Mi hijo / *(2)* Nuestro hijo (*[3]* mayor / *[4]* menor) tiene ___ años de edad. *(1)* **Here** / *(2)* **This is a picture of** *(3)* **my** / *(4)* **our son(s).** *(1)* Aquí está… / *(2)* Esta es… una foto de *(3)* mi(s) / *(4)* nuestro(s) hijo(s).

song *n* canción *f* **folk** ~ canción tradicional **love** ~ canción de amor **melody of a** ~ la melodía de una canción **new** ~ canción nueva **old** ~ canción antigua **our (favorite)** ~ nuestra canción (favorita) **popular** ~ canción popular **sing a** ~ cantar una canción **words of a** ~ la letra de una canción **your favorite** ~ *su (Fam: tu)* canción favorita **I** *(1)* **like** / *(2)* **love that song.** Me *(1)* gusta / *(2)* encanta esa canción. **That's my favorite song.** Esa es mi canción favorita. **Do you know that song?** ¿Se sabe usted (Fam: ¿ Te sabes) esa canción? **What's the name of that song?** ¿Cómo se llama esa canción? **The name of that song is** *(name).* Esa canción se llama ___. **That song has a nice melody.** Esa canción tiene una bonita melodía. **Do you know the words to that song?** ¿Se sabe usted (Fam: ¿Te sabes) la letra de esa canción? **Teach me the words to that song.** *Enséñeme (Fam: Enséñame)* la letra de esa canción. **You put a song in my heart.** Tú pusiste una canción en mi corazón.

son-in-law *n* yerno *m*

soon *adv* pronto **as** ~ **as** tan pronto como, en cuanto **sooner** más pronto **I want to see** *(1,2)* **you (again)** *(3)* **soon.** / *(4)* **as soon as possible.** Quiero (volver a) *(1)* verlo *m* / *(2)* verla *f (Fam: verte)* *(3)* pronto. / *(4)* lo más pronto posible. **Let's get together soon.** Véamonos pronto. *(1)* **I** / *(2)* **We have to** *(3)* **leave** / *(4)* **return soon.** *(1)* Tengo que… / *(2)* Tenemos que…

Spanish "o" is pronounced like "o" in "note".

(3) salir / *(4)* regresar pronto. **How soon can you** *(1)* **be there?** / *(2)* **come?** / *(3)* **do it?** / *(4)* **get it?** ¿Qué tan pronto *puede usted (Fam: puedes)* *(1)* estar ahí? / *(2)* venir? / *(3)* hacerlo? / *(4)* conseguirlo? **The sooner, the better.** Mientras más pronto, mejor. **See** *(1,2)* **you soon!** Nos vemos pronto.

soothing *adj* tranquilizante *m&f*, relajante *m&f* **That's very soothing. (Don't stop.)** Eso es muy relajante. (No te detengas.)

sophisticated *adj* sofisticado *m*, -da *f*

sophomore *n* estudiante *m&f* de segundo año ~ **in college** segundo año en la universidad ~ **in high school** segundo año en la prepa

sore *adj* irritado *m*, -da *f* ~ **throat** garganta irritada

sorry *adj* arrepentido *m*, -da *f* **be** ~ estar arrepentido, -da **feel** ~ arrepentirse *(1,2)* **I'm (very) sorry.** *(1)* Estoy (muy) arrepentido *(-da)*. / *(2)* Lo siento (mucho). *(1,2)* **We're (very) sorry.** *(1)* Estamos (muy) arrepentidos. / *(2)* Lo sentimos (mucho). **I'm sorry for what I said.** Lamento lo que dije. **I'm sorry to hear that.** Lamento oír eso. **I'm sorry to say...** Lamento decir…

sort *n* clase *f*, tipo *m* ~ **of** algo, en cierto modo **What sort of job do you have?** ¿Qué tipo de trabajo *tiene usted (Fam: tienes)*? **I was sort of worried.** Estaba algo preocupado. **We were sort of worried.** Estábamos algo preocupados. **It's sort of** *(1)* **cold.** / *(2)* **difficult.** / *(3)* **expensive.** / *(4)* **far.** Está algo *(1)* frío. / *(2)* difícil. / *(3)* caro. / *(4)* lejos.

so-so *adv* más o menos

soul *n* alma *f* **adventurous** ~ alma aventurera **artist's** ~ alma de artista **beautiful** ~ alma hermosa **good** ~ alma buena **happy** ~ alma feliz **honest** ~ alma honesta **passionate** ~ alma apasionada **poet's** ~ alma de poeta **sensitive** ~ alma sensible **simple** ~ alma sencilla **timid** ~ alma tímida **your** ~ *su (Fam: tu)* alma **Your beauty and charm are an elixir to my soul.** Tu belleza y tu encanto son el elixir de mi alma. **I gave my soul to you as soon as I saw you.** Desde que te vi te entregué mi alma. **I want you to open your soul to me.** Quiero que me abras tu corazón. **You bring out the poetry in my soul.** *Usted despierta (Fam: Tú despiertas)* al poeta que hay en mi alma. **I love you with all my heart and soul.** Te amo con toda el alma y todo el corazón. **I guess there's a little bit of gypsy in my soul.** Algo de gitano tiene mi alma.

soulmate *n* alma gemela **You're the perfect soulmate for me.** Tú eres mi alma gemela.

sound *vi* sonar **How does that sound (to you)?** *(1)* ¿Qué tal suena eso? / *(2)* ¿Qué tal *le (Fam: te)* suena eso? **That sounds like** *(1)* **fun.** / *(2)* **a good idea.** / *(3)* **okay (to me).** Suena *(1)* divertido. / *(2)* a que es una buena idea. / *(3)* bien. (Me suena bien.) **That music sounds (so)** *(1)* **beautiful.** / *(2)*

Numbers in parentheses always signal choices.

cool. / (3) **great.** / (4) **melancholy.** / (5) **nice.** / (6) **terrific.** Esa música
suena (tan) (1) hermosa. / (2) buena onda. / (3) súper. / (4) melancólica. /
(5) bonita. / (6) maravillosa.

sound n sonido m **beautiful** ~ sonido hermoso **nice** ~ sonido agradable ~ **of
your laughter** el sonido de *su (Fam: tu)* risa ~ **of your name** el sonido de
su (Fam: tu) nombre ~ **of your voice** el sonido de *su (Fam: tu)* voz **I
savor the sound of your name on my lips.** Me gusta saborear tu nombre.

sour adj agrio m, agria f, ácido m, -da f ~ **grapes** uvas verdes

source n fuente f

sourpuss n (slang) amargado m, -da f, aguafiestas m&f

south adv sur **go** ~ ir al sur

south n sur m **in the** ~ en el sur **to the** ~ al sur

southeast adj sureste m&f, sudeste m&f ~ **part** en la parte sureste

southeast adv sureste, sudeste

southeast n sureste, sudeste **in the** ~ en el sureste

southern adj sureño m, -ña f

southwest adj suroeste m&f, sudoeste m&f ~ **part** en la parte suroeste

southwest adv suroeste, sudoeste

southwest n suroeste m, sudoeste m **in the** ~ en el suroeste

souvenir n souvenir m, recuerdo m **buy some** ~s comprar unos recuerdos

spa n (resort) balneario m, spa m

space n 1. (room; place) espacio m ; 2. (slang) (freedom) espacio m ; 3.
(cosmos) espacio m **I believe in giving a person their space.** Yo pienso
que hay que darles su espacio a las personas.

spacy adj (slang: scatter-brained) andar en la luna, despistado m, -da f

spades n, pl (card) espadas fpl

Spanish adj español m –ñola f

Spanish n (language) español m **I speak Spanish a little.** Hablo un poco de
español. **I don't speak Spanish** (1) **very well.** / (2) **at all.** No hablo español
(1) muy bien. / (2) para nada. **I just know a few words of Spanish.** Solo
sé algunas palabras en español. **What is this called in Spanish?** ¿Cómo
se llama eso en español? **How do you say** _(word)_ **in Spanish?** ¿Cómo
dices ___ en español? **Could you help me learn Spanish?** ¿Me *puede
usted (Fam: puedes)* ayudar a aprender español? **You could help me learn
Spanish (and I could help you learn English).** Tú me ayudas a aprender
español y yo te ayudo a aprender inglés. **Spanish is a beautiful language.**
El español es un bonito idioma.

spare adj de más, de repuesto ~ **tire** llanta de repuesto

spark n chispa f

sparkle vi chispear **I love the way your eyes sparkle when you talk.** Me

---

Spanish "a" is mostly like "a" in "mama".

encanta como te chispean los ojos cuando hablas.

sparkling *adj* chispeante *m&f* **You have such a sparkling personality.** *Tiene usted (Fam: Tú tienes)* una personalidad tan chispeante.

spark plug *n* bujía *f*

speak *vt & vi* hablar **Could you speak a little *(1)* louder, / *(2)* slower, please?** *¿Podría usted (Fam: Podrías)* hablar un poco *(1)* más alto, / *(2)* más despacio, por favor? **Could I speak with you in private?** ¿Podría hablar *con usted (Fam: contigo)* en privado? **Could I speak to *(name)*?** ¿Podría hablar con (___)?. **Do you speak *(1)* English? / *(2)* French? / *(3)* German? / *(4)* Portuguese?** *¿Habla usted (Fam: ¿Hablas) (1)* inglés? / *(2)* francés? / *(3)* alemán? / *(4)* portugués? **I speak a little bit of Spanish.** Hablo un poquito de español. **I don't speak Spanish (very well).** No hablo español (muy bien). **Speak for yourself.** Cuéntame de ti. **Speak of the devil!** ¡Hablando del rey de Roma!

special *adj* especial *m&f* ~ **case** un caso especial ~ **prize** un premio especial ~ **request** una solicitud especial **You are (very) special to me.** Tú eres (muy) especial para mí. **What are you doing tonight?** *(Reply:)* **Nothing special.** ¿Qué *va usted (Fam: vas)* a hacer esta noche? *(R:)* Nada en especial.

specialist *n* especialista *m&f* **You need a specialist for that. And you're in luck - I'm a specialist.** Para eso *necesita usted (Fam: necesitas)* un especialista. Y *está usted (Fam: estás)* de suerte: yo soy especialista.

specialize *vi* especializarse **I specialize in leg massages.** Yo me especializo en masajes para las piernas.

specialty *n* especialidad *f* **Back massages are my specialty.** Los masajes en la espalda son mi especialidad. **That happens to be my specialty.** Sucede que esa es mi especialidad.

spectacular *adj* espectacular *m&f* **That was spectacular!** ¡Eso fue espectacular! **You look spectacular.** *Se ve usted (Fam: Te ves)* espectacular.

spectator *n* espectador *m*, -dora *f*

spectrum *n* espectro *m*, gama *f* ~ **of feelings** una gama de sentimientos

speechless *adj* sin habla **I'm speechless (with awe).** Me dejaste sin habla (de asombro).

speed *n* velocidad *f* ~ **limit** límite de velocidad **Watch your speed.** Cuidado con la velocidad.

speedy *adj* veloz *m&f*, pronto *m*, -ta *f* ~ **recovery** pronta recuperación

spell *vt* deletrear, escribir **How do you spell it?** ¿Cómo lo *deletrea usted (Fam: deletreas)*? **Could you spell it for me?** ¿Me lo *puede usted (Fam: puedes)* deletrear? **You spell it like this...** Se escribe así...

spelunker *n* espeleólogo *m*, -ga *f*

Articles: m = el, f = la, mpl = los, fpl = las

spelunking *n* espeleología *f*

spend *vt* 1. *(money)* gastar; 2. *(time)* pasar ~ **money** gastar dinero ~ **the (whole) night** pasar (toda) la noche ~ **time (together)** pasar tiempo (juntos) **I love to spend time together with you.** Me encanta pasar el tiempo con *usted (Fam: contigo). (1)* **We could spend...** / *(2)* **We're going to spend... the whole week** *(3)* **enjoying each other.** / *(4)* **lying in the sun.** / *(5)* **sightseeing.** / *(6)* **traveling around.** *(1)* Podemos pasar... / *(2)* Vamos a pasar... toda la semana *(3)* disfrutándonos. / *(4)* echados bajo el sol. / *(5)* visitando lugares de interés. / *(6)* viajando.

spender *n* derrochador *m*, -dora *f* **The last of the big-time spenders.** El *(La)* último *(-ma)* de los *(las)* grandes derrochadores *(-ras).*

sphinx *n* esfinge *f*

spice *n* especia *f* **Put a little spice in your life.** Ponle un poco de sabor a tu vida. **They say that girls are made of sugar and spice and everything nice. Is that true of you?** Dicen que las chicas están hechas de azúcar y de especias y de todo lo bonito. ¿Es eso cierto en *su (Fam: tu)* caso?

spice up *idiom* dar sabor **You need someone like me to spice up your life.** Necesitas a alguien como yo para darle sabor a tu vida. **You really spice up my life.** En verdad le das sabor a mi vida.

spider *n* araña *f* ~ **web** telaraña *f*

spiffy *adj* 1. *(smart, dapper, elegant)* elegante *m&f*; 2. *(stylish)* con estilo

spin *vi* dar vueltas **You make my head spin.** Usted hace *(Fam: Tú haces)* que me dé vueltas la cabeza.

spine *n* espina *f* dorsal **Shivers go up and down my spine.** Me suben y bajan escalofríos por la espalda.

spinster *n* solterona *f*

spirit *n* 1. *(animating / vital force)* espíritu *m* ; 2. *(activating / essential principle influencing a person)* espíritu *m* ; 3. *(mood, temper)* ánimo *m* ; 4. *(person with characteristics referred to)* alma *f*; 5. *(supernatural being)* espíritu *m* **adventurous** ~ espíritu aventurero **Christmas** ~ espíritu navideño **evil** ~ espíritu malévolo **free** ~ espíritu libre **holiday** ~ espíritu festivo **human** ~ espíritu humano **in good** ~**s** de buen ánimo **in high** ~**s** con el ánimo elevado **kindred** ~ alma gemela **nomadic** ~ espíritu de nómada **youthful** ~ espíritu jovial **You are such a blithe spirit.** Usted tiene *(Fam:Tú tienes)* un espíritu risueño. **You are sunshine to my spirit.** Usted es *(Fam: Tú eres)* como un sol para mi alma. **You've lifted my spirits** *(1)* **a lot.** / *(2)* **more than I can tell you.** Usted me ha *(Fam: Tú me has)* elevado el espíritu *(1)* bastante. / *(2)* más de lo que puedo contarte.

spiritual *adj* espiritual *m&f* **deeply** ~ profundamente espiritual ~ **awakening** despertar espiritual

---

Spanish "z" is pronounced like "s" in "safe".

spitfire *n (slang)* cascarrabias *m&f*

spite *n*: **in ~ of** a pesar de

splash *vt* salpicar **Don't splash water all over.** No salpiques todo.

splendid *adj (great, fine, wonderful)* espléndido *m*, -da *f* **That's a splendid** *(1)* **idea.** / *(2)* **suggestion.** Esa es una *(1)* idea. / *(2)* sugerencia espléndida.

split up *vi (slang: separate)* separar

splurge *vi* derrochar, darse gusto **Let's splurge tonight. (And have hamburgers.)** Esta noche vamos a derrochar. (Y a comernos unas hamburguesas.)

spoil *vt* 1. *(ruin; mar)* echar a perder, arruinar; 2. *(pamper)* chiquear **I'm sorry. I've spoiled everything.** Lo lamento. Lo he arruinado todo. **You spoiled everything.** Lo arruinaste todo. **I'm going to spoil you** *(1)* **all the time.** / *(2)* **beyond your wildest dreams.** Te voy a chiquear *(1)* todo el tiempo. / *(2)* hasta decir basta. **You spoil me too much.** Me chiqueas demasiado.

spoiled *adj (pampered)* chiqueado *m*, -da *f* **You're a spoiled brat!** ¡Eres un(a) mocoso *(-sa)* chiqueado *(-da)*!

sponsor *vt* patrocinar, respaldar **Perhaps** *(1)* **I** / *(2)* **we could sponsor you.** Tal vez *(1)* yo pueda / *(2)* podamos patrocinarte / respaldarte.

sponsor *n* patrocinador *m*, -dora *f*

spontaneous *adj* espontáneo *m*, -nea *f*

spooky *adj* espeluznante *m&f*, espantoso *m*, -sa *f* **~ house** una casa embrujada **~ place** un lugar espeluznante

spoon *n* cuchara *f*

sport *n* deporte *m* **outdoor ~s** deportes al aire libre **spectator ~s** deportes para espectadores **~ coat** abrigo deportivo **~s car** carro deportivo **~s equipment** equipo deportivo **~ shirt** camisa deportiva **What sports do you** *(1)* **like best?** / *(2)* **play?** ¿Cuáles deportes *(1)* le *(Fam: te)* gustan más? / *(2)* juegas?

sporting *adj* deportivo *m*, -va *f* **~ goods** artículos deportivos **~ goods store** tienda de artículos deportivos

sports-minded *adj* dado *(-da)* al deporte

spot *n* 1. *(place)* zona *f*; *(in the heart)* lugar *m*; 2. *(restaurant; club)* lugar *m*; 3. *(situation)* posición *f*; 4. *(stain, soiled place)* mancha *f* **bald ~** zona de calvicie **cozy ~** lugar acogedor **difficult ~** posición difícil **nice little ~** lugarcito rico **soft ~** *(in the heart)* punto vulnerable **tender ~** *(in the heart)* punto sensible **tight ~** posición apretada **tough ~** posición difícil

spouse *n* esposo *m*, -sa *f* **former ~** el ex-esposo *(m)* la ex-esposa *(f)*

sprain *vt* torcer **I sprained my** *(1)* **ankle.** / *(2)* **wrist.** Me torcí *(1)* el tobillo. / *(2)* la muñeca.

A tilde ~ in terms stands for the main entry word.

spread *vt (lay out)* extender; untar **Spread the blanket** *(1)* **here.** / *(2)* **there.** Extiende la cobija *(1)* aquí. / *(2)* allá. **Let me spread suntan lotion on your back.** Déjame untarte el bronceador en la espalda.

spring *n (season)* primavera *f* **in the** ~ en la primavera **last** ~ la primavera pasada **next** ~ la próxima primavera **the magic of the** ~ la magia de la primavera

springtime *n* en primavera *f* **There is springtime in my heart because of you.** Hay primavera en mi corazón por causa tuya.

spry *adj* lleno *m* (–na *f*) de vida, activo *m*, -va *f* **You're pretty spry for an old** *(1)* **man.** / *(2)* **woman.** Estás muy lleno *(-na)* de vida para ser una *(1,2)* persona mayor.

spunk *n (slang: ardor, spirit)* chispa *f* **You really have a lot of spunk.** De veras tienes mucha chispa.

spy *vi* espiar **I'm spying on you.** Te estoy espiando.

spy *n* espía *m & f* **It's part of my mission as a spy.** Es parte de mi misión como espía. **I'm asking you all these questions because I'm a spy.** Te pregunto todo esto porque soy espía.

square *adj* cuadrado *m*, -da *f*

square *n* 1. *(equilateral rectangle)* cuadrado *m* ; 2. *(town plaza)* plaza *f*

squawk *vi* rezongar, chillar **What are you squawking about?** ¿Por qué rezongas?

squeamish *adj* delicado *m*, -da *f* **Don't be so squeamish.** No seas tan delicado *(-da)*.

squeeze *vt* apretar, estrechar **I love squeezing you.** Me encanta estrecharte. **I like it when you squeeze my hand like that.** Me gusta que me aprietes así la mano.

stable *adj* estable *m&f* **financially** ~ económicamente estable ~ **relationship** una relación estable

stable *n (horses)* establo *m*

stack *n (orderly pile)* pila *f*, montón *m*

stadium *n* estadio *m*

staff *n (personnel)* personal *m*

stage *n (theater platform)* foro *m*

stairs *n, pl* escaleras *fpl* **Let's take the stairs.** Vámonos por la escalera.

stake *n (money bet)* apuesta *f* **We'll play for stakes, okay?** Vamos a jugar por apuestas, ¿está bien? **Those are high stakes.** Esas son grandes apuestas.

stall *vi (delay)* demorarse, dar largas **You're stalling, aren't you?** Me estás dando largas, ¿verdad? **Enough stalling!** ¡Ya deja de darme largas!

stamina *n* resistencia *f*, aguante *m* **You have remarkable stamina.** Tienes tremendo aguante.

Spanish "ch" is pronounced like ours
(e.g., "cheese," "charge").

stamp *n (postage)* timbre *m* postal **collect ~s** filatelia *f*, coleccionar timbres postales **commemorative ~s** timbres postales conmemorativos ~ **collection** colección de timbres postales ~ **collector** filatelista *m&f*, coleccionista de timbres postales **trade ~s** cupones comerciales

stand *vt (tolerate, endure)* soportar **I can't stand the thought of leaving you.** No soporto la idea de dejarte. **I can't stand it!** ¡No lo soporto!

stand *vi* pararse **Stand** *(1)* **closer.** / *(2)* **further back.** / *(3)* **here.** / *(4)* **over there.** / *(5)* **still.** *Párese (Fam: Párate) (1)* más cerca. / *(2)* más atrás. / *(3)* aquí. / *(4)* allá. / *(5)* quieto. **Don't just stand there. (Do something.)** No te quedes ahí parado *(-da)*. (Haz algo).

★ **stand up** *vt idiom (make someone wait in vain)* plantar, dejar plantado *(-da)* **I'm sorry I stood you up.** Disculpa que te planté. **I didn't mean to stand you up.** No era mi intención plantarte. **I won't stand** *(1,2)* **you up, I promise.** No *(1)* lo *m* / *(2)* la *f (Fam: te)* voy a plantar, *se (Fam: te)* lo prometo.

★ **stand up** *vi idiom* ponerse de pie **Stand up (for a minute).** *Póngase (Fam: Ponte)* de pie (un momento).

stand *n (slang: liaison)* relación *f* **I don't like one-night stands.** No me gustan las relaciones de una sola noche. **I don't want (this to be) a one-night stand.** No quiero (que esto sea) una relación de una sola noche.

star *n* estrella *f* **bright ~** estrella brillante **falling ~** estrella fugaz **gaze at the ~s** ver las estrellas **look at the ~s** mirar a las estrellas **lucky ~** estrella de la buena suerte **shooting ~** estrella fugaz **~ of my life** la estrella de mi vida **Aren't the stars beautiful tonight?** ¿No están hermosas las estrellas esta noche? **Let's go outside and gaze at the stars.** Salgamos para ver las estrellas. **Do you know that you have stars in your eyes?** ¿Sabes que tienes estrellas en los ojos? **When I look into your eyes, I see the stars.** Cuando miro tus ojos, veo las estrellas. **I thank my lucky stars that** *(1)* **I met you (in this world).** / *(2)* **you came into my life.** Doy gracias a mi buena estrella *(1)* que te encontré (en este mundo). / *(2)* que llegaste a mi vida. **We say that you can make a wish on the first star you see at night.** Nosotros decimos que al ver la primera estrella de la noche se puede pedir un deseo.

stare *vi* ver, mirar **Forgive me for staring. It's just that you're so beautiful.** Perdóneme que la esté mirando. Es que usted es tan hermosa.

start *vi* empezar **What time does it start?** ¿A qué hora empieza? **It starts at** *(time).* Empieza a las ___. **Let's start.** ¡Comencemos! **They've already started.** Ya comenzaron.

start *n* iniciar **head ~** ventaja inicial *(1)* **I'll** / *(2)* **We'll give you a head start.** Te*(1)* voy a dar / *(2)* vamos a dar una ventaja inicial. **Give** *(1)* **me /**

Stress rule #1: The last syllable is stressed if the word ends in a consonant (except "n" and "s").

(2) **us a head start, okay?** *(1)* Dame / *(2)* Danos una ventaja inicial. ¿Sale?

starting *adj* de arranque, inicial *m&f* ~ **line** línea de arranque ~ **point** punto de arranque

startle *vt* asustar **You startled me.** *Me asustó usted (Fam: Me asustaste).* **I didn't mean to** *(1,2)* **startle you.** No quise *(1)* asustarlo m / *(2)* asustarla f *(Fam: asustarte).*

starved *adj* muerto *(-ta)* de hambre **I'm starved.** Me muero de hambre. **We're starved.** Nos morimos de hambre. **I'm (really) starved for** *(1)* **you.** / *(2)* **love.** / *(3)* **your (sweet) kisses.** Tengo (verdadera) hambre *(1)* de ti. / *(2)* de tu amor. / *(3)* de tus (dulces) besos.

state *n* 1. *(condition)* estado *m* ; 2. *(U.S.)* estado *m* **in a ~ of** *(1,2)* **flux** en estado *(1)* fluctuante / *(2)* fluido *(1)* I / *(2)* **We live in the state of California.** *(1)* Vivo / *(2)* Vivimos en el estado de California. *(1)* **I'm / *(2)* We're from the state of New York.** *(1)* Soy / *(2)* Somos del estado de Nueva York.

station *n* estación *f* **bus ~** terminal *f* de autobuses **metro ~** estación de metro **service ~** *(automot.)* estación de servicio **train ~** estación de trenes **What station are you getting off at?** ¿En cuál estación *se va (Fam: te vas)* a bajar? **I'm getting off at the next station.** Me bajo en la siguiente estación. **What's the next station?** ¿Cuál es la siguiente estación? **The next station is** *(name).* La siguiente estación es ___. **Your station is** *(1)* **the next one.** / *(2)* **the one after next.** / *(3)* **the third** / *(4)* **fourth stop** / *(5)* **still along way.** *Su (Fam: Tu)* estación es (1) la siguiente. / (2) la segunda / (3) la tercera / (4) la cuarta parada. / (5) Falta mucho todavía.

stationed *adj (mil.)* apostado *m* **be ~** estar apostado **I'm stationed at** *(name of base / city).* Estoy apostado en ___.

statue *n* estatua *f (1)* **Who** / *(2)* **What is this statue for?** ¿ *(1)* De quién / *(2)* de qué es esa estatua?

status *n* estado *m* **marital ~** estado civil

stay *vi* quedarse **How long are you going to stay (***[1]* **here** / *[2]* **there** / *[3]* **in** *[place]***)?** ¿Cuánto tiempo *se va usted (Fam: te vas)* a quedar (*[1]* aquí / *[2]* allá / *[3]* en ___)? *(1)* **I'm going to...** / *(2)* **I plan to... stay (***[3]* **here** / *[4]* **there** / *[5]* **in** *[place]***) for** *(amount of time).* *(1)* Me voy a... / *(2)* Pienso.... quedarme (*[3]* aquí / *[4]* allá / *[5]* en ___.) por ___. **Please stay.** Por favor *quédese (Fam: quédate).* **Stay** *(1)* **a (little) longer.** / *(2)* **at my place.** / *(3)* **here.** / *(4)* **with me.** *Quédese (Fam: Quédate) (1)* un (poco) más. / *(2)* en mi casa. / *(3)* aquí. / *(4)* conmigo. **Can you stay?** *¿Se puede usted (Fam: ¿Te puedes)* quedar? **Can you stay** *(1)* **a little longer?** / *(2)* **for another day?** / *(3)* **two more days?** / *(4)* **another week?** *¿Puede usted quedarse (Fam: ¿Puedes quedarte) (1)* un poco más? / *(2)* otro día?

Spanish "i" is mostly "ee", but can also be shorter, like "i" in "sit," when together with other vowels.

/ *(3)* dos días más? / *(4)* otra semana? **Would it be possible for you to stay (with me)** *(1)* **overnight?** / *(2)* **all night?** ¿Sería posible que *se quedara usted (Fam: te quedaras)* (conmigo) *(1)* por la noche? / *(2)* toda la noche? **Would it be possible to stay at your** *(1)* **apartment?** / *(2)* **house?** ¿Sería posible que me quedara en *su (Fam: tu)* *(1)* departamento? / *(2)* casa? **You can(not) stay at my** *(1)* **apartment.** / *(2)* **house.** / *(3)* **hotel.** *Usted (no) puede quedarse (Fam: Tú [no] puedes quedarte)* en mi *(1)* departamento. / *(2)* casa. / *(3)* hotel. **I can(not) stay (a little longer).** (No) Me puedo quedar (más tiempo). **I can stay another** *(1)* **day** / *(2)* **week (if you want).** Puedo quedarme otro *(1)* día / *(2)* semana (si tú quieres). **Let's stay here. Where are you staying?** ¿Dónde *se está quedando usted (Fam: te estás quedando)*? *(1)* **I'm** / *(2)* **We're staying at the** *(hotel name)*. *(1)* Yo me estoy hospedado… / *(2)* Nos estamos hospedados... en el hotel ___. **Where's a good place to stay?** ¿Dónde hay un buen lugar para quedarse? **A good place to stay is** *(hotel name)*. Un buen lugar para quedarse es ___. **You certainly stay in good shape.** De veras que te mantienes en buena forma. **I try to stay** *(1)* **fit.** / *(2)* **in shape.** Trato de mantenerme *(1)* bien . / *(2)* en forma.

★ **stay away** *idiom* mantenerse lejos, alejarse **Stay away from me.** No te me acerques.

★ **stay up** *idiom* quedarse despierto *(1)* **I** / *(2)* **We stayed up all night.** *(1)* Me quedé / *(2)* Nos quedamos despiertos toda la noche.

stay *n* estancia *f* **pleasant ~** estancia agradable *(1)* **I'm** / *(2)* **We're here just for a short stay.** *(1)* Estoy / *(2)* Estamos aquí sólo por una estancia corta.

steady *adj (regular)* estable *m&f* **~ job** un empleo estable

steal *vt* robar **~ a kiss** robar un beso **Someone stole my** *(1)* **bag.** / *(2)* **camera.** / *(3)* **pack.** / *(4)* **passport.** / *(5)* **purse.** / *(6)* **suitcase.** / *(7)* **wallet.** Alguien se robó mi *(1)* bolsa. / *(2)* cámara. / *(3)* paquete. / *(4)* pasaporte. / *(5)* monedero. / *(6)* maleta. / *(7)* cartera. **You've stolen my heart (completely) away.** Me has robado el corazón (por completo.)

steamer, steamship *n* vapor *m*, barco *m* de vapor

steep *adj* empinado *m*, -da *f* **~ cliff** un risco empinado **~ hill** un cerro empinado **~ trail** una vereda empinada **It's too steep (for** *[1]* **me** / *[2]* **us).** Está demasiado empinado (para *[1]* mí / *[2]* nosotros.)

steer *vt* manejar, guiar, conducir **~ around** sacar la vuelta **~ to the left** doblar a la izquierda **~ to the right** doblar a la derecha **Do you want to steer it?** ¿Quiere usted *(Fam:* ¿Quieres) manejarlo?

step *vi* pisar, dar paso **Step carefully (around here).** Pisa con cuidado (por aquí). **Step back.** Paso atrás. **Step forward.** Paso adelante.

step *n* escalón *m*, peldaño *m* **go down the ~s** bajar los escalones **go up the ~s**

subir los escalones

stepbrother *n* hermanastro *m*

stepdaughter *n* hijastra *f*

stepfather *n* padrastro *m*

stepmother *n* madrastra *f*

stepsister *n* hermanastra *f*

stepson *n* hijastro *m*

stern *n (ships)* popa *f*

stick *vt* poner **Could you stick this in your** *(1)* **bag** *(=purse)?* / *(2)* **pocket?** / *(3)* **purse?** / *(4)* **suitcase?** ¿Podrías poner esto en tu *(1)* bolsa? / *(2)* bolsillo? / *(3)* monedero? / *(4)* maleta?

stick *n* bastón *m* **hiking** ~ bastón de excursionismo **walking** ~ bastón

still *adj* 1. *(quiet)* en silencio; 2. *(motionless)* quieto *m*, -ta *f*, en calma *(1,2)* **Be still!** *(1)* ¡Estate quieto! / *(2)* ¡Cállate! **Sit still!** ¡Quédate quieto! **Still waters flow deep.** Las aguas mansas van a lo profundo.

still *adv* aún, todavía **Do you still** *(1)* **love me?** / *(2)* **want to go?** ¿Todavía *(1)* me amas? / *(2)* quieres ir?

stimulating *adj* estimulante *m&f* ~ **conversation** una conversación estimulante

sting *vt* picar **A bee stung me.** Me picó una abeja.

stingy *adj* tacaño *m*, -ña *f* **Don't be stingy (with your kisses).** No seas tacaño (-ña) (con tus besos.)

stink *vi* apestar, heder **It stinks (terribly).** Hiede (horrible.)

stir (up) *vt (feelings)* conmover ~ **feelings** despertar sentimientos de piedra.

stirrup *n* estribo *m*

stock *n (shares in a corporation)* acciones *fpl* **buy** ~ comprar acciones **shares of** ~ valores *m, pl* bursátiles ~ **market** mercado *m* de valores

stocking(s) *n (pl)* media(s) *f (pl)*

stomach *n* estómago *m*, panza *f*, barriga *f* **bare** ~ barriga al desnudo **big** ~ gran barriga **fat** ~ mucha barriga **flat** ~ barriga plana **hard** ~ abdomen *m* duro **little** ~ barriguita **small** ~ poca barriga **scar on my** ~ una cicatriz en la barriga **You have such a flat stomach.** Tienes un abdomen bien plano.

stomachache *n* dolor *m* de estómago ese arroyo?

stone *n* piedra *f* **precious** ~ piedra preciosa **I'm not made of stone.** No soy de piedra.

stool *n* banco *m*, taburete *m* **bar** ~ taburete de bar **small** ~ banquito *m*

stop *vt* dejar **I stopped** *(1)* **drinking** / *(2)* **smoking** *(number)* **years ago.** Dejé *(1)* de beber / *(2)* de fumar hace ___ años. **You really should try to stop smoking. It's the best thing you can do for your health.** En serio, trata de dejar de fumar. Es lo mejor que puedes hacer por tu salud. **I don't**

Spanish "j" is pronounced like "h".

want to stop kissing you. No quiero dejar de besarte. **I will never stop loving you.** Nunca dejaré de amarte. **Stop it!** ¡Déjalo! **Stop doing that!** ¡Deja de hacer eso!

stop *vi* pararse, detenerse **Does the bus for** *(place name)* **stop here?** ¿Esta es la parada del camión que va a ___? **My watch stopped. What time is it?** Mi reloj se detuvo. ¿Qué hora es? **Please stop** *(1)* **here.** / *(2)* **(over) there.** Por favor *deténgase (Fam: détente) (1)* aquí. / *(2)* allá.

stop *n* parada *f* **This is my stop.** Esta es mi parada. **The next stop is mine.** Me bajo en la siguiente .

stoplight *n* semáforo *m*

stopover *n* hacer escala **I** *(1)* **had** *(2)* **will have a stopover in Miami.** *(1)* Hice / *(2)* Voy a hacer una escala en Miami. **We** *(1)* **had** / *(2)* **will have a stopover in Miami.** *(1)* Hicimos / *(2)* Vamos a hacer una escala en Miami.

storage *n* almacenaje *m* *(1)* **Leave** / *(2)* **Put it in (the hotel's) storage.** *(1)* Déjalo / *(2)* Ponlo en almacenaje (en el hotel). *(1)* **I** / *(2)* **We left it in storage.** Lo *(1)* dejé / *(2)* dejamos en el almacenaje.

store *vt* guardar **Where can I store my suitcase?** ¿Dónde puedo guardar mi maleta? **Where can we store our suitcases?** ¿Dónde podemos guardar nuestras maletas?

store *n* tienda *f (See also* **shop***)* **auto parts** ~ tienda de repuestos para auto **clothing** ~ tienda de ropa **department** ~ tienda de departamentos **grocery** ~ tienda de abarrotes **hardware** ~ ferretería *f* **liquor** ~ licorería **music** ~ tienda de música **shoe** ~ zapatería *f* **sporting goods** ~ tienda de artículos deportivos **toy** ~ juguetería *f* **video rental** ~ video centro

storm *n* tormenta *f* ~ **of sensations** un mar de sensaciones **There's a storm coming.** Viene una tormenta.

story *n* cuento *m*, historia *f*, chiste *m* **dirty** ~ chiste pelado **fascinating** ~ historia fascinante **funny** ~ *(amusing)* cuento divertido **interesting** ~ historia interesante **love** ~ historia de amor **sad** ~ historia triste **short** ~ cuento breve ~ **with a happy ending** cuento con un final feliz **strange** ~ historia extraña *(1)* **I want to hear...** / *(2)* **Tell me... the story of your life.** *(1)* Quiero conocer … / *(2)* Cuéntame … la historia de tu vida. **That's the story of my life.** *(ironic)* Esa es la historia de mi vida. **It's a long story.** Es largo de contar. **To make a long story short...** Para no hacer el cuento largo... **That's a different story.** Ese es otro cuento.

stove *n* estufa *f* **camping** ~ estufa de campismo **gas** ~ estufa de gas **wood** ~ estufa de leña

straight *adj* 1. *(not curved)* recto *m*, -ta *f* ; 2. *(direct, candid)* directo *m*, directa *f*; 3. *(slang) (not homosexual)* heterosexual *m&f* **It's straight ahead.** Es aquí recto. **Give me a straight answer.** Dame una respuesta directa.

Familiar "tu" forms in parentheses can replace italicized polite forms.

straight *adv* en línea recta **Go straight (ahead).** Sigue (adelante) en línea recta .

strain *n* tensión *f*, preocupación *f* **That's too much of a strain (for you).** Es demasiada tensión (para ti). **I've been under a lot of strain.** He estado bajo mucha tensión.

strait jacket *n* camisa *f* de fuerza **I'm ready for a strait jacket.** Estoy listo para la camisa de fuerza. **I think we need to get you into a strait jacket.** Creo que necesitamos ponerte una camisa de fuerza.

stranded *adj* varado *m*, -da *f* *(1)* **I was...** / *(2)* **We were... stranded there for** *(3)* **two** / *(4)* **three** / *(5)* **four** *(6)* **hours.** / *(7)* **days.** / *(8)* **a week.** *(1)* Me quedé varado… / *(2)* Nos quedamos varados... allí por *(3)* dos / *(4)* tres / *(5)* cuatro *(6)* horas. / *(7)* días. / *(8)* una semana.

strange *adj (1. odd, bizarre; 2. unfamiliar)* raro *m*, -ra *f*, extraño *m*, -ña *f* ~ **country** país extraño ~ **place** lugar extraño **A strange thing happened.** Pasó algo raro. **How strange.** Qué raro. **Strange as it may seem...** Por extraño que parezca… **You want to hear something strange?** ¿Quiere usted *(Fam: Quieres)* oír algo raro? **Everything is so strange.** Todo es tan extraño.

strangely *adv* de modo raro **act** ~ actuar raro

stranger *n* extraño *m*, -ña *f*, desconocido *m*, -da *f* ; *(from another place)* extranjero *m*, -ra *f*, forastero *m*, -ra *f* **complete** ~ completamente desconocido *(-da)* **perfect** ~ perfecto desconocido *(-da)* **~s in the night** extraños en la noche **total** ~ total extraño *(-ña)*

strap *n* 1. *(general)* cinta *f*; 2. *(shoulder strap)* correa *f*; 3. *(undergarments)* tirante *m* **pack** ~ correa de la maleta **My (pack) strap is torn.** Se rompió la correa de mi maleta.

streak *n* 1. *(characteristic; disposition)* lado *m* ; 2. *(hair with color)* rayo *m* **blonde** ~ rayo rubio **grey** ~ rayo gris **mean** ~ lado mezquino **nervous** ~ lado nervioso **reddish** ~ rayo rojizo **romantic** ~ lado romántico **wild** ~ lado loco

stream *n* 1. *(small river)* arroyo *m*; 2. *(copious flow)* torrente *m* **cross a** ~ cruzar un arroyo **~ of kisses** un torrente de besos **~ of sensations** un torrente de sensaciones **Can we fish in that stream?** ¿Podemos pescar en ese arroyo?

street *n* calle *f* **Which street** *(1)* **do you live on?** / *(2)* **is it located on?** ¿En qué calle *(1)* vive usted *(Fam: vives)*? / *(2)* se encuentra ubicado?

streetcar *n* tranvía *m*

strength *n* fuerza *f*, fortaleza *f* **emotional** ~ fortaleza emocional **great** ~ una gran fuerza **inner** ~ fortaleza interior **physical** ~ fuerza física **spiritual** ~ fortaleza espiritual **I admire** *(1,2)* **you for your strength.** *(1)* Lo *m* / *(2)* La *f (Fam: Te)* admiro por *su (Fam: tu)* fortaleza. **You have a lot of**

Spanish "e" is pronounced like English "e" in "get"

strength. *Tiene usted (Fam: Tú tienes)* mucha fuerza. **My strength is gone.** Se me acabaron las fuerzas. **Give me strength.** *(humorous)* Dame fuerzas.

strenuous *adj* agotador *m*, -dora *f* ~ **climb** escalada agotadora ~ **hike** caminata agotadora ~ **trail** sendero agotador

stress *n* estrés *m* **I'm under a lot of stress (in my work).** Estoy bajo mucho estrés (en mi trabajo).

stretch *vt* estirar, retorcer ~ **the truth** retorcer la verdad

stretch out *idiom* estirarse **I want to stretch out for a little bit.** Quiero estirarme un poco.

strict *adj* estricto *m*, -ta *f*

strictly *adv* estrictamente **This will be strictly by the rules. (My rules.)** Esto será en estricto apego a las reglas. (Mis reglas.) **That's strictly forbidden.** Está estrictamente prohibido.

strike *vt* golpear **Strike the ball like this.** Golpea la pelota así. **I was instantly struck by your** *(1)* **beauty.** / *(2)* **charm.** Yo quedé inme-diatamente impactado por *su (Fam: tu) (1)* belleza. / *(2)* encanto.

striking *adj* impactante *m&f* **You're a woman of striking beauty.** *Es usted (Tú eres)* una mujer de belleza impactante. **That's a striking outfit (that you're wearing).** Ese atuendo (que *usted trae(Fam: tú traes)* es impactante.

string *n* 1. *(for tying)* cordel *m* ; 2. *(thread)* sarta *f* ; 3. *pl (conditions)* compromisos *m, pl* ~ **of beads** sarta de cuentas ~ **of pearls** sarta de perlas **No strings attached.** Sin compromisos.

striptease *n* striptease *m* **Will you do a striptease for me?** ¿Me haces un striptease? **If you want, I'll do a striptease for you.** Si quieres, te hago un striptease.

stroke *vt* acariciar

stroll *vi* pasearse **I like to stroll with you like this.** Me gusta pasear así contigo. **Let's stroll around the** *(1)* **park** / *(2)* **town.** Vamos a pasear por *(1)* el parque. / *(2)* la ciudad.

stroll *n* paseo *m* **moonlight** ~ paseo a la luz de la luna **Would you like to go for a stroll?** ¿Le *(Fam: ¿Te)* gustaría dar un paseo? **Let's take a stroll along the beach.** Vamos a pasear por la playa.

strong *adj* fuerte *m&f*, firme *m&f* ~ **belief** creencia firme ~ **faith** mucha fe ~ **enough** suficientemente fuerte **You're very strong.** *Usted es (Fam: Tú eres)* muy fuerte. **My love for you grows stronger every day.** Mi amor por ti se fortalece cada día.

struggle *n* lucha *f* **What a struggle!** ¡Qué lucha!

stubborn *adj* necio *m*, -cia *f*, testarudo *m*, -da *f* **Don't be so stubborn.** No seas tan necio. **You're (*[1]* awfully / *[2]* so) stubborn.** Eres (*[1]*

Stress rule # 2: The next-to-last syllable is stress in words ending in "n", "s" or a vowel.

terriblemente / *[2]* tan) necio.

stuck *adj* 1. *(jammed)* atascado *m*, -da *f*; 2. *(bogged down)* atorado *m*, -da *f*; 3. *(stranded)* atorado *m*, -da *f* **It's stuck. (It won't *[1]* move. / *[2]* open. / *[3]* work.)** Está atorado. (No *[1]* se mueve. / *[2]* se abre. / *[3]* funciona.) **The car is stuck (in the *[1]* mud / *[2]* sand / *[3]* snow).** El carro está atascado (en *[1]* el lodo / *[2]* la arena / *[3]* la nieve.) **We're stuck here (for today).** Estamos atorados aquí (por hoy).

stuck-up *adj (colloq.)* estirado *m*, -da *f*, creído *m*, -da *f*

student *n* estudiante *m&f* **high school** ~ estudiante de prepa **university** ~ estudiante universitario

studio *n* estudio *m* **photo** ~ foto estudio

study *vt* 1. *(a subject)* estudiar; 2. *(observe)* estudiar *(1)* **What... / *(2)* What subjects... are you studying (at the university)?** *(1)* ¿Qué… / *(2)* ¿Cuáles materias… *está usted (Fam: estás)* estudiando (en la universidad)? **I'm studying *(1)* architecture. / *(2)* art. / *(3)* business. / *(4)* chemical engineering. / *(5)* computer science. / *(6)* dentistry. / *(7)* economics. / *(8)* education. / *(9)* English. / *(10)* history. / *(11)* law. / *(12)* mathematics. / *(13)* mechanical engineering. / *(14)* medicine. / *(15)* music./ *(16)* physics. / *(17)* psychology. / *(18)* sociology. / *(19)* (subject).** Estoy estudiando *(1)* arquitectura. / *(2)* arte. / *(3)* comercio. / *(4)* ingeniería química. / *(5)* ciencias de la computación. / *(6)* odontología. / *(7)* economía. / *(8)* educación. / *(9)* inglés. / *(10)* historia. / *(11)* derecho. / *(12)* matemáticas. / *(13)* ingeniería mecánica. / *(14)* medicina. / *(15)* música. / *(16)* física. / *(17)* psicología. / *(18)* sociología. / *(19)* ___ . **I was studying *(1,2)* you from across the room.** *(1)* Lo *m* / *(2)* La *f (Fam: Te)* estaba estudiando desde el otro lado del salón.

study *vi* estudiar **What university *(1)* did / *(2)* do you study at?** ¿En qué universidad *(1) estudió usted (Fam: estudiaste)*? / *(2) estudia usted (Fam: estudias)*? **I study at (name) university.** Estudio en la universidad de ___.

stuff *n* 1. *(things)* cosas *fpl* ; 2. *(merchandise)* cosas *fpl*; 3. *(matters)* cosas *fpl* **Whose stuff is this?** ¿De quién son estas cosas? **I have to get my stuff.** Tengo que traer mis cosas. *(1)* **I / *(2)* We need to buy some stuff.** *(1)* Tengo / *(2)* Tenemos que comprar unas cosas. **I've got some stuff to take care of.** Tengo unas cosas que atender.

stuffed *adj (slang: full of food)* lleno *m*, -na *f* **I can't eat anymore. I'm stuffed.** Ya no puedo comer más. Estoy lleno *(-na)*.

stuffy *adj* sofocante *m&f* **Does it seem stuffy in here to you?** ¿Le *(Fam: ¿Te)* parece que está muy sofocante aquí?

stumbler *n* tropezoso *m*, -sa *f* **A good stumbler never falls.** Quien bien

---

Spanish "x" is always like "ks", as in our word "taxi".

tropieza jamás se cae.

stunning *adj* despampanante *m&f* **You look (absolutely) stunning (in that**
[1] **dress /** *[2]* **outfit).** *Se ve (Fam: Te ves)* (absolutamente) despampanante
(con ese *[1]* vestido / *[2]* atuendo).

stunt *n* proeza *f* **acrobatic** ~ proeza acrobática

stupid *adj* tonto *m*, -ta *f* ~ **idea** idea *f* tonta ~ **mistake** error *m* tonto ~
remark comentario *m* tonto ~ **thing** cosa *f* tonta **That was a stupid thing
I** *(1)* **said. /** *(2)* **did.** *(1)* Dije… / *(2)* Hice ... una tontería. **That was a
stupid thing you** *(1)* **said. /** *(2)* **did.** Eso que *(1)* dijiste / *(2)* hiciste fue una
tontería. **I'm so stupid.** Soy tan tonto *(-ta).*

style *n* 1. *(way)* estilo *m*; 2. *(chic, class)* estilo *m*; *(taste)* estilo *m*; 3. *(fashion)* estilo *m* **elegant** ~ estilo elegante **hair** ~ estilo de peinado **latest** ~ el
último estilo **modern** ~ estilo moderno **new** ~ nuevo estilo **nice** ~ estilo
bonito **old** ~ estilo antiguo **simple** ~ estilo simple ~ **of living** estilo de vida
I (really) like your style. Me gusta (mucho) tu estilo.

stylish *adj* elegante *m & f*, con estilo

suave *adj* sofisticado *m*, -da *f*, elegante *m&f* ~ **manner** forma sofisticada

subconscious *adj* subconsciente *m&f*

subconsciously *adv* subconscientemente **Subconsciously you want to throw
yourself at me.** Subconscientemente te me quieres tirar encima.

subdued *adj* deprimido *m*, -da *f* ~ **mood** ánimo deprimido

subject *n* 1. *(topic)* tema *m*, asunto *m* ; 2. *(course of study)* materia *f*
dangerous *(1,2)* ~ *(1)* tema / *(2)* asunto peligroso **deep** *(1,2)* ~ *(1)* tema /
(2) asunto profundo **delicate** *(1,2)* ~ *(1)* tema / *(2)* asunto delicado **favorite**
~ tema favorito, materia favorita **great** ~ gran tema **interesting** *(1,2)* ~ *(1)*
tema / *(2)* asunto interesante **main** ~ tema principal **required** ~ materia
obligada **safe(r)** *(1,2)* ~ *(1)* tema / *(2)* asunto (más) seguro **taboo** ~ tema
tabú **touchy** *(1,2)* ~ *(1)* tema / *(2)* asunto delicado **unpleasant** ~ asunto
desagradable **What subjects are you taking?** ¿Qué materias estás
tomando? **What's your favorite subject?** ¿Cuál es tu materia favorita?
My favorite subject is *(name)*. Mi materia favorita es ___.

submit *vt (present)* presentar ~ **an application** presentar una solicitud

substitute *vi* sustituir *(1)* **I'll /** *(2)* **You'll substitute for** *(name)*. *(games) (1)*
Yo sustituyo... / *(2)* Tú sustituyes... a ___.

substitute *n* sustituto *m*, -ta *f*

subtle *adj* sutil *m&f* ~ **difference** la diferencia sutil

subway *n* metro *m* ~ **fare** tarifa del metro ~ **line** línea del metro ~ **station**
estación del metro ~ **ticket** boleto del metro ~ **train** ferrocarril subterráneo
Let's take the subway. Vamos a tomar el metro. **How much does the
subway cost?** ¿Cuánto cuesta el metro? **Which subway line do** *(1)* **I /** *(2)*

---

*Stress rule # 3: Syllables with accent marks
have the stress there.*

we take? ¿Cuál línea del metro *(1)* tomo? / *(2)* tomamos?

succeed *vi* 1. *(achieve a certain goal)* tener éxito; 2. *(achieve success)* tener éxito **I'm sure you'll succeed in your effort.** Estoy seguro de que *usted tendrá (Fam: tendrás)* éxito en *su (Fam: tu)* esfuerzo. **If at first you don't succeed, try, try again.** Si al principio no puedes, intenta una y otra vez. **I hope our plan succeeds.** Espero que nuestro plan funcione. **Congratulations! You succeeded (in waking me up)!** ¡Te felicito! ¡Pudiste (despertarme)!

success *n* éxito *m* **achieve ~** lograr éxito **great ~** gran éxito **have ~** tener éxito **~ in life** éxito en la vida **Did you have any success?** ¿Tuvo *(Fam: ¿Tuviste)* éxito? **No success.** Sin éxito. **I wish you success.** Le *(Fam: Te)* deseo éxito.

successful *adj* exitoso *m*, -sa *f*

successfully *adv* exitosamente

succulent *adj* suculento *m*, -ta *f*

such *adj & adv* tal, tan **~ as** tal como **You're such a nice person.** Usted es *(Fam: Tú eres)* una persona tan agradable. **It's such a pleasure talking with you.** Es tan agradable platicar *con usted (Fam: contigo)*. **It's such a beautiful day.** Es un día tan bonito. **It's such a pity you can't go. Are you sure?** Es una lástima que no puedas ir. ¿Estás seguro *(-ra)*? **Have you ever seen such a thing?** ¿Alguna vez *había usted (Fam: ¿Habías)* visto tal cosa? **I've never heard of such a thing.** Nunca había oído tal cosa.

sucker *n (slang) (dupe)* imbécil *m&f* **I guess I'm a sucker for a pretty face.** Creo que me pongo imbécil ante una cara bonita. **What a sucker I was!** ¡Qué imbécil fui yo!

sudden *adj* repentino *m*, -na *f* **~ decision** decisión repentina **Why the sudden change of mind?** ¿Por qué el cambio tan repentino?

suddenly *adv* de repente, repentinamente **It all happened suddenly.** Todo sucedió de repente.

suffer *vi* sufrir, padecer **You don't want me to suffer (from a broken heart), do you?** Tú no quieres que me muera (de amor), ¿verdad? **I'm suffering terribly.** Sufro terriblemente. **If you don't want me to suffer, you'll meet me (for dinner) tonight.** Si *usted no quiere (Fam: tú no quieres)* que yo sufra, *se reunirá (Fam: te reunirás)* conmigo (para cenar) esta noche.

sugar *n* 1. *(sweet substance)* azúcar *m or f*; 2. *(slang) (kisses)* cariñito *m* **Do you want some sugar?** ¿Quieres un cariñito? **Give me some sugar.** Hazme un cariñito.

suggest *vt* sugerir **What do you suggest?** ¿Qué *sugiere usted (Fam: sugieres tú)*? **I suggest...** Yo sugiero…

suggestion *n* sugerencia *f* **brilliant ~** sugerencia brillante **good ~** buena

Spanish pronunciation rules are on pages 407-408.

sugerencia **great** ~ sugerencia genial **wonderful** ~ sugerencia maravillosa **I'd like to make a suggestion.** Me gustaría hacer una sugerencia.

suit *vt* quedar **How does that suit you?** ¿Cómo *le (Fam: te)* queda? **That suits me (fine).** Me queda (bien.)

suit *n* traje *m* **bathing** ~ traje de baño **beautiful** ~ traje bonito **black** ~ traje negro **dark** ~ traje oscuro **dark blue** ~ traje azul oscuro **swim(ming)** ~ traje de natación **wet** ~ traje de neopreno

suitable *adj* adecuado *m*, -da *f*

suitcase *n* maleta *f* **I have to get my** *(1)* **suitcase.** / *(2)* **suitcases.** Tengo que ir por *(1)* mi maleta. / *(2)* mis maletas. **Let's put our suitcases in storage.** Vamos a poner nuestras maletas en resguardo.

suite *n* suite *f* **honeymoon** ~ suite nupcial

suited *adj* adecuado *m*, -da *f* **I think you and I are perfectly suited to each other.** Creo que tú y yo estamos hechos el uno para el otro.

sulk *vi* enfurruñarse **What are you sulking about?** ¿De qué te enfurruñas? **Stop sulking!** ¡Deja de enfurruñarte!

sullen *adj* malhumorado *m*, -da *f* **What a sullen expression!** ¡Qué expresión tan malhumorada!

sultry *adj* voluptuoso *m*, -sa *f*

summer *n* verano *m* **in the** ~ en el verano **last** ~ verano pasado **next** ~ próximo verano

summertime *n* verano *m*

sump *n* pozo *m (1)* negro / *(2)* séptico

sun *n* sol *m* **in the** ~ en el sol ~ **hat** sombrero *m* para el sol ~ **screen** bloqueador *m* solar ~ **umbrella** parasol *m* **Let's lie in the sun for a while.** Vamos a echarnos bajo el sol un rato. **That sun feels (so) good.** El sol se siente (tan) rico. **Don't** *(1)* **lie /** *(2)* **stay in the sun too long.** No *(1)* se eche usted *(Fam: te eches)* / *(2)* se quede usted *(Fam: te quedes)* mucho rato al sol. **Let's get up early and watch the sun rise.** Vamos a levantarnos temprano a ver la salida del sol.

sunbathe *vi* darse baños de sol **Let's go sunbathe for a while.** Vamos un rato a darnos un baño de sol .

sunblock *n* bloqueador *m* solar

sunburn *n* quemadura *f* de sol **bad** ~ tremenda quemadura de sol **slight** ~ leve quemadura de sol **I've got a sunburn (on my** *[1]* **back /** *[2]* **shoulders).** Tengo una quemadura de sol (en *[1]* la espalda / *[2]* los hombros). **You've got a sunburn (on your** *[1]* **back /** *[2]* **shoulders).** *Usted tiene (Fam: Tú tienes)* una quemadura de sol (en *[1]* la espalda / *[2]* los hombros). **Do you have any** *(1)* **lotion /** *(2)* **salve for a sunburn?** ¿*Tiene usted (Fam: ¿Tienes) (1)* alguna loción / *(2)* algún ungüento para una

---

Some Spanish words have accented and unaccented forms to differentiate their meanings (e.g., el = the, él = he).

quemadura de sol? **Here, put some of this on your sunburn.** *Tenga (Fam: Ten), póngase (Fam: ponte) un poco de esto en su (Fam: tu) quemadura de sol.*

sunburned, sunburnt *adj:* **be ~** tener quemaduras del sol **Your back is sunburned.** *Tiene usted (Fam: Tienes) la espalda quemada del sol.* **Be careful** *(1,2)* **you don't get sunburned.** *Cuidado se quema usted (Fam: te quemas) con el sol.*

Sunday *n* domingo *m* **last ~** el domingo pasado **next ~** el próximo domingo **on ~** el domingo

sunglasses *n, pl* lentes *mpl* para el sol **stylish ~** lentes para el sol elegantes **You'd better wear sunglasses.** *Será mejor que se ponga usted (Fam: te pongas) lentes para el sol.*

sunlight *n* luz *f* solar

sunny *adj* soleado *m*, -da *f* **~ day** día soleado **~ disposition** disposición alegre **~ smile** sonrisa radiante **~ weather** clima soleado **I love your sunny smile.** *Me encanta su (Fam: tu) radiante sonrisa.*

sunrise *n* amanecer *m*, salida *f* del sol **What a glorious sunrise!** *¡Qué espléndido amanecer!*

sunset *n* atardecer *m*, puesta *f* del sol, ocaso *m* **What a** *(1)* **beautiful /** *(2)* **magnificent sunset!** *¡Qué (1) hermoso / (2) magnífico atardecer!*

sunshine *n* sol *m*, luz *f* de sol **Let's take advantage of this beautiful sunshine.** *Aprovechemos este sol tan precioso.* **You are my sunshine.** *Tú eres mi sol.* **You bring so much sunshine into my life.** *Tú le has dado tanta luz a mi vida.* **I love the sunshine of your smile.** *Me encanta la luz de su (Fam: tu) sonrisa.* **I want to bask forever in the warmth of your sunshine.** *Quiero gozar para siempre el calor de tu luz.* **The sunshine of your love has melted away all my loneliness.** *La luz de tu amor ha derretido mi soledad.*

suntan *n* bronceado *m* **~ lotion** loción *f* bronceadora **You've got a great suntan.** *Tiene usted (Fam: Tienes) un bronceado muy bonito.* **Let me put some suntan lotion on you.** *Déjame ponerte loción bronceadora.* **Let me put some suntan lotion on your** *(1)* **back. /** *(2)* **shoulders.** *Déjame ponerte loción bronceadora en (1) la espalda. / (2) los hombros.*

suntanned *adj* bronceado *m*, -da *f*

super *adj* súper *m&f*, genial *m&f* **That's super!** *¡Eso es genial!* **That would be super!** *¡Eso sería súper!*

superb *adj* magnífico *m*, -ca *f* **~ body** un cuerpo magnífico **~ physique** un físico magnífico

superior *adj* superior *m&f*, mejor *m&f* **~ skill** habilidad superior **~ technique** técnica superior

---

*Spanish ' g" is like "h" in front of "e" and "i".
In front of other vowels it's like our "g" in "gun".*

superiority *n* superioridad *f* **Time to demonstrate** *(1)* **my /** *(2)* **our superiority again.** Es hora de volver a demostrar *(1)* mi /*(2)* nuestra superioridad.

supermarket *n* supermercado *m* **Is there a supermarket around here?** ¿Hay algún supermercado por aquí?

supernatural *adj* sobrenatural *m&f*

superstition *n* superstición *f* **We have an old superstition about knocking three times on wood to chase away evil spirits who might be listening and might become envious and cause us harm.** Tenemos una vieja superstición que es tocar madera tres veces para alejar a los malos espíritus que pudieran estar escuchando con envidia y hacernos un mal.

superstitious *adj* supersticioso *m*, -sa *f* **Are you superstitious?** ¿Es usted *(Fam: ¿Eres)* supersticioso *(-sa)*? **I'm (not) superstitious.** (No) Soy supersticioso *(-sa)*.

supervise *vt* supervisar **I'll supervise.** Yo superviso.

supervisor *n* supervisor *m*, -sora *f*

supper *n* merienda *f* **Time for supper.** Hora de merendar. **Let's go have supper.** Vamos a merendar.

supple *adj* ágil *m&f*, flexible *m&f* **You're so lithe and supple.** *Usted es (Fam: Tú eres)* tan ágil y flexible.

supplies *n, pl (provisions)* provisiones *fpl* **We'll need supplies for** *(1)* **three /** *(2)* **four days. /** *(3)* **a week. /** *(4)* **two weeks.** Vamos a necesitar provisiones para *(1)* tres / *(2)* cuatro días. / *(3)* una semana. / *(4)* dos semanas.

support *vt* 1. *(hold up)* sostener, apoyar; 2. *(provide for)* mantener ~ **a child** apoyar a un hijo ~ **a family** mantener una familia ~ **children** mantener a los hijos **I have to support my** *(1)* **father. /** *(2)* **son. /** *(3)* **daughter. /** *(4)* **mother. /** *(5)* **children. /** *(6)* **parents.** Tengo que mantener a *(1)* mi padre. / *(2)* mi hijo. / *(3)* mi hija. / *(4)* mi madre. / *(5)* mis hijos. / *(6)* mis padres.

support *n* 1. *(holding up)* soporte *m* ; 2. *(financial)* ayuda *f*, apoyo *m* **child ~** ayuda para menores **financial ~** apoyo financiero **moral ~** apoyo moral **Thanks for your (moral) support.** Gracias por tu apoyo (moral).

suppose *vt* suponer, creer **What do you suppose will happen?** ¿Qué supones *or* crees que va a pasar? **I suppose…** Supongo… **I** *(1,2)* **suppose so.** Así lo *(1)* supongo. / *(2)* creo.

supposed *adj (expected, should)* supuesto *m*, -ta *f* **You're supposed to laugh.** Se supone que *le (Fam: te)* da risa. **What am I supposed to do?** ¿Qué se supone que debo hacer? **What are we supposed to do?** ¿Qué se supone que debemos hacer? **You're supposed to…** Se supone que *usted (Fam: tú)*… **You're not supposed to look.** Se supone que no debes mirar. **It's supposed to** *(1)* **be nice. /** *(2)* **rain.** Se supone que va *(1)* a estar bien. / *(2)* a llover.

English-Spanish and Spanish-English glossaries of food and drink are on pages 420-427.

supreme *adj* supremo *m*, -ma *f* ~ **achievement** logro supremo ~ **delight** deleite supremo ~ **mastery** maestría suprema

surcharge *n* recargo *m*

sure *adj* seguro *m*, -ra *f* **for** ~ seguramente **know for** ~ saber con seguridad **make** ~ asegurarse *(1,2)* **Sure!** *(1)* ¡Seguro! / *(2)* ¡Claro! **Are you sure?** ¿Está usted (Fam: ¿Estás) seguro *(-ra)*? **I'm (not) sure.** (No) Estoy seguro *(-ra)*. **We're (not) sure.** (No) Estamos seguros *(-ras)*.

surely *adv* seguramente, sin duda **slowly but** ~ lento pero seguro

surf *vi* navegar, hacer surf ~ **the internet** navegar por Internet **Let's go surfing.** Vamos a hacer surf. **I'll teach you how to surf.** Yo le *(Fam: te)* enseño a hacer surf.

surf *n* oleaje *m*

surface *n* superficie *f* **on the** ~ en apariencia

surfboard *n* tabla *f* de surf

surfing *n* surf(eo) *m*

surprise *vt* sorprender, dar una sorpresa *(1)* **I** / *(2)* **We want to** *(3,4)* **surprise you.** *(1)* Quiero / *(2)* Queremos *(3)darle* / *(4)* *(Fam: darte)*una sorpresa. **You surprised** *(1)* **me.** / *(2)* **us.** *(1)* Me / *(2)* Nos *sorprendió usted (Fam: sorprendiste)*.

surprise *n* sorpresa *f* ~ **party** fiesta sorpresa **Here's a little surprise for you.** Esta es una pequeña sorpresa para *usted (Fam: ti)*. **What a** *(1)* **big** / *(2)* **delightful** / *(3)* **lovely** / *(4)* **nice** / *(5)* **pleasant** / *(6)* **wonderful surprise!** ¡Qué sorpresa tan *(1)* grande! / *(2)* deliciosa! / *(3)* encantadora! / *(4)* bonita! / *(5)* agradable! / *(6)* maravillosa! **You're full of surprises.** Eres un estuche de sorpresas. **It's a surprise.** Es una sorpresa. **You took me by surprise.** *Usted me tomó (Fam: Me tomaste)* de sorpresa.

surprised *adj* sorprendido *m*, -da *f* **Are you surprised?** ¿Te sorprende? **I'm (really) surprised.** Estoy (de veras) sorprendido *(-da)*. **I was completely surprised.** Estaba sorprendido *(-da)* por completo. **You'll be surprised.** *Le (Fam: Te)* va a sorprender.

surprising *adj* sorprendente *m&f* **That's (not) surprising.** Eso (no) es sorprendente.

surrounding *adj* circundante *m&f* ~ **area** la zona circundante ~ **countryside** el campo circundante

survive *vt* sobrevivir **Believe it or not, we survived the** *(1)* **climb.** / *(2)* **hike.** / *(3)* **hill.** Aunque no lo creas, sobrevivimos la *(1)* escalada. / *(2)* caminata. / *(3)* colina.

survive *vi* sobrevivir **Somehow we managed to survive.** De algún modo nos las arreglamos para sobrevivir.

survivor *n* sobreviviente *m&f*

---

suspect *vt* sospechar **Surely you don't suspect me!** ¡No vas a sospechar de mí! **How could you possibly suspect me?** ¿Cómo pudiste sospechar de mí?

suspense *n* suspenso *m* **The suspense is killing** *(1)* **me.** / *(2)* **us.** El suspenso *(1)* me / *(2)* nos está matando. **Don't keep** *(1)* **me** / *(2)* **us in suspense.** No *(1)* me / *(2)* nos tengas en suspenso.

suspicion *n* sospecha *f* **You realize you're under suspicion.** Te das cuenta de que estás bajo sospecha.

suspicious *adj* suspicaz *m&f*, sospechoso *m*, -sa *f* **You have a suspicious look on your face.** Tienes una mirada sospechosa. **There's something suspicious going on here.** Ahí está pasando algo sospechoso. **Don't be so suspicious.** No seas tan suspicaz.

svelte *adj* esbelto *m*, -ta *f*, refinado *m*, -da *f*

swamp *n* pantano *m*, ciénaga *f*

swap *vt* cambiar **Do you want to swap places?** ¿*Quiere usted (Fam: ¿Quieres)* cambiar lugares?

swear *vi* 1. *(solemnly assert)* jurar; 2. *(use profanity)* decir palabrotas **I swear** *([1]* **it's true.** / *[2]* **it wasn't me.).** Juro *([1]* que es verdad. / *[2]* que yo no fui.) **It's not necessary to swear.** No hay necesidad de decir palabrotas.

sweat *vi* sudar **I'm sweating.** Estoy sudando.

sweat *n* sudor *m*

sweater *n* suéter *m* **Better bring a sweater.** Mejor trae un suéter.

sweatshirt *n* sudadera *f*

sweaty *adj* sudoroso *m*, -sa *f* **I'm all sweaty.** Estoy todo *(-da)* sudoroso *(-sa)*. **You're all sweaty.** Estás todo *(-da)* sudoroso *(-sa)*.

sweep *vt* 1. *(s.o. off their feet)* mover el piso; 2. *(win all games / matches)* barrer **You (really) swept me off my feet.** (De veras) me *movió usted (Fam: moviste)* el piso. **We swept them, three matches to zero.** Los barrimos, tres a cero.

sweet *adj* encantador *m*, -dora *f*, dulce *m&f*, lindo *m*, -da *f* ~ **disposition** disposición encantadora ~ **lips** labios encantadores ~ **nature** de naturaleza encantadora ~ **tooth** afición por los dulces **That's (really) sweet of you.** Eso fue (muy) lindo de *su (Fam: tu)* parte. **How sweet of you!** ¡Qué lindo! **That was a sweet thing to say.** Ese fue un comentario encantador. **You're the sweetest** *(1)* **guy** / *(2)* **man I've ever met.** Tú eres el *(1)* tipo / *(2)* hombre más dulce que haya conocido jamás. **You're the sweetest** *(1)* **girl** / *(2)* **woman** / *(3)* **person I've ever met.** Tú eres la *(1)* chica / *(2)* mujer / *(3)* persona más dulce que haya conocido jamás. **What a sweet smile you have.** Qué sonrisa tan dulce tienes. **I have a sweet tooth.** Tengo debilidad

---

A slash always means "or".

por los dulces.

sweetheart *n* mi amor *m&f*, querido *m*, -da *f* **You're my sweetheart.** Tú eres mi amor.

sweet-natured *adj* de naturaleza dulce

sweetness *n* dulzura *f* **enchanting** ~ dulzura encantadora ~ **of your lips** la dulzura de tus labios **How can there be so much sweetness in one person?** ¿Cómo puede existir tanta dulzura en una persona? **The sweetness of your lips is heavenly.** La dulzura de tus labios es la gloria.

sweets *n, pl* dulces *mpl* **I don't care for sweets.** No me gustan los dulces.

sweet-smelling *adj* de olor dulce

sweet-talk *vt (slang: make seductive compliments)* lisonjear **You really know how to sweet-talk a person.** Sabes muy bien cómo lisonjear a una persona.

swim *vi* nadar *(See also phrases under* **like** *and* **love**.*)* **Do you know how to swim?** ¿Sabe usted (Fam: ¿Sabes) nadar? **I can(not) swim.** Yo (no) sé nadar. **I'll teach you how to swim.** Yo *le (Fam: te)* enseño a nadar. **Let's go swim (in the** *[1]* **ocean /** *[2]* **pool).** Vámonos a nadar *[1]* al mar *[2]* a la piscina. **Can we swim here?** ¿Podemos nadar aquí? **Is it safe to swim here?** ¿Es seguro nadar aquí?

swim *n* nadar **Let's go for a swim.** Vamos a nadar.

swimmer *n* nadador *m*, -dora *f* **I'm a** *(1)* **good /** *(2)* **poor swimmer.** Soy un*(a)* *(1)* buen*(a)* / *(2)* mal*(a)* nadador *(-dora)*. **You're a good swimmer.** *Usted es (Fam: Tú eres)* un*(a)* buen*(a)* nadador *(-dora)*.

swimming *n* natación *f (See phrases under* **go, like** *and* **love**.*)* **go** ~ ir a nadar **Where can we go swimming?** ¿Adónde podemos ir a nadar?

swimsuit *n* traje *m* de baño

swindle *n* engaño *m* **This is an outrageous swindle!** ¡Este es un engaño vil!

swine *n* marrano *m*, cerdo *m*

swing *vt (around)* hacer girar **Swing the racket like this.** Haz girar así la raqueta.

switch *vt (exchange)* cambiar ~ **seats** cambiar asientos ~ **sides** cambiar de lado **Okay, let's switch sides.** Está bien, vamos cambiando de lado.

swollen *adj* inflamado *m*, -da *f* ~ **head** engreído *m*, -da *f*

swordfish *n* pez *m* espada

syllable *n* sílaba *f*

symbol *n* símbolo *m* **This ring is a symbol of our (enduring) love.** Este anillo es símbolo de nuestro (eterno) amor.

symbolize *vt* simbolizar **What does it symbolize?** ¿Qué simboliza eso? **It symbolizes...** Simboliza...

sympathetic *adj* comprensivo *m*, -va *f* **be** ~ ser comprensivo *m*, -va *f*

Spanish "v" is pronounced like a soft "b".

sympathize *vi* compadecerse, comprender **I** (*[1]* **deeply** / *[2]* **truly**) **sympathize with** *(3)* **you.** / *(4)* **your situation.** Me compadezco (*[1]* profundamente / *[2]* verdaderamente) *(3)* de *usted (Fam: ti)*. / *(4)* de *su (Fam: tu)* situación.

sympathy *n* simpatía *f*, compasión *f*

symphony *n* sinfonía *f* ~ **of pleasure** sinfonía de placer ~ **orchestra** orquesta sinfónica

synagogue *n* sinagoga *f*

synonym *n* sinónimo *m*

system *n* sistema *m* **bus** ~ sistema de autobuses **clever** ~ sistema inteligente **foolproof** ~ sistema a prueba de tontos **good** ~ buen sistema **new** ~ sistema nuevo **old** ~ sistema antiguo **poor** ~ sistema malo **postal** ~ sistema postal **subway** ~ sistema del metro **transportation** ~ sistema de transportes **I know a great system for betting on horses. (That's why I'm so rich.)** Yo conozco un gran sistema para apostar a los caballos. (Por eso soy tan rico.)

Time expressions are given on page 413.

T

table *n* mesa *f* **billiard** ~ mesa de billar   **card** ~ mesa para jugar cartas   **coffee** ~ mesa cafetera   **extra** ~ mesa adicional   **find a** ~ encontrar una mesa   **night** ~ buró *m*   **ping-pong** ~ mesa de ping-pong   **pool** ~ mesa de billar   **reserve a** ~ reservar una mesa   **We'd like a table for** *(1)* **two** / *(2)* **three** / *(3)* **four, please.** Una mesa para *(1)* dos / *(2)* tres / *(3)* cuatro, por favor.   **Please come to the table.** Sírvanse pasar a la mesa.   **Come join** *(1)* **me** / *(2)* **us at** *(3)* **my** / *(4)* **our table.** Ven *(1)* conmigo / *(2)* con nosotros a *(3)* mi / *(4)* nuestra mesa.   **Let's get a table outdoors.** Vamos a tomar una mesa afuera.

tablet *n* 1. *(pad of paper)* bloc *m* ; 2. *(medicine)* tableta *f*

taboo *n* tabú *m*   **That's strictly taboo.** Eso es estricto tabú.

tackle *n* *(fishing gear)* equipo *m*, aparejos *mpl*   **fishing** ~ aparejos *mpl* de pesca

tacky *adj* *(slang)* naco *m*, -ca *f*, chabacano *m*, -cana *f*

tact *n* tacto *m*   ★   **tactful** *adj* discreto *m*, -ta *f*

tactic *n* táctica *f*   **That's a clever tactic.** Esa es una táctica inteligente.   **Those tactics won't work.** Esas tácticas no van a funcionar.

tactless *adj* indiscreto *m*, -ta *f*

tag *n* etiqueta *f*   **price** ~ etiqueta de precio

tail *n* 1. *(of an animal)* cola *f*; 2. *(slang: buttocks)* cola *f*, nalgas *f, pl*

take *vt* 1. *(acquire, obtain)* tomar; 2. *(occupy)* ocupar; 3. *(convey, drive)* llevar; 4. *(time: require)* tomar   **You'd better take along** *(1)* **a coat.** / *(2)* **a sweater.** / *(3)* **an umbrella.** / *(4)* **your passport.** Será mejor que *se lleve (Fam: te lleves)* *(1)* un abrigo. / *(2)* un suéter. / *(3)* un paraguas. / *(4)* su *(Fam: tu)* pasaporte.   **Take some.** Toma unas.   **Is this seat taken?** ¿Está ocupado este asiento?   **This seat is taken.** Este asiento está ocupado.   **Where are you taking** *(1)* **me?** / *(2)* **us?** ¿A dónde *(1)* me / *(2)* nos *lleva usted (Fam: llevas)*?   *(1)* **I can** *(2,3)* **take you...** / *(4)* **I'll take** *(5,6)* **you...**

Spanish "qu" is pronounced like "k".

home (in my car). *(1)* Yo puedo *(2) llevarlo m / (3) llevarla f (Fam: llevarte)*… / *(4)* Yo *(5) lo m / (6) la f (Fam: te)* llevo… a *su (Fam: tu)* casa (en mi carro). **We can *(1,2)* take you... / *(2)* We'll take *(5,6)* you... home (in our car).** *(1)* Nosotros podemos *(2) llevarlo m / (3) llevarla f (Fam: llevarte)*… / *(4)* Nosotros *(5) lo m / (6) la f (Fam: te)* llevamos… a *su (Fam: tu)* casa (en nuestro carro). **Would you mind if I took your picture?** ¿*Le (Fam: Te)* importa si *le (Fam: te)* tomo una foto? **Could you take our picture?** ¿*Podría usted (Fam: Puedes)* tomarnos una foto? **How long does it take (to get there)?** ¿Cuánto tiempo toma (llegar ahí)? **It takes about** *(1)* **five** / *(2)* **ten** / *(3)* **fifteen minutes.** / *(4)* **a half hour.** / *(5)* **an hour.** / *(6)* **two** / *(7)* **three hours.** Toma aproximadamente *(1)* cinco / *(2)* diez / *(3)* quince minutos. / *(4)* una media hora. / *(5)* una hora. / *(6)* dos / *(7)* tres horas. **How long will it take?** ¿Cuánto tiempo toma eso? **It will take** *(amount of time).* Eso se toma ____ .

★ **take after** *idiom (resemble)* parecerse **I take after my** *(1)* **father.** / *(2)* **mother.** Me parezco a mi *(1)* padre. / *(2)* madre.

★ **take back** *idiom* 1. *(return)* devolver; 2. *(retract)* retractarse **I'll take it back (to the office).** Lo voy a devolver a la oficina. **I take back what I said (about you).** Me retracto de lo que dije (de ti).

★ **take care of** *idiom* cuidar **Could you take care of it (for *[1]* me / *[2]* us)?** ¿*Podría usted (Fam: ¿Podrías tú)* *[1]* cuidármelo / *[2]* cuidárnoslo)?

★ **take down** *idiom (tents: disassemble)* desarmar **I'll take down the tent and pack it.** Voy a desarmar y a empacar la tienda .

★ **take off** *idiom* 1. *(get off work)* retirarse, salirse del trabajo; 2. *(remove)* quitarse **Please take off your** *(1)* **coat.** / *(2)* **shoes.** Por favor, *quítese (Fam: quítate)* *(1)* el abrigo / *(2)* los zapatos.

★ **take out** *idiom* 1. *(food: carry out)* para llevar; 2. *(escort on a date)* llevar **Let's order something to take out.** Ordenemos algo para llevar. *(1)* **I'd** / *(2)* **We'd like to take *(3,4)* you out to dinner (*[5]* tonight** / *[6]* **tomorrow night).** *(1)* Me / *(2)* Nos gustaría *(3)* llevarlo m / *(4)* llevarla f (Fam: llevarte) a cenar (*[5]* esta noche / *[6]* mañana por la noche.)

take-charge *adj* emprendedor *m*, -dora *f*

talent *n* talento *m* **You really have a lot of talent.** *Usted tiene (Fam: Tú tienes)* de veras mucho talento. **You have quite a talent for** *(1)* **music.** / *(2)* **painting.** *Usted tiene (Fam: Tú tienes)* bastante talento para *(1)* la música. / *(2)* la pintura.

talented *adj* talentoso *m*, -sa *f* **You're very talented.** *Es usted (Fam: Eres)* muy talentoso *(-sa).*

Words in parentheses (not italicized) are optional.

talk *vi* hablar, platicar **Please talk (a little) *(1)* louder. / *(2)* slower.** Por favor, *hable usted (Fam: habla)* (un poco) más *(1)* fuerte. / *(2)* despacio. **You talk *(1)* kind of fast. / *(2)* too fast.** *Usted habla (Fam: Tú hablas) (1)* un poco rápido. / *(2)* demasiado rápido. **What are you talking about?** ¿De qué *está usted (Fam: estás)* hablando? **I'm talking about...** Estoy hablando de... **I enjoy talking with you.** Me gusta platicar *con usted (Fam: contigo). (1)* **I / *(2)* We enjoyed talking with you.** *(1)* Me / *(2)* nos dio gusto platicar *con usted (Fam: contigo).* **It's so nice to talk with you.** Es tan agradable platicar *con usted (Fam: contigo).* **I could spend hours talking with you.** Me podría pasar horas platicando *con usted (Fam: contigo).* **Let's go somewhere where we can sit and talk.** Vamos a donde podamos sentarnos y platicar. **Could I talk with you (for a moment)?** ¿Podría hablar *con usted (Fam: contigo)* (un momento)? **We have to talk.** Tenemos que hablar. **We need to meet and talk together.** Necesitamos reunirnos a platicar.

talk *n* plática *f* **We need to have a nice long talk together.** Necesitamos tener una larga plática.

talkative *adj* platicador *m*, -ra *f*, parlanchín *m*, -china *f*

tall *adj* alto *m*, -ta *f (1,2)* **How tall are you?** *(1)* ¿Qué tan alto *(-ta)* eres? / *(2)* ¿Qué estatura tienes? **I'm *(number)* centimeters tall.** Mido __ centímetros.

tame *adj* dócil *m&f*

tampon(s) *n(pl)* tampón(es) *m(pl)*

tan *vi* broncearse **I (don't) tan easily.** Yo (no) me bronceo fácilmente.

tan *n* bronceado *m* **golden ~** bronceado dorado **You have a *(1)* gorgeous / *(2)* nice tan.** Tienes un bronceado *(1)* fabuloso. / *(2)* bonito. **I'm going to work on my tan.** Voy a mejorar mi bronceado.

tango *vi* bailar tango **Teach me how to tango.** Enséñame a bailar tango.

tango *n* tango *m*

tank *n* tanque *m*

tanned *adj* bronceado *m*, -da *f* **get ~** broncearse

tantalizing *adj* tentador *m*, -dora *f*

tape *vt* 1. *(seal with tape)* pegar con cinta (adhesiva); 2. *(tape-record)* grabar

tape *n* cinta *f* **adhesive ~** cinta adhesiva **cassette ~** cinta en cassette **measuring ~** flexómetro *m* **music ~s** cintas de música **video ~** cinta de vídeo **Let's play some tapes.** Vamos a tocar unas cintas. **I want you to hear this tape.** Quiero que oigas esta cinta. **Can I copy your tape?** ¿Puedo copiar tu cinta?

tape-record *vt* grabar

target *n* blanco *m* **Did I hit the target?** ¿Le di al blanco? **You hit the target.** Le *dio (Fam: diste)* al blanco. **You missed the target.** Le *falló*

A single Spanish "r" should be lightly trilled;
double "r" ("rr") should be strongly trilled.

(Fam: fallaste) al blanco.

task *n* tarea *f* **difficult** ~ tarea difícil **easy** ~ tarea fácil

taste *vt* probar **Taste this.** Prueba esto. **Let me taste.** Déjame probar.

taste *vi* saber **How does it taste?** ¿Qué tal sabe? **It tastes** *(1)* **awful.** / *(2)*
good. / *(3)* **great.** / *(4)* **strange.** / *(5)* **terrible.** / *(6)* **wonderful.** Sabe *(1)*
horrible. / *(2)* bueno. / *(3)* buenísimo. / *(4)* raro. / *(5)* espantoso. / *(6)*
maravilloso. **Your lips taste like honey.** Tus labios saben a miel.

taste *n* 1. *(sense)* sabor *m* ; 2. *(preference)* gusto *m* **bad** ~ 1. *(preference)* mal
gusto; 2. *(food)* mal sabor **good** ~ 1. *(preference)* buen gusto; 2. *(food)*
buen sabor **in bad** ~ de mal gusto **in good** ~ de buen gusto **nice** ~ *(food)*
buen sabor **same** ~s los mismos gustos **strange** ~ *(food)* sabor raro
sweet ~ *(food)* sabor dulce **wonderful** ~ *(food)* sabor maravilloso **You
have** *(1)* **good** / *(2)* **excellent taste in** *(3)* **art.** / *(4)* **clothes.** / *(5)* **decorat-
ing.** / *(6)* **music.** / *(7)* **wine.** Tienes *(1)* buen gusto... / *(2)* un gusto
excelente... en *(3)* arte. / *(4)* ropa. / *(5)* decoración. / *(6)* música. / *(7)* vinos.
I have simple tastes. Tengo gustos sencillos.

tasty *adj* sabroso *m*, -sa *f*

tattoo *n* tatuaje *m* **That's a** *(1)* **beautiful** / *(2)* **fantastic** / *(3)* **unique** / *(4)*
wild tattoo! ¡Ese es un tatuaje *(1)* hermoso! / *(2)* fantástico! / *(3)* único! /
(4) brutal! **I have a small tattoo on my** *(1)* **back.** / *(2)* **buttock.** / *(3)* **leg.**
/ *(4)* **shoulder.** / *(5)* **stomach.** Tengo un tatuaje pequeño en *(1)* la espalda.
/ *(2)* la nalga. / *(3)* la pierna. / *(4)* el hombro. / *(5)* el estómago. **Do you want
to see my tattoo?** ¿Quieres ver mi tatuaje?

tattooed *adj* tatuado *m*, -da *f*

Taurus *(Apr. 20 - May 20)* Tauro

tavern *n* taberna *f*; cantina *f*

tax *n* impuesto *m* **airport** ~ impuesto de uso de aeropuertos **federal** ~
impuesto federal **income** ~ impuesto sobre la renta **property** ~ impuesto
sobre la propiedad **sales** ~ impuesto sobre ventas **state** ~ impuesto
estatal **value-added** ~ impuesto al valor agregado **What's the rate of the
sales tax?** ¿Cuál es la tasa del impuesto sobre ventas?

taxi(cab) *n* taxi *m* ~ **fare** tarifa *f* de taxi ~ **meter** taxímetro *m* **Let's take a
taxi.** Tomemos un taxi. **Where can** *(1)* **I** / *(2)* **we get a taxi?** ¿Dónde *(1)*
puedo / *(2)* podemos tomar un taxi? **What's the usual taxi fare from
here to** *(1)* **the airport?** / *(2)* **the train station?** / *(3)* *(place)***?** ¿Cuál es la
tarifa normal de aquí *(1)* al aeropuerto? / *(2)* a la estación del ferrocarril? /
(3) ___? **Could you call a taxi for** *(1)* **me?** / *(2)* **us?** *(1)* ¿Me / *(2)* ¿Nos
pides un taxi?

tea *n* té *m* **iced** ~ té helado **How about a cup of tea?** ¿Qué te parece un té?
Let's go somewhere and have a cup of tea. Vamos a alguna parte a tomar

---

*Familiar "tu" forms in parentheses can replace
italicized polite forms.*

un té.

teach *vt* enseñar **Can you teach me (Spanish)?** ¿Me *puede usted (Fam: puedes)* enseñar (español)? **I'll teach you (how to *[1]* dance / *[2]* drive / *[3]* play / *[4]* swim.)** Yo *le (Fam: te)* enseño a (*[1]* bailar / *[2]* manejar / *[3]* jugar / *[4]* nadar.) **Teach me (how to *[1]* dance / *[2]* play / *[3]* swim).** *Enséñeme (Fam: Enséñame)* (a *[1]* bailar / *[2]* jugar / *[3]* nadar). **Could you teach me how to play the guitar?** ¿Podría usted (Fam: Podrías) enseñarme a tocar la guitarra? **I want to teach you how to *(1)* ride rainbows. / *(2)* soar through the cosmos.** Quiero enseñarte a *(1)* montar en arco iris. / *(2)* volar por el cosmos. **What do you teach?** ¿Qué *enseña usted (Fam: enseñas tú)*? **I teach *(1)* English. / *(2)* history. / *(3)* math. / *(4)* science. / *(5)* (subject).** Enseño *(1)* inglés. / *(2)* historia. / *(3)* matemáticas. / *(4)* ciencias. / *(5)* ____ .

team *n* equipo *m* **form ~s** formar equipos **opposing ~** equipo rival **our ~** nuestro equipo **You be on my team.** Tú vente a mi equipo. **I want to be on your team.** Quiero estar en tu equipo.

tear *vt* romper **I tore it.** Lo rompí.

★ **tear up** *idiom* romper **I tore it up (and threw it away).** Lo rompí (y lo tiré).

tear *n (from crying)* lágrima *f* **Why the tears?** ¿A qué se deben las lágrimas? **Let me dry your tears.** Déjame secar tus lágrimas.

tease *vt* molestar **I'm just teasing you.** Nomás te estoy molestando. **Stop teasing me.** Deja de molestarme.

technical *adj* técnico *m*, -ca *f*

technique *n* técnica *f* **Let me show you the proper technique.** Déjame mostrarte la técnica correcta. **You have great technique.** Tienes una técnica estupenda.

tedious *adj* tedioso *m*, -sa *f*

tee *n (golf: peg)* tee *m*

teenage(d) *adj* adolescente *m&f* ★ **teenager** *n* adolescente *m&f*

tee off *idiom (golf)* dar el primer golpe

television *n* televisión *f*, tele *f* **cable ~** televisión por cable **on ~** en la tele **watch ~** ver la tele **I saw a program on television about (subject).** Vi un programa en la tele sobre ____ .

tell *vt* decir, contar **~ a lie** decir una mentira **~ a story** contar un cuento **You told me...** Tú me dijiste... **I told you...** Yo te dije... **What did *(1)* he / *(2)* she / *(3)* they tell you?** ¿Qué te *(1)* dijo él? / *(2)* dijo ella? / *(3)* dijeron ellos? ***(1)* He / *(2)* She told me...** *(1)* Él / *(2)* Ella me dijo... **They told me...** Ellos me dijeron... **Tell me *(1)* about it. / *(2)* about yourself. / *(3)* the truth. / *(4)* what happened.** Cuénteme (Fam: Cuéntame) *(1)* de eso. /

Spanish "ll" is pronounced like "y" in "yes".

(2) de *usted (Fam: ti. / (3)* la verdad. / *(4)* qué pasó. **Could you tell** *(1)* **me** / *(2)* **us** *(3)* **how to get to** *(place)***?** / *(4)* **where** *(place)* **is?** *¿Podría usted (Fam: ¿Podrías tú) (1)* decirme / *(2)* decirnos *(3)* cómo llegar a __? / (4)* dónde es ___?

temper *n* carácter *m*, paciencia *f* **bad ~** mal carácter **hot ~** carácter explosivo **I'm sorry I lost my temper.** Lo siento, perdí la paciencia. **Temper, temper!** ¡Paciencia, paciencia!

temperature *n* temperatura *f* **What's the temperature?** ¿Cuál es la temperatura?

temple *n (religious)* templo *m* **Aztec ~** templo azteco **Buddhist ~** templo budista **Maya(n) ~** templo maya

temporary *adj* temporal *m&f* **~ insanity** demencia temporal **~ job** trabajo temporal

tempt *vt* tentar, provocar **You tempt me.** *Usted me provocó (Fam: Tú me provocaste).* **Don't tempt me.** No me *tiente (Fam: tientes).*

temptation *n* tentación *f* **big ~** gran tentación **enormous ~** tentación enorme **resist the ~** resistir la tentación **I couldn't resist the temptation of** *(1,2)* **calling you.** / *(3)* **coming to** *(4,5)* **see you.** No pude resistir la tentación de *(1)* llamarlo *m* / *(2)* llamarla *f (Fam: llamarte). / (3)* venir a *(4)* verlo *m* / *(5)* verla *f (Fam: verte).*

tempting *adj* tentador *m*, -dora *f* **It's a tempting** *(1)* **idea.** / *(2)* **suggestion.** Es una *(1)* idea / *(2)* sugerencia tentadora.

temptress *n* tentadora *f*

tend (to) *vi* tender **I tend to** *(1)* **avoid** / *(2)* **ignore such** *(3)* **people.** / *(4)* **things.** Tiendo a *(1)* evitar / *(2)* ignorar *(3)* a esa gente. / *(4)* esas cosas.

tendency *n* tendencia *f* **have a ~ to** tener tendencia a

tender *adj* tierno *m*, -na *f*

tenderly *adv* con ternura

tennis *n* tenis *m* (★ *See also phrases under* **like, love** *and* **play***.)* **table ~** tenis de mesa, ping-pong *m* **~ ball** pelota de tenis **~ court** cancha de tenis **~ raquet** raqueta de tenis

tense *adj* tenso *m*, -sa *f* **You're too tense.** Estás demasiado tenso *(-sa).* **Don't be so tense.** No estés tan tenso *(-sa).*

tent *n* tienda *f* de campaña **~ space** espacio para la tienda de campaña **Help me** *(1)* **fold** / *(2)* **put up** / *(3)* **take down the tent.** Ayúdame a *(1)* doblar / *(2)* poner / *(3)* desarmar la tienda de campaña. **Where shall we put up the tent?** ¿Dónde ponemos la tienda de campaña?

term *n* 1. *(expression)* término *m* ; 2. *pl (relations)* relaciones *fpl* **technical ~** término técnico **We're still on friendly terms.** Todavía somos amigos.

terminal *n (station)* terminal *f* **air ~** terminal aérea **bus ~** terminal de

---

Common occupations are listed on pages 415-416.

autobuses

terrace *n* terraza *f*

terrain *n* terreno *m* **rough / rugged** ~ terreno agreste / breñal

terrible *adj* terrible *m&f*, espantoso *m*, -sa *f* **That's terrible!** ¡Eso es espantoso! **How terrible!** ¡Qué espantoso! **It was terrible.** Fue espantoso. **I'm a terrible player.** Soy un*(a)* jugador *(-dora)* malísimo *(-ma)*. **I feel terrible.** Me siento muy mal.

terribly *adv* muy, tremendamente **I'm terribly sorry.** Estoy muy apenado. **I want terribly to kiss you right now.** Tengo unas ganas horribles de besarte ya.

terrific *adj* maravilloso *m*, -sa *f*, tremendo *m*, -da *f* *(1-3)* **Terrific!** *(1)* ¡Magnífico! / *(2)* ¡Estupendo! / *(3)* ¡Fenomenal! **You look (absolutely) terrific.** Te ves (absolutamente) maravillosa. **You are terrific.** *Usted es (Fam: Eres)* maravilloso *(-sa)*.

terrified *adj* aterrorizado *m*, -da *f* **I'm terrified of heights.** Me aterrorizan las alturas.

terror *n* terror *m*

terrorism *n* terrorismo *m* **act of** ~ un acto de terrorismo

terrorist *adj* terrorista *m&f* ~ **attack** un ataque terrorista

terrorist *n* terrorista *m&f*

test *n* 1. *(trial)* prueba *f* ; 2. *(school exam)* examen *m* ; 3. *(med. analysis)* análisis *m* **AIDS** ~ prueba del sida *m* **blood** ~ análisis de sangre **final** ~ examen final ~ **of strength** prueba de fuerza

than *conj* más **That's more than enough.** Eso es más que suficiente. **You're bigger than I am.** *Usted es (Fam: Tú eres)* más grande que yo.

thank *vt* agradecer **Thank you (very much).** (Muchas) Gracias. *(1)* **Thank you...** / *(2)* **I want to thank you... for** *(3)* **everything.** / *(4)* **your (kind) hospitality.** / *(5)* **your help.** / *(6)* **giving me a ride.** *(1)* Gracias... / *(2)* Quiero *agradecerle (Fam: agradecerte)…* por *(3)* todo. / *(4)* su *(Fam: tu)* (amable) hospitalidad. / *(5)* su *(Fam: tu)* ayuda. / *(6)* darme un aventón.

thanks *n, pl* gracias *fpl* **Thanks (a lot).** (Muchas) Gracias. **No, thanks.** No, gracias.

Thanksgiving *n (U.S. holiday)* Día de Acción de Gracias.

that *adj* ese, esa ~ **bus** ese camión ~ **place** ese lugar ~ **station** esa estación ~ **street** esa calle ~ **train** ese tren

that *dem. pron* eso **What's that?** ¿Qué es eso? **Whose is that?** ¿De quién es eso? **That's really nice of you.** Eso es muy amable de *su (Fam: tu)* parte. **That's** *(1)* **mine.** / *(2)* **ours.** / *(3)* **yours.** Eso es *(1)* mío. / *(2)* nuestro. / *(3)* suyo *(Fam: tuyo)*.

theater *n* 1. *(drama)* teatro *m* ; 2. *(movie)* cine *m* **movie** ~ cine ~ **tickets**

Spanish "y" is "ee" when alone or at the end of words.

boletos para el teatro

then *adv* 1. *(afterward, next)* después; 2. *(at that time)* entonces; 3. *(in that case)* entonces **by ~** para entonces **now and ~** de vez en cuando **since ~** desde entonces **till ~** hasta entonces **Then what did you do?** ¿Qué *hizo usted (Fam: hiciste)* después? **We can take a swim and then go downtown.** Podemos ir a nadar y después al centro. **I was** *(1)* **married /** *(2)* **single then.** Entonces *(1)* estaba casado. / *(2)* era soltero. **Then you'll call me?** ¿Entonces *usted me llama (Fam: tú me llamas)*?

theory *n* teoría *f*

there 1. *(location)* ahí; 2. *(motion to)* allá; 3. *(motion from)* allá; 4. *(exclamation)* ahí; 5. *(with is and are)* hay **It's (over) there.** Está por allá. **How long will you stay there?** ¿Cuánto tiempo *se va usted (Fam: te vas)* a quedar allá? *(1)* **I'm /** *(2)* **We're going to stay there for** *(3)* **a few days. /** *(4)* **a week.** *(1)* Me voy… / *(2)* Nos vamos… a quedar allá por *(3)* unos días. / *(4)* una semana. **When are you going there?** ¿Cuándo te vas para allá? *(1)* **I'm /** *(2)* **We're going there** *(3)* **today. /** *(4)* **tomorrow. /** *(5)* **day after tomorrow.** *(1)* Voy / *(2)* Vamos a ir allá *(3)* hoy. / *(4)* mañana. / *(5)* pasado mañana. **Where are you going from there?** ¿De allí a dónde te vas? **From there** *(1)* **I'll /** *(2)* **we'll probably go to** *(place)*. De allí probablemente *(1)* me voy… / *(2)* nos vamos… a ____. *(1,2)* **There you are!** *(1)* ¡Allí estás! / *(2)* ¡Ahí tienes! **There they are!** ¡Allí están! **There** *(1)* **he /** *(2)* **she is!** ¡Allí está *(1)* él! / *(2)* ella! **There it goes!** ¡Ahí va! **Is there another** *(1)* **bus /** *(2)* **train today?** ¿Hay otro *(1)* camión / *(2)* tren el día de hoy? **There's a show at nine o'clock.** Hay una presentación a las nueve. **There's no hope.** No hay esperanza. **Are there any seats left?** ¿Hay asientos libres? **There are some seats in the back.** Hay unos asientos en la parte de atrás. **There are no more tickets.** Ya no hay boletos.

★ **there + be:** hay, haber **Is there a** *(what)* **there?** ¿Hay allí un ___? **Is there an Internet café around here?** ¿Hay algún café de Internet por aquí? **There's plenty of time.** Hay bastante tiempo. **There's not enough time.** Ya no hay tiempo. **Are there any** *(1)* **seats /** *(2)* **tickets available?** ¿Hay *(1)* asientos / *(2)* boletos disponibles? **There are so many things about you that I like.** Hay tantas cosas de ti que me gustan. **There aren't any more.** Ya no hay.

therefore *adv* por lo tanto

thermal *n (paragliding)* térmica *f*

thermometer *n* termómetro *m*

these *adj & dem. pron, pl* estos *mpl*, estas *fpl* **Are these seats taken?**

Feminine forms of words in phrases
are usually given in parentheses (italicized).

¿Están ocupados estos asientos? **These are** *(1)* **mine.** / *(2)* **ours.** / *(3)* **yours.** Estos son *(1)* míos. / *(2)* nuestros. / *(3)* tuyos.

thick *adj* grueso *m*, -sa *f*

thief *n* ladrón *m*, -drona *f*

thigh *n* muslo *m*

thin *adj* delgado *m*, -da *f* **get** ~ adelgazar

thing *n* (1. *object*; 2. *matter*; 3. *creature*) cosa *f* **a couple** ~s un par de cosas **a few** ~s unas cuantas cosas **another** ~ otra cosa **innocent** ~ cosa inocente **my** ~s mis cosas **poor (little)** ~ pobrecito *(-ta)* **real** ~ *(slang)* 1. *(true love)* lo genuino; 2. *(meaningful relationship)* cosa seria **the first** ~ la primera cosa **the last** ~ la última cosa **the most important** ~ la cosa más importante **the only** ~ la única cosa **young** ~ chamaco *(-ca)* **your** ~s sus *(Fam: tus)* cosas **I need to pick up a few things at a store.** Necesito recoger unas cosas en una tienda. **I've got a couple things to take care of.** Tengo un par de cosas que atender. **How are things?** ¿Cómo van las cosas? **You're a sweet little thing.** Eres una cosita linda.

think *vi* pensar, creer **What do you think?** ¿Qué *piensa usted (Fam: piensas)*? **I (don't) think…** Yo (no) pienso… **Do you think so?** ¿Cree usted? *(Fam: ¿Tú crees?)* **I (don't) think so.** No creo. / Yo (no) pienso así. **Think about it and let** *(1)* **me** / *(2)* **us know.** Piénselo *(Fam: Piénsalo)* y *(1)* me *avisa (Fam: avisas)* / *(2)* nos *avisa (Fam: avisas)*. **I thought about you a lot** *(1)* **all day.** / *(2)* **last night.** / *(3)* **yesterday.** Pensé mucho en ti *(1)* todo el día. / *(2)* anoche. / *(3)* ayer.

thirst *n* sed *f* **I have a** *(1)* **monstrous** / *(2)* **raging thirst.** Tengo una sed *(1)* tremenda. / *(2)* loca.

thirsty *adj* sediento *m*, -ta *f* **be** ~ tener sed **Are you thirsty?** ¿Tiene usted *(Fam: Tienes)* sed? **I'm (really) thirsty.** Tengo (mucha) sed.

this *adj* este *m*, esta *f* ~ **bus** este camión ~ **place** este lugar ~ **station** esta estación ~ **street** esta calle ~ **time** esta hora, esta vez ~ **train** este tren

this *dem. pron* esto **What's this?** ¿Qué es esto? **This is really nice.** Esto es muy bonito. **Does this belong to you?** ¿Es suyo *(Fam: tuyo)* esto? **This is** *(1)* **mine.** / *(2)* **ours.** / *(3)* **yours.** Esto es *(1)* mío. / *(2)* nuestro. / *(3)* suyo *(Fam: tuyo)*. **This is for you.** Esto es para *usted (Fam: ti)*.

those *adj & dem. pron* esos *mpl*, esas *fpl* **Whose are those?** ¿De quién son esos? **Those are** *(1)* **mine.** / *(2)* **ours.** / *(3)* **yours.** Esos son *(1)* míos. / *(2)* nuestros. / *(3)* suyos *(Fam: tuyos)*.

though *conj* aunque **even** ~ aún cuando

thought *n* pensamiento *m*, idea *f* **nice** ~ pensamiento bonito **original** ~ idea original **warm** ~s pensamientos entusiastas **The thought of it** *(1)* **fills me with dread.** / *(2)* **makes my mouth water.** Sólo de pensarlo *(1)*

Spanish "c" before "e" and "i" is pronounced like "s".

me da terror. / *(2)* se me hace agua la boca. **A penny for your thoughts.** ¿En qué piensas? **I'll give it some thought.** Voy a pensarlo.

thoughtful *adj (considerate)* considerado *m*, -da *f* **That** *(1)* **is** / *(2)* **was very thoughtful of you.** Eso *(1)* es / *(2)* fue muy considerado de *su (Fam: tu)* parte. **You're such a thoughtful person.** *Usted es (Fam: Tú eres)* una persona tan considerada.

thoughtfulness *n* amabilidad *f*, solicitud *f* *(1)* **I** / *(2)* **We appreciate your thoughtfulness (very much).** *(1)* Aprecio / *(2)* Apreciamos (mucho) *su (Fam: tu)* amabilidad.

thoughtless *adj* desatento *m*, -ta *f*, desconsiderado *m*, -da *f* **That was thoughtless of me. I apologize.** Qué desatento *(-ta)* soy. Perdón.

thrill *vt* emocionar

thrill *n* emoción *f* **incredible** ~s emociones increíbles *(1)* **Paragliding** / *(2)* **Skydiving** / *(3)* **Windsurfing really gives you a thrill.** *(1)* Planear en paracaídas… / *(2)* Lanzarse en paracaídas… / *(3)* Hacer surf … te emociona de verdad. **It's a thrill a minute being with you.** Estar contigo es una emoción constante.

thrilled *adj* emocionado *m*, -da *f* *(1)* **I'm** / *(2)* **We're thrilled to have you come along.** *(1)* Estoy emocionado porque vienes conmigo. / *(2)* Estamos emocionados porque vienes con nosotros.

thrilling *adj* emocionante *m&f* ~ **experience** experiencia emocionante

throat *n* garganta *f*

through *prep* a través de

through *adj (finished)* terminado *m*, -da *f* **Are you through?** ¿Terminó usted (Fam: ¿Terminaste)? **Are you through playing?** ¿Terminó usted (Fam: ¿Terminaste) de jugar? **I'm through.** Terminé. **We're through.** Terminamos.

through *adv (finished)* terminado **get** ~ terminar **When you get through,** *(1)* **come over.** / *(2)* **give** *(3)* **me** / *(4)* **us a call.** Cuando *usted termine (Fam: termines)*, *(1)* venga *(Fam: vienes)*. / *(2)* llámeme *(Fam: llámame)* / *(3)* llámenos *(Fam: llámanos)*.

throw *vt* lanzar **Throw it to me.** Lánzamelo.
   ★ **throw away** *idiom* botar, tirar **Don't throw it away.** No lo tires. **I threw it away.** Lo tiré.
   ★ **throw up** *idiom* vomitar **I feel like I'm going to throw up.** Siento que voy a vomitar.

thumb *n* pulgar *m*

thunder *n* trueno *m*

Thursday *n* jueves *m* **last** ~ el jueves pasado **next** ~ el próximo jueves **on** ~ el jueves

---

Numbers in Spanish are given on pages 411-412.

ticket *n* boleto *m* **ballet ~(s)** boleto(s) para el ballet **bus ~(s)** boleto(s) de autobús **circus ~(s)** boleto(s) para el circo **concert ~(s)** boleto(s) para el concierto **cruise ~(s)** boleto(s) para un crucero **exhibition ~(s)** boleto(s) para la exposición **flight ~(s)** boleto(s) de avión **game ~(s)** boleto(s) para el juego **movie ~(s)** boleto(s) para el cine **skilift ~(s)** boleto(s) para el telesquí **soccer ~(s)** boleto(s) para el futbol **theater ~(s)** boleto(s) para el teatro **tour ~(s)** boleto(s) para el paseo / tour **train ~(s)** boleto(s) para el tren **Where can I get a ticket?** ¿Dónde puedo conseguir un boleto? **Where can we get tickets?** ¿Dónde podemos conseguir boletos? **How much does a ticket cost?** ¿Cuánto cuesta un boleto? **I'll go get tickets. (You wait here).** Yo voy por los boletos. (Tú espera aquí). **Go get tickets. (/[1] I / [2] We will wait here.)** Ve por los boletos. (/[1] yo espero / [2] nosotros esperamos aquí.) **Can you (1) get / (2) book (3) a ticket / (4) tickets (for [5] me / [6] us)?** ¿Puede usted (Fam: ¿Puedes) (1) conseguir / (2) reservar (3) un boleto / (4) boletos (para [5] mí / [6] nosotros)? **I'll book tickets for (all of) (1) us. / (2) you.** Voy a reservar boletos para (todos) (1) nosotros. / (2) ustedes. **I booked tickets (for us) already.** Ya reservé (nuestros) boletos. **(1) I'll / (2) We'll pay for your ticket.** (1) Yo pago... / (2) Nosotros pagamos... tu boleto. **Tickets are sold out.** Ya se agotaron los boletos.

tickle *vt* hacer cosquillas

ticklish *adj* cosquilloso *m*, -sa *f* **Are you ticklish?** ¿Eres cosquilloso *(-sa)*? **I'm (not) (very) ticklish.** Yo (no) soy (muy) cosquilloso *(-sa)*.

tide *n* marea *f* **high ~** marea alta **low ~** marea baja **The tide is (1) coming in. / (2) going out.** La marea está (1) subiendo. / (2)bajando. **We'll wait for (1) high / (2) low tide.** Vamos a esperar la marea (1) alta. / (2) baja.

tie *vt* 1. *(fasten)* amarrar; 2. *(score even)* empate **Can you tie this for me?** ¿Puede usted (Fam:Puedes) amarrarme esto? **Tie it down.** Amár-ralo. **Tie it tightly.** Amárralo fuerte. **Tie it to (1) this. / (2) that.** Amárralo a (1) esto. / (2) eso. **Where shall I tie the horse?** ¿Dónde amarro el caballo? **The score is tied.** El marcador está empatado. **We tied them, 3-3.** Empatamos, tres a tres.

tie *n* 1. *(necktie)* corbata *f*; 2. *(even score)* empate *m* ; 3. *pl (bonds)* ataduras *fpl* **Do I need to wear a tie?** ¿Necesito ponerme corbata? **It was a tie.** Fue un empate. **I have family ties.** Tengo mis ataduras familiares. **I have no ties.** No tengo ataduras.

tight *adj* 1. *(tightly closed)* bien cerrado *m*, -da *f*; *(stomach)* apretado *f*, -da *f*; 2. *(tight-fitting)* apretado *m*, -da *f*; 3. *(slang) (drunk)* bien borracho *m*, -cha *f*

tight *adv (firmly)* firme **Hold tight!** ¡Agárrate bien! **I like it when you**

Spanish "h" is always silent.

hold me tight. Me gusta cuando me abrazas fuerte.

tigress *n* tigresa *f* **You're a little tigress.** Tú eres una pequeña tigresa.

time *n* 1. *(amount, period)* tiempo *m*; 2. *(hour)* hora *f*; 3. *(repetition)* vez *f*; 4. *(episode, occasion, experience)* ocasión **couple ~s** un par de veces **a few ~s** unas cuantas veces **all the ~** todas las veces / siempre **a long ~** un largo rato **a long ~ ago** hace mucho rato / hace mucho tiempo **a lot of ~** mucho tiempo **ample ~** tiempo de sobra **another ~** otra ocasión **any ~** cualquier momento **any ~ now** en cualquier momento **arrival ~** hora de llegada **a short ~** poco tiempo **bad ~** mal momento **certain ~** cierta ocasión **convenient ~** momento conveniente **departure ~** hora de salida **difficult ~** momento difícil **each ~** cada vez **enough ~** tiempo suficiente **every ~** cada vez **extra ~** tiempo extra **first ~** primera vez **for the ~ being** por el momento **free ~** tiempo libre **from ~ to ~** ocasionalmente, de vez en cuando **good ~** buen tiempo **great ~** gran ocasión **have ~** tener tiempo **have a good ~** pasar un buen momento **how many ~s** cuántas veces **lack of ~** falta de tiempo **last ~** 1. *(final)* última vez; 2. *(previous)* última vez **leisure ~** tiempo de ocio **little ~** poco tiempo **local ~** hora local **long ~** largo rato, largo tiempo **lots of ~** mucho tiempo **lots of ~s** muchas veces **lovely ~** momento delicioso **many ~s** muchas veces **next ~** la próxima vez **nice ~** momento agradable **not enough ~** no hay tiempo **not have ~** no tener tiempo **not much ~** no mucho tiempo **on ~** a tiempo **one ~** una vez **pleasant ~** momento agradable **plenty of ~** mucho tiempo **rest ~** tiempo de descanso **save ~** ahorrar tiempo **second ~** segunda vez *(1,2)* **short ~** *(2)* ratito / *(2)* poco tiempo **some other ~** en otra ocasión **spare ~** tiempo libre **spend ~** pasar el tiempo **the whole ~** todo el tiempo **this ~** esta vez **~ difference** diferencia de horario **~ limit** límite de tiempo **~ of day** hora del día **~ of the month** fecha del mes **two ~s** dos veces **vacation ~** tiempo de vaca-ciones **waste of ~** pérdida de tiempo **waste ~** perder el tiempo **work(ing) ~** horas de trabajo **wonderful ~** momento maravilloso **What time is it (now)?** ¿Qué hora es? **What time** *(1)* **do you have to go?** / *(2)* **does your train leave?** / *(3)* **does your flight depart?** / *(4)* **does it start?** / *(5)* **finish?** / *(6)* **open?** / *(7)* **close?** / *(8)* **do you want to meet?** ¿A qué hora *(1)* se tiene *(Fam: te tienes)* que ir? / *(2)* sale su *(Fam: tu)* tren? / *(3)* sale *su (Fam: tu)* vuelo? / *(4)* empieza? / *(5)* acaba? / *(6)* abre? / *(7)* cierra? / *(8)* quiere usted *(Fam: quieres)* que nos veamos? **What time** *(1)* **will you come?** / *(2)* **shall I come?** / *(3)* **do you finish work?** / *(4)* **will you be there?** / *(5)* **shall I call?** ¿A qué hora *(1)* vendrá usted *(Fam: vienes)*? / *(2)* vengo? / *(3)* termina su *(Fam: terminas tu)* trabajo? / *(4)* estará usted *(Fam: estarás)* allí? / *(5)* llamo? **What's a good time for you?** *(Answer:* **How about** *[time]***?)** ¿Qué hora es buena para ti? *(Answer:*

Questions about the metric system? See page 417.

¿Qué te parece a las __?). **Do you have time?** ¿*Tiene usted (Fam: Tienes)* tiempo? *(1)* **I** / *(2)* **We (don't) have time.** *(1)* Yo (no) tengo... / *(2)* Nosotros (no) tenemos... tiempo. **How much time do** *(1)* **you** / *(2)* **we have?** ¿Cuánto tiempo *(1) tiene usted (Fam: tienes)*? / *(2)* tenemos? *(1)* **I** / *(2)* **We have (about)** *(number)* *(3)* **minutes.** / *(4)* **hours.** *(1)* Yo tengo... / *(2)* Nosotros tenemos... (aproxima-damente) __ *(3)* minutos. / *(4)* horas. *(1,2)* **Have a good time!** *(1)* ¡Que te vaya bien! / *(2)* ¡Que te diviertas! *(1,2)* **Did you have a good time?** *(1)* ¿Lo pasaste bien? / *(2)* ¿Te divertiste? *(1)* **I** / *(2)* **We had a** *(3)* **nice** / *(4)* **great** / *(5)* **wonderful** / *(6)* **terrific time.** *(1)* Pasé... / *(2)* Pasamos... un rato *(3)* agradable. / *(4)* fenomenal. / *(5)* maravilloso. / *(6)* súper. **Take your time.** *Tómese su (Fam: Tómate tu)* tiempo.

time-consuming *adj* que requiere mucho tiempo
time-out *n* tiempo *m* de receso **take a ~** tomarse un receso
timid *adj* tímido *m*, -da *f*
timing *n* sentido *m* del tiempo **Timing is everything.** El sentido del tiempo lo es todo. **That was** *(1)* **bad** / *(2)* **good** / *(3)* **great** / *(4)* **horrible** / *(5)* **perfect timing.** Ese fue un *(1)* mal / *(2)* buen / *(3)* magnífico / *(4)* mal / *(5)* perfecto sentido del tiempo.
tiny *adj* diminuto *m*, -ta *f*
tip *vt (give a gratuity)* dar propina **How much should I tip** *(1)* **her** / *(2)* **him?** ¿Cuánto le doy de propina?
tip *n* 1. *(point; end)* punta *f*; 2. *(gratuity)* propina *f* **leave a ~** dejar propina
tipsy *adj* achispado *m*, -da *f* **be ~** estar achispado *m*, -da *f* **get ~** achisparse **Are you tipsy?** ¿Estás un poquito borracho *(-cha)*? **(I think) I'm tipsy.** (Creo que) Estoy un poco borracho *(-cha)*. **I think I'm getting tipsy.** Creo que me estoy emborrachando. **I was tipsy.** Yo estaba un poco borracho *(-cha)*. **I get tipsy easily.** Me emborracho fácil.
tire *n* llanta *f* **change the ~** cambiar la llanta **fix the ~** reparar la llanta **flat ~** llanta ponchada **spare ~** llanta de repuesto
tired *adj* cansado *m*, -da *f* **be ~** estar cansado, -da **be ~ of** estar cansado *(-da)* de **get ~** cansarse **I'm getting tired.** Me estoy cansando. **Are you tired?** ¿Estás cansado *(-da)*? *(1)* **I'm** / *(2)* **We're (not) tired.** (No) *(1)* Estoy cansado *(-da)*. / *(2)* Estamos cansados *(-das)*. **You look tired.** Te ves cansado *(-da)*. **You must be tired.** Debes estar cansado *(-da)*.
tissue *n* kleenex *m*
title *n* título *m*
TLC *abbrev* = **tender, loving care** cuidado *m* tierno y amoroso
toast *n* 1. *(salute)* brindis *m*; 2. *(toasted bread)* pan *m* tostado **I propose a toast.** Propongo un brindis.

The letter "ñ" sounds like the "ny" in "canyon".

tobacco *n* tabaco *m*

today *n & adv* hoy **later ~** más tarde el día de hoy **Today is** *(1)* **my /** *(2)* **our last day (here).** Hoy es *(1)* mi / *(2)* nuestro último día (aquí).

toe *n* dedo *m* del pie *m*

toenail *n* uña *f* del pie **beautiful ~s** lindas uñas de los pies

together *adv* junto, juntos **Let's go together.** Vamos juntos. **I like doing things together with you.** Me gusta hacer cosas junto contigo. **It's so** *(1)* **nice /** *(2)* **wonderful being together with you.** Es tan *(1)* agradable / *(2)* maravilloso estar junto a ti.

toilet *n* baño *m* **~ paper** papel *m* higiénico **Where's the toilet?** ¿Dónde es el baño? **I have to go to the toilet.** Tengo que ir al baño.

token *n (symbol)* muestra *f* **This is just a small token of** *(1)* **my love for you. /** *(2)* **my /** *(3)* **our appreciation.** Esta es una pequeña muestra de *(1)* mi amor por ti. / *(2)* mi / *(3)* nuestro aprecio.

tolerant *adj* tolerante *m&f*

tomb *n* tumba *f*

tomboy *n* marimachona *f*

tomorrow *n & adv* mañana *m* **by ~** para mañana **day after ~** pasado mañana **See you tomorrow!** ¡Hasta mañana!

tongue *n* lengua *f* **sharp ~** lengua filosa **silver ~** pico de oro **~ twister** trabalenguas *m* **It's on the tip of my tongue.** Lo tengo en la punta de la lengua.

tongue-tied *adj* cohibido *m*, -da *f*, con la lengua trabada **be ~** tener la lengua trabada **You've got me tongue-tied.** *Usted me tiene (Fam: Tú me tienes)* cohibido *(-da)*.

tonic *n* tónico *m* **You're a tonic for my soul.** Tú eres el tónico de mi alma.

tonight *adv* esta noche

too *adv* 1. *(also)* también; 2. *(too much)* demasiado **You, too?** ¿Tú también? **Me too.** Yo también.

tooth *n* diente *m* **I have a sweet tooth.** Soy aficionado *(-da)* a lo dulce.

toothache *n* dolor *m* de muelas

toothbrush *n* cepillo *m* de dientes ★ **toothpaste** *n* pasta *f* de dientes

top *n* 1. *(peak)* cima *f*; 2. *(upper part)* tope *m* ; 3. *(highest position / rank)* el primero *m*, la primera *f*, el mejor *m*, la mejor *f*; 4. *(upper outer garment)* top *m;* blusa *f*; suéter *m* ; 5. *(car roof)* capota *f* **on ~** *adv* arriba; *prep* encima de **Let's climb to the top.** Vamos a escalar a la cima.

topic *n* tema *f*

topless *adj* topless, con los pechos al aire **go around ~** andar topless, andar con los pechos al aire **~ beach** playa para mujeres en monoquini

topsy-turvy *adj* patas arriba **You've turned my whole world topsy-turvy.**

Meet Mexicans online!
See pages 428-430 for websites.

Tú has puesto mi mundo todo patas arriba.

torment *vt* atormentar **Do you enjoy tormenting me?** ¿Te gusta atormentarme?

torment *n* tormento *m* **be in ~** estar en un tormento

torn *adj* roto *m*, -ta *f*

torrid *adj* tórrido *m*, -da *f*, apasionado *m*, -da *f*

torture *vt* torturar **You torture me.** Me torturas. **Why do you torture me like this?** ¿Por qué me torturas así?

torture *n* tortura *f* **This is absolute torture.** Esta es una verdadera tortura.

total *adj* total *m&f* **~ disappointment** total decepción **~ waste of time** total pérdida de tiempo **What's (1) my / (2) our / (3) your total score?** ¿Cuál es *(1)* mi / *(2)* nuestro / *(3)* tu puntaje total?

total *n* total *m* **What's the total?** ¿Cuál es el total?

totally *adv* totalmente **You are totally beautiful.** Tú eres totalmente bella. **I'm totally wiped out.** *(slang: exhausted)* Estoy totalmente agotado *(-da)*.

touch *vt* 1. *(with the hand)* tocar; 2. *(emotionally)* conmover; 3. *(come in contact with)* tocar **~ my heart** conmover mi corazón **Don't let anybody touch this.** No dejes que nadie toque esto. **Don't touch me.** No me toques.

touch *n* 1. *(physical contact)* tacto *m* ; 2. *(contact)* contacto *m* **feminine ~** toque femenino **magic ~** toque mágico **How can (1) I / (2) we get in touch with you?** ¿Cómo *(1)* puedo ponerme... / *(2)* podemos ponernos... en contacto *con usted (Fam:* contigo)? **You can get in touch with (1) me / (2) us at (number or address).** Usted puede ponerse *(Fam: Tú puedes ponerte)* en contacto *(1)* conmigo / *(2)* con nosotros en ___. *(1)* **I'll / (2) We'll get in touch with you (3) as soon as (4) I / (5) we can. / (6) tomorrow. / (7) on Monday / etc.** *(1)* Me pondré... / *(2)* Nos pondremos... en contacto *con usted (Fam: contigo) (3)* en cuanto *(4)* pueda. / *(5)* podamos. / *(6)* mañana. / *(7)* el lunes. **Please keep in touch.** Por favor *manténgase (Fam: man-tente)* en contacto.

touched *adj (affected emotionally)* conmovido *m*, -da *f* **I'm deeply touched by your (1) concern. / (2) gift. / (3) thoughtfulness.** Estoy profundamente conmovido *(-da)* por tu *(1)* preocupación. / *(2)* regalo. / *(3)* consideración.

touching *adj* conmovedor *m*, -dora *f* **How touching.** Qué conmovedor *(-ra)*.

touchy *adj* 1. *(irritable)* irritable *m & f*; 2. *(highly sensitive)* delicado *m*, -da *f* **~ subject** tema *m* delicado **Touchy, touchy!** ¡Uy qué delicado *(–da)*!

tough *adj* 1. *(rugged)* escabroso *m*, -sa *f*; 2. *(difficult)* difícil *m & f* **~ time** momento difícil

---

Spanish "o" is pronounced like "o" in "note"

tour *n* tour *m*, recorrido *m* **go on a** ~ ir en un tour **guided** ~ tour guiado **sightseeing** ~ recorrido por los lugares turistícos **take a** ~ tomar un tour ~ **bus** autobús para turistas ~ **guide** guía del tour ~ **program** programa del tour **walking** ~ paseo a pie **Come on the tour with** *(1)* **me.** / *(2)* **us.** Ven al tour *(1)* conmigo. / *(2)* con nosotros. **How much does the tour cost?** ¿Cuanto cuesta el tour?

tourist *adj* turístico *m*, -ca *f*, para turistas, ~ **prices** precios para turistas ~ **trap** trampa para turistas

tourist *n* turista *m&f*

toward *prep* hacia

towel *n* toalla *f* **bath** ~ toalla de baño **beach** ~ toalla de playa

tower *n* torre *f*

towing *n* remolque *m*

town *n* población *f* **home** ~ el lugar donde nací **small** ~ poblado pequeño

toy *n* juguete *m*

track *n* 1. *(trains)* vía *f*; 2. *(sport)* pista *f* ~ **meet** competencia de atletismo en pista **Which track does** *(1)* **my** / *(2)* **our train arrive on?** ¿En cuál vía llega *(1)* mi / *(2)* nuestro tren? **Which track does** *(1)* **my** / *(2)* **our train depart from?** ¿De cuál vía sale *(1)* mi / *(2)* nuestro tren? **I ran track in** *(1)* **high school.** / *(2)* **college.** Fui corredor de pista en la *(1)* prepa. / *(2)* universidad.

trade *vt* cambiar ~ **places** cambiar lugares ~ **stamps** cambiar timbres

tradition *n* tradición *f* **by** ~ por tradición **old** ~ vieja tradición

trail *n* sendero *m* **easy** ~ sendero fácil **good** ~ buen sendero **horse** ~ sendero para caballos **poor** ~ mal sendero **rocky** ~ sendero rocoso **steep** ~ sendero empinado **well-maintained** ~ sendero bien mantenido **Stay on the trail.** Manténgase en el sendero. **How far does the trail go?** ¿Hasta dónde va el sendero? **What kind of trail is it?** ¿Qué tipo de sendero es? **Does the trail have signs?** ¿Tiene señales el sendero? **What should** *(1)* **I** / *(2)* **we look out for on the trail?** ¿De qué *(1)* debo estar atento… / *(2)* debemos estar atentos… en el sendero?

trailer *n* remolque *m*, trailer *m* **boat** ~ remolque para bote **camping** ~ remolque para acampar **horse** ~ remolque para caballos ~ **hitch** gancho para remolque

train *vt* entrenar **I can see I have to train you.** Ya veo que te tengo que entrenar.

train *n* tren *m* ~ **schedule** itinerario del tren **What time does your train leave?** ¿A qué hora sale *su (Fam: tu)* tren? *(1)* **My** / *(2)* **Our train leaves at** *(time)*. *(1)* Mi / *(2)* Nuestro tren sale a las __. *(1)* **I** / *(2)* **We have to catch a train** (at *time*). *(1)* Tengo / *(2)* Tenemos que tomar un tren (a las __).

Numbers in parentheses always signal choices.

When is the next train to *(place)***?** ¿A qué hora sale el próximo tren a __?

Do *(1)* **I** / *(2)* **we have to change trains?** *(1)* ¿Tengo / *(2)* ¿Tenemos que cambiar de tren?

trainer *n (fitness)* entrenador *m*, -dora *f* **personal ~** entrenador personal

trait(s) *n (pl)* rasgo(s) *m (pl)* **family ~(s)** rasgo(s) familiar(es) **You have many fine traits (that I admire).** *Usted tiene (Fam: Tú tienes) muchos bellos rasgos (que yo admiro).*

trampoline *n* cama *f* elástica, trampolín *m*

tramway *n (cable railway)* funicular *m* **Let's take the tramway (to the top).** Tomemos el funicular (a la cima.)

trance *n* trance *m* **in a ~** en trance

tranquil *n* tranquilo *m*, -la *f*

transfer *vt (funds)* transferir **~ money** transferir dinero

transfer *vi (change buses / trains)* transferir **Where do** *(1)* **I** / *(2)* **we have to transfer?** ¿Dónde *(1)* tengo / *(2)* tenemos que transferir?

transfer *n (funds)* transferencia *f* **bank ~** transferencia bancaria **money ~** transferencia de dinero

transformer *n (elec.)* transformador *m*

translate *vt* traducir **~ from English to Spanish** traducir del inglés al español. **~ from Spanish to English** traducir del español al inglés. **Could you translate this (into** *[1]* **English** / *[2]* **Spanish) for me?** ¿Podrías traducirme esto (al *[1]* inglés / *[2]* español)? *(1)* **Is there somebody...** / *(2)* **Do you know somebody... who could translate it?** *(1)* ¿Hay alguien… / *(2)* ¿Conoces a alguien… que pudiera traducirlo? *(1)* **I** / *(2)* **We need to have this translated (into** *[3]* **English** / *[4]* **Spanish).** *(1)* Necesito / *(2)* Necesitamos que se traduzca esto (al *[3]* inglés / *[4]* español.) **Thank you for translating this for** *(1)* **me** / *(2)* **us.** Gracias por *(1)* traducirme / *(2)* traducirnos esto.

translation *n* traducción *f* **accurate ~** traducción fiel **incorrect ~** traducción incorrecta **literal ~** traducción literal **notarized ~** traducción notariada **~ from English into Spanish** traducción del inglés al español **~ from Spanish into English** traducción del español al inglés **How much is the translation fee?** ¿Cuál es el costo de la traducción?

translator *n* traductor *m*, -tora *f* **find a ~** encontrar un *(a)* traductor *(-tora)* **hire a ~** contratar un *(a)* traductor *(-tora)*

transmission *n (automot.)* transmisión *f* **The transmission is out.** La transmisión no sirve.

transportation *n* transporte *m* **arrange for ~** arreglar el transporte **public ~** transporte público *(1)* **I** / *(2)* **We need transportation** *(3)* **downtown.** / *(4)* **to** *(place)*. *(1)* Necesito / *(2)* Necesitamos transporte *(3)* al centro. / *(4)*

Spanish "a" is mostly like "a" in "mama".

a ___.

trap *vt* atrapar **You trapped me!** ¡Me atrapaste! **I trapped you!** ¡Te atrapé!

trap *n* trampa *f* **This must be some kind of trap.** Esto debe ser alguna clase de trampa.

trash *n* basura *f* ~ **can** bote de basura **Where can I throw this trash?** ¿Dónde puedo tirar esta basura?

travel *adj* de viaje(s) ~ **agency** agencia *f* de viajes ~ **agent** agente *m & f* de viajes ~ **companion** compañero *(-ra)* de viaje ~ **diary** diario *m* de viaje ~ **itinerary** itinerario de viaje ~ **plans** planes *m, pl* de viaje ~ **site** *(www)* sitio *m* de viajes en la red

travel *vi* viajar *(See also phrases under* **like** *and* **love.**) **Do you travel (1) often? / (2) a lot?** ¿Usted viaja (1) seguido? / (2) mucho? **I travel (1) often. / (2) sometimes. / (3) a lot.** Yo viajo (1) seguido. / (2) a veces. / (3) mucho. **Have you travelled a lot?** ¿Ha viajado usted (Fam: ¿Has viajado) mucho? **(1) I've / (2) We've travelled (3) quite a lot. / (4) to many countries. / (5) a little.** (1) Yo he viajado… / (2) Nosotros hemos viajado… (3) mucho. / (4) a muchos países. / (5) poquito. **(1) I / (2) We haven't travelled (3) much. / (4) before.** (1) Yo no he viajado… / (2) Nosotros no hemos viajado… (3) mucho / (4) antes. **(1) I've / (2) We've never travelled to Mexico before.** (1) Yo nunca había viajado… / (2) Nosotros nunca habíamos viajado… a México. **Have you ever travelled to (1) America? / (2) Australia? / (3) Canada? / (4) England? / (5) (country)?** ¿Nunca ha viajado usted (Fam: has viajado) a (1) Estados Unidos? / (2) Australia? / (3) Canadá? / (4) Inglaterra? / (5) ___? **1) I / (2) We love to travel.** (1) Me encanta… / (2) Nos encanta … viajar. **(1) Would you like to... / (2) Could you ... travel with me?** (1) ¿Le (Fam: ¿Te) gustaría ... / (2) ¿Podría usted (Fam: Podrías)... viajar conmigo? **Let's travel (there) together.** Viajemos (allá) juntos. **I would love to travel with you.** Me encantaría viajar *con usted (Fam: contigo).*

travel *n* viaje *m* **world** ~ viaje por el mundo

traveler *n* viajero *m*, –ra *f* **experienced** ~ viajero *(-ra)* experimentado *(-da)* **world** ~ viajero *(-ra)* del mundo

treasure *vt* atesorar **I will always treasure (1) this. / (2) the memories of this wonderful time with you.** Siempre atesoraré (1) esto. / (2) los recuerdos de este maravilloso momento contigo.

treasure *n* tesoro *m* **go ~ hunting** ir a buscar tesoros **hunt for ~** buscar tesoros **You are the treasure of my heart** Eres el tesoro de mi corazón. **What a treasure you are.** Eres un tesoro. **You're a treasure chest of brilliant ideas.** Eres todo un tesoro de ideas brillantes.

treat *vt* 1. *(have as a guest)* convidar; 2. *(act toward)* tratar **(1) I / (2) We**

Articles: m = el, f = la, mpl = los, fpl = las

want to *(3,4)* **treat you.** *(1)* Yo quiero… / *(2)* Nosotros queremos… *(3)* convidarlo *m* / *(4)* convidarla *f (Fam: convidarte).* **I'm sorry for the way I treated you.** Lamento la manera en que te traté. **I treated you badly and I apologize.** Te traté mal y me disculpo. **Treat others the same way you want to be treated.** Trata a los demás como quieras que te traten.

treat *n* gusto *m*   **nice ~** gusto rico   **special ~** gusto especial

tree *n* árbol *m*   **Christmas ~** árbol de Navidad   **climb the ~** subirse al árbol   **family ~** árbol genealógico   **shady ~** árbol frondoso   **Let's have our picnic under that tree.** Tengamos nuestro día de campo bajo ese árbol. **Let's sit under that tree.** Vamos a sentarnos bajo ese árbol.

trekking *n* caminata *f,* trekking *m*

tremendous *adj* tremendo *m,* -da *f*

tremendously *adv* tremendamente

trick *vt* engañar   **You tricked me!** ¡Me engañaste!

trick *n* 1. *(skillful act)* travesura *f,* truco *m* ; 2. *(cards won)* baza *f*   **card ~** truco *m* de naipes   **play a ~** *(on someone)* hacer una travesura   **take a ~** *(cards)* hacerse una baza   **win a ~** *(cards)* ganar una baza   **No tricks!** ¡Sin trucos! **What a dirty trick!** ¡Qué truco tan sucio! **You're full of tricks, aren't you?** Estás lleno de bromas, ¿no es cierto? **You don't miss a trick, do you?** No se te va una broma, ¿o sí? **Let me show you a card trick.** Déjame mostrarte un truco de naipes.

tricky *adj (devious, sly)* tramposo *m,* -sa *f*

trim *adj (slender)* delgado *m,* -da *f*

trinket *n* chuchería *f*

trip *n* viaje *m*   **bike ~** viaje en bicicleta   **boat ~** viaje en barco   **bus ~** viaje en autobús   **business ~** viaje de negocios   **camping ~** ir de campamento   **field ~** viaje de estudio   **go on a ~** ir de viaje   **honeymoon ~** viaje de luna de miel   **long ~** viaje largo   **motorcycle ~** viaje en motocicleta   **nice ~** viaje agradable   **on this ~** en este viaje   **short ~** viaje corto   **take a ~** hacer un viaje   **train ~** viaje en tren   **Would you like to go on a trip (with *[1]* me / *[2]* us)?** ¿Te gustaría ir de viaje (*[1]* conmigo / *[2]* con nosotros)? **Let's go on a trip (together) to** *(place).* Viajemos (juntos) a __. **Enjoy your trip!** ¡Que disfrute usted su *(Fam: disfrutes tu)* viaje! **Have a *(1)* good / *(2)* safe trip!** ¡Que tenga usted *(Fam: tengas)* un *(1)* buen viaje! / *(2)* viaje seguro!

triumph *vi* triunfar   *(1)* **I** / *(2)* **We triumphed again!** *(1)* ¡Triunfé / *(2)* ¡Triunfamos otra vez!

trolley *n* carrito *m,* carretilla *f*

trophy *n* trofeo *m*

trouble *vt (bother)* molestar   **I'm sorry to trouble you.** Disculpe *(Fam: Disculpa* la molestia.

Spanish "z" is pronounced like "s" in "safe".

trouble *n* 1. *(unpleasantness)* problema *f*; 2. *(difficulties, inconvenience, bother)* molestia *f* *(1)* **I** / *(2)* **We don't want to make any trouble (for you).** No *(1)* quiero / *(2)* queremos dar(-*le* (*Fam: -te*)) molestias. **Please don't go to a lot of trouble.** Por favor, no te metas en tantos problemas. **You shouldn't have gone to so much trouble.** *No debió usted tomarse (Fam: No debiste tomarte)* tanta molestia. **That's too much trouble.** Eso es demasiada molestia. **It's no trouble at all.** No es molestia. **I don't want to get in trouble.** No quiero meterme en problemas. **Try to stay out of trouble, okay?** Trata de no meterte en problemas, ¿sí?

troublemaker *n* alborotador *m*, -dora *f*

trounce *vt (completely defeat)* vapulear

trousers *n, pl* pantalones *mpl* **pair of** ~ unos pantalones

trout *n* trucha *f*

truck *n* camión *m* **tow** ~ grúa *f*

true *adj* 1. *(not false)* cierto *m*, -ta *f*; 2. *(loyal)* fiel *m & f* **Is that (really) true?** ¿Es cierto (de veras)? **It's (not) true. (I swear.)** (No) Es cierto. (Lo juro.) **Tell me true.** Dime la verdad. **I will always be true to you.** Siempre te seré fiel.

truly *adv (sincerely)* sinceramente, de veras

trump *vt* vencer, ganar

trump *n* triunfo *m* **What's trump?** ¿Qué triunfa?

trust *vt* confiar **(Please) trust me.** (Por favor) confía en mí. **Don't you trust me?** ¿No *confía usted (Fam: confías tú)* en mí? **I (don't) trust you.** (No) confío en *usted (Fam: ti)*.

trust *n* confianza *f* **I would never betray your trust.** Nunca traicionaría *su (Fam: tu)* confianza. **You have shattered my trust in you.** Has perdido mi confianza.

trusted *adj* fiable *m&f*, de confianza **Can you be trusted?** ¿Se puede confiar en ti?

trusting *adj* confiado *m*, -da *f* ~ **soul** alma cándida

trustworthy *adj* digno *m*, -na *f* de confianza, confiable *m&f*

truth *n* verdad *f* **absolute** ~ verdad absoluta **honest** ~ la verdad neta **plain** ~ la pura verdad **real** ~ la mera verdad **simple** ~ simple verdad **tell the** ~ decir la verdad **whole** ~ toda la verdad **Are you telling me the truth?** ¿Me estás diciendo la verdad? **You're not telling me the truth.** No me estás diciendo la verdad. **I'm telling you the truth.** *Le (Fam: Te)* estoy diciendo la verdad. **Tell me the truth.** Dime la verdad. **I'll tell you the whole truth.** *Le (Fam: Te)* diré toda la verdad. **Is that the truth?** ¿Es esa la verdad? **That's (not) the truth.** Esa (no) es la verdad. **The truth is** *(1)* **I love you very much.** / *(2)* **I'm married.** La verdad es que *(1)* te amo

---

A tilde ~ *in terms stands for the main entry word.*

muchísimo. / *(2)* estoy casado *(-da)*.

try *vt* probar **I'll try (almost) anything once.** Probaré (casi) todo una vez. **Go ahead, try** *(1)* **it.** / *(2)* **some.** Anda, *(1)* pruébatelo. / *(2)* prueba unos. **I want to try everything with you.** Quiero probarlo todo contigo.

try *vi* intentar, tratar **Please try.** Por favor, inténtalo. **I'll try.** Lo voy a intentar. **We'll try.** Lo vamos a intentar. **I tried.** Lo intenté

T-shirt *n* playera *f*

tub *n* tina *f* hot ~ tina caliente

Tuesday *n* martes *m* **last ~** el martes pasado **next ~** el próximo martes **on ~** en martes

tune *n (melody)* tonada *f* **whistle the ~** silbar la tonada **Do you know the tune?** ¿Se sabe usted *(Fam: ¿Te sabes)* la tonada?

turbulent *adj* turbulento *m*, -ta *f*

turn *vt* dar vuelta **Turn it** *(1)* **this way.** / *(2)* **to the left** / *(3)* **right.** Dale vuelta *(1)* hacia acá. / *(2)* a la izquierda. / *(3)* a la derecha.

turn *vi* dar vuelta **Turn** *(1)* **left** / *(2)* **right (at the next street).** Da vuelta a la *(1)* izquierda / *(2)* derecha (en la próxima calle).

★ **turn around** *idiom* voltearse **Turn around.** *Voltéese usted (Fam: Voltéate)*.

★ **turn back** *idiom (go back)* regresar **I think we ought to turn back.** Creo que debemos regresar. *(1)* **I'm** / *(2)* **We're going to turn back.** *(1)* Voy / *(2)* Vamos a regresar. **Let's turn back.** Regresemos.

★ **turn down** *idiom* 1. *(reduce volume)* bajar (el volumen); 2. *(refuse, decline)* rechazar **Turn it down.** Bájale. **Turn down the** *(1)* **CD.** / *(2)* **radio.** / *(3)* **TV.** Bájale al volumen *(1)* del CD. / *(2)* del radio. / *(3)* de la tele. **I was afraid you'd turn me down.** Temía que me rechazaras.

★ **turn off** *idiom* 1. *(switch off)* apagar; 2. *(exit)* salir **Turn it off.** Apágale. **Turn off the** *(1)* **light.** / *(2)* **TV.** Apaga la *(1)* luz / *(2)* tele. **Turn off** *(1)* **on that road.** / *(2)* **over there.** Salte en ese *(1)* camino. / *(2)* por allí.

★ **turn on** *idiom* 1. *(switch on)* encender; 2. *(excite)* excitar **Turn it on.** Enciéndelo. **Turn on the** *(1)* **light.** / *(2)* **TV.** Enciende la *(1)* luz. / *(2)* tele. *(1,2)* **You (really) turn me on.** *(1)* Tú (realmente) me excitas. / *(2)* Tú me vuelves loco *(-ca)*.

★ **turn out** *idiom (result, develop, come out)* resultar **How did it turn out?** ¿Cómo resultó? **Everthying turned out okay.** Todo resultó bien. **It didn't turn out so well.** No resultó tan bien.

★ **turn over** *idiom* 1. *(cards: uncover)* voltear; 2. *(roll over)* rodar, dar

---

*Spanish "ch" is pronounced like ours
(e.g., "cheese," "charge").*

la vuelta **Turn over a card.** Voltea una carta. **Turn over. (I'll put some lotion on your back.)** Date la vuelta. (Voy a ponerte loción en la espalda.)

★ **turn up** *idiom (increase volume)* subir (el volumen) **Turn it up.** Súbele. **Turn up the** *(1)* **CD.** / *(2)* **radio.** / *(3)* **TV.** Súbele *(1)* al CD. / *(2)* al radio. / *(3)* a la tele.

turn *n (occasion, opportunity)* turno *m* **Whose turn is it?** ¿De quién es el turno? **It's** *(1)* **her** / *(2)* **his** / *(3)* **my** / *(4)* **your turn.** Es *(1,2)* su / *(3)* mi / *(4)* su *(Fam: tu)* turno. **You played out of turn.** Jugaste fuera de turno. **Everybody take turns.** Túrnense todos.

turtle *n* tortuga *f* **sea ~** tortuga de mar **slow as a ~** lento como una tortuga

tutor *vt* dar clases **Could you tutor me?** ¿Me podrías dar clases? **I'd be more than happy to tutor you.** Me encantaría darte clases.

tutor *n* profesor *m*, -sora *f* **Would you like to be my tutor?** ¿Le *(Fam: ¿Te)* gustaría ser mi profesor *(-sora)*? **I'll be your tutor.** Yo seré *su (Fam: tu)* profesor *(-sora)*.

tweezers *n, pl* pinzas *fpl*

twice *adv* dos veces

twin *adj* gemelo *m*, -la *f* **~ bed** cama gemela **~ brother** hermano gemelo **~ sister** hermana gemela

twins *n, pl* mellizos *mpl*, -zas *fpl*

twine *n* cordel *m*

twist *vt* torcer **Twist it.** Tuércelo.

two-faced *adj* de dos caras, falso *m*, -sa *f*

type *vt & vi (on a keyboard)* teclear

type *n* tipo *m* **body ~** tipo de cuerpo **my ~** mi tipo **silent ~** tipo callado **that ~** ese tipo **this ~** este tipo **what ~** qué tipo

typical *adj* típico *m*, -ca *f*

Stress rule #1: The last syllable is stressed if the word ends in a consonant (except "n" and "s").

U

ugly *adj* feo *m*, fea *f* ~ **duckling** patito *m* feo **You're not ugly! You're beautiful!** ¡No eres fea! ¡Eres hermosa!

umbrella *n* paraguas *m* **beach** ~ sombrilla *f* de playa **sun** ~ quitasol *m*

unable *adj* incapaz, no poder **be** ~ ser incapaz **I'm unable to stay longer.** No puedo quedarme más tiempo. **We're unable to go.** No podemos ir.

unaccustomed *adj* desacostumbrado *m*, -da *f* **be** ~ estar desacostumbrado *(-da)*

unattached *adj* libre *m&f*, soltero *m*, -ra *f* **I'm unattached (at the present time).** (Por ahora) Estoy libre. **I hope you're unattached. Are you?** Espero que estés libre. ¿Lo estás?

unaware *adj*: **be** ~ **(of)** no ser consciente (de), estar ajeno *(-na)* (de)

unbearable *adj* insoportable *m&f*

unbelievable *adj* increíble *m&f*

unbelievably *adv* increíblemente

unbounded *adj* infinito *m*, -ta *f*

unbutton *vt* desabotonar, desabrochar

uncalled-for *adj* 1. *(unnecessary; undeserved)* innecesario *m*, -ria *f*; 2. *(out of place)* fuera de lugar

uncanny *adj* asombroso *m*, -sa *f* **You have uncanny luck.** Tiene usted *(Fam. Tienes)* una suerte asombrosa.

uncertain *adj* incierto *m*, -ta *f*

uncivilized *adj* incivilizado *m*, -da *f* **Your behavior is uncivilized.** Tu comportamiento es incivilizado.

uncle *n* tío *m* **rich** ~ tío rico

uncomfortable *adj* incómodo *m*, -da *f* **It makes me uncomfortable when you** *(1)* **talk like that.** / *(2)* **do that.** Me incomoda cuando *(1)* hablas así. / *(2)* haces eso.

uncommon *adj* raro *m*, -ra *f*, inusual *m&f*, poco común

Spanish "i" is mostly "ee", but can also be shorter, like "i" in "sit," when together with other vowels.

unconscious *adj* 1. *(having lost consciousness)* inconsciente *m&f*; 2. *(involuntary)* involuntario *m*, -ria *f*

unconsciously *adv* inconscientemente, involuntariamente

uncontrollable *adj* incontrolable *m&f* ~ **desire** deseo incontrolable ~ **impulse** impulso incontrolable

undecided *adj* indeciso *m*, -sa *f* **I'm (still) undecided.** (Todavía) Estoy indeciso *(-sa)*. **We're (still) undecided.** (Todavía) Estamos indecisos.

undemanding *adj* cómodo *m*, -da *f*, poco exigente *m&f*

under *prep* bajo, debajo de ~ **the water** bajo el agua

underage(d) *adj* menor *m&f* de edad

underbrush *n* maleza *f*, breña *f*

underestimate *vt* subestimar **I underestimated** *(1,2)* **you.** *(1) Lo m / (2) La f (Fam. Te)* subestimé. **Don't underestimate me.** No me subestimes.

underhanded *adj* clandestino *m*, -na *f*, encubierto *m*, -ta *f*

underpants *n, pl* calzones *mpl*

understand *vt* entender **Do you understand (**[1] **me /** [2] **it)?** *(*[1] *¿Me... [2] ¿Lo...) entiende usted (Fam. entiendes tú)?* **I (don't) understand (**[1,2] **you /** [3] **it).** Yo (no) *(*[1] *lo m /* [2] *la f (Fam. te) /* [3] *lo)* entiendo. **I didn't understand what you said.** Yo no entendí lo que *usted dijo (Fam. tú dijiste)*. **I hope you understand.** Espero que *usted entienda (Fam. tú entiendas)*.

understandable *adj* comprensible *m&f*

understanding *adj* comprensivo *m*, -va *f* **You're very understanding.** *Usted es (Fam. Tú eres)* muy comprensivo *(-va)*.

understatement *n* declaración *(1)* mesurada / *(2)* comedida **That's the understatement of the year.** Esa es la declaración más mesurada del año.

undertow *n* trasfondo *m*

undoubtedly *adv* indudablemente

undress *vt* desvestir **slowly** ~ *(s.o.)* desvestir lentamente

undress *vi* desvestirse

undying *adj* imperecedero *m*, -dera *f*, perpetuo *m*, -tua *f*, eterno *m*, -na *f* ~ **love** amor eterno

unemployed *adj* desempleado *m*, -da *f*

unenthusiastic *adj* poco entusiasta *m&f*, indolente *m&f*

unequal *adj* desigual *m&f*

unexpected *adj* inesperado *m*, -da *f* **That was unexpected.** Eso fue inesperado.

unfair *adj* injusto *m*, -ta *f*

unfaithful *adj* infiel *m&f* **I will never be unfaithful to you.** Nunca te seré infiel.

unfamiliar *adj* desconocido *m*, -da *f*

Help us improve our book!
Send us the feedback form on page 431.

unfasten *vt* desabrochar, desatar **Can you unfasten this (for me)?** ¿Puedes desatar(me) esto?

unforgettable *adj* inolvidable *m&f*

unforgivable *adj* imperdonable *m&f*

unfortunate *adj* desafortunado *m*, -da *f*

unfortunately *adv* desafortunadamente **Unfortunately, (1) I / (2) we can't make it.** Desafortunadamente, *(1)* yo no puedo... / *(2)* nosotros no podemos... llegar.

unfriendly *adj* poco amistoso *m*, -sa *f*, antipático *m*, -ca *f*

ungrateful *adj* desagradecido *m*, -da *f*

unhappiness *n* desdicha *f*

unhappy *adj* infeliz *m&f*, disgustado *m*, -da *f* **I'm sorry I made (1,2) you unhappy.** Lamento *(1) haberlo m / (2) haberla f (Fam. haberte)* disgustado. **Why are you unhappy?** ¿Por qué *está usted (Fam: estás)* disgustado *(-da)*? **I don't want you to be unhappy.** No quiero que *esté usted (Fam. estés)* disgustado *(-da)*.

unharmed *adj* ileso *m*, -sa *f*, intacto *m*, -ta *f*

unhealthy *adj* malsano *m*, -na *f*, enfermizo *m*, -za *f*

uniform *n (mil.)* uniforme *m* **in ~** de uniforme

unimaginable *adj* inimaginable *m&f*

uninhabited *adj* deshabitado *m*, -da *f*

uninhibited *adj* desinhibido *m*, -da *f*

uninvited *adj* no invitado, sin invitación **come ~** venir sin invitación

unique *adj* único *m*, -ca *f*, singular *m&f*

United States of America *n, pl* Estados Unidos de Norteamérica.

universal *adj* universal *m&f*

universe *n* universo *m*

university *n* universidad *f* **enter the ~** entrar a la universidad **Which university do you go to?** ¿A qué universidad *va usted (Fam. vas tú)*? **I go to (name) University.** Voy a la Universidad de ___. **What are you studying at the university?** ¿Qué *estudia usted (Fam: estudias)* en la universidad? **I graduated from the university (1) in (year). / (2) last year.** Me gradué de la universidad *(1)* en ___. / *(2)* el año pasado.

unkind *adj* poco amable *m & f*, descortés *m & f*

unless *conj* a menos que **...unless it rains.** ...a menos que llueva.

unlike *adj* distinto *m*, -ta *f*, diferente *m & f* **You're unlike anyone I've ever met.** *Usted es (Fam. Tú eres)* distinto *(-ta)* a las personas que he conocido.

unlikely *adj* improbable *m & f*

unlock *vt* abrir una cerradura

unloved *adj* sin amor **Until I met you, I felt (completely) unloved.** Hasta

Spanish "j" is pronounced like "h".

que te conocí, me sentía (totalmente) sin amor.

unlucky *adj* desdichado *m*, -da *f*, desafortunado *m*, -da *f*

unmarried *adj* soltero *m*, -ra *f*, no casado *m*, -da *f*

unmerciful *adj* despiadado *m*, -da *f*, cruel *m&f* **You're unmerciful.** Tú eres despiadado *(-da)*.

unnatural *adj* poco natural *m&f*, antinatural *m&f*

unnecessary *adj* innecesario *m*, -ria *f*

unpack *vt & vi* desempacar ~ *(1)* **my** / *(2)* **your suitcase** desempacar *(1)* mi / *(2)* su *(Fam: tu)* maleta ~ **our suitcases** desempacar nuestras maletas *(1)* **I** / *(2)* **We (still) have to unpack.** (Todavía) *(1)* Tengo / *(2)* Tenemos que desempacar.

unpleasant *adj* desagradable *m&f*

unpredictable *adj* impredecible *m&f* **You're really unpredictable.** *Usted es (Fam. Tú eres)* verdaderamente impredecible.

unreal *adj* irreal *m&f*

unreasonable *adj* irrazonable *m&f*

unsaddle *vt* desensillar, derribar al jinete

unsafe *adj* inseguro *m*, -ra *f*, peligroso *m*, -sa *f*

unshaven *adj* sin rasurar

unsociable *adj* insociable *m&f*, huraño *m*, -ña *f*

unsophisticated *adj* sencillo *m*, -lla *f*, poco sofisticado *m*, -da *f*

unspeakable *adj* indecible *m&f*

unsuccessful *adj* fracasado *m*, -da *f*, desafortunado *m*, -da *f*

unthinking *adj* irreflexivo *m*, -va *f*, precipitado *m*, -da *f*

untie *vt* desatar

until 1. *prep* hasta; 2. *conj* hasta **Until tomorrow!** ¡Hasta mañana!

untrue *adj* falso *m*, -sa *f*, infiel *m&f*

unused *adj (never used)* sin estrenar, nuevo *m*, -va *f*

unusual *adj* inusual *m&f*

unwelcome *adj* inoportuno *m*, -na *f*, poco grato *m*, -ta *f*

unwind *vi (relax)* relajarse *(1)* **I** / *(2)* **We just want to unwind for a few days.** Sólo *(1)* quiero relajarme… / *(2)* queremos relajarnos… unos días.

unwise *adj* imprudente *m&f*, necio *m*, -cia *f*

unzip *vt* abrir *(1)* el cierre / *(2)* el zíper

up *adv (upward)* arriba **go ~ the mountain** subir la montaña

upbeat *adj (slang: positive)* optimista *m & f*

up *adv* arriba **What's up?** Qué pasa?

★ **up for** 1. *(slang: ready, willing to try)* listo *m*, -ta *f*; 2. *(motivated, fired up)* entusiasmado *m*, -da *f* **I'm up for (almost) anything.** Yo estoy listo *(-ta)* para (casi) todo. **I'm up for this match.** Estoy

---

Familiar "tu" forms in parentheses can replace italicized polite forms.

entusiasmado *(-da)* con este partido.

★ **up on** *idiom (informed, knowledgeable)* informado *m*, -da *f* **I try to stay up on current events.** Trato de estar informado *(-da)* de los acontecimientos actuales.

★ **up to** *idiom* 1. *(engaged in)* hacer, andar; 2. *(depend on)* corresponder, depender **What are you up to?** ¿Qué haces? / ¿En qué andas? **You're up to no good, I know.** No andas en nada bueno, yo lo sé. **That's up to you**. Eso, como tú quieras. **It's not up to me.** No me corresponde.

up-front *adj (slang: forthright)* directo *m*, -ta *f*

uphill *adv* cuesta arriba, en subida

upper *adj* superior *m&f*, de arriba ~ **berth** la litera *f* de arriba

uproar *n* alboroto *m* **What's all the uproar?** ¿Qué es ese alboroto?

upset *adj* disgustado *m*, -da *f* **get** ~ disgustarse **What are you upset about?** ¿Por qué estás disgustado *(-da)*? **You sound (a little) upset.** Se te oye (un poco) disgustado *(-da)*. **I'm (not) upset.** (No) Estoy disgustado *(-da)*.

upside down *idiom* de cabeza, patas arriba **You've turned my world upside-down.** Has puesto mi mundo de cabeza.

upstairs *adv* arriba **go** ~ subir (las escaleras) *(1)* **He / (2) She / (3) It is... / (4) They are... upstairs.** *(1)* Él está / *(2)* Ella está / *(3)* Está *(4)* Están ...arriba.

uptight *adj (slang: tense)* tenso *m*, -sa *f*

urge *n* ganas *fpl*, impulso *m* **overpowering** ~ impulso irresistible **tremendous** ~ tremendas ganas **I have an uncontrollable urge to** *(1)* **bop you on the head. / (2) kiss you. / (3) scream.** Tengo unas ganas incontenibles de *(1)* darte un coscorrón. *(2)* besarte. *(3)* gritar.

urgent *adj* urgente *m&f* ~ **matter** asunto *m* urgente ~ **message** mensaje *m* urgente ~ **request** solicitud *f* urgente

use *vt* usar **Could I (please) use** *(1)* **this? / (2) that?** ¿Puedo usar *(1)* esto / *(2)* eso (por favor)? **Could I (please) use your** *(1)* **bathroom? / (2) computer? / (3) dictionary? / (4) map? / (5) pen? / (6) telephone?** ¿Puedo usar *su (Fam. tu)* *(1)* baño / *(2)* computadora / *(3)* diccionario / *(4)* mapa / *(5)* lapicero / *(6)* teléfono (por favor)? **Here, use** *(1)* **this. / (2) mine.** Ten, *(1)* usa esto *(2)* usa el mío. **Could you show me how to use this?** ¿Me *puede usted (Fam. puedes tú)* enseñar cómo se usa esto? **I'll show you how to use it.** Yo *le (Fam. te)* enseño a usarlo.

used *adj* usado *m*, -da *f* ~ **car** un carro *m* usado

used to *idiom* 1. *(accustomed to)* acostumbrado *m*, -da *f* ; 2. *(formerly)* acostumbraba **get** ~ acostumbrarse **I'm not used to** *(1)* **this. / (2) the food.** No estoy acostumbrado *(-da)* a *(1)* esto. / *(2)* esta comida. **We're not used to** *(1)* **that. / (2) the weather.** No estamos acostumbrados a *(1)* eso. / *(2)*

Spanish "e" is pronounced like English "e" in "get"

al clima. **I used to go camping a lot, but I don't anymore.** Antes iba
mucho a acampar, pero ya no voy.

useful *adj* útil *m & f* **Take it along, it might be useful.** Llévatelo, te puede
ser útil.

useless *adj* inútil *m & f*, inservible *m & f*

usual *adj* usual *m & f*, acostumbrado *m*, -da *f*

usually *adv* usualmente

utensil *n* utensilio *m* **eating ~s** utensilios para comer

vacancy *n* vacante *f* **There's a vacancy.** Hay una vacante.
vacant *adj* desocupado *m*, -da *f* ~ **apartment** departamento *m* desocupado ~ **cabin** cabina *f* desocupada ~ **house** casa *f* desocupada ~ **room** habitación *f* desocupada
vacation *n* vacaciones *f*, *pl* **go on a** ~ ir de vacaciones **nice** ~ bonitas vacaciones **one-month** ~ un mes de vacaciones **one-week** ~ una semana de vacaciones **school** ~ vacaciones de la escuela **summer** ~ vacaciones de verano **take a** ~ tomar unas vacaciones **three-week** ~ tres semanas de vacaciones **two-week** ~ dos semanas de vacaciones **wonderful** ~ vacaciones maravillosas **Are you on vacation?** ¿Está usted (Fam: ¿Estás) de vacaciones? *(1)* **I'm** */ (2)* **We're on vacation.** *(1)* Estoy */ (2)* Estamos de vacaciones. **How long is your vacation?** ¿De cuánto tiempo son *sus (Fam. tus)* vacaciones? *(1)* **My** */ (2)* **Our vacation is for** *(number)* **weeks.** *(1)* Mis */ (2)* Nuestras vacaciones son por ___ semanas.
vague *adj* vago *m*, -ga *f* ~ **idea** idea *f* vaga ~ **recollection** recuerdo *m* vago
vaguely *adv* vagamente ~ **recall** recordar vagamente
vain *adj* 1. *(futile)* vano *m*, -na *f*, inútil *m&f*; 2. *(conceited)* vano *m*, -na *f*
Valentine *n* 1. *(sweetheart)* enamorado *m*, -da *f*; 2. *(Valentine's Day card)* tarjeta del día de San Valentín
Valentine's Day Día de San Valentín.
valley *n* valle *m*
valuable *adj* valioso *m*, -sa *f* **Is it valuable?** ¿Es valioso *(-sa)*? **It's (**[1]**) very** */* [2]**) not) valuable.** *(1)* Es muy valioso *(-sa)*. (2) No es valioso *(-sa)*.
value *vt* apreciar **I value your** *(1)* **friendship** */ (2)* **opinion.** Aprecio *su (Fam: tu)* (1) amistad */ (2)* opinión.
value *n* valor *m* **artistic** ~s valores artísticos **family** ~s valores familiares **good moral** ~s buenos valores morales **old-fashioned** ~s valores anticuados **spiritual** ~s valores espirituales **strong** ~s valores sólidos **traditional** ~s

---

Spanish "x" is always like "ks", as in our word "taxi".

valores tradicionales **It seems we share the same values.** Parece que compartimos los mismos valores.

vampire *n* vampiro *m*

van *n* vagoneta *f*

vanish *vi* desvanecer

variety *n* variedad *f* **a lot of** ~ mucha variedad **not much** ~ no mucha variedad **wide** ~ amplia variedad **Variety is the spice of life.** En la variedad está el gusto.

various *adj* diversos *mpl*, -sas *fpl*

vast *adj* vasto *m*, -ta *f*, gran *m&f* ~ **difference** gran diferencia

vegetable *n* verdura *f*

vegetarian *n* vegetariano *m*, -na *f*

velvet(y) *adj* de terciopelo, aterciopelado *m*, -da *f*

vendor *n* vendedor *m*, -dora *f* **ice cream** ~ heladero *m*, -ra *f*

vengeance *n* venganza *f* **Vengeance is mine!** ¡La venganza es mía!

verb *n* verbo *m* **Excuse me, could you tell me how to conjugate this verb (in the** *[1]* **future** / *[2]* **past** / *[3]* **present tense)?** *Disculpe (Fam: Disculpa), ¿podría usted (Fam: podrías) decirme cómo conjugar este verbo (en tiempo [1] futuro / [2] pasado / [3] presente)?*

versatile *adj* versátil *m&f* **You're quite versatile.** *Es usted (Fam. Eres)* bastante versátil.

verse *n (music: stanza)* verso *m*

versus *prep* contra **It's the good guys versus the bad guys.** Son los buenos contra los malos.

vertical *adj* vertical *m&f*

very *adv* muy ~ **much** mucho **That's very nice of you.** Eso es muy amable de tu parte. **Thank you very much.** Muchísimas gracias.

veteran *n* veterano *m*, -na *f* **military** ~ veterano *(-na)* del ejército **war** ~ veterano *(-na)* de guerra

via *prep* por

vice versa viceversa

vicinity *n* vecindario *m*, alrededores *mpl* **in the** ~ **of** en los alrededores de **What do they have in this vicinity?** ¿Qué tienen en este vecindario?

vicious *adj* vicioso *m*, -sa *f*, depravado *m*, -da *f*

victim *n* víctima *f*

victorious *adj* victorioso *m*, -sa *f* **Victorious again!** ¡Otra vez victorioso *(-sa)*!

victory *n* victoria *f* **Another victory for the champion.** Otra victoria para el campeón.

video *n (tape)* video *m* **return the** ~ devolver el video ~ **camera** cámara de

---

Stress rule # 3: Syllables with accent marks have the stress there.

video ~**cassette recorder (VCR)** grabadora de videocintas ~**shop** tienda de video ~**tape** videocinta **Where can we rent a video?** ¿Dónde podemos rentar un video? **Let's watch a video.** Vamos a ver un video.

view *n* 1. *(sight, panorama)* vista *f*; 2. *(conception)* opinión *f* **beautiful** ~ vista hermosa **great** ~ gran vista **liberal** ~**s** opiniones liberales **magnificent** ~ vista magnífica **panoramic** ~ vista panorámica **personal** ~ opinión personal ~ **of the ocean** vista del océano **Let's look at the view from there.** Vamos a ver la vista desde aquí. **What a** *(1)* **beautiful /** *(2)* **great view!** ¡Qué vista tan *(1)* hermosa / *(2)* fenomenal!

vigor *n* 1. *(energy)* vigor *m*; 2. *(strength)* vigor *m* **full of** ~ lleno *(-na)* de vigor

villa *n* villa *f* **rent a** ~ rentar una villa ~ **by the sea** villa junto al mar

village *n* pueblo *m* **small** ~ un pueblito

villain *n* villano *m*, -na *f*

vineyard *n* viñedo *m*

vintage *n* cosecha *f* **What vintage is this wine?** ¿De qué cosecha es este vino?

violence *n* violencia *f* **No violence, please.** Sin violencia, por favor. **I abhor violence (in any form).** Aborrezco la violencia (en cualquier forma).

violin *n* violín *m* **I play the violin.** Yo toco el violín.

virgin *n* virgen *f* **Are you a virgin?** ¿Eres virgen? **I'm (not) a virgin.** (No) Soy virgen.

virtue *n* virtud *f* **It's one of my many virtues.** Es una de mis muchas virtudes.

visa *n* visa *f* **business** ~ visa de negocios **entry** ~ visa de ingreso **exit** ~ visa de salida **fiancee** ~ visa de prometido **tourist** ~ visa de turista **visitor('s)** ~ visa de visitante

visit *vt* visitar *(1)* **I /** *(2)* **We want to visit** *(place).* *(1)* Quiero / *(2)* Queremos visitar ___. *(1)* **I /** *(2)* **We visited** *(place).* *(1)* Visité / *(2)* Visitamos ___. **Let's go visit** *(place).* Vamos a visitar ___. **Can I come visit you (in your home)?** ¿Puedo venir a visitarte (a tu casa)? **Please come visit** *(1)* **me /** *(2)* **us.** Por favor ven a *(1)* visitarme / *(2)* visitarnos.

visit *n* visita *f* **first** ~ primera visita **long** ~ visita larga **my** ~ mi visita **next** ~ próxima visita **nice** ~ visita agradable **our** ~ nuestra visita **pleasant** ~ visita agradable **second** ~ segunda visita **short** ~ visita breve **social** ~ visita social **your** ~ *su (Fam: tu)* visita *(1)* **I /** *(2)* **We want to pay a visit to** *(place).* Yo quiero / *(2)* Nosotros queremos hacer una visita a ___.

visitor *n* visitante *m&f*

vitality *n (liveliness)* vitalidad *f*; *(energy)* vitalidad *f* **full of** ~ lleno *(-na)* de vitalidad

vivacious *adj* vivaz *m&f* ~ **personality** de personalidad vivaz **You're the**

Spanish pronunciation rules are on pages 407-408.

most vivacious woman I've ever met. *Usted es (Fam: Tú eres)* la mujer más vivaz que he conocido.

vixen *n* zorra *f*, arpía *f*

vocabulary *n* vocabulario *m* **large** ~ vocabulario extenso **My Spanish vocabulary is small.** Mi vocabulario en español es muy escaso. **I need to build my vocabulary.** Necesito aumentar mi vocabulario.

voice *n* voz *f* **deep** ~ voz profunda **gentle** ~ voz suave **good** ~ buena voz **melodic** ~ voz melodiosa **my** ~ mi voz **silky** ~ voz de seda **soft** ~ voz suave **sweet** ~ voz dulce **warm** ~ voz afectuosa **You have a** *(1)* **beautiful** */ (2)* **nice** */ (3)* **sexy voice.** *Tiene usted (Fam. Tienes)* una voz *(1)* hermosa. */ (2)* bonita. */ (3)* sensual. **I like to listen to your voice.** Me gusta escuchar *su (Fam. tu)* voz. **Your voice is so soothing.** *(Su (Fam. Tu)* voz es tan tranquilizante.

volcano *n* volcán *m*

volleyball *n* volibol *m (See also phrases under* **like, love** *and* **play**.*)*

volume *n (loudness)* volumen *m* **Please turn the volume down.** Por favor, bájale al volumen.

volunteer *vi* ofrecerse como voluntario *m*, -ria *f* **I volunteer.** Yo me ofrezco como voluntario *(-ria)*.

volunteer *n* voluntario *m*, -ria *f* **We need a volunteer. I pick you.** Necesito un voluntario. Te elijo a ti.

voluptuous *adj* voluptuoso *m*, -sa *f*

vote *vi* votar **I vote for ___.** Yo voto por ___.

vote *n* voto *m* **Let's take a vote.** Vamos a someterlo a votación. **You have my vote.** Tienes mi voto.

voyage *n* viaje *m* **long** ~ viaje largo **short** ~ viaje corto

vulgar *adj* vulgar *m&f* **How vulgar!** ¡Qué vulgar!

vulture *n* buitre *m*

Some Spanish words have accented and unaccented forms to differentiate their meanings (e.g., el = the, él = he).

W

wackiness *n* excentricidad *f*, extravagancia *f* **There's no limit to your wackiness, is there?** Tu excentricidad no tiene límites, ¿verdad?

wacko, wacky *adj (slang: zany, foolish)* absurdo *m* -da *f*, loco *m*, -ca *f*

wade *vi* vadear ~ **across the stream** vadear el arroyo ~ **into the ocean** adentrarse en el mar

wagon *n* vagón *m* **horse-drawn** ~ carromato *m*

waist *n* talle *m* **slim** ~ talle delgado **trim** ~ talle esbelto

waistline *n* cintura *f*

wait *vi* esperar **(Please) Wait (a *[1]* minute / *[2]* moment).** Espera (un *(1)* minuto / *(2)* momento) (por favor). **Wait, I'll be right over.** Espérame, voy para allá. **Where shall *(1)* I / *(2)* we wait (for *[3,4]* you)?** ¿Dónde (*[3]* lo *m* / *[4]* la *f* [Fam: te]) *(1)* espero? / *(2)* esperamos? **Where will you wait for *(1)* me? / *(2)* us?** ¿Dónde *va usted (Fam: vas)* a *(1)* esperarme? / *(2)* esperarnos? *(1)* **Please wait for *(2)* me / *(3)* us... / *(4)* I'll wait for *(5,6)* you...** (*[7]* **here.** / *[8]* **there.** / *[9]* **by the *(place)* entrance.** / *[10]* **in the lobby.** / *[11]* **outside.** / *[12]* **on the corner.** / *[13]* **at *(name of café or club)*.** / *[14]* **at the airport** / *[15]* **train station** / *[16]* **bus station.).** *(1)* Por favor, *(2)* espérame / *(3)* espéranos... / *(4)* Yo *(5)* lo *m* / *(6)* la *f* [Fam: te] espero (*[7]* aquí. / *[8]* allá. / *[9]* por la entrada de ___. / *[10]* en el vestíbulo. / *[11]* afuera. / *[12]* en la esquina. / *[13]* en ___. / *[14]* en el aeropuerto. / *[15]* en la estación del tren. / *[16]* en la terminal de autobuses.) **We'll wait for *(1,2)* you** *(See choices above.)*. Nosotros *(1)* lo *m* / *(2)* la *f* *(Fam: te)* esperamos. **I'll be waiting *(1)* for your letter / *(2)* call. / *(3)* to hear from you. / *(4,5)* for you.** Estaré *(1)* esperando *su (Fam: tu)* carta. / *(2)* llamada. / *(3)* saber de *usted(Fam: ti)*. / *(4)* esperándolo *m* / *(5)* esperándola *f (Fam: esperándote)*. **I hope you'll wait for me.** Ojalá me esperes. **I can hardly wait.** Apenas puedo esperar. *(1)* **I / *(2)* We waited for *(3,4)* you (*[5]* 30 minutes. / *[6]* one hour. / *[7]* a long time.).** *(3)* Lo

---

*Spanish "g" is like "h" in front of "e" and "i".
In front of other vowels it's like our "g" in "gun".*

m / *(4)* La *f (Fam: Te) (1)* esperé / *(2)* esperamos / *([5]* treinta minutos. / *[6]* una hora. / *[7]* mucho tiempo.). *(1)* I / *(2)* **We couldn't wait (any longer).** *(1)* No pude / *(2)* No pudimos esperar (más). **What are we waiting for?** ¿Qué estamos esperando? **You are the person I've been waiting for all my life.** Tú eres la persona que he estado esperando toda mi vida.

wait *n* espera *f*   **long** ~ larga espera   **short** ~ corta espera   **It's going to be a long wait.** Va a ser una larga espera. **The wait was worth it.** Valió la pena esperar.

waiter *n* mesero *m*   ★   **waitress** *n* mesera *f*

wake up *vt* despertar   **Wake** *(1)* **me** / *(2)* **us up at** *(time)*. *(1)* Despiértame / *(2)* Despiértanos a las __ de la mañana. *(1)* **I'll** / *(2)* **We'll wake you up at** *(time)*. *(1)* Yo te despierto / *(2)* Nosotros te despertamos a las __ de la mañana.

wake up *vi* despertar   **Wake up!** ¡Despierta!   **What time did you wake up?** ¿A qué hora *despertó usted (Fam: despertaste)*? *(1)* **I** / *(2)* **We woke up at** *(time)*. *(1)* Me desperté / *(2)* Nos despertamos a las __ de la mañana.

walk *vt (escort)* encaminar, acompañar   **Can I walk you home?** ¿Te puedo encaminar a tu casa? **I'll walk you** *(1)* **home.** / *(2)* **there.** Te acompaño a *(1)* tu casa. / *(2)* allá.

walk *vi* caminar *(See also phrases under* **like** *and* **love***.)*   **I like to walk (**[1] **in the countryside. /** [2] **park. /** [3] **woods. /** [4] **downtown. /** [5] **on the beach.)** Me gusta caminar (*[1]* en el campo / *[2]* en el parque / *[3]* en el bosque / *[4]* en el centro / *[5]* en la playa). **Can I walk with you?** ¿Puedo caminar con usted *(Fam: contigo)*? **Let's walk (there).** Caminemos (para allá). **Can we walk there?** ¿Podemos ir allá caminando? **We can(not) walk there.** (No) Podemos ir allá caminando.

walk *n* paseo *m* ; caminata *f (See phrases under* **go, like** *and* **love***.)*   **Let's go for a walk.** Vamos a caminar. **Would you like to go for a walk?** ¿*Le (Fam: Te)* gustaría ir a caminar? **Do you like to take walks?** ¿*Le (Fam: Te)* gusta caminar? **I like to take (long) walks (**[1] **in the countryside.** / [2] **park. /** [3] **woods. /** [4] **downtown. /** [5] **on the beach.)** Me gustan las (grandes) caminatas (*[1]* por el campo / *[2]* en el parque / *[3]* en el bosque / *[4]* en el centro/ *[5]* en la playa.)

wall *n* pared *f*, muro *m*   **on the** ~ en la pared   **stone** ~ muro de piedra

wallet *n* cartera *f*

waltz *vi* valsear, bailar vals   **I love to waltz.** Me encanta bailar vals.

waltz *n* vals *m*   *(1)* **dance** / *(2)* **do a** ~ *(1,2)* bailar un vals

wand *n* vara *f*   **magic** ~ varita mágica

wander *vi* andar   **Let's wander around (town) for a while.** Vamos a andar (por la ciudad) un rato. **Let's wander over the fields.** Vamos a andar por

---

English-Spanish and Spanish-English glossaries of food and drink are on pages 420-427.

los campos.

wanderlust *n* ganas *fpl* de viajar **I often get wanderlust.** Muchas veces me entran ganas de viajar.

want *vt* querer **What do you want?** ¿Qué quiere usted *(Fam: quieres)*? **What do you want to do?** ¿Qué quiere usted *(Fam: quieres)* hacer? **I (don't) want...** (No) quiero… **We (don't) want...** (No) queremos.... **Is that what you (really) want?** ¿Eso es lo que usted quiere *(Fam: quieres)* (de veras)? **That's (not) what I want.** Eso (no) es lo que quiero. **I want (so much) to** *(1)* **hold /** *(2)* **kiss you.** Quiero *(1)* abrazarte / *(2)* besarte *(tanto).* **I want you more than anything.** Te quiero más que nada. **I'll do whatever you want.** Haré lo que tú quieras.

war *n* guerra *f* **after the** ~ después de la guerra **during the** ~ durante la guerra **in the** ~ en la guerra **I fought in the** *(name)* **war.** Peleé en la guerra de ___.

warm *adj* 1. *(day, water)* templado *m*, -da *f*, tibio *m*, -bia *f* ; *(food, drink)* caliente *m&f*; *(clothes)* abrigador *m*, -dora f, calientito *m*, -ta *f*, cómodo *m*, -da *f* ; 2. *(cordial; affectionate)* calido *m*, -da *f*, cariñoso *m*, -sa *f* **get** ~ calentarse ~ **clothes** ropa abrigadora ~ **coat** abrigo calientito ~ **day** ~ dia templado **drink** bebida caliente ~ **friendship** cálida amistad ~ **heart** corazón afectuoso ~ **water** agua templada ~ **welcome** cálida bienvenida **You're so warm and cuddly.** Eres tan cariñoso *(sa)* y adorable. **You'd better wear** *(1)* **something warm. /** *(2)* **warm clothes.** Será mejor que *se ponga usted (Fam: te pongas) (1)* algo calientito. / *(2)* ropa calientita. **This will keep** *(1,2)* **you warm.** Esto *(1)* lo *m* / *(2)* la *f (Fam: te)* mantendrá calientito *(-ta).*

warm *vt* calentar *(1)* **Your words... /** *(2)* **The things you say... warm my heart.** *(1)* Tus palabras… / *(2)* Las cosas que dices… confortan mi corazón.

★ **warm up** *idiom (get ready)* calentarse **Let's warm up first.** Vamos a calentarnos primero. **That's nothing. I'm just warming up.** No es nada. Sólo me estoy calentando.

warm-hearted *adj* afectuoso *m*, -sa *f*, bondadoso *m*, -sa *f*

warmth *n* calor *m*, simpatía *f*, entusiasmo *m*, cordialidad *f* **genuine** ~ genuina simpatía

warn *vt* advertir **I'm warning you (for the last time).** Te lo advierto (por última vez). **I warned you.** Te lo advertí.

warning *n* advertencia *f* **fair** ~ advertencia justa

wary *adj* precavido *m*, -da *f* **I'm wary of things like that.** No me fío de esas cosas.

wash *vt* lavar ~ **dishes** lavar los platos **I have to wash my hair.** Tengo que lavarme el pelo. *(1)* **I /** *(2)* **We have to wash clothes.** *(1)* Tengo / *(2)* Tenemos que lavar la ropa. **Where can** *(1)* **I /** *(2)* **we wash clothes?**

A phrasebook makes a great gift!
Use the order form on page 432.

¿Dónde *(1)* puedo / *(2)* podemos lavar ropa?

★ **wash up** *idiom* lavar, lavarse *(1)* **I'm /** *(2)* **We're going to go wash up.** *(1)* Voy a lavarme. / *(2)* Vamos a lavarnos.

washcloth *n* toallita *f* para lavarse la cara

wasp(s) *n(pl)* avispa(s) *f(pl)*

waste *vt* desperdiciar ~ **money** desperdiciar dinero ~ **time** desperdiciar tiempo **We're wasting time.** Estamos perdiendo tiempo. *(1)* **I /** *(2)* **We don't want to waste time.** No *(1)* quiero / *(2)* queremos perder tiempo.

waste *n* desperdicio *m* **That's a waste of** *(1)* **money. /** *(2)* **time.** Eso fue un desperdicio de *(1)* dinero. / *(2)* tiempo.

watch *vt* 1. *(look at)* ver, mirar; 2. *(take care of)* cuidar **Do you like to watch** *(1)* **ballet? /** *(2)* **movies? /** *(3)* **sports? /** *(4)* **videos? /** *(5)* **TV?** ¿Te gusta ver *(1)* ballet? / *(2)* películas? / *(3)* deportes? / *(4)* videos? / *(5)* tele? **I (don't) like to watch...** *(See above choices.)* (No) Me gusta ver .... **Let's watch a** *(1)* **movie. /** *(2)* **video.** Vamos a ver *(1)* una película. / *(2)* un video. **Could you watch this for me?** ¿Podrías cuidarme esto? **Watch it!** ¡Cuidado! **Watch out!** ¡Cuidado!

watch *n* reloj *m*

water *adj* de agua *m&f* ~ **bottle** botella *f* de agua ~ **faucet** llave *f* de agua

water *n* agua *f* **bottle of** ~ botella de agua **drink of** ~ agua de beber **drinking** ~ agua potable **fresh** ~ agua dulce **glass of** ~ vaso *m* de agua **play in the** ~ jugar en el agua **salt** ~ agua salada **Let's go in the water.** Vamos a meternos al agua. **Is the water deep** *(1)* **here? /** *(2)* **there?** ¿Está honda el agua *(1)* aquí? / *(2)* allá? **The water is (not) deep.** El agua (no) está honda. **The water is (not)** *(1)* **clean. /** *(2)* **cold. /** *(3)* **dirty. /** *(4)* **warm.** El agua (no) está *(1)* limpia. / *(2)* fría. / *(3)* sucia. / *(4)* caliente. **Is the water okay to drink?** ¿Esta agua se puede beber?

waterfall *n* cascada *f*

waterfowl *n* acuática *f* **hunt for** ~ buscar acuática

waterfront *n* zona *f* costera, costa *f* **Let's walk along the waterfront.** Vamos a caminar por la costa.

waterski *vi* esquiar en el agua **Teach me how to water-ski.** *Enséñeme (Fam: Enséñame)* a esquiar en el agua. **I want to learn how to water-ski.** Quiero aprender a esquiar en agua. **I'll teach** *(1,2)* **you how to water-ski.** Yo *(1)* lo *m* / *(2)* la *f (te)* enseño a esquiar en agua.

waterskiing *n* esquí *m* acuático **go** ~ ir a esquiar en el agua **Let's go waterskiing.** Vamos a esquiar en el agua.

wave *n* ola *f*, onda *f*

wavelength *n* longitud *f* de onda *f* **You and I are truly on the same wavelength.** *Usted (Fam: Tú)* y yo estamos de veras en la misma longitud

---

A slash always means "or".

de onda.

way *n* 1. *(route)* camino *m*; 2. *(direction)* dirección *f*; 3. *(distance)* distancia *f*; 4. *(manner)* manera *f*, modo *m*; *(method)*; 5. *(characteristic)* carácterística *f* ; *(tradition, custom)* costumbres *fpl*, tradiciones *fpl*, cosas *fpl* **a long ~** una gran distancia **better ~** mejor manera **different ~** 1. *(route)* camino diferente; 2. *(method)* manera diferente **different ~s** diferentes modos **in a different ~** de un modo diferente **in a family ~** estar embarazada **in** *(1)* **this /** *(2)* **that ~** de *(1)* esta / *(2)* esa manera **shorter ~** camino más corto **some ~** de alguna manera **the same ~** de la misma manera **~ of life** modo de vida **Do you know the way?** ¿Conoces el camino? *(1)* **I /** *(2)* **We (don't) know the way.** *(1)* Yo (no) conozco... / *(1)* Nosotros (no) conocemos... el camino. **Which way should** *(1)* **I /** *(2)* **we go?** ¿En qué dirección *(1)* debo / *(2)* debemos de ir? **Is this the right way to the post office?** ¿Es este el camino correcto a la oficina de correos? **Are you sure this is the right way?** ¿Estás seguro *(-ra)* de que vamos por buen camino? **This is the** *(1)* **right /** *(2)* **wrong way.** Este es el camino *(1)* correcto. / *(2)* equivocado. **Let's go this way.** Vamos por ese camino / en esta dirección. **Let's go back the way we came.** Vamos a regresar por donde vinimos. **This way.** En esta dirección. / Por aquí. **I'm on my way to** *(place)***.** Voy en camino a ___. **We're on our way to** *(place)***.** Vamos en camino a ___. **Lead the way.** Dirige el camino. **Which way is the city center?** ¿Por dónde se llega al centro de la ciudad? **Which way are you going?** ¿En qué dirección vas? **Do you have a long way to go?** ¿Tienes que ir lejos? *(1)* **I /** *(2)* **We have a long way to go.** *(1)* Tengo / *(2)* Tenemos que llegar lejos. **I like the way you** *(1)* **talk. /** *(2)* **smile. /** *(3)* **kiss. /** *(4)* **hold me. /** *(5)* **walk. /** *(6)* **move. /** *(7)* **look at me. /** *(8)* **wear your hair.** Me gusta tu modo de *(1)* hablar. / *(2)* sonreír. / *(3)* besar. / *(4)* abrazarme. / *(5)* caminar. / *(6)* moverte. / *(7)* mirarme. / *(8)* peinarte. **In what way?** ¿De qué modo? **I'll show you the way to do it.** Yo te enseño el modo de hacerlo. **We'll find a way (to do it).** Encontraremos el modo (de hacerlo). **Is there some way I can** *(1)* **contact /** *(2)* **reach you?** ¿Hay alguna manera en que pueda *(1)* ponerme en contacto contigo? / *(2)* alcanzarte? **You can't always have your own way.** No siempre puedes salirte con la tuya. **Make way for** *(1)* **Her Majesty! /** *(2)* **His Majesty!** ¡Abran paso a *(1,2)* Su Majestad! **No way!** ¡Ni hablar! **By the way, ...** Por cierto,… **Way to go!** ¡Qué bien!

way *adv (far)* allá lejos **It's way out in the** *(1)* **country. /** *(2)* **mountains.** Está allá lejos en *(1)* el campo. / *(2)* la montañas. **It's way on the other side of the city.** Está allá lejos al otro lado de la ciudad. **They're way** *(1)* **ahead of us. /** *(2)* **behind us.** Van lejos por *(1)* delante de nosotros. / *(2)* detrás de nosotros. **That's way beyond me.** Eso está fuera de mi

---

Spanish "v" is pronounced like a soft "b".

comprensión.

we *pron* nosotros **We** *(1,2)* **are.** Nosotros *(1)* somos. / *(2)* estamos. **We** *(1,2)* **were.** Nosotros *(1)* fuimos. / *(2)* estuvimos. **We** *(1,2)* **will be.** Nosotros *(1)* seremos. / *(2)* estaremos.

weak *adj* débil *m&f* ~ **excuse** una excusa poco convincente **You make me weak in the knees.** Tú haces que se me aflojen las rodillas. **You're taking advantage of my weak will.** Tú te aprovechas de mi débil voluntad.

weakling *n* debilucho *m*, -cha *f*

weakness *n* debilidad *f* **You've discovered my weakness.** Has descubierto mi debilidad. **It's a weakness of mine.** Es una de mis debilidades.

weak-willed *adj* de poca voluntad *m&f*

wealth *n* riqueza *f*

wealthy *adj* rico *m*, -ca *f*

weapon *n* arma *f* **Careful, my hands are registered as lethal weapons.** Cuidado, mis manos están registradas como armas mortales.

wear *vt* ponerse (ropa) **What should** *(1)* **I** / *(2)* **we wear?** ¿Qué *(1)* debo de ponerme *(2)* debemos de ponernos? **What are you going to wear?** ¿Qué te vas a poner? *(1)* **I think I'll wear...** / *(2)* **You should wear...** *(3)* **a coat.** / *(4)* **a dress.** / *(5)* **a long gown.** / *(6)* **shorts.** / *(7)* **a skirt.** / *(8)* **slacks.** / *(9)* **a sport coat.** / *(10)* **a suit.** / *(11)* **a sweater** / *(12)* **a tie.** *(1)* Creo que me voy a poner... / *(2)* Debes de ponerte... *(3)* un abrigo. / *(4)* un vestido. / *(5)* un vestido largo. / *(6)* shorts. / *(7)* una falda. / *(8)* ropa holgada. / *(9)* chaqueta informal. / *(10)* un traje. / *(11)* un suéter. / *(12)* una corbata.

weary *adj* cansado *m*, -da *f* **I'm weary of this place.** Estoy cansado de este lugar.

weather *n* clima *m* **bad** ~ mal clima **good** ~ buen clima **ideal** ~ clima ideal **lousy** ~ pésimo clima **perfect** ~ clima perfecto ~ **forecast** pronóstico del clima **What's the weather going to be tomorrow?** ¿Cómo va a estar mañana el clima? **I hope we have good weather.** Espero que tengamos buen clima. **The weather** *(1)* **here** / *(2)* **there is (very)** *(3)* **nice.** / *(4)* **beautiful.** / *(5)* **pleasant.** / *(6)* **warm.** / *(7)* **hot.** / *(8)* **cool.** / *(9)* **cold.** / *(10)* **rainy.** / *(11)* **terrible.** El clima *(1)* aquí / *(2)* allá es (muy) *(3)* agradable. / *(4)* lindo. / *(5)* placentero. / *(6)* tibio. / *(7)* caliente. / *(8)* fresco. / *(9)* frío. / *(10)* lluvioso. / *(11)* terrible.

web *n* 1. *(spider's)* telaraña *f*; 2. *(Internet)* Internet *f* **search the** ~ buscar en Internet **surf the** ~ navegar por Internet ~ **page** página de Internet ~ **site** sitio de Internet

wedding *n* boda *f* **call off the** ~ cancelar la boda **celebrate the** ~ celebrar la boda **church** ~ boda religiosa **have the** ~ tener la boda **outdoor** ~ boda al aire libre **perform the** ~ oficiar la boda **plan the** ~ planear la boda **post-**

Time expressions are given on page 413.

pone the ~ posponer la boda **~ ceremony** ceremonia de boda **~ dress** vestido de boda **witness the ~** atestiguar la boda *(See also* **We need to plan the wedding.** Necesitamos planear la boda. **What kind of wedding do you want to have?** ¿Qué tipo de boda quieres tener? **Do you want to have a small wedding or a large one?** ¿Quieres tener una boda pequeña o grande? **I want to have a(n)** *(1)* **small** / *(2)* **intimate** / *(3)* **large wedding.** Quiero tener una boda *(1)* pequeña. / *(2)* íntima. /*(3)* grande. *(1)* **When** / *(2)* **Where shall we have the wedding?** *(1)* ¿Cuándo / *(2)* Dónde será la boda? **Who should we invite to the wedding?** ¿A quién debemos de invitar a la boda? **Who will perform the wedding?** ¿Quién va a oficiar la boda? **Who will witness the wed-ding (for us)?** ¿Quiénes serán (nuestros) testigos de boda? **We can't have the wedding until...** No podemos tener la boda hasta…

Wednesday *n* miércoles *m* **last ~** el miércoles pasado **next ~** el próximo miércoles **on ~** en miércoles

week *n* semana *f* **all ~** toda la semana **a ~ ago** hace una semana **a ~ from now** dentro de una semana **a whole ~** toda una semana **during the ~** durante la semana **every ~** cada semana **for a (whole) ~** por (toda) la semana **for** *(1)* **two** / *(2)* **three** / *(3)* **four ~s** por *(1)* dos / *(2)* tres / *(3)* cuatro semanas **in** *(1)* **a** / *(2)* **one ~** 1. *(after)* después de *(1,2)* una semana; 2. *(in the space of)* en *(1,2)* una semana **in** *(1)* **two** / *(2)* **three** / *(3)* **four ~s** 1. *(after)* después de *(1)* dos / *(2)* tres / *(3)* cuatro semanas; 2. *(in the space of)* en *(1)* dos / *(2)* tres / *(3)* cuatro / *(4)* cinco semanas **last ~** semana pasada **next ~** próxima semana **once a ~** una vez por semana **this ~** esta semana **the whole ~** toda la semana **this coming ~** la semana entrante **two ~s ago** hace dos semanas **two ~s from now** dentro de dos semanas~ **after ~** semana tras semana **wonderful ~** semana maravillosa

weekend *n* fin *m* de semana **for** *(1)* **a** / *(2)* **the ~** por *(1)* un / *(2)* el fin de semana. **next ~** el próximo fin de semana **on the ~** en el fin de semana **on ~s** en los fines de semana **this (coming) ~** este fin de semana (que viene)

weekly *adj* semanalmente *m & f*

weigh *vi* pesar **How much do you weigh?** ¿Cuánto pesas? **I weigh about 140 pounds.** *(2.2 lbs = 1 kilogram)* Peso unos 63 kilos. *(1 kg = 2.2 lb)*

weight *n* 1. *(quantity)* peso *m*; 2. *pl (barbells)* pesas *f, pl* **gain ~** subir de peso **lose ~** bajar de peso **perfect ~** el peso perfecto **put on ~** subir de peso **I'm trying to lose weight.** Estoy tratando de bajar de peso. **I want to lose some more weight.** Quiero bajar más de peso. **I try to watch my weight.** Trato de cuidar mi peso. **I gained weight (lately).** Subí de peso (últimamente). **I lift weights.** Levanto pesas.

weightlifting *n* levantamiento *m* de pesas

Spanish "qu" is pronounced like "k".

weird *adj* raro *m*, rara *f*, extraño *m*, -ña *f* **It was totally weird.** Fue totalmente extraño.

weirdly *adv* extrañamente ~ **dressed** vestido *(-da)* de un modo extraño

weirdo *n (slang: strange-acting person)* persona rara **What are you, some kind of weirdo?** ¿Quién eres, alguna clase de raro *(-ra)*?

welcome *n* bienvenida *f* **friendly** ~ bienvenida amistosa **nice** ~ cordial bienvenida **warm** ~ bienvenida cálida **That's the kind of welcome you give me, huh?** ¿Y esa es la bienvenida que me das, eh?

welcome *interj.* bienvenido; de nada **You're welcome.** *(Response to thanks.)* De nada. **Welcome!** ¡Bienvenido! **Welcome to Guadalajara!** ¡Bienvenido a Guadalajara!

welfare *n (govt support of the poor)* asistencia social *m* **be on** ~ estar bajo asistencia social

well *adj (not sick)* bien *m&f* **I don't feel well.** No me siento bien. **I hope you get well soon.** Espero que pronto *se ponga (Fam: te pongas)* bien.

well *adv (in a good way)* bien ~ **done** *(fully cooked)* bien *(1)* hecho / *(2)* cocido **You *(1)* play / *(2)* sing very well.** Usted *(Fam: Tú) (1)* juega *(Fam: juegas / (2)* canta *(Fam: cantas)* muy bien. **Everything went well.** Todo salió bien.

well *n* pozo *m* **oil** ~ pozo petrolero

well-built *adj* bien construido *m*, -da *f*

well-dressed *adj* bien vestido *m*, -da *f*

well-educated *adj* bien educado *m*, -da *f*

well-informed *adj* bien informado *m*, -da *f*

well-off *adj* adinerado *m*, -da *f*, acomodado *m*, -da *f*

well-ordered *adj* bien ordenado *m*, -da *f*

well-organized *adj* bien organizado *m*, -da *f*

well-read *adj* muy leído *m*, -da *f*

well-rounded *adj* polifacético *m*, -ca *f*

west *adj* oeste *m & f* *n* oeste *m*

western *adj* occidental *m&f* ★ *n (cowboy movie)* película *f* de vaqueros

wet *adj* mojado *m*, -da *f* **My clothes are all wet.** Mi ropa está toda mojada. **My *(1)* pants / *(2)* shoes / *(3)* socks are all wet.**Mis *(1)* pantalones / *(2)* zapatos / *(3)* calcetines están todos mojados.

whale(s) *n (pl)* ballena(s) *f (pl)*

wharf *n* muelle *m*, embarcadero *m*

what *pron* qué, cuál **What is it?** ¿Qué es? **What is *(1)* this? / *(2)* that?** ¿Qué es *(1)* esto? / *(2)* eso? **What are they?** ¿Qué son? **What happened?** ¿Qué pasó? **What do you want?** ¿Qué *quiere usted (Fam: quieres)*? **What do you have?** ¿Qué *tiene usted (Fam: tienes)*? **What's a good restaurant?**

Words in parentheses (not italicized) are optional.

¿Cuál restaurante es bueno? **What's your name?** ¿Cuál es *su (Fam: tu)* nombre?

what *adj* qué *m&f*, cuál **What time is it?** ¿Qué hora es? **What kind do you want?** ¿De cuál quieres? **For what reason?** ¿Por qué razón? **What days are you off?** ¿Qué días *tiene usted (Fam: tienes)* libres? **What beautiful eyes you have.** Qué bonitos ojos tienes. **What a surprise!** ¡Qué sorpresa! **What's in it for me?** ¿Y en eso qué hay para mí?

what *adv* que **about ~ (***or* **~ about)** acerca de qué (o qué con) **for ~ (***or* **~ for)** para qué **with ~ (***or* **~with)** con qué **What did you say?** ¿Qué *dijo usted (Fam: dijiste)*? **What did you do?** ¿Qué *hizo usted (Fam: hiciste)*? **I'll tell you what...** Yo te digo qué…

whatever *pron* cualquier cosa **Whatever.** Lo que sea.

wheel *n* rueda *f*

wheelchair *n* silla *f* de ruedas

when *adv & conj* cuándo; cuando **When?** ¿Cuándo? **When are you going?** ¿Cuándo vas a ir? **When will it be?** ¿Cuándo será? **When is your birthday?** ¿Cuándo es tu cumpleaños? **Call *(1)* me / *(2)* us when you get home.** *(1)* Llámame / *(2)* Llámanos cuando llegues a casa.

where *adv* dónde; donde **Where?** ¿Dónde? **Where shall we meet?** ¿Dónde nos vamos a encontrar? **Where shall I meet you?** ¿Dónde te voy a encontrar? **Where do you *(1)* live? /*(2)* work?** ¿Dónde *(1)* vive usted *(Fam: vives)*? / *(2)* trabaja usted *(Fam: trabajas)*? **Where are you staying?** ¿Dónde *se está usted (Fam: te estás)* quedando? **Where *(1)* is it? / *(2)* are they?** ¿Dónde *(1)* está? / *(2)* están? **Where are we?** ¿Dónde estamos? **Where's the nearest *(1)* bank? / *(2)* cash machine? / *(3)* Internet café? / *(4)* shopping center? / *(5)* supermarket?** ¿Dónde está el *(1)* banco / *(2)* cajero automático / *(3)* café de Internet / *(4)* centro comercial / *(6)* súper... más cercano? **Where's the nearest pharmacy?** ¿Dónde está la farmacia más cercana? **Where to?** ¿A dónde? **Where are you going?** ¿A dónde *va usted (Fam: vas)*? **Where (are you) from?** ¿De dónde *(es usted (Fam: eres)*? **Where are you coming from?** ¿De dónde *viene usted (Fam: vienes)*? **Where is the *(1)* bus / *(2)* subway / *(3)* train station?** ¿Dónde está la estación del *(1)* camión? /*(2)* metro? / *(3)* tren?

wherever *adv & conj (it is)* donde sea; *(desired)* donde quiera que **We can go wherever you want.** Podemos ir a donde *usted quiera (Fam: tú quieras)*.

whether *conj* si **I don't know whether *(1)* I / *(2)* we can or not.** No sé si *(1)* yo pueda o no. / *(2)* podamos o no.

which *pron & adj* cuál; cual **Which one would you like?** ¿Cuál *le gustaría a usted (Fam: te gustaría)*? **Which hotel are you staying in?** ¿En cuál hotel *se está usted (Fam: te estás)* quedando? **Which way should *(1)* I /

A single Spanish "r" should be lightly trilled;
double "r" ("rr") should be strongly trilled.

(2) **we go?** ¿En cuál dirección *(1)* debo de / *(2)* debemos de ir?

while *conj* mientras **Wait here while I** *(1)* **get it.** / *(2)* **go to the bank.** Espera aquí mientras *(1)* lo consigo. / *(2)* voy al banco. *(1)* **I'll** / *(2)* **We'll sit outside while you're getting ready.** *(1)* Me voy a sentar / *(2)* Nos vamos a sentar afuera mientras te arreglas. **While** *(1)* **I'm** / *(2)* **we're there I'd like to visit the** *(place)*. Mientras *(1)* esté / *(2)* estemos allí me gustaría visitar ___.

while *n* rato *m*, momento *m* **a little ~ ago** hace un rato **for a ~** por un momento **once in a ~** de vez en cuando

whim *n* capricho *m* **crazy ~** capricho loco **feminine ~s** caprichos femeninos

whip *n* látigo *m* **Where's my whip?** ¿Dónde está mi látigo?

whisper *vt & vi* susurrar **Why are you whispering?** ¿Por qué susurras?

whisper *n* susurro *m* **in a ~** en un susurro

whistle *vt* silbar **I'll whistle a tune outside your window.** Te voy a silbar afuera de tu ventana.

whistle *n* silbato *m*

white *adj* blanco *m*, -ca *f*

who *pron* quién **Who?** ¿Quién? **Who is** *(1)* **he?** / *(2)* **she?** ¿Quién es *(1)* él? / *(2)* ella? **Who are they?** ¿Quiénes son ellos? **Who knows?** ¿Quién sabe? **Who's there?** ¿Quién es? **Who did you give it to?** ¿A quién se lo diste? **Who wants to** *(1)* **come?** / *(2)* **go?** / *(3)* **play?** ¿Quién quiere *(1)* venir? / *(2)* ir? / *(3)* jugar? **Do you know someone who has a car?** ¿Conoces a alguien que tenga carro?

whoever *pron* quienquiera que **Whoever wants to go, let's go!** ¡Quien quiera ir, vámonos!

whole *adj* completo *m*, -ta *f*, todo *m*, -da *f* **a ~ month** todo un mes **a ~ week** toda una semana **the ~ day** todo el día **the ~ time** todo el tiempo

wholehearted *adj* sincero *m*, -ra *f*, entusiasta *m&f*

whose *pron* de quién **Whose is it?** ¿De quién es? **Whose are they?** ¿De quién son? **Whose is** *(1)* **this?** / *(2)* **that?** ¿De quién es *(1)* esto? / *(2)* eso? **Whose car are we going in?** ¿En el carro de quién vamos a ir? **Whose side are you on?** ¿De qué lado estás?

why *adv* por qué **Why (not)?** ¿Por qué (no)? **Why do you say that?** ¿Por qué dices eso? **Why did you do that?** ¿Por qué hiciste eso? **I don't know why I love you.** No sé por qué te amo. **Why can't you** *(1)* **come?** / *(2)* **go?** ¿Por qué no puedes *(1)* venir? / *(2)* ir? **Why don't we go to** *(place)*? ¿Por qué no vamos a ___?

wicked *adj* malvado *m*, -da *f*, malo *m*, -la *f*, **~ thoughts** malos pensamientos **You wicked girl!** ¡Niña malvada!

wide *adj* amplio *m*, -plia *f*, ancho *m*, -cha *f*

Familiar "tu" forms in parentheses can replace italicized polite forms.

wide *adv* despierto *m*, -ta *f* **I'm wide awake.** Estoy bien despierto *(-ta)*.

widow *n* viuda *f*

widower *n* viudo *m*

wife *n* esposa *f* **my ex-wife** mi ex-esposa **perfect ~** la esposa perfecta **your ~** su *(Fam: tu)* esposa **Do you have a wife?** ¿Tienes esposa? **I (don't) have a wife** (No) Tengo esposa. **This is my wife,** *(name)*. Esta es mi esposa ___. **This is a picture of my wife.** Esta es una foto de mi esposa. **Your wife is very attractive.** *(photo)* Su *(Fam: Tu)* esposa es muy atractiva. **My wife passed away (in** *[year]*). Mi esposa falleció (en __).

wild *adj* salvaje *m&f*, loco *m*, -ca *f* **~ idea** idea loca **~ party** fiesta alocada **~ time** momento salvaje **Are you always this wild?** ¿Siempre eres así de salvaje?

wild *adv* loco *m*, -ca *f* **You drive me wild.** Me vuelves loco *(-ca)*. **I'm going to drive you wild.** Te voy volver loco *(-ca)*.

wildcat *n (slang: wildly dangerous girl)* fiera *f*

wildlife *n* flora *f* y fauna *f*

wiles *n, pl* ardid *m*, astucia *f* **womanly ~** astucia femenina

will *n (desire, volition, power)* voluntad *f* **against** *(1)* **my /** *(2)* **your ~** contra *(1)* mi / *(2)* tu voluntad **good ~** buena voluntad **iron ~** voluntad de hierro **of** *(1)* **my /** *(2)* **your own free ~** por *(1)* mi / *(2)* tu propia y libre voluntad **strong ~** firme voluntad **weak ~** voluntad débil **~ power** fuerza de voluntad **Where there's a will, there's a way.** Si se quiere, se puede. **You've found my weak spot - my will power.** Has descubierto mi lado débil: mi fuerza de voluntad. **Come on, use a little will power.** Vamos, pon un poco de voluntad.

willing *adj* dispuesto *m*, -ta *f* **Would you be willing to share the cost?** ¿Estarías dispuesto *(-ta)* a compartir el costo? *(1)* **I'd /** *(2)* **We'd be willing to share the cost.** *(1)* Estaría dispuesto *(-ta)...* / *(2)* Estaríamos dispuestos... a compartir el costo. **I'm willing to try.** Estoy dispuesto *(-ta)* a intentarlo.

wimp *n (slang: weak person)* pelele *m&f*

win *vt* ganar **Who's winning?** ¿Quién va ganando? *(1)* **I'm /** *(2)* **You're /** *(3)* **He's /** *(4)* **She's /** *(5)* **They're /** *(6)* **We're winning**. *(1)* Yo voy / *(2)* Tú vas / *(3)* Él va / *(4)* Ella va / *(5)* Ellos van / *(6)* Nosotros vamos ganando. **Who won?** ¿Quién ganó? *(1)* **I /** *(2)* **You /** *(3)* **He /** *(4)* **She /** *(5)* **They /** *(6)* **We won.** *(1)* Yo gané. / *(2)* Tú ganaste. / *(3)* Él ganó. / *(4)* Ella ganó. / *(5)* Ellos ganaron. / *(6)* Nosotros ganamos.

wind *n* viento *m* **strong ~** viento fuerte

window *n* ventana *f* **sit by the ~** sentarse junto a la ventana **table by the ~** una mesa junto a la ventana *(1)* **Close /** *(2)* **Open the window.** *(1)* Cierra

---

Spanish "ll" is pronounced like "y" in "yes".

/ *(2)* Abre la ventana. **Can we get a table by the window?** ¿Podemos tomar una mesa junto a la ventana?

windsurf *vi* hacer windsurf(ing)

windsurfing *n* windsurf(ing) *m*, surf(eo) *m* a vela

windy *adj* ventoso *m*, -sa *f*

wine *n* vino *m* **bottle of** ~ botella *f* de vino **red** ~ vino tinto **white** ~ vino blanco **Would you care for a glass of wine?** ¿Te gustaría una copa de vino?

winery *n* vinatería *f*

winner *n* ganador *m*, -dora *f* **You're the winner!** ¡Tú eres el ganador!

winning *adj* ganador *m*, -dora *f* ~ **number** número *m* ganador ~ **streak** línea *f* ganadora ~ **team** equipo *m* ganador ~ **ticket** boleto *m* ganador

winter *adj* de invierno *m&f* ~ **sports** deportes de invierno

winter *n* invierno *m* **in the** ~ en el invierno **last** ~ el invierno pasado **next** ~ el próximo invierno

wipe *vt* limpiar, quitar, secar ~ **off** quitar, limpiar, secar ~ **up** limpiar, quitar, secar

wire *n* alambre *m* **electrical** ~ alambre eléctrico **You're really a live wire.** Eres una persona súper eléctrica.

wisdom *n* sabiduría *f*

wise *adj* inteligente *m&f*, sabio *m*, -bia *f* ~ **decision** decisión inteligente ~ **thing to do** la decisión más sabia **I think that's very wise of you.** Creo que es muy inteligente de tu parte. **That would (not) be wise.** Eso (no) sería inteligente.

wish *vi* desear *(1)* **I** / *(2)* **We wish you** *(3)* **(lots of) luck.** / *(4)* **all the luck in the world.** / *(5)* **all the best.** / *(6)* **happiness (always).** / *(7)* **success.** Te *(1)* deseo / *(2)* deseamos *(3)* (mucha) suerte. / *(4)* toda la suerte del mundo. / *(5)* todo lo mejor. / *(6)* felicidad (por siempre). / *(7)* éxito.

wish *n* deseo *m* **best** ~**es** los mejores deseos **my fervent** ~ mis deseos fervientes **my only** ~ mi único deseo **sincere** ~ deseo sincero **your (every)** ~ (todos) tus deseos **Make a wish. (Then blow out the candles.)** Pide un deseo. (Luego apaga las velas.) **My secret wish is...** Mi deseo secreto es… **Your wish is my command.** Tus deseos son órdenes.

wishful *adj* deseoso *m*, -sa *f* **That's wishful thinking.** Eso es hacerse ilusiones.

wishy-washy *adj* aguado *m*, -da *f*, insípido *m*, -da *f*

wit *n* 1. *(cleverness at humor)* humor *m*, agudeza *f*; 2. *(intelligence, sense)* *(often pl)* ingenio *m* ; 3. *(witty person)* ingenioso *m*, -sa *f* **You really have a** *(1)* **quick** / *(2)* **sarcastic** / *(3)* **sharp wit.** Tienes un humor muy *(1)* ágil / *(2)* sarcástico / *(3)* agudo.

Common occupations are listed on pages 415-416.

witch *n* bruja *f*

with *prep* 1. *(together with)* con; 2. *(by means of)* con

without *prep* sin ~ **a doubt** sin duda **What would** *(1)* **I /** *(2)* **we do without you?** ¿Qué *(1)* haría yo / *(2)* haríamos sin ti? **Without you I would be totally bored.** Sin ti estaría totalmente aburrido. **We can get along without it.** Podemos prescindir de eso.

witness *n* testigo *m&f* **You're my witness.** Tú eres mi testigo. **We need two witnesses.** Necesitamos dos testigos.

witty *adj* ingenioso *m*, -sa *f*, agudo *m*, -da *f*; chistoso *m*, -sa *f*, gracioso *m*, -sa *f* **You and your witty remarks.** Tú y tus comentarios graciosos.

wizard *n* hechicero *m*, brujo *m*

woman *n* mujer *f* **another** ~ otra mujer **good** ~ buena mujer **good-hearted** ~ mujer de buen corazón **good-looking** ~ mujer bien parecida **married** ~ mujer casada **nice** ~ mujer bonita ~ **friend** mujer amiga **You're a very beautiful woman.** Tú eres una mujer muy hermosa. **What a wonderful woman you are.** Qué mujer tan maravillosa eres. **You're the nicest woman I've ever met.** Tú eres la mujer más bonita que he conocido. **I've always wanted to meet a woman like you.** Siempre quise conocer una mujer como tú. **You're the woman for me.** Tú eres la mujer para mí. **I want to be your woman always.** Quiero ser tu mujer por siempre. **What woman could resist you?** ¿Qué mujer se te podría resistir? **Do you say such things to every woman you meet?** ¿Les dices eso a todas las mujeres? **What kind of a woman do you think I am?** ¿Qué clase de mujer crees que soy? **My woman's intuition tells me that...** Mi intuición de mujer me dice que…

womanizer *n* mujeriego *m*

women's *adj* de mujer *f* ~ **clothing** ropa de mujer ~ **restroom** baño de mujeres

wonder *vi* preguntarse **I wonder** *(1)* **what that is. /** *(2)* **what they're doing. /** *(3)* **why they stopped. /** *(4)* **when it will start. /** *(5)* **how long we'll have to wait.** Me pregunto *(1)* qué es eso. / *(2)* qué están haciendo. / *(3)* por qué se detuvieron. / *(4)* cuándo comienza. / *(5)* cuánto tiempo tenemos que esperar.

wonder *n* 1. *(miracle)* milagro *m* ; 2. *(surprise)* sorpresa *f* **no** ~ con razón **Wonders never cease.** Siempre hay sorpresas. **No wonder you're still single - you work all the time.** Con razón *sigue usted (Fam: sigues)* soltera: *trabaja usted (Fam: trabajas)* todo el tiempo.

wonderful *adj* maravilloso *m*, -sa *f* **How wonderful!** ¡Qué maravilloso! *(1)* **I /** *(2)* **We had a wonderful time.** *(1)* Yo pasé / *(2)* Nosotros pasamos un rato maravilloso. **What a wonderful place!** ¡Qué lugar tan maravilloso!

Spanish "y" is "ee" when alone or at the end of words.

You're wonderful. Tú eres maravilloso *(-sa)*. **I've never known anyone as wonderful as you.** Nunca conocí a nadie tan maravilloso *(-sa)* como tú.

wood(en) *adj* de madera *m&f*

wood *n* madera *f*, leña *f* **gather** *(1,2)* ~ recoger *(1)* leña / *(2)* madera **work with** ~ trabajar con madera **Put some more wood on the fire.** Ponle más leña al fuego.

woods *n, pl* bosque *m* **in the** ~ en el bosque

wool(en) *adj* de lana ★ *n* lana *m&f*

word *n* palabra *f* **beyond** ~s más allá de las palabras **dirty** ~ palabra obscena **English** ~ palabra en inglés **exact** ~s palabras exactas **express in** ~s expresar en palabras **fancy** ~s palabras rebuscadas **find the** ~s encontrar las palabras **flowery** ~s palabras floridas **kind** ~ palabras amables **my** ~ **of honor** mi palabra de honor **put into** ~s ponerlo en palabras **right** ~ palabra correcta **slang** ~ palabra de jerga / caliche *m* **Spanish** ~ palabra en español **such** ~s tales palabras **swear** ~ decir palabrotas **sweet** ~s palabras dulces **the** ~s **to the music** la letra de la música ~s **of love** palabras de amor **your** ~s tus palabras **That's a word I don't** *(1)* **know.** / *(2)* **understand.** Esa es una palabra que no *(1)* conozco. / *(2)* entiendo. **Is that the right word?** ¿Es esa la palabra correcta? **What does the word ___ mean?** ¿Qué significa la palabra ___? **Wait, I have to look up a word (in the dictionary).** Espera, tengo que buscar una palabra (en el diccionario). **Those are fighting words!** ¡Esas son palabras ofensivas! **You took the words right out of my mouth.** Me quitaste las palabras de la boca. **You have a** *(1)* **great** / *(2)* **marvelous** / *(3)* **wonderful way with words.** Tienes un modo *(1)* genial / *(2)* maravilloso / *(3)* asombroso de usar las palabras. **Don't say a word of this to anyone.** No digas una palabra de esto a nadie. **I give you my word.** Te doy mi palabra. **You gave me your word.** Me diste tu palabra. **In other words...** En otras palabras…

work *vi* 1. *(labor)* trabajar; 2. *(function)* funcionar ~ **fulltime** trabajar a tiempo completo ~ **hard** trabajar duro ~ **part-time** trabajar medio tiempo **Where do you work?** ¿En dónde *trabaja usted (Fam: trabajas)*? **I work** *(1)* **for** *(company)* . / *(2)* **at** / *(3)* **in a** *(type of business)*. Yo trabajo *(1)* para___. / *(2)* en ___. / *(3)* en un*(a)* ___ . **I work as a** *(job title)*. Yo trabajo como ___. **What hours do you work?** ¿Qué horas trabajas? **How long have you worked there?** ¿Cuánto tiempo has trabajado allí? **I've worked there for** *(number)* **years.** He trabajado allí por ___ años. **How does it work?** ¿Cómo funciona? **It doesn't work.** No funciona.

★ **work out** *idiom* 1. *(exercise)* hacer ejercicio; 2. *(turn out)* resultar; 3. *(turn out successfully)* salir bien **I hope everything works out okay for you.** Espero que todo *le (Fam: te)* resulte bien. **Don't**

---

*Feminine forms of words in phrases
are usually given in parentheses (italicized).*

worry, everything will work out. No te preocupes, todo saldrá
bien. **I like to work out.** Me gusta hacer ejercicio. **I work out**
(1) **regularly** / *(2)* **almost every day** *([3]* **at home.** / *[4]* **at a**
health club.) Yo hago ejercicio *(1)* con regularidad / *(2)* casi todos
los días *([3]* en la casa. / *[4]* en un club de salud. **Let's go work**
out (together). Vamos a hacer ejercicio (juntos). **Do you want to**
go work out *([1]* **tomorrow morning?** / *[2]* **this afternoon?** /
[3] **this evening?)?** ¿Quieres hacer ejercicio *([1]*mañana por la
mañana? / *[2]* esta tarde? / *[3]* esta noche?)? **Where's a (good)**
place to work out? ¿Dónde hay un (buen) lugar para hacer
ejercicio?

work *n* trabajo *m* **out of** ~ sin empleo **What kind of work do you do?** ¿Qué
clase de trabajo *hace usted (Fam: haces)*? *(For replies, see under* **be** *and*
work *[vi])* **What time do you** *(1)* **start** / *(2)* **finish** / *(3)* **get off work?** ¿A
qué hora *(1)* comienza usted *(Fam: comienzas)* a... / *(2)* termina usted
(Fam: terminas) de... / *(3)* sale usted *(Fam: sales)* de... trabajo? **I have to**
go to work *([1]* **now** / *[2]* **at** *[time].)* Me tengo que ir al trabajo *([1]* ahora
/ *[2]* a las ___). **I** *(1)* **finish** / *(2)* **get off work at** *(time).* Yo *(1)* termino / *(2)*
salgo del trabajo a la una (treinta). **I'm going to work.** Voy a trabajar. **Are**
you *(1)* **busy** / *(2)* **free after work?** ¿Estás *(1)* ocupado *(-da)* / *(2)* libre
después del trabajo? **What are you doing** *(1)* **after work?** / *(2)* **after you**
get off work? ¿Qué vas a hacer *(1)* después del trabajo? / *(2)* cuando salgas
del trabajo?

workaholic *n* adicto *m (-ta) f* al trabajo

worker *n* obrero *m*, -ra *f*, trabajador *m*, -dora *f* **hard** ~ muy trabajador *(-dora)*

world *n* mundo *m* **big** ~ gran mundo **crazy** ~ mundo loco **crowded** ~ mundo
sobrepoblado **entire** ~ mundo entero **goofy** ~ mundo loco **in the whole**
~ en todo el mundo **mixed-up** ~ mundo enredado **nothing in the** ~ nada
en el mundo **out of this** ~ fuera de este mundo **wacky** ~ mundo loco ~
champion campeón mundial **I'd like to travel around the world with**
you. Me gustaría viajar contigo alrededor del mundo. **I want to share the**
world with you. Quiero compartir el mundo contigo. **My world is a** *(1)*
better / *(2)* **happier place because of you.** Por ti mi mundo es un lugar *(1)*
mejor. / *(2)* más feliz. **You mean the world to me.** Tú eres el mundo para
mí. **You are all I want in this world.** Tú eres todo lo que quiero en este
mundo. **You're the** *(1)* **nicest** / *(2)* **sweetest person in the whole world.**
Tú eres la persona *(1)* más linda / *(2)* más dulce del mundo. **The food is**
out of this world! ¡La comida es algo fuera de este mundo! **I'm King of**
the World! ¡Yo soy el Rey del Mundo! **And now, ladies and gentleman,**
the world's greatest *(1)* **diver.** / *(2)* **player.** / *(3)* **swimmer.** Y ahora,

Spanish "c" before "e" and "i" is pronounced like "s".

damas y caballeros, *(1)* el clavadista / *(2)* el jugador / *(3)* el nadador más grande del mundo.

worm(s) *n(pl)* lombriz *f(pl:* lombrices)

worn out *adj (exhausted)* agotado *m*, -da *f*, exhausto *m*, -ta *f* **You must be worn out.** Debes estar agotado *(-da)*. **I'm (totally) worn out.** Estoy (completamente) exhausto *(-ta)*.

worried *adj* preocupado *m*, -da *f* **Are you worried?** ¿Estás preocupado *(-da)*? **I'm (not) worried (about...).** (No) estoy prepocupado *(-da)* (por…). **What are you worried about?** ¿Qué te preocupa? **Don't be worried.** No te preocupes.

worry *vi* preocuparse **I (don't) worry (about** *[1]* **you /** *[2]* **him /** *[3]* **her /** *[4]* **us /** *[5]* **them).** (No) me preocupo (por *[1]* ti / *[2]* él / *[3]* ella / *[4]* nosotros / *[5]* ellos). **Don't worry.** No te preocupes. **There's nothing to worry about.** No hay de qué preocuparse.

worry-wart *n (slang: person who constantly worries)* preocupón *m*, -na *f*

worse *adj* peor *m&f* **It could have been worse.** Pudo haber sido peor. **Finally I found someone who** *(1)* **plays /** *(2)* **sings worse than I do.** Al fin encontré a alguien que *(1)* juega / *(2)* canta peor que yo. **I'm bad, but your worse.** Soy malo, pero tú eres peor.

worship *vt* idolatrar **I worship you.** Te idolatro.

worst *adj* lo peor *m&f* **~ case scenario** el peor de los casos **What's the worst thing that could happen?** ¿Qué es lo peor que puede pasar? **I'm the worst** *(1)* **dancer /** *(2)* **swimmer you ever saw.** Yo soy el *m* / la *f* peor *(1)* bailarín *(-rina)* / *(2)* nadador *(-dora)* que hayas visto.

worth *adj* valer *m&f* **What's it worth?** ¿Qué vale eso? **It's worth** *(value)*. Eso vale ___. **It's not worth it.** No vale la pena. **It was worth it.** Valió la pena.

worthless *adj* sin ningún valor *m&f*, despreciable *m&f* **absolutely ~** absolutamente despreciable

would *v aux* **I would** *(1)* **do it... /** *(2)* **go... /** *(3)* **stay..., if I could.** *(1)* Lo haría…, / *(2)* Iría..., / *(3)* Me quedaría..., si pudiera. **Would you care to join** *(1)* **me? /** *(2)* **us?** ¿Te gustaría *(1)* acompañarme? / *(2)* acompañarnos? **I wouldn't mind.** No me importaría. **I wouldn't do that if I were you.** Yo no haría eso si fuera tú.

wrap *vt* envolver **~ a gift** envolver un regalo *m* **~ a package** envolver un paquete *m*

wrapping *adj*: **~ paper** papel *m* de envoltura

wrecked *adj* arruinado *m*, -da *f* **All** *(1)* **my /** *(2)* **our plans are wrecked.** Todos *(1)* mis / *(2)* nuestros planes se arruinaron.

wrench *n* llave *f* inglesa **socket ~** llave de tubo

Numbers in Spanish are given on pages 411-412.

wrestle *vi* luchar   **wrestler** *n* luchador *m*, -dora *f*

wrestling *n* lucha *f*   ~ **match** torneo *m* de lucha   **pro(fessional)** ~ lucha profesional

wrinkled *adj* arrugado *m*, -da *f* **My clothes are all wrinkled.** Mi ropa está toda arrugada.

wrist *n* muñeca *m*

write *vt* escribir, anotar   ~ **in** *(1)* **English** / *(2)* **Spanish** escribir en *(1)* inglés / *(2)* español **(I promise) I'll write to you (**[1] **often.** / [2] **soon.** / [3] **every day /** [4] **week. /** [5] **as soon /** [6] **often as I can. /** [7] **[at least] one or twice a week. /** [8] **every chance I get.).** (Prometo que) Te voy a escribir (*[1]* con frecuencia. / *[2]* pronto. / *[3]* todos los días. / *[4]* todas las semanas. / *[5]* tan pronto como pueda. / *[6]* tan seguido como pueda. / *[7]* (al menos) una o dos veces por semana. *[8]* cada vez que pueda.) **Write to me (**[1]**often /** [2] **soon), okay?** Escríbeme (*[1]* con frecuencia / *[2]* pronto), ¿sí? **I wrote (a** [1] **letter /** [2] **postcard) to you (from ...). Did you get it?** Te escribí (*[1]* una carta / *[2]* una postal*)* (desde ...). ¿La recibiste? **Write down your** *(1)* **address /** *(2)* **phone number /** *(3)* **e-mail address for me.** *Anóteme su (Fam: Anótame tu) (1)* domicilio. / *(2)* número telefónico. / *(3)* dirección electrónica. **How do you write your name?** ¿Cómo *escribe usted (Fam:* escribes) tu nombre?

writer *n* escritor *m*, -tora *f*

wrong *adj* 1. *(incorrect)* equivocado *m*, -da *f*; 2. *(inappropriate)* mal *m&f*; 3. *(amiss, not normal)* contrario *m*, -ria *f*   ~ **time** mal momento   **You're wrong.** Estás equivocado *(-da).* **I'm sorry, I was wrong.** Perdón, me equivoqué. **(1) My /** *(2)* **Your watch is wrong.** *(1)* Mi / *(2)* Su *(Fam: Tu)* reloj está mal. **We're going the wrong way.** Vamos por el camino equivocado. *(1)* **I /** *(2)* **We took the wrong** *(3)* **bus /** *(4)* **subway. /** *(5)* **train.** *(1)* Tomé / *(2)* Tomamos el *(3)* camión / *(4)* metro / *(5)* tren equivocado. **We got on the wrong** *(1)* **highway. /** *(2)* **road. /** *(3)* **street.** Entramos *(1)* a la autopista equivocada. / *(2)* al camino equivocado. / *(3)* a la calle equivocada. **Don't get the wrong idea.** No tengas una idea equivocada. **What's wrong?** ¿Qué está mal? **Nothing is wrong.** Nada está mal. **Something is wrong.** Algo anda mal.

wrong *adv* mal **You're doing it wrong. Let me show you.** Lo estás haciendo mal. Déjame mostrarte. **Don't get me wrong.** No me tomes a mal. **I hope nothing goes wrong (with our plans).** Espero que nada salga mal (con nuestros planes.) **Everything went wrong.** Todo salió mal. **I read the schedule wrong.** Leí mal el programa.

wry *adj* irónico *m*, -ca *f*, sardónico *m*, -ca *f*   ~ **sense of humor** humor *m* sardónico   ~ **wit** ingenio *m* burlón

---

Spanish "h" is always silent.

Y

yacht *n* yate *m* **yachting** *n* navegación *f* a vela

yard *n* 1. *(of a house)* patio *m* ; 2. *(36 inches)* yarda *f* **front ~** patio frontal **back ~** patio trasero

yarn *n* hilaza *f* **ball of ~** bola de hilaza

yawn *vi* bostezar **No yawning!** ¡Sin bostezar! **I'm sorry, I can't stop yawning.** Perdón, no puedo dejar de bostezar.

year *n* año *m* **a ~ ago** hace un año **all ~** todo el año **every ~** cada año **in a ~** en un año; dentro de un año **last ~** el año pasado **next ~** el año próximo **once a ~** una vez al año **this ~** este año **two ~s ago** hace dos años **In what year?** ¿En qué año? **How many years have you** *(1)* **lived /** *(2* **worked** *(3)* **here? /** *(4)* **there?** ¿Cuántos años *(1)* ha vivido usted (Fam: has vivido) / *(2)* ha trabajado usted (Fam: has trabajado) *(3)* aquí? / *(4)* allí? **I've** *(1)* **lived /** *(2)* **worked there for** *(number)* **years.** He *(1)* vivido / *(2)* trabajado allí por __ años. **We've lived there for** *(number)* **years.** Hemos vivido allí por __ años. **I'm** *(number)* **years old.** Yo tengo __ años. *(1)* **He /** *(2)* **She is** *(3)* **one year old. /** *(4)* *(number)* **years old.** *(1)* Él / *(2)* Ella tiene *(3)* un año. / *(4)* __ años. **Happy New Year!** ¡Feliz Año Nuevo!

yearly *adj* anual *m&f* **~ salary** salario *m* anual

yearn *vi* ansiar **I yearn to** *(1)* **hold /** *(2)* **kiss you.** Ansío *(1)* abrazarte. / *(2)* besarte.

yell *vi* gritar **Don't yell!** ¡No grites!

yellow *adj* amarillo *m*, -lla *f*

yes *adv* sí **Yes, I do.** Sí. **Yes, I** *(1,2)* **was.** Sí, yo *(1)* era. / *(2)* estuve. **Yes, I will.** Sí, lo haré. **Say yes.** Dí que sí. **I'll take that as a yes.** Tomaré eso como un sí.

yesterday *n & adv* ayer *m* **day before ~** anteayer *m*, antier *m*

yet *adv* aún, todavía **Aren't you ready yet?** ¿Todavía no estás listo *(-ta)*? **Have you seen it yet?** ¿Todavía no lo ves? *(1)* **I /** *(2)* **We haven't seen it**

Questions about the metric system? See page 417.

yet. Todavía no lo *(1)* he / *(2)* hemos visto. **Have you been there yet?** ¿Todavía no has estado ahí? *(1)* **I** / *(2)* **We haven't been there yet.** Todavía no *(1)* he… / *(2)* hemos… estado ahí.

yoga *n* yoga *m* **I practice yoga** (*[1]* **everyday** / *[2]* **often**). Hago yoga (*[1]* diario / *[2]* con frecuencia.)

you *pron (Pol:)* usted; *(Fam:)* tú; *(Pl:)* ustedes **You** *(1,2)* **are.** Usted *(1)* es. *(2)* está. *(Fam:* Tú *(1)* eres. / *(2)* estás).* **You** *(1,2)* **were.** Usted *(1)* era. *(2)* estaba. *(Fam:* Tú *(1)* eras. / *(2)* estabas).* **You** *(1,2)* **will be.** Usted *(1)* será. *(2)* estará. *(Fam:* Tú *(1)* serás. / *(2)* estarás).* **I want (very much) to speak to you with "familiar you".** Quiero (mucho) hablarle de "tú." **Would you mind if I used "familiar you" with you?** ¿Le molestaría si le hablo de "tú"? **I** *(1)* **need** / *(2)* **want you.** Te *(1)* necesito. / *(2)* quiero. **I missed you.** Te extrañé. **It's so nice to be with you.** Es tan rico estar con usted *(Fam: contigo).*

young *adj* joven *m&f* ~ **boy** muchacho joven ~ **girl** muchacha joven ~ **man** hombre joven ~ **woman** mujer joven *(1)* **My** / *(2)* **Our children are still young.** *(1)* Mis / *(2)* Nuestros hijos todavía están jóvenes. **You're still young.** Todavía estás joven. **You look so young.** Te ves tan joven. **I'm still (very) young at heart.** Todavía estoy (muy) joven de corazón.

younger *comp adj* más joven *m&f* **You're younger than I am.** Tú eres más joven que yo. **I'm younger than you are.** Yo soy más joven que tú. *(1)* **He** / *(2)* **She is younger than** *(3)* **he** / *(4)* **she (is).** *(1)* Él / *(2)* Ella es más joven que *(3)* él. / *(4)* ella.

your *poss. adj (Pol:)* su *sing.,* sus *pl; (Fam:)* tu *sing.,* tus *pl* ~ **apartment** *su (Fam: tu)* departamento ~ **car** *su (Fam: tu)* carro ~ **house** *su (Fam: tu)* casa ~ **job** *su (Fam: tu)* empleo ~ **parents** *sus (Fam: tus)* padres ~ **school** *su (Fam: tu)* escuela **Is this your bag?** ¿Es esta *su (Fam: tu)* bolsa? **What's your address?** ¿Cuál es *su (Fam: tu)* dirección? **Write down your phone number.** Anóteme *su (Fam: Anótame tu)* número telefónico. **I like your** *(1)* **blouse.** / *(2)* **dress.** / *(3)* **sweater.** Me gusta *su (Fam: tu)* *(1)* blusa / *(2)* vestido / *(3)* suéter.

yours *poss. pron (Pol:)* suyo *m sing.,* suya *f sing; (Fam:)* tuyo *m sing,* tuya *f sing; (Pol:)* suyos *mpl,* suyas *fpl (Fam:)* tuyos *mpl,* tuyas *fpl* **Is this yours?** ¿Es *suyo (Fam: tuyo)* esto? **I believe this is yours.** Creo que esto es *suyo (Fam:* tuyo). **Is** *(1)* **he** / *(2* **she a friend of yours?** *(1)* ¿Él es amigo *suyo (Fam: tuyo)*? / *(2)* ¿Ella es amiga *suya (Fam:* tuya)?

yourself *pers. pron (reflexive) (Pol:)* se, sí mismo *m,* sí misma *f; (Fam:)* te, ti mismo *m,* ti misma *f* **Don't hurt yourself.** No *se lastime (Fam: te lastimes).* **Did you hurt yourself?** ¿*Se lastimó usted? (Fam:* ¿*Te lastimaste?)* **You should be ashamed of yourself.** Debería *darle (Fam: dar-*

The letter "ñ" sounds like the "ny" in "canyon".

te) vergüenza. **You have to believe in yourself.** *Tiene usted (Fam: Tienes)* que creer en *sí (Fam: ti)* mismo *(-ma)*. **Are you going by yourself?** *¿Va usted (Fam: Vas)* por *su (Fam: tu)* cuenta? **Did you make that yourself?** *¿Lo hizo usted (Fam: hiciste tú)* mismo *(-ma)*?

youth *n* juventud *f* in my ~ en mi juventud

youthful *adj* juvenil *m&f*

Z

zealot *n* fanático *m*, -ca *f*
zenith *n* cenit *m*
zero *n* cero *m* ~ **chance** sin oportunidad ~ **points** a cero puntos
zest *n* gusto *m*, ganas *fpl* **with** ~ con ganas ~ **for life** gusto por la vida ~
   for living ganas de vivir
zip (up) *vt* subirse el cierre
zipper *n* cierre *m*
zit *n (slang: blackhead, pimple)* espinilla *f*, barro *m*
zodiac *n* zodiaco *m* **What's your zodiac sign?** ¿Cuál es *su (Fam: tu)*
   signo zodiacal? **My (zodiac) sign is** *(1)* **Capricorn** *(Dec. 22 - Jan. 19)*
   / (2) **Aquarius** *(Jan. 20 - Feb. 18) / (3)* **Pisces** *(Feb. 19 - Mar. 20) / (4)*
   Aries *(Mar. 21 - Apr. 19) / (5)* **Taurus** *(Apr. 20 - May 20) / (6)* **Gemini**
   (May 21 - Jun. 20) / (7) **Cancer** *(Jun. 21 - Jul. 22) / (8)* **Leo** *(Jul. 23 -*
   Aug. 22) / (9) **Virgo** *(Aug. 23 - Sep. 22) / (10)* **Libra** *(Sep. 23 - Oct. 22) /*
   (11) **Scorpio** *(Oct. 24 - Nov. 21) / (12)* **Sagittarius** *(Nov. 22 - Dec. 21)*.
   Mi signo zodiacal es *(1)* Capricornio. / *(2)* Acuario. / *(3)* Piscis. / *(4)*
   Aries. / *(5)* Tauro. / *(6)* Géminis. / *(7)* Cáncer. / *(8)* Leo. / *(9)* Virgo. / *(10)*
   Libra. / *(11)* Escorpión. / *(12)* Sagitario.
zombie *n* zombi(e) *m&f*
zone *n* zona *f* **erogenous** ~ zona erógena **time** ~ huso *m* horario
zoo *n* zoológico *m*

Spanish "o" is pronounced like "o" in "note".

Spanish Alphabet

Letter	Name	Phonetic Value
A	*ah*	*"ah" in "mama" or "papa"*
B	*beh*	*Similar to "b" in "best", often sounds much softer*
C	*seh*	*"s" as in "sister"*
D	*deh*	*"d" as in "dog"*
E	*eh*	*"eh" as in* "get"
F	*eh-feh*	*"f" as in "free"*
G	*kheh*	*1. "h" as in "hat" in front of e and i;* *2. Elsewhere like "g" in "gate"*
H	*ah-cheh*	*Always silent*
I	*ee*	*"ee" in "meet"*
J	*khoh-ta*	*A heavy "h", close to Scottish "ch" in "loch"*
K	*kah*	*"k" as in "king"*
L	*eh-leh*	*"l" as in "list" or "garlic"; ll is like "y" in "yes"*
M	*eh-meh*	*"m" as in "summer"*
N	*ayn-neh*	*"n" as in "never"*

Letter	Name	Phonetic Value
Ñ	**en**-*yeh*	*Like "ny" in "canyon"*
O	*oh*	*"o" in "vote"*
P	*peh*	*"p" as in "past"*
Q	*koo*	*"k" as in "kiss"*
R	**er**-*reh*	*A hard "r", softly trilled; double* **rr** *is strongly trilled*
S	**eh**-*seh*	*"s" as in "sweet"*
T	*teh*	*"t" as "top"*
U	*oo*	*"oo" as in "boot"*
V	*beh*	*A very soft "b"*
W	**doh**-*leh beh*	*"w" (used mostly in foreign words like "web")*
X	**eh**-*kees*	*1. "ks" as in "taxi"* *2. "s" in front of consonants*
Y	*ee gree-***yeh***-gah*	*"ee" when alone or at the end of a word*
Z	**se**-*tah*	*"s" as in "sick"*

Spanish Grammar

A rich and beautiful language, Spanish, like any other language, requires considerable study and practice in order to become fluent in it. What follows here is a very cursory overview of its main characteristics-

Gender: Most nouns and adjectives in Spanish are either masculine (*m*) or feminine (*f*). A good number, however, can be either (*m&f*).

Articles: Like English, Spanish has articles that correspond to "a" and "the," with masculine and feminine forms of each. Thus, "a" in Spanish is either **un** (*m*) or **una** (*f*), and "the" is either **el** (*m*) or **la** (*f*). Further, Spanish "the" can also be plural, both feminine and masculine: **las** (*fpl*) and **los** (*mpl*).

Nouns: Spanish nouns that end in **o** are usually masculine, those that end in **a**, **d** or **-ción** are generally feminine. There are exceptions to this rule. Other nouns need to be learned one by one.

Plural forms of nouns are commonly formed by adding **s** or **es** to the end of the word. Even though plural, they retain their genders.

Adjectives: In Spanish, adjectives must agree with nouns in gender and number. This means that they can be masculine singular, feminine singular, masculine plural, and feminine plural. Some adjectives can be either feminine or masculine, both in their singular and plural forms. An **s** or **es** is added on the end to make them plural.

Adjectives usually follow the nouns they modify, but sometimes they go in front.

Verbs: Spanish verbs have many tenses. (We'll leave that hot potato for textbooks.) Suffice it to say that they conjugate with different endings for the different "persons" (I, polite and familiar you, he/she/it, we, plural you, they). Thus, the word for "go" in Spanish looks different in the present tense for "I" (**voy**) than it does for "we" (**vamos**). This rule applies to the other tenses as well.

There are also reflexive verbs in Spanish. These would be akin to such things as "I hurt myself" in English. The infinitives of reflexive verbs have **se** on the end.

Pronouns: The Spanish pronouns, with their forms for direct and indirect objects in parentheses, are as follows: "I" = **yo** (**me - me**), polite "you" = usted (**le** *m*, **la** *f* - **le** *m&f*), familiar "you" = **tú** (**te - ti**), "he" = **él** (**le, lo - le**), "she" = **ella** (**la - le**), "it" = (**la - le**), "we" = **nosotros** (**nos - nos**), plural "you" = **ustedes** (**los** *mpl*, **las** *fpl* - **les**), "they" = **ellos** *mpl,* **ellas** *fpl* (**los** *mpl,* **las** *fpl* - **les**).

Demonstrative adjectives and pronouns: This group, which features "this," "that," "these," and "those," also incorporates masculine and feminine forms, both singular and plural. Example: "this" - **este** (*m*), **esta** (*f*); "these" - **estos** (*mpl*), **estas** (*fpl*).

Possession. Whereas we have apostrophe-s in English, Spanish uses **de** ("of") as their workhorse. In front of singular masculine nouns it's **del**, with no further **el** needed.

The other way of expressing possession is with possessive pronouns **mi** (my), **su** (polite your, his, her & its), **tu** (familiar your), **nuestro** & **nuestra** (our, *m & f*), and **su** (plural your & their). These all have plurals, formed with **s** on the end.

A note about possession: Spanish is not as liberal in its use of possessive pronouns as English is. Often, an article is used instead of a possessive.

Word order is much the same as in English.

Questions can be formed (1), by inflecting the voice with a regular sentence, (2) by inverting the subject and the predicate (like we do with "Did you see it?"), often with a lead-off question word, and (3) by making a statement and then putting a tag question on the end (like we do in "It's a nice day, isn't it?"). Two common Spanish tag questions are ¿**no?** and ¿**verdad?**.

Negatives. Just add a **no** and you've got it.

Numbers

0	cero	40	cuarenta
1	uno	45	cuarenta y cinco
2	dos	50	cincuenta
3	tres	55	cincuenta y cinco
4	cuatro	60	sesenta
5	cinco	65	sesenta y cinco
6	seis	70	setenta
7	siete	75	setenta y cinco
8	ocho	80	ochenta
9	nueve	85	ochenta y cinco
10	diez	90	noventa
11	once	95	noventa y cinco
12	doce	100	cien
13	trece	110	ciento diez
14	catorce	120	ciento veinte
15	quince	130	ciento treinta
16	dieciséis	140	ciento cuarenta
17	diecisiete	150	ciento cincuenta
18	dieciocho	160	ciento sesenta
19	diecinueve	170	ciento setenta
20	veinte	180	ciento ochenta
21	veintiuno	190	ciento noventa
22	veintidós	200	doscientos
23	veintitrés	300	trescientos
24	veinticuatro	400	cuatrocientos
25	veinticinco	500	quinentos
26	veintiséis	600	seiscientos
27	veintisiete	700	setecientos
28	veintiocho	800	ochocientos
29	veintinueve	900	novecientos
30	treinta	1,000	mil
31	treinta y uno	5,000	cinco mil
32	treinta y dos	10,000	diez mil
33	treinta y tres	100,000	cien mil
34	treinta y cuatro	500,000	quinentos mil
35	treinta y cinco	1,000,000	un millión

Ordinal Numbers

first	primero
second	secundo
third	tercero
fourth	cuarto
fifth	quinto
sixth	sexto
seventh	séptimo
eighth	octavo
ninth	noveno
tenth	decimo
eleventh	undécimo
twelfth	duodécimo

Fractions

1/4	un cuarto	**1/3**	un tercio
1/2	un mitad	**2/3**	dos tercios
3/4	tres cuartos		

When counting things with **1** in Spanish, remember to use **un** for masculine things, and **una** for feminine. Other numbers take plurals.

Clock Time

1:00	la una	**7:00**	las siete
1:15	la una y cuarto	**7:15**	las siete y cuarto
1:30	la una y media	**7:30**	las siete y media
1:45	la una menos cuarto	**7:45**	las siete menos cuarto
2:00	las dos	**8:00**	las ocho
2:15	las dos y cuarto	**8:15**	las ocho y cuarto
2:30	las dos y media	**8:30**	las ocho y media
2:45	las dos menos cuarto	**8:45**	las ocho menos cuarto
3:00	las tres	**9:00**	las nueve
3:15	las tres y cuarto	**9:15**	las nueve y cuarto
3:30	las tres y media	**9:30**	las nueve y media
3:45	las tres menos cuarto	**9:45**	las nueve menos cuarto
4:00	las cuatro	**10:00**	las diez
4:15	las cuatro y cuarto	**10:15**	las diez y cuarto
4:30	las cuatro y media	**10:30**	las diez y media
4:45	las cuatro menos cuarto	**10:45**	las diez menos cuarto
5:00	las cinco	**11:00**	las once
5:15	las cinco y cuarto	**11:15**	las once y cuarto
5:30	las cinco y media	**11:30**	las once y media
5:45	las cinco menos cuarto	**11:45**	las once menos cuarto
6:00	las seis	**12:00**	las doce
6:15	las seis y cuarto	**12:15**	las doce y cuarto
6:30	las seis y media	**12:30**	las doce y media
6:45	las seis menos cuarto	**12:45**	las doce menos cuarto

5 minutes after	y cinco	**5 minutes till**	menos cinco
10 minutes after	y diez	**10 minutes till**	menos diez
20 minutes after	y veinte	**20 minutes till**	menos veinte
25 minutes after	y veinticinco	**25 minutes till**	menos veinticinco

What time is it? ¿Que hora es?
(For replies with 1:) Es la... *(For other numbers:)* Son las...

Calendar Time

Days of the week:

Monday	lunes	**on Monday**	el lunes
Tuesday	martes	**since Monday**	desde lunes
Wednesday	miércoles	**this Monday**	este lunes
Thursday	jueves	**last Monday**	el lunes pasado
Friday	viernes	**next Monday**	el próximo lunes
Saturday	sábado	**every Monday**	todos los lunes
Sunday	domingo	**by Monday**	ante del lunes

Monday morning	el lunes por la mañana
Monday afternoon	el lunes por la tarde
Monday evening	el lunes por la noche
Monday night	el lunes por la noche

Months of the year:

January	enero	**in May**	en mayo
February	febrero	**since May**	desde mayo
March	marzo	**this May**	este mayo
April	abril	**last May**	el mayo pasado
May	mayo	**next May**	el próximo mayo
June	junio	**by May**	para mayo
July	julio	**at the end of May**	a finales de mayo
August	agosto		
September	septiembre	**during the month of May**	durante el mes de mayo
October	octubre		
November	noviembre		
December	diciembre		

in the spring	en primavera *f*
in the summer	en verano *m*
in the fall	en otoño *m*
in the winter	en invierno *m*

Common Occupations

accountant contador *m*, -dora *f*
accounting clerk empleado *m*, -da *f* de la contabilidad
administrative assisstant auxiliar *m&f* administrativa
airport worker trabajador *m*, -dora *f* del aeropuerto
apartment manager administrador *m*, -dora *f* del apartamento
architect arquitecto *m*, -ta *f*
artist / painter artista *m&f*
assembler assemblador *m*, -ra *f*
automechanic
baker panadero *m*, -ra *f*
bank employee bancario *m*, -ria *f*, empleado *m*, -da *f* de banco
bank teller cajero *m*, -ra *f*
barber peluquero *m*
bartender barman *m*, mesera *f*
bookkeeper tenedor *m*, -dora *f* de libros
bus driver conductor *m*, -ra *f* de autobús, camionero *m*, -ra *f*
businessman empresario, hombre de negocios
businesswoman empresaria, mujer de negocios
butcher carnicero *m*, -ra *f*
car dealer / salesman
carpenter carpintero *m*, -ra *f*
cashier cajero *m*, -ra *f*
caterer persona *f* que se encarga del servicio de comida y bebida para fiestas
clergyman clérigo *m*
construction worker trabajador *m*, -ra *f* de la construccion
cook cocinero *m*, -ra *f*
delivery person persona *f* de la entrega

dental assistant auxiliar *m&f* odontologo *m*, -ga *f*
dentist odontologo *m*, -ga *f*
designer disenador m, -ra *f*
director directivo *m*, -va *f*
doctor doctor *m*, -tora *f*
electrician electriscista *m&f*
engineer ingeniero *m*, -ra *f*
factory worker trabajador *m*, -ra *f* de la fabrica
farmer ranchero *m*, -ra *f*
fashion designer disenador *m*, -ra *f* de la moda
financial advisor consejero *m*, -ra f de financiero
firefighter bombero *m*
fisherman pescador *m*
flight attendant auxiliar *m&f* de vuelo
florist florista *m&f*
gardener jardinero *m*, -ra *f*
glazier vidriero *m*, -ra *f*
government employee empleado *m*, -da *f* del gobierno *or* estado
hairstylist peinador *m*, -ra *f*
interior decorator interiorista *m&f*
hotel manager administrador *m*, -dora *f* del hotel
housekeeper ama de llaves *f*
human resources manager administrador *m*, -dora *f* de los recursos humanos
inspector inspector *m*, -ra *f*
insurance agent agente *m&f* del seguro
interpreter interprete *m&f*
investigator (private) inspector *m*, -tora *f* (privado *m*, -da *f*)
jeweler joyero *m*, -ra *f*
journalist periodista *m&f*

kitchen worker trabajador *m*, -dora *f* de la cocina
landscaper jarddinero *m*, -ra *f* paisajista
lawyer abogado *m*, -da *f*
librarian bibliotecario *m*, -ria *f*
loan processor contador *m*, -dora *f* del credito
machinist maquinista *m&f*
magazine editor redactor *m*, -tora *f* de la revista
mailman cartero *m*
manager director *m*, -tora *f*; administrador *m*, -dora *f*
metalworker obrero metalúrgico *m*, obrera metalúrgica *f*
miner minero *m*
model modelo *m&f*
musician músico *m&f*
newspaper editor director *m*, -tora *f* del periodico
nurse emfermero *m*, -ra *f*
office clerk empleado *m*, -da *f* de la oficiana
oilfield worker trabajador *m*, -dora *f* del petrolifero *or* de petroleo
optician óptico *m*, -ca *f*
painter pintor *m*, -tora *f*
pharmacist farmaceutico *m*, -ca *f*
photographer fotografo *m*, -fa *f*
pilot piloto *m&f*
planner planificador *m*, -dora *f*
plumber plomero *m*, -ra *f*
police officer policia *m&f*
postal worker trabajador *m*, -dora *f* postal
principal director *m*, -tora *f*
printer impresor *m*, -sora *f*
professor prefesor universitario *m*, -sora -ria *f*
programmer programador *m*, -dora *f*
psychologist (p)sicologo *m*, -ga *f*
publisher editor *m*, -tora *f*

railroad worker trabajador *m*, -dora *f* del ferrocarril
real estate agent agente *m&f* de bienes raíces
receptionist recepcionista *m&f*
repair(wo)man técnico *m*, -ca *f*
reporter periodista *m&f*, reportero *m*, -ra *f*
restaurant manager encargado *m*, -da *f* (de restaurante)
salesclerk venedor *m*, -dora *f*
scientist científico *m*, -ca *f*
seamstress costurera *f*
secretary secretario *m*, -ria *f*
singer cantante *m&f*
social service worker trabajador *m*, -dora *f* de la asistencia
sport instructor instructor *m*, -tora *f* del deporte
stockbroker corredor *m*, -dora *f* de valores
supervisor supervisor *m*, -sora *f*
surgeon cirujano *m*, -na *f*
system analyst analista *m&f* del sistema
tailor sastre *m&f*
taxi driver taxista *m&f*
teacher profesor *m*, -ra *f*
techinician técnico *m*, -ca *f*
trainer *(sports)* entrenador *m*, -dora *f*; *(horses)* preparador *m*, -dora *f*; (animals) amaestrador *m*, -dora *f*
translator traductor *m*, -tora *f*
travel agent agente *m&f* de viajes
truck driver camionero *m*, -ra *f*
typist mecanógrafo *m*, -fa *f*
veternarian medico veterinario *m*, -ca -ria *f*
waiter mesero *m*
waitress mesera *f*
warehouse worker trabajador *m*, -dora *f* del deposito
writer escritor *m*, -tora *f*

Metric Measurements

Length
1 millimeter, mm (milímetro *m*, mm) = 0.04 inches
10 mm = 1 centimeter, cm (centímetro *m*, cm) = 0.4 inches
1000 mm = 100 cm = 1 meter, m (metro *m*, m) = 3.3 feet
1000 m = 1 kilometer, km (kilómetro *m*, km) = 0.6 miles
8 km = 5 miles

1 inch = 2.5 centimeters = 25 millimeters
1 foot = 30 centimeters = 300 millimeters
1 yard = 90 centimeters = 0.9 meters
1 mile = 1.6 kilometers = 1609 meters

Weight
1 gram, g (gramo *m*, g) = 0.035 ounces
500 g = ½ kilogram (medio *m* kilogramo, ½ kg) = 1.1 pounds
1000 g = 1 kilogram, kg (kilogramo *m*, kg) = 2.2 pounds

1 ounce = 28 grams
1 pound = 450 grams = 0.45 kilograms

Volume
1 liter, l (litro *m*, l) = 1.06 quarts
4 liters = 1.06 U.S. gallons

1 quart = 0.95 liters
1 U.S. gallon = 3.8 liters

Temperature
Fahrenheit, F = °Centigrade x 9/5 + 32   *(9/5 = 1.8)*
Centigrade, C = (°Fahrenheit - 32) x 5/9   *(5/9 = 0.5555)*

Boiling point: 212°F = 100°C
Body temperature: 98.6°F = 37°C
Pleasant temperature: 72°F = 22°C
Freezing point: 32°F = 0°C

Common Adult Heights

The following height equivalents are approximate. 1 inch = 2.54 cm

Metric	U.S.	Metric	U.S.
150 cm	4' 11"	175 cm	5' 9"
151 cm	4' 11 ½"	176 cm	5' 9"
		177 cm	5' 9 ½"
152 cm	5' 0'		
153 cm	5' 0"	178 cm	5' 10"
154 cm	5' ½"	179 cm	5' 10 ½"
155 cm	5' 1"	180 cm	5' 11"
156 cm	5' 1 ½"	181 cm	5' 11"
		182 cm	5' 11 ½"
157 cm	5' 2"		
158 cm	5' 2"	183 cm	6' 0"
159 cm	5' 2 ½"	184 cm	6' ½"
160 cm	5' 3"	185 cm	6' 1"
161 cm	5' 3 ½"	186 cm	6' 1"
		187 cm	6' 1 ½"
162 cm	5' 4"		
163 cm	5' 4"	188 cm	6' 2"
164 cm	5' 4 ½"	189 cm	6' 2 ½"
165 cm	5' 5"	190 cm	6' 3"
166 cm	5' 5 ½"	191 cm	6' 3"
		192 cm	6' 3 ½"
167 cm	5' 6"		
168 cm	5' 6"	193 cm	6' 4"
169 cm	5' 6 ½"	194 cm	6' 4 ½"
170 cm	5' 7"	195 cm	6' 5"
171 cm	5' 7 ½"	196 cm	6' 5"
		197 cm	6' 5 ½"
172 cm	5' 8"		
173 cm	5' 8"	198 cm	6' 6"
174 cm	5' 8 ½"	199 cm	6' 6 ½"

Common Adult Weights

The following height equivalents are approximate. 1 kg = 2.2 lbs and 1 lb = 0.455 kg.

Metric	U.S.	U.S.	Metric
40 kg	88 lbs	90 lbs	41 kg
42 kg	92 lbs	95 lbs	43 kg
45 kg	99 lbs	100 lbs	45 kg
47 kg	103 lbs	105 lbs	48 kg
50 kg1	10 lbs	110 lbs	50 kg
52 kg	114 lbs	115 lbs	52 kg
55 kg	121 lbs	120 lbs	55 kg
57 kg	125 lbs	125 lbs	57 kg
60 kg	132 lbs	130 lbs	59 kg
62 kg	136 lbs	135 lbs	61 kg
65 kg	143 lbs	140 lbs	64 kg
67 kg	147 lbs	145 lbs	66 kg
70 kg	154 lbs	150 lbs	68 kg
72 kg	158 lbs	155 lbs	70 kg
75 kg	165 lbs	160 lbs	73 kg
77 kg	169 lbs	165 lbs	75 kg
80 kg	176 lbs	170 lbs	77 kg
82 kg	180 lbs	175 lbs	80 kg
85 kg	187 lbs	180 lbs	82 kg
87 kg	191 lbs	185 lbs	84 kg
90 kg	198 lbs	190 lbs	86 kg
92 kg	202 lbs	195 lbs	89 kg
95 kg	209 lbs	200 lbs	91 kg
97 kg	213 lbs	205 lbs	93 kg
100 kg	220 lbs	210 lbs	95 kg
102 kg	224 lbs	215 lbs	98 kg
105 kg	231 lbs	220 lbs	100 kg
107 kg	235 lbs	225 lbs	102 kg
110 kg	242 lbs	230 lbs	105 kg
112 kg	246 lbs	235 lbs	107 kg
115 kg	253 lbs	240 lbs	109 kg
117 kg	257 lbs	245 lbs	111 kg
120 kg	264 lbs	250 lbs	114 kg

Food & Drink
English-Spanish Glossary

abalone abulón *m*
almonds almendras *fpl*
anchovies anchoas *fpl*
appetizer entrada *f*
apple manzana *f*
apricots chabacanos *mpl*
asparagus espárragos *mpl*
artichokes alcachofas *fpl*
avacado aguacate *m*
bacon tocino *m*
baked al horno
banana plátano *m*
barbacued en barbacoa
bass mero *m*
beans frijoles *mpl*
  black ~ frijoles negros
  green ~ ejotes *mpl*
beef carne *m* de res
beer cerveza *f*
blackberries moras *fpl*
blueberries arándanos *mpl*
boiled cocido *m*, -da *f*
brandy coñac *m*
bread pan *m*
bream besugo *m*
broccoli brócoli *m*
brussels sprouts coles *fpl* de Bruselas
  butter montequilla *f*
cabbage col , repollo *m*
cake pastel *m*
cantaloupe cantalupo *m*
capers alcaparras *fpl*
carrot zanahoria *f*
catsup ketchup *m*, catsup *m*
cauliflower coliflor *f*
celery apio *m*
cereal cereales *mpl*

cheese queso *m*
cherries cerezas *fpl*
chestnuts castañas *fpl*
chicken pollo *m*
chives cebollinos *mpl*
chocolate, hot chocolate *m* caliente
cinnamon canela *f*
clams almejas *fpl*
cloves clavos *mpl*
coconut coco *m*
cod bacalao *m*
cognac coñac *m*
coffee café *m*
cola coca *f*
cookies galletas *fpl*
corn elote *m*
crab cangrejo *m*
crackers galletas *fpl* saladas
cream crema *f*
  whipped ~ crema batida
creamed en crema
cucumber pepino *m*
cutlet costilla *f*
decaffeinated descafeinado
dessert postre *m*
doughnut rosquilla *f*
dressing, salad aliño *m* de ensalada, aderezo *m* de ensalada
duck pato *m*
eel anguila *f*
eggplant berenjena *f*
eggs huevos *mpl*
  fried ~ huevos fritos
  hard-boiled ~ huevo duro
  scrambled ~ huevos revueltos
figs higos *mpl*

French fries papas *fpl* a la francesca

fried frito *m*, -ta *f*

fruit frutas *fpl*

  passion ~ granadilla *f*

garlic ajo *m*

gin gin *m*

grapefruit toronja *f*

grapes uvas *fpl*

grilled a la parrilla

guava guayaba *f*

hake merluza *f*

ham jamón *m*

hamburger hamburguesa *f*

herring boquerones *mpl*

honey miel *f*

ice hielo *m*

ice cream helado *m*

jam mermelada *f*

juice hugo *m*

  grapefruit ~ hugo de toronja

  orange ~ hugo de naranja

  tomato ~ hugo de jitomate

lamb cordero *m*

lemon limón *m*

lemonade limonada *f*

lentils lentejas *fpl*

lettuce lechuga *f*

liqueur licor *m*

liver hígado *m*

lobster langosta *f*

macaroni macarrones *mpl*

mackerel caballa *f*

mango mango *m*

margarine margarina *f*

meat *m* carne

medium a medio cocinar

melon melón *m*

milk leche *f*

milkshake batido *m* de leche

mint menta *f*

monkfish rape *m*

mullet mújol *m*

  red ~ salmonetes *mpl*

mushrooms champiñones *mpl*

mussels cholgas *fpl*

mustard mostaza *f*

mutton carnero *m*

noodles fideos *mpl*

octopus pulpo *m*

oil aceite *m*

  olive ~ aceite de oliva

  vegetable ~ aceite vegetal

olives aceitunas *fpl*

omelet(te) omelette *f*

onions cebollas *fpl*

  green ~ cebolletas *fpl*

orange naranja *f*

oysters ostiones *mpl*

papaya papaya *f*

parsley perejil *m*

pasta pasta(s) *f(pl)*

peach durazno *m*

peanuts cacahuates *mpl*

peas chícharos *mpl*

pepper pimienta *f*

  black ~ pimienta *f* negra

  green ~ pimiento *m* verde

  hot ~ ají picante

  red ~ ají *m*

pie pai *m*

pineapple piña *f*

plantain plátano *m*

plum ciruela *f*

pomegranate granada *f*

pork (carne de) puerco *m*

port oporto *m*

potato papa *f*

  mashed ~es puré *m* de papa

  sweet ~ batata *f*, boniato *m*, camote *m*

prunes ciruelas *fpl* secas

radish rábano *m*

raisins pasas *fpl*

rare a la inglesa
raspberries frambuesas *fpl*
rice arroz *m*
roasted asado *m*, -da *f*
roll(s) bollilo(s) *m(pl)*
rum ron *m*
salad ensalada *f*
  fruit ~ ensalada de fruta
  potato ~ ensalada de papas
  shrimp ~ ensalada de camarones
salmon salmón *m*
salt sal *f*
sandwich sándwich *m*, emparedado *m*
sardines sardinas *fpl*
sauce salsa *f*
  soy ~ salsa de soya
sausage salchicha *f*
sherry jerez *m*
shrimp *(small)* gambas *fpl*; *(large)* camarones *mpl* grandes
smoked ahumado *m*, -da *f*
snapper, red huachinango *m*
sole lenguado *m*
sorbet nieve *f*
soup sopa *f*
spaghetti spaghetti *mpl*
spinach espinacas *fpl*
squash calabaza *f*
squid calamares *mpl*
starfruit carambola *f*
steak bistec *m*, filete *m*
  T-bone ~ bife *m* de costilla
steamed al vapor
stew guiso *m;* guisado *m*
  seafood ~ cazuela *f* de mariscos
strawberries fresas
stuffed relleno *m*, -na *f*
sugar azúcar *m or f*
sugar cane caña *f* de azúcar
swordfish pez *m* espada
tangarine mandarina *f*

tea té *m,*
toast pan *m* tostado
  French ~ torrejas *fpl*
tomato jitomate *m*
trout trucha *f*
tuna atún *m*
  striped ~ bonito *m*
turbot rodaballo *m*
turkey pavo *m*
vanilla vainilla *f*
veal ternera *f*
vegetable verdura *f*
vinegar vinagre *m*
vodka vodka *m*
walnuts nueces *fpl*
water agua *m&f*
  mineral ~ agua mineral
watermelon sandía *f*
well-done bien cocinado *m*, -da *f*
whiskey whisky *m*
wine vino *m*
  dry ~ vino seco
  red ~ vino tinto
  róse ~ vino rosado
  sparkling ~ vino espumoso
  sweet ~ vino dulce
  white ~ vino blanco
yam yame *m*
yogurt yogur *m*, yougurt *m*
zucchini zapallitos *mpl*

Food & Drink
Spanish-English Glossary

abulón *m* abalone
aceite *m* oil
 ~ **de oliva** olive oil
 ~ **vegetal** vegetable oil
aceitunas *fpl* olives
aderezo *m* **de ensalada** salad
 dressing
adobo *m* a type of chili sauce
agua *m&f* water
 ~ **mineral** mineral water
aguacate avacado
ahumado *m*, **-da** *f* smoked
ají red pepper
ajo *m* garlic
a la inglesa rare
a la parrilla grilled
albóndiga *f* meatball
alcachofas *fpl* artichokes
alcaparras *fpl* capers
al horno baked
aliño *m* **de ensalada** salad
 dressing
almejas *fpl* clams
almendras *fpl* almonds
al vapor steamed
a medio cocinar medium
anchoas *fpl* anchovies
anguila *f* eel
ante *m* pastry made of coconut and
 almonds
antojitos *mpl* appetizers, snacks
apio *m* celery
arándanos *mpl* blueberries
arroz *m* rice
 ~ **con leche** rice pudding

asadero *m* a soft, creamy cheese
asado *m*, **-da** *f* roasted
atole *m* hot maize drink
atún *m* tuna
azúcar *m or f* sugar
bacalao *m* cod
barbacoa *f* barbacue
batata *f* sweet potato
batido *m* **de leche** milkshake
berenjena *f* eggplant
besugo *m* bream
bien cocinado *m*, **-da** *f* well-done
bife *m* **de costilla** T-bone steak
bistec *m* steak
bollilo(s) *m(pl)* roll(s)
boniato *m* sweet potato
bonito *m* striped tuna
boquerones *mpl* herring
brócoli *m* broccoli
budín *m* pudding
buñuelos *mpl* fritters with sugar
 and cinnamon
burrito *m* wheat flour tortilla
 filled with meat or cheese
caballa *f* mackerel
cacahuates *mpl* peanuts
café *m* coffee
 ~ **solo** black coffee
cajeta *f* desert of milk and vanilla
calabaza *f* squash
calamares *mpl* squid
caldo *m* **verde** kale soup
camarones *fpl* **grandes** shrimp,
 prawns *(large)*

camote *m* sweet potato
canela *f* cinnamon
cangrejo *m* crab
cantalupo *m* cantaloupe
caña *f* **de azúcar** sugar cane
capirotada *f* bread pudding with fruit, nuts and cheese
carambola *f* starfruit
carne *m* meat
~ **a la tampiqueña** steak strips with guacamole, tacos and **fried beans**
~ **de res** beef
carnero *m* mutton
castañas *fpl* chestnuts
cazuela *f* **de mariscos** seafood stew
cebollas *fpl* **encurtidos** pickled onion rings
cebollas *fpl* onions
cebolletas *fpl* green onions
cebollinos *mpl* chives
cereales *mpl* cereal
cerezas *fpl* cherries
cerveza *f* beer
~ **rubia** light beer
ceviche *m* raw fish marinated in lemon juice
chabacanos *mpl* apricots
champiñones *mpl* mushrooms
chayote *m* vegetable like an avocado
chicha *f* strong drink made from fermented corn and fruit
chícharos *mpl* peas
chilaquiles *mpl* corn tortilla filled with beef in tomato & chili sauce
chirimoya *f* custard apple
chocolate *m* **caliente** hot chocolate

cholgas *fpl* mussels
chorizo *m* smoked pork sausage
churros *m* fried strips of dough
ciruelas *fpl* plums
~ **secas** prunes
clavos *mpl* cloves
coca *f* cola
cochinillo *m* suckling pig
~ **pibil** suckling pig baked in banana leaf wrapping
cocido *m*, **-da** *f* boiled
coco *m* coconut
col *f* cabbage
~**es de Bruselas** brussels sprouts
coliflor *f* cauliflower
coñac *m* brandy, cognac
cordero *m* lamb
costilla *f* cutlet
crema *f* cream
~ **batida** whipped cream
en ~ creamed
descafeinado decaffeinated
dulce de camote puréed yam with nuts and dried fruit
durazno *m* peach
ejotes *mpl* green beans
elote *m* corn
empanada *f* turnover with various kinds of fillings
emparedado *m* sandwich
enchilada *f* tortilla filled with meat and sauce
~ **de pollo** chicken enchilada
~ **suiza** enchilad with sour cream
enfrijolada *f* tortilla with cheese, onions and bean sauce
ensalada *f* salad
~ **de camarones** shrimp salad
~ **de fruta** fruit salad

~ de papas potato salad

entomatada *f* tortilla with cheese, onions and tomato sauce

entrada *f* appetizer

espárragos *mpl* asparagus

espinacas *fpl* spinach

fideos *mpl* noodles

filete *m* steak

frambuesas *fpl* raspberries

fresas *fpl* strawberries

frijoles *mpl* beans

  ~ negros black f/beans

frito *m*, **-ta** *f* fried

frutas *fpl* fruit

galletas *fpl* cookies

  ~ saladas (salt) crackers

gambas *fpl* shrimp *(small)*

gazpacho *m* cold soup of tomatoes and peppers

granada *f* pomegranate

granadilla *f* passion fruit

guayaba *f* guava

guisado *m* stew

guiso *m* stew **b**

  ~ de puerco pork stew

hamburguesa *f* hamburger

helado *m* ice cream

hielo *m* ice

hígado *m* liver

higos *mpl* figs

horchata *f* drink made from ground melon seeds

huachinango *m* red snapper

huauzontles *mpl* vegetable filled with cheese

huevo(s) *m(pl)* egg(s)

  ~ duro hard-boiled egg

  ~s fritos fried eggs

  ~s revueltos scrambled eggs

hugo *m* juice

  ~ de jitomate tomato juice

  ~ de naranja orange juice

  ~ de toronja grapefruit juice

jamón *m* ham

jerez *m* **sherry**

jitomate *m* tomato

langosta *f* lobster

leche *f* milk

lechuga *f* lettuce

lenguado *m* sole

lentejas *fpl* lentils

licor *m* liqueur

licuado *m* fruit shake

limón *m* **lemon**

limonada *f* lemonade

macarrones *mpl* macaroni

mandarina *f* tangerine

manzana *f* apple

margarina *f* margarine

melón *m* melon

menta *f* mint

menudo *m* tripe in chili pepper sauce

merluza *f* hake

mermelada *f* jam

mero *m* bass

mescal *m* alcoholic drink similar to tequila

miel *f* honey

milanesa *f* breaded steak

mole *m* 1. a kind of chili sauce; 2. a meat or poultry dish made with this sauce

montequilla *f* butter

moras *fpl* blackberries

mustard mostaza *f*

mostaza *f* mustard

mújol *m* mullet

naranja *f* orange
nieve *f* sorbet, flavored ice
nopal *m* prickly pear
nueces *fpl* walnuts
oporto *m* port
ostiones *mpl* oysters
pai *m* pie
pan *m* bread
~ **tostado** toast
panecillos *mpl* bread rolls
panqué *m* sponge cake
papa *f* potato
~s **a la francesca** French fries
papaya *f* papaya
pasas *fpl* raisins
pasta(s) *f(pl)* pasta
pastel *m* cake
pato *m* duck
pavo *m* turkey
pepino *m* cucumber
perejil *m* parsley
pez *m* **espada** swordfish
pimienta *f* pepper
~ **negra** black pepper
pimiento *m* **verde** green pepper
piña *f* pineapple
plátano *m* banana
pollo *m* chicken
~ **en adobo** chicken in red pepper sauce
~ **en mole** chicken in mole sauce
ponche *m* fruit and rum punch
postre *m* dessert
pozole *m* pork and maize soup
puerco *m* pork
~ **en naranja** pork loin with orange sauce
pulpo *m* octopus
pulque *m* milky beer made from fermented cactus

puré *m* **de papa** mashed potatoes
quesadilla *f* cheese tortilla
queso *m* cheese
~ **añejo** a sharp, salty cheese
~ **de bola** soft cheese in a ball
~ **fresco** a fresh white cheese
rábano *m* radish
rape *m* monkfish
refrescos *mpl* cold drinks
relleno *m*, **-na** *f* stuffed
repollo *m* cabbage
rodaballo *m* turbot
ron *m* rum
rosquilla *f* doughnut
sal *f* salt
salchicha *f* sausage
salmón *m* salmon
salmonetes *mpl* red mullet
salsa *f* sauce
~ **de soya** soy sauce
sandía *f* watermelon
sardinas *fpl* sardines
sincronizada *f* ham and cheese tortilla
solomillo *m* fillet steak; pork fillet
sopa *f* soup
~ **de ajo** soup with fried bread
~ **de arroz** rice soup
~ **de cebolla** onion soup
~ **de elote** corn soup
~ **de frijoles** bean soup
~ **de mariscos** seafood soup
~ **de papas** potato soup
~ **de pescado** fish soup
~ **de verdures** green vegetable soup
taco tortilla with beef, chicken or cheese filling

tamal *m* ground maize with chopped pork wrapped in a banana leaves
~ **asado** corn flour cake

té *m* tea

tepache *m* drink made from pineapple, pulque and chives

ternera *f* veal

tocino *m* bacon

toronja *f* grapefruit

torrejas *fpl* French toast

torta *f* **del cielo** almond sponge cake

tostada *f* fried tortilla with various fillings

trucha *f* trout

uvas *fpl* grapes

vainilla *f* vanilla

verdura *f* vegetable

vinagre *m* vinegar

vino *m* wine
~ **blanco** white wine
~ **dulce** sweet wine
~ **espumoso** sparkling wine
~ **rosado** róse wine
~ **seco** dry wine
~ **tinto** red wine

yame *m* yam

yogur *m* / **yougurt** *m* yogurt

zanahoria *f* carrot

zapallitos *mpl* zucchini

Websites to Meet Mexicans

To give you a little help in meeting people from Mexico, we've compiled a list of websites that offer introduction services and opportunities for correspondence. The list is by no means complete.

(Disclaimer: The inclusion of the websites in this list by no means constitutes any endorsement of them, explicit or implied, nor can Rodnik Publishing Company assume any responsibility for any communications or transactions resulting therefrom. As with all sites and offers on the Internet, you are cautioned to exercise caution and good judgement in dealing with them.)

Name of Website	Website Address (URL)
CyberFriends Amigos por correspondencia	http://www.geocities.com/SunsetStrip/Palms/8198/miem.html
Foros Mexico – Amistades y Parejas	http://www.forosmexico.com/cgi-bin/foros/ultimatebb.cg
Enfoque on line	http://www.enfoqueonline.com/amigos1.html
Mexico Web	http://mexico.web.com.mx/Paginas_Personales/pagina6.html
El Laberinto Secreto de los Jaguares	http://gbooks1.melodysoft.com/app?ID=unguerreronuncaesvictima
Grancanariaweb – El rincon de Amistad	http://www.grancanariaweb.com/amistad/
Netmio.com – Amigos y más	http://www.netmio.com/
Angelfire – Club de Amigos	http://www.angelfire.com/mb/CLUBDEAMIGOS/ultimos.html
Yo soy de México	http://www.chicos.net/chicosnet/html/la-tela/yo-soy/iamex.htm
Top100Latino.com	http://www.top100latino.com/
Chat Mejicano (El Club del amor)	http://www.chatmejicano.com/
The International Friendship Club	http://www.hypermex.com/html/lvg_ifc.htm

Name of Website	Website Address (URL)
Friendship Exchange – Mexico City	http://www.wantabe.com/~andy/Friendship%20Exchange.htm
America-Mexico Foundation	www.puerto-vallarta.com/amf/
Do Dating.com	http://www.spiralgarden.com/
International Penpals	http://www.mylanguageexchange.com/penpals.asp
Penpals & Dating	http://www.penpalsanddating.com/penpals/
Signal Penpals	http://www.sci.fi/~signal/
2747.com – Penpals	http://www.2747.com/2747/contact/penpals/latinamerica/index.htm
Lovers or Friends	http://www.loversorfriends.com
Hands Across the World	http://hatw.net/
Andy's Penpals Worldwide	http://www.andys-penpals.com/
Penpals From All Over the World	http://koti.mbnet.fi/~kakoskin/penpal/index.html
Worldwide Penpals	http://www.worldwidepenpals.com/
E-mail Penpals.com	http://www.email-penpals.com/
Sassociations Pen Pal Links	http://www1.domaindlx.com/penpals/scripts/links.asp
Pen Pals Net	http://www1.domaindlx.com/penpals/scripts/links.asp
Mexican Singles	http://www.mexicansingles.com
Dating Review	http://www.dating-review.co.uk/International_Dating/Mexico_Singles.htm
Dating Place	http://www.datingplace.com/
Mexican Matchmakers	http://www.mexicanmatchmakers.com/
Parejas-Encuentros	http://www.parejas-encuentros.com/textos2/mexican-singles.html
Latin Match	http://www.latinmatch.com/

Name of Website	Website Address (URL)
Latinas International Introductions	http://www.latinas-intro.com/
Singles List	http://www.singleslist.net/latina.html
Global Singles	http://www.globalsingles.com/guadalajara.htm
Dating Services 4U	http://www.dating-services4u.com/latin.html
Pippin US	http://match-site.pippin.hot-springs.ar.us/
A World of Romance.com	http://www.aworldofromance.com/
Latin Marriage Agency	http://www.latin-marriage-agency.com/
Mexican Brides	http://www.mexican-brides.com/
Mexican Ladies	http://www.mexicanladies.com/
South of the Border Introductions	http://www.sotb.com/
TLC Worldwide, Inc.	http://www.tlcworldwide.com/
Viking Fishing	http://vikingfishing.f.se/top6.htm
Marry Me In Mexico	http://www.marrymeinmexico.com/
Amigos.com	http://amigos.com/
Singlesburg Dot Net	http://www.singlesburg.net/MEXICAN_Mexico.html
Friend Finder.com	http://guest.friendfinder.com/
I Want U.com	http://my.iwantu.com/
Hispanic Matchmaker	http://hispanic.matchmaker.com/
LoveListings.com	http://www.lovelistings.com/
Mexican Dates	http://www.mexican-dates.com/index.htm
Fire & Passion	http://www.firepassion.com/

Have any comments or contributions?
Please send them to us.

If you have any comments you'd like to make concerning our phrasebook or if you wish to contribute any material for the next edition, please write them in the spaces provided below and send them to us at:

Rodnik Publishing Company
P.O. Box 46956
Seattle, WA 98146-0956
U.S.A.

Comments and Contributions

_____
_____
_____
_____
_____
_____
_____
_____
_____
_____

Name & address *(optional)*:
_____
_____

e-mail address: _____

Thank you!

Phrasebooks make great presents for Christmas and birthdays!

Surprise your traveling friends and relatives with one of our unique language guides!

I'd like to order the following phrasebook(s):

1. **Making Friends in Mexico;**
   A Spanish Phrasebook, C 2003, 432 pp   **$9.95**   ___ cys
2. **Making Friends in Russia;**
   A Russian Phrasebook, C 2003, 460 pp   **$10.95**   ___ cys
3. **English-Russian Dictionary-Phrasebook**
   of Love, C 2000, 800 pp   **$24.95**   ___ cys

Shipping & handling:
1 and # 2: $2.00 USA; $3.00 Canada; $5.00 airmail overseas.
#3: $3.00 USA; $5.00 Canada; $10.00 airmail overseas.
(Residents of Washington state please add 8.6% state sales tax.)

The total for my order is: **$** _____

I wish to pay for this order by:

  ☐ **check** (enclosed)   ☐ **Visa**   ☐ **MasterCard**

Number: _____   Exp: _____

Authorized signature: _____

Name: _____

Address: _____

_____

Mail to: **Rodnik Publishing Company**
P.O. Box 46956
Seattle, WA 98146-0956, USA